Fodor's 05

COSTA RICA

Where to Stay and Eat
for All Budgets

Must-See Sights
and Local Secrets

Ratings You Can Trust

Fodor's Travel Publications   New York, Toronto, London, Sydney, Auckland
www.fodors.com

COSTA RICA 2005

Editor: Shannon Kelly

Editorial Production: Jacinta O'Halloran
Editorial Contributors: David Dudenhoefer, Dorothy MacKinnon, Joy Rothke, Ryan Sarsfield, Jeffrey Van Fleet, Carol Weir
Maps: David Lindroth, *cartographer;* Bob Blake and Rebecca Baer, *map editors*
Design: Fabrizio La Rocca, *creative director;* Guido Caroti, *art director;* Moon Sun Kim, *cover designer;* Melanie Marin, *senior picture editor*
Production/Manufacturing: Angela L. McLean
Cover Photo (Red-eyed tree frog): © Turco

SPECIAL SALES

This book is available for special discounts for bulk purchases for sales promotions or premiums. Special editions, including personalized covers, excerpts of existing books, and corporate imprints, can be created in large quantities for special needs. For more information, write to Special Markets/Premium Sales, 1745 Broadway, MD 6-2, New York, New York 10019, or e-mail specialmarkets@randomhouse.com.

AN IMPORTANT TIP & AN INVITATION

Although all prices, opening times, and other details in this book are based on information supplied to us at press time, changes occur all the time in the travel world, and Fodor's cannot accept responsibility for facts that become outdated or for inadvertent errors or omissions. So **always confirm information when it matters,** especially if you're making a detour to visit a specific place. Your experiences—positive and negative—matter to us. If we have missed or misstated something, **please write to us.** We follow up on all suggestions. Contact the Costa Rica editor at editors@fodors.com or c/o Fodor's at 1745 Broadway, New York, NY 10019.

PRINTED IN THE UNITED STATES OF AMERICA

10 9 8 7 6 5 4 3 2 1

DESTINATION COSTA RICA

osta Rica's beauty would flatter a land 10 times as large. The sheer plenty of flora and fauna packed into this tiny nation, combined with a wild variety of climates and landscapes, can make the senses reel. Enchanting eco-zones, beach resorts, and surf sites dot both shores, mixing revelry and relaxation. Almost every trip begins and ends in Costa Rica's urban hub, the feisty capital of San José, where dining and nightlife abound. Within day-tripping distance are volcanoes and rivers prime for white-water adventures. For some serious rest and relaxation, experience the Pacific side of the country, with untouched nature and massive Volcán Arenal in the north, and unspoiled beaches, world-class surfing, abundant wildlife, and virgin rain forests in the south. Or set out for Costa Rica's eastern coast, where life marches more to Caribbean drummers than to the Central American rhythms of the rest of the country. Riding horseback toward simmering volcanoes, tramping through the rain forest, or surfing the long waves, you'll discover why Costa Rica has become one of the hottest destinations in the Western Hemisphere. *¡Pura vida!*

Tim Jarrell, Publisher

CONTENTS

ABOUT THIS BOOK

The best source for travel advice is a like-minded friend who's just been where you're headed. But with or without that friend, you'll be in great shape to find your way around your destination once you learn to find your way around your Fodor's guide.

SELECTION

Our goal is to cover the best properties, sights, and activities in their category, as well as the most interesting communities to visit. We make a point of including local food-lovers' hot spots as well as neighborhood options, and we avoid all that's touristy unless it's really worth your time. You can go on the assumption that everything in this book is recommended wholeheartedly by our writers and editors. Flip to On the Road with Fodor's to learn more about who they are. It goes without saying that no property pays to be included.

RATINGS

Orange stars ☆ denote sights and properties that our editors and writers consider the very best in the area covered by the entire book. These, the best of the best, are listed in the Fodor's Choice section in the front of the book. Black stars ★ highlight the sights and properties we deem Highly Recommended, the don't-miss sights within any region. In cities, sights pinpointed with numbered map bullets ❶ in the margins tend to be more important than those without bullets.

SPECIAL SPOTS

Pleasures & Pastimes and text on the chapter title pages focus on types of experiences that reveal the spirit of the destination. Also watch for Off the Beaten Path sights. Some are out of the way, some are quirky, and all are worthwhile. When the munchies hit, look for Need a Break? suggestions.

TIME IT RIGHT

Check On the Calendar up front and chapters' Timing sections for weather and crowd overviews and best days and times to visit.

SEE IT ALL

Use Fodor's exclusive Great Itineraries as a model for your trip. Either follow those that begin the book, or mix regional itineraries from several chapters. In cities, Good Walks guide you to important sights in each neighborhood; ▶ indicates the starting points of walks and itineraries in the text and on the map.

BUDGET WELL

Hotel and restaurant price categories from ¢ to $$$$ are defined in the opening pages of each chapter—expect to find a balanced selection for every budget. For attractions, we always give standard adult admission fees; reductions are usually available for children, students, and senior citizens. Look in Discounts & Deals in Smart Travel Tips for information on destination-wide ticket schemes.

BASIC INFO

Smart Travel Tips lists travel essentials for the entire area covered by the book; city- and region-specific basics end each chapter. To find the best way to get around, see the transportation section; see individual modes of travel (for example, "By Car") for details. We assume you'll check Web sites or call for particulars.

ON THE MAPS	Maps throughout the book show you what's where and help you find your way around. Black and orange numbered bullets ❶ ❶ in the text correlate to bullets on maps.
BACKGROUND	We give background information within the chapters in the course of explaining sights as well as in CloseUp boxes and in Understanding Costa Rica at the end of the book. To get in the mood, review Books & Movies. The Spanish Vocabulary can be invaluable.
FIND IT FAST	Within the book, chapters are arranged in a roughly counterclockwise direction starting with San José, in the center of the country. Chapters are divided into small regions, within which towns are covered in logical geographical order; attractive routes and interesting places between towns are flagged as En Route. Heads at the top of each page help you find what you need within a chapter.
DON'T FORGET	Restaurants are open for lunch and dinner daily unless we state otherwise; we mention dress only when there's a specific requirement and reservations only when they're essential or not accepted—it's always best to book ahead. Hotels have private baths, phones, TVs, and air-conditioning and operate on the European Plan (a.k.a. EP, meaning without meals) unless otherwise stated. We always list facilities but not whether you'll be charged extra to use them, so when pricing accommodations, find out what's included.
SYMBOLS	

Many Listings

★ Fodor's Choice
★ Highly recommended
⊠ Physical address
⌒⫐ Mailing address
☎ Telephone
⎙ Fax
⊕ On the Web
✉ E-mail
🎟 Admission fee
☉ Open/closed times
► Start of walk/itinerary
⊟ Credit cards

Outdoors

⅄ Golf
⛺ Camping

Hotels & Restaurants

🏨 Hotel
🛏 Number of rooms
♨ Facilities
🍽 Meal plans
✕ Restaurant
⌁ Reservations
🎩 Dress code
↘ Smoking
🍺 BYOB
✕🏨 Hotel with restaurant that warrants a visit

Other

☺ Family-friendly
🛈 Contact information
⇨ See also
⊠ Branch address
☞ Take note

Our success in showing you every corner of Costa Rica is a credit to our extraordinary writers. Although there's no substitute for travel advice from a good friend who knows your style, our contributors are the next best thing—the kind of people you would poll for travel advice if you knew them.

Writer and photographer David Dudenhoefer spent most of the 1990s based in San José and traveling much of Central and South America. He is a biologist by training, and as a writer he specializes in the environment and travel. David has worked in 20 countries on three continents and has written about everything from migratory birds to intransigent politicians. He has written and updated material for Fodor's guides to Cuba, Panama, Colombia, Ecuador, Belize, and Guatemala, and for five editions of *Fodor's Costa Rica*. David updated the Central Costa Rica and Central Pacific chapters for this edition and wrote the essay "A Biological Superpower."

Seasoned traveler and journalist Dorothy MacKinnon took up a post in San José from which to contribute to the *Tico Times* on ecotourism, restaurants, and nonprofit development stories—and to update the Nicoya Peninsula and Southern Pacific chapters of this guide. She has written on travel and other topics for several North American newspapers, including the *Washington Post*.

Joy Rothke lives in La Fortuna de San Carlos, Costa Rica, where she's learned to love birds and ignore insects. Joy has published nonfiction in numerous publications, including the *Chicago Tribune, Fort Worth Star-Telegram, San Francisco Examiner, Tico Times, New York Times* syndicate, Salon.com, *Diablo*, and *San Francisco Focus*, where she also served as an editor. Joy lent her expertise to the "Destination: Costa Rica" and "Understanding Costa Rica" sections of the book.

Ryan Sarsfield, a biologist and naturalist, travels extensively in Central and South America. He has studied insect dung in Guanacaste, Costa Rica; birds in Pohnpei, Micronesia; and rattlesnakes in Sonora, Mexico. He has also honed his Spanish in Golfito, Costa Rica; taught English in Brazil; and led tours in Brazil and Venezuela. Ryan, who considers Costa Rica his first home away from home, updated the wildlife glossary and wrote the CloseUp box, "Top Wildlife-Viewing Tips."

San José–based freelance writer Jeffrey Van Fleet has spent the better part of the last decade enjoying Costa Rica's long rainy seasons and Wisconsin's winters. (Most people would try to do it the other way around.) He saw his first Resplendent Quetzal, that bird-watcher's Holy Grail, while researching this guide. Jeff is a regular contributor to Costa Rica's English-language newspaper, the *Tico Times*, and has written for Fodor's guides to Chile, Argentina, Peru, and Central and South America. Jeff updated the San José, Northern Zone, and Caribbean chapters.

Carol Weir, who updated the Smart Travel Tips section, divides her time between Costa Rica and South Carolina, where she writes for a daily newspaper. A former managing editor of the *Tico Times*, she is married to a Costa Rican biologist and has two young sons.

Central America

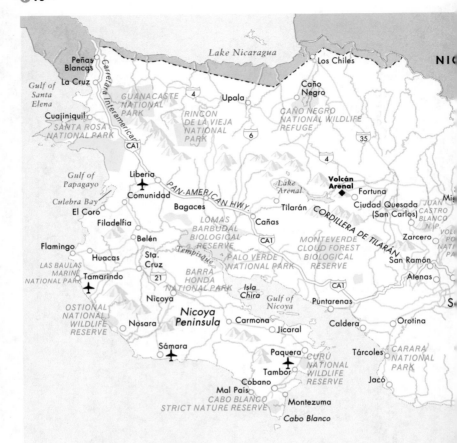

Peñas Blancas
Gulf of Santa Elena
La Cruz
Carretera Interamericana
Lake Nicaragua
Los Chiles
NI
Cuajiniquil
GUANACASTE NATIONAL PARK
4
Upala
Caño Negro
CAÑO NEGRO NATIONAL WILDLIFE REFUGE
SANTA ROSA NATIONAL PARK
RINCON DE LA VIEJA NATIONAL PARK
CA1
6
35
4
Gulf of Papagayo
Liberia
Comunidad
PAN-AMERICAN HWY.
Lake Arenal
Volcán Arenal
Fortuna
Ciudad Quesada (San Carlos)
JUAN CASTRO BLANCO N.P.
Mie
Culebra Bay
El Coro
Bagaces
Tilarán
CORDILLERA DE TILARÁN
Zarcero
VOL PO NATI PA
Filadelfia
LOMAS BARBUDAL BIOLOGICAL RESERVE
Cañas
CA1
MONTEVERDE CLOUD FOREST BIOLOGICAL RESERVE
San Ramón
Flamingo
Belén
Tempisque
PALO VERDE NATIONAL PARK
Atenas
LAS BAULAS MARINE NATIONAL PARK
Huacas
Tamarindo
Sta. Cruz
BARRA HONDA NATIONAL PARK
Isla Chira
Gulf of Nicoya
Puntarenas
CA1
S
21
Nicoya
Nicoya Peninsula
Carmona
Caldera
Orotina
OSTIONAL NATIONAL WILDLIFE RESERVE
Nosara
Jicaral
Sámara
Paquera
CURÚ NATIONAL WILDLIFE RESERVE
Tárcoles
CARARA NATIONAL PARK
Tambor
Jacó
Cobano
Mal País
CABO BLANCO STRICT NATURE RESERVE
Montezuma
Cabo Blanco

PACIFIC OCEAN

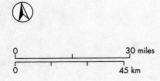

0 ———————————— 30 miles
0 ———————————— 45 km

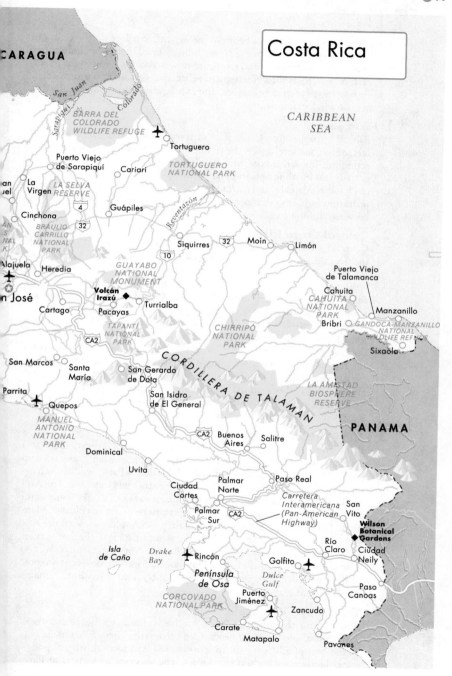

Costa Rica

NICARAGUA

San Juan

Sarapiquí

Colorado

BARRA DEL COLORADO WILDLIFE REFUGE

✈ Tortuguero

CARIBBEAN SEA

Puerto Viejo de Sarapiquí

Cariari

TORTUGUERO NATIONAL PARK

an uel

La Virgen

LA SELVA RESERVE

4

Guápiles

Cinchona

Reventazón

ÁN S NAL K

BRAULIO CARRILLO NATIONAL PARK

32

Siquirres 32 Moín Limón

10

Alajuela Heredia

GUAYABO NATIONAL MONUMENT

Puerto Viejo de Talamanca

Cahuita

CAHUITA NATIONAL PARK

Manzanillo

Volcán Irazú ◆

n José

Cartago Pacayas Turrialba

Bribri *GANDOCA-MANZANILLO NATIONAL WILDLIFE REFUGE*

TAPANTÍ NATIONAL PARK

CA2

CHIRRIPÓ NATIONAL PARK

Sixaola

San Marcos Santa María

San Gerardo de Dota

C O R D I L L E R A   D E   T A L A M A N

LA AMISTAD BIOSPHERE RESERVE

PANAMA

Parrita

✈ Quepos

MANUEL ANTONIO NATIONAL PARK

San Isidro de El General

CA2 Buenos Aires Salitre

Dominical

Uvita

Ciudad Cortés

Palmar Norte Paso Real

Carretera Interamericana (Pan-American Highway) San Vito

Wilson Botanical Gardens ◆

Palmar Sur CA2

Río Claro Ciudad Neily

Isla de Caño

Drake Bay ✈ Rincón

Península de Osa

Golfito ✈

Dulce Gulf

Paso Canoas

CORCOVADO NATIONAL PARK

Puerto Jiménez

Zancudo

Carate

Matapalo

Pavones

Most trips to Costa Rica begin in the capital, San José, at the center of the country. Day trips to the surrounding Central Valley include coffee plantations, volcanoes, and river canyons. An hour's flight to the north, east, or west transports you to pristine beaches, verdant rain forest, sleepy surfing towns, active volcanoes, and exhilarating snorkeling, scuba diving, or windsurfing waters.

1 San José

Ringed by mountains, Costa Rica's capital is more than 1,150 m (3,773 feet) above sea level and is the center of national political, cultural, and economic life. A third of Costa Rica's 4 million people live in busy, congested, and bustling San José, its suburbs, and in the neighboring cities of Heredia, Alajuela, and Cartago. Since the capital is the country's transportation hub, it's often necessary to return to San José when traveling between destinations.

2 Central Costa Rica

Central Costa Rica consists of the Central Valley (*Meseta Central*), which includes the capital and is the most densely populated region of the country, and the surrounding ring of impressive volcanoes and mountains. The region has active volcanic craters, luxuriant cloud forests, and some of the country's best hotels and restaurants. West of San José is the upscale suburb of Escazú, to the north are the cities of Heredia and Alajuela, and to the southeast is Cartago, the colonial capital until 1823. Costa Rica's most accessible volcanoes, Poás and Irazú, define the valley's northern edge. Southeast of the Central Valley lies the smaller Orosi Valley, a coffee-growing region with historic monuments and lovely scenery, and the agricultural community of Turrialba, near the country's preeminent archaeological site, the Guayabo National Monument. Coffee, *grano d'oro*, or the "golden bean," is the country's economic backbone, and Central Costa Rica is the heart of the industry.

3 The Northern Zone

Birds and birders flock to the Monteverde Cloud Forest, the Caño Negro Wildlife Refuge in the far north, and many other preserves and parks. Down by the sea, at Santa Rosa National Park, wildlife-watching is sublime. Volcanoes loom large on the ethereal landscape. The Arenal Observatory Lodge gives you the closest views of smoke spirals and lava flows of Volcán Arenal, the world's third most active volcano. Man-made Lake Arenal, in the shadow of the volcano, has some of the best windsurfing in the Americas. Nearby, you can soak in the hot springs at the beautifully landscaped Tabacón Resort. Northern Guanacaste and Alajuela provinces—including La Fortuna and Monteverde—contain some of the least developed regions of the country, and agriculture remains the dominant way of life.

4 The Nicoya Peninsula

With top-notch surfing at Playa Avellanas, the lively beach resorts of Tamarindo, and waves of nesting sea turtles, the Nicoya Peninsula may be the best of all Costa Rican worlds. At Playa Ocotal, surreal underwater landscapes beckon snorkelers. The spectacular sunsets at Playa

Pelada draw spectators on foot and on horseback. Many large, all-in-clusive beach resorts are increasingly focusing on golf. And private cabanas concealed in the forest are not hard to come by. For something a little more wild, visit the popular party town of Montezuma, near the private reserve Curú National Wildlife Refuge and the isolated Cabo Blanco Nature Reserve, Costa Rica's first protected area.

5 The Central Pacific

Some of the country's most popular destinations are in this region—from the surfing town of Jacó to Manuel Antonio National Park, two of Costa Rica's top tourist destinations. Quepos, a town adjacent to Manuel Antonio, is a mecca for visitors, and has several discos, decent restaurants, and hotels that are cheaper than those in Manuel Antonio. Just north, the overdeveloped surf town of Jacó has plenty of activity day and night—it's funky, fun, and unabashedly tacky, with casinos, discos, and bars. And as the closest beach resort to San José, it's popular with locals as well as gringos.

6 The Southern Pacific

Even by local standards, the sheer number of plant and animal species in the southern Pacific is astonishing. In the lush and enormous Corcovado National Park—sometimes called the "Amazon of Costa Rica"—hikers scamper past swamplands, jungle-thick riverbanks, unspoiled beaches, and heavenly primary rain forest. Lodges in the heart of the Osa Peninsula accommodate those who want to bond with nature but aren't ready to sleep outdoors in it. A boat ride in Drake Bay shows you the rugged coastline that Sir Francis saw when he paid a call, and some of the country's most beautiful underwater scenery is at Isla del Caño. Luxurious lodges in Drake Bay cater to amateur naturalists, anglers, and scuba divers. Puerto Jiménez and Golfito are air transportation hubs, with a few hotels and restaurants and some good fishing. Some of Costa Rica's most remote beaches and best surfing destinations are south of Golfito.

7 The Caribbean

The Afro-Caribbean influence is apparent on Costa Rica's Atlantic side. You find reggae, johnnycakes, and fluent English-speakers in Limón. Natural sights explode here, both above and below sea level. Cahuita National Park is a popular stop for budget travelers and backpackers, who enjoy snorkeling the coral reef or strolling the snowy-white, forest-edged beach. At Tortuguero National Park, majestic Green Sea Turtles come ashore to nest; the park also provides 11 distinct ecological habitats for crocodiles, manatees, amphibians, and reptiles. Rustic Barra del Colorado is popular with sport anglers, who fish for tarpon and snook. Although visitors to Costa Rica tend to favor the Pacific coast, partly because the Atlantic has fewer luxury accommodations and more rain, many of Costa Rica's most beautiful spots—and true bargains—are found here.

You can get virtually *anywhere* in Costa Rica via public bus, and cheaply. However, there is no central bus terminal in San Jose, written schedules are rare, many bus stops are unmarked, and itineraries are subject to frequent changes. If you're planning to use public transportation to get around Costa Rica, the key is to check and double-check for the latest information. Ask at your hotel or visit a tourist center to get the most up-to-date information.

Costa Rica Classic
5 to 7 days

Rugged topography and iffy road conditions (less than 20% of the country's roads are paved) mean destinations appearing close on the map in Costa Rica are actually a half day's drive apart. To avoid the frustration of packing too much in, follow this itinerary that hits the highlights, from spectacular volcanoes and misty cloud forests to golden beaches, leaving you time to relax and enjoy each region in the process.

THE CENTRAL VALLEY 1 day. Don't spend much time in San José. Go straight to one of the small or large luxury hotels in Alajuela or Heredia. Xandari Plantation, near Alajuela, and the Marriott Hotel and Resort in San Antonio de Belén are luxurious, attractive, and close to the Juan Santamaría International Airport.

ARENAL 1 day. In the morning, drive to La Fortuna, visit Arenal Volcano, and soak in Tabacón Hot Springs. Spend the night at one of the nature lodges near the volcano. Arenal Observatory Lodge affords the best view, whereas the Tilajari Resort Hotel, in Muelle de San Carlos, has quiet rooms beside a river and its own large forest preserve. In the morning, go for a horseback ride to La Fortuna's *Catarata* (waterfall) just a few miles outside of town.

MONTEVERDE CLOUD FOREST 3 days. Make the daylong drive to Monteverde via Lake Arenal. Stop for lunch at one of the restaurants that ring the lake; most are inside hotels. In Monteverde, check into an inn near the private cloud-forest reserve. After a casual dinner at Pizzería de Johnny or another local eatery, turn in early—unless you're up for a night of salsa dancing at La Catarata, a lively nightspot that draws locals and visitors. In the morning, get to the reserve as early as possible, and hire a local guide to hike with you. Spend two days in Monteverde visiting the town's butterfly and orchid gardens, seeing a slide show of spectacular nature photography by Michael and Patricia Fogden—and, for the adventurous, zipping through the forest on a canopy tour.

THE NICOYA COAST 2 days. If you have a couple more days, drive to Tamarindo or other beaches along the coast of the Nicoya Peninsula and spend the rest of your time in the sun.

A Walk in the Clouds
5 to 8 days

This itinerary takes you from an impressive active volcano to the Osa Peninsula—the country's most remote region—and back to warm sands and rolling waves.

THE CENTRAL VALLEY **1 or 2 days.** When you arrive, check in to one of the Central Valley inns for a night or two to acclimate to Costa's Rica's *pura vida*—the good life—philosophy. After you've rested, get up early and drive to the Poás Volcano. Mornings are usually best—before the clouds roll in. There is a hot sulfur lake at the bottom of the volcano with active fumaroles. Warm up with a steaming cup of hot chocolate or coffee at the park's café. Then head to nearby La Paz Waterfall Gardens. After hiking to the pounding waterfalls and visiting the butterfly and hummingbird gardens, eat lunch at the open-air restaurant. Resplendent Quetzals nest here between December and February, and wild orchids bloom along the property's many kilometers of well-kept trails. Spend the night close to the airport.

THE OSA PENINSULA **2 to 5 days.** The next day, fly to the gorgeous and remote Osa Peninsula for jungle living. Choose a lodge such as Lapa Ríos or Corcovado Lodge Tent Camp, which include meals, bird-watching, and guided nature walks. End your trip here or head north for a relaxing stint on a Nicoya beach.

NICOYA BEACHES **2 to 3 days.** From the Osa Peninsula, fly back to San José and then to the upscale beach areas of Tamarindo, or Manuel Antonio National Park, or one of the less-touristed areas along the northern Pacific.

A Caribbean Caper
7 to 9 days

On the Caribbean coast, living is easy and the ocean is crystal-clear and warm. Prices are lower than on the Pacific side of the country, and the culture—shaped by descendants of mainly Jamaican immigrants—has a distinctly Afro-Caribbean flavor.

THE NORTHERN LOWLANDS **2 to 3 days.** After your first night at a Central Valley inn, drive east on the Braulio Carrillo Highway, passing through the majestic cloud forest in the national park by the same name. Stop at the Rain Forest Aerial Tram, part of an 850-acre private nature reserve, for a breathtaking tram ride through the treetops, lunch, and a short guided hike. Continue another hour to Puerto Viejo de Sarapiquí, and check into the comfortable Selva Verde Lodge on the banks of the Río Sarapiquí. You can raft on the gently rolling river, go bird-watching with one of the Selva Verde's expert local guides, and visit the La Selva Biological Station. Also in the area, and worth a visit, are the Jewels of the Rainforest insect museum housed at La Quinta de Sarapiquí Country Inn, and Centro Neotrópico Sarapiquís, which includes ornamental and tropical fruit gardens and a replica of a pre-Columbian Indian village.

COASTAL TALAMANCA **2 days.** Leave this lush lowland region and continue on to Puerto Viejo de Talamanca, where you check into one of the small nature lodges tucked behind the palm trees along the road to Manzanillo, or at one of the small hotels in town. Spend your days snorkeling, biking down the dirt road to Manzanillo Beach, and sampling jerk chicken, johnnycake, coconut-flavored rice and beans, and other Caribbean treats. At night, check out a reggae bar. The Gandoca–Manzanillo National Wildlife Refuge is about 65% tropical rain forest, and also has a 9-km (5½-mi) stretch of beach where four turtle species—including Giant Leatherbacks—lay their eggs. January through April is the best time to see turtles.

SAN JOSÉ **1 day.** Return to San José and spend a night at the Hotel Grano de Oro or other historic hotel. Visit one of the capital's many museums—the Jade, the Gold, and National museums are all within walking distance of one another. In the evening, attend the symphony or another production at the Teatro Nacional, a national monument built in 1894. Even if nothing is scheduled, visit the Teatro—widely regarded as the most beautiful building in Costa Rica.

TORTUGUERO **2 to 3 days.** The next morning, having made reservations at Mawamba Lodge or Laguna Lodge or another jungle lodge in Tortuguero, journey to this remote natural paradise in a motorized pontoon boat driven by a local guide. Along the way, you might see sloths, caimans, iguanas, White-faced Capuchin and Howler monkeys, and maybe a boa constrictor sleeping on the banks of the canals. Tortuguero is the largest nesting area in the Western Hemisphere for the Green Sea Turtle. Leatherbacks also nest there, and a turtle walk by a local guide is a must. Rent a dugout canoe and explore the canals yourself. From Tortuguero, fly back to the capital. Depending on your time and interests, visit Monteverde, Volcán Arenal, or a Central Pacific or Guanacaste beach before you head home.

Light Adventure: Arenal, Monteverde & Tamarindo
7 days

Even with just a week to spare, you can see a lot of Costa Rica: the volcanic plains; the cloud forest; and the Pacific beaches. This week offers days of action combined with evenings of luxury and relaxation.

ARENAL **2 days.** Arrive at Juan Santamaría International airport. A shuttle from the luxury Xandari Plantation nearby will pick you up at the airport. Enjoy a spa treatment, then dinner and the view from the outdoor terrace restaurant, and a good night's rest in your villa. The next day, pick up a four-wheel-drive rental vehicle and drive to La Fortuna (about four hours) to spend the night. If the skies are clear, take a volcano tour in the afternoon to experience up close the rumbling wonders of Volcán Arenal. Spend evening hours soaking in Tabacón's volcanic hot springs and watching lava flow down Arenal's flanks.

MONTEVERDE **2 days.** Drive to Monteverde (about four hours) and check into the Monteverde Lodge or Trapp Family Lodge, and head to Santa Elena for *almuerzo* (lunch). If it's clear, make reservations for the Sky Walk, where you explore five suspension bridges and platforms, from ground to tree canopy level. For dinner, there's elegant dining at Monteverde Lodge's restaurant, or American-style pizza and beer at the always-popular Pizzería de Johnny. The following day, enjoy some Monteverde coffee and cheese for breakfast at Stella's Bakery, then visit the Monteverde Reserve and the Butterfly Garden and maybe the Sky

Walk. Take the time to visit Montev
the local cheeses or an ice cream con
iting Monteverde's many art galleries.

TAMARINDO **3 days.** On Day 5, drive th
beach area known as Costa Rica's "G
Hotel Capitán Suizo. Head for the beach
ing around the hotel's large free-form sw
take a half-day sailing trip, which gives y   ˌs,
puffer fish, trigger fish, dolphins, and—from   ˌn April—
whales. Or, alternatively, take a tour to Play   ˌe, which focuses
on the natural history and protection of the Giant Leatherback Turtle—
the world's largest reptile. If you're more of a land person, try an ATV
ride through the hills, a shoreline horseback ride, or birding in the estuary. On your final day, return to San José (driving time is four to five
hours) and spend the night at Orquídeas Inn, a tranquil yet architecturally quirky Alajuela hotel close to the airport.

A Family Affair
7 days

If you're going to take the time and spend the money to haul your family all the way to Central America, how about showing them something
they won't see back home? Giant turtles. Tortuguero National Park is
one of the most important hatcheries in the western Caribbean for
Green Sea Turtles, as well as Hawksbills, Loggerheads, and Giant
Leatherbacks.

SAN JOSÉ **2 days.** Arrive in San José and overnight at Hotel Bougainvillea. Take the next day to get acclimated and see a bit of the capital. IN-
Bioparque, an educational and recreational center, has interactive
exhibits, multimedia, audiovisuals, and guided natural trails. After
lunch, visit the Café Britt coffee *finca* (plantation) and explore 6 acres
of coffee fields, tropical gardens, and a coffee processing plant. If you
visit between November and January, you can watch the harvest in
progress. A buffet Costa Rican dinner is available, accompanied by live
Tico folk music and dancing.

TORTUGUERO **5 days.** Take a half-hour flight to Tortuguero on Day 3. Dine
and spend the night at Tortuga Lodge. Early morning is the best time to
see birds, and a bird walk is scheduled for 5:30 AM. If you'd rather wake
a bit later, lodge guides lead tours of Tortuguero National Park. Its almost 52,000 acres are home to the endangered Great Green Macaw,
White-faced Capuchin, Howler, and Spider monkey, Chestnut-mandibled
Toucan, and Slatey-tailed Trogon. After dinner, walk the beach to see turtles nesting. Leatherbacks nest in March and April; Green Turtles in July;
Hawksbills from July through September. The following day, visit the village of Tortuguero, where the Caribbean Conservation Corporation operates a visitor center and a turtle museum. After breakfast on your last
day in Tortuguero depart by boat to the canals of Caño Palma (Palm Canal)
for a half day of exploring via canoes, kayaks, or hydro-bikes, and return
in the late afternoon. Take a flight to San José the next morning.

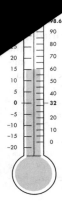

e dry season on the Pacific coast runs from mid-December through April. From mid-December until early February, you have the combined advantages of good weather and lush vegetation. Some areas, especially Guanacaste, are dry and dusty by April. The Caribbean coast is always unpredictable when it comes to rain, but enjoys a short "dry" season in September and October. Both coasts get some sunny weather in July, August, and early September. Hotels are most likely to be full during dry seasons, so plan several months in advance. To avoid crowds and high prices, visit in the rainy season. Vegetation is lush and gorgeous then, but some roads are washed out, and beaches are often wet in the afternoon but sunny and dry in the morning. You can find deals in July or August, when the storms let up a bit, or mid-December, when rains are tapering off. September and October are a quiet time to visit—some hotels are virtually empty, and you might have the beaches to yourself.

Climate

The climate varies greatly between the lowlands and the mountains. Tropical temperatures generally hover between 20°C (70°F) and 30°C (85°F). High humidity, especially in the dense jungle of the Caribbean coast and in the northern lowlands, is the true culprit in any discomfort. Guanacaste, on the more arid Pacific coast, is Costa Rica's hottest region, with frequent temperatures in the 90s during the dry season.

⚅ Forecasts **Weather Channel Connection** ☎ 900/932-8437, 95¢ per minute from a Touch-Tone phone ⊕ www.weather.com.

The following are the average daily maximum and minimum temperatures for San José, whose weather is typical of other highland towns, and Golfito, which has a climate similar to that of most coastal and lowland towns.

SAN JOSÉ

Jan.	75F	24C	May	80F	27C	Sept.	79F	26C
	58	14		62	17		61	16
Feb.	76F	24C	June	79F	26C	Oct.	77F	25C
	58	14		62	17		60	16
Mar.	79F	26C	July	77F	25C	Nov.	77F	25C
	59	15		62	17		60	16
Apr.	79F	26C	Aug.	78F	26C	Dec.	75F	24C
	62	17		61	16		58	14

GOLFITO

Jan.	91F	33C	May	91F	33C	Sept.	91F	33C
	72	22		73	23		72	22
Feb.	91F	33C	June	90F	32C	Oct.	90F	32C
	72	22		73	23		72	22
Mar.	91F	33C	July	90F	32C	Nov.	91F	32C
	73	23		72	22		72	22
Apr.	91F	33C	Aug.	90F	32C	Dec.	91F	33C
	73	23		72	22		72	22

From parades and pilgrimages to rodeos and *topes* (horse parades) to the hedonistic excess of Carnival, every month in the Costa Rican calendar includes a wide variety of festivals and events. Many are linked to the Roman Catholic calendar, since Roman Catholicism is Costa Rica's official religion. Easter is the biggest holiday of the year in Costa Rica, and from Holy Thursday through Easter Sunday, the country essentially shuts down. Other festivals celebrate the heroes of Tico history as well as its ethnic diversity. Winter

Dec.–Jan.	In Boruca, 10 km (6 mi) south of Paso Real in southern Costa Rica, is the indigenous Fiesta de los Diablitos (Festival of the Little Devils), December 31–January 2, which celebrates the defeat of the Spanish. Men dress in burlap sacks and carved masks and act out a "fight" between the Indians (*diablitos*, or "little devils") and the Spaniards, represented by one or two men dressed as bulls.
Jan.	The Fiesta Patronales de Alajuelita, during the week of January 15, is an oxcart parade and pilgrimage in honor of the Black Christ of Esquipulas, the patron saint of Alajuela.
	At the Fiesta de Santa Cruz, the week of January 16 there are folk dances, rodeo, music, and bullfights in Santa Cruz, Guanacaste, in honor of the Black Christ of Esquipulas.
	During the first two weeks of January are the Palmares Fiestas, in Palmares (about 56 km [35 mi] west of San José), with folk dances, music, rides, and bullfights.
	The Copa del Café, an international tennis tournament, takes place at the Costa Rican Country Club in San José in mid-January.
Feb.	The first week of February brings the San Isidro de el General Fiestas, which include an agricultural fair, cattle shows, bullfights, and a flower show.
	Parades, floats, dancing, and music take place at the Puntarenas Carnival the last week of the month.
	A Fiesta de los Diablitos (Festival of the Little Devils), much like the one held in Boruca from late December to early January, takes place in the indigenous community of Rey Curré, 5 km (3 mi) south of Paso Real, in late February.
	February 25 is the Sun Festival, held to honor the Maya New Year with a fire ceremony.
Feb.–Mar.	Costa Rican musicians perform at the Monteverde Music Festival in this small town in northern Puntarenas Province.
	The last week of February are the Liberia Fiestas, with Guanacaste folklore and concerts, in Costa Rica's second-largest city.

Mar.	On the second Sunday in March, the Día del Boyero (Oxcart-Driver Day) is marked with a colorful procession of carts through San Antonio de Escazú.
	At San José's cattle show there are bullfights, a rodeo, and horse races.
	In San José, the International Festival of the Arts, the second week of March, has theater, dance, concerts, and art exhibits from Costa Rica and other Central American countries.
	San José Day, on March 19, brings fairs and Masses to cities and neighborhoods called San José throughout Costa Rica. It's a tradition to visit Poás Volcano on this day.
	The National Orchid Show in mid-March brings displays of more than 1,500 local and foreign orchid varieties and hybrids.
	A daylong religious procession winds from Cartago to the ruins of Costa Rica's first church, at Ujarrás, in mid-March.

SPRING

Apr.	April 11 is Día de Juan Santamaría (Juan Santamaría Day)—honoring a national hero—which is celebrated in Alajuela with a parade and other festivities.
	During Easter week, the Semana Santa (Holy Week), most of the country shuts down from Thursday through Sunday. A series of Masses, processions, and parades take place throughout the country. The largest and most well known are in Cartago, Heredia, Escazú, and San José.
	The last week in April is University Week in San José, with parades, concerts, and exhibits at the University of Costa Rica in San Pedro.
Apr.–May	The Artisans Fair in Costa Rica, with crafts from across the country, takes place the last week of April through the first week of May.
May	May 1 is Labor Day, when parades take place throughout the nation and congressional elections are held. In Puerto Limón, the day is celebrated with cricket matches, music, dancing, and parades.
	The Carrera de San Juan on May 17 is a 22.5-km cross-country race beginning in San Jose.
	Religious celebrations take place nationwide on May 29, Corpus Christi Day, which is a national holiday.

SUMMER

June	Namesake towns (San Pedro and San Pablo) have religious celebrations on June 29, Saints Peter and Paul Day.
July	Alajuela's Festival de los Mangoes pays tribute to that tropical fruit with nine days of music, parades, and markets.

Guanacaste Day, commemorating the annexation of Guanacaste from Nicaragua, is celebrated on July 25 in Liberia and Santa Cruz with music, folk dancing, rodeos, and bullfights.

On the Saturday closest to July 16 in Puntarenas is the Virgin of the Sea Festival. Boats in the Golfo de Nicoya are decorated in preparation for a colorful regatta, and parades, concerts, sporting events, and fireworks take place to honor the town's patron saint, the Virgin of Mount Carmel.

Aug.

Throughout August the Teatro Nacional in San José is loaded with performances by classical musicians from all over the world, part of the Costa Rica International Music Festival (⊕ www.costaricamusic.com).

The Día de la Virgen de Los Angeles, which honors Costa Rica's patron saint, called "La Negrita," is celebrated in Cartago on August 2 with processions and a well-attended Mass. The night before, tens of thousands of faithful worshippers walk *la romaría*, a 22-km (14-mi) trek east down the highway from San José to Cartago.

August 30 is San Ramón Day, with parades and "Saint Ramón" dancing in the streets.

Aug.–Sept.

The Semana Afro–Costarricense (Afro–Costa Rican Week) is a celebration of Afro–Costa Rican culture in Puerto Limón and San José that takes place August 22–September 4.

FALL

Sept.

September 15 is the Día del Independencia (Independence Day). On the 14th, students carry a *farole*, a "freedom torch," in a relay race from Guatemala to the colonial capital of Cartago. It arrives at precisely 6 PM on the 14th, when all of Costa Rica stops to sing the national anthem. There are nationwide parades on the 15th.

Oct.

The weeklong Mardi Gras–style Limón Carnival comes to the center of Costa Rica's Afro-Caribbean community in Puerto Limón in early to mid-October.

Christopher Columbus, Limón's first tourist, set foot on nearby Uvita Island in 1504. The city celebrates the encounter of Old and New Worlds with parades and music during Carnival week bracketing the October 12 holiday, commemorated in Costa Rica as the Día de las Culturas (Day of the Cultures). There are sometimes indigenous protests on this day.

It's all hail to corn at the Fiesta del Maíz (Corn Festival) in Upala near the Nicaraguan border on October 12. Residents dressed in costumes made entirely of corn parade down the street, and a corn queen is named.

Nov.	Día de los Muertos (Day of the Dead, or All Soul's Day) is observed nationwide on November 2 with special church services and people visiting family graves.
	The International Theater Festival brings plays and companies from all over the Americas to San José. The Fiesta de Café (Coffee Festival) in the Central Valley announces the beginning of the harvest with music, dancing, and a coffee-picking contest.
	At the end of November an Oxcart Parade, with hand-painted oxcarts from all over the country, files down the Paseo de Colón in San José.
Dec.	The Fiesta de La Luz (Festival of Lights) starts at the beginning of December, when decorations and lights fill San José streets. It culminates with a carnival on December 27 with dancing, music, competitions, float parades, and fireworks.
	December 8 is the Fiesta de la Inmaculada Concepción de la Virgen María (Festival of the Immaculate Conception of the Virgin Mary), celebrated with fireworks nationwide.
	In Boruca, a tiny Indian community near Paso Real, the weeklong Fiesta de los Negritos takes place around the Festival of Immaculate Conception. Ancient rituals are performed with elaborate costumes, music, and dancing.
	The Fiesta de la Yeguita (Festival of the Little Mare), honoring the Virgin of Guadelupe, takes place in Nicoya on December 12. There are fireworks, parades, bullfights, and concerts.
	Christmas festivals are held throughout the month. In many towns, residents and business owners compete for the best Nativity scene, usually judged on December 22. Beginning December 15, carolers go from house to house and are given food and drink. A *Misa del Gallo* (Midnight Mass) is given on December 24.
	On December 26, Ticos come from all over the country to downtown San José to participate in the Tope, a parade of horses and costumed riders, as well as some of Costa Rica's famous oxcarts.
	December 25–31 are the Festejos Populares (Year-End Festivals). The celebrations at the Zapote fairgrounds south of San José are regarded as the best in Costa Rica, with rides, games, bullfighting, music, food, and fireworks.

PLEASURES & PASTIMES

Bird-Watching Many of Costa Rica's creatures are named after their homes: for example, the wild turkey (Highland Tinamou), the melodious Riverside Wren, or the Volcano Hummingbird. You may be surprised to encounter a Canadian Warbler, Baltimore Oriole, or Kentucky Warbler—some of the 200 North American bird species found in Costa Rica. Some of these species stay year-round, and others come and go during the winter migration. Costa Rica also has the requisite tropical birds, including 6 kinds of toucans, 16 parrots and parakeets, and more than 50 hummingbirds. Other tropical groups, such as ant birds, are well represented. The birds of Costa Rica represent close to 10 percent of the total bird species in the world.

Fishing Costa Rica is a freshwater and saltwater angler's dream. Marlin, sailfish, tuna, and dorado abound in the Pacific, and fishing folk fill Golfito-area lodges all the way up the coast. Experienced captains, small and medium-size marinas, and charter fishing companies compete for business, so prices remain reasonable. Fishing-and-lodging packages are common. Tarpon and snook are the highlights of the Caribbean. The Barra del Colorado River, in the heart of the rain forest, gets more than 200 inches of annual rainfall and has its best fishing from December to early May, and late July to late August. *Guapote* (sea bass), catfish, and *gaspar* (Alligator Gar) can also be caught here. Lake Arenal has many rainbow bass, tilapia, and gaspar, and several mountain lodges offer trout fishing in tumbling streams. Good fishing is also found in the Río Frío, which passes through Los Chile, a northern town on the border with Nicaragua. Tarpon, snook, White Drum, gar, and more bite here. You can fish from the municipal dock in Los Chiles or rent a *panga* (small boat) driven by a local guide.

Rain Forests The lowland rain forests of Costa Rica and the rest of the New World tropics are complex biological communities. A typical hectare (2½ acres) of Costa Rican rain forest might be home to nearly 100 species of trees, whereas 30 is typical in the richest forests of the United States. In addition to trees, you'll see epiphytes and giant rain forest versions of orchids, as well as sloths, monkeys, copious birds, and more. Good places for hiking are Braulio Carrillo National Park, near San José, which contains rain forest and cloud forest, and the hot and humid rain forest in La Selva Biological Station. On the Pacific coast, Corcovado National Park and Marenco Wildlife Refuge have well-maintained—but often muddy and steep—trails where you can meander for hours through impressive primary forests. Filled with giant strangler figs and dripping with moss, Monteverde's private reserve is a good place to hike through cool and misty primeval cloud forests. Even a quick walk through forest trails on the way to the beach in Manuel Antonio National Park can reveal squirrel monkeys, white-faced coatis, and iguanas. For a closer look at the canopy, ride the Rain Forest Aerial Tram, near the Guápiles Highway or, for an adventurous angle, take a canopy tour. It's best to walk or hike with a local guide—a good one points out plants and animals you would surely miss on your own.

Shopping

Many of the colorful goods sold in Costa Rica are actually made in Guatemala, Nicaragua, or Panama, but some local crafts are still practiced. The oxcart is the national symbol of Ticos' hardworking, self-reliant character and rural roots. Brightly painted carts come in all dimensions—from the size of a matchbook to full size. In Sarchí, in the Western Central Valley, the art of making oxcarts has been passed down through generations. Sarchí's artisans also work native hardwoods into bowls, boxes, toys, platters, and jewelry. In the capital, art and crafts galleries near the Parque Morazón and the northern suburb of Moravia have the best shopping. Wood-framed mirrors in the shape of forest creatures, bamboo mobiles of tropical fish, and leather rocking chairs are good buys. The outdoor crafts market beside the Museo Nacional is a fun place to browse, although most items are overpriced. A good place to buy anything from local music recordings to hand-painted ceramic tiles is the Annemarie Souvenir shop inside the Hotel Don Carlos, near the National Library. Coffee and rum make good gifts, too. Buy yours at any supermarket, where it's much cheaper than gift shops. Café Britt is one of the country's most popular brands; Volio, SunBurst, and Café Rey Tarrazú are also good, as is coffee roasted in Monteverde. Ron Centenario rum is good, but Flor de Caña, from Nicaragua, is even better.

Snorkeling & Scuba Diving

Along the Caribbean coast, the areas from Puerto Viejo de Talamanca to Gandoca-Manzanillo Wildlife Refuge and from Limón to Isla Uvita are good for snorkeling or diving. The Caribbean is clearest in October and November, when visibility can reach 30 m (100 feet). The country's largest reef, which has been severely damaged but still has plenty to admire, is protected within the Parque Nacional Cahuita. Pacific excursions depart from the southern zone's Drake Bay, and Flamingo, Ocotal, and Playa del Coco in the northern province of Guanacaste. The Pacific coast has less colorful coral but more big animals, such as manta rays, sea turtles, and even Whale Sharks. The best Pacific coast diving spot is Isla del Caño, near Drake Bay. The snorkeling is excellent around the rocky points that flank Bajo del Diablo and Paraíso, where you are guaranteed to encounter thousands of big fish. In the northwest, there are dozens of dive spots around Santa Catalina. Costa Rica's best dive spot, Cocos Island, must be visited on 9- or 10-day scuba trips aboard either the *Okeanos Aggressor* or the *Undersea Hunter*. For experienced divers only, this remote destination 600 km (375 mi) southwest of the mainland has waters teeming with manta rays and eight shark species, including Hammerhead and Whale sharks. Dive schools in San José offer PADI open-water diving courses, and some beach hotels allow noncertified divers to use scuba equipment for shallow dives of 15 m (49 feet) or less.

Surfing

Costa Rica is one of the world's most popular surfing destinations, but the waves—from the radical, experts-only reef break at Puerto Viejo de Talamanca to the mellower waves off Tamarindo on the Pacific—remain relatively uncrowded. The water is deliciously warm on both coasts and there are good waves year-round. The Central Pacific is the most popular surfing destination because it's close to San José and has plenty of diversity. The party town of Jacó has a fun beach break and is home to some of Costa Rica's best surfers and surfing facilities. It's an ideal base for trips to nearby Playa Hermosa, with a long beach and surfing competitions, and less-crowded Playa Panama. Near Puntarenas, the sand spit at the mouth of the Barranca River produces one of the world's longest left-breaking waves, although the water is polluted. If you surf, watch out for the all-too-common riptides. Lifeguards are rare.

About a dozen popular surf spots are scattered along the coast south of Tamarindo, and because of its excellent surf shop and many hotels and restaurants, it is a base for trips to Playas Langosta, Avellanas, and Negra. Playa Avellanas has eight surf spots ranging from beach breaks to rock-reef breaks to river-mouth sandbar breaks. A spectacular and well-known break is Witches Rock at Playa Naranjo, inside Parque Nacional Santa Rosa. Those willing to make the journey to Pavones and Matapalo, on Costa Rica's southern Pacific coast, can ride some of the world's longest waves. Dominical has also long drawn surfers to its consistent beach breaks, and a surf shop here rents, sells, and repairs surfboards. Puerto Viejo de Talamanca's Salsa Brava is one of the country's best breaks and one of the Atlantic coast's few surf spots. The water starts deep and runs quickly onto a shallow reef, forming seriously huge waves.

Volcanoes

Costa Rica has 100 or so volcanoes, seven of which are active today. Near San José, paved roads run right to the summit of Poás and Irazú volcanos. Volcán Irazú, Costa Rica's highest at 3,753 m (12,313 feet), last erupted on the day of U.S. President John F. Kennedy's visit in 1963. Ash showers followed by rain left the Central Valley covered in black soot and sludge for months. Dormant Volcán Barva, north of San José and cloaked in cloud forest, has two crater lakes and spectacular scenic overlooks as rewards for a steep all-day hike to the summit. A tough hike to the steaming crater at Rincón de la Vieja National Park, in the country's northern zone, reveals steaming fumaroles bubbling on the ground, and a cold river that collides with a warm sulfur spring. However, nothing in Costa Rica rivals the sheer mass and power of Volcán Arenal. By day, it is veiled in clouds, but at night, red hot molten lava can be seen oozing from the cone, a flirtatious dance with disaster. In August 2000, an eruption sent poisonous gases spilling down the eastern side of the mountain, killing three people who were watching from a supposedly safe distance. Geologists later found the popular Tabacón Hot Springs Resort and a campground to be in a high-risk zone. The government has since posted warning signs at the hot springs and various other points around the volcano.

White-Water Rafting

Half a dozen Olympic kayak teams spend the winter on the wild rivers of Costa Rica. Single- and multi-day trips are marked by gorgeous scenery, various difficulty levels, and year-round warm water. The country's rafting center is Turrialba, a hospitable, medium-size town on the banks of the Reventazón River and home to some of the country's best guides. The Reventazón and nearby Pacuare river are popular for their exciting runs and proximity to San José. Outfitters in La Fortuna, near Volcán Arenal, lead Class III and IV white-water trips on the narrow Río Peñas Blanca and Río Toro. Nearby, you can take half-day trips on the tamer but gorgeous Sarapiquí River, through verdant rain forest and tranquil towns. Near Quepos, rafting companies run three white rivers during rainy season—the Parrita, Naranjo, and Savegre. The country's longest white-water run is the Río General, a rousing raft or kayak trip that has long stretches of flat water and starts in San Isidro.

Wildlife

Costa Rica covers less than .03% of the Earth's surface but contains nearly 4% of the planet's animal species. The country has 4 species of monkeys, 6 types of wild cats, and 876 bird species, which is more than are found in the United States and Canada combined. About half of the country's mammals are bats; Costa Rica has 103 bat species, including Honduran White Bats—with a wingspan of ½ m (2 feet)—and 2 species of vampire bats, 1 that favors birds and 1 that prefers mammals. This abundance of wildlife is due in part to the country's geographical position on a land bridge between North America and South America. Flitting around Costa Rica are more than 2,000 species of butterflies, including the huge and incandescent Blue Morpho. Five of the world's 7 species of sea turtles nest in Costa Rica, including the Green Sea, Giant Leatherback, Loggerhead, Olive Ridley, and Hawksbill. More than 30 of the world's 80 species of dolphins, whales, and porpoises inhabit Costa Rican waters, and tour companies in Quepos and near the Gandoca-Manzanillo National Wildlife Refuge lead dolphin- and whale-watching excursions.

If you expect a National Geographic–style safari, you will be disappointed. Forests with dense foliage combined with the animals' skittish nature and excellent camouflage make them hard to see. Realistically, you can expect to see coatis, monkeys, and perhaps a sloth or agouti. Sightings of large mammals like wildcats and tapirs are extremely rare. You may see one of Costa Rica's 18 species of poisonous snakes if you wander off trail, but that's rare. (Snakes try to flee unless cornered or protecting a nest.) Seeing wildlife is mostly a matter of luck and patience, although talking with locals and hiring local guides increases your chances of being at the right place at the right time.

Windsurfing

Champion windsurfers have called Costa Rica's Lake Arenal one of the world's top five windsurfing spots. The man-made lake, which has spectacular views of one of the world's most active volcanos, is 35 km (22 mi) long, and the water temperature averages 23°C (73°F) from December to April. Unusually stable winds average 40 kph (25 mph); windsurfers can typically sail one sail all day. The best windsurfing is on the north and northwest sides of the lake. Coto Lake, a small, remote lake north of Arenal, has excellent conditions during the same months. Bolaños Bay, in Guanacaste near the border with Nicaragua, is the place for ocean windsurfing, with winds as strong and consistent as Arenal's. The closed bay combined with side-onshore winds makes it very safe. Conditions are best from November to April. Also near the border with Nicaragua, the waters off the beautiful beaches Cuajiniquil and Puerto Soley are tranquil, with direct offshore winds during the December-to-April dry season. Farther south, Tamarindo and Playa Flamingo also have good windsurfing conditions. Ocean windsurfing is not very popular in Costa Rica, so bring your own equipment unless you're staying at Bolaños Bay Resort, which rents everything you need.

FODOR'S CHOICE

The sights, restaurants, hotels, and other travel experiences on these pages are our editors' and writers' top picks—our Fodor's Choices. They're the best of their type in Costa Rica—not to be missed and always worth your time. In the destination chapters that follow, you will find all the details.

LODGING

$$$$ **Hotel Punta Islita,** Punta Islita. Overlooking the Pacific, this secluded resort offers luxurious rooms, splendid views, sybaritic spa treatments, and abundant peace and quiet.

$$$$ **Lapa Ríos,** Cabo Matapalo. Perched on a ridge in a private rain forest reserve, with views of the surrounding jungle and the ocean beyond, Lapa Ríos is a small hotel that brings you close to nature without skimping on the amenities.

$$$$ **Makanda by the Sea,** Manuel Antonio. This secluded Central Pacific retreat has gorgeous, luxury villas and a multicolored pool scattered through the rain forest, with ocean views, excellent food, abundant bird song, and a private beach down the hill.

$$$–$$$$ **Bosque del Cabo,** Cabo Matapalo. The rustic and yet world-class bungalows (love the garden showers) afford breathtaking views of the ocean, and the lodge's nonstop activities in and around the private nature reserve make a humdrum vacation unlikely.

$$$–$$$$ **Club del Mar,** Jacó. Spacious one- and two-story condominiums at this luxury resort are just steps from the beach in a quiet cove surrounded by huge tropical trees.

$$$–$$$$ **Finca Rosa Blanca Country Inn,** Volcán Barva. An enticing mix of Gaudíesque architecture, tropical hardwoods, verdant grounds, and attention to detail make this one of the Central Valley's nicest bed-and-breakfasts.

$$$–$$$$ **La Mariposa,** Manuel Antonio. The villas, deluxe rooms, and suites of this hilltop hotel are set between tropical gardens and the rain forest, and share one of the best views in the country—a sweeping panorama of forested hills, aquamarine Pacific, and offshore islands.

$$$–$$$$ **Peace Lodge,** Volcán Poás. The spacious, whimsical rooms here, at the edge of the cloud forest, are like something out of a fairy tale; they're a short walk away from spectacular waterfalls, butterfly gardens, and hordes of hummingbirds.

$$$–$$$$ **Xandari,** Alajuela. Whether you fix your vision on the clever design of the spacious villas, their sweeping Central-Valley views, or the birds and butterflies flitting through the surrounding tropical gardens, it's hard not to be enchanted by this unique inn and spa.

$$$ | **Hotel Capitán Suizo,** Tamarindo. Many consider this Swiss-run gem the finest beachfront lodging in Guanacaste. Its lush gardens provide a wonderful sense of seclusion not far from Tamarindo's resort-town amusements and gorgeous beach.

$$$ | **Sueño del Mar,** Playa Langosta. A sweet little white adobe B&B, with Balinese outdoor showers, fantastic breakfasts, charming gardens, and a perfect beach, sleeps just a handful for an intimate getaway. It can also accommodate a larger gathering of family or friends.

$$ | **Aviarios del Caribe,** Limón. See hundreds of bird species before breakfast at this nature-heavy B&B and wildlife refuge, where injured animals are nursed back to health. Service is highly personalized.

$$ | **Corcovado Lodge Tent Camp,** Corcovado National Park. Truly isolated from civilization, this collection of rustic tents facing the sea is literally steps from the beach and the rain forest. It's a fabulous place to end your Costa Rican adventure.

$$ | **Fonda Vela,** Monteverde. Built with local hardwoods, these spacious rooms have plenty of windows, the better to enjoy the surrounding forest and distant Gulf of Nicoya. The restaurant serves food to match the view.

$$ | **Hotel Grano de Oro,** San José. A welcome change from Costa Rica's standard "tear it down" approach is this restored lodging in a pair of early-20th-century houses, a quiet respite from the commotion of the city.

$$ | **Villa Decary,** Nuevo Arenal. Attentive service is just the icing on the cake at this lodging fixed to the side of a hill overlooking Lake Arenal. Enormous picture windows and private balconies mean stupendous views and great bird-watching.

$-$$ | **Cariblue Bungalows,** Puerto Viejo de Talamanca. Lovely wooden bungalows with thatched roofs near a palm-lined white-sand beach are designed to slow your internal clock to Caribbean time.

$-$$ | **El Encanto Bed & Breakfast,** Cahuita. An ultimate relaxation destination that realizes the owners' Zen Buddhist ideals, El Encanto has a serene tropical garden, yoga classes, and large healthful breakfasts.

$-$$ | **Le Bergerac,** San José. Deluxe rooms and extensive gardens have long kept this quiet, friendly hotel a notch above the competition, and the presence of L'Ile de France, one of the city's best restaurants, makes it that much more compelling.

$-$$ | **Pura Vida Hotel,** Alajuela. Perched on a ridge in the countryside north of town, this small collection of bungalows and rooms offers views of tropical gardens and distant Poás Volcano, a mere 10 minutes from the international airport.

$-$$ El Sol, Monteverde. Every spot is a vantage point in the two wooden cabins at this place, secluded even by Monteverde's standards.

BUDGET LODGING

$ Casa Pura Vida, Playa Hermosa. The three apartments in this Spanish-style building just steps away from the beach share a green-tile pool, a large patio, a playground, and a fully equipped kitchen, making it quite the deal.

$ Chalet Nicholas, Nuevo Arenal. The owners' gracious hospitality and ample bird-watching are yours at this quintessential B&B that overlooks Lake Arenal and its volcano.

¢-$ Hotel Aranjuez, San José. Lush gardens, abundant common areas, hearty breakfasts, and low prices make this little B&B in the quiet barrio of Aranjuez a real bargain.

¢-$ Hotel Vela Bar, Manuel Antonio. Nestled in the jungle a short walk from the beach, this tasteful little inn has small but attractive rooms and a good restaurant, all at very reasonable prices.

RESTAURANTS

$-$$$$ El Invernadero, Escazú. Hanging ferns, orchids, and candlelight provide the perfect setting to enjoy what is some of the country's best food—an inventive mix of Mediterranean dishes.

$-$$$ El Gran Escape, Quepos. Succulent and fresh seafood—from sashimi and *ceviche* (fish, shrimp, or octopus marinated in lime juice) to surf and turf—is the reason to visit this restaurant and bar. Bring in your own catch of the day to be prepared any way you like.

$$ L'Ile de France, San José. Costa Rica is not known for its fine dining, but this elegant spot, with its brilliant French cuisine, is a notable exception to the rule.

$-$$ Café Mundo, San José. From its lovely old wooden house in historic Barrio Amón, this popular café serves pastas, salads, meat, and seafood dishes at reasonable prices. The pastries are to die for.

$-$$ El Camarón Dorado, Brasilito. Beachside seating, plentiful portions of fresh seafood, and spectacular sunset vistas make this an excellent choice for a romantic evening or a relaxing end to your day.

$-$$ La Casona del Cafetal, Orosi Valley. On a coffee farm at the edge of a lake, this airy brick restaurant is a popular lunch stop, thanks to its inventive variation on Costa Rican cuisine.

$-$$ Cha Cha Chá, Cahuita. Simple but masterful international and eclectic cuisine is expertly prepared at this low-key place in the center of town.

| $-$$ | **Karolas,** Manuel Antonio. This collection of tables nestled in the rain forest offers one of the country's most enchanting dining experiences, thanks to abundant candles, illuminated foliage, and excellent food. |

| $-$$ | **La Pecora Nera,** Puerto Viejo de Talamanca. Light Tuscan fare is dished up with style and flamboyance in this roadside setting on the beach road outside of town. |

| $-$$ | **Playa de los Artistas,** Montezuma. Imaginative Mediterranean cuisine combines with a dramatic, sea-splashed setting to create one of the most romantic and memorable restaurants in the country. |

| $-$$ | **Tin Jo,** San José. The best of Asia—east, southeast, and south—is proffered at this restaurant a short walk southeast of downtown. |

BUDGET RESTAURANTS

| $ | **Chubascos,** Volcán Poás. It's a winning combination: brisk mountain air, delicious *refrescos* (fresh fruit drinks), green surroundings, and platters packed with traditional Costa Rican taste treats. |

| $ | **Lazy Wave Food Company,** Tamarindo. Don't miss these seriously irresistible lunches, dinners, and desserts at prices that are just as laughably irresistible. |

| ¢–$ | **Mirador del Cafetal,** Atenas. An obligatory stop on your way from San José to the Central Pacific coast, this open-air eatery perched above steep coffee fields offers an ample mix of Costa Rican and Mexican dishes to complement an impressive view. |

ARCHAEOLOGY

Guayabo National Monument, Turrialba. This is Costa Rica's most significant archeological site. The partially excavated ancient city was once home to 20,000 people. Abandoned in the 15th century, it was rediscovered in the late 19th century, and restoration began in 1968.

Museo de Jade and **Museo del Oro Precolombino,** San José. Costa Rica's most interesting archaeological artifacts are found in these museums in the capital.

BEACHES

Playa Carrillo, Sámara. This half-moon, palm-fringed beach is one of the most perfectly picturesque in the country.

Playa Guiones and **Playa Pelada,** near Nosara. These wild and wonderful beaches are so immense that both surfers and strollers can stake out private territory.

Playa Manuel Antonio, Manuel Antonio. In Manuel Antonio National Park this crescent of pale sand backed by lush foliage combines calm waters for swimming and snorkeling with exposure to rain-forest fauna.

Puerto Viejo de Talamanca. It's really a series of palm-fringed beaches (Negra, Cocles, Chiquita, and Punta Uva). All sway to a wonderfully laid-back Caribbean rhythm.

OUTDOOR ACTIVITIES

Bird-watching on the Osa Peninsula. If you already own a few field guides, then you've probably planned your trip with our feathered friends in mind. If you don't, sign up for a tour, borrow some binoculars, and get up at dawn—you won't regret your search for a Baird's Trogon or a Scarlet Macaw.

Caribbean jungle river trips. Slip into the rain forest the old-fashioned way. Adventures range from heart-stopping paddles down the hair-raising rapids of the Pacuare to lazy navigation of Caribbean canals. With luck you'll spot a Roseate Spoonbill, Purple Gallinule, Howler Monkey, crocodile, or caiman along the way.

Diving at Caño Island. The best diving in Costa Rica (apart from Cocos Island) is 20 km (12 mi) offshore from Drake Bay, in the Southern Pacific.

Monkeying around on a Canopy Tour, Monteverde. Do as the monkeys, and swing from tree to tree on a canopy tour, with locations in Monteverde and around the country. With mountain climbing gear fastening you in, you'll have a perspective of the Costa Rican rain forest from the top down.

Soaking in the Tabacón hot springs. From the Tabacón Resort's gorgeously landscaped series of hot springs, you can soak away your cares and take in views of magnificent and rumbling Volcán Arenal. Check safety conditions at this active volcano before going.

Surfing in Nicoya. The best spots to surf on the Nicoya Peninsula are Witch's Rock, Tamarindo, and Playa Negra.

White-water rafting on the Pacuare River, Turrialba. The boulder-strewn Pacuare churns and winds its way past some of Costa Rica's most spectacular scenery—lush canyons, waterfalls, and pristine rain forest—which makes the Class III–IV rafting trip down its rapids a mix of an adrenaline rush and contemplation of tropical nature.

PARKS

Volcan Poás National Park, Volcán Poás. Costa Rica's most visited park, because of its proximity to San José, Poás protects the top of a mildly active volcano, with its massive, smoking crater, lush cloud forest, and blue-green crater lake.

QUINTESSENTIAL COSTA RICA

Bird-watching. With 876 bird species—more than are found in the United States and Canada combined—Costa Rica has few spots where you don't see some interesting feathered creatures. Bring binoculars, hire a guide, and feast your eyes on the colors of the trogons, tanagers, toucans, parrots, and any of more than 50 species of hummingbirds.

Britt Coffee Tour, Heredia. Coffee is the crop on which Costa Rica was built, and this entertaining tour offers a fun and informative introduction to the history and cultivation of the "golden bean."

Pacific sunsets. There's something about the cloud formations, colors, and settings that makes these exemplary crepuscular productions. Flocks of diving pelicans scarfing up sardines often add foreground action.

Volcán Arenal erupting at night. Arenal's conical profile dominates the southern end of a lake, and thrills onlookers with regular incendiary performances. (Check safety conditions at this active volcano before going.)

ROMANTIC HIDEAWAYS

Cabinas El Sano Banano, Montezuma. Play castaways in your comfortable, cozy beach bungalows stranded on a beach, half a mile away from the nearest town.

Colores del Pacífico, Playa Flamingo. Chic and contemporary, this lodge clings to a cliff overlooking Flamingo Bay. Float in the infinity pool, laze in a hammock on a private veranda, and luxuriate in the exquisitely designed, very private bedrooms.

Makanda by the Sea, Manuel Antonio. This secluded Central Pacific retreat has gorgeous, luxury villas and a multicolored pool scattered through the rain forest, with ocean views, excellent food, abundant bird song, and a private beach down the hill.

La Paloma, Drake Bay. Live a tropical island fantasy on a forested headland that juts out onto Drake Bay, where breezy, secluded casitas are surrounded by garden and ocean.

Villa Caletas, Punta Leona. The elegant suites and villas sequestered in the rain forest of this mountaintop resort south of Punta Leona offer luxury, seclusion, and some of Costa Rica's most amazing views.

Xandari, Alajuela. These spacious, cleverly designed villas surrounded by tropical gardens offer seclusion and gorgeous Central-Valley views, and a short walk away is a full spa.

Curú National Wildlife Refuge, Paquera. Spider Monkeys, Jesus Christ Lizards, and birds abound at this Nicoya Peninsula refuge. You can walk the jungle trails or kayak the refuge's shores.

Manuel Antonio National Park. The small national park here may lack the diversity of other areas, but its animals have had enough exposure to people to make it easy to get close to them, and because there is as much forest outside the park as in it, you will see plenty of wildlife around the area's hotels and restaurants.

Marina Las Baulas National Park, Tamarindo. Set out in the darkness to witness a 500-pound Giant Leatherback Turtle struggling to shore to dig a deep hole with her flippers in which to lay close to 100 eggs in Nicoya's Playa Grande.

Monteverde Cloud Forest Reserve, Monteverde. Get up early in the morning to beat the crowds, and birds galore are yours for the viewing. And if the avian fates smile upon you, you just might catch a glimpse of Costa Rica's famed Resplendent Quetzal.

San Gerardo de Dota Valley. Nothing in the birding world rivals the sight of a male Resplendent Quetzal in full breeding plumage. Sightings of this colorful bird are almost guaranteed in this high-altitude valley.

Santa Rosa National Park, Guanacaste. Here, at one of the best places in Costa Rica to view mammals, you can see monkeys (Spider, White-faced Capuchin, and Howler), tapirs, coatis, and ocelots.

La Selva Biological Station, Puerto Viejo de Sarapiquí. The folks at this working field station throw open their gates and accompany you on some of the country's top guided nature walks.

Tortuguero National Park, Tortuguero. The name ("Turtle Region") says it all, and this is the country's premier site for watching the thousands-year-old ritual of egg laying, hatching, and return to the sea of four turtle species.

SMART TRAVEL TIPS

Finding out about your destination before you leave home means you won't squander time organizing everyday minutiae once you've arrived. You'll be more streetwise when you hit the ground as well, better prepared to explore the aspects of Costa Rica that drew you here in the first place. The organizations in this section can provide information to supplement this guide; contact them for up-to-the-minute details, and consult the A to Z sections that end each chapter for facts on the various topics as they relate to Costa Rica's many regions. Happy landings!

ADDRESSES

In Costa Rica, addresses are usually given in terms of how many meters the place is from a landmark. Street names and building numbers are not commonly used. Churches, stores, even large trees that no longer exist—almost anything can be a landmark, as long as everyone knows where it is, or where it used to be. A typical address in San José is *100 metros este y 100 metros sur de Más x Menos* (100 meters east and 100 meters south from the Más x Menos supermarket).

In towns and cities in Costa Rica, each block is assumed to be 100 meters, although some blocks may be much longer and some may be shorter. So, if someone tells you *"sigue recto 500 metros, y despues dobla a la izuierda 100 metros,"* they mean you should go straight five blocks, then turn left and go one block. In the countryside, people will estimate the distance between points and give it in meters (if close by) or in kilometers. These estimates are usually not very accurate.

Street numbers are used in downtown San José, where streets are laid out in a logical system, with odd-numbered streets east of Calle Central and even-numbered avenues south of this main thoroughfare. In other parts of the city, a business may have an "official" address with a street number, and an "unofficial" address like the one above. Ticos, as Costa Ricans call themselves, spend a lot of time asking people to describe where things are and are usually happy to help lost visitors.

AIR TRAVEL

Most people who come to Costa Rica fly to San José, though more and more flights are heading directly to Liberia. In the United States, Miami has the highest number of direct flights, but New York, Chicago, Los Angeles, Washington, D.C., and some other major cities also have direct flights. Flights from London usually stop in Madrid, Miami, Washington, D.C., or Mexico City. Flights from Canada usually connect through Chicago, Miami, or New York. From New Zealand and Australia, consult a travel agent, who will probably send you first to Los Angeles and then on to Costa Rica.

Heavy rains in the afternoons and evenings during the May-to-November green (rainy) season sometimes cause flights coming into San José to be rerouted to Panama City, where you may be forced to spend the night. In the rainy season, always take the earliest departure available.

Given Central America's often difficult driving conditions, distances that appear short on a map can represent hours of driving on dirt roads pocked with craters, so **consider domestic flights.** Because car-rental rates are so steep, flying can often actually be cheaper than driving.

Domestic flights impose a luggage weight limit of 13.6 kilograms (30 pounds)—*including* carry-ons, as the planes are tiny. Excess weight, if safety permits, is charged by the pound.

Don't buy a one-way ticket to Costa Rica—Costa Rican customs officials may ask you to prove you have a return ticket to leave the country.

CARRIERS

Continental flies twice daily from Houston and once from Newark. American flies daily from Miami and Dallas. Delta flies nonstop from Atlanta daily. United flies from Chicago and Los Angeles. You can also fly from Los Angeles via Mexico City on Mexicana. Central American airline Grupo TACA has flights from San Fran-

cisco, Los Angeles, Dallas, Houston, New Orleans, Miami, Washington, D.C., New York's JFK, Montréal, and Toronto. Some flights are direct. Martinair flies nonstop between Orlando, Florida, and San José both ways every Monday.

American Airlines flies from Heathrow to Miami, and Virgin Atlantic flies from Gatwick to Miami, where you can connect with flights to San José. You can fly from London to San José on Iberia, but you have to change planes in Madrid and Miami. United Airlines flies from Heathrow to Washington, D.C., connecting to Costa Rica via Mexico City.

Costa Rica has two domestic airlines, SANSA and NatureAir. SANSA flies from Juan Santamaría International Airport to Barra del Colorado, Coto 47, Drake Bay, Golfito, Liberia, Nosara, Palmar Sur, Puerto Jiménez, Punta Islita, Quepos, Samara, Tamarindo, Tambor, and Tortuguero. SANSA also flies between Quepos and Palmar Sur.

NatureAir has daily flights from Tobias Bolaños Airport, in the San José suburb of Pavas, to Barra del Colorado, Carrillo, Drake Bay, Golfito, Puerto Jiménez, Liberia, Nosara, Palmar Sur, Punta Islita, Quepos, Tamarindo, Tambor, and Tortuguero. More than a dozen flights run between those destinations, saving you the trouble of returning to San José. Copa, and Grupo TACA airlines have flights to Panama City, Panama, and Managua, Nicaragua.

Major Airlines American ☎ 800/433-7300 in U.S., 0208/222-8900 in U.K. ⊕ www.aa.com. **Continental** ☎ 800/231-0856 in U.S. ⊕ www.continental.com. **Delta** ☎ 800/221-1212 in U.S. ⊕ www.delta.com. **Iberia** ☎ 0208/222-8900 in the U.K. ⊕ www.iberia.com. **United Airlines** ☎ 800/241-6522 in U.S., 0845/844-4777 in U.K. **Virgin Atlantic** ☎ 0208/897-5040 in U.K. ⊕ www.virgin-atlantic.com.

Regional Airlines Copa ☎ 506/222-6640 ⊕ www.copaair.com. **Grupo TACA** ☎ 506/296-9353, 800/535-8780 in U.S. ⊕ www.grupotaca.com. **NatureAir** ☎ 506/220-3054 ⊕ www.natureair.com. **SANSA** ☎ 506/221-9414 or 506/441-8035 ⊕ www.flysansa.com.

CHARTER FLIGHTS

Charter flights within Costa Rica are not as expensive as one might think and can be an especially good deal if you are traveling with a group of four to eight people. If a group this size charters a small plane, the price per person will be only slightly more than taking a regularly scheduled domestic flight, and you can set your own departure time. Also, the country has dozens of airstrips that are accessible only by charter planes. Note that the charter companies listed here do not have English-speaking staff. Remote eco-lodges often arrange charter flights for their guests, and in most cases, it's worth the extra money and saves you valuable time.

Several charter companies in San José—including commercial airline NatureAir, which has some charter flights—offer flights to places not served by scheduled flights. Helinorte provides helicopter service. During the dry season, weekly charter flights serve Costa Rica from half a dozen American and Canadian cities, most landing in Liberia, Guanacaste. These flights are sold only as part of packages that include hotel stays. Departure cities for charters include Miami, Detroit, Philadelphia, Minneapolis, Atlanta, Dallas, and others. Ask a travel agent about charter options.

🛦 Charter Companies **Aerolineas Turisticas** ☎ 506/290-8413. **Aeronaves** ☎ 506/282-4033 in San José, 506/775-0278 in Golfito. **Helinorte** ☎ 506/232-7534. **NatureAir** ☎ 506/220-3054.

CHECK-IN & BOARDING

Always **ask your carrier about its check-in policy.** Plan to arrive at the airport about 2 hours before your scheduled departure time for domestic flights and 2½ to 3 hours before international flights. You may need to arrive earlier if you're flying from one of the busier airports or during peak air-traffic times. Arrive at least an hour before a domestic flight within Costa Rica. Note that when you fly out of Costa Rica, you'll have to pay a $26 airport departure tax at Juan Santamaría Airport.

Airlines routinely overbook planes. After volunteers, the first passengers to get bumped are those who checked in late and those flying on discounted tickets, so **get to the gate and check in as early as possible,** especially during peak periods.

CUTTING COSTS

Depending on the time of year and what airline specials are available, the cheapest way to arrive may be to combine a round-trip ticket from Miami with a separate round-trip ticket from your departure city in the United States or elsewhere. Airlines run specials throughout the year, but you can usually get the best deals from May to November, the rainy season in most of Costa Rica. Fares from Canada typically cost 25 to 50 percent more than those from the United States.

The least expensive airfares to Costa Rica are priced for round-trip travel and must usually be purchased in advance. Airlines generally allow you to change your return date for a fee; most low-fare tickets, however, are nonrefundable. **Call a number of airlines and check the Internet;** when you are quoted a good price, **book it on the spot**—the same fare may not be available the next day, or even the next hour. Always **check different routings** and look into using alternate airports. Also, price off-peak flights, which may be significantly less expensive than others. Travel agents, especially low-fare specialists (⇨ Discounts & Deals), are helpful.

Consolidators are another good source. They buy tickets for scheduled flights at reduced rates from the airlines, then sell them at prices that beat the best fare available directly from the airlines. Sometimes you can even get your money back if you need to return the ticket. Carefully read the fine print detailing penalties for changes and cancellations, purchase the ticket with a credit card, and **confirm your consolidator reservation with the airline.**

🛦 Consolidators **AirlineConsolidator.com** ☎ 888/468-5385 ⊕ www.airlineconsolidator.com; for international tickets. **Best Fares** ☎ 800/576-8255 or 800/576-1600 in U.S. ⊕ www.bestfares.com; $59.90 annual membership. **Cheap Tickets** ☎ 800/377-1000 or 888/922-8849 in U.S. ⊕ www.cheaptickets.com. **Expedia** ☎ 404/728-8787, 800/397-3342 in U.S. ⊕ www.expedia.com. **Hotwire** ☎ 920/330-9418 or 866/468-9473 ⊕ www.

hotwire.com. **Now Voyager Travel** ✉ 315 W. 49th St., Plaza Arcade, New York, NY 10019 ☎ 212/459-1616 🖶 212/243-2711 ⊕ www.nowvoyagertravel. com. **Onetravel.com** ⊕ www.onetravel.com. **Orbitz** ☎ 888/656-4546 ⊕ www.orbitz.com. **Priceline. com** ⊕ www.priceline.com. **Tico Travel** ☎ 800/493-8426 in U.S. **Travelocity** ☎ 888/709-5983 in U.S., 877/282-2925 in Canada, 0870/876-3876 in U.K. ⊕ www.travelocity.com.

ENJOYING THE FLIGHT

State your seat preference when purchasing your ticket, and then repeat it when you confirm and when you check in. For more legroom, you can request one of the few emergency-aisle seats at check-in, if you are capable of lifting at least 50 pounds—a Federal Aviation Administration requirement of passengers in these seats. Seats behind a bulkhead also offer more legroom, but they don't have underseat storage. Don't sit in the row in front of the emergency aisle or in front of a bulkhead, where seats may not recline.

Ask the airline whether a snack or meal is served on the flight. If you have dietary concerns, request special meals when booking. On long flights, try to maintain a normal routine, to help fight jet lag. At night, get some sleep. By day, eat light meals, drink water (not alcohol), and **move around the cabin** to stretch your legs. For additional jet-lag tips consult *Fodor's FYI: Travel Fit & Healthy* (available at bookstores everywhere). Smoking is prohibited on flights to Costa Rica.

FLYING TIMES

From New York, flights to San José are 5½ hours nonstop or 6–7 hours via Miami. From Los Angeles, flights are 8½ hours via Mexico; from Houston, 3½ hours nonstop; from Miami, 3 hours. Flying times to San José from Chicago, Toronto, London, and Sydney vary widely, depending on the routing and the number of connections.

HOW TO COMPLAIN

If your baggage goes astray or your flight goes awry, complain right away. Most carriers require that you **file a claim immediately.** The Aviation Consumer Protection Division of the Department of Transportation publishes *Fly-Rights,* which discusses airlines and consumer issues and is available on-line. You can also find articles and information on mytravelrights.com, the Web site of the nonprofit Consumer Travel Rights Center.

🔲 Airline Complaints **Aviation Consumer Protection Division** ✉ U.S. Department of Transportation, C-75, Room 4107, 400 7th St. SW, Washington, DC 20590 ☎ 202/366-2220 ⊕ airconsumer.ost.dot.gov. **Federal Aviation Administration Consumer Hotline** ✉ for inquiries: FAA, 800 Independence Ave. SW, Washington, DC 20591 ☎ 800/322-7873 ⊕ www.faa.gov.

RECONFIRMING

Always confirm international flights at least 72 hours ahead of the scheduled departure time. Check the status of your flight before you leave for the airport. You can do this on your carrier's Web site, by linking to a flight-status checker (many Web booking services offer these), or by calling your carrier or travel agent.

Once in Costa Rica, call your airline's office in San José about three days before your return flight to reconfirm, and again the day before you are scheduled to return home to make sure your flight time hasn't changed.

AIRPORTS

Juan Santamaría International Airport (SJO) is Costa Rica's main airport. It's about 15 mi (30 minutes by car) north of downtown San José, in the suburb of Alajuela. The SANSA terminal for domestic flights is here. The tiny Tobías Bolaños airport, in the San José suburb of Pavas, serves domestic airline NatureAir and domestic charter companies. The country's other international airport is the Daniel Oduber International Airport (LIR), a small airport near Liberia. This airport is about five hours by car from San José.

If you are visiting several regions of the country, flying into San José, in the center of the country, is the best option. Flying into Liberia makes sense if you are planning to spend your whole vacation in Guanacaste. Charter companies from the United States and Canada fly into the Liberia airport and take clients directly to all-inclusive resorts in Guanacaste. For this purpose, the Liberia airport is wonderful, since bus travel time between the airport and most of the resorts is less than two hours. Liberia itself has decent hotels, but the city is not much of a tourist destination. It's better to head straight from the airport to the beaches to start your vacation.

At this writing, the airlines using the Liberia airport are charters booked as part of packages and major airlines Delta (five arrivals weekly from Atlanta), Continental (five arrivals weekly from Houston), Northwest (one arrival weekly from Minneapolis), and American (three arrivals weekly from Miami).

At Juan Santamaría Airport in San José you need to get to the airport two hours before your flight, and expect long lines to check in. Liberia is a tiny airport, so check-in times are usually shorter than at Juan Santamaría, but airlines still request that you arrive 90 minutes before international departures. Juan Santamaría is a full-service airport with many arrivals and departures each day, so if you miss your flight or have some other unexpected mishap, you're better off there. Fares are usually lower to San José than to Liberia, but airlines occasionally offer specials, so always check rates to both airports.

Besides the larger airports listed here, other places where planes land aren't exactly airports. They more resemble a carport with a landing strip, at which a SANSA or NatureAir representative arrives just minutes before a plane is due to land or take off. The informality of domestic air service means you might want to **purchase your domestic airplane tickets in advance,** although you can buy them once you're in the country. You can buy tickets from SANSA and NatureAir via their Web sites (⇨ Air Travel).

🛈 Airport Information **Aeropuerto Internacional Daniel Oduber** ☎ 506/668–1010. **Aeropuerto Internacional Juan Santamaría** ☎ 506/443–2622 or 506/443–2942. **Aeropuerto Internacional Tobías Bolaños** ✉ 3 km (2 mi) west of San José, Pavas ☎ 506/232–2820.

AIRPORT TRANSFERS

At Juan Santamaría Airport, all international passengers are funneled out one tiny doorway to an underground fume-filled parking area, which is flanked with hordes of tour operators waiting for arriving visitors and cabdrivers calling out "Taxi?" If you're with a tour, you need only look for a representative of your tour company with a sign that bears your name. Others should **take an orange or red cab,** called *taxi unidos,* which work only from the airport; avoid *collectivos,* or minivans—they're almost the same price as a taxi, but the van is often crammed with other passengers, and you'll have to make stops at their hotels, which in San José traffic can really make your transfer another journey in itself. Also avoid *piratas* (pirates), or unregulated cabs. Take any red or orange cab identified with a number and that has a meter.

At Daniel Oduber Airport in Liberia, official red taxis, piratas, and hotel vans wait to meet each flight. When making a hotel reservation for the first night, ask if the hotel will provide a cab or shuttle. If not, ask how much you should expect to pay for ground transportation from the airport. Fares vary widely, depending on how far away the hotel is and how many people are traveling together. In Guanacaste, it's usually safe to take pirata taxis, but always negotiate the price before getting into the cab.

Most travelers to Costa Rica spend the first night in San José and leave for their domestic destination the next morning out of the SANSA terminal next to the international airport or out of tiny Tobias Bolaños airport. Rarely does an international flight get into San José early enough to make a domestic connection, as the weather for flying is typically clear until about noon only. When given a choice, **always take the earliest morning flight.** Also, domestic flights to the far south may not be direct. You might stop in Golfito first, then continue on to Puerto Jiménez, for example.

DUTY-FREE SHOPPING

San José's Juan Santamaría International Airport is a good place to buy souvenirs, including Costa Rican coffee, wood and leather crafts, bottled sauces for cooking, and T-shirts. Prices in the airport are higher than at other souvenir shops, but the extra money may be worth it to avoid carrying souvenirs around during your vacation. Unlike many Latin American countries, Costa Rica does not have a large artisan community and doesn't produce spectacular crafts. The types and quality of souvenirs you find in the airport are generally the same as the products you find elsewhere in the country.

BIKE TRAVEL

Costa Rica has fantastic mountain biking trails, but they are hard to find on your own. Bad road conditions, bad weather, and erratic drivers can make biking on your own in Costa Rica problematic. The best option if you want to cycle seriously is to sign up with a tour company that specializes in bike tours (⇨ Tours & Packages). Multiday road bike tours and mountain biking tours are available.

Bikes are used for transportation by Ticos who live in flat rural areas. However, cyclists are killed each year by motorists, and roads don't have shoulders or bike lanes. Bikes are available for rent in beach towns and La Fortuna, usually for $5 to $10 per day. They're a great way to get around small towns and explore off-road trails, and the terrain is flat and not too difficult. The topographical maps (not biking maps per se) sold at the San José department stores Universal and Lehmann include unpaved roads that are often perfect for mountain biking.

Inspect your bike carefully before you leave the rental shop: often the equipment is not in good repair. Always lock your bike, even in the sleepiest-looking towns. If you value your life, don't try biking in San José.

F Bike Maps **Lehmann** ⊠ Avda. Central between Cs. 1 and 3, Centro Colón, San José. **Universal** ⊠ Avda. Central between Cs. 0 and 1, Centro Colón, San José.

BIKES IN FLIGHT

Most airlines accommodate bikes as luggage, provided they are dismantled and boxed; check with individual airlines about packing requirements. Some airlines sell bike boxes, which are often free at bike shops, for about $15 (bike bags can be considerably more expensive). International travelers often can substitute a bike for a piece of checked luggage at no charge; otherwise, the cost is about $100. U.S. and Canadian airlines charge $40–$80 each way.

BOAT & FERRY TRAVEL

Regular passenger and car ferries connect Puntarenas with Playa Naranjo, Tambor, and Pacquera, on the south end of the Nicoya Peninsula. These ferries take you to the southern and mid-Nicoya Peninsula. Ferries are also an important part of the transportation in the Southern Pacific zone. The Taiwan Friendship Bridge (also called the Río Tempisque Bridge), which opened in 2003, has eliminated the time-consuming ferry trip that used to be the only way to cross the Tempisque River. The toll bridge costs 400 colónes ($0.95) at this writing, and spans the section of the river near Puerto Nípero, crossing the mouth of the river to end near Barra Honda National Park. It is the preferred travel route to Guanacaste.

FARES & SCHEDULES

Cash is the only method of payment accepted by ferries. Ferries cost $1–$2 for passengers and $8–$12 for cars. Printed schedules are usually posted at the ticket offices on the docks where ferries embark. No other printed schedules are available.

The Puntarenas–Playa Naranjo Ferry leaves the ferry terminal in Puntarenas at 6 AM, 10 AM, 2:20 PM, and 7 PM and returns from Naranjo at 7:30 AM, 12:50 PM, 5 PM, and 9 PM. Two ferries leave Puntarenas for Paquera, on the southern tip of the Nicoya Peninsula eight times daily, roughly every two hours between 4:30 AM and 7 PM.

F Boat & Ferry Information **Asociación Desarrollo Integral de Paquera** ☎ 506/641-0118 or 641-0515. **Coontramar** ☎ 506/661-1069. **Naviera Tambor** ☎ 506/661-2084.

BUS TRAVEL

Reliable, inexpensive bus service covers much of the country. Most Costa Ricans don't have cars, so buses go almost everywhere. Several private companies leave San José from a variety of departure points—there is no main bus station. Buses range from huge, modern, air-conditioned beasts with lead-foot drivers, bathrooms, and an occasional movie to something a little less new and a whole lot more sweaty and crowded. Tall people may be uncomfortable, because there isn't much legroom; some of the vehicles are converted school buses. Buses usually leave and arrive on time and sometimes even leave a few minutes early, so get to your stop before the scheduled departure time. Buses are inexpensive and usually well maintained. Fares for long-distance routes on public buses are usually $5–$10 one way. For schedules and bus terminal information, *see* Bus Travel *in* the A to Z sections at the end of each chapter.

Bus routes to popular beach destinations sell out quickly, so buy your ticket in advance. In rural areas and on city bus routes in San José, standing in the aisles is permitted, but on long-distance routes from San José, everyone must have a seat. Sometimes tickets include seat numbers, which are usually printed on the tops of the chairs. Smoking is not permitted on buses.

Watch your luggage on the bus. Don't put your belongings in the overhead bin unless you have to, and if you do, keep your eye on them. If someone—even a person who looks like an employee of the bus line—offers to put your luggage on the bus or in the luggage compartment underneath for you, politely decline. If you must put your luggage underneath the bus, try to get off quickly when you arrive at your destination and go around to retrieve it.

The main inconvenience of buses is that you usually have to return to San José to travel between outlying regions. For example, if you want to take public buses between Quepos/Manuel Antonio and Playa Tamarindo, you have to connect in San José, which is significantly out of the way. Two private bus companies, Gray Line Tours Fantasy Bus and Interbus, offer an alternative to traveling through the capital. These buses, which are much more expensive than public buses, cost about $15–$55 one-way but can take hours off your trip. Within San José, taxis are inexpensive and much faster than city buses. City buses are crowded and uncomfortable if you have a lot of luggage.

Car seats are permitted but aren't practical because most of the buses are former school buses that don't have seat belts. Most have bench-style seats rather than individual bucket-style seats, and many bus seats aren't wide enough to accommodate a car seat.

CLASSES

There are no classes of bus service in Costa Rica. Usually, only one company serves each destination. Several companies serve destinations in the Central Valley, including Heredia, Cartago, and Alajuela, but service on all of them is similar. Bus travel in Costa Rica is formal, meaning no pigs or chickens inside and no people or luggage on the roof. Buses are in good repair but not air-conditioned.

FARES & SCHEDULES

Bus companies don't have printed bus schedules to give out, although departure times may be printed on a sign at the bus company's office and ticket window. Hotels usually know where bus stops are, when buses leave, and how much they cost. Otherwise, visit or call the bus company's office. Be prepared for bus-company employees and bus drivers to speak Spanish only.

Buses to popular beach and mountain destinations often sell out on the weekends and the day before and after a holiday. It's also difficult to get tickets back to San José on Sunday afternoon. Some bus companies take reservations over the phone, but others require you to buy a ticket in person. Tickets are sold at bus stations and on the buses themselves; you must pay with cash. Buy your ticket at the ticket window if there is one. The only way to reserve a seat is to buy your ticket ahead of time. On longer routes, buses stop midway at modest restaurants. Near the ends of their runs many nonexpress buses turn into large taxis, dropping passengers off one by one at their destinations; to save time, take a *directo* (express) bus.

There are no multiday or multitrip bus passes in Costa Rica. Infants and children younger than three years of age travel free when they sit on their parents' laps.

PAYING
Cash is the only form of payment accepted for bus trips.

RESERVATIONS
Buy your tickets a day or more ahead of time for popular beach destinations such as Jaco and Manuel Antonio. Bus tickets must be bought in person by going to the company's office with cash. A few hotels in smaller resort towns sell bus tickets or serve as bus stops, and some hotels in San José buy tickets for their guests. Outside of San José, always ask at your hotel for the local bus schedule and bus stop locations, because both change frequently. Arrive at the bus station or bus stop at least half an hour before your bus is scheduled to depart. It's common for buses to depart early, especially in rural areas. Many buses sell out before the day of departure, so play it safe and buy your ticket ahead of time.

✈ Atlantic Lowlands & Pacific Coast Bus Companies **Autotransportes Sarapiquí** ☎ 506/257-6854. **Empresarios Guapilenos** ☎ 506/710-7780. **Transportes Caribeños** ☎ 506/257-6854. **Transportes Mepe** ☎ 506/257-8129.

✈ Central Pacific Bus Companies **Transportes Delio Morales** ☎ 506/223-5567. **Transportes Jacó** ☎ 506/223-1109.

✈ Central Valley Bus Companies **Empresarios Unidos** ☎ 506/222-0064. **Sacsa** ☎ 506/223-5350. **Transtusa** ☎ 506/222-4464. **Tuasa** ☎ 506/222-5325.

✈ Nicoya Peninsula Bus Companies **Empresa Alfaro** ☎ 506/685-5032. **Empresarios Unidos** ☎ 506/222-0064. **Pulmitan** ☎ 506/222-1650.

✈ Northern Guanacaste & Alajuela Bus Companies **Tralapa** ☎ 506/221-7202. **Transportes La Cañera** ☎ 506/222-3006. **Transportes Tilarán** ☎ 506/695-5611, 222-3854 in San José.

✈ Private Bus Companies **Gray Line Tours Fantasy Bus** ☎ 506/220-2126. **Interbus** ☎ 506/283-5573 ⊕ www.interbusonline.com.

✈ Southern Pacific Bus Companies **Musoc** ☎ 506/222-2422. **Tracopa-Alfaro** ☎ 506/222-2666. **Transportes Blanco Lobo** ☎ 506/257-4121.

BUSINESS HOURS
Business hours are about the same from region to region and don't differ much from cities to rural areas and resorts. Most shops and offices are open 8–6. Government offices, except for the Tourism Institute, close at 4 PM. In rural areas and smaller cities, some shops and offices close at lunch for an hour or more. This practice is going out of fashion in San José. Businesses usually close only on legal holidays, some of which are religious holidays. In small towns and rural areas, nothing is open on Sunday. In San José and resorts, supermarkets and some restaurants are open Sunday.

BANKS & OFFICES
Most state banks are open weekdays 9–3, and some are open Saturday morning. Several branches of Banco Nacional are open until 6. Private banks—Scotia, Banco Banex, and Banco de San José—tend to keep longer hours and are usually the best places to change U.S. dollars and traveler's checks. At Juan Santamaría International Airport, a branch of the Banco de San José is open every day from 5 AM to 10 PM.

GAS STATIONS
There are 24-hour gas stations near most cities, especially along the Pan-American Highway. Most other stations are open from about 7 to 7, sometimes until midnight.

MUSEUMS & SIGHTS
Museums open at 8:30, 9, or 10 AM. and close at 4, 4:30, or 5 PM. Some of Costa Rica's public museums are closed Monday.

PHARMACIES
Pharmacies throughout the country are generally open from 8 to 8, though it's best to consult with your hotel's staff to be sure. Some pharmacies in San José affiliated with clinics stay open 24 hours. In the Central Valley, the Fischel Pharmacy (⇨ Emergencies) stays open until midnight.

SHOPS
In rural areas, supermarkets are usually not open on Sunday. Throughout the country, other stores and offices, and many restaurants, are closed on Sunday. Most shops are open weekdays 8–6 and Saturday 8–1.

CAMERAS & PHOTOGRAPHY

Photographic opportunities abound in Costa Rica, but don't expect to take pictures of jaguars or tapirs. Large animals are very elusive; you could live your whole life in Costa Rica and not see them. Consider bringing a macro lens, because some of the best shots are of insects, leaves, flowers, and other tiny wonders. You should be able to find monkeys and toucans willing to appear in your photos. Sunsets off Pacific beaches, panoramas of the forest canopy, and pictures of people are obligatory shots. Always ask permission before taking pictures of locals. You will not be allowed to take pictures when watching turtles nest, as any light can deter them from nesting. The *Kodak Guide to Shooting Great Travel Pictures* (available at bookstores everywhere) is loaded with tips.

 Photo Help **Kodak Information Center** ☎ 800/242-2424 ⊕ www.kodak.com.

EQUIPMENT PRECAUTIONS

Humidity and rain are the biggest problems facing photographers in Costa Rica. Take plenty of resealable plastic bags for lenses and other camera equipment, and consider buying a dry bag, sold in outdoors stores, for your camera. **Don't pack film and equipment in checked luggage,** where it is much more susceptible to damage. X-ray machines used to view checked luggage are extremely powerful and therefore are likely to ruin your film. Try to **ask for hand inspection of film,** which becomes clouded after repeated exposure to airport X-ray machines, and **keep videotapes and computer disks away from metal detectors.** Always **keep film, tape, and computer disks out of the sun.** Carry an extra supply of batteries, and **be prepared to turn on your camera, camcorder, or laptop** to prove to airport security personnel that the device is real.

FILM & DEVELOPING

Although travelers are technically allowed to bring only six rolls of film into the country, customs agents almost never check. Kodak, Fuji, Mitsubishi, and AGFA film is widely available. In rural areas and smaller shops, check the expiration date of film. Most film costs at least 20% more in Costa Rica than in the United States, so try to **bring along enough film for your trip.** Plenty of shops in San José develop film, usually the same day, but they tend to change the chemicals less often than they should, so you risk getting prints of poor quality.

 Local Labs **Dima Color** ⊠ 300 m east of U.S. Embassy, Pavas ☎ 506/231-4130. **Rapi Foto** ⊠ C. Central at Avda. 5, Centro Colón, San José ☎ 506/223-7640.

VIDEOS

The system used in Costa Rica is NTSC—the same as in North America. Prices for blank videotapes and DV tapes are slightly higher than in the United States and Canada.

CAR RENTAL

Most rental car companies use late-model imported economy cars such as Hyundai Excel and four-wheel-drive vehicles including Gran Vitara and Suzuki Samurai. Midsize and luxury sedans are not usually available. Most cars in Costa Rica have manual transmissions; you should specify when making the reservation if you want an automatic transmission. Many travelers shy away from renting a car in Costa Rica, if only for fear of the road conditions. Indeed, this is not an ideal place to drive: in San José, traffic is bad and car theft is rampant (look for guarded parking lots or hotels with lots); in rural areas, roads are often unpaved or potholed. The greatest deterrent of all might be the extremely high rental rates.

Still, having your own wheels gives you more control over your itinerary and the pace of your trip. If you decide to go for it, you'll have to choose which type of vessel to rent: a standard vehicle, fine for most destinations, or a *doble-tracción* (four-wheel drive), often essential to reach the more remote parts of the country, especially during the rainy season. These can cost roughly twice as much as an economy car and should be booked well in advance. If you plan to rent any kind of vehicle between December 15 and January 3, or during Holy Week, **reserve several months ahead of time.**

Costa Rica has around 50 international and local car-rental firms, the larger of which have several offices around San José. At least a dozen rental offices line San José's Paseo Colón, and most large hotels have representatives. For a complete listing, look in the local phone directory once you arrive, under *alquiler de automóviles*.

It is not common for travelers to hire a car with a driver, but at $75 per day plus the driver's food, it is almost the same price as renting a four-wheel drive. Some drivers are also knowledgeable guides; others just drive. To find a list of these services, check the *Tico Times* classified ads. The *Tico Times* is published on Friday and is available at supermarkets, souvenir shops, bookstores, and hotels.

CUTTING COSTS

Most car rental firms are in San José and at the Juan Santamaría International Airport. It is easier to pick up and return rental cars at the airport, and the price is the same. You may be able to save money by renting cars from private individuals who advertise in classified ads in the *Tico Times*, but there are no guarantees on the condition of the cars. Most local firms are affiliated with international car-rental chains and offer the same guarantees and services as their branches abroad. Check cars thoroughly for damage before you sign the rental contract. Even tough-looking four-wheel-drive vehicles should be coddled because they can be damaged by potholes, fresh and salt water, and other common Costa Rican road hazards. The charges levied by rental companies for damage—no matter how minor—are outrageous even by U.S. or European standards. For a good deal, **call directly to Costa Rica or book through a travel agent who will shop around.**

Do **look into wholesalers,** companies that do not own fleets but rent in bulk from those that do and often offer better rates than traditional car-rental operations. Prices are best during off-peak periods. Rentals booked through wholesalers often must be paid for before you leave home.

🚗 Rental Agencies **Alamo** ☎ 506/233-7733, 800/ 522-9696 in U.S. ⊕ www.alamo.com. **Avis** ☎ 506/ 293-2222, 800/331-1084 in U.S., 800/879-2847 in Canada, 0870/606-0100 in U.K., 02/9353-9000 in Australia, 09/526-2847 in New Zealand ⊕ www. avis.com. **Budget** ☎ 506/223-3284, 800/527-0700 in U.S., 0870/156-5656 in U.K. ⊕ www.budget.com. **Dollar** ☎ 506/257-1585, 800/800-6000 in U.S., 0124/622-0111 in U.K. (where it's affiliated with Sixt), 02/9223-1444 in Australia ⊕ www.dollar.com. **Economy** ☎ 506/231-5410. **Elegante** ☎ 506/257-0026. **Hertz** ☎ 506/221-1818, 800/654-3001 in U.S., 800/ 263-0600 in Canada, 0870/844-8844 in U.K., 02/ 9669-2444 in Australia, 09/256-8690 in New Zealand ⊕ www.hertz.com. **Hola** ☎ 506/231-5666. **National** ☎ 506/290-8787, 800/227-7368 in U.S., 0870/600-6666 in U.K. ⊕ www.nationalcar.com. **Pan American** ☎ 506/223-5959.
🚗 Wholesalers **Auto Europe** ☎ 207/842-2000, 800/223-5555 in U.S. 🖷 207/842-2222 ⊕ www. autoeurope.com.

INSURANCE

When driving a rented car you are generally responsible for any damage to or loss of the vehicle as well as for any property damage or personal injury that you may cause. Insurance issued by car-rental agencies in Costa Rica usually has a very high deductible. Before you rent, see what coverage your personal auto-insurance policy and credit cards provide.

RATES

High-season rates in San José begin at $45 a day and $290 a week for an economy car with air-conditioning, manual transmission, unlimited mileage, and obligatory insurance; but rates fluctuate considerably according to demand, season, and company. Rates for a four-wheel-drive vehicle during high season are $60–$90 a day and $400–$500 per week. Smaller Tico companies tend to be cheaper than international franchises. The *Tico Times* English-language newspaper has good deals, but conditions vary greatly and insurance is not always an option. When renting a car, **ask whether the rate includes the mandatory $15 daily fee for collision insurance.** Some firms don't charge the fee for economy cars but do for four-wheel-drive vehicles. Often companies will also require a $1,000 deposit, payable by credit card.

REQUIREMENTS & RESTRICTIONS

Car seats are compulsory for children under four years old, but many Costa Rican drivers don't use them. Make sure you specify that you need a car seat when booking a rental car. Rental cars may not be driven across borders to Nicaragua and Panama. Seat-belt use is compulsory in the front seat. To rent a car with an international agency you need a driver's license, a valid passport, and a credit card; you must also be at least 25 years of age. If you use a local company, you must be 21.

SURCHARGES

Before you pick up a car in one city and leave it in another, **ask about drop-off charges or one-way service fees,** which can be substantial. Note, too, that some rental agencies charge extra if you return the car before the time specified in your contract. To avoid a hefty refueling fee, **fill the tank just before you turn in the car,** but be aware that gas stations near the rental outlet may overcharge. It's almost never a deal to buy the tank of gas that's in the car when you rent it; the understanding is that you'll return it empty, but some fuel usually remains. Car seats cost about $3–$5 per day. Additional drivers are about $5–$10 per day.

CAR TRAVEL

You can use your own driver's license in Costa Rica, but you must carry your passport showing that you entered the country less than 90 days ago. Driving can be a challenge, but it's a great way to explore certain regions, especially Guanacaste, the Atlantic Lowlands, and the Caribbean coast (apart from Tortuguero and Barra del Colorado). Keep in mind that mountains and poor road conditions make most trips longer than you'd normally expect. If you want to visit a few different far-flung areas and have a short amount of time, domestic flights are a better option.

In the rainy season, you must have a four-wheel-drive vehicle to reach Monteverde and some destinations in Guanacaste. Car trips to Northern Guanacaste from San José can take an entire day, so flying is probably better if you don't have long to spend in the country. Flying is definitely better than driving for visiting the Southern Pacific zone of Puerto Jiménez, Golfito, Drake Bay, and so on.

When visiting the Atlantic coast by car, remember that fog often covers the Braulio Carrillo mountains after noon, making driving hazardous. Don't plan to cross this area in the afternoon. The same holds true for trips to the Southern Zone, where the Cerro de la Muerte mountain is often covered with fog in the afternoons. Driving to the Central Pacific beaches, Arenal Volcano, and destinations in the Central Valley is pleasant, but be alert, because roads are in poor condition and winding, and drivers tend to pass on blind curves. Driving at night throughout the country is not recommended, because roads are poorly lighted and many don't have painted center lines or shoulder lines.

🚗 Auto Clubs **American Automobile Association** (AAA) ☎ 800/564-6222 in North America. **Australian Automobile Association** ☎ 02/6247-7311 in Australia. **Automobile Association** (AA) ☎ 0870/600-0371 in U.K. **Canadian Automobile Association** (CAA) ☎ 613/247-0117 in North America. **New Zealand Automobile Association** ☎ 09/377-4660 in New Zealand. **Royal Automobile Club** (RAC) ☎ 0800/015-4435 in U.K.

EMERGENCY SERVICES

Costa Rica has no highway emergency service organization. In Costa Rica, 911 is the nationwide number for accidents. Traffic police are scattered around the country, but Costa Ricans are very good about stopping for people with car trouble. Local car-rental agencies can give you a list of numbers to call in case of accidents or car trouble.

GASOLINE

Gas is more expensive in rural areas, and gas stations can be few and far between. Try to fill your tank in cities. Major credit cards are widely accepted. There are no self-service pumps or pumps that accept credit cards. It is customary to tip the attendant 100 colones. Ask the attendant if you want a receipt, which is called a *factura*. Regular unleaded gasoline is called *regular* and high-octane unleaded is called *super*. Gas is sold by the liter. Cost at this writing is 66¢ per liter ($2.50 per gallon) for regular and 69¢ per liter ($2.62 per gallon) for super.

PARKING
A parking lot is always better than street parking. If you must park on the street, try to park where you can see your car. Always lock your car, and don't leave valuables in sight. Accept the services of local men or boys who offer to watch your car, and pay them the equivalent of $1 per hour when you return. There are very few parking meters, almost none outside San José. They take 50- and 100-colón coins. Parking lots are easy to find in San José and other cities. Parking costs about $1 per hour. Most lots close between 9 and 11 PM, so always inquire about closing times before leaving your car.

Parking regulations are strictly enforced in San José, and police may tow your car or give you a ticket for up to $30. In rural areas, parking regulations are less strictly enforced. If you get a ticket in a rental car, always give the ticket to the company. **Park overnight in a locked garage or guarded lot,** as Central American insurance may hold you liable if your rental car is stolen. Most hotels, barring the least expensive, offer secure parking with a guard or locked gates, as car theft is rife.

ROAD CONDITIONS
San José is terribly congested during the week during morning and afternoon rush hours (7–9 AM and 4–6 PM). Avoid returning to the city on Sunday evening, when traffic to San José from the Pacific-coast beaches backs up for hours. In San José, roads are generally in good condition, but in the countryside conditions vary. During the rainy season, roads are in much worse shape throughout the city.

San José has many one-way streets and traffic circles. Streets in the capital are narrow. Pedestrians are supposed to have the right of way but do not in reality, so be alert when walking. The local driving style is erratic and aggressive but not fast, because road conditions don't permit too much speed. Frequent fender benders tie up traffic. Keep your windows rolled up in the center of the city, because thieves will reach into your car at stoplights and snatch your purse, jewelry, and so on.

Outside of San José, you'll run into long stretches of unpaved road. Frequent hazards in the countryside are potholes, landslides during the rainy season, and cattle on the roads. Drunk drivers are a hazard throughout the country on weekend nights.

ROAD MAPS
Local road maps are available at gas stations and tourist information offices for about $10. Bookstores in San José that sell maps include Librería Universal, Librería Lehmann, and Seventh Street Books (⇨ Shopping *in* Chapter 1.)

RULES OF THE ROAD
The highway speed limit in Costa Rica is usually 90 kph (54 mph), which drops to 60 kph (36 mph) in residential areas. Speed limits are rigorously enforced in all regions of the country. Seat belts are required, though this is not rigorously enforced. *Alto* means "stop" and *Ceda* means "yield." Right turns on red are permitted except where signs indicate otherwise, but in San José this is usually not possible because of one-way streets and pedestrian crossings.

Local drunk driving laws are strict. Policemen who stop drivers for speeding and drunk driving are often looking for payment on the spot—essentially a bribe. Whether you're guilty or not, you'll get a ticket if you don't give in. Ask for a ticket instead of paying the bribe. It discourages corruption, and if you bring the ticket to your car-rental company, they might pay it on your behalf. If you think it's in your best interest to pay the bribe, $20 is usually enough to get out of a speeding ticket and $50 is usually acceptable for a drunk driving charge.

Car seats are required for children ages four and under, but car-seat laws are not rigorously enforced. Many Tico babies and children ride on their parents' laps. Children are allowed in the front seat.

There are plenty of questionable drivers on Costa Rican highways; **be prepared for harebrained passing on blind corners, tail-**

gating, and failing to signal. Watch, too, for two-lane roads that feed into one-lane bridges with specified rights-of-way. Look out for potholes, even in the smoothest sections of the best roads.

You can drive over Costa Rica's borders into Panama and Nicaragua, but not in a rental car—vehicles rented in one country cannot be taken into the next.

CHILDREN IN COSTA RICA

Costa Ricans are very fond of children and are tolerant of them at restaurants, museums, and other attraction. Thanks to high safety and health standards, Costa Rica is popular with traveling families. Most of the health problems you might associate with the tropics are rare or nonexistent in Costa Rica (though they do exist in neighboring Nicaragua), and the country's most popular destinations have plenty to offer kids. Beware of dangerous currents at many popular beaches when the surf is up.

The *Tico Times,* published (in English) on Friday, lists activities for children in the "Weekend" section. The daily Spanish-language newspaper, *La Nación,* publishes a section called "Viva" on Friday and Sunday listing events and activities for families.

If you are renting a car, don't forget to **arrange for a car seat** when you reserve. For general advice about traveling with children, consult *Fodor's FYI: Travel with Your Baby* (available in bookstores everywhere).

Sights and attractions throughout this book that are especially appealing to children are indicated by a rubber-duckie icon (Ⓒ) in the margin.

FLYING

If your children are two or older, **ask about children's airfares.** As a general rule, infants under two not occupying a seat fly at greatly reduced fares or even for free. But if you want to guarantee a seat for an infant, you have to pay full fare. Consider flying during off-peak days and times; most airlines will grant an infant a seat without a ticket if there are available seats.

When booking, **confirm carry-on allowances** if you're traveling with infants. In general, for babies charged 10%–50% of the adult fare you are allowed one carry-on bag and a collapsible stroller; if the flight is full, the stroller may have to be checked or you may be limited to less.

Experts agree that it's a good idea to use safety seats aloft for children weighing less than 40 pounds. Airlines set their own policies: If you use a safety seat, U.S. carriers usually require that the child be ticketed, even if he or she is young enough to ride free, because the seats must be strapped into regular seats. And even if you pay the full adult fare for the seat, it may be worth it, especially on longer trips. Do **check your airline's policy about using safety seats during takeoff and landing.** Safety seats are not allowed everywhere in the plane, so get your seat assignments as early as possible.

When reserving, **request children's meals or a freestanding bassinet** (not available at all airlines) if you need them. But note that bulkhead seats, where you must sit to use the bassinet, may lack an overhead bin or storage space on the floor.

FOOD

U.S fast-food chains are plentiful in San José but not elsewhere in the country. Typical Costa Rican restaurants will serve plain grilled chicken, fish, or beef and french fries to tykes.

LODGING

Most midprice and higher-price hotels offer cribs; some offer cots. For cheaper hotels, ask in advance but be prepared to share a bed with your child or have him or her sleep in a regular single bed. Baby-sitters and children's programs are available only in the largest resorts, and usually only in the December–April high season.

Hotels that are especially good for children include Selva Verde in the Atlantic lowlands, Mawamba Lodge in Tortuguero, Sapo Dorado in Monteverde, Hotel Grano de Oro in San José, and Sí Como No in Manuel Antonio. The Punta Leona Beach Resort is also great for kids; it's close to San José, and caters to upper-class Tico families. It has a playground, beach umbrellas, a children's pool, and high chairs and cribs. It's also less than two hours' driving time from San José and has tranquil, shallow waters and a wide sandy beach. The high-end Marriott, Melía, and Barceló hotel chains are also good for children because they have cots, cribs, and children's discounts. Most hotels in Costa Rica allow children under a certain age to stay in their parents' room at no extra charge, but others charge for them as extra adults; be sure to **find out the cutoff age for children's discounts.**

⚑ Best Choices Barceló Tambor Beach ⊠ Tambor ☎ 506/683-0303 ⊕ www.barcelo.com. **Corcovado Lodge Tent Camp** ⊠ Corcovado National Park ☎ 506/222-0333 ⊕ www.costaricaexpeditions. com**Hotel Grano de Oro** ⊠ San José ☎ 506/255-3322 ⊕ www.hotelgranodeoro.com. **Hotel Punta Leona** ⊠ Punta Leona ☎ 506/231-3131 ⊕ www. hotelpuntaleona.com. **Hotel El Sapo Dorado** ⊠ Monteverde ☎ 506/645-5010 ⊕ www. sapodorado.com. **Hotel Sí Como No** ⊠ Manuel Antonio ☎ 506/777-0777 ⊕ www.sicomono.com. **Marriott Costa Rica Hotel** ⊠ San Antonio de Belén ☎ 506/298-0000, 800/228-9290 in U.S. ⊕ www. marriott.com. **Mawamba Lodge** ⊠ Tortuguero ☎ 506/293-8181 ⊕ www.grupomawamba.com. **Selva Verde Lodge** ⊠ Puerto Viejo de Sarapiquí ☎ 506/776-6800 ⊕ www.selvaverde.com.

PRECAUTIONS

Sunburn and dehydration are problems commonly experienced by children. Slather on the sunscreen and make sure they swim in T-shirts and wear hats. Give them plenty to drink, and try to take bus trips, which can be very hot, early in the morning or late in the afternoon. Never let a child swim unattended in the ocean or go deeper than his or her waist.

SUPPLIES & EQUIPMENT

Baby formula and disposable diapers are widely available in supermarkets and pharmacies around the country. Usually only powder formula is available, and specialty types of formula (i.e., lactose-free) are available only in pharmacies. Major U.S. brands of disposable diapers are sold. Prices are about the same as or slightly higher than in the United States.

COMPUTERS ON THE ROAD

Many hotels in Costa Rica have data ports. Batteries and stabilizers are hard to come by, however, and since the electrical current fluctuates significantly, a stabilizer is usually necessary. It's best to call your hotel in advance for details. Cybercafés are available all over metropolitan San José and in some other places as well; ask around for the one nearest you. For addresses of Internet cafés, *see* Mail & Shipping *in* the A to Z sections at the end of each chapter.

CONSUMER PROTECTION

Get receipts for your purchases, and check that the correct amount has been written in on credit-card receipts. When paying with a credit card in restaurants, make sure the slip is totaled, whether or not you are leaving a tip. It is helpful to carry a pocket calculator so you can convert to your home currency when checking prices. Whether you're shopping for gifts or purchasing travel services, **pay with a major credit card** whenever possible, so you can cancel payment or get reimbursed if there's a problem (and you can provide documentation). If you're doing business with a particular company for the first time, **contact your local Better Business Bureau and the attorney general's offices** in your state and (for U.S. businesses) the company's home state as well. Have any complaints been filed? Finally, if you're buying a package or tour, always **consider travel insurance** that includes default coverage (⇨ Insurance).

⚑ BBBs Council of Better Business Bureaus ⊠ 4200 Wilson Blvd., Suite 800, Arlington, VA 22203 ☎ 703/276-0100 🖷 703/525-8277 ⊕ www. bbb.org.

CRUISE TRAVEL

Large cruise ships usually spend only one day in Costa Rica. To spend more time cruising the waters of Costa Rica and visiting destinations within the country by ship, consider Lindblad Expeditions and Cruisewest, two smaller lines that offer weeklong cruises around the country.

The U.S.–Costa Rica cruise season runs September–May, with trips lasting from three days to a week. A travel agent can explain prices, which range from $1,000 to $5,000. Luxury liners equipped with pools and gyms sail from Fort Lauderdale, Florida, to Limón, or through the Panama Canal to Caldera, south of Puntarenas. Some cruises sail from Los Angeles to Caldera, continuing to the canal. On board the ship you can sign up for shore excursions and tours. Cruise packages include the cost of flying to the appropriate port.

To learn how to plan, choose, and book a cruise-ship voyage, consult *Fodor's FYI: Plan & Enjoy Your Cruise* (available in bookstores everywhere).

🚢 Cruise Lines **Carnival** ☎ 800/327–9501 in U.S. ⊕ www.carnival.com. **Cruisewest** ☎ 800/580–0072 in U.S. ⊕ www.cruisewest.com. **Cunard** ☎ 800/221–4770 in U.S. ⊕ www.cunard.com. **Holland America** ☎ 800/426–0327 in U.S. ⊕ www.hollandamerica.com. **Lindblad Expeditions** ☎ 212/765–7740, 800/397–3348 in U.S. ⊕ www.lindblad.com. **Seabourn** ☎ 800/351–9595 in U.S. ⊕ www.seabourn.com.

CUSTOMS & DUTIES

When shopping abroad, **keep receipts** for all purchases. Upon reentering the country, **be ready to show customs officials what you've bought.** Pack purchases together in an easily accessible place. If you think a duty is incorrect, appeal the assessment. If you object to the way your clearance was handled, note the inspector's badge number. In either case, first ask to see a supervisor. If the problem isn't resolved, write to the appropriate authorities, beginning with the port director at your point of entry.

IN COSTA RICA

It usually takes about 10–30 minutes to clear customs when arriving in Costa Rica. Visitors entering Costa Rica may bring in 500 grams of tobacco, 3 liters of wine or spirits, 2 kilograms of sweets and chocolates, and the equivalent of $100 worth of merchandise. Two cameras, six rolls of film, binoculars, and electrical items for personal use only are also allowed. Customs officials at San José's international airport rarely examine tourists' luggage, but if you enter by land, they'll probably look through your bags.

Pets are not quarantined if you bring a health certificate obtained from a Costa

Rican consulate in your home country and filled out by a veterinarian before you arrive. Contact a Costa Rican consulate for more information about bringing pets to the country.

IN AUSTRALIA

Australian residents who are 18 or older may bring home A$400 worth of souvenirs and gifts (including jewelry), 250 cigarettes or 250 grams of cigars or other tobacco products, and 1,125 ml of alcohol (including wine, beer, and spirits). Residents under 18 may bring back A$200 worth of goods. Members of the same family traveling together may pool their allowances. Prohibited items include meat products. Seeds, plants, and fruits need to be declared upon arrival.

🚢 **Australian Customs Service** 📠 Regional Director, Box 8, Sydney, NSW 2001 ☎ 02/9213–2000 or 1300/363263, 02/9364–7222 or 1800/803–006 quarantine-inquiry line 📠 02/9213–4043 ⊕ www.customs.gov.au.

IN CANADA

Canadian residents who have been out of Canada for at least seven days may bring in C$750 worth of goods duty-free. If you've been away fewer than seven days but more than 48 hours, the duty-free allowance drops to C$200. If your trip lasts 24 to 48 hours, the allowance is C$50. You may not pool allowances with family members. Goods claimed under the C$750 exemption may follow you by mail; those claimed under the lesser exemptions must accompany you. Alcohol and tobacco products may be included in the seven-day and 48-hour exemptions but not in the 24-hour exemption. If you meet the age requirements of the province or territory through which you reenter Canada, you may bring in, duty-free, 1.5 liters of wine *or* 1.14 liters (40 imperial ounces) of liquor *or* 24 12-ounce cans or bottles of beer or ale. Also, if you meet the local age requirement for tobacco products, you may bring in, duty-free, 200 cigarettes and 50 cigars. Check ahead of time with the Canada Customs and Revenue Agency or the Department of Agriculture for policies regarding meat products, seeds, plants, and fruits.

You may send an unlimited number of gifts (only one gift per recipient, however) worth up to C$60 each duty-free to Canada. Label the package UNSOLICITED GIFT—VALUE UNDER $60. Alcohol and tobacco are excluded.

🇨🇦 **Canada Customs and Revenue Agency** ✉ 2265 St. Laurent Blvd., Ottawa, Ontario K1G 4K3 ☎ 204/983-3500, 506/636-5064, or 800/461-9999 ⊕ www.ccra.gc.ca.

IN NEW ZEALAND

All homeward-bound residents may bring back NZ$700 worth of souvenirs and gifts; passengers may not pool their allowances, and children can claim only the concession on goods intended for their own use. For those 17 or older, the duty-free allowance also includes 4.5 liters of wine or beer; one 1,125-ml bottle of spirits; and either 200 cigarettes, 250 grams of tobacco, 50 cigars, *or* a combination of the three up to 250 grams. Meat products, seeds, plants, and fruits must be declared upon arrival to the Agricultural Services Department.

🇳🇿 **New Zealand Customs** ✉ Head office: The Customhouse, 17–21 Whitmore St., Box 2218, Wellington ☎ 04/473-6099 or 0800/428-786 ⊕ www.customs.govt.nz.

IN THE U.K.

From countries outside the European Union, including Costa Rica, you may bring home, duty-free, 200 cigarettes or 50 cigars; 1 liter of spirits or 2 liters of fortified or sparkling wine or liqueurs; 2 liters of still table wine; 60 ml of perfume; 250 ml of toilet water; plus £145 worth of other goods, including gifts and souvenirs. Prohibited items include meat products, seeds, plants, and fruits.

🇬🇧 **HM Customs and Excise** ✉ Portcullis House, 21 Cowbridge Rd. E, Cardiff CF11 9SS ☎ 0845/010-9000 or 0292/038-6423 ⊕ www.hmce.gov.uk.

IN THE U.S.

U.S. residents who have been out of the country for at least 48 hours may bring home, for personal use, $800 worth of foreign goods duty-free, as long as they haven't used the $800 allowance or any part of it in the past 30 days. This exemption may include 1 liter of alcohol (for travelers 21 and older), 200 cigarettes, and 100 non-Cuban cigars. Family members from the same household who are traveling together may pool their $800 personal exemptions. For fewer than 48 hours, the duty-free allowance drops to $200, which may include 50 cigarettes, 10 non-Cuban cigars, and 150 ml of alcohol (or 150 ml of perfume containing alcohol). The $200 allowance cannot be combined with other individuals' exemptions, and if you exceed it, the full value of all the goods will be taxed. Antiques, which the U.S. Customs Service defines as objects more than 100 years old, enter duty-free, as do original works of art done entirely by hand, including paintings, drawings, and sculptures. This doesn't apply to folk art or handicrafts, which are in general dutiable.

You may also send packages home duty-free, with a limit of one parcel per addressee per day (except alcohol or tobacco products or perfume worth more than $5). You can mail up to $200 worth of goods for personal use; label the package PERSONAL USE and attach a list of its contents and their retail value. If the package contains your used personal belongings, mark it AMERICAN GOODS RETURNED to avoid paying duties. You may send up to $100 worth of goods as a gift; mark the package UNSOLICITED GIFT. Mailed items do not affect your duty-free allowance on your return.

To avoid paying duty on foreign-made high-ticket items you already own and will take on your trip, register them with customs before you leave the country. Consider filing a Certificate of Registration for laptops, cameras, watches, and other digital devices identified with serial numbers or other permanent markings; you can keep the certificate for other trips. Otherwise, bring a sales receipt or insurance form to show that you owned the item before you left the United States.

🇺🇸 **U.S. Customs Service** ✉ for inquiries and equipment registration, 1300 Pennsylvania Ave. NW, Washington, DC 20229 ⊕ www.customs.gov ☎ 202/354-1000 ✉ for complaints, Customer Satisfaction Unit, 1300 Pennsylvania Ave. NW, Room 5.5D, Washington, DC 20229.

DISABILITIES & ACCESSIBILITY

The best way for people with disabilities to see Costa Rica is to go with a specialized tour. Accessibility in Central America is extremely limited. Wheelchair ramps are practically nonexistent, and streets are often unpaved outside major cities, making wheelchair travel difficult. Exploring most attractions involves walking down cobblestone streets, steep trails, or muddy paths. Buses are not equipped to carry wheelchairs, so people using wheelchairs should hire a van to get around and bring someone along to help out. There is some growing awareness of the needs of people with disabilities, and some hotels and attractions in Costa Rica have made the necessary provisions; the Costa Rican Tourist Institute, known locally as the ICT, has more information.

▣ Local Resources **Costa Rican Tourist Institute** ✉ Avda. 4, between Cs. 5 and 7, 11th fl., Centro Colón, San José, Costa Rica ☎ 506/223-1733.

LODGING

Very few hotels in Costa Rica are equipped for travelers in wheelchairs. The Hampton Inn and the Marriott, near the San José international airport, and the Aurola Holiday Inn in downtown San José have some wheelchair accommodations. Vista del Valle and El Rodeo are wheelchair-accessible hotels in the Central Valley. La Selva, Centro Neotrópico Sarapiquís, or La Quinta are wheelchair-accessible choices in Sarapiquí. Other wheelchair-accessible lodgings are Río Colorado Lodge in Barra del Colorado; Tabacón Resort, Arenal Observatory Lodge, or La Pradera in Arenal; and Marriott Los Sueños Beach, El Paraíso Escondido, or Hotel Villa Lapis in the Central Pacific. Wilson Botanical Gardens, in the Southern Pacific, has one room equipped for a wheelchair.

▣ Best Choices **Arenal Observatory Lodge** ✉ La Fortuna ☎ 506/692-2070 or 506/290-7011 ⊕ www. arenal-observatory.co.cr. **Aurola Holiday Inn** ✉ San José ☎ 222-2424, 800/465-4329 in U.S. ⊕ www.aurola-holidayinn.com **Centro Neotrópico Sarapiquís** ✉ Puerto Viejo de Sarapiquí ☎ 506/761-1004 ⊕ www.sarapiquis.org. **Hotel Villa Lapas** ✉ Tárcoles ☎ 506/637-0232 ⊕ www.villalapas.

com. **Marriott Costa Rica** ✉ San Antonio de Belén ☎ 506/298-0000, 800/228-9290 in U.S. ⊕ www. marriott.com. **Marriott Los Sueños Beach** ✉ Playa Herradura ☎ 506/630-9000, 800/228-9290 in U.S. ⊕ www.marriott.com. **La Pradera** ✉ La Fortuna ☎ 506/479-9597. **Río Colorado Lodge** ✉ Barra del Colorado ☎ 506/232-4063, 800/243-9777 in U.S. ⊕ www.riocoloradolodge.com. **El Rodeo** ✉ San Antonio de Belén ☎ 506/293-3909. **La Selva** ✉ La Selva Biological Station ☎ 506/766-6565 or 506/240-6696. **Tabacón Resort** ✉ La Fortuna ☎ 506/460-2020 or 506/256-1500 ⊕ www.tabacon.com. **Vista del Valle Plantation Inn** ✉ Grecia ☎ 506/450-0800 ⊕ www.vistadelvalle.com. **Wilson Botanical Garden** ✉ San Vito ☎ 506/240-6696 ⊕ www.ots.ac.cr.

RESERVATIONS

When discussing accessibility with an operator or reservations agent, **ask hard questions.** Are there any stairs, inside *or* out? Are there grab bars next to the toilet *and* in the shower/tub? How wide is the doorway to the room? To the bathroom? For the most extensive facilities meeting the latest legal specifications, **opt for newer accommodations.** If you reserve through a toll-free number, consider also calling the hotel's local number to confirm the information from the central reservations office. Get confirmation in writing when you can.

SIGHTS & ATTRACTIONS

Most Costa Rican attractions are inaccessible for travelers with wheelchairs, as are restaurant bathrooms. Volcán Poás National Park is probably the most wheelchair-friendly site, with Volcán Irazú the runner-up. INBioparque, on the road leading from San José to Santo Domingo de Heredia, is a good choice for people using wheelchairs. It has ramps to exhibits, plenty of room for wheelchairs to maneuver, and wheelchair-accessible bathrooms and trails. The Orosi Valley and Sarchí also have limited exploring options for travelers using wheelchairs. The Rain Forest Aerial Tram and its coffee shop are wheelchair accessible, but the facility's rest rooms, trails, and main restaurant are not. Other wheelchair-accessible attractions: Café Britt coffee tour, in Heredia; Butterfly Farm, near Alajuela; Zoo Ave in the

Central Valley; Tabacón Hot Springs in La Fortuna; and parts of Carara National Park, in the Central Pacific.

TRANSPORTATION

There are no wheelchair facilities on public buses. Call a taxi to pick you up instead. Juan Santamaría International Airport has wheelchair ramps. Developed areas, especially San José and the Central Valley, can be managed in a wheelchair more easily than rural areas. The tour company Vaya con Silla de Ruedas (Go with Wheelchairs) provides transportation and guided tours.

▨ Complaints Aviation Consumer Protection Division ⊠ U.S. Department of Transportation, C-75, Room 4107, 400 7th St. NW, Washington, DC 20590 ☎ 202/366-2220 ⊕ www.dot.gov/airconsumer. **Departmental Office of Civil Rights** ⊠ for general inquiries, U.S. Department of Transportation, S-30, 400 7th St. SW, Room 10215, Washington, DC 20590 ☎ 202/366-4648 🖷 202/366-9371 ⊕ www.dot. gov/ost/docr/index.htm. **Disability Rights Section** ⊠ NYAV, U.S. Department of Justice, Civil Rights Division, 950 Pennsylvania Ave. NW, Washington, DC 20530 ☎ ADA information line 202/514-0301, 800/514-0301, 202/514-0383 TTY, 800/514-0383 TTY ⊕ www.ada.gov. **U.S. Department of Transportation Hotline** 🖷 for disability-related air-travel problems, 800/778-4838 or 800/455-9880 TTY.

▨ Tour Companies & Travel Agencies Access Adventures/B. Roberts Travel ⊠ 206 Chestnut Ridge Rd., Scottsville, NY 14624 ☎ 585/889-9096 ⊕ www.brobertstravel.com ✍ dltravel@prodigy. net, run by a former physical-rehabilitation counselor. **CareVacations** ⊠ No. 5, 5110-50 Ave., Leduc, Alberta, Canada, T9E 6V4 ☎ 780/986-6404 or 877/478-7827 🖷 780/986-8332 ⊕ www.carevacations. com, for group tours and cruise vacations. **Flying Wheels Travel** ⊠ 143 W. Bridge St., Box 382, Owatonna, MN 55060 ☎ 507/451-5005 🖷 507/451-1685 ⊕ www.flyingwheelstravel.com. **Vaya con Silla de Ruedas** ☎ 506/391-5045 ⊕ www. gowithwheelchairs.com.

DISCOUNTS & DEALS

Some local tour companies offer one-day tours to multiple attractions, usually for about $80 per person for up to five stops. These tours may sound like great deals, but be aware that you won't stay very long at any of the attractions and that your day may be very long and tiring.

Be a smart shopper and **compare all your options** before making decisions. A plane ticket bought with a promotional coupon from travel clubs, coupon books, and direct-mail offers or purchased on the Internet may not be cheaper than the least expensive fare from a discount ticket agency. And always keep in mind that what you get is just as important as what you save.

DISCOUNT RESERVATIONS

To save money, **look into discount reservations services** with Web sites and toll-free numbers, which use their buying power to get a better price on hotels, airline tickets (⇨ Air Travel), even car rentals. When booking a room, always **call the hotel's local toll-free number** (if one is available) rather than the central reservations number—you'll often get a better price. Always ask about special packages or corporate rates.

When shopping for the best deal on hotels and car rentals, **look for guaranteed exchange rates,** which protect you against a falling dollar. With your rate locked in, you won't pay more, even if the price goes up in the local currency.

▨ Airline Tickets Air 4 Less ☎ 800/AIR4LESS in the U.S.; low-fare specialist.

▨ Hotel Rooms Accommodations Express ☎ 800/444-7666 or 800/277-1064 in the U.S. ⊕ www.accommodationsexpress.com. **Hotels.com** ☎ 214/369-1246, 800/246-8357 in U.S. ⊕ www. hotels.com. **Turbotrip.com** ☎ 800/473-7829 in U.S. ⊕ www.turbotrip.com.

PACKAGE DEALS

Don't confuse packages and guided tours. When you buy a package, you travel on your own, just as though you had planned the trip yourself. Fly-drive packages, which combine airfare and car rental, are often a good deal. In cities, ask the local visitor's bureau about hotel packages that include tickets to major museum exhibits or other special events.

EATING & DRINKING

Many travelers expect Costa Rican food to be spicy and similar to Mexican food. They are surprised to be served, over and over again, plates of delicately seasoned black beans, steamed white rice, and relatively unadorned broiled fish, chicken, or pan-fried steak called *casados*. These foods—plus a breakfast dish of rice and black beans mixed together and accompanied by eggs and perhaps meat—make up the typical Costa Rican diet. The monotony is broken by a cornucopia of tropical fruits, fruit drinks, and vegetables finely chopped, sautéed, and seasoned with spices.

In recent years, San José has experienced a flowering of international restaurants, and the city now has an exciting and varied restaurant scene for all budgets. From sushi to Lebanese food to Peruvian *ceviche* (fish, shrimp, or octopus marinated in lime juice), the capital can satisfy any craving. It is difficult to find typical Costa Rican food at upscale restaurants in San José. The rice, beans, and meat plate described above is served at more humble establishments called *sodas* (informal eateries) and at hotels that cater to foreign travelers. Outside of San José, casados are served everywhere and typically cost less than $5. *Bocas* (literally "tastes") are appetizers or snacks, which are served free with drinks at some bars, though usually you have to pay for them.

U.S. chains McDonald's, KFC, Burger King, Pizza Hut, and Hardees are well represented in the Central Valley. Chinese restaurants—most of them inexpensive—are plentiful because of the large number of immigrants. Local restaurant chains include Princesa Marina, which serves inexpensive seafood in a family-friendly setting and has several locations throughout the Central Valley; and Pollo Ranchera, a fast-food carry-out-only restaurant that serves rotisserie chicken, black beans, and other local fare.

The restaurants we list are the cream of the crop in each price category. Properties indicated by a ✕🏠 are lodging establishments whose restaurant warrants a special trip.

WHAT IT COSTS (at dinner)	
$$$$	over $25
$$$	$20–$25
$$	$10–$20
$	$5–$10
¢	under $5

Prices are per-person for a main course.

MEALS & SPECIALTIES

Desayuno (breakfast) is served at sodas and hotels. Eggs are prevalent, as is *gallo pinto* ("spotted rooster," a mix of black beans and rice), often topped with a dollop of *natilla* (sour cream), and squeezed juices from carrot to fresh-picked star fruit. Always at *almuerzo* (lunch), and sometimes at *cena* (dinner), you can depend on a casado, the *típico* (typical) Costa Rican meal. Salads with *aguacate* (avocado) and *palmito* (heart of palm) are also common. Note that lettuce is almost always served shredded.

MEALTIMES

In San José and surrounding cities, sodas are usually open daily 7 AM to 7 or 9 PM, though some close on Sunday. Other restaurants are usually open 11 AM–9 PM. In rural areas, restaurants are usually closed on Sunday, except around resorts. In resort areas, some restaurants may be open late. The only all-night restaurants are in downtown San José casinos. Normal dining hours in Costa Rica are noon–3 and 6–9. Unless otherwise noted, the restaurants listed in this guide are open daily for lunch and dinner.

PAYING

Credit cards are not accepted at most restaurants in rural areas. Always ask before you order to find out if your credit card will be accepted. Visa and MasterCard are the most commonly accepted cards; American Express and Diners Club are less widely accepted. In Costa Rica, 23% is added to all menu prices—13% for tax and 10% for service. An additional tip is not expected, but always appreciated.

RESERVATIONS & DRESS

Reservations are always a good idea; we mention them only when they're essential or not accepted. Book as far ahead as you can, and reconfirm as soon as you arrive. (Large parties should always call ahead to check the reservations policy.)

We mention dress only when men are required to wear a jacket or a jacket and tie. However, Costa Ricans generally dress more formally than North Americans. For dinner, long pants and closed-toed shoes are standard for men except for beach locations, and women tend to wear dressy clothes that show off their figures, with high heels. Shorts, flip-flops, and tank tops are not acceptable, except at inexpensive restaurants in beach towns.

WINE, BEER & SPIRITS

Costa Rica's one brewery makes half a dozen brands of beer, including the popular Imperial, a dark brew called Steinbrau, and a local version of Heineken, with the same name. All wine is imported; the best deals are usually from Chile and Argentina, particularly the Chilean Castillero del Diablo and Sangre de Toro. Costa Rica's best rum is Centenario, but most Ticos drink a rot-gut rum called *guaro*. All of the above is served at restaurants and bars and sold in supermarkets and liquor stores. Café Britt makes a refined coffee liqueur that is sold at supermarkets and liquor stores, as well as the airport.

ECOTOURISM

Ecotourism, green tourism, environmental tourism: the buzzwords have been flying around Costa Rica for more than a decade. Many tour companies have incorporated a high level of environmental awareness into their business practices. **Find out whether or not your prospective tour company has "eco-friendly" policies,** such as hiring and training locals as guides, drivers, managers, and office workers; teaching people as much as possible about the plant and animal life, geography, and history that surrounds them; controlling the numbers of people allowed daily onto a given site; restoring watersheds and anything else damaged by trail building, visiting, or general overuse; and discouraging wildlife feeding or any other unnatural or disruptive behavior (such as making loud noises to scare birds into flight). All these practices can mitigate the effects of intense tourism. After all, it's better to have 100 people walking through a forest than to cut the forest down.

Whether you travel on your own or with a tour group (⇨ Tours & Packages), try to make your visit beneficial to those who live near protected areas: **use local guides**

or services, eat in local restaurants, and buy local crafts or produce. To ensure land preservation for future generations, you can donate to local conservation groups or a few foreign environmental organizations—including Conservation International, The Nature Conservancy, and the World Wide Fund for Nature—that aid ecological efforts in Costa Rica.

Don't remove plants, rocks, shells, or animals from their natural environment. Take only pictures; leave only footprints. It's illegal to take anything, alive or dead, out of a national park or any other protected area. To see turtles nesting, go with a guide. If you go on your own, you will disrupt them. Most national parks have trash cans, but pack out your trash when doing backcountry camping. Do not feed wildlife, even when animals appear tame. Do not stray from the trails for any reason.

The official government rating system for eco-lodges is the Costa Rican Tourism Board's Certification for Sustainable Tourism. It rates tourism companies and lodges in four categories: interaction with the surrounding habitat; policies and steps taken to be more sustainable; actions taken to encourage clients to participate in the company's sustainability policy; and interaction with the local community. Hotels that have received five leaves—the highest rating—include El Rodeo Country Inn (San Antonio de Belén), Arenal Observatory Lodge and Tabacón Resort in La Fortuna, Laguna del Lagarto Lodge (San Carlos), and Vista del Valle (Grecia). However, many people think that the program is politicized and that certain hotels do not deserve such high ratings. For example, several Barcelo hotels were rated highly despite the chain's many past violations of environmental laws.

In our opinion, some of the best eco-lodges in the country are Lapa Ríos (near Puerto Jiménez), Villa Lapas (near Carara), Hotel Si Como No (Manuel Antonio), Laguna del Lagarto Lodge (San Carlos), and Tiskita Lodge (Playa Pavones).

🖪 **Local Conservation Groups** ANAI ☎ 506/224–3570. APREFLOFAS ☎ 506/240–6087. **Monteverde**

Institute ☎ 506/645-5053. **Neotropica Foundation** ☎ 506/253-2130.

International Conservation Groups Conservation International ✉ 1919 M St. NW, Suite 600, Washington, DC 20036 ☎ 202/973-2227 or 800/429-5660 ⊕ www.conservation.org. **The Nature Conservancy** ✉ 4245 N. Fairfax Dr., Suite 100, Arlington, VA 22203 ☎ 800/628-6860 ⊕ www.tnc.org. **World Wide Fund for Nature** ✉ Av. du Mont-Blanc, CH 1196 Gland, Switzerland ☎ 4122/364-9111 ⊕ www.panda.org.

NATIONAL PARKS

For specific information on Costa Rican parks and protected areas, call the regional offices (⇨ Park listings *in* Chapters 1–7) or the national-park information line at the Ministry of Environment and Energy. For specific requests, such as reserving camping or cabin space, call the regional office of the park in question. Practical information on parks, including limited literature, is available at the Fundación de Parques Nacionales. The price of admission to Costa Rica's national parks is $4–$8 per day.

Costa Rica Park Contacts Fundación de Parques Nacionales ✉ 300 m north and 300 m east of Church of Santa Teresita, San José ☎ 506/257-2239. **Ministry of Environment and Energy (MINAE)** ☎ 506/233-4533, 192 in Costa Rica.

WILDLIFE

Travelers are often surprised by how hard it can be to see animals in the rain forest. Despite their frequent appearances in advertisements and brochures, many endangered species are practically impossible to spot. Between the low density of mammals, their shyness, and the fact that thick vegetation often obstructs your view, you must **be patient and stay attentive.** Because the tropical dry forest is less overgrown than the rain forest, it's one of the best life zones for animal observation; river trips, too, can make for great viewing. **Don't give up hope:** if you take the time to explore a few protected areas, you're almost certain to spy dozens of interesting critters.

ELECTRICITY

The electrical current in Central America is 110 volts (AC). Costa Rica has standard North American two-prong outlets. Adapters are required for three-prong plugs, which are not common in Costa Rica. If your appliances are dual voltage, you'll need only an adapter. If they aren't, use a 220-volt to 110-volt transformer. Don't use 110-volt outlets marked FOR SHAVERS ONLY for high-wattage appliances such as blow-dryers unless you use a transformer. Most laptops operate equally well on 110 and 220 volts and so require only an adapter, but you should bring a surge protector for your computer. Blackouts are common in some rural areas.

EMBASSIES

Citizens of Australia and New Zealand should contact the British Embassy.

In Canada Embassy of Costa Rica ✉ 208-135 York St. Ottawa, ON K1N 5T4 ☎ 613/562-2855. **In Costa Rica British Embassy (Embajada Británica)** ✉ 11th fl., Centro Colón, between Cs. 38 and 40, Paseo Colón, San José ☎ 506/258-2025 ⊕ www.embajadabritanica.com. **Canadian Embassy (Embajada Canadiense)** ✉ next to Tennis Club, Sabana Sur, Oficentro Ejecutivo La Sabana, Torre No. 5, 3rd fl., San José ☎ 506/242-4400. **United States Embassy (Embajada de los Estados Unidos)** ✉ C. 120 and Avda. 0, Pavas, San José ☎ 506/220-3939 ⊕ usembassy.or.cr. **In the U.K. Costa Rican Embassy** ✉ Flat 1, 14 Lancaster Gate, London W2 3LH ☎ 020/7706-8844. **In the U.S. Embassy of Costa Rica** ✉ 2114 S St. NW, Washington, DC 20008 ☎ 202/234-2945 or 202/234-2946 ⊕ costarica-embassy.org.

EMERGENCIES

Dial ☎ 911 for an ambulance, the fire department, or the police. Costa Ricans are usually quick to respond to emergencies. In a hotel or restaurant, the staff will usually offer immediate assistance, and in a public area, passersby can be counted on to stop and help.

Traffic Police ☎ 222-9245.

ENGLISH-LANGUAGE MEDIA

English is practically everywhere in Costa Rica, from abundant publications to the cable TV beamed into most San José hotels.

BOOKS

The Biblioteca Mark Twain in the lower level of the Centro Cultural

Costarricense–Norteamericano is San José's only library with an American and English-language focus. The book collection is moderate, but there's an extensive selection of magazines from the United States, as well as day-old editions of the *Miami Herald*, the *New York Times*, and *USA Today*. Librería Chunches in Santa Elena on the Nicoya Peninsula maintains a good selection of books, magazines, and day-old U.S. newspapers in English. Some large hotels and other shops also sell English-language books, particularly titles on the tropical outdoors.

🖪 Bookstores **Biblioteca Mark Twain** ⊠ Avda. 1 and C. 37, Barrio Dent San Pedro ☎ 207-7500. **Lehmann** ⊠ Avda. Central between Cs. 1 and 3, Centro Colón, San José ☎ 506/223-1212. **Librería Chunches** ⊠ 45 m south of Banco Nacional, Santa Elena ☎ 645-5147. **Librería Internacional** ⊠ 300 m west of Taco Bell Barrio Dent, San José ☎ 506/253-9553. **7th Street Books** ⊠ C. 7 between Avdas. Central and 1, Centro Colón, San José ☎ 506/256-8251.

NEWSPAPERS & MAGAZINES

Founded in 1956, English-language weekly *The Tico Times* hits the newsstands every Friday with solid reporting in English of Costa Rican news, and is especially strong on coverage of the environment, an area often ignored by the Spanish-language press. An abridged Web version includes updates each weekday.

American newspapers and magazines are widely distributed at newsstands and hotels in San José and sold in some resorts outside the capital. In San José, gift shops in large hotels, bookstores with English-language publications, and the shops at Juan Santamaría Airport have a few newspapers and magazines from the United States: The *Miami Herald* arrives in San José in the afternoon; the *New York Times* and *USA Today,* the day following publication. The Latin American editions of *Time* and *Newsweek* arrive a few days after their U.S. counterparts.

🖪 English-Language Newspaper **The Tico Times** ⊕ www.ticotimes.net.

RADIO & TELEVISION

Radio 107.5 (107.5 FM) broadcasts in English 24 hours a day with news reports

from the BBC World Service at 6 and 8 AM and 5 PM. Radio Dos (99.5 FM) broadcasts in English from 6 to 8 AM daily with news reports in English every two hours during the day beginning at 8 AM. U.S. and British pop and rock music are the staple of both stations.

Most large San José hotels offer cable or satellite television with a few English-language channels. CNN is a staple, but prime-time programming from the U.S. broadcast networks is blocked because of a lack of licensing rights for Latin America. Sony, Warner, and Fox cable-satellite services to Latin America show many hours of U.S. programming in English with Spanish subtitles.

ETIQUETTE & BEHAVIOR

If invited to someone's home, take a hostess gift such as flowers or a bottle of wine, or some memorabilia from your home country. If offered food at someone's home, accept it and eat it even if you aren't hungry. You will be offered coffee and should accept, although it's not necessary to finish the whole cup. Know that Costa Ricans don't like to say no and will often avoid answering a question or simply say *gracias* when they really mean no.

On the whole, Costa Ricans are extremely polite, quick to shake hands and place a kiss on the left cheek. Ticos tend to use formal Spanish, preferring, for example, *con mucho gusto* (with much pleasure) instead of *de nada* for "you're welcome." At the same time, a large portion of Costa Rican men make a habit of ogling or making gratuitous comments when young women pass on the street. Women should wear a bra at all times. Family is very important in Costa Rica. It is considered polite to ask about one's marital status and family—don't confuse this with prying.

As you would anywhere, **dress and behave respectfully when visiting churches.** In churches, men and women should not wear shorts, sleeveless shirts, or sandals; women should wear skirts below the knee.

BUSINESS ETIQUETTE

Dress in San José is more formal than in the countryside. Men do not wear shorts outside of beach areas. Women do not wear short skirts during the day. Most Costa Ricans wear leather dress shoes instead of tennis shoes unless they are engaged in sports. Most men do not wear a tie to work. Northerners are bound to find business meetings friendlier and more relaxed in Costa Rica than at home. Dress is usually casual, and tardiness is common.

FLIGHTSEEING
San José–based pilot Jenner Rojas will take you anywhere in Costa Rica for flightseeing and picture taking. The rate is $230 per hour, or less if you arrange a trip of several hours' duration.

🛪 Flightseeing Companies **Jenner Rojas** ☎ 506/ 385–5425.

GAY & LESBIAN TRAVEL
Although harassment of gays and lesbians is infrequent in Costa Rica, so are public displays of affection. Discretion is advised. Same-sex couples won't have problems at hotel check-in desks unless they engage in public displays of affection. Ticos, for whom religion and family are very important, tend simply to assume that everyone is straight. Relative to most other Latin American countries, Costa Rica is quite tolerant. Although the country has had some instances of intolerance in the recent past—a gay and lesbian festival was canceled in 1998, and religious protesters have blocked the arrival of gay and lesbian tour groups—the official government position seems to be one of tolerance.

Costa Rica has attracted many gay people from other Latin American nations and consequently has a large gay community. San José and Manuel Antonio are probably the most gay-friendly towns, and they have some gay and lesbian bars and hangouts. The beach at the northern end of Playa Espadilla in Manuel Antonio National Park is a small, secluded cove known to be a gay nude beach. There are no anti-gay laws.

GAY & LESBIAN RESOURCES
San José's 1@10 Café Internet serves as a gay and lesbian resource center. Its Web page is a wealth of information on whom to contact and where to go. *Gente 10* magazine is a bimonthly Costa Rican magazine that has bilingual, LGBT-friendly tour and hotel listings. You can find it, and the community paper, *Gayness,* in gay-friendly hotels, bars, and bookshops. The informal online Gay and Lesbian Guide to Costa Rica has some good travel information, including hotels that are listed with the Costa Rican Gay Business Association. GayCostaRica.com is a Web site with information on gay-friendly hotels, tour agencies, pharmacies, wedding planners, and real estate companies.

🛪 **1@10 Café Internet** Uno@Diez ⊠ C. 3 and Avda. 7, Barrio Amón ☎ 506/258–4561 ⊕ www.1en10.com. **GayCostaRica.com** ⊕ www.costaricagay.net. **Gay and Lesbian Guide to Costa Rica** ⊕ www. hometown.aol.com/gaycrica/guide.html.

🛪 Gay- & Lesbian-Friendly Travel Agencies **Different Roads Travel** ⊠ 8383 Wilshire Blvd., Suite 902, Beverly Hills, CA 90211 ☎ 323/651–5557 or 800/ 429–8747 (Ext. 14 for both) 🖷 323/651–3678 ✉ lgernert@tzell.com. **Kennedy Travel** ⊠ 130 W. 42nd St., Suite 401, New York, NY 10036 ☎ 212/840–8659, 800/237–7433 🖷 212/730–2269 ⊕ www. kennedytravel.com. **Now, Voyager** ⊠ 4406 18th St., San Francisco, CA 94114 ☎ 415/626–1169 or 800/ 255–6951 🖷 415/626–8626 ⊕ www.nowvoyager. com. **Skylink Travel and Tour** ⊠ 1455 N. Dutton Ave., Suite A, Santa Rosa, CA 95401 ☎ 707/546–9888 or 800/225–5759 🖷 707/636–0951, serving lesbian travelers.

GUIDEBOOKS
Plan well and you won't be sorry. Guidebooks are excellent tools—and you can take them with you. You may want to check out color-photo-illustrated *Fodor's Exploring Costa Rica,* which is thorough on culture and history and is available at online retailers and bookstores everywhere.

HEALTH
Many of the doctors at San José's Clínica Bíblica and Clínica Católica, and Escazú's CIMA Hospital (⇨ Emergencies) speak English well, and some studied medicine in the United States. These clinics have 24-hour pharmacies.

DIVERS' ALERT
Do not fly within 24 hours of scuba diving.

FOOD & DRINK

Most food and water is sanitary in Costa Rica. In rural areas, you run a mild risk of encountering drinking water, fresh fruit, and vegetables contaminated by fecal matter, which causes intestinal ailments known variously as Montezuma's Revenge (traveler's diarrhea) and leptospirosis (another disease borne in contaminated food or water that can be treated by antibiotics if detected early). Although it may not be necessary, you can stay on the safe side by avoiding ice, uncooked food, and unpasteurized milk (including milk products) and drinking bottled water. Mild cases of Montezuma's Revenge may respond to Imodium (known generically as loperamide) or Pepto-Bismol (not as strong), both of which can be purchased over the counter. Drink plenty of purified water or tea; chamomile is a good folk remedy. In severe cases, rehydrate yourself with a salt-sugar solution (½ teaspoon salt and 4 tablespoons sugar per quart of water).

MEDICAL PLANS

No one plans to get sick while traveling, but it happens, so **consider signing up with a medical-assistance company.** Members get doctor referrals, emergency evacuation or repatriation, hotlines for medical consultation, cash for emergencies, and other assistance.

⚡ Medical-Assistance Companies **International SOS Assistance** ⊕ www.internationalsos.com ⊠ 8 Neshaminy Interplex, Suite 207, Trevose, PA 19053 ☎ 215/244–1500 or 800/523–8930 ⬜ 215/244–9617 ⊠ 12 Chemin Riantbosson, 1217 Meyrin 1, Geneva, Switzerland ☎ 4122/785–6464 ⬜ 4122/785–6424 ⊠ 331 N. Bridge Rd., 17-00, Odeon Towers, Singapore 188720 ☎ 65/338–7800 ⬜ 65/338–7611.

OVER-THE-COUNTER REMEDIES

Farmacia is Spanish for "pharmacy," and the names for common drugs *aspirina*, Tylenol, and *ibuprofen* are basically the same as they are in English. Pepto-Bismol is widely available. Many drugs for which you need a prescription back home are sold over the counter in Costa Rica. Antibiotics do require a prescription.

PESTS & OTHER HAZARDS

Altitude sickness is not a problem unless you are climbing Chirripó, the country's highest peak (14,000 feet). Heat stroke and dehydration are real dangers, especially for hikers, so drink lots of water. Take at least 1 liter per person for every hour you plan to be on the trail. Sunburn is the most common traveler's health problem. Use sunscreen with SPF 30 or higher. Most pharmacies and supermarkets carry sunscreen in a wide range of SPFs, though it is relatively pricey.

Repelente (insect repellent spray) and *espirales* (mosquito coils) are sold in supermarkets and small country stores. U.S. insect repellent brands with DEET are sold in pharmacies and supermarkets. Mosquito nets are available in some remote lodges; you can buy them in camping stores in San José. Mild insect repellents, like the ones in some skin softeners, are no match for the intense mosquito activity in the hot, humid regions of the Atlantic Lowlands, Osa Peninsula, and Southern Pacific. Moreover, perfume, aftershave, and other lotions and potions can actually attract mosquitoes. Malaria is not a problem in Costa Rica except in some remote northern Caribbean areas near the Nicaraguan border. Poisonous snakes, scorpions, and other pests pose a small (often overrated) threat.

The greatest danger to your person actually lies off Costa Rica's popular beaches—riptides are common wherever there are waves, and several tourists drown in them every year. If you see waves, ask the locals where it's safe to swim; and if you're uncertain, don't go in deeper than your waist. If you get caught in a rip current, swim parallel to the beach until you're free of it, and then swim back to shore.

SHOTS & MEDICATIONS

According to the U.S. Centers for Disease Control, travel to Costa Rica poses some risk of malaria, hepatitis A and B, dengue fever, typhoid fever, rabies, Chagas' disease, and *E. coli*. The CDC recommends getting vaccines for hepatitis A and typhoid fever, especially if you are going to be in remote areas or plan to stay for more than six weeks. Check with the CDC for detailed health advisories and recommended vaccinations. In areas with malaria and dengue, both of which are carried by mosquitoes, **bring mosquito nets, wear clothing that covers your body, and apply repellent containing DEET** in living and sleeping areas. There are some pockets of malaria near the Nicaraguan border on the Caribbean coast. You probably won't need to take malaria pills before your trip unless you are staying for a prolonged period in the north, camping on northern coasts, or crossing the border into Nicaragua or Panama. You should discuss the option with your doctor. Children traveling to Central America should have current inoculations against measles, mumps, rubella, and polio.

🔳 Health Warnings **National Centers for Disease Control and Prevention** (CDC) ✉ National Center for Infectious Diseases, Division of Quarantine, Travelers' Health, 1600 Clifton Rd. NE, Atlanta, GA 30333 ☎ 877/394-8747 international travelers' health line, 800/311-3435 other inquiries 🖨 888/232-3299 ⊕ www.cdc.gov/travel.

HOLIDAYS

National holidays are known as *feriados*. On these days government offices, banks, and post offices are closed, and public transport is restricted. Religious festivals are characterized by colorful processions.

Except for those in hotels, most restaurants and many attractions close between Christmas and New Year's Day and during Holy Week (Palm Sunday to Easter Sunday). Those that do stay open may not sell alcohol between Holy Thursday and Easter Sunday.

Major national holidays are New Year's Day; Juan Santamaría Day (Apr. 11); Good Friday–Easter Sunday (Mar. 25–27, 2005); Labor Day (May 1); Corpus Christi Day (May 29); Annexation of Guanacaste (July 25); Virgin of the Angels (Costa Rica's patron saint; Aug. 2); Independence Day (Sept. 15); *Día de las Culturas* (Columbus Day; Oct. 12); and Christmas.

INSURANCE

The most useful travel-insurance plan is a comprehensive policy that includes coverage for trip cancellation and interruption, default, trip delay, and medical expenses (with a waiver for preexisting conditions).

Without insurance you'll lose all or most of your money if you cancel your trip, regardless of the reason. Default insurance covers you if your tour operator, airline, or cruise line goes out of business. Trip-delay covers expenses that arise because of bad weather or mechanical delays. Study the fine print when comparing policies.

If you're traveling internationally, a key component of travel insurance is coverage for medical bills incurred if you get sick on the road. Such expenses aren't generally covered by Medicare or private policies. U.K. residents can buy a travel-insurance policy valid for most vacations taken during the year in which it's purchased (but check preexisting-condition coverage). British and Australian citizens need extra medical coverage when traveling overseas.

Always **buy travel policies directly from the insurance company**; if you buy them from a cruise line, airline, or tour operator that goes out of business you probably won't be covered for the agency or operator's default, a major risk. Before making any purchase, **review your existing health and homeowner's policies** to find what they cover away from home.

🔳 Travel Insurers In the U.S.: **Access America** ✉ Box 90315, Richmond, VA 23286 ☎ 800/284-8300 🖨 804/673-1491 or 800/346-9265 ⊕ www.accessamerica.com. **Travel Guard International** ✉ 1145 Clark St., Stevens Point, WI 54481 ☎ 715/345-0505 or 800/826-4919 🖨 800/955-8785 ⊕ www.travelguard.com.

🔳 In the U.K.: **Association of British Insurers** ✉ 51 Gresham St., London EC2V 7HQ ☎ 020/7600-3333 🖨 020/7696-8999 ⊕ www.abi.org.uk. In Canada: **RBC Insurance** ✉ 6880 Financial Dr., Mississauga, Ontario L5N 7Y5 ☎ 800/565-3129 🖨 905/813-4704 ⊕ www.rbcinsurance.com. In Australia: **Insurance Council of Australia** ✉ Insurance Enquiries and Complaints, Level 3, 56 Pitt St., Sydney, NSW 2000 ☎ 1300/363683 or 02/9251-4456 🖨 02/9251-4453 ⊕ www.iecltd.com.au. In New Zealand: **Insurance Council of New Zealand** ✉ Level 7, 111-115 Customhouse Quay, Box 474, Wellington ☎ 04/472-5230 🖨 04/473-3011 ⊕ www.icnz.org.nz.

LANGUAGE

Spanish is the official language, although many tour guides and locals in heavily touristed areas speak English. You'll have a better time if you learn some basic Spanish before you go and bring a phrase book with you. When possible, choose the more formal phrasing, such as *¿Cómo está usted?* (How are you?) rather than the North American or Mexican *¿Cómo está?*, which is not used here. At the very least, **learn the rudiments of polite conversation**—niceties such as *por favor* (please) and *gracias* (thank you) will be warmly appreciated. *See* the brief Costa Rican Spanish glossary *in* the Understanding Costa Rica chapter. Spanish-language learning vacations are popular in Costa Rica (⇨ Tours and Packages).

In the Caribbean province of Limón a creole English called Mekatalyu is widely spoken by older generations. English is understood by most everyone in these parts.

LANGUAGES FOR TRAVELERS

A phrase book and language-tape set, such as *Fodor's Spanish for Travelers* (available at bookstores everywhere), can help get you started.

LODGING

At Costa Rica's popular beach and mountain resorts **reserve well in advance for the dry season** (mid-December–April everywhere except the Caribbean, which has a short September–October "dry" season). You'll need to give credit-card information or send a deposit to confirm the reservation. Try to do this with the hotel and not a third-party reservations network. During the rainy season (May–mid-December except on the Caribbean coast, where it's almost always rainy) most hotels drop their rates considerably, which sometimes sends them into a lower price category than the one we indicate.

Luxury hotels are found mainly in San José, Guanacaste, and the Central Valley. Except at the most popular Pacific beaches, lodging in outlying areas is usu-ally in simple *cabinas* (cabins). Cabinas range from basic concrete boxes with few creature comforts to flashier units with all the modern conveniences. Costa Rica also has an abundance of nature lodges (often within private biological reserves) with an emphasis on ecology; most of these are entirely rustic, but a few of the newest are quite luxurious. About half the national parks in this region have campgrounds with facilities.

Nature lodges may be less expensive than they initially appear, as the price of a room usually includes three hearty meals a day. One or more guided hikes also may be included, but always ask about meals and hikes when making your reservation. Since many of the hotels are remote and have an eco-friendly approach (even to luxury), air-conditioning, in-room telephones, and TVs are exceptions to the rule. We mention air-conditioning and phones only when they're not offered.

Many hotels, even pricier ones, do not have hot water, and sometimes what is billed as "hot" water is actually lukewarm. If it's important to you, be very specific when you reserve.

The lodgings we list are the cream of the crop in each price category. We always list the facilities that are available, but we don't specify whether they cost extra; when pricing accommodations, always ask what's included and what costs extra. Properties are assigned price categories based on the range from the least-expensive standard double room at high season (excluding holidays) to the most expensive. Properties marked ✕▥ are lodging establishments whose restaurants warrant a special trip.

Assume that hotels operate on the European Plan (EP, with no meals) unless we specify that they use the Continental Plan (CP, with a Continental breakfast), Breakfast Plan (BP, with a full breakfast), Modified American Plan (MAP, with breakfast and dinner), Full American Plan (FAP, with all meals), or are All-inclusive (AI, including all meals and most activities).

WHAT IT COSTS (for two people)	
$$$$	over $200
$$$	$125–$200
$$	$75–$125
$	$35–$75
¢	under $35

Prices are for two people in a standard double room in high season, excluding service and tax (16.4%).

APARTMENT & VILLA RENTALS

If you want a home base that's roomy enough for a family and comes with cooking facilities, **consider a furnished rental.** In addition to accommodating your crowd, these can save you money. Look through classified ads in the Real Estate section of Costa Rica's English-language weekly, the *Tico Times.* Home-exchange directories sometimes list rentals as well as exchanges. The paper is sold in Costa Rican bookstores, supermarkets, souvenir shops, and hotel gift shops. Costa Rica Rentals International has rental homes and apartments in the San José area and elsewhere. Tropical Waters arranges short-term rentals in the Dominical area. Marina Trading Post, an affiliate of Century 21, arranges house and condominium rentals near Playa Flamingo.

🚩 International Agents **Hideaways International** ✉ 767 Islington St., Portsmouth, NH 03802 ☎ 603/430–4433 or 800/843–4433 🖷 603/430–4444 🌐 www.hideaways.com, membership $145. **Vacation Home Rentals Worldwide** ✉ 235 Kensington Ave., Norwood, NJ 07648 ☎ 201/767–9393 or 800/633–3284 🖷 201/767–5510 🌐 www.vhrww.juneau.com. **Villas and Apartments Abroad** ✉ 183 Madison Ave., Suite 201, New York, NY 10016 ☎ 212/213–6435 or 800/433–3020 🖷 212/755–8316 🌐 www.ideal-villas.com. **Villas International** ✉ 4340 Redwood Hwy., Suite D309, San Rafael, CA 94903 ☎ 415/499–9490 or 800/221–2260 🖷 415/499–9491 🌐 www.villasintl.com.

🚩 Local Agents **Costa Rica Rentals International** ✆ Apdo. 1136–1250, Escazú ☎ 506/228–6863. **Century 21** ✉ Suites Presidenciales, Playa Flamingo, Guanacaste ☎ 506/654–4004. **Tropical Waters** ✉ 3½ km (2¼ mi) north of Dominical ☎ 506/258–1558.

🚩 Rental Listings **The Tico Times** ☎ 506/233–6378 🌐 www.ticotimes.net.

CAMPING

Most commercial campgrounds in Costa Rica are at the beaches and cater to Tico families who want an economical alternative to staying in a hotel. Thus campgrounds are extremely crowded on weekends in the dry season and on national holidays. Typically the sites are small, and when the campground is full, the tents and campers will be close together and noise may be a problem. Ticos like to bring radios when they camp, and party hard. Some beach campgrounds have spectacular views of the ocean. Expect cold showers and shared water access. Fires are not permitted; most people eat out or bring butane camp stoves. Campgrounds usually start out clean but can get trashy if they are crowded.

Some private mountain reserves have campgrounds, which are similar to the beach ones described above but in cold climates may allow fires at the sites. Again, expect cold showers. Some national parks, including Rincon de la Vieja and Guayabo National Monument, have campgrounds, which are similarly rustic with shared water and cold showers. It's best to contact the park rangers for information. Chirripó National Park has a modern lodge where campers sleep on cots in a dorm, and in Corcovado National Park, campers stay at the ranger stations (reservations required). Camping is especially pleasant at the beaches of Guanacaste if you go during the week (and not on a holiday) in the dry season. Camping in the rainy season is probably not a good idea, because your equipment will get drenched and not have enough time to dry out before it rains again. It is not legal to camp outside of campgrounds, but landowners in rural areas often allow it if you ask. Do not pitch your tent without getting permission first. Some popular beaches, including Manuel Antonio, Jacó, Sámara, Tamarindo, and Puerto Viejo, have private camping areas with bathrooms and showers. If you camp on the beach or in other unguarded areas, **don't leave belongings unattended in your tent.**

HOME EXCHANGES

If you would like to exchange your home for someone else's, **join a home-exchange organization,** which will send you its updated listings of available exchanges for a year and will include your own listing in at least one of them. It's up to you to make specific arrangements.

Exchange Clubs HomeLink International Box 47747, Tampa, FL 33647 ☎ 813/975-9825 or 800/638-3841 ⊟ 813/910-8144 ⊕ www.homelink. org, $110 yearly for a listing, on-line access, and catalog, $40 without catalog. **Intervac U.S.** ✉ 30 Corte San Fernando, Tiburon, CA 94920 ☎ 800/ 756-4663 ⊟ 415/435-7440 ⊕ www.intervacus.com, $105 yearly for a listing, on-line access, and a catalog, $50 without catalog.

HOSTELS

No matter what your age, you can **save on lodging costs by staying at hostels.** In some 4,500 locations in more than 70 countries around the world, Hostelling International (HI), the umbrella group for a number of national youth-hostel associations, offers single-sex, dorm-style beds and, at many hostels, rooms for couples and family accommodations. In Costa Rica, information and reservations for some hostels are available at the Hostal Toruma in San José. Membership in any HI national hostel association, open to travelers of all ages, allows you to stay in HI-affiliated hostels at member rates; one-year membership is about $28 for adults (C$35 for a two-year minimum membership in Canada, £13.50 in the United Kingdom, A$52 in Australia, and NZ$40 in New Zealand); hostels charge about $10–$30 per night. Members have priority if the hostel is full; they're also eligible for discounts around the world, even on rail and bus travel in some countries.

Organizations Hostelling International–USA ✉ 8401 Colesville Rd., Suite 600, Silver Spring, MD 20910 ☎ 301/495-1240 ⊟ 301/495-6697 ⊕ www. hiayh.org. **Hostelling International–Canada** ✉ 400–205 Catherine St., Ottawa, Ontario K2P 1C3 ☎ 613/237-7884 or 800/663-5777 ⊟ 613/237-7868 ⊕ www.hihostels.ca. **YHA England and Wales** ✉ Trevelyan House, Dimple Rd., Matlock, Derbyshire DE4 3YH, U.K. ☎ 0870/870-8808 ⊟ 0870/770-6127 ⊕ www.yha.org.uk. **YHA Australia** ✉ 422

Kent St., Sydney, NSW 2001 ☎ 02/9261-1111 ⊟ 02/9261-1969 ⊕ www.yha.com.au. **YHA New Zealand** ✉ Level 3, 193 Cashel St., Box 436, Christchurch ☎ 03/379-9970 or 0800/278-299 ⊟ 03/365-4476 ⊕ www.yha.org.nz.

HOTELS

Aire condicionado (air-conditioning) is not standard in Costa Rica, and some hotels charge extra for rooms with air-conditioning. Almost all hotels in Costa Rica have private bathrooms, though *tinas* (bathtubs) are not available except in the most expensive large hotels. All hotels listed in this book have private bathrooms unless we indicate otherwise.

Many hotels have only *camas individuales* (single beds) and *camas matrimoniales* (double beds). At more expensive hotels, *camas queen* (queen-size beds) and *camas king* (king-size beds) may be available, but always ask about bed size.

Costa Rica also has a local environmental rating system for hotels, resorts, and beaches. Contact the ICT (⇨ Visitor Information) for details. There are a few large hotels on the outskirts of San José and on some of the more popular beaches, but most Costa Rican hotels are smaller, with more personalized service. Outside San José, rooms are in great demand between the week after Christmas and the week before Easter; reserve one to three months in advance for those times. Most hotels drop their rates during the "green season" (May to mid-December), and during this time—barring July—it's quite feasible to show up without reservations and haggle over rates, a process that can bring your hotel budget down to nearly half what it might be in the high season.

RESERVING A ROOM

Here's a sample letter requesting a room: *Estimados senores Hotel [insert name]: Es de mi interes el alquiler de una habitación en su hotel. Me interesa en particular saber que tipo de habitaciones tienen, y a la vez reservar una habitación doble con baño privado.* (Dear Sirs, at Hotel [insert name]: I am interested in reserving a room at your hotel. Specifically, I would like to know what types of rooms you have, and also to reserve a double room with a private bath.) You might also request *una habitación doble con baño compartido* (a double room with a shared bath); *una habitación con baño en un piso elevado con vista* (a double room with bath on higher floor with a view); *una habitación doble con baño en el primer piso* (a double room with bath on the ground floor); or *una habitación doble tranquila* (a quiet double room).

Most hotels, especially those in San José, require that you **reconfirm your reservation 24 to 48 hours before you arrive.** If you don't reconfirm, you may find yourself without a room.

MAIL & SHIPPING

Mail from the United States or Europe can take two to three weeks to arrive in Costa Rica (occasionally it never arrives at all). Within the country, mail service is even less reliable. Outgoing mail is marginally quicker, with delivery in five days to two weeks, especially when sent from San José. **Always use airmail for overseas cards and letters.** Mail theft is a chronic problem, so **do not mail checks, cash, or anything else of value.**

OVERNIGHT SERVICES

If you need to send important documents, checks, or other noncash valuables, you can use an international courier service, such as UPS, DHL, FedEx, or Jetex, or any of various local courier services with offices in San José. FedEx and DHL are the most widely used. (Look in the yellow pages under "Courier," in English.) If you've worked with international couriers before, you won't be surprised to hear that, for any place farther away than Miami, "overnight" is usually a misnomer—shipments to most North American cities take two days, to Britain three, and to Australia and New Zealand four or five.

🏢 Major Services **DHL** ☎ 506/210-3838. **Federal Express** ☎ 0800/052-1090. **Jetex** ☎ 506/293-0505. **United Parcel Service** (UPS) ☎ 506/290-2828.

POSTAL RATES

Letters from **Costa Rica** to the United States and Canada cost the equivalent of U.S. 26¢, postcards to the United States 23¢; to the United Kingdom, letters cost 31¢, postcards 23¢; and to Australia or New Zealand, letters cost 33¢, postcards 30¢.

RECEIVING MAIL

You can have mail sent poste restante (*lista de correos*) to any Costa Rican post office. There is no house-to-house mail service—indeed, no house numbers—in Costa Rica; most residents pick up their mail at the post office itself. In written addresses, *apartado,* abbreviated *apdo.,* indicates a post office box. Anyone with an American Express card or traveler's checks can receive mail at the American Express office in San José.

SHIPPING PARCELS

Shipping parcels through the post office is not for those in a hurry, because packages to the United States and Canada can take weeks, to the United Kingdom, Australia, and New Zealand months. Also, packages may be pilfered. If you must ship parcels, use a courier service, which is expensive but safe. Some stores offer shipping, which is usually quite expensive. It is best to carry your packages home with you. Packages can be sent from any post office, with rates spanning $6–$12 per kilogram and shipping time ranging from weeks to months, depending on the destination. Quicker, more expensive alternatives are DHL, FedEx, Jetex, and UPS, which have offices in Costa Rica—prices are about 10 times what you'd pay at the post office, but packages arrive in a matter of days.

MONEY MATTERS

Costa Rica is more expensive than other destinations in Central America, and prices are rising as more foreigners visit and relocate here. Food in modest restaurants and public transportation are inexpensive. A 1-mi taxi ride costs about $1.50. Here are some sample prices to give you an idea of the cost of living in Costa Rica: 750-ml (¾-liter) bottle of Coca-Cola, 65¢–95¢; cup of coffee, 50¢–95¢; bottle of beer, $1–$1.50; sandwich, $2–$3; daily U.S. newspaper, $1.25–$2.25.

Prices throughout this guide are given for adults. Substantially reduced fees are almost always available for children, students, and senior citizens.

ATMS

Don't count on using an ATM outside of San José. ATMs that supposedly accept Cirrus (a partner with MasterCard) and Plus (a partner with Visa) cards often don't. Get most or all of the cash you need in San José and carry some U.S. dollars in case you run out of colónes. Even in San José, it's helpful to have both a Visa and a MasterCard, as many machines accept only one or the other. ATMs are sometimes out of order and sometimes run out of cash on weekends. Only four-digit PIN numbers are accepted at ATMs in Costa Rica. The term for ATM is *cajero automático*. In San José, the main Banco Popular, which accepts Plus cards, is at Avda. 2 and C. 1, near the National Theater. Cash advances are also available in the Credomatic office, on C. Central between Avdas. 3 and 5, or the Banco de San José, across the street, which also has an American Express office on the 3rd floor. The Banco de San José has ATMs on the Cirrus system, and the bank has more than a dozen locations in San José, including the Centro Omni, one block north of the Gran Hotel Costa Rica. ScotiaBank ATMs and ATH (A Todas Horas) machines also accept international debit cards.

CREDIT CARDS

Credit cards are accepted at most major hotels and restaurants in this book. As the phone system improves and expands, many budget hotels, restaurants, and other properties have begun to accept plastic; but plenty of properties still require payment in cash. **Don't count on using plastic all the time**—once you venture outside San José, **carry enough cash or traveler's checks** to patronize the many businesses without credit-card capability. Note that some hotels, restaurants, tour companies, and other businesses add a surcharge (around 5%) to the bill if you pay with a credit card, or give you a 5%–10% discount if you pay in cash.

Throughout this guide, the following abbreviations are used: **AE,** American Express;

DC, Diners Club; **MC,** MasterCard; and **V,** Visa.

🔢 Reporting Lost Cards **American Express** ☎ 0800/012-3211 collect to U.S. **Diners Club** ☎ 702/797-5532 collect to the U.S. **MasterCard** ☎ 0800/011-0184 toll-free to U.S. **Visa** ☎ 0800/011-0030 toll-free to U.S.

CURRENCY

All prices in this book are quoted in U.S. dollars. The Costa Rican currency, the colón (plural: colónes), is subject to continual, small devaluations. At this writing, the colón is 443 to the U.S. dollar, 536 to the Euro, 323 to the Canadian dollar, 803 to the pound sterling, 314 to the Australian dollar, and 274 to the New Zealand dollar.

CURRENCY EXCHANGE

For the most favorable rates, **change money through banks or use local ATMs.** Although ATM transaction fees may be higher than at home, ATM rates are excellent because they are based on wholesale rates offered only by major banks. Exchange rates are not as good at hotels, restaurants, or stores, though their hours are often more convenient than those of the banks. Costa Rican colónes are sold abroad at terrible rates, so you should wait until you arrive in Costa Rica to get local currency. Private banks—Scotia, Banco Banex, and Banco de San José—are the best places to change U.S. dollars and traveler's checks. There is a branch of the Banco de San José in the airport that is open daily 5 AM–10 PM where you can exchange money when you arrive, but taxi and van drivers who pick up at the airport do take U.S. dollars. Currencies other than U.S. dollars are not widely accepted and may be difficult to exchange, so bring U.S. dollars. Australian and New Zealand dollars can't be changed at all in Costa Rica, even at banks.

Avoid people on the city streets who offer to change money. San José's outdoor money changers are notorious for short-changing people and passing counterfeit bills. The guys who change money at the airport aren't quite as shady, but they might not be above shortchanging you, and they don't offer great rates in any case.

🖪 Exchange Services International Currency Express ✉ 427 N. Camden Dr., Suite F, Beverly Hills, CA 90210 ☎ 888/278-6628 orders 🖷 310/278-6410 ⊕ www.foreignmoney.com. Thomas Cook Currency Services ☎ 800/287-7362 orders and retail locations ⊕ www.us.thomascook.com.

TRAVELER'S CHECKS

Do you need traveler's checks? It depends on where you're headed. If you're going to rural areas and small towns, go with cash; traveler's checks are best used in cities. Lost or stolen checks can usually be replaced within 24 hours. To ensure a speedy refund, buy your own traveler's checks—don't let someone else pay for them: irregularities like this can cause delays. The person who bought the checks should make the call to request a refund. If you have an American Express card and can draw on a U.S. checking account, you can buy U.S.-dollar traveler's checks at the American Express office in San José for a 1% service charge.

PACKING

Pack light, as you will probably end up having to carry your bag for some distance. Plus, domestic airlines have tight weight restrictions (at this writing 25 pounds [11.3 kilograms] for NatureAir and 30 pounds [13.6 kilograms] for SANSA) and not all buses have luggage compartments. It's a good idea to pack essentials in one bag and extras in another, so you can leave one bag at your hotel in San José or at the airport if you exceed weight restrictions. Frameless backpacks and duffel bags are good luggage choices—they can be squeezed into tight spaces and are less conspicuous than fancier luggage. Bring comfortable, hand-washable clothing. T-shirts and shorts are acceptable near the beach and in tourist areas; long-sleeve shirts and pants protect your skin from ferocious sun and, in some regions, mosquitoes. In less-touristed areas, women should avoid tops that show cleavage or part of the stomach and shorts and skirts much above the knee.

Leave your jeans behind—they take forever to dry and can't be worn out in the evenings. **Bring a large hat** to block the sun from your face and neck. **Pack a waterproof, lightweight jacket** and a light sweater for cool nights, early mornings, trips up volcanoes, and to the Atlantic coast; you'll need even warmer clothes for trips to Chirripó National Park or Volcán Baru and overnight stays in San Gerardo de Dota or La Providencia Lodge. Sturdy sneakers or hiking boots are essential for sightseeing on foot. Waterproof hiking sandals such as Tevas are good for boat rides, beach walks, streams (should you need to ford one), and light hiking trails. Bring at least one good (and wrinkle-free) outfit for going out at night. Costa Ricans tend to dress up a bit more than Americans. Remember to bring a small day-trip backpack or bag.

Insect repellent (especially if you're going to Tortuguero), sunscreen, sunglasses, and umbrellas (during the rainy season) are crucial. Women might have a tough time finding tampons, so bring your own. Other handy items—especially if you'll be roughing it—include toilet paper, facial tissues, a plastic water bottle, and a flashlight (for occasional power outages or inadequately lighted walkways at lodges). Toilet paper is not usually available in public rest rooms unless there is an attendant. For almost all toilet articles, including contact lens supplies, a pharmacy is your best bet. **Don't forget binoculars** and a comfortable carrying strap. Snorkelers staying at budget hotels should consider bringing their own equipment; otherwise, you can rent gear at most beach resorts. If you're surfing, consider buying your board here; Tamarindo has a good shop. Some beaches, such as Playa Grande, do not have shade trees, so if you're planning to linger at the beach, you might consider investing in a sturdy tarpaulin.

In your carry-on luggage, **pack an extra pair of eyeglasses or contact lenses and enough of any medication** you take to last a few days longer than the entire trip. You may also ask your doctor to write a spare prescription using the drug's generic name, as brand names may vary from country to country. In luggage to be checked, **never pack prescription drugs, valuables, or un-**

developed film. And don't forget to carry with you the addresses of offices that handle refunds of lost traveler's checks. Check *Fodor's How to Pack* (available at online retailers and bookstores everywhere) for more tips.

To avoid customs and security delays, carry medications in their original packaging. Don't pack any sharp objects in your carry-on luggage, including knives of any size or material, scissors, and corkscrews, or anything else that might arouse suspicion.

To avoid having your checked luggage chosen for hand inspection, don't cram bags full. The U.S. Transportation Security Administration suggests packing shoes on top and placing personal items you don't want touched in clear plastic bags.

CHECKING LUGGAGE

The tiny, domestic passenger planes (seating about 6 to 12 people) in Costa Rica require that you pack light. A luggage weight limit of 25 or 30 pounds (11 or 14 kilograms), *including* carry-ons, is almost always enforced. For the same reason, two lighter bags are preferable to one heavy bag.

On international flights, you're allowed to carry aboard one bag and one personal article, such as a purse or a laptop computer. Make sure what you carry on fits under your seat or in the overhead bin. Get to the gate early, so you can board as soon as possible, before the overhead bins fill up.

Baggage allowances vary by carrier, destination, and ticket class. On international flights, you're usually allowed to check two bags weighing up to 70 pounds (32 kilograms) each, although a few airlines allow checked bags of up to 88 pounds (40 kilograms) in first class. Some international carriers don't allow more than 66 pounds (30 kilograms) per bag in business class and 44 pounds (20 kilograms) in economy. Check baggage restrictions with your carrier before you pack.

Airline liability for baggage is limited to $2,500 per person on flights within the United States. On international flights it amounts to $9.07 per pound or $20 per kilogram for checked baggage (roughly $640 per 70-pound bag) and $400 per passenger for unchecked baggage. You can buy additional coverage at check-in for about $10 per $1,000 of coverage, but it often excludes a rather extensive list of items, shown on your airline ticket.

Before departure, **itemize your bags' contents** and their worth, and label the bags with your name, address, and phone number. (If you use your home address, cover it so potential thieves can't see it readily.) Include a label inside each bag and **pack a copy of your itinerary.** At check-in, **make sure each bag is correctly tagged** with the destination airport's three-letter code. Because some checked bags will be opened for hand inspection, the U.S. Transportation Security Administration recommends that you leave luggage unlocked or use the plastic locks offered at check-in. TSA screeners place an inspection notice inside searched bags, which are resealed with a special lock.

If your bag has been searched and contents are missing or damaged, file a claim with the TSA Consumer Response Center as soon as possible. If your bags arrive damaged or fail to arrive at all, file a written report with the airline before leaving the airport.

⊞ Complaints U.S. Transportation Security Administration Consumer Response Center ☎ 866/ 289-9673 ⊕ www.tsa.gov.

PASSPORTS & VISAS

When traveling internationally, **carry your passport** even if you don't need one (it's always the best form of ID) and **make two photocopies of the data page** (one for someone at home and another for you, carried separately from your passport). If you lose your passport, promptly call the nearest embassy or consulate and the local police.

U.S. passport applications for children under age 14 require consent from both parents or legal guardians; both parents must appear together to sign the application. If only one parent appears, he or she must submit a written statement from the other parent authorizing passport issuance for the child. A parent with sole authority must present evidence of it when applying;

acceptable documentation includes the child's certified birth certificate listing only the applying parent, a court order specifically permitting this parent's travel with the child, or a death certificate for the nonapplying parent. Application forms and instructions are available on the Web site of the U.S. State Department's Bureau of Consular Affairs (⊕ www.travel.state.gov).

Citizens of Australia and New Zealand need only a valid passport to enter Costa Rica for stays of up to 30 days. You are presented with a 30-day tourist visa when you arrive. Once you're here, you can go to the Migracion office in La Uruca and extend the visa to 90 days. Canadians, U.S. citizens, and citizens of the U.K. need only a valid passport to enter Costa Rica for stays of up to 90 days.

REST ROOMS

Rest rooms in Costa Rica are similar to those in the United States, except toilet paper is usually not provided. Carry some in your bag or pocket. There are no pay toilets in Costa Rica, but some public rest rooms have attendants whom you have to pay (usually around 25¢) to get a few sheets of toilet paper, particularly at bus stations. Some restaurants and bars require a fee to use the rest room, usually about 10¢–25¢. Gas stations do have rest rooms. Cleanliness standards for all rest rooms, including public rest rooms, vary widely. Sinks everywhere but at the most expensive hotels do not have hot water, and sinks in public restaurants often don't have soap.

SAFETY

For many English-speaking tourists, standing out like a sore thumb can't be avoided in Costa Rica. But there are some precautions you can take. Don't wear a waist pack or a money belt, because thieves can cut the strap. Instead, distribute your cash and any valuables (including credit cards and passport) among a deep front pocket, an inside jacket or vest pocket, and a hidden money pouch. Carry some cash in your purse or wallet so you don't have to reach for the money pouch in public.

Violent crime is not a serious problem in Costa Rica, but thieves can easily prey on tourists, so be alert. Roll up car windows and lock car doors when you leave your car, and keep windows rolled up and doors locked all the time in cities. Crimes against property are rife in San José. In rural areas theft is on the rise. Park in designated parking lots, or if that's not possible, accept the offer of men or boys who ask if they can watch your car while you're gone. Give them the equivalent of a dollar per hour when you return. **Never leave valuables visible in a car,** even in an attended parking lot. Take them inside with you whenever possible, or lock them in the trunk. Padlocks are a good idea for all luggage. Talk with locals or your hotel's staff about crime whenever you arrive in a new location. They will be able to tell you if it's safe to walk around after dark and what areas to avoid.

Don't wear expensive jewelry or watches. Backpacks should be carried on your front; thieves can slit your backpack and run away with its contents before you notice. Likewise, your wallet goes in your front pocket, and you should keep your hand on it if you are in a crowd or on a crowded bus. In cities women shouldn't let purses dangle from their shoulders; always hold on to your purse with your hand, and if it has a shoulder strap, cross it over your chest. If you put your luggage on the luggage rack in the bus, you're in danger of it being hooked and dragged to the back of the bus, where someone can exit with it. Attach your bag to the luggage rack with a caribiner or padlock it with a small chain.

Never walk in a narrow space between a building and a car parked on the street close to it; thieves can be hiding there. If you are involved in an altercation with a mugger, immediately surrender your possessions and walk away quickly. Do not walk in parks in San José or other cities at night. Muggers abound, and are not above knocking you on your head with a piece of wood or other weapon to steal your shoes! Men should be suspicious of overly friendly or sexually aggressive females. At best they are probably a prostitute; at worst they have targeted you for a scam.

Scams involving date-rape drugs have become common in the past few years; the incapacitating drug Rohypnol is still afoot and is used on men and women, so never leave a drink unattended in a club or bar. When on a crowded bus, keep your hand on your wallet or your eyes on your purse. Never leave your belongings unattended anywhere, including at the beach or in a tent. Many hotel rooms have safes, which should be used (even if it's an extra charge). If your room doesn't have one, ask the manager to put your valuables in the hotel safe. Ask him or her to sign a list of what you put in the safe. Do not carry expensive cameras or much cash in cities. Most important, **don't bring anything you can't stand to lose.**

LOCAL SCAMS

Scams are common in San José, where a drug addict may tell tales of having recently been robbed, then ask you for donations; a distraction artist might squirt you with cream or chocolate sauce, then try to clean you off while his partner steals your backpack; pickpockets and bag slashers work buses and crowds; and street money changers pass off counterfeit bills. To top it all off, car theft is rampant. Beware of anyone who seems overly friendly, aggressively helpful, or disrespectful of your personal space.

WOMEN IN COSTA RICA

If you carry a purse, choose one with a zipper and a thick strap that you can drape across your body; adjust the length so that the purse sits in front of you at or above hip level. Store only enough money in the purse to cover casual spending. Distribute the rest of your cash and any valuables among deep front pockets, inside jacket or vest pockets, and a concealed money pouch.

Lone women travelers will get a fair amount of attention from men, but in general should be safe. Women should not hitchhike alone or in pairs. Blondes and redheads will get more grief than brunettes. To avoid hassles, avoid wearing short shorts, short skirts, or sleeveless tops. On the bus, try to take a seat next to a woman. Women should not walk alone

in San José at night or venture into dangerous areas of the city at all. Ask at your hotel which neighborhoods to avoid. Ignore unwanted comments. If you are being harassed on a bus, in a restaurant or other public place, tell the manager. In taxis, sit in the backseat.

SENIOR-CITIZEN TRAVEL

Older travelers flock to Costa Rica, and many businesses are making an effort to cater to the specific comforts of this demographic. Some senior citizens may encounter more challenges to mobility than they do at home—especially on those muddy jungle trails—but should otherwise find Costa Rica most hospitable.

To qualify for age-related discounts, **mention your senior-citizen status up front** when booking hotel reservations (not when checking out) and before you're seated in restaurants (not when paying the bill). Be sure to have identification on hand. When renting a car, ask about promotional car-rental discounts, which can be cheaper than senior-citizen rates.

🏫 Educational Programs **Elderhostel** ✉ 11 Ave. de Lafayette, Boston, MA 02111-1746 ☎ 877/426-8056, 978/323-4141 international callers, 877/426-2167 TTY 📠 877/426-2166 🌐 www.elderhostel.org. **Interhostel** ✉ University of New Hampshire, 11 Garrison Ave., Durham, NH 03824 ☎ 603/862-2015 or 800/313-5327 📠 603/862-1113 🌐 www.learn.unh.edu.

SHOPPING

Shopping is not a main reason to visit Costa Rica, but some high-quality wooden and leather handicrafts are available. San José has the best shopping opportunities, in small gift stores in the city center, an outdoor market near the Museo Nacional, and a whole neighborhood called Moravia in the northern part of the city devoted to souvenir stores. Bargaining is possible in outdoor markets, where you should expect to pay about 80% of the first price the vendor gives. Souvenir stores usually give discounts if you pay cash.

KEY DESTINATIONS

The town of Sarchí in the Central Valley, the Moravia neighborhood in San José, and Hotel Don Carlos and La Casona artisan's market in Central San José are good places to shop. Also, there is an outdoor handicraft market in the Plaza de la Democracia, contiguous to the Museo Nacional. All offer the same types of leather and wooden handicrafts, including miniature oxcarts, which are the unofficial national symbol of Costa Rica.

SMART SOUVENIRS

Attractive souvenirs from Costa Rica include wooden bowls and boxes, wooden mobiles, and wood and leather rocking chairs. All of these can be found at souvenir shops in San José, in crafts stores in the town of Sarchi, and at gift shops in larger hotels. Prices are varied depending on the size of the bowls and boxes. The rocking chairs, which fold for shipping, cost about $100. The mobiles cost $15–$20 and also fold for shipping.

Coffee is a good souvenir, and if you choose a high-quality Costa Rica brand with no sugar added, there's no need to pay inflated prices for export brands marketed at foreigners. Local brands Cafe Volio and Cafe Rey sold at ordinary grocery stores and neighborhood shops (*pulperias*) are good. Other popular food items that make great souvenirs include Salsa Alfaro (formerly Salsa Lizano, as it is still commonly known), a tangy cooking sauce used to season beans, meat, and chicken, and Costa Rican cookies and candy. Local cookie factory Gallito produces many different varieties. Buy them at grocery stores and pulperias.

WATCH OUT

Cuban cigars are available in Costa Rica but won't be allowed in the country if you take them back to the United States. Don't buy products made of animal skins or tortoiseshell. Indian pottery that is sold on the street as authentic is not. Instead, buy pottery in Guiatil, Santa Cruz in Nicoya, or in upscale art galleries and hotel gift shops in and around San José. Hotel Grano de Oro and Hotel Don Carlos in San José, the Marriott in San Antonio de Belén, and Hotel Bougainvillea in Heredia are good bets.

SIGHTSEEING GUIDES

Guides are organized through tour companies or private nature reserves and are hired at the reserves or through local travel agencies and tour companies. Freelance guides don't approach travelers at destinations. If you are approached by someone who is persistent, go into the nearest hotel, restaurant, or park office and complain to the management.

SPORTS & THE OUTDOORS

BICYCLING

Costa Rica is a combination of mountainous terrain and cycle-friendly flatlands. A number of tour operators run bike tours (⇨ Tours & Packages). You can rent bikes in most Costa Rican mountain and beach resorts. No national biking organizations exist. Inquire in local bike shops about recommendations for trails and routes, equipment purchases, and repair. One good bike shop is on the Paseo Colon in San José near the Hospital de Niños, another is in San Pedro next to the Fuji photo store.

BIRD-WATCHING

Costa Rica is one of the world's most popular birding destinations, because of the more than 800 species that live in the country for all or part of the year. In a full week of birding and traveling around the country, an experienced birder can expect to see 300 species including many "life birds" (first of a species you see in your life). The best way to do birding in Costa Rica is to go with an experienced, bilingual naturalist guide. Although it is possible for independent travelers with binoculars to see birds on their own in the wild, it's difficult to discern them in dense rain forest or cloud forest. Some private reserves and lodges employ resident guides, some of whom are excellent birders. Some of the best birding areas are Monteverde, the Atlantic Lowlands—including the area around Puerto Viejo de Sarrapiqui—and Carara National Park. There are birds everywhere in Costa Rica—it is truly a birder's paradise.

Veteran birder, freelance guide, and long-time Costa Rica resident Richard Garrigues keeps his Gone Birding Web site updated with a complete Costa Rican bird list. It is more up-to-date than most field guides, and reflects recent additions and deletions approved by the National Museum of Costa Rica's Ornithology Department. You can sign up to receive Garrigues' e-mail newsletter, which comes out four times a year and includes rare sightings, activities of the Costa Rican Ornithological Association (Spanish only) and of the Birding Club of Costa Rica (English), plus the Audubon Society's Christmas Bird Count and other bird happenings in Costa Rica.

Bird-watching Resources Gone Birding ⊕ www.angelfire.com/bc/gonebirding. **Birding Club of Costa Rica** ✉ crbirdingclub@hotmail.com.

HIKING

You will have no problem finding lots of hiking opportunities in Costa Rica. Ask at your hotel for directions to hiking trails, and make sure you ask about the difficulty of the trail, how much time it will take, and any special conditions or warnings. Hikes range from relaxing strolls on well-marked trails to strenuous, multiday backpacking trips through the rain forest. National parks have long and short hiking routes that in many cases include stepping-stones and handrails. Stick to clearly marked trails, and avoid venturing out on your own into natural areas. Every year travelers are lost in the wilderness (often deep in national parks) after they strayed from the trails, and some have died. Many tour companies that specialize in hiking visit sites off the beaten track (⇨ Tours & Packages).

Start your hike early to see wildlife; try to be on the trail by 6:30 AM to see the most birds. Dangers to hikers in Costa Rica include dehydration, sunstroke, snakes, and weather conditions such as cold—in Chirripo, Monteverde, and Cerro de la Muerte—and rain. It is essential to take rain gear and drinking water, and to wear good walking shoes. Arenal Volcano, Monteverde, Tapanti National Park, and Corcovado National Park are popular hiking destinations for day trips. There are three major long-distance hikes within Corcovado National Park, with camping available at ranger stations along the way. Make reservations months ahead to hike overnight in Corcovado.

Climbing Chirripó, Costa Rica's highest peak, is a fantastic multiday trip for serious hikers.

There are several camping gear stores in San José that sell hiking equipment, but at much higher prices than in the United States. These stores tend to have a small selection of merchandise and are usually staffed by people who don't know much about hiking. It's better to bring your own hiking boots and other essential equipment from home.

SCUBA DIVING

Costa Rica's best dive spot is Cocos Island. The only way to get there is on a 10-day trip aboard the *Okeanos Aggressor* or *Undersea Hunter* (⇨ Tours & Packages).

Most Costa Rican dive shops are part of the PADI system. Apart from the world-class Cocos Island, Costa Rica does not have top scuba diving locations. But the warm, clear waters make it a good place for an introduction to the sport. Especially popular are day trips to Guanacaste's Catalina and Murcielago islands. Caño Island, off Drake Bay, is the best destination for a daylong scuba and snorkeling trip, and all of the Drake Bay lodges run dive tours to the island. Among the sea creatures scuba divers usually see are white-tipped reef sharks, spotted eagle rays, sea turtles, angelfish, octopus, stingrays, and sometimes whale sharks (prevalent around Cocos Island).

On the Pacific side of the country, the best months for diving are December to April, and July, which are the dry months. Heavy rains during the rest of the year cause river runoff to cloud waters at popular diving spots. On the Atlantic side of the country, diving conditions are more unpredictable, but October is usually considered the best month to go. Prices for PADI diving certification courses are lower than in the United States. Most major beach towns on both coasts have scuba diving shops.

Divers looking for sites off the beaten track can contact Shawn Larkin, a freelance dive guide and columnist who writes about sea life and diving conditions for the

Tico Times, for information or to sign up for a dive trip.

🎿 Scuba Diving Resources **Pacific Coast Dive Center** ☎ 506/653-0267 Tamarindo, 506/654-444, Ext. 264 Playa Flamingo. **Shawn Larkin** ✉ Near Gandoca-Manzanillo National Wildlife Refuge ☎ 506/770-8021 or 506/391-3417 ✍ shawn@costacetacea.com.

SNORKELING

You can make skin-diving excursions from Drake Bay, Playa Flamingo, Playa Ocotal, and Playa del Coco.

Inquire about snorkeling locations and rental of snorkel gear at scuba diving shops. Scuba diving tour companies often give snorkeling tours as well (⇨ Tours & Packages). Snorkeling is common at beach locations, but Costa Rica doesn't have much live coral reef close to shore. The exception is in Cahuita, on the Atlantic Coast, where Cahuita National Park has a beautiful reef for snorkeling. Several tour and souvenir shops in Cauhita and Puerto Viejo de Talamanca rent snorkeling equipment, but it is not the best quality or in the best shape. If you want to do some serious snorkeling, bring your own equipment. Your hotel might also rent or lend equipment.

Other good snorkeling spots include Manuel Antonio National Park, Mal Pais near the Pacific beach town of Montezuma, and Flamingo Beach in Guanacaste.

SURFING

Costa Rica is famous for its awesome waves. Surfing conditions are best in Gaunacaste and the Central Pacific in the November to March windy season. On the Atlantic, the best waves are December–February. Popular surfing beaches include Tamarindo, Jacó, Hermosa, Dominical, and Pavones. Playa Naranjo, in Santa Rosa National Park, is famous for incredible tubular waves at Witches Rock. Puerto Viejo de Talamanca is known for "Salsa Brava," huge waves that are not for amateurs. In Guanacaste, try Playa Negra, which is a favorite with Tico surfers. There are surf shops in Tamarindo, Jacó, San José, Puerto Viejo de Talamanca, Dominical, and Puntarenas.

Many travelers bring their own boards and sell them at these surf shops when they leave. Surfers say the best way to take a surfing vacation is to get several buddies together, rent a four-wheel-drive vehicle for a week or more, put the boards on the top, and hit several different surfing beaches. Wavehunters Surf Travel and CR-Surf.com offer lots of information. Tico Travel and Costa Rica Surfing Adventures organize surfing vacations.

Airlines generally allow surfboards on board for a fee of around $15. Surfing vacation packages are available (⇨ Tours & Packages).

🏄 Surfing Resources **Costa Rica Surfing Adventures** ☎ 800/948-3770 ⊕ www.centralamerica.com/cr/surf. **CRSurf.com** ⊕ www.crsurf.com. **Iguana Surf Aquatic Outfitters** ✉ Road to Playa Langosta, Tamarindo ☎ 506/653-0148. **Mango Surf Shop** ✉ Mall San Pedro, San Pedro ☎ 506/224-1775. **Quique** ✉ Avda. Central, between Cs. 5 and 7, San José ☎ 506/222-9463. **Tico Travel** ☎ 800/493-8426 in North America. **Wavehunters Surf Travel** ☎ 760/433-3078, 888/899-8823 in North America ⊕ www.wavehunters.com.

WHITE-WATER RAFTING

Wild rivers churn plenty of white water for rafting. The Pacuare, Sarapiquí, and Peñas Blancas rivers are some of the best for rafting. Some sections of the Río Reventazón are still used by commercial companies, although a hydroelectric dam has destroyed what was the best section. Try to consider yourself fortunate if your company cancels your trip because of high or low water levels. There have been several deaths on commercial white-water rafting trips in the last few years, and the government and a steering committee of rafting company representatives are in the process of developing new standards. The largest rafting companies, Ríos Tropicales, Costa Rica Expeditions, and Aventuras Naturales, observe rigorous safety standards and treat the country's rivers with respect.

Commercial rafting trips range from Class I (floating) to Class III (a couple of wild rapids in the Pacuare). Class IV and V rapids are not run on commercial trips.

🚣 White-Water Rafting Outfitters **Aventuras Naturales** ✉ San Pedro, Costa Rica ☎ 506/225-3939.

Costa Rica Expeditions ✉ Avda. 3, 25 m east of the Oficina Central de Correos San José, Costa Rica ☎ 506/222-0333. **Ríos Tropicales** ✉ C. 38, between Avdas. Central and 2 San José, Costa Rica ☎ 506/233-6455.

WINDSURFING

Lake Arenal is one of the world's best places to windsurf because of strong winds year-round. The lake also has warm water, moderate temperatures, and good accommodations nearby.

⚑ **Windsurfing Outfitters Tilawa** ✉ Lake Arenal ☎ 506/695-5050 ⊕ www.hotel-tilawa.com.

STUDENTS IN COSTA RICA

Although prices are on the rise, you can still travel on $25–$30 a day if you put your mind to it. There are youth hostels and hotels affiliated with Hostelling International all over Costa Rica, though one of the cheapest ways to spend the night in this region is to camp; as long as you have your own tent, it's easy to set up house almost anywhere. It illegal to camp outside of campgrounds, but many land owners in rural areas will allow you to camp on their land. Do not pitch your tent without getting permission first. Don't ever leave your belongings or a campfire unattended.

⚑ **IDs & Services STA Travel** ✉ 10 Downing St., New York, NY 10014 ☎ 212/627-3111 or 800/777-0112 🖷 212/627-3387 ⊕ www.statravel.com. **Travel Cuts** ✉ 187 College St., Toronto, Ontario M5T 1P7, Canada ☎ 416/979-2406, 800/592-2887, 866/246-9762 in Canada 🖷 416/979-8167 ⊕ www.travelcuts.com.

TAXES

When you fly out of Costa Rica, you'll have to pay a $26 airport departure tax at Juan Santamaría airport. Although people may offer to sell it to you the moment you climb out of your taxi, it's best to **buy your exit stamp inside the airport**; look for airport-employee identification. If you buy elsewhere, you'll have no recourse if someone sells you fake stamps or gives you the wrong change or conversion rate.

VALUE-ADDED TAX

All Costa Rican businesses charge a 13% sales tax, and hotels charge an extra 4% tourist tax. Tourists do not get refunds on sales tax paid in Central American countries.

TELEPHONES

Local telephone numbers have seven digits. If your cell phone or pager company has service to Costa Rica, you theoretically can use it here, but expect reception to be impossible in many areas of this mountainous country. The Costa Rican phone system is very good by the standards of other developing countries. However, phone numbers change often and are handed out willy-nilly.

AREA & COUNTRY CODES

The country code for Costa Rica is 506. There are no area codes. Phoning home: the country code for the United States and Canada is 001, Australia 61, New Zealand 64, and the United Kingdom 44.

DIRECTORY & OPERATOR ASSISTANCE

International information is 124. The international operator is 175. Calling cards from the United States or Canada with 800 numbers don't work in Costa Rica. In Costa Rica, dial ☎ 113 for domestic directory inquiries and ☎ 110 for domestic collect calls.

INTERNATIONAL CALLS

Costa Rica's *guía telefónica* (phone book) lists the rates for calling various countries. To call overseas directly, dial 00, then the country code, the area code, and the number. Calls to the United States and Canada are the same price at all times; calls to the United Kingdom are discounted only on weekends, from Friday at 10 PM to Monday at 7 AM.

It's cheapest to either call from a pay phone using an international phone card, sold in shops; call from a pay phone using your own long-distance calling card; or call from a telephone office. Dialing directly from a hotel room is very expensive, as is recruiting an international operator to connect you.

LOCAL CALLS

Making a local call in Costa Rica is pretty straightforward, because all telephone numbers in the country are seven digits.

Using a phone card from a pay phone can be frustrating because different phones operate somewhat differently. In some you put the card in first and then dial; in the more modern phones, you don't insert the card.

For long-distance calls within Costa Rica, you don't have to dial anything extra. All phone numbers in Costa Rica have seven digits, whether you are calling within the same town or to the other side of the country.

LONG-DISTANCE SERVICES

AT&T, MCI, and Sprint access codes make calling long-distance relatively convenient, but you may find the local access number blocked in many hotel rooms. First ask the hotel operator to connect you. If the hotel operator balks, ask for an international operator, or dial the international operator yourself. To reach an English-speaking operator, dial 116. To make a collect call from any phone, dial 09, the international access code of the country being called, and then the number. One way to improve your odds of getting connected to your long-distance carrier is to travel with more than one company's calling card (a hotel may block Sprint, for example, but not MCI). If all else fails, call from a pay phone.

✆ Access Codes AT&T Direct ☎ 0800/011-4114. **British Telecom** ☎ 0800/044-1044. **Canada Direct** ☎ 0800/015-1161. **MCI WorldPhone** ☎ 0800/012-2222. **Sprint International Access** ☎ 0800/013-0123.

✆ Telephone Offices Radiográfica Costarricense ✉ Avda. 5 between Cs. 1 and 3.

PHONE CARDS

Most phone cards have codes (revealed by scratching off a section on the back) that you have to punch into the telephone. Scratch-off cards are called *tarjetas telefónicas de raspar.* They are sold in an array of shops, including Más x Menos supermarkets, post offices, offices of the Costa Rican Electricity Institute (ICE), and at any business displaying the gold-and-blue TARJETAS TELEFÓNICAS sign. Phone cards can be purchased in different amounts; with *tarjetas para llamadas na-*

cionales (domestic calling cards), the card denominations are 500 colónes, 1,000 colónes, and 3,000 colónes. Cards for international calls are sold in $10, $20, 3,000 colónes, and 10,000 colónes amounts (denominations are inexplicably split between dollars and colónes). *Tarjeta para llamadas internacionales* (international calling cards) can be used at any nonrotary public telephone in Costa Rica, including residential phones, cell phones, and hotel phones. The cost of calling to the United States is about a dollar a minute. Ask about international calling rates before you call from your hotel room; some hotels charge much more than you would pay by buying a phone card.

To use an international phone card purchased in Costa Rica, first dial 199, then the PIN on the back of your card (revealed after scratching off a protective coating), then the phone number. Follow the same procedure to use a domestic phone card, but dial 197 instead of 199.

Some public phones accept only *tarjetas chip* ("chip" cards), which record what you spend, though they're a dying breed. Avoid buying chip cards: they malfunction, you can use them only at the few-and-far-between chip phones, and they are sold in small denominations that are not sufficient for international calls.

PUBLIC PHONES

Pay phones are abundant, though they always seem to be in use. Some older-style phones accept coins, but most accept only phone cards, which are sold in various shops. Local calls are charged by the minute. Rates are different depending on how far away in the country you are calling.

Watch out for pay phones marked CALL USA/CANADA WITH A CREDIT CARD. They are *wildly* expensive.

TIME

Costa Rica is six hours behind GMT; the country does not observe daylight saving time.

TIPPING

Taxi drivers aren't tipped. Tip gas station attendants 100 colónes. Do not use American change to tip, because there is no way for locals to exchange it. Chambermaids get 400–800 colónes per day. Concierges are usually not tipped. Room-service waiters should be tipped about 400 colónes, as should bell caps (more in the most expensive hotels). Restaurant bills include a 13% tax and 10% service charge—sometimes these amounts are included in prices on the menu, and sometimes they aren't. The menu should say or you should ask. Additional gratuity is not expected, especially in cheap restaurants, but people often leave something extra when service is good. Leave a tip of about 200 colónes per drink for bartenders, too.

At some point on a trip, most visitors to Costa Rica are in the care of a naturalist guide, who can show you the sloths and special hiking trails you'd never find on your own. **Give $10 (4,500 colónes) per day per person to guides** if they've transported and guided you individually or in small groups. Give less to guides on bigger tours, or if they're affiliated with the hotel or lodge where you're staying.

TOURS & PACKAGES

Because everything is prearranged on a prepackaged tour or independent vacation, you spend less time planning—and often get it all at a good price.

BOOKING WITH AN AGENT

Travel agents are excellent resources. But it's a good idea to collect brochures from several agencies, as some agents' suggestions may be influenced by relationships with tour and package firms that reward them for volume sales. If you have a special interest, **find an agent with expertise in that area**; the American Society of Travel Agents (ASTA; ⇨ Travel Agencies) has a database of specialists worldwide.

Make sure your travel agent knows the accommodations and other services of the place being recommended. Ask about the hotel's location, room size, beds, and whether it has a pool, room service, or programs for children, if you care about these. Has your agent been there in person or sent others whom you can contact?

Do some homework on your own, too: local tourism boards can provide information about lesser-known and small-niche operators, some of which may sell only direct.

BUYER BEWARE

Each year consumers are stranded or lose their money when tour operators—even large ones with excellent reputations—go out of business. So **check out the operator**. Ask several travel agents about its reputation, and try to **book with a company that has a consumer-protection program.** (Look for information in the company's brochure.) In the United States, members of the National Tour Association and the United States Tour Operators Association are required to set aside funds to cover payments and travel arrangements in the event that the company defaults. It's also a good idea to choose a company that participates in the American Society of Travel Agents' Tour Operator Program; ASTA will act as mediator in any disputes between you and your tour operator.

Remember that the more your package or tour includes, the better you can predict the ultimate cost of your vacation. Make sure you know exactly what is covered, and **beware of hidden costs.** Are taxes, tips, and transfers included? Entertainment and excursions? These can add up.

📝 Tour-Operator Recommendations **American Society of Travel Agents (** ⇨ Travel Agencies). **National Tour Association (NTA)** ✉ 546 E. Main St., Lexington, KY 40508 ☎ 859/226–4444 or 800/682–8886 ⊕ www.ntaonline.com. **United States Tour Operators Association (USTOA)** ✉ 275 Madison Ave., Suite 2014, New York, NY 10016 ☎ 212/599–6599 or 800/468–7862 🖷 212/599–6744 ⊕ www.ustoa.com.

BIKING TOURS

Most bike tour operators cater to travelers who are in moderately good shape and do some biking at home. The operators provide top-notch equipment, including bikes, helmets, water bottles, and so forth. Most use mountain bikes and require a lot of downhill and some uphill pedaling. All of the companies can design custom tours for extreme cyclists if requested.

F Bike Tour Operators **BiCosta Rica** ⊠ Atenas 🚲 506/446-7585. **Coast to Coast** ⊠ San José ☎ 506/280-8054. **Coasts and Mountains** ⊠ Apdo. 317051, Cartago ☎ 506/395-5216. **Jungle Man Adventures** ⊠ Hotel Don Fadrique, San José ☎ 506/225-8186. **Río Escondido Mountain Bikes** ⊠ Rock River Lodge, Tilarán ☎ 506/692-1180.

BIRD-WATCHING TOURS

You will almost definitely get more out of your time in Costa Rica by taking a tour rather than trying to find birds on your own. Bring your own binoculars but don't worry about a spotting scope; if you go with a tour company that specializes in birding tours, your guide will have one. Expect to see about 300 species during a weeklong tour. Many U.S. travel companies that offer bird-watching tours subcontract with the Costa Rican tour operators listed below. By arranging your tour directly with the Costa Rican companies, you avoid the middleman and save money.

F Bird-Watching Tour Operators **Costa Rica Expeditions** ⊠ San José, Costa Rica ☎ 506/222-0333. **Horizontes** ⊠ San José, Costa Rica ☎ 506/222-2022.

CANOPY TOURS

If you not only want to see monkeys in Costa Rica but also want the perspective of one, **take a canopy tour.** Using rock-climbing equipment, you slide along cables strung between treetops in the canopy. It's a unique experience that's easier to manage than you might think—even for the slightly fearful. Heavier people should ask about weight limits ahead of time. One reputable company is the Original Canopy Tour, with branches in Monteverde, Tabacón (near Arenal), Drake Bay, and four other destinations. Its well-trained guides are bilingual and its safety record is good. **Don't go with the less-expensive competitors** unless you've acquainted yourself with their safety practices and feel comfortable; and **be prepared to walk away** if the trip doesn't look or feel professionally handled. It's still an unregulated business, and many companies cut corners on safety to save a buck.

Sky Trek tours are similar to canopy tours but may include suspension bridges, cable flights across valleys, and a hilltop tower (not necessarily in the rain or cloud forest). Sky Walk tours are for those not necessarily up for the "Me Tarzan, you Jane" routine, with less strenuous canopy exploration options. Here you can tiptoe through the treetops on a series of six suspension bridges, which provide a monkey's-eye view of the aerial garden of the cloud-forest canopy. Get here early if you're into bird-watching.

F Canopy Tour Contacts **The Original Canopy Tour** ☎ 506/257-5149 ⊕ www.canopytour.com. **Sky Trek and Sky Walk** ☎ 506/645-5238 ⊕ www.skytrek.com.

DIVING TOURS

Cocos Island, Costa Rica's best dive spot, can be visited only on a 10-day scuba safari on the *Okeanos Aggressor* or *Undersea Hunter*. Diving Safaris, in Playa Hermosa, has trips to dive sites in Guanacaste. It is a good alternative if you can't afford the money or time for Cocos Island.

F Dive Operators **Diving Safaris** ☎ 506/672-0012. **Okeanos Aggressor** ☎ 506/257-8686. **Undersea Hunter** ☎ 506/228-6613.

ECO TOURS

If you park yourself at a beach hotel or an all-inclusive, you'll miss what Costa Rica does best: nature. To get the most out of your trip, **pair up with a professional bilingual nature guide** who knows the country's diverse landscapes, birds, animals, and where you'll see them. Costa Rica Expeditions, known for its commitment to conservation, has high-quality tours led by knowledgeable, professional guides. Horizontes is also a top-notch natural-history tour operator with some of the country's best guides. Aventuras Naturales runs terrific adventure tours (including whitewater rafting and bicycling) either as a one-day trip or multiday package. Sun Tours trips are well organized and guides are informative and friendly; they do a superb job of planning trips that hit all the country's highlights. There are many tour companies and guides out there (and many lodges staff their own naturalist).

"Soft adventure" travelers are well catered to aboard the 185-foot M.V. *Pacific Explorer*, run by Cruise West, with multiday natural-history cruises along the Southern Pacific coast. Lindblad Expeditions runs cruises aboard the larger *Sea Voyager*.

Costa Rica Aventuras Naturales ⬧ Box 10736-1000, San José ☎ 506/225-3939, 800/514-0411 in North America 📠 506/253-6934 ⊕ www.toenjoynature.com. **Costa Rica Expeditions** ☎ 506/222-0333 📠 506/257-1665 ⊕ www.costaricaexpeditions.com. **Horizontes** ☎ 506/222-2022 📠 506/255-4513 ⊕ www.horizontes.com. **Lindblad Expeditions** ☎ 212/765-7740, 800/397-3348 in North America ⊕ www.lindblad.com. **Sun Tours** ☎ 506/296-7757 📠 506/296-4307 ⊕ www.crsuntours.com. **Temptress Adventure Cruises** ✉ Cruise West, 2401 4th Ave., Suite 700, Seattle, WA 98121-1438 ☎ 800/580-0072 in North America 📠 206/441-4757 ⊕ www.cruisewest.com.

HIKING TOURS

Most nature tour companies include hiking as part of their itineraries, but these hikes may be short and not strenuous enough for serious hikers. Ask a lot of questions about hike lengths and difficulty levels before booking the tour or you may be disappointed with the amount of time you get to spend on the trails. The following companies cater to serious hikers.

Hiking Tour Companies Gap Adventures ☎ 800/465-5600 ⊕ wwwgapadventures.com. **Serendipity Adventures** ☎ 877/507-1358 in North America ⊕ www.serendipityadventures.com. **The Walking Connection** ☎ 602/978-1887, 800/295-9255 in North America ⊕ www.walkingconnection.com.

TRAIN TRAVEL

Costa Rica's countrywide train system has been defunct since 1986 because of recurring earthquakes and lack of profits. But a tour company called AmericaTravel now gives weekend day trips in 1940s passenger railcars from San José to the inland Pacific towns of Caldera and Orotina.

Train Information AmericaTravel ☎ 506/233-3300 ✍ americatravel@msn.com.

TRANSPORTATION AROUND COSTA RICA

The most common form of public transportation is bus. All Costa Rican towns are connected by regular, inexpensive bus service. For example, tickets cost $5–$10 from the capital to Quepos and $5–$9 to Monteverde; the more expensive rates are for *directo* (express) service. Buses between major cities are modern and air-conditioned, but once you get into the rural areas, you may get the school-bus equivalent. Because buses can be a slow and uncomfortable way to travel, domestic flights are a desirable and practical option. Most major destinations are served by daily domestic flights; prices range from $40 to $90 one-way (round-trips are double the one-way fare). Renting a car gives you the most freedom, but rates can be expensive, especially since you need four-wheel drive in most parts of the country.

TRAVEL AGENCIES

A good travel agent puts your needs first. Look for an agency that has been in business at least five years, emphasizes customer service, and has someone on staff who specializes in your destination. In addition, **make sure the agency belongs to a professional trade organization.** The American Society of Travel Agents (ASTA)—the largest and most influential in the field with more than 20,000 members in some 140 countries—maintains and enforces a strict code of ethics and will step in to help mediate any agent-client disputes involving ASTA members if necessary. ASTA (whose motto is "Without a travel agent, you're on your own") also maintains a Web site that includes a directory of agents. (If a travel agency is also acting as your tour operator, *see* Buyer Beware *in* Tours & Packages.)

Local Agent Referrals American Society of Travel Agents (ASTA) ✉ 1101 King St., Suite 200, Alexandria, VA 22314 ☎ 703/739-2782 or 800/965-2782 24-hr hotline 📠 703/684-8319 ⊕ www.astanet.com. **Association of British Travel Agents** ✉ 68-71 Newman St., London W1T 3AH ☎ 020/7637-2444 📠 020/7637-0713 ⊕ www.abtanet.com. **Association of Canadian Travel Agents** ✉ 130 Albert St., Suite 1705, Ottawa, Ontario K1P 5G4 ☎ 613/237-3657 📠 613/237-7052 ⊕ www.acta.ca. **Australian Federation of Travel Agents** ✉ Level 3, 309 Pitt St., Sydney, NSW 2000 ☎ 02/9264-3299 📠 02/9264-1085 ⊕ www.afta.com.au. **Travel Agents' As-**

sociation of New Zealand ✉ Level 5, Tourism and Travel House, 79 Boulcott St., Box 1888, Wellington 6001 ☎ 04/499-0104 🖷 04/499-0786 ⊕ www. taanz.org.nz.

VISITOR INFORMATION

Instituto Costarricense de Turismo in San José staffs a tourist information office beneath the Plaza de la Cultura, next to the Museo de Oro. Pick up free maps, bus schedules, and brochures weekdays 9–12:30 and 1:30–5. The Costa Rican National Chamber of Tourism Web site is a good starting point for your trip. Visitor information is provided by the Costa Rica Tourist Board in Canada and the United States and by Costa Rica Tourist Services in the United Kingdom.

Learn more about foreign destinations by checking government-issued travel advisories and country information. For a broader picture, consider information from more than one country.

🚩 Tourist Information **Costa Rican National Chamber of Tourism** ⊕ costarica.tourism.co.cr. **Costa Rica Tourist Board** ☎ 506/234-6222 or 800/343-6332 in North America. **Costa Rica Tourist Services** ✉ 47 Causton St., London SW1P 4AT ☎ 020/7976-5511 🖷 020/7976-6908. **Instituto Costarricense de Turismo (ICT)** ✉ C. 5 between Avdas. Central and 2, Barrio La Catedral, San José ☎ 222-1090 ⊕ www.tourism-costarica.com.

🚩 Government Advisories **U.S. Department of State** ✉ Overseas Citizens Services Office, Room 4811, 2201 C St. NW, Washington, DC 20520 ☎ 202/647-5225 interactive hotline or 888/407-4747 ⊕ www.travel.state.gov; enclose a cover letter with your request and a business-size SASE. **Consular Affairs Bureau of Canada** ☎ 613/944-6788 or 800/267-6788 ⊕ www.voyage.gc.ca. **U.K. Foreign and Commonwealth Office** ✉ Travel Advice Unit, Consular Division, Old Admiralty Building, London SW1A 2PA ☎ 08/7060-60290 ⊕ www.fco.gov.uk/travel. **Australian Department of Foreign Affairs and Trade** ☎ 02/6261-1299 Consular Travel Advice Faxback Service ⊕ www.dfat.gov.au. **New Zealand Ministry of Foreign Affairs and Trade** ☎ 04/439-8000 ⊕ www.mft.govt.nz.

VOLUNTEER & EDUCATIONAL TRAVEL

Tag sea turtles as part of a research project, build trails in a National Park, or volunteer at an orphanage. Costa Rica has an abundance of volunteer opportunities for diverse interests. Many of the organizations require at least rudimentary Spanish. Most of the programs for volunteers who don't speak Spanish charge a daily fee for room and board. The Institute for Central American Development Studies (ICADS) is a non-profit institute that runs a language school and arranges internships and field study (college credit is available); some programs are only available to college students. ICADS places you with local social service organizations, environmental groups, and other organizations, depending on your interests.

Real Places, Real People, a tour company based in San José, specializes in taking you off the beaten path to see rural Costa Ricans doing traditional crafts such as weaving baskets and baking home-style bread. If you wish, you can work side by side with them for short periods of time. Mesoamerica, a nonprofit organization devoted to peace and social justice, has long- and short-term exchange programs for high school and college students, newswriting internships for young journalists, and volunteer opportunities working on the Interoceanic Biological Corridor, stretching from the Central Pacific Conservation Area to the La Amistad International Park.

For other volunteer opportunities, do a Web search for the type of organization you'd like to work with, then contact them directly and describe your skills and what you'd like to do. Allow several months lead time for correspondence, and if at first they don't respond, be persistent by e-mail, fax, and phone. For college credit, semester- and year-long exchange programs through the University of Kansas and other U.S. universities also accept students from other universities and colleges.

🚩 Volunteer & Educational Programs **Institute for Central American Development Studies (ICADS)** ✉ Dept. 826, Box 025216, Miami, FL 33102-5216 ☎ 506/225-0508 ⊕ www.icadscr.com. **Mesoamerica** ✉ Box 1524-2050, San Pedro ☎ 506/253-3195 ⊕ www.mesoamericaonline.net. **Real Places, Real People** ☎ 506/810-4444 ⊕ www.realplaces.net.

SPANISH-LANGUAGE PROGRAMS

Thousands of people travel to Costa Rica every year to study Spanish. Dozens of schools in and around San José offer professional instruction and home stays, and there are several smaller schools outside the capital. Conversa has a school in San José and in Santa Ana, west of the capital. Mesoamerica is a low-cost language school that is part of a nonprofit organization devoted to peace and social justice. La Escuela D'Amore is in beautiful Manuel Antonio. Language programs at the Institute for Central American Development Studies include optional academic seminars in English about Central America's political, social, and economic conditions. It also runs an internship program for college students.

F Spanish-Language Programs **Conversa** ⌂ Apdo. 17–1007, Centro Colón, San José ☎ 506/221–7649, 800/354–5036 in North America ⊕ www.conversa.net. **ILISA** ⌂ Dept. 1420, Box 25216, Miami, FL 33102 ☎ 506/280–0700. **Institute for Central American Development Studies** (ICADS) ⌂ Dept. 826, Box 025216 ☎ 506/225–0508 ⊕ www.icadscr.com. **La Escuela D'Amore** ⌂ Apdo. 67, Quepos ☎ 506/777–1143 ⊕ www.escueladamore.com. **Mesoamerica** ⌂ Apdo. 1524–2050, San Pedro ☎ 506/253–3195 ⊕ www.mesoamericaonline.net.

VOLUNTEER PROGRAMS

In recent years, more and more Costa Ricans have realized the need to preserve their country's precious biodiversity. Both Ticos and far-flung environmentalists have founded volunteer and educational concerns to this end: Caribbean Conservation Corporation (CCC) is devoted to the preservation of sea turtles. Earthwatch Institute leads science-based trips, and Talamancan Association of Ecotourism and Conservation (ATEC) designs short group and individual outings centered on Costa Rican wildlife and indigenous culture. Follow their lead, and you, too, can have an effect.

F Volunteer Programs **Caribbean Conservation Corporation (CCC)** ⌂ 4424 N.W. 13th St., Suite A-1, Gainesville, FL 32609 ☎ 800/678–7853 ⊕ www.cccturtle.org. **Earthwatch Institute** ⌂ 3 Clock Tower Pl., Suite 100, Box 75, Maynard, MA 01754 ☎ 800/776–0188 ⊕ www.earthwatch.org. **Talamancan Association of Ecotourism and Conservation (ATEC)** ⌂ Puerto Viejo de Limón ☎ 506/750–0191 ⊕ http://greencoast.com/atec/htm.

WEB SITES

Do check out the Web when planning your trip. You'll find everything from weather forecasts to virtual tours of famous cities. Be sure to **visit Fodors.com** (⊕ www.fodors.com), a complete travel-planning site. You can research prices and book plane tickets, hotel rooms, rental cars, vacation packages, and more. In addition, you can post your pressing questions in the Travel Talk section. Other planning tools include a currency converter and weather reports, and there are loads of links to travel resources.

Info Costa Rica (⊕ www.infocostarica.com) has a Web site with maps, photos, news articles, and chat rooms. For current events, check out the English-language newspaper *Tico Times* (⊕ www.ticotimes.net) online. Horizontes (⊕ www.horizontes.com) is a tour operator that offers nature vacations but also has extensive general information on its Web site. Similar is the site by competing nature tour company Costa Rica Expeditions (⊕ www.expeditions.co.cr), which offers ecologically minded trips. The Costa Rican National Chamber of Tourism's comprehensive site (⊕ http://costarica.tourism.co.cr) has maps, a real estate section, health information, a section devoted to volunteer opportunities, and much more.

SAN JOSÉ

(1)

Updated by
Jeffrey Van
Fleet

SHADY PARKS, QUIET MUSEUMS, LIVELY PLAZAS, and a cobblestone pedestrian boulevard that cuts through downtown make up for the city's less attractive attributes—its disproportionate share of potholes, traffic jams, and unimpressive gray office blocks that dominate the downtown grid. Fortunately, many of San José's older neighborhoods and its more affluent suburbs are downright charming. Some 1 million Ticos (as Costa Ricans call themselves) live and work in the greater metropolitan area, where such urban activities as fine dining and nightlife exist alongside such urban problems as petty crime and exhaust fumes.

Downtown San José is a mere 40-minute drive from verdant, tranquil countryside. The city stands in a broad, fertile bowl referred to as the Valle Central (central valley) or Meseta Central (central plateau), at an altitude of 1,149 meters (3,770 feet) bordered to the southwest by the jagged Cerros de Escazú (Escazú Hills), to the north by Volcán Barva (Barva Volcano), and to the east by lofty Volcán Irazú. In the dry season (mid-December–April), these green uplands are almost never out of sight, and during rainy-season afternoons they're usually enveloped in cloudy mantles. Temperatures ranging from 15°C to 26°C (59°F to 79°F) create cool nights and pleasant days, making San José one of those fabled "cities of eternal springtime." The rainy season lasts from May to mid-December, though mornings during this time are often sunny and brilliantly clear.

San José was founded in 1737 and replaced nearby Cartago as the capital of Costa Rica in 1823, shortly after the country won independence from Spain. The city grew relatively slowly during the following century, as revenues from the coffee and banana industries financed the construction of stately homes, theaters, and a trolley system that was later abandoned. As recently as the mid-1900s, San José was no larger than the present-day downtown area; vast coffee and sugarcane plantations extended beyond its borders. The city started to mushroom after World War II, when many old buildings were razed to make room for concrete monstrosities, and it eventually sprawled to the point of connection to nearby cities. Industry, agribusiness, the national government, and the international diplomatic corps are headquartered in San José, and all the institutions required of a capital city—good hospitals, schools, the country's main university, theaters, restaurants, and nightclubs—flourish in close quarters. Ticos come to San José to shop, take care of official business, and seek medical attention, and you should tend to those needs here as well. The rest of the country lags behind in modernity and convenience.

EXPLORING SAN JOSÉ

Numbers in the text correspond to numbers in the margin and on the San José map.

Costa Rica's capital is laid out on a grid: *avenidas* (avenues) run east–west, and *calles* (streets) run north–south. Avenidas north of the Avenida Central have odd numbers, and those to the south have even ones. On the western end of downtown, at Calle 14, Avenida Central

If you're like most visitors, you'll spend the first day of your Costa Rica visit in San José, and then head out to the hinterlands, not returning until the night before your flight home. (Rain forests, beaches, and volcanoes do beckon, after all.) But the capital has enough items of interest to keep you occupied for a few days, and makes a wonderful base for numerous easy day or half-day excursions. San José has several interesting museums and theaters, more shops than you can shake a credit card at, and pleasant sidewalk amenities such as newsstands and ice cream vendors. If you're here during the rainy season, head out to the countryside in the morning and return to the city to shop and visit museums in the afternoon.

If you have 1 day

Spend most of the day in downtown San José. Wander down the Avenida Central pedestrian mall. Pop into the Teatro Nacional at the southwest corner of the Plaza de la Cultura. Then head to the neoclassic Catedral Metropolitana just east of Parque Central. Double back to take in one of three museums: the Museo del Oro Precolombino at the Plaza de la Cultura, the Museo Nacional, or the Museo de Jade in Barrio El Carmen. If you're traveling with children, consider visiting the Jardín de Mariposas Spyrogyra (Butterfly Garden) north of downtown in Barrio Tournón.

If you have 3 days (city)

Three days in the city lets you expand on the one-day itinerary outlined above. Spend your second morning browsing the shops and souvenir stores loosely clustered around Parque Morazán, being sure to take in the phenomenal Galería Namu. Or take a taxi to the northern suburb of Moravia, and browse the artisan shops there. If you're here during the rainy season, take refuge from the afternoon showers inside one of the museums you didn't have time for the day before. The Museo Nacional and the Museo para la Paz, just one block apart, can be done in one afternoon. Spend your third morning soaking up the student-fueled energy of the University of Costa Rica, browsing the area's bookstores, and stopping for a quick bite at one of the inexpensive dining places. Head back downtown in the afternoon, and take in the Museo de Jade on the top floor of the INS building. Or if you're traveling with children, visit the exhibits designed with kids in mind at the Museo de los Niños.

If you have 3 days (city & central valley)

After you've surveyed the sights in the one-day itinerary above, you should get out of the capital on the morning of Day 2. Take in nearby sights in the Central Valley (⇨ Chapter 2) such as the La Paz Waterfall Gardens on the road to Volcán Poás and INBioparque near Heredia. Tour the Café Britt coffee plantation in Heredia, saving the afternoon for shopping. On Day 3 head up a volcano, take a trip to the Rain Forest Aerial Tram near Santa Clara (⇨ Chapter 7), or explore the historic Orosí Valley southeast of town. Consider a white-water rafting trip on the Class III and IV rapids of the Río Pacuare (thrilling, but not so thrilling as to induce heart failure), with swimmable warm water and spectacular scenery.

becomes Paseo Colón; on the eastern end, at about Calle 31, it becomes an equally busy, though nameless, four-lane boulevard as it enters the suburb of San Pedro. Streets to the east of Calle Central have odd numbers; those to the west are even. This would be straightforward enough, except that Costa Ricans do not use street addresses. They rely instead on an archaic system of directions that makes perfect sense to them but tends to confuse foreigners. A typical Tico address could be "200 meters north and 50 meters east of the post office." The key to interpreting such directions is to keep track of north, south, east, and west, and remember that 100 meters designates a city block, regardless of how long it actually is.

Beyond the block and street level, downtown San José is divided into numerous *barrios* (neighborhoods), which are also commonly cited in directions. Some barrios are worth exploring; others you should avoid. Barrio Amón and Barrio Otoya, northeast of the town center, are two of the city's oldest sections; some of their historic buildings have been transformed into charming hotels and restaurants. Los Yoses and Barrio Escalante, east of downtown, are basically residential neighborhoods with some nice restaurants and galleries and a few bed-and-breakfasts. San Pedro—technically a suburb outside the capital even farther east, although it's hard to tell where it ends and San José begins—is the home of the University of Costa Rica and numerous youth-oriented bars and restaurants.

Downtown San José's northwest quarter (everything west of Calle Central and north of Avenida 3) is a very different story. Called the Zona Roja, or red-light district, it's a rough area, frequented by prostitutes and alcoholics. It is best avoided unless you're headed to one of the bus companies there, in which case you should take a taxi. Much of the city's southern half—south of Avenida 4 between Calles Central and 14—is equally undesirable. If you follow Avenida Central west to where it becomes Paseo Colón, you'll enter an affluent area, with plenty of restaurants and hotels. The farther west you head, the more exclusive the neighborhoods become. Escazú, in the hills west of San José, is a traditional town that has become a favorite among U.S. expatriates. Surrounding neighborhoods are packed with relatively upscale, U.S.-style restaurants and a few cozy inns.

Most museums, shops, and restaurants in the city center are within walking distance of each other. If you're headed for a far-flung spot, or need to get from one end of the city to another, grab a taxi—they're abundant and inexpensive ($3–$4 for most trips). On the whole, San José is a relatively safe city, but a growing influx of tourists has resulted in an increase in the number of thieves to prey on them, such as bag and backpack slitters, pickpockets, and distraction artists who usually work in pairs—one person hassles you, or sprays something on you and helps you clean it off, while his or her partner gets your purse, wallet, backpack, camera, and so on. Make sure you keep a photocopy of your passport and a list of credit-card phone numbers in your luggage, and never leave anything in an unguarded car.

Excursions

San José's central position in the Central Valley and its relative proximity to both the Pacific coast and the mountains invites day trips—you can be out in the countryside in just 20 to 30 minutes. The Central Valley is a boon for quick outdoor adventures, among them treks to waterfalls and volcanoes, horseback tours on private ranches, mountain hikes, and white-knuckle rafting excursions down the Sarapiquí, Reventazón, and Pacuare rivers. Most tours will pick you up at your San José hotel and drop you off the same day.

Festivals

Every other year the two-week Festival Internacional de las Artes brings dancers, theater groups, and musicians from Costa Rica and elsewhere to a dozen city venues in late March. During Semana Universitaria (University Week), usually in April, students at the University of Costa Rica put their studies on hold to concentrate on drinking and dancing. San José becomes a ghost town during Semana Santa (Holy Week) in March or April, when everyone flees to the mountains or beach. The city is refreshingly free of traffic that week, save for a few religious processions. Don't expect to find anything except your hotel open on Holy Thursday or Good Friday.

The Festival Internacional de Música enlivens July and August. The Día de la Virgen de Los Angeles honors Costa Rica's patron saint every August 2 with processions and a well-attended mass. On the eve of this holiday, crowds walk la romería, a 22-km (14-mi) trek along the road from San José to Cartago. The city blazes with blue-white-red-white-blue Costa Rican flags during September in honor of Independence Day on the 15th. The real treat comes the night before when people all over the city stop what they're doing at 6 PM to sing the national anthem, a touching tribute to the land they love.

City sidewalks, busy sidewalks . . . December and throngs of festive but determined shoppers mean it's Christmastime in the city. The Teatro Nacional inaugurates its portal (nativity scene) the first Monday of the month, followed by Christmas carols in front of the theater each night that week. The Festival de Coreógrafos, a dance festival, takes place in mid-December. Plan to get covered with confetti if you walk down Avenida Central most December evenings through Christmas Eve. The Festival de la Luz (Festival of Light) parade passes down Paseo Colón and Avenida 2 the second Saturday evening before Christmas. A carnival parade heads down Avenida 2 every December 26, and a tope (horse parade) gets under way December 27.

Soccer

The capital's beloved fútbol team, Saprissa, holds court at its stadium in the northern suburb of Tibás. But you don't need to attend a match to partake of the excitement. Clusters of fans decked out in purple-and-white team colors gather around any spare television set on game days, usually Sunday and Wednesday, and yell "¡Gooooooooooooool!" with each score. Everyone takes to the streets after a win and cars parade with team flags streaming out the windows. Passion reaches fever pitch during match-ups with archrival La Liga, based in nearby Alajuela. The town is close enough to San José that the capital counts many of its fans, too. (They'll be the ones dressed in red and black.)

Downtown San José

a good walk

Start at the eastern end of the **Plaza de la Cultura ❶ ▶**, where wide stairs lead down to the **Museo de Oro Precolombino ❷**, whose gold collection deserves a good hour or two. Wander around the bustling plaza and slip into the **Teatro Nacional ❸** for a look at the elegant interior and perhaps a cup of coffee in the lobby café. Leaving the theater, you'll be facing west, with the city's main eastbound corridor, Avenida 2, to your left. Walk 1½ blocks west along Avenida 2 to the **Parque Central ❹** and **Catedral Metropolitana ❺**. The ornate **Teatro Popular Melico Salazar ❻** sits on the north side of the park. The interior is most easily viewed by attending a performance. Cross Avenida 2 and head north one block on Calle Central to Avenida Central, where you should turn left and follow the pedestrian zone to the small plaza next to the **Banco Central ❼**. Continue west along the pedestrian zone to the **Mercado Central ❽**, and shop or browse at your leisure. Head back east two blocks on the Avenida Central pedestrian zone, then turn left on Calle 2, and walk one block north to the green-and-gray–stuccoed **Correos de Costa Rica ❾**, the central post office. Pop into the Instituto Costarricense de Turismo (ICT tourist office) in the same building for a free map, bus schedule, and brochures. From there, return to Avenida Central and walk east along the mall back to the Plaza de la Cultura.

From the eastern end of the Plaza de la Cultura, near the Museo de Oro, walk two blocks north on Calle 5 to **Parque Morazán ❿**. Walk across the park—be careful crossing busy Avenida 3—and head along the yellow metal school building to shady **Parque España ⓫**. On the north side of the park, on Avenida 7, is the modern Instituto Nacional de Seguros (INS) building, whose 11th-floor **Museo de Jade ⓬** has an extensive American-jade collection and great city views. Pass through the entrance to the **Centro Nacional de la Cultura ⓭**, the former National Liquor Factory complex, now renovated as a cultural center, on the east side of Parque España.

The southeast entrance of the Centro Nacional de la Cultura emerges onto **Parque Nacional ⓮**. Take a look at the Monumento Nacional at the center of the park, and then head a block east to the **Museo de Formas, Espacios y Sonidos ⓯**, formerly the Atlantic Railway Station, and explore new dimensions in spaces and sounds. Two blocks beyond lies the **Antigua Aduana ⓰**, the old customhouse, scheduled to open as a cultural center in 2005. Head back four blocks on Avenida Central to the entrance of the **Museo Nacional ⓱**, housed in the old Bellavista Fortress. On the west side of the fortress lies the terraced **Plaza de la Democracia ⓲**; from here you can walk west on Avenida 2 to the **Museo para la Paz ⓳**, a museum dedicated to the cause of peace and social justice. Another three blocks east on Avenida 2 and north on Calle 3 returns you to the Plaza de la Cultura.

TIMING & PRECAUTIONS　This walk can take an entire day if you pause to absorb each museum and monument and stop to shop here and there. You can, however, easily split the tour in half: see all the sights west of the Plaza de la Cultura (❶–❾) one day and the remaining places (❿–⓳) on another. Every stop on this tour is open from Tuesday to Friday; check the hours listed below to make sure the sights you want to see are open on Mondays or weekends. Note that downtown traffic is legendarily heavy and that drivers rarely give way to pedestrians.

What to See

16 **Antigua Aduana** (Old Customhouse). A once bustling customs facility just east of downtown served trains arriving from Limón on the former Atlantic Railway. The Ministry of Culture plans to restore and refurbish the building to its former glory and open it as a Costa Rican cultural center in 2005. ✉ *C. 23, Barrio La California* ☎ *255–3188.*

7 **Banco Central** (Central Bank). The grandiose monuments so typical of Latin America are nowhere to be found in Costa Rica, a country that instead prizes its smallness. Witness Fernando Calvo's sculpture *Presentes*: 10 sculpted, smaller-than-life figures of bedraggled *campesinos* (peasants) stand outside the western end of Costa Rica's modern federal reserve bank building. The small, shady plaza south of the bank, an extension of Avenida Central, is popular with hawkers, money changers, and retired men and can be a good place to get a shoe shine and listen to street musicians. Beware: the money changers here are notorious for circulating counterfeit bills and using doctored calculators to short-change unwitting tourists. It is better to change money at banks or through cash machines, where you get the best rate. In fact, you can stop by a money-exchange kiosk right here operated by Banco Nacional, one of the state banks, and open seven days a week. ✉ *Bordered by Avdas. Central and 1 and Cs. 2 and 4, Barrio La Merced.*

5 **Catedral Metropolitana** (Metropolitan Cathedral). Built in 1871, and completely refurbished in the late 1990s to repair earthquake damage, this neoclassic structure east of the park with a corrugated tin dome is not terribly interesting outside, but inside you find patterned floor tiles and framed polychrome bas-reliefs. The renovation did away with one small time-honored tradition: rather than purchase and light a votive candle, the faithful now deposit a 50-colón coin illuminating a bulb in a row of tiny electric candles. The interior of the small chapel (Sagrario) on the cathedral's north side is much more ornate than the cathedral itself, but it's usually closed. Masses are held throughout the day on Sunday starting at 7 AM. ✉ *Bordered by Avdas. 4 and 2 and Cs. Central and 1, Barrio La Merced* ☎ *221–3820* ⊙ *Weekdays 6 AM–noon and 3–6 PM, Sun. 6 AM–9 PM.*

13 **Centro Nacional de la Cultura** (National Cultural Center). Costa Rica cherishes its state enterprises. Here the government is your light and water utility, your phone company, your Internet service provider, your bank, your insurance agent, and your hospital. It is also your distillery, and this complex served as the headquarters of the Fábrica Nacional de Licores (FANAL, or National Liquor Factory) until 1981, when it moved to a modern facility west of Alajuela. In a heartwarming exception to the usual "tear it down" mentality so prevalent in San José, the Ministry of Culture converted the sloped-surface, double-block 1853 factory into a 14,000-square-meter center of its own offices, two theaters, and a museum. The metal **Teatro FANAL** (☎ 222–2974), once the fermentation area, now hosts frequent theater and music performances. The

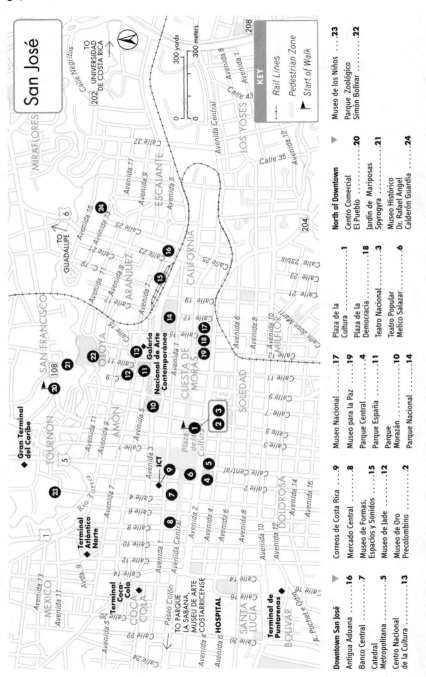

clay-brick **Teatro 1887** (☎ 222–2974) served as the factory's personnel office, and today dedicates itself to performances by the National Dance Company. What is now the theater's lobby was once the chemical testing lab. The stone-block storage depot next to the water towers at the southeast side of the complex became the **Museo de Arte y Diseño Contemporáneo** (Museum of Contemporary Art and Design; ☎ 257–7202 ⊕ www.madc.ac.cr), a wonderfully minimalist space perfect for serving as the country's premier modern-art venue. The MADC, as it is known around town, hosts changing exhibits of work by artists and designers from all over Latin America. The museum is open Tuesday through Saturday 10–5; admission is $1. You can arrange for a guided visit with a couple of days' advance notice. A stone gate and sun clock grace the entrance nearest the museum. ✉ *C. 13 between Avdas. 3 and 5, Barrio Otoya* ☎ *257–5524* ⊙ *Weekdays 8–5, Sat. 10–5.*

need a break?

Cafeteando, a small café on the first floor of the Correos, overlooks the bustling pedestrian boulevard and a small park shaded by massive fig trees. Behind the park is the marble facade of the exclusive, members-only Club Unión. ✉ *Correos, C. 2, between Avdas. 1 and 3, 1st fl., Barrio La Merced* ☎ *No phone.*

❾ Correos de Costa Rica (Central Post Office). The handsome, carved seagreen exterior of the post office, dating from 1917, is hard to miss among the bland buildings surrounding it. Stamp collectors should stop at the **Museo Filatélico** (Philatelic Museum; ☎ 223–6918) upstairs for its display of first-day stamp issues. It's a worthwhile visit for anyone interested in seeing how the country's history has been portrayed through the issuance of stamps. Early-20th-century telegraphs and telephones are also on display. The museum is open weekdays 8–5; admission is free. From the second-floor balcony, you can see the loading of *apartados* (post-office boxes) going on below: Ticos covet these hard-to-get boxes, as the city's lack of street addresses makes mail delivery a challenge. The large building behind the Correos is the headquarters of Banco Nacional, a state-run bank. ✉ *C. 2, between Avdas. 1 and 3, Barrio La Merced* ⊙ *Weekdays 7:30–6, Sat. 7:30–noon.*

off the beaten path

INSTITUTO CLODOMIRO PICADO (Clodomiro Picado Institute) – Of the 600 to 700 people bitten by poisonous snakes each year in the country, only one or two die, thanks to this institution affiliated with the University of Costa Rica, and named for the country's foremost biologist. Picado pioneered a method of extracting venom from live snakes, a so-called "milking" process—which you can see when you visit—and the production of the antivenin serum that supplies most of Central America. (Picado, minus the snakes, appears on Costa Rica's 2,000-colón note.) The complex, which sits in the far-eastern suburb of Coronado, plans to open visitor facilities in 2005. (Admission prices have not been determined at this writing.) Until then, informal talks and visits can be arranged with a few days' advance notice. ✉ *Dulce Nombre, Coronado* ☎ *229–0344* ⊕ *www. icp.ucr.ac.cr* ⊙ *By appointment.*

❽ Mercado Central (Central Market). This block-long melting pot is a warren of dark, narrow passages flanked by stalls packed with spices (some purported to have medicinal value), fish, fruit, flowers, pets, and wood and leather crafts. But the 1880 structure is a kinder, gentler introduction to a Central American market; there are no pigs or chickens or their accompanying smells to be found here. A few stands selling tourist souvenirs congregate near the entrances, but this is primarily a place where the average Costa Rican comes to shop. There are also dozens of cheap restaurants and snack stalls, including the country's first ice cream vendor. (Even President Abel Pacheco has been spotted lunching at the restaurants here on occasion.) This is a great place to stop for ceviche. Be warned: the concentration of shoppers makes this a hot spot for pickpockets, purse snatchers, and backpack slitters. You'll most likely enter at the southeast corner of the building (Avda. Central at C. 6). Try to leave the same way you came in. The green-and-white SALIDA signs will direct you to any exit, but the other doors spill onto slightly less safe streets. The image of the Sacred Heart of Jesus, the market's patron and protector, near the center of the building, faces that safer corner by which you should exit. (Things probably weren't planned that way.) ⊠ *Bordered by Avdas. Central and 1 and Cs. 6 and 8, Barrio La Merced* ☉ *Mon.–Sat. 6–6.*

need a break? **Pop's** dishes out the crème de la cream of locally made Costa Rican ice cream. And after a long walk on crowded sidewalks, it may just save your sanity. This prolific chain is everywhere, and you'll find four outlets downtown. Mango is a favorite flavor. ⊠ *Avda. Central, between Cs. 11 and 13* ⊠ *Avda. Central, between Cs. 1 and 3* ⊠ *C. 4, between Avdas. Central and 1* ⊠ *Avda. 2, between Cs. 4 and 6.*

Museo de Arte Costarricense (Museum of Costa Rican Art). The vast westside Parque La Sabana once served as the country's international airport. Its terminal and control tower were whitewashed and became an art museum when the airport moved to its present-day site near Alajuela. The building houses a splendid collection of 19th- and 20th-century Costa Rican art in its 12 exhibition halls. Be sure to visit the top-floor Salón Dorado to see the stucco, bronze-plated bas-relief mural depicting Costa Rican history, created by French sculptor Louis Feron. A sculpture garden in back opened in 2003 and is a work in progress. ⊠ *C. 42 and Paseo Colón, Paseo Colón* ☎ *222–7155* ⊠ *$1, free Sun.* ☉ *Tues.–Sun. 10–5.*

☾ ⓯ Museo de Formas, Espacios y Sonidos (Museum of Forms, Spaces and Sounds). The old Atlantic Railway Station once bustled with passengers leaving and arriving on trains to and from Limón. The Ministry of Culture has refurbished the 1871 structure and converted it into an interactive museum ideal for children (and adults) who want to learn more about conceptions of sound and space. The museum takes special pride in its exhibits designed to accommodate visitors with disabilities. The project is a work in progress, and exhibits are expected to be completed by 2005. In back are a couple of former trains that once served the Caribbean route. A bust outside honors Tomás Guardia, one of the few dictators in this peaceful country's history. He launched construction of the railroad. ⊠ *Avda. 3 between Cs. 19 and 21, Barrio La California* ☎ *223–4173* ⊠ *$1* ☉ *Jan. and Feb., weekdays 9:30–3; Mar.–Dec., Tues.–Fri. 9:30–3.*

★ ⑫ **Museo de Jade** (Jade Museum). This is the world's largest collection of American jade—that's "American" in the hemispheric sense. Nearly all the items on display were produced in pre-Columbian times, and most of the jade (pronounced *jah*-day in Spanish) dates from 300 BC to AD 700. In the spectacular Jade Room, pieces are illuminated from behind so you can appreciate their translucency. A series of drawings explains how this extremely hard stone was cut using string saws with quartz-and-sand abrasive. Jade was sometimes used in jewelry designs, but it was most often carved into oblong pendants. The museum also has other pre-Columbian artifacts, such as polychrome vases and three-legged *metates* (small stone tables for grinding corn), and a gallery of modern art. The final room on the tour has a startling display of ceramic fertility symbols. A photo-filled, glossy guide in English to the museum sells for $17. ⊠ *INS building, Avda. 7 between Cs. 9 and 11, 11th fl., Barrio El Carmen* ☎ *287–6034* ⊠ *$2* ☉ *Weekdays 8:30–3:30.*

★ ❷ **Museo del Oro Precolombino** (Pre-Columbian Gold Museum). The dazzling, modern museum of gold, in a three-story underground building beneath the Plaza de la Cultura, contains the largest collection of pre-Columbian gold jewelry in Central America—20,000 troy ounces in more than 1,600 individual pieces—all owned by the Banco Central. Many pieces are in the form of frogs and eagles, two animals perceived by the region's pre-Columbian cultures to have great spiritual significance. Most spectacular are the varied shaman figurines, which represent the human connection to animal deities. One of the halls houses the **Museo Numismática** (Coin Museum; admission included with Gold Museum), a repository of historic coins and bills and other objects used as monetary units throughout the country's history. Another level of the complex houses rotating art exhibitions. ⊠ *Eastern end of Plaza de la Cultura, C. 5 between Avdas. Central and 2, Barrio La Soledad* ☎ *243–4202* ⊕ *www.museosdelbancocentral. org* ⊠ *$5* ☉ *Tues.–Sun. 10–4:30.*

⑰ **Museo Nacional** (National Museum). In the whitewashed Bellavista Fortress, which dates from 1870, the National Museum gives you a quick and insightful lesson in Costa Rican culture from pre-Columbian times to the present. Some of the country's foremost ethnographers and anthropologists are on the museum's staff. Glass cases display pre-Columbian artifacts, period dress, colonial furniture, religious art, and photographs. Outside are a veranda and a pleasant, manicured courtyard garden. A former army headquarters, this now-tranquil building saw fierce fighting during the 1948 revolution, as the bullet holes pocking its turrets attest. ⊠ *C. 17, between Avdas. Central and 2, Barrio La Soledad* ☎ *257–1433* ⊕ *www.museocostarica.com* ⊠ *$4* ☉ *Tues.–Sun. 9–4.*

⑲ **Museo para la Paz** (Peace Museum). Former president Oscar Arias won the 1987 Nobel Peace Prize for his tireless efforts to bring reconciliation to a war-torn Central America, and today he remains a vocal force for international peace and social justice. His Arias Foundation operates this museum, with bilingual exhibits documenting the isthmus's turbulent history and promoting the cause for peace. Messages from other Nobel laureates—the Dalai Lama, Lech Walesa, Rigoberta Menchú, and Henry Kissinger among them—adorn one room. Begin your visit in the auditorium watching a 12-minute video in English, *The Dividends of Peace*. There's also an hour-long video that delves into the topic if you have the time. The museum is a work in progress, expected to be completed by 2006. It may not appear to be open when you walk by. Knock on the gate or, better yet, call and let the attendant know you're coming. ✉ *Avda. 2 and C. 13, Barrio La Soledad* ☎ 223–4664 ⚰ *Free* ⊘ *Weekdays 8–noon and 1:30–4:30.*

❹ **Parque Central** (Central Park). At the city's nucleus, this simple tree-planted square—it's more a plaza than a park—has a gurgling fountain and concrete benches, and a life-size bronze statue of a street sweeper cleaning up some bronze litter. In the center of the park is a spiderlike, mango-color gazebo donated by former Nicaraguan dictator Anastasio Somoza. Several years ago a referendum was held to decide whether to demolish the despot's gift, but Ticos voted to preserve the bandstand for posterity. The city's cathedral fronts the square on Calle 2 to the east, and nondescript stores and office buildings are across Calle 4 to the west and Avenida 4 to the south. The Teatro Popular Melico Salazar stands across the street on Avenida 2. The Burger King and KFC restaurants next door were once the Palace movie theater and, on the outside at least, maintain that film-house-of-yesteryear appearance. ✉ *Bordered by Avdas. 2 and 4 and Cs. 2 and Central, Barrio La Merced.*

⓫ **Parque España.** One of the most pleasant spots in the capital is this shady little park. A bronze statue of Costa Rica's Spanish founder, Juan Vásquez de Coronado, overlooks an elevated fountain on its southwest corner; the opposite corner has a lovely tiled guardhouse. A bust of Queen Isabella of Castile stares at the yellow compound to the east of the park, the Centro Nacional de la Cultura (National Center of Culture).

Just west of the park is a two-story, metal-sided school made in Belgium and shipped to Costa Rica in pieces more than a century ago. Local lore holds that the intended destination was really Chile, but that Costa Rica decided to keep the mistakenly shipped building components. The yellow colonial-style building to the east of the modern INS building is the **Casa Amarilla** (☎ 223–7555), home of Costa Rica's Foreign Ministry. The massive ceiba tree in front, planted by John F. Kennedy and the presidents of all the Central American nations in 1963, gives you an idea of how quickly things grow in the tropics. The building is rarely open to the public. A garden around the corner on Calle 13 contains a 2-meter-wide section of the Berlin Wall donated by Germany's Foreign Ministry after reunification. Ask the guard to let you into the garden if you want a closer look. A few doors east is the elegant Mexican Embassy, once a private home and the site of the signing of the truce ending Costa Rica's brief 1948 civil war. ✉ *Bordered by Avdas. 7 and 3 and Cs. 11 and 17, Barrio El Carmen* ☎ 257–7202.

Parque Metropolitano La Sabana. Though it isn't centrally located, La Sabana (the savannah) comes the closest of San José's green spaces to achieving the same function and spirit as New York's Central Park. A statue of 1930s president León Cortes greets you at the park's principal entrance at the west end of Paseo Colón. Behind the statue, a 5-meter-tall menorah serves as a gathering place for San José's small Jewish community during Hanukkah. La Sabana was once San José's airport, and the whitewashed Museo de Arte Costarricense, just south of the Cortes statue, served as terminal and control tower. The round Gimnasio Nacional (National Gymnasium) sits at the southeast corner of the park and hosts sporting events and the occasional concert. The Estadio Nacional (National Stadium) near the park's northwest corner is the site of important soccer matches, and is one of the country's major outdoor concert venues. The unattractive building headquarters of the Instituto Costarricense de Electricidad, the state electricity and telecommunications monopoly, fronts the park's north side. In between are acres of space for soccer, basketball, tennis, swimming, aerobics, jogging, picnicking, and kite flying. The park hums with activity on weekend days. Like most of San José's green spaces, it should be avoided at night. ⊠ *Bordered by C. 42, Avda. de las Américas, and Autopista Próspero Fernández, Paseo Colón.*

⑩ Parque Morazán. Anchored by the Templo de Música (Temple of Music), a neoclassic bandstand that has become the symbol of the city, the largest park in downtown San José is somewhat barren, though the Pink and Golden Trumpet trees on its northwest corner brighten things up when they bloom in the dry months. The park is named for Honduran general Francisco Morazán, whose dream for a united Central America failed in the 1830s. The general's bust near the north entrance to the park is easy to miss. Much more prominent here are monuments to South American liberators Simón Bolívar and Bernardo O'Higgins, and 1970s Costa Rican president Daniel Oduber. Avoid the park late at night, when a rough crowd and occasional muggers appear. Along the southern edge are a public school and two lovely old mansions, both with beautiful facades—one is a private home, the other a prostitute pickup bar. There's a park annex with a large fountain to the northeast, across busy Avenida 3, in front of the metal school building. ⊠ *Avda. 3, between Cs. 5 and 9, Barrio El Carmen.*

⑭ Parque Nacional (National Park). A bronze monument commemorating Central America's battles against American invader William Walker in 1856 forms the centerpiece of this large and leafy park. Five Amazon women, representing the five nations of the isthmus, attack Walker, who shields his face from the onslaught. Costa Rica maintains the lead and shelters a veiled Nicaragua, the country most devastated by the war. Guatemala, Honduras, and El Salvador might dispute this version of events, but this is how Costa Rica chose to commission the work by French sculptor Louis Carrier Belleuse, a student of Rodin, in 1895. Bas-relief murals on the monument's pedestal depict key battles in the war against the Americans. The park paths are made of cobblestone rescued from downtown streets, and tall trees shading concrete benches often hide colorful parakeets in their branches. The modern pink building west of the park houses the Registro Civil (Civil Registry) and the Tribunal Supremo de Elecciones (Supreme Electoral Tribunal), which keep track of voters—as well as their births, marriages, divorces, deaths, and *cédulas* (the national identity cards carried by all citizens)—and oversee elections. The tall gray building to the north is the Biblioteca Nacional (National Library), beneath which, on the western side, is the **Galería Nacional de Arte Contemporáneo** (☎ 257–5524), a small gallery affiliated with the west-side Museo de Arte Costarricense that exhibits the work of contemporary artists, mostly Costa Rican. Quality varies, but since admission is free, it's always worth taking a peek. Don't confuse it with the larger Museo de Arte y Diseño Contemporáneo just down the street. The walled complex to the northwest is the Centro Nacional de Cultura. Across from the park's southwest end is the Moorish Asamblea Legislativa (Legislative Assembly), where Costa Rica's congress meets. Next door is the Casa Rosada, a colonial-era residence now used for congressional offices, and behind that is a more modern house used by the government for parties and special events. One block northeast of the park is the former Atlantic Railway Station, now the Museum of Forms, Spaces and Sounds. The park is best avoided at night, despite ample lighting and security patrol. ⊠ *Bordered by Avdas. 1 and 3 and Cs. 15 and 19, Barrio El Carmen.*

► **❶ Plaza de la Cultura.** A favored spot for local marimba bands, clowns, jugglers, and colorfully dressed South Americans playing Andean music, this somewhat sterile, large concrete square is surrounded by shops and fast-food restaurants. It's a nice place to feed pigeons and buy some souvenirs. The stately Teatro Nacional dominates the plaza's southern half, and its western edge is defined by the Gran Hotel Costa Rica, with its 24-hour Café Parisienne. ⊠ *Bordered by Avdas. Central and 2 and Cs. 3 and 5, Barrio La Soledad.*

⓲ Plaza de la Democracia. President Oscar Arias built this terraced open space west of the Museo Nacional to mark 100 years of democracy and to receive dignitaries during the 1989 hemispheric summit. The view west toward the dark-green Cerros de Escazú is nice in the morning and fabulous at sunset. The plaza is dominated by a statue of José "Don Pepe" Figueres, three-time president and leader of the 1948 revolution. Jewelry, T-shirts, and crafts from Costa Rica, Guatemala, and South America are sold in a string of stalls along the western edge. ⊠ *Bordered by Avdas. Central and 2 and Cs. 13 and 15, Barrio La Soledad.*

Pueblo Antiguo. A Tico version of Colonial Williamsburg west of the city depicts Costa Rica between 1880 and 1930. Actors in period costumes staff a turn-of-the-century general store, sugar and coffee mill, and stores all arranged around a central park with requisite church and bandstand. All the buildings were constructed in the late 20th century. *Típico* restaurants dish up hearty Costa Rican food. Ticket prices include admission to the adjoining Parque de Diversiones amusement park. Noches Costarricenses (Costa Rican Nights) performances take place on Friday and Saturday nights from 6:30 to 9 with dinner and music and dance performances. The $40 tour price includes transportation to and from San José hotels and English-speaking guides. ⊠ *2 km (1½ mi) west of Hospital México, Barrio La Uruca* ☎ *231–2001* ⊕ *www.parquediversiones.com* 🖾 *$7* ⊙ *Mon.–Thurs. 9–5, Fri.–Sun. 9–7.*

★ ❸ **Teatro Nacional** (National Theater). This is easily the most enchanting building in Costa Rica. Chagrined that touring prima donna Adelina Patti bypassed San José in 1890, wealthy coffee merchants raised import taxes to hire Belgian architects to design this building, lavish with cast iron and Italian marble. The sandstone exterior is marked by Italianate arched windows, marble columns with bronze capitals, and statues of strange bedfellows Ludwig van Beethoven (1770–1827) and 17th-century Spanish golden-age playwright Pedro Calderón de la Barca (1600–1681). The Muses of Dance, Music, and Fame are silhouetted in front of an iron cupola. Given the provenance of the building funds, it's not surprising that frescoes on the stairway inside depict coffee and banana production. Note Italian painter Aleardo Villa's famous ceiling mural *Alegoría del Café y Banano* (Allegory of Coffee and Bananas), a joyful harvest scene that also appears on Costa Rica's old five-colón note. (The bill is prized by collectors and by tourists as a souvenir.) The theater was inaugurated in 1897 with a performance of Gounod's *Faust,* featuring an international cast. The sumptuous neo-Baroque interior sparkles thanks to an ongoing restoration project. The best way to see the inside is to attend one of the performances, which take place several nights a week; ticket prices are much less than you'd pay in a comparable venue in North America or Europe. Alternatively, a nominal admission fee gets you in beyond the lobby for a self-guided daytime visit. The theater is sometimes closed for rehearsals, so call before you go. The stunning Café del Teatro Nacional just off the vestibule serves upscale coffee concoctions, good sandwiches, and exquisite pastries. ⊠ *Plaza de la Cultura, Barrio La Soledad* ☎ *221–1329* 🖾 *$3, performance tickets $4–$40* ⊙ *Mon.–Sat. 9–5.*

❻ **Teatro Popular Melico Salazar** (Melico Salazar Theater). Across Avenida 2 on the north side of Parque Central stands San José's second major performance hall (after the Teatro Nacional). The 1928 building is on the site of a former 19th-century military barracks felled by an earthquake. The venue was later named for Costa Rican operatic tenor Manuel "Melico" Salazar (1887–1950). It was constructed specifically to provide a less highbrow alternative to the Teatro Nacional. But these days, the Melico is plenty cultured and provides the capital with a steady diet of music and dance performances. Something goes on nearly every night of the week, and the Café Bohemia off the lobby is a quiet place to stop for a pre- or post-performance drink. ⊠ *Avda. 2 and C. 2, Barrio La Merced* ☎ *221–4952* 🖾 *Performance tickets $2–$20.*

Universidad de Costa Rica. The University of Costa Rica, or "La U," in San Pedro just east of San José, is a great place to hang out and meet people, especially if your Spanish is pretty good. Oxford or Harvard with their ivy-covered buildings this is not. Most of the boxy structures date from the 1940–1950s and are painted a riot of tropical pastels: the library is sea green; General Studies, orange; Social Science, beige. Medicine is red, yellow, and blue, the only primary colors you'll find here. The open-air gallery at the **Facultad de Bellas Artes** (College of Fine Arts), on the east side of campus, hosts free music recitals on Tuesday nights when classes are in session. Scurry on over to the agronomy department's **Museo de Insectos** (☒ North of Bellas Artes, in the basement of the Artes Musicales building ☎ 207–5318 ⊕ www.insectos.ucr.ac.cr), open weekdays 1–4:45. The $2 admission buys you a good look at dead insects in re-created habitats and information in English and Spanish on everything from insect sex to the diseases these little buggers cause.

Aficionados of Spanish literature should browse around the many off-campus bookstores. Anyone who appreciates cheap grub can revel in the vast selection of inexpensive lunch places around the university. Weeknights at the university are mellow, but nearby bars are packed with students and intellectuals on weekends. To get to San Pedro, walk a few miles east along Avenida Central's strip of shops and bars or take a $2 taxi ride from downtown and get off in front of Banco Nacional, just beyond the rotunda with the fountain at its center. ☒ *Avda. Central and C. Central, San Pedro* ⊕ *www.ucr.ac.cr.*

North of Downtown

> a good
> tour

Take a taxi to the **Centro Comercial El Pueblo** ㉘ ⌐, in Barrio Tournón. One block east and half a block south of El Pueblo is the **Jardín de Mariposas Spyrogyra** ㉑, a butterfly garden overlooking the greenery of Costa Rica's zoo, the **Parque Zoológico Simón Bolívar** ㉒. The best way to reach the zoo, however, is to walk north from the bandstand in the Parque Morazán along Calle 7 to the bottom of the hill, then turn right. The **Museo de los Niños** ㉓, a children's museum and scientific and cultural center housed in an old jail, lies several blocks to the west. It's surrounded by dubious neighborhoods, so take a taxi.

TIMING You can visit all four of these sights in one morning.

What to See

⌐ ㉘ **Centro Comercial El Pueblo** (El Pueblo Shopping Center). This shopping center was built to resemble the kind of colonial village that Costa Rica lacks. *Pueblo* means "town," and the cobbled passages, adobe walls, and tiny plazas are surprisingly convincing. Most of the commercial spaces are occupied by bars, restaurants, and discos that attract a twentysomething crowd. El Pueblo gets very busy at night, especially on weekends—but there are a few shops worth checking out during the day. ☒ *Avda. 0, Barrio Tournón* ☎ *221–9434* ☉ *Daily 8 AM–3 AM.*

★ ☺ ㉑ **Jardín de Mariposas Spyrogyra** (Spyrogyra Butterfly Garden). An hour or two at this magical garden is entertaining and educational for nature lovers of all ages. Self-guided tours enlighten you on butterfly ecology and give you a chance to see the winged creatures close up. After an 18-minute video introduction, you're free to wander screened-in gardens along a numbered trail. Some 30 species of colorful butterflies flutter about, accompanied by 6 types of hummingbirds. Try to come when it's sunny, as butterflies are most active then. A small, moderately priced café borders the garden and serves sandwiches and Tico fare. Spyrogyra abuts the northern edge of Parque Zoológico Simón Bolívar, but you enter on the outskirts of Barrio Tournón, near El Pueblo Shopping Center. ⊠ *100 m east and 150 m south of main entrance to El Pueblo, Barrio Tournón* ☎ *222–2937* ⌑ *$6* ⊙ *Daily 8–4.*

㉔ Museo Histórico Dr. Rafael Angel Calderón Guardia (Dr. Rafael Angel Calderón Guardia Historical Museum). A physician and Costa Rica's president from 1940 to 1944, Rafael Angel Calderón Guardia (1900–70) oversaw some of the most important developments of Costa Rica's modern history. He was instrumental in the founding of the University of Costa Rica and is revered for his role in the establishment of the Código de Trabajo (labor code) and the Garantías Sociales (social guarantees), which created the country's modern welfare state. But his support for the losing side in Costa Rica's brief 1948 civil war led to a 10-year exile in Mexico. Calderón's home houses exhibits about his public and private life, and an adjoining gallery hosts rotating art exhibitions. The museum is several blocks off the standard tourist circuit, and deals with somewhat esoteric subject matter unless you are a student of Costa Rican history. ⊠ *C. 25, between Avdas. 11 and 13, Barrio Escalante* ☎ *255–1218* ⌑ *Free* ⊙ *Mon.–Sat. 9–5.*

㉓ Museo de los Niños. San José's Children's Museum is housed in a former jail, and big kids may want to check it out just to marvel at the castle-like architecture and the old cells that have been preserved in an exhibit about prison life. Three halls in the complex are filled with eye-catching seasonal exhibits for kids, ranging in subject from local ecology to outer space. The exhibits are annotated in Spanish, but most are interactive, so language shouldn't be much of a problem. The museum's most popular resident is the Egyptian exhibit's sarcophagus; the mummy draws the "oohs" and "ewws." The museum's **Galería Nacional,** adjoining the main building, is more popular with adults; it usually shows fine art by Costa Rican artists free of charge. Adjoining the museum is the **Auditorio Nacional,** in which the National Symphony plays Sunday-morning concerts at 10 from March to November. ⊠ *North end of C. 4, Barrio El Carmen* ☎ *258–4929* ⌑ *$2* ⊙ *Daily 9:30–5.*

㉒ Parque Zoológico Simón Bolívar. Considering Costa Rica's mind-boggling diversity of wildlife, San José's zoo is rather modest in scope. It does, however, provide an introduction to some of the animals you might see in the jungle. The park is set in a forested ravine in historical Barrio Amón, offering soothing green space in the heart of the city. ⊠ *Avda. 11 and C. 11, Barrio Amón* ☎ *233–6701* ⌑ *$2* ⊙ *Daily 9–4:30.*

WHERE TO EAT

Wherever you eat in San José, be it a small *soda* (café) or a sophisticated restaurant, dress is casual. Meals tend to be taken earlier than in other Latin American countries; few restaurants serve past 10 PM. Local cafés usually open for breakfast at 7 AM and remain open until 7 or 9 in the evening. Restaurants serving international cuisine are usually open from 11 AM to 9 PM. Some cafés that serve mainly San José office workers are closed Sunday. Restaurants that do open on Sunday do a brisk business: it's the traditional family day out (and the maid's day off.) Casino restaurants in downtown San José are open 24 hours.

Note that 23% is added to all menu prices—13% for tax and 10% for service. Because a gratuity is included, there's no need to tip, but if your service is good, it's nice to add a little money to the obligatory 10%. Except for those in hotels, most restaurants close between Christmas and New Year's Day and during Holy Week (Palm Sunday to Easter Sunday). Call before heading out. Those that do stay open may not sell alcohol between Maundy Thursday and Easter Sunday. Even if you keep your base in San José, consider venturing to the Central Valley towns for a meal or two.

WHAT IT COSTS				
	$$$$	$$$	$$	$	¢
AT DINNER	over $25	$20–$25	$10–$20	$5–$10	under $5

Prices are per-person for a main course.

Downtown San José

AMERICAN/
CASUAL
$–$$

✕ **News Café.** Had your fill of rice and beans? You can get a Caesar salad and other American dishes here. Breakfasts and dinner fare are hearty, but the café is most popular at lunchtime and cocktail hour. It's one of the few eateries in the city with covered outdoor seating, and it's in the perfect place for it—right off the pedestrian boulevard's east end. Inside, the wrought-iron chairs, wood beams, and brick walls give the place an old-town tavern feel, though it's actually on the first floor of the 1960s landmark Hotel Presidente. ⊠ C. 7 and Avda. Central, Barrio La Soledad ☎ 222–3022 ☰ AE, DC, MC, V.

CAFÉS
$–$$
Fodor'sChoice
★

✕ **Café Mundo.** You could easily walk by this corner restaurant without noticing its tiny sign behind the foliage. Walk in and upstairs, however, and you discover an elegant eatery serving meals on the porch, on a garden patio, or in two dining rooms. Start with the soup of the day and some fresh-baked bread; then opt for penne in a shrimp and vegetable cream sauce or lomito en salsa de vino tinto (tenderloin in a red-wine sauce). Save room for the best chocolate cake in town, drizzled with homemade blackberry sauce. ⊠ C. 15 and Avda. 9, Barrio Otoya ☎ 222–6190 ☰ AE, MC, V ☉ Closed Sun. No lunch Sat.

¢–$

✕ **Café del Teatro Nacional.** Not only will the Teatro Nacional satisfy your cultural needs, but the café off the lobby quenches those midday hunger pangs as well. Have a cup of mocha with hazelnut and rest your weary head against cool marble while gazing at the frescoes on the ceiling. Atmosphere comes at a reasonable price here—coffees run anywhere from $1 to $2, depending on how much alcohol or ice cream is added. Sandwiches and cakes set you back $3 to $4. ⊠ Teatro Nacional, Plaza de la Cultura, Barrio La Soledad ☎ 221–3262 ⊕ www.cafebritt.com ☉ Closed Sun.

¢–$

✕ **Café de la Posada.** The owners of this small café come from Argentina, and they know how to make a great cappuccino. Salads, quiches, and empanadas are the specialties. The best bargains are the four rotating platos del día (daily specials), with entrée, salad, beverage, and dessert for $5. The café is at the Calle 17 pedestrian mall and on warm days has tables out front, a rarity among San José restaurants. The place closes at 7 on weeknights. ⊠ *C. 17, between Avdas. 2 and 4* ☎ *257–9414 or 258–1027* ▤ *AE, DC, MC, V* ⊘ *No dinner Sat. and Sun.*

★ ¢–$ ✕ **Kafé Ko.** Glass tables, wrought-iron chairs, and lots of candles fill this cozy, upscale restaurant just two blocks east of Museo Nacional. Choose from sandwiches, quiches, pastas, penne, and nachos. Top off your meal with a tiramisu or a dessert crepe. The café has no liquor license, but serves a full range of coffees and teas. The television is going—it might be an *I Love Lucy* episode or an Indian Bollywood video—but the sound will be off, with soft jazzy music playing in the background. ⊠ *C. 21, 25 m south of Primavera gas station, Barrio La California* ☎ *302–7026* ▤ *No credit cards* ⊘ *Closed Sun. and Mon.*

¢ ✕ **Café Hanna.** Coffee, tea, sandwiches, quiches, croissants, and the chance to while away a quiet afternoon are the draw at this irregularly laid-out building on a rounded street corner near Parque España. Or you can opt for a buffet lunch and salad bar and top it off with desserts. If you opt for dinner, make it an early one; the café closes at 7 PM. ⊠ *C. 13, between Avdas. 7 and 9, Barrio Otoya* ☎ *233–0843* ▤ *AE, DC, MC, V* ⊘ *Closed Sun.*

CHINESE ✕ **Don Wang.** In a country where "Chinese cuisine" often means rice and
$–$$ vegetables bearing a suspicious resemblance to *gallo pinto* ("spotted rooster," a typical Costa Rican dish of black beans and rice) Don Wang's authenticity comes as a real treat. Cantonese cuisine is the mainstay here—the owner comes from that region of China—but these folks will spice your dishes up if you ask. Mornings give way to the immensely popular dim sum, called *desayuno chino* (literally "Chinese breakfast"). The dining area is built around a stone garden and small waterfall. There's no television blaring here, a refreshing change from many Costa Rican restaurants. ⊠ *C. 11, between Avdas. 6 and 8* ☎ *233–6484 or 223–5925* ▤ *AE, DC, MC, V.*

COSTA RICAN ✕ **La Cocina de Leña.** La Cocina serves traditional Costa Rican fare sur-
★ $–$$ rounded by old tools and straw bags hung on walls to make you feel like you're down on the farm. Popular Tico dishes such as black-bean soup, ceviche, tamales, oxtail with cassava, and plantains are served, and the restaurant has live marimba music several nights a week during high season. Although the kitchen closes at 11, you're welcome to stay as long as the band keeps playing. It is one of the few places that doesn't close during Holy Week. ⊠ *Centro Comercial El Pueblo, Barrio Tournón* ☎ *223–3704* ▤ *AE, DC, MC, V.*

¢–$ ✕ **La Criollita.** Start your day with breakfast at this emerald green–colored restaurant. Mornings are the perfect time to snag one of the precious tables in the back garden, an unexpected refuge from busy downtown San José. Choose from the *americano*, with pancakes and toast; the *tico*, with bread, fried bananas, and *natilla* (sour cream); or the huge *criollita*, with ham or pork chops; all have eggs on the side. Workers from nearby government office buildings begin to pour in late in the morning, and the lunchtime decibel level increases appreciably. They filter out about 2 PM and once again you have a quiet place for

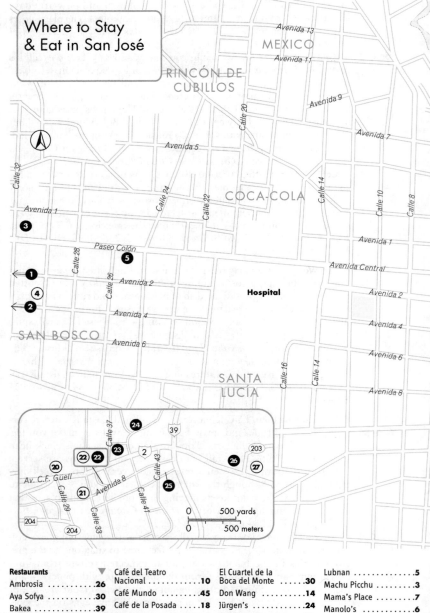

Where to Stay
& Eat in San José

Avenida 13
MEXICO
Avenida 11
RINCÓN DE
CUBILLOS
Avenida 9
Calle 20
Avenida 7
Avenida 5
Calle 32
Calle 24
Calle 22
COCA-COLA
Calle 14
Avenida 1
Calle 10
Calle 8
Calle 28
Paseo Colón
5
Avenida 1
3
Avenida Central
Calle 26
Avenida 2
Hospital
Avenida 2
1
4
2
Avenida 4
Avenida 4
SAN BOSCO
Avenida 6
Avenida 6
Calle 16
Calle 14
SANTA
LUCÍA
Avenida 8

24
Calle 37
39
23
2
22 22
203
20
26
27
Av. C.F. Güell
Calle 43
Calle 29
21
Avenida 8
25
Calle 41
204
Calle 33
204

0   500 yards
0   500 meters

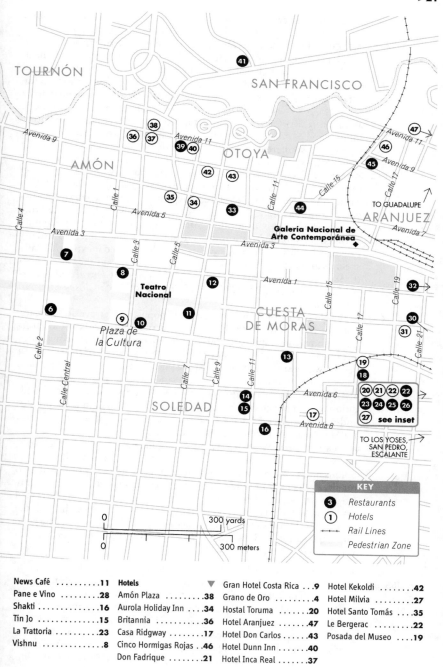

TOURNÓN

SAN FRANCISCO

❹❶

Avenida 9

❸❽ *Avenida 11*
❸❻ ❸❼   OTOYA
❸❾❹⓿

AMÓN

❹❷   ❹❸

Calle 1

❸❺ ❸❹

Avenida 5

❸❸

Calle 4

Avenida 3

Calle 3

Calle 5

**Galería Nacional de
Arte Contemporánea** ◆

Avenida 3

❼

❽

**Teatro
Nacional**

❶❷

Avenida 1

Calle 15

❸❷

❻

❾ ❿

*Plaza de
la Cultura*

❶❶

CUESTA
DE MORAS

Calle 17

❸⓿
❸❶

Calle 2

Calle Central

Calle 7

Calle 9

Calle 11

❶❸

❶❾
❶❽

❷⓿ ❷❶ ❷❷ ㉒

❷❸ ㉔ ㉕ ㉖

㉗ **see inset**

SOLEDAD

❶❹
❶❺

Avenida 6

❶❼
Avenida 8

❶❻

TO LOS YOSES,
SAN PEDRO,
ESCALANTE →

Avenida 9

❹❼ →

❹❻
❹❺ *Avenida 9*

TO GUADALUPE
ARANJUEZ

Avenida 7

Calle 19

Calle 21

0		300 yards

0		300 meters

KEY

❸	Restaurants
①	Hotels
┼┼┼	Rail Lines
	Pedestrian Zone

coffee and dessert. ⊠ *Avda. 7, between Cs. 7 and 9 Barrio Amón* ☎ *256–6511* ⊟ *AE, DC, MC, V* ✆ *Closed Sun. No dinner Sat.*

¢–$ ✗ **El Cuartel de la Boca del Monte.** Although it's one of San José's more popular late-night bars, El Cuartel is actually a nice place to have a meal, too. The restored brick walls, wood beams, and simple wood tables lend a rustic feel in one room, and you'll find a more finished room to the left of the entrance, decorated with original art. Best on the menu is arroz con pollo, but you can also order plates of delicious *bocas* (snacks), such as the *plato de gallos* (corn tortillas topped with beef, potatoes, and other fillings) and *piononos* (sweet plantains stuffed with cheese or beans and served with sour cream). ⊠ *Avda. 1, between Cs. 21 and 23, Barrio La California* ☎ *221–0327* ⊟ *AE, DC, MC, V* ✆ *No lunch weekends.*

¢–$ ✗ **Mama's Place.** Mama's is a Costa Rican restaurant with a difference: the owners are Italian, so in addition to corvina *al ajillo* (sautéed with garlic) and other staple Tico fare, they serve homemade seafood chowder, traditional Italian pastas, and meat dishes with delicate wine sauces. The brightly decorated coffee shop opens onto busy Avenida 1; the more subdued restaurant is upstairs. At lunchtime, it's usually packed with business types drawn to the delicious and inexpensive daily specials and perhaps the macrobiotic fruit shakes, another menu item that sets this place apart. ⊠ *Avda. 1, between Cs. Central and 2, Barrio El Carmen* ☎ *223–2270* ⊟ *AE, DC, MC, V* ✆ *Closed Sun. No dinner Sat.*

¢–$ ✗ **Manolo's.** This 24-hour eatery has been popular with travelers for years, both for its location on the bustling pedestrian thoroughfare and for its great sandwiches, espressos, and *churros con chocolate* (fried dough with hot fudge sauce). A few outdoor tables allow for some of the city's best people-watching. Inside, however, the place feels more like a diner than a café, down to its plastic-coated menu and its promise of breakfast food at any hour. The owner always prepares a few Spanish favorites in addition to the typical Tico fare, such as *tortilla española* (a thick potato-and-onion omelet). ⊠ *Avda. Central, between Cs. Central and 2, Barrio La Merced* ☎ *221–2041* ⊟ *AE, DC, MC, V.*

¢–$ ✗ **Nuestra Tierra.** With its relaxed atmosphere and rough-hewn tables, Nuestra Tierra is an upscale alternative to "soda" dining. Bunches of onions and peppers dangle from the ceiling, recalling a provincial Tico ranch. The generous homemade meals are delicious, and the incredibly friendly waitstaff, who epitomize Costa Rican hospitality and dress in traditional folkloric clothing, prepare your coffee filtered through the traditional cloth *chorreador*. The place is open 24 hours, just in case gallo pinto pangs hit at 3 AM. ⊠ *Avda. 2 and C. 15, Barrio La Soledad* ☎ *258–6500* ⊟ *AE, DC, MC, V.*

ECLECTIC ✗ **Jürgen's.** Decorated in gold and terra-cotta with leather and wood
$$–$$$ accents, the dining room of this contemporary restaurant feels more like a lounge than a fine restaurant. In fact, the classy bar, with a large selection of good wine and good cigars, is a prominent feature. The inventive menu, with such delicacies as medallions of roast duck and tuna fillet encrusted with sesame seeds, sets this place apart from the city's more traditional venues. Jürgen's is a common haunt for *politicos* and San José's elite. ⊠ *¾ km (½ mi) north of the Subaru dealership,*

on Barrio Dent Blvd., Barrio Dent ☎ *283–2239* ▭ *AE, DC, MC, V* ◷ *Closed Sun. No lunch Sat.*

$–$$ ✕ **Ambrosia.** The navy-blue canopy in an open-air shopping plaza heralds this chic restaurant. The international menu draws the customers. Expect inventive salads, soups, pasta, and fish dishes. Start with *sopa Neptuna* (a creamy fish soup with tomato and bacon), and follow with either the light fettuccine ambrosia (in a rich cream sauce with ham and oregano) or the corvina *troyana* (with a shrimp and tarragon sauce). The dining room is relaxed, with plants, subdued watercolors, crisp white tablecloths, and wood-and-cane chairs. ⊠ *Centro Comercial de la C. Real, 50 m east of Banco Popular, San Pedro* ☎ *253–8012* ▭ *AE, DC, MC, V* ◷ *No dinner Sun.*

$–$$ ✕ **Bakea.** Trendy, right down to its small art gallery and whimsical rest
FodorśChoice rooms, this restaurant in a restored Barrio Amón mansion is the place
★ to see and be seen, and is one of the few upscale places in town to grab a very-late-night bite. Le Cordon Bleu–trained chef Camille Ratton-Pérez takes French and Costa Rican cuisine and spices it with Thai and Middle Eastern influences. Top off your meal with a *Cahuita caramelo*, a scrumptious chocolate-banana-butterscotch concoction, or, if you can't decide, go for the *paleta Bakea*, a dessert sampler platter. ⊠ *C. 7 and Avda. 11, Barrio Amón* ☎ *248–0303* ▭ *AE, DC, MC, V* ◷ *Closed Sun. and Mon. No lunch Sat.*

FRENCH ✕ **Le Chandelier.** Formal service and traditional sauce-heavy French
$$–$$$$ dishes are part of the experience at the city's classiest restaurant, Le Chandelier. The dining room is elegant, with wicker chairs, a tile floor, and original paintings. The Swiss chef, Claude Dubuis, might start you off with saffron ravioli stuffed with ricotta cheese and walnuts. His main courses include such unique dishes as corvina in a *pejibaye* (peach palm) sauce, hearts of palm and veal chops glazed in a sweet port-wine sauce, and the more familiar *pato a la naranja* (duck à l'orange). ⊠ *50 m west and 100 m south of the ICE building, San Pedro* ☎ *225–3980* ▭ *AE, DC, MC, V* ◷ *Closed Sun. No lunch Sat.*

$$ ✕ **L'Ile de France.** Long one of San José's most popular restaurants, L'Ile
FodorśChoice de France is in the Le Bergerac hotel in Los Yoses, where you can dine
★ in a tropical garden courtyard. The fairly traditional French menu has some interesting innovations. Start with the classic onion soup or with *pâté de lapin* (rabbit liver pâté); then sink your teeth into a pepper steak, broiled lamb with seasoned potatoes, or corvina in a spinach sauce. Save room for the profiteroles filled with vanilla ice cream and smothered in chocolate sauce. ⊠ *Le Bergerac hotel, C. 35, between Avdas. Central and 2, first Los Yoses entrance, Los Yoses, San Pedro* ☎ *283–5812* ⌕ *Reservations essential* ▭ *AE, DC, MC, V* ◷ *Closed Sun. No lunch.*

ITALIAN ✕ **Balcón de Franco.** With old sepia photos and a strolling guitarist who
$–$$ seems to have been working the room for years, Balcón de Franco—the sign out front says BALCÓN DE EUROPA—transports you to the year of its inception, 1909. Pasta specialties such as the *plato mixto* (mixed plate with lasagna, tortellini, and ravioli) are so popular that they haven't changed much, either. For something lighter, try the scrumptious heart-of-palm salad or sautéed corvina. ⊠ *Avda. Central and C. 9, Barrio La Soledad* ☎ *221–4841* ▭ *AE, DC, MC, V* ◷ *Closed Sat.*

$ ✕ **La Trattoria.** Excellent homemade pasta dishes are reasonably priced at this popular lunch spot. The blond-wood tables and Tuscan yellow walls lend levity. Begin your meal with fresh bread and any number of excellent antipastis, continuing on with your favorite pasta dish. And for dessert, who can resist tiramisu? ✉ *Behind Auto-Mercado Los Yoses in Barrio Dent, San Pedro* ☎ *224–7065* ▭ *AE, DC, MC, V.*

$ ✕ **Pane e Vino.** Look closely at the extensive menu here: there are 40 varieties of the capital's best thin-crust pizza. This lively two-level restaurant rounds out its offerings with a complete selection of pastas. You can dine until midnight daily, expect on Sunday, when you'll have to finish dinner by 10 PM. ✉ *50 m west and 15 m south of Más X Menos, San Pedro* ☎ *280–2869* ▭ *AE, DC, MC, V.*

JAPANESE ✕ **Matsuri.** This two-in-one Japanese restaurant counts a downstairs sushi
★ $-$$ bar with lots of varnished wood and chrome. The chefs here have created 48 recipes for original rolls, sushi, and sashimi using imported high-quality ingredients. Bento boxes are the weekday lunch specials. The oohing and aahing goes on upstairs around the chefs performing at the teppanyaki grills to the delight and applause of patrons. ✉ *Plaza Cristal, 600 m south of Pop's ice cream shop, Curridabat* ☎ *280–5522* ▭ *AE, DC, MC, V.*

MIDDLE EASTERN ✕ **Lubnan.** The Lebanese owners here serve a wide variety of dishes from
$-$$ their native region, so if you can't decide, the *mezza* serves two people and gives you a little bit of everything. For your own individual dish, try the juicy shish kebab *de cordero* (of lamb), or if you're feeling especially adventurous, the raw-ground meat *kebbe naye* (with wheat meal) and *kafta naye* (without wheat meal). Tapestries and drawings decorate the walls, and you'll negotiate a wicker revolving door at the entrance. ✉ *Paseo Colón, between Cs. 22 and 24, Paseo Colón* ☎ *257–6071* ▭ *AE, DC, MC, V* ☺ *Closed Mon. No dinner Sun.*

PAN-ASIAN ✕ **Tin Jo.** You can eat in the Japan, India, China, or Thailand room at
$-$$ this wide-ranging Asian restaurant with a menu to match its varied din-
Fodor'sChoice ing areas. Tin Jo stands out with always exceptional food and quirky
★ decorations that add color to this former residence. Start with a powerful Singapore sling (brandy and fruit juices) before trying such treats as *kaeng* (Thai shrimp and pineapple curry in coconut milk), *mu shu* (a beef, chicken, or veggie stir-fry with crepes), samosas (stuffed Indian pastries), and sushi rolls. The vegetarian menu is extensive. ✉ *C. 11, between Avdas. 6 and 8, Barrio La Soledad* ☎ *257–3622* ▭ *AE, DC, MC, V.*

PERUVIAN ✕ **Machu Picchu.** A few travel posters and a fishnet holding crab and
★ $-$$ lobster shells are the only props used to evoke Peru, but no matter: the food is anything but plain, and the seafood is excellent at both the east- and west-side branches of this mainstay. The *pique especial de mariscos* (special seafood platter), big enough for two, presents you with shrimp, conch, and squid cooked four ways. The ceviche here is quite different from and better than that served in the rest of the country. A blazing Peruvian hot sauce served on the side adds zip to any dish, but be careful—apply it by the drop. ✉ *C. 32, 130 m north*

of KFC, Paseo Colón ☎ *222–7384* ✉ *150 m south of Ferretería El Mar, San Pedro* ☎ *283–3769* 🖃 *AE, DC, MC, V* ⊘ *Paseo Colón location closed Sun.*

SPANISH ✕ **La Masía de Triquell.** San José's most traditional Spanish restaurant is
$$–$$$ appropriately housed in the Casa España, a Spanish cultural center. The dining room follows the theme with a tile floor, wood beams, white tablecloths, leather-and-wood Castilian-style chairs, and red, green, and yellow walls. *Champiñones al ajillo* (mushrooms sautéed with garlic and parsley) make a fine appetizer; *camarones Catalana* (shrimp in a tomato-and-garlic cream sauce) is a standout entrée. The long wine list is strongest in the Spanish and French departments. ✉ *45 m west and 130 m north of Burger King, Sabana Norte* ☎ *296–3528* ◬ *Reservations essential* 🖃 *AE, DC, MC, V* ⊘ *Closed Sun.*

$–$$ ✕ **Casa Luisa.** The moment you enter this homey, upscale Catalan restaurant, you sense you're in for a special evening. It is eclectic and artful, with wood floors, arresting artwork, soft lighting, and flamenco music in the background. Start the meal with gazpacho or eggplant pâté, accompanied by a glass of top Spanish wine. The wonderful main dishes include rosemary lamb chops, suckling pig, and grilled lobster. Finish with a platter of nuts, dates, and figs drizzled with a wine sauce or the decadent *crema catalana* with a *brûlée* glaze. ✉ *400 m south and 40 m west of the Contraloría, Sabana Sur* ☎ *296–1917* 🖃 *AE, DC, MC, V* ⊘ *No dinner Sun.*

TURKISH ✕ **Aya Sofya.** Natives of Istanbul, the chef and one of the owners have
¢–$ imported excellent recipes for red peppers stuffed with spicy beef and rice, eggplant-tomato salad, and other Mediterranean treats. The selection of vegetarian salads is good. Desserts include a scrumptious yogurt-and-honey *revani* cake and the beloved baklava. Beyond the obligatory evil-eye motif and a few wall hangings, this is a no-frills place, but good food and a friendly staff make it a find. ✉ *Avda. Central and C. 21, Barrio La California* ☎ *221–7185* 🖃 *AE, DC, MC, V* ⊘ *Closed Sun.*

VEGETARIAN ✕ **Shakti.** Amidst the baskets of fruit and vegetables at the entrance and
¢–$ the wall of herbal teas, health food books, and fresh herbs for sale by the register, there's no doubt you're in a vegetarian-friendly joint. The bright and airy restaurant serves breakfast and lunch: homemade bread, soy burgers, pita sandwiches (veggie or, for carnivorous dining companions, chicken), macrobiotic fruit shakes, and a hearty plato del día that comes with soup, green salad, and a fruit beverage. The *ensalada mixta* is a meal in itself, packed with root vegetables native to Costa Rica. The restaurant closes at 7 PM daily. ✉ *Avda. 8 and C. 13, Barrio La Soledad* ☎ *222–4475* ◬ *Reservations not accepted* 🖃 *AE, DC, MC, V* ⊘ *Closed Sun.*

¢ ✕ **Vishnu.** Named after the Hindu god who preserves the universe, Vishnu has become a bit of an institution in San José. Even its dining area looks institutional—sterile booths with Formica tables and posters of fruit on the walls—but the attraction is the inexpensive vegetarian food. Your best bet is usually the plato del día, which includes soup, beverage, and dessert, but the menu also offers soy burgers, salads, fresh fruit juices, and a yogurt smoothie called *morir soñando* (literally, "to die dreaming"). ⊠ *Avda. 1, west of C. 3, Barrio El Carmen* ☎ *233–9976* ⌒ *Reservations not accepted* ⊟ *AE, DC, MC, V.*

WHERE TO STAY

San José packs every kind of accommodation, from luxury to bare necessity. You can find massive hotels with all the modern conveniences and amenities, historic buildings with traditional architecture but fewer creature comforts, and smaller establishments with the simplicity (and prices) beloved of backpackers. Dozens of former homes in the city's older neighborhoods, such as Barrio Amón and Barrio Otoya, and surrounding towns such as San Pedro have been converted to moderately priced B&Bs. Confirm all reservations 24 hours ahead.

For the rather luxurious business-oriented Marriott and Meliá hotels northwest of the capital near the airport, *see* San Antônio de Belén *in* Chapter 2.

WHAT IT COSTS				
	$$$$	$$$	$$	$	¢
FOR 2 PEOPLE	over $200	$125–$200	$75–$125	$35–$75	under $35

Prices are for two people in a standard double room in high season, excluding service and tax (16.4%).

Downtown San José

Staying in the downtown area allows you to travel around the city as most Ticos do: on foot. Stroll the city's parks, museums, and shops, and then retire in one of many small or historic hotels that have plenty in the way of character.

$$–$$$ 🏨 **Aurola Holiday Inn.** The upper floors of this 17-story mirrored-glass building, three blocks north of the Plaza de la Cultura, have the best views in town. Ignoring the view of downtown San José and its surroundings, however, you could just as soon be in Ohio, as the interior decoration betrays no local influence. The high-ceiling lobby is modern and airy, with lots of shiny marble. The good restaurant and casino are on the top floor, making full use of their vantage points. ⊠ *Avda. 5 and C. 5, Barrio Amón* ⌂ *Apdo. 7802–1000, San José* ☎ *222–2424, 800/ 465–4329 in U.S.* 🖷 *255–1171* ⊕ *www.aurola-holidayinn.com* ⇆ *200 rooms, 12 suites* ⌂ *Restaurant, coffee shop, in-room data ports, in-room safes, minibars, cable TV, indoor pool, gym, hot tub, sauna, spa, bar, casino, shop, laundry service, concierge, Internet, business services, meeting rooms, car rental, travel services, free parking, no-smoking floors* ⊟ *AE, DC, MC, V* ⏀ *BP.*

★ $$ 🏨 **Amón Plaza.** Here's the perfect alternative if you seek the Barrio Amón experience, but need the services of a international-class hotel, without opting for the Aurola Holiday Inn up the hill. The pink Amón Plaza doesn't overpower the surrounding neighborhood, and takes pride that each of its 80-plus rooms are slightly different. But all the amenities of a high-rise business-class hotel are yours here. Friday night sees cocktails and a buffet dinner at the hotel's open-air café to the accompaniment of light music. ⊠ *Avda. 11 and C. 3 Bis, Barrio Amón* ☎ *257–0191 or 257–8686, 800/575–1253 in U.S., 866/845–3763 in Canada* 📠 *257–0284* ⊕ *www.hotelamonplaza.com* 🛏 *84 rooms, 3 suites* ⚐ *Restaurant, coffee shop, in-room data ports, in-room safes, some refrigerators, gym, hot tub, massage, sauna, spa, bar, casino, shop, dry cleaning, laundry service, meeting rooms, travel services, free parking, no-smoking rooms* ☰ *AE, DC, MC, V* ⦿ *BP.*

$$ 🏨 **Britannia.** Except for the addition of some rooms and the conversion of the old cellar into an intimate international restaurant, this stately pink home with a tiled porch has changed little since its construction in 1910. Rooms in the newer wing are slightly small, with carpeting and hardwood furniture. Deluxe rooms and junior suites in the original house are spacious, with high ceilings and windows on the street side; they're worth the extra money but are close enough to the street that noise might be a problem if you're a light sleeper. ⊠ *C. 3 and Avda. 11, Barrio Amón* 🏤 *Apdo. 3742–1000, San José* ☎ *223–6667, 800/263–2618 in U.S.* 📠 *223–6411* ⊕ *www.hotelbritanniacostarica.com* 🛏 *19 rooms, 5 suites* ⚐ *Restaurant, fans, in-room safes, cable TV, bar, shop, dry cleaning, laundry service, Internet, airport shuttle, travel services, free parking; no a/c in some rooms* ☰ *AE, DC, MC, V.*

$$ 🏨 **Hotel Grano de Oro.** Two turn-of-the-20th-century wooden houses on
Fodor'sChoice San José's western edge have been converted into one of the city's most
★ charming inns. New rooms have been added to the attractive space, which is decorated with old photos of the capital and paintings by local artists. A modest restaurant, run by a French-trained chef, is surrounded by a lovely indoor patio and gardens. The old rooms are the nicest, especially the Garden Suite, with hardwood floors, high ceilings, and private garden. The hotel's sundeck has a view of both the city and the far-off volcanoes. ⊠ *C. 30, between Avdas. 2 and 4, Paseo Colón* 🏤 *1701 N.W. 97th Ave., SJO 36, Box 025216, Miami, FL 33102-5216* ☎ *255–3322* 📠 *221–2782* ⊕ *www.hotelgranodeoro.com* 🛏 *32 rooms, 3 suites* ⚐ *Restaurant, room service, in-room safes, minibars, cable TV, outdoor hot tub, shop, laundry service, free parking, no-smoking rooms; no a/c* ☰ *AE, MC, V.*

★ **$–$$** 🏨 **Hotel Don Carlos.** One of the city's first guesthouses, Don Carlos has been in the same family for four generations. Most rooms in the rambling villa have ceiling fans and big windows. Those in the Colonial Wing have a bit more personality, and several newer rooms on the third floor have volcano views. Abundant public areas are adorned with orchids and pre-Columbian statues. Complimentary cocktails and breakfast are served on the garden patio; the small restaurant serves lunch and dinner. ⊠ *C. 9 and Avda. 9, Barrio Amón* 🏤 *Box 025216, Dept. 1686, Miami, FL 33102-5216* ☎ *221–6707* 📠 *255–0828* ⊕ *www. doncarloshotel.com* 🛏 *33 rooms* ⚐ *Restaurant, in-room safes, outdoor hot tub, shop, dry cleaning, laundry service, Internet, airport shuttle, free parking; no a/c in some rooms* ☰ *AE, MC, V* ⦿ *CP.*

★ **$–$$** 🏨 **Hotel Santo Tomás.** Don't be put off that the front of this century-old, former coffee-plantation house butts up against the sidewalk on a busy street; the lobby and rooms are set back, pleasantly removed from the noise of traffic. The spacious rooms have wood or tile floors, and lots of deep, varnished wood furnishings. Some of the tiled bathrooms have skylights. A bright breakfast room adjoins an interior patio, and if you keep traveling back into the interior of the building, you'll find a small outdoor pool, a rarity in this size hotel in the capital. Rates include 30 minutes of free Internet access per day, and the friendly, helpful staff makes this a real find. ⊠ *Avda. 7 between Cs. 3 and 5, Barrio Amón* ☎ *255–0448* 🖷 *222–3950* ⊕ *www.hotelsantotomas.com* ⇙ *20 rooms* ⌂ *Restaurant, dining room, pool, gym, hot tub, bar, travel services, parking (fee); no a/c* ⊟ *AE, MC, V* ¹⊙¹ *CP.*

$ 🖼 **Gran Hotel Costa Rica.** Opened in 1930, the grande dame of San José hotels remains a focal point of the city and is the first choice of travelers who want to be where the action is. It's a good deal for the money, but the flow of nonguests who frequent the 24-hour casino, Café Parisienne, restaurant, and bar reduces the intimacy quotient to zero. Rooms are large and somewhat lackluster, with small windows and tubs in the tiled baths. Most overlook the Plaza de la Cultura, which can be a bit noisy, and the quieter, interior rooms are pretty dark. ⊠ *Avda. 2 and C. 3, Barrio La Soledad* ⌀ *Apdo. 527–1000, San José* ☎ *221–4000, 800/949–0592 in U.S.* 🖷 *221–3501* ⊕ *www.granhotelcr.com* ⇙ *98 rooms, 1 suite* ⌂ *Restaurant, café, fans, cable TV, bar, casino, shop, laundry service, travel services, parking (fee)* ⊟ *AE, MC, V* ¹⊙¹ *CP.*

$ 🖼 **Hotel Dunn Inn.** Adjoining 1926 and 1933 houses fuse to create the cozy Barrio Amón experience at bargain prices, so the Dunn Inn is justifiably immensely popular. Pinewood dominates in one section; brick in the other. Sun-filled rooms bear indigenous Bribri names. One room has a balcony, but a few do not have outdoor windows. All have terracotta floors, and the staff adds little touches such as fresh flowers in the rooms. The delightful, skylight-covered central patio serves as a bar–breakfast room combo. ⊠ *Avda. 11 at C. 5, Barrio Amón* ☎ *222–3232 or 222–3426* 🖷 *221–4596* ⊕ *www.hoteldunninn.com* ⇙ *24 rooms* ⌂ *Restaurant, fans, minibars, bar, Internet, travel services, parking (fee)* ⊟ *V* ¹⊙¹ *BP.*

$ 🖼 **Hotel Inca Real.** The Ecuadorian owners have constructed a modern Spanish-colonial-style hotel that evokes South, rather than Central America. Rooms congregate around a bright, skylight-covered, plant-filled central patio with wrought-iron gates around the second- and third-floor passageways. All rooms are ample in size. Those on the first floor are tiled; those on the second and third floors are carpeted. Some of the rooms have three beds. All have orthopedic mattresses. ⊠ *Avda. 11, between Cs. 3 and 5, Barrio Amón* ☎ *222–5318* 🖷 *223–8883* ⊕ *www. hotelincareal.com* ⇙ *33 rooms* ⌂ *Fans, bar, shop, laundry service, Internet, car rental, travel services, free parking; no a/c* ⊟ *V* ¹⊙¹ *CP.*

$ 🖼 **Hotel Kekoldi.** You'd think you were in Miami Beach with all the tropical Florida-like pastels, but the art-deco, pink-and-white Kekoldi sits right in the center of Barrio Amón. The secluded interior garden with umbrella-covered tables is a pleasant respite from the hustle and bustle of the city. The enormous, so-called "master queen" room overlooks the garden. The drapes, spreads, and pillows in all rooms echo the bright tropical prints throughout the hotel. ⊠ *Avda. 9, between Cs. 5 and 7,*

Barrio Amón ☎ *248–0804* 📠 *248–0767* 🌐 *www.kekoldi.com* 🛏 *10 rooms* ♿ *Fans, in-room safes, travel services, parking (fee); no a/c* ▭ *AE, MC, V* ⚟ *BP.*

$ 🏨 **Hotel Rincón de San José.** Never mind that the interior looks more European than Latin American. This elegant little inn has comfortable rooms in a charming area near the Parque España. Rooms have carved doors, custom-made furniture, and small bathrooms. Most have hardwood window frames and floors; several have bathtubs. Complimentary breakfast is served in the garden courtyard, which doubles as a bar. Rates include Internet access. ✉ *Avda. 9 and C. 15, Barrio Otoya* ☎ *221–9702* 📠 *222–1241* 🌐 *www.hotelrincondesanjose.com* 🛏 *27 rooms* ♿ *Fans, bar, parking (fee); no a/c* ▭ *AE, DC, MC, V* ⚟ *CP.*

$ 🏨 **Posada del Museo.** Here's a great place to stay if you're bound for San José's museums, hence the name. This converted 1928 house sits diagonally from Museo Nacional. The friendly Argentine owners live on-site. Each room is different. In the restoration, the owners have maintained the original tiles, wooden double doors, and artfully painted ceilings. The hallway on the second floor overlooks the two-story lobby from what the owners call their "Romeo and Juliet balcony." ✉ *Avda. 2 and C. 17* ☎ *257–9414* 📧 *posadadelmuseo@racsa.co.cr* 🛏 *7 rooms, 1 suite* ♿ *Restaurant, fans, in-room data ports, shop, free parking; no a/c* ▭ *AE, DC, MC, V* ⚟ *CP.*

¢–$

FodorśChoice

★

🏨 **Hotel Aranjuez.** Several 1940s-era houses, with extensive gardens and cozy common areas, constitute this family-run B&B. Each room is different; some have private gardens or small sitting rooms. Aranjuez is a short walk from most San José attractions and offers such perks as discount tour services. The complimentary breakfast buffet is a substantial spread of eggs, pastries, tropical fruit, good Costa Rican coffee, and more, served on a pretty, palm-shaded patio. Reserve well in advance during high season. ✉ *C. 19, between Avdas. 11 and 13, Barrio Aranjuez* ☎ *256–1825, 877/898–8663 in U.S.* 📠 *223–3528* 🌐 *www. hotelaranjuez.com* 🛏 *35 rooms, 25 with bath* ♿ *Dining room, fans, in-room safes, cable TV, babysitting, laundry service, Internet, travel services, free parking; no a/c* ▭ *MC, V* ⚟ *BP.*

¢

🏨 **Casa Ridgway.** Affiliated with the Quaker Peace Center next door, Casa Ridgway is the budget option for itinerants concerned with peace, the environment, and social issues in general. In an old villa on a quiet street, the bright, clean premises include a planted terrace, a lending reference library, and a kitchen where you can cook your own food. There are three rooms with two bunk beds each, three rooms with single beds, and one with a double bed. ✉ *Avda. 6 Bis and C. 15, Barrio Gonzalez Laman* 📪 *Apdo. 1507–1000* ☎ *222–1400* 📠 *233–6168* 📧 *friends@racsa.co.cr* 🛏 *8 shared rooms without bath* ♿ *Library, laundry service, meeting room, parking (fee); no a/c, no room phones, no room TVs* ▭ *No credit cards.*

¢

🏨 **Cinco Hormigas Rojas.** The name of this whimsical little lodge translates as "five red ants." Behind the wall of vines that obscures it from the street is a wild garden—it's an unexpected urban bird-watching venue—leading to an interior space filled with original artwork. Color abounds, from the bright hues on the walls right down to the toilet seats.

Sure enough, the resident owner is an artist—Mayra Güell turned the house she inherited from her grandmother into San José's most original B&B–cum–art gallery. She tosses in thoughtful touches such as a healthful boxed breakfast if you're heading out on an early-morning excursion, and coffee and tea 24/7. ☒ *C. 15, between Avdas. 9 and 11, Barrio Otoya* ☎ *357–8872* 🖶 *257–8581* ⊕ *www.crtimes.com/ tourism/cincohormigasrojas/maincinco.htm* 🛏 *6 rooms, 1 with bath* ⌂ *Fans, laundry service, parking (fee); no a/c, no room phones, no room TVs* 🖃 *AE, MC, V* ⦿⧉ *BP.*

East of San José

The small properties beyond downtown, toward the university, offer personalized service and lots of peace and quiet. Plenty of restaurants and bars are within easy reach, although downtown is just a 10-minute cab ride away.

$–$$ ✕🖭 **Le Bergerac.** Le Bergerac, surrounded by extensive green grounds,
Fodor'sChoice is the cream of a growing crop of small, upscale San José hotels. It oc-
★   cupies two former private homes and is furnished with antiques. All rooms have custom-made wood-and-stone dressers and writing tables; deluxe rooms have two beds, private garden terraces or balconies, and large bathrooms. The hotel's restaurant, L'Ile de France, is one of the city's best, so dinner reservations are essential, even for guests. Breakfast is served on a garden patio. ☒ *C. 35, between Avdas. Central and 2, first entrance to Los Yoses, Los Yoses, San Pedro* ⊕ *Apdo. 1107–1002, San José* ☎ *234–7850* 🖶 *225–9103* ⊕ *www.bergerachotel. com* 🛏 *25 rooms* ⌂ *Restaurant, fans, in-room data ports, in-room safes, cable TV, bar, dry cleaning, laundry service, Internet, airport shuttle, travel services, free parking, no-smoking rooms; no a/c* 🖃 *AE, DC, MC, V* ⦿⧉ *BP.*

$ 🖭 **Don Fadrique.** This tranquil, family-run B&B on the outskirts of San José was named after Fadrique Guttiérez, an illustrious great-uncle of the owners. A collection of original Costa Rican art decorates the lobby and rooms, most of which have hardwood floors, peach walls, and pastel bedspreads. Several carpeted rooms downstairs open onto the garden. There is also an enclosed garden patio, where meals are served. ☒ *C. 37 at Avda. 8, Los Yoses, San Pedro* ☎ *225–8186* 🖶 *224–9746* ⊕ *www. hoteldonfadrique.com* 🛏 *20 rooms* ⌂ *Restaurant, fans, cable TV, laundry service, Internet, car rental, travel services, free parking; no a/c* 🖃 *AE, MC, V* ⦿⧉ *BP.*

$ 🖭 **Hotel Milvia.** Once a militia-arms depository, this 100-year-old house-turned-B&B on a San Pedro back street has charming small rooms and volcano views from the second-story balcony. There is a small pond out front in the lush meditation garden. Inside are gorgeous tropical paintings—manager Florencia Urbina belongs to the local art consortium Bocaracá, and the group's art adorns the hotel's common areas—a breakfast salon and small bar area, and classic Tico furniture. The bathrooms have lovely hand-painted tiles. ☒ *50 m north and 200 m east of Centro Comercial Muñoz y Nanne, San Pedro* ⊕ *Apdo. 1660–2050, San Pedro* ☎ *225–4543 or 283–9548* 🖶 *225–7801* ⊕ *www.hotelmilvia.com* 🛏 *9 rooms* ⌂ *Fans, in-room safes, cable*

TV, pond, bar, library, laundry service, Internet, free parking, no-smoking rooms; no a/c ⊟ *AE, DC, MC, V* ⦸ *BP.*

¢ ⊞ **Hostal Toruma.** The headquarters of RECAJ, Costa Rica's expanding Hostelling International network, is housed in an elegant colonial bungalow, built around 1900, in the tranquil Barrio La California. The tiled lobby and veranda are ideal places for backpackers to hang out and exchange travel tales. Beds on the ground floor are in little compartments with doors; rooms on the second floor have standard bunks. There are also three private rooms for couples. The on-site information center offers discounted tours. ⊠ *Avda. Central, between Cs. 29 and 31, Barrio La California* ⊘ *Apdo. 1355–1002, San José* ☎ *234–8186* ⊟⊟ *224–4085* ⊕ *www.hicr.org* ⤴ *80 beds in 17 dormitory rooms with shared baths, 3 private rooms without bath* ⚭ *Dining room, Internet, travel services, free parking; no a/c, no room phones, no room TVs* ⊟ *MC, V* ⦸ *CP.*

NIGHTLIFE & THE ARTS

The Arts

San José might be a small capital of a small Latin American country, but events pack its cultural calendar most of the year, and ticket prices pale in comparison to what you'd pay back home. The downside? The selection of theater and art offerings becomes sparse during school vacations from mid-December until early February, which coincides with prime tourist season.

The best source for theater, dance, film, and arts information is the "Viva" entertainment section of the Spanish-language daily *La Nación. San José Volando* is a free monthly magazine found in many hotels, and publishes features about what's going on around town. Listings in both publications are in Spanish, but are easy to decipher. The "Weekend" section of the English-language weekly *The Tico Times* lists information about arts and culture, much of it events of interest to the expatriate community. The paper comes out each Friday.

Art Galleries

San José's art galleries, public or private, museum or bohemian, keep daytime hours only, but all kick off a new show with an evening exhibit opening. They're free and open to the public, and offer a chance to rub elbows with Costa Rica's art community (and to sip wine and munch on appetizers). Listings appear in *La Nación*'s "Viva" section. Your time in the capital might coincide with one of these by happenstance. Look for the term *inauguración* (inauguration).

Cultural Centers

The cultural centers of five nations give an added spark to San José's arts scene, although their art exhibitions, plays, or discussions are just as likely to be Costa Rican in focus as they are to deal with their home countries. There's usually something going on two or three nights a week. Check *La Nación* for listings.

The **Alliance Française** (⊠ Avda. 7 and C. 5, Barrio Amón ☎ 222–2283 ✉ 200 m south of Librería Universal, Sabana Sur ☎ 290–2705) teaches French courses, hosts occasional art exhibitions, and screens French films. In addition to being one of the city's foremost English-language schools, the **Centro Cultural Costarricense–Norteamericano** (Costa Rican–American Cultural Center; ⊠ Avda. 1 and C. 37, Barrio Dent San Pedro ☎ 207–7500 ✉ 200 m north, 100 m east, 100 m north, and 100 m east of the ICE building, Sabana Norte ☎ 290–2540 ⊕ www.cccncr. com) holds plays and concerts at its Eugene O'Neill Theater and art shows at its Sophia Wanamaker gallery. The **Centro Cultural de México** (Mexican Cultural Center; ⊠ 250 m south of the Subaru dealership, Los Yoses ☎ 283–2333) hosts a packed schedule of lectures, concerts, and art exhibitions. The **Centro Cultural Dante Alighieri** (Dante Alighieri Cultural Center; ⊠ 200 m south of KFC, Barrio La California ☎ 283–5632) brings a bit of la dolce vita to San José and showcases art, teaches Italian courses, and has a small lunch restaurant. Spain's **Centro Cultural de España** (Spanish Cultural Center; ⊠ 100 m west of the Farolito, Barrio Escalante ☎ 257–2919 ⊕ www.centrocultural-es.or.cr) is the most active of the cultural centers—it's the mother country, after all—with lectures, art exhibitions, films, book releases, and workshops.

Theater & Music

San José has an active theater scene. More than a dozen theater groups (many of which perform slapstick comedies) hold forth in smaller theaters around town. If your Spanish is up to it, call for a reservation. The curtain rises at 8 PM, Thursday through Sunday.

The baroque **Teatro Nacional** (⊠ Plaza de la Cultura, Barrio La Soledad ☎ 221–1329) is the home of the excellent National Symphony Orchestra, which performs on Friday evenings and Sunday mornings between April and December. The theater also hosts visiting musical groups and dance companies. San José's second-most popular theater, the **Teatro Popular Melico Salazar** (⊠ Avda. 2, between Cs. Central and 2, Barrio La Merced ☎ 221–4952) has a full calendar of music and dance, as well as a few offbeat productions.

There are frequent dance performances and concerts in the **Teatro FANAL** and the **Teatro 1887**, both in the **Centro Nacional de la Cultura** (⊠ C. 13, between Avdas. 3 and 5, Barrio Otoya ☎ 257–5524). The **Eugene O'Neill Theater** (⊠ Centro Cultural Costarricense–Norteamericano, Avda. 1 and C. 37, Barrio Dent San Pedro ☎ 207–7554) has chamber concerts and plays most weekend evenings. The cultural center is a great place to meet expatriate North Americans.

Nightlife

Bars

No one could accuse San José of having too few watering holes, but outside the hotels, there aren't many places to have a quiet drink, especially downtown—Tico bars tend to be on the lively side. Bars congregate in the Centro Comercial El Pueblo, north of downtown, and near the University of Costa Rica in San Pedro, especially on the Calle de la Amargura.

Intensely Bohemian **Café Expresivo** (⊠ Avda. 9, between Cs. 29 and 31, Barrio Escalante ☎ 224–1202) hosts poetry readings and acoustic guitar concerts and serves light pastas and sandwiches. For a decidedly uptown experience, head to the oh-so-chic **Café Loft** (⊠ Avda. 11 at C. 3, in front of Hotel Britannia, Barrio Amón ☎ 221–2303), a popular late-night eating spot with a modern lounge feel. It's closed Monday. The highly recommended restaurant **Café Mundo** (⊠ C. 15 and Avda. 9, Barrio Otoya ☎ 222–6190) is also quiet spot for a drink frequented by gay and bohemian crowds. University students tend to hang out on San Pedro's **Calle Amargura**, which has tons of bars with "binge drinking specials."

The second floor of the **Casino Colonial** (⊠ Avda. 1, between Cs. 9 and 11, Barrio El Carmen ☎ 258–2807) is a good place to watch a soccer game on television. The **Centro Comercial El Pueblo** (⊠ Avda. 0, Barrio Tournón) has a bar for every taste, from quiet pubs to thumping discos. Several bars have live music on weekends; it's best to wander around and see what sounds good. Open 24 hours, **Chelles** (⊠ Avda. Central and C. 9, Barrio La Soledad ☎ 221–1369) is a brightly lighted downtown bar that serves monster sandwiches.

A trendy place to see and be seen is **El Cuartel de la Boca del Monte** (⊠ Avda. 1, between Cs. 21 and 23, Barrio La California ☎ 221–0327), a large bar where young artists and professionals gather to sip San José's fanciest cocktails and share plates of tasty bocas (snacks). It has live music ★ Monday and Wednesday night. The **Jazz Café** (⊠ Avda. Central next to Banco Popular, San Pedro ☎ 253–8933) draws big crowds, especially for live jazz on Tuesday and Wednesday nights. Costa Rica's only microbrewery, **K & S Brewery** (⊠ Centro Comercial Cristal, 600 m south of Pop's ice cream shop, Curridabat ☎ 283–7583) serves its own pilsners and lagers in an "oom-pah-pah" German-style bar and restaurant.

You can imagine Che Guevara plotting the revolution in a corner of **La Villa** (⊠ Calle de la Amargura, San Pedro ☎ 280–9541), a laid-back, alternative bar popular with politically active students. Trendy **Luna Roja** (⊠ C. 3, between Avdas. 9 and 11, Barrio Amón ☎ 222–5944) doubles as café and dance floor with occasional live music. **Mac's Bar** (⊠ South side of La Sabana Park, next to the Tennis Club, Sabana Sur ☎ 234–3145) usually has a sporting event playing on the television.

A restaurant with strolling mariachi groups, **Rancho Guanacaste** (⊠ Rotonda de Alajuelita, Hatillo ☎ 254–7942) also hosts comedians many nights. You need good Spanish and a knowledge of Costa Rican culture to get all the jokes. San José's large Argentine community packs the smoky **Rincón del Tango Che Molinari** (⊠ Centro Comercial El Pueblo, Barrio Tournón) after 9 PM Friday and Saturday nights to belt out their favorite tangos to the accompaniment of the mournful accordionlike *bandoleón*. In the same complex as the Sala Garbo and Laurence Olivier theaters, the **Shakespeare Bar** (⊠ Avda. 2 and C. 28, Paseo Colón ☎ 257–1288) is a quiet place to go for a pre- or post-movie drink. The mammoth, bilevel, semi-open-air **Terra U** (⊠ Calle de la Amargura, San Pedro ☎ 225–4261) rocks with college-age students, many of them foreigners, who come to dance, drink, and converse.

COLORFUL COSTA RICAN SPANISH

EVEN WITH SEVERAL YEARS OF
SPANISH-LANGUAGE TRAINING
*under your belt you may be
shocked when you get to Costa
Rica—first by Ticos responding in near-
perfect English, and second by Spanish so
localized and particular to Costa Rica that
it is difficult to understand. Although every
country has its own particular ways of
saying things, Costa Rica is a land where
eloquent speech and creative verbal
expression is highly valued, and San José,
with its convergence of ethnicities,
nationalities, and lifestyles, is where one
hears the most interesting speech.*

*Some colorful expressions still in use have
rural roots that date back to the last
century. Others, employed mostly by
young people, blend English and Spanish,
often with a sarcastic twist. English-based
expressions include "watching pupilas"
(sleeping—literally, "watching pupils"),
tuanis (a contraction of "too nice," used
like "cool" in the United States), la birra
(beer), and tenis (tennis shoes or
sneakers).*

*Colorful expressions abound to describe
people, their actions, and their physical
and social characteristics. Most Costa
Ricans have nicknames based on their
physical or social characteristics or their
actions: Chino or China for anyone of
Asian descent or with almond-shape eyes,
Gordo or Gorda for the plump, Flaco or
Flaca for the thin. A neighbor of mine in
the north of San José is called Pichon de
Zoncho (baby vulture) because he's bald
and has a hooked nose, and another is
known as Gusano (worm) because he's
always begging to borrow things but
doesn't return them.*

*Colorful expressions put spice in everyday
life. Death is colgar las tenis (hang up the
tennis shoes), and to smile is pelar los
dientes (peel the teeth). An unhappy*

*person jode mas que abuela recien
operada (complains more than a
grandmother who just had surgery), and a
nervous person parece un burro en lancha
(looks like a burro struggling to keep its
balance in an open boat). Someone who's
stingy mas agarrado que un mono en
ventilero (holds on tighter than a monkey
in a windstorm).*

*The courtly tradition of paying elaborate
compliments to women still survives in
San Jose among older men. When a
beautiful girl hurries by on the sidewalk
on a rainy day, a gentleman might say,
"No corra mi amor, porque la lluvia es
hecha para las flores." (Don't run, my
love, because rain is made for flowers.)
Comments made by younger men tend to
be much more sexual and less creative.
Despite the high-tech, cosmopolitan
lifestyle that is rapidly overtaking San
José and the influence of many
nationalities converging on the capital,
slang shows no signs of waning. If
anything, Costa Ricans are more proud
than ever of their unique ways of
expressing themselves, and continue to
invent new expressions to describe new
situations that modern life presents.*

— Carol Weir

Cafés

In a country so economically dependent on coffee, and one that takes its afternoon coffee breaks at home or work religiously, the European-style cafe concept is only beginning to catch on.

Near the university, **Fezcafé** (✉ Calle de la Amargura, San Pedro ☎ 280–6982) is a quiet alternative to the noisy bars nearby, at least until 8 PM on weeknights. Restaurant **Kafé Ko** (✉ C. 21, 25 m south of the Promavera gas station, Barrio La California) morphs into central San José's only true late-night coffee spot. It's a quiet place for conversation, with soft, jazzy music playing.

Casinos

The 24-hour **Casino Colonial** (✉ Avda. 1, between Cs. 9 and 11, Barrio El Carmen ☎ 258–2807) has a complete casino, bar, restaurant, and cable TV, and a betting service for major U.S. sporting events. **Jungle Casino** (✉ Avda. Central, between Cs. 7 and 9, Barrio La Soledad ☎ 222–5022) in the Balmoral Hotel downtown is a casino, bar, and restaurant in one. Most of the city's larger hotels have casinos, including the Amón Plaza, the Aurola Holiday Inn (the view from the casino is breathtaking), the Meliá Cariari, and the Gran Hotel Costa Rica.

Dance Clubs

Many of San José's live-music dance halls not listed here populate rougher neighborhoods on the city's south side and are best avoided.

Partyers in their early twenties fill **Bash** (✉ 75 m north of Cine Magaly, Barrio La California ☎ 281–0163), which has a good assortment of Latin and techno rhythms. **Cocoloco** (✉ Centro Comercial El Pueblo, Avda. 0, Barrio Tournón ☎ 222–8782) has Latin music. **Friends** (✉ Centro Comercial El Pueblo, Avda. 0, Barrio Tournón ☎ 233–5283) plays mostly pop and Latin music. For an international scene, head to **Planet Mall** (✉ Mall San Pedro, C. 42 and Avda. 2 ☎ 280–4693) on the top floor of the massive San Pedro Mall, which bills itself as the largest disco in Central America. Dress to impress; this is one of the city's most expensive dance bars.

Merecumbé (✉ 100 m south and 25 m west of former Banco Popular San Pedro ☎ 224–3531) is the most established of San José's dance schools, with eight branches around the metropolitan area. Month-long intensive courses (in Spanish) might not fit into the average visitor's schedule. But the folks here can hook you up with English-speaking instructors who will give you private dance lessons for as little as an hour, tailored to your needs, at one of their studios. If your hips are up to the task, bring your dancing shoes along with you and learn a few salsa and merengue steps to wow your friends back home. For a dance hall experience in a good neighborhood, the enormous **El Tobogán** (✉ 200 m north and 100 m east of La República, Barrio Tournón ☎ 223–8920) provides an alternative to the postage-stamp-size floors of most discos. Live Latin bands get everyone on their feet Friday and Saturday nights.

Gay & Lesbian

San José has a few bars, restaurants, and dance places patronized primarily by a gay and lesbian clientele, although all are welcome. Another tier of businesses, exemplified by the venerable Café Mundo, draws a mixed gay-straight crowd. The gay-and-lesbian resource center **1@10 Café Internet** (⊠ C. 3 and Avda. 7, Barrio Amón ☎ 258-4561 ⊕ www.1en10.com) can provide you with information on gay and lesbian San José.

Al Despiste (⊠ Across from Mudanzas Mundiales, Zapote ☎ 283-7164) is a gay bar that serves yummy light bocas. A gay and lesbian crowd frequents **La Avispa** (⊠ C. 1, between Avdas. 8 and 10, Barrio La Soledad ☎ 223-5343), which has two dance floors with videos and karaoke, and a quieter upstairs bar with pool tables. The last Wednesday of each month is women's night.

El Bochinche (⊠ C. 11, between Avdas. 10 and 12, Barrio La Soledad ☎ 221-0500) is a gay bar that doubles as a restaurant. **Déjà Vu** (⊠ C. 2, between Avdas. 14 and 16A, Barrio El Pacífico ☎ 223-3758) is a mostly gay, techno-heavy disco with two dance floors. Take a taxi to and from here; the neighborhood's sketchy. Restaurant and bar **.G** (⊠ 50 m east of the higuerón [fig tree], San Pedro ☎ 280-3726) draws a primarily gay and lesbian clientele.

SPORTS & THE OUTDOORS

Sports mean one thing in San José: soccer. Very young boys (and a slowly increasing number of girls) will kick around a ball—or some other object if no ball is available—in a street pickup game, and will grow into fans passionate about their local team. Everyone puts aside regional differences when Costa Rica's reputation is on the line, as it was during its 2002 World Cup appearance.

Traffic, bus fumes, potholed streets, uneven sidewalks, and scarcity of green space conspire to make the city an outdoor sports participant's nightmare. That explains the popularity of the vast acres of green space of La Sabana Park and the University of Costa Rica. Take care of your running and outdoor exercise needs in the early morning; that's the best way to avoid the heat of midday and afternoon rains during the May–December wet season.

Running

Once San José's airport but now a eucalyptus-shaded park, **Parque Metropolitano La Sabana** (⊠ Bordered by C. 42, Avda. de las Américas and Autopista Próspero Fernández, Paseo Colón) at the end of the Paseo Colón, is the city's best place to run, with 5-km (3-mi) routes on concrete paths. Within the park are a sculpture garden and duck ponds. Free **aerobics classes** on La Sabana's west end start at 9 on Sunday morning and usually draw scores.

Soccer

Consult the Spanish-language daily *La Nación* or ask at your hotel for details on upcoming games—you simply buy a ticket at the stadium box office. Prices range from $2 to $12. *Sombra numerado* (shaded seats) are the most expensive.

Professional soccer matches are usually played on Sunday morning or Wednesday night in either of two San José stadiums, one of which is the **Estadio Nacional** (⊠ Western end of La Sabana park). The **Estadio Ricardo Saprissa** (⊠ Next to the Clínica Interada de Tibás) hosts professional soccer matches and is in the northern suburb of Tibás. Despite its name, the **Gimnasio Nacional** (National Gymnasium; ⊠ Southeast corner of La Sabana park) is just as likely to host concerts, beauty pageants, and large kids' parties as it is the occasional basketball game.

White-Water Rafting

White-water trips down the Reventazón, Pacuare, Sarapiquí, and General rivers all leave from San José. Nearly half a dozen licensed, San José–based tour companies operate similar rafting and kayaking trips of varying lengths and grades. The Reventazón's Class III and IV–V runs are day trips, as are the Sarapiquí's Class II–IV runs. You descend the General (Class III–IV) on a three-day camping trip. You can run the Pacuare (Class III–IV) in one, two, or three days.

Accommodations for overnight trips on the General or Pacuare River are usually in tents, but Aventuras Naturales, Costa Rica Sun Tours, and Ríos Tropicales have comfortable lodges on the Pacuare, making them the most popular outfitters for overnight trips on that river. The cost ranges from $75 to $95 per day, depending on the river. Two- and three-day river-rafting or kayaking packages with overnight stays are considerably more expensive.

Aventuras Naturales (⊠ 300 m north of Bagelmens, Barrio Escalante ☎ 225–3939 or 224–0505 ☎ 253–6934 ⊕ www.toenjoynature.com) is a popular outfitter with high-adrenaline rafting adventures on the Pacuare and Sarapiquí rivers. **Costa Rica Expeditions** (⊠ Avda. 3 and C. Central, Barrio Catedral ☎ 257–0766 ☎ 257–1665 ⊕ www.costaricaexpeditions.com) has been offering rafting tours to the Pacuare, Reventazón, and Sarapiquí rivers for more than 20 years. The outfitter has day trips only.

Costa Rica Sun Tours (⊠ 100 m south of Agromec, on the corner, Urupa ☎ 296–7757 ☎ 296–4307 ⊕ www.crsuntours.com) is a high-class operation with trips on the three major rivers. It also offers mountain-bike and horseback tours. **Ríos Tropicales** (⊠ 45 m south of Centro Colón, Paseo Colón ☎ 233–6455 ☎ 255–4354 ⊕ www.riostropicales.com) is the largest outfitter running white-water tours in the area.

SHOPPING

San José provides the answer to all those "Did you bring me anything?" questions you're sure to get upon your return home. It's all here—everything from original art to mass-produced, miniature oxcart paperclip holders. Although it might seem more "authentic" to buy your souvenirs at their out-country source, you can find everything in the city, a real bonus if you're pressed for time. Shops such as San Jose's venerable Galería Namu have assembled an amazing collection of folkloric and indigenous art from around Costa Rica. And there is indeed native San José–area art. Kaltak Artesanías in the suburb of Moravia deals in Pefi and Osenbach ceramics, trademark products of two well-known artisans in the capital.

Major Shopping Districts

If the capital has any real tourist shopping district, it's found loosely in the cluster of streets around Parque Morazán, just north of downtown, an area bounded roughly by Avenidas 1 and 7 and Calles 5 and 9. Stroll and search, because many other businesses congregate in the area as well. The northeastern suburb of Moravia contains a cluster of high-quality crafts and artisan shops in the three blocks heading north from the Colegio María Inmaculada. The street is two blocks behind the city's church.

Specialty Stores

Antiques
Antigüedades Chavo (⊠ C. Central, between Avdas. Central and 1, Barrio El Carmen ☏ 258–3966) sells mostly furniture but has some smaller antiques. **Antigüedades El Museo** (⊠ C. 3 Bis and Avda. 7, Barrio Amón ☏ 223–9552) sells antique paintings, cerñ mics, jewelry, and other small items.

Art Galleries
Amir Art Gallery (⊠ C. 5 and Avda. 5, Barrio El Carmen ☏ 256–9445) has a selection of Costa Rican oils and watercolors. **Galería Artes Bis** (⊠ C. 3 Bis, between Avdas. 7 and 9, Barrio Amón ☏ 248–0244) sells paintings by Costa Rican artists. **Galería Zukia** (⊠ Avda. 3, between Cs. 5 and 7, Barrio El Carmen ☏ 258–2404) specializes in paintings and sculpture by Costa Rican artists. The adjoining store has more standard tourist souvenir fare, primarily wood, leather, and ceramics.

Books & Maps
Casa de las Revistas (⊠ C. 5, between Avdas. 3 and 5, Barrio El Carmen ☏ 256–5092 ⊠ Plaza del Sol, Curridabat ☏ 283–0822 ⊠ Plaza Mayor, Blvd. de Rohrmoser, Rohrmoser ☏ 296–7943) stores, with several locations around San José, have the best selection of magazines in English. **Lehmann** (⊠ Avda. Central, between Cs. 1 and 3, Barrio El Carmen ☏ 223–1212) has some books in English and a stock of large-scale topographical maps. **Librería Internacional** (⊠ 300 m west of Taco Bell, Barrio Dent ☏ 253–9553) has English translations of Latin American literature and myriad coffee-table books on Costa Rica. **Mora Books** (⊠ Avda. 1, between Cs. 3 and 5, ☏ 255–4136) has a good selection of used books, maps, and CDs in English. **7th Street Books** (⊠ C. 7, between Avdas. Central and 1, Barrio La Soledad ☏ 256–8251) has an excellent selection of new books in English and is particularly strong on Latin America and tropical ecology.

Crafts

★ A must-stop shop, **Galería Namu** (✉ Avda. 7, between Cs. 5 and 7, behind Aurola Holiday Inn, Barrio Amón ☎ 256–3412) has Costa Rican folkloric art and some of the best indigenous crafts in town. Its inventory brims with colorful creations by the Guaymí, Boruca, Bribri, Chorotega, Huetar, and Maleku peoples from Costa Rica. You can also find exquisitely carved ivory nut "Tagua" figurines made by Wounan Indians from Panama's Darien region. Take note of carved balsa masks, woven cotton blankets, and hand-painted ceramics. A real standout from all the Moravia shops is **Kaltrak Artesanías** (✉ 50 m north of Colegio María Inmaculada, Moravia ☎ 297–2736). The friendly staff can help you find that perfect gift among the selection of ceramics—Pefi and Osenbach designs are well represented here—or wood-and-leather rocking chairs, oxcarts of all sizes, orchids, and carvings from native *cocobolo* and *guápinol* woods and ash wood.

Food & Beverages

You can buy coffee in any supermarket—where you'll get the best price—or souvenir shop. Café Rey Tarrazú and Café Britt are quality brands. Costa Rica's best rum is the aged Centenario—pick up a bottle for about $8. There are also several brands of coffee liqueurs, including Café Rica and Golden Cream, but the best is Britt. Buy these at any of San José's abundant supermarkets and liquor stores. Any self-respecting Tico home or restaurant keeps a bottle of Salsa Lizano, one of the country's signature products, on hand. Its tang brightens up meat, vegetable, and rice dishes, and a bottle fits nicely into your carry-on. **Más X Menos** (✉ Avda. Central, between Cs. 11 and 13 ☎ 233–7811) has a wide selection of liquor, coffee, and food items.

Shopping Malls

Old-timers lament the malling over of San José, but five huge enclosed shopping centers anchor the metro area, complemented by dozens of smaller malls. Expect all the comforts of home—food courts and movie theaters included. **Mall San Pedro** (✉ Rotonda de la Hispanidad, San Pedro ☎ 283–7540) sits in its namesake suburb, a short 10-minute taxi ride from downtown San José. **Multiplaza del Este** (✉ Across from Registro Público, Curridabat ☎ 289–9300) lies east of San José, and is the counterpart to the west-side Multiplaza. **Terramall** (✉ Autopista Florencio del Castillo, Tres Ríos ☎ 278–6970) opened in late 2003 and has quickly become the far eastern suburbs' prime shopping destination.

Souvenirs

Boutique Annemarie (✉ C. 9 and Avda. 9, Barrio Amón ☎ 221–6063) in the Don Carlos hotel has a huge selection of popular souvenirs and CDs of Costa Rican musicians, including Grammy-winning Editus. The boutique carries comical figurines, cards, stationery, and standard, kitschy tourist gear. Café Britt operates **El Cafetal** and the **Casa Tica** airport gift shops (✉ Aeropuerto Internacional Juan Santamaría) for those last-minute purchases. Choose from Britt coffee ($5 per pound) and a terrific selection of good-quality merchandise, such as hand-carved bowls and jewelry, aromatherapy candles, banana-paper stationery, and Costa Rica travel books. There's nary another store in the country carrying such a variety of desirable items all in one place. The catch is that the shops charges U.S. prices for this luxury.

Some 100 souvenir vendors congregate and offer some real bargains in hammocks, wood carvings, and clothing in the **Calle Nacional de Artesanía y Pintura** (⊠ C. 13, between Avdas Central and 2, Barrio), a block-long covered walkway on the western side of the Plaza de la Democracia. Dozens of souvenir vendors set up shop on the two floors of **La Casona** (⊠ C. 2, between Avdas. Central and 1, Barrio El Carmen), an old downtown mansion. The rickety building is a fun place to browse.

Diagonal from the National Museum, **Congo** (⊠ C. 17 and Avda. 2, Barrio La Soledad ☏ 258–8904) has a terrific selection of high-quality ceramics, woods, banana papers, oxcarts, and figurines in an attractive shop. Downtown San José's **Mercado Central** (⊠ Bordered by Avdas. Central and 1 and Cs. 6 and 8, Barrio La Merced) doesn't bill itself for souvenir shopping, but a few stands of interest to tourists congregate near the entrances. The **Mundo de Recuerdos** (⊠ Across from Colegio María Inmaculada, Moravia ☏ 240–8990) is the largest of the Moravia shops with simply everything you could ask for under one roof.

Toys
Kids' toys in Costa Rica are much the same as you'd find back home. **Rincón Educativo** (⊠ 225 m east of Church of San Pedro, San Pedro ☏ 283–5810) distinguishes itself for its educational-activity toys—books, coloring books, flash cards, stickers—ideal for that child you know who is beginning to learn Spanish.

SAN JOSÉ A TO Z

To research prices, get advice from other travelers, and book travel arrangements, visit www.fodors.com.

AIRPORTS & TRANSFERS
Two airports serve San José: Aeropuerto Internacional Juan Santamaría (SJO) is the destination for all international flights as well as those of domestic airline SANSA; domestic NatureAir flights depart from Aeropuerto Internacional Tobías Bolaños (SYQ).

Immigration lines can be long at Juan Santamaría if you arrive in the evening with most of the large flights from North America. You'll find free luggage carts in the baggage-claim area downstairs. Customs officials will often wave you through if you're obviously a tourist, although they might ask you to put your suitcase through an X-ray machine. Those same flights turn around and depart early the next morning. If you're on one of them, expect equally long lines at check-in. You're required to arrive at the airport three hours in advance of your international flight's departure time. Stop first at the airport-tax desk inside the terminal before getting in line at your airline's counter. To comply with post–September 11 security procedures, only ticketed passengers are permitted inside the building, and your checked luggage will be hand-searched if you're flying to the United States.

Arrival and departure at the tiny Tobías Bolaños Airport is very informal.

⚡ Airport Information Aeropuerto Internacional Juan Santamaría ⊠ 16 km (10 mi) northwest of downtown San José just outside Alajuela ☎ 443-2942. **Aeropuerto Internacional Tobías Bolaños** ⊠ 3 km (2 mi) west of the city center, Pavas ☎ 232-2820. **⚡ Carriers Air Canada** ☎ 800/052-1988 in Costa Rica. **America West** ☎ 430-1679. **American** ☎ 257-1266. **Continental** ☎ 296-4911. **Copa** ☎ 220-6640. **Delta** ☎ 257-4141 or 800/560-2002 in Costa Rica. **Iberia** ☎ 257-8266. **Martinair** ☎ 220-4111. **Mexicana** ☎ 295-6969. **NatureAir** ☎ 220-3054. **SANSA** ☎ 221-9414. **TACA** ☎ 296-9353. **Thomas Cook-Condor** ☎ 221-7444. **United** ☎ 220-4844. **US Airways** ☎ 430-6690.

AIRPORT
TRANSFERS
A taxi from Juan Santamaría Airport to downtown San José costs $12. Stop at the Taxis Unidos stand immediately outside the airport customs exit. Tell the attendant where you need to go and pay your fare. A driver will take you to your destination in one of the company's orange vehicles. Other taxis, official and not so legal, wait in a startling mass at the airport exit beyond the velvet rope, along with all the families and friends who show up to greet arriving passengers. Drivers do not expect tips, but beware of those eager to take you to a particular hotel—their only motive is a hefty commission. Far cheaper (about 50¢), but not nearly as fast, is the bus marked RUTA 200 SAN JOSÉ, which drops you at the west end of Avenida 2, a few blocks from the heart of the city, an iffy neighborhood at night. If you rent a car at the airport, driving time to San José is about 20 minutes; 40 minutes if traffic is heavy or you get lost. Note that some hotels provide a free shuttle service—inquire when you reserve.

The domestic airline NatureAir operates vans from its Tobías Bolaños Airport to take you anywhere in or around San José. Expect to pay $7.

BUS TRAVEL TO & FROM SAN JOSÉ

A handful of private companies operate from San José, providing reliable, inexpensive bus service throughout much of Costa Rica from several departure points. San José has no central bus terminal, and buses to many destinations depart from street corners. The four largest bus stations—the Gran Terminal del Caribe, the Terminal Atlántico Norte, the Terminal de Puntarenas, and the Terminal Coca-Cola—are all in dicey neighborhoods. Always take a taxi to and from the bus station, and at the Coca-Cola, never take your eyes off your belongings. Consider the comfort of a shuttle van service in an air-conditioned minivan for travel around Costa Rica. (⇨ For bus and shuttle van information and departure points from San José to other areas of the country, *see* A to Z sections *in* Chapters 2–7.)

For international services, use Tica Bus, which plies the Central American axis from southern Mexico to Panama, and Transnica, which travels to Nicaragua.

⚡ Bus Terminals Gran Terminal del Caribe ⊠ C. Central and Avda. 13, Barrio Tournón ☎ 222-0610. **Terminal Atlántico Norte** ⊠ C. 12 and Avda. 9, Barrio México ☎ 225-4318. **Terminal Coca-Cola** ⊠ C. 16, between Avdas. 1 and 3, Barrio México. **Terminal de Puntarenas** ⊠ C. 16, between Avdas. 10 and 12, Barrio Cuba ☎ 222-1867.
⚡ International Bus Companies Tica Bus ⊠ C. 9 and Avda. 4, Barrio La Soledad ☎ 221-8954. **Transnica** ⊠ C. 22 and Avda. 5, Barrio México ☎ 223-4242.

BUS TRAVEL WITHIN SAN JOSE

Bus service within San José is absurdly cheap (30¢–50¢) and easy to use. For Paseo Colón and La Sabana, take buses marked SABANA-CEMENTERIO from stops on the southern side of the Parque Morazán, or on Avenida 3 next to the Correos (Post Office). For the suburbs of Los Yoses and San Pedro near the university, take one marked SAN PEDRO, CURRIDABAT, or LOURDES from Avenida Central, between Calles 9 and 11.

CAR RENTAL

Contact any of the major agencies below to rent a car in San José. It's virtually impossible to rent a car in Costa Rica between December 20 and January 3 because of the exodus from the city for the holidays. If you want to rent a car during this time, reserve far in advance. At any other time of year, shop around for the best rate.

🚗 **Major Agencies** **Alamo** ⊠ Avda. 18, between Cs. 11 and 13, Barrio González-Víquez ☎ 233–7733, 800/570–0671 in U.S., 800/462–5266 in Costa Rica ⊕ www.alamo.com. **Budget** ⊠ Paseo Colón and C. 30, Paseo Colón ☎ 223–3284, 800/224–4627 in U.S. ⊕ www.budget.com. **Dollar** ⊠ Paseo Colón and C. 32, Paseo Colón ☎ 257–1585, 800/ 800–4000 in U.S. ⊕ www.dollar.com. **Hertz** ⊠ Paseo Colón and C. 38, Paseo Colón ☎ 221–1818, 800/654–3001 in U.S. ⊕ www.hertz.com. **National** ⊠ 1 km (½ mi) north of Hotel Best Western Irazú, Barrio La Uruca ☎ 290–8787, 800/227–7368 in U.S. ⊕ www.nationalcar.com.

CAR TRAVEL

San José is the hub of the national road system. Paved roads fan out from Paseo Colón west to Escazú and northwest to the airport and Heredia. For the Pacific coast, Guanacaste, and Nicaragua, take the Carretera Interamericana (Pan-American Highway) north (CA1). Calle 3 runs north into the highway to Guápiles, Limón, and the Atlantic coast through Braulio Carrillo National Park, with a turnoff to the Sarapiquí region. If you follow Avenida Central or 2 east through San Pedro, you'll enter the Pan-American Highway south (CA2), which has a turnoff for Cartago, Volcán Irazú, and Turrialba before it heads southeast over the mountains toward Panama.

Almost every street in downtown San José is one-way. Try to avoid driving at peak hours (7–9 AM and 5–6:30 PM), as traffic gets horribly congested. Parking lots, scattered throughout the city, charge around $1 an hour. Outside the city center, you can park on the street, where *wachimen* ("watchmen" or car guards) usually offer to watch your car for a 300-colón tip, more if you're going to be away from the car for a few hours. Even so, never leave shopping bags or valuables inside your parked car.

EMERGENCIES

You can dial ☎ 911 for just about any emergency nationwide. Your embassy can provide you with a list of recommended doctors and dentists. All hospitals are open to foreigners. Government facilities—the so-called "Caja" hospitals (short for Caja Costarricense de Seguro Social, or Costa Rican Social Security System)—and clinics, such as the San Juan de Dios, Calderón Guardia, and México hospitals, are of acceptable quality, but notoriously overburdened, a common complaint in socialized-medicine systems anywhere. Private hospitals are more accustomed to serving foreigners. They include Hospital CIMA (⇨ Central Valley A to Z *in* Chapter 2), Clínica Bíblica, and Clínica Católica, which all have 24-hour pharmacies. The long-established and ubiquitous Fischel pharmacies are a great place for your prescription needs. Antibiotics and psychotropic medications (for sleep, anxiety, or pain) require prescriptions in Costa Rica. Little else does. But plan ahead and bring an adequate supply with you from home; matches may not be exact.

🚩 Emergency Services **Ambulance** ☎ 128. **Fire** ☎ 118. **Police** ☎ 117, 127 outside major cities. **Traffic Police** ☎ 222-9245.

🚩 Hospitals **Clínica Bíblica** ⊠ Avda. 14, between Cs. Central and 1, Barrio El Pacífico ☎ 257-0466 emergencies. **Clínica Católica** ⊠ Guadalupe, attached to San Antonio Church on C. Esquivel Bonilla, Guadalupe ☎ 283-6616.

🚩 Late-Night Pharmacies **Fischel Pharmacy** (Farmacia Fischel) ⊠ Centro Comercial Feria del Norte, Tibás ☎ 240-8598 ⊠ Across from Banco Popular, San Pedro ☎ 253-5121.

MAIL & SHIPPING

It is best not to send important packages via the Correos de Costa Rica, the Tico postal system, as it is infamous for losing letters. But if you must, head to the Central Postal Office, open weekdays 7:30–6 and Saturday 7:30–noon. Routine mail, such as postcards to the folks back home, takes about two weeks to reach the United States and Canada, three weeks to Europe. You can also post letters from large hotels. For important packages, rely on DHL, FedEx, and UPS for shipping.

There are Internet cafés on almost every block in downtown San José. Many of those just south of the Universidad de Costa Rica in San Pedro are open 24 hours.

🚩 Internet Cafés **1@10 Café Internet** ⊠ C. 3 and Avda. 7, Barrio Amón ☎ 258-4561. **Café Net California** ⊠ Avda. 1, between Cs. 19 and 21, Barrio La California, ☎ 258-2324. **Cafenet** ⊠ C. 19 at Avda. 10, Barrio La Soledad, ☎ 255-1910. **CepiaNet** ⊠ Avda. Central and C. 5, Barrio La Soledad, ☎ 258-5050. **CyberCafé Las Arcadas** ⊠ Avda. 2, between Cs. 1 and 3, ground floor of Las Arcadas building, Barrio La Soledad ☎ 233-3310. **Estudio Net Café** ⊠ C. de la Armargura, San Pedro ☎ No phone. **Internet Café Costa Rica** ⊠ 50 m west of Banco Popular, San Pedro ☎ 283-5375 ⊠ Avda. Central, between Cs. 7 and 9, Barrio La Soledad ☎ 255-1154 ⊠ Avda. Central and C. 4, Barrio La Merced ☎ No phone ⊠ Paseo Colón, between Cs. 38 and 40, Paseo Colón ☎ No phone. **RACSA office** ⊠ C. 1 at Avda. 5, Barrio La Merced ☎ 287-0087. **SuperNet** ⊠ C. de la Armargura, San Pedro ☎ 234-8200.

🚩 Post Office **Correos de Costa Rica** ⊠ C. 2, between Avdas. 1 and 3, Barrio La Merced

🚩 Shipping Services **DHL** ⊠ C. 34, between Paseo Colón and Avda. 2, Paseo Colón ☎ 210-3838. **FedEx** ⊠ Paseo Colón, between Cs. 40 and 42, Paseo Colón ☎ 293-3157 or 800/052-1090 in Costa Rica. **UPS** ⊠ East of Pizza Hut offices, Zona Industrial, Pavas ☎ 290-2828

MONEY MATTERS

Before you head out of San José, get all the cash you need. Outside the capital, there are few banks and ATMs, and it's difficult to change money. It is virtually impossible to change currency other than U.S. dollars or traveler's checks outside of San José. Lines at the state banks—Banco Nacional, Banco de Costa Rica (BCR), Bancrédito, and Banco

Popular—move very slowly, but you can change cash dollars and traveler's checks. The private ScotiaBank and BAC San José (formerly Banco San José) perform the same services with more palatable lines. They have many fewer outlets. You can get local currency using your MasterCard or Visa at the Juan Santamaría Airport; one machine accepts only MasterCard and the other only Visa—not unusual in Costa Rica. It's handy to have both types of card. The ATH (A Todas Horas) and Red Total networks accept Plus- and Cirrus-affiliated cards. A few Red Total machines give cash against an American Express and Diners Club card as well. Ask at your hotel for the location of the nearest bank or *cajero automático* (ATM), and specify whether you need a MasterCard- or Visa-friendly machine.

🏦 Banks **BAC San José** ⊠ Avda. 2, between Cs. Central and 2, Barrio El Carmen ☎ 295-9595. **Banco Nacional** ⊠ Avda. 1, between Cs. 2 and 4, Barrio La Merced ☎ 212-2000. **ScotiaBank** ⊠ Avda. 1, between Cs. Central and 2, Barrio La Merced ☎ 287-8700

TAXIS

Taxis are a good deal within the city. You can hail one on the street (all taxis are red with a gold triangle on the front door) or have your hotel or restaurant call one for you, as cabbies tend to speak only Spanish and addresses are complicated. (Have someone write down the address to show to the driver if you wish.) A 3-km (2-mi) ride costs around $2, and tipping is not the custom. Taxis parked in front of expensive hotels charge about twice the normal rate. By law, all cabbies must use their meters—called *marías*—when operating within the metropolitan area; if one refuses, negotiate a price before setting off, or hail another. The surest way to antagonize a driver is to slam the door; be gentle. Cab companies include San Jorge, Coopetaxi, and, if you need to go to the airport, Taxis Unidos. Many unofficial taxis (*piratas*) ply the streets as well. They might be red cars with a margarine container on the dashboard painted to resemble a taxi sign. Some locals use them, but they have no meters, are illegal and often unsafe, and carry no insurance in the event of an accident.

🚕 Taxi Companies **Alfaro** ☎ 221-8466. **Coopetaxi** ☎ 235-9966. **Coopetico** ☎ 224-7979. **Taxis Unidos** ☎ 221-6865.

TOURS

The Tren Tico gives you a 25-minute city tour without commentary, from 10 to 4 on Sundays and holidays. Pick up the ride at the Gran Hotel Costa Rica. Aventuras Naturales and Eclipse Tours lead rafting and mountain-biking tours. Costa Rica Expeditions is one of the country's most experienced rafting outfitters. Expediciones Tropicales arranges horseback-riding tours. Horizontes customizes natural-history and adventure trips with expert guides to any Costa Rican itinerary. Costa Rica's Temptations organizes a variety of tours around the Central Valley and throughout the country. Ríos Tropicales offers rafting, sea-kayaking, and mountain-biking tours. The Rain Forest Aerial Tram takes you floating through the treetops on a modified ski lift. Tropical Bungee runs bungee-jump trips daily from San José to an old bridge on the way to the Central Pacific. For a day trip to the beach at Punta Coral and Isla Tortuga, try Calypso.

Most of San José's travel agencies can arrange one-day horseback tours to farms in the surrounding Central Valley.

🗹 Tour Operators **Aventuras Naturales** ✉ 300 m north of Bagelmans, Barrio Escalante ☎ 225-3939 🖷 253-6934 ⊕ www.toenjoynature.com. **Calypso** ✉ Arcadas building, 3rd fl., next to Gran Hotel Costa Rica, Barrio La Soledad ☎ 256-2727 🖷 256-6767 ⊕ www. calypsocruises.com. **Costa Rica Expeditions** ✉ Avda. 3 at C. Central, Barrio El Carmen ☎ 222-0333 🖷 257-1665 ⊕ www.costaricaexpeditions.com. **Costa Rica's Temptations** ☎ 220-4437 🖷 220-2792 ⊕ www.crtinfo.com. **Eclipse Tours** ✉ Villa Tournón, Avda. 0, east side of traffic circle, Barrio Tournón ☎ 223-7510 🖷 233-3672. **Expediciones Tropicales** ✉ C. 3, between Avdas. 11 and 13, Barrio Amón ☎ 257-4171 🖷 257-4124 ⊕ www.costaricainfo.com. **Horizontes** ✉ 130 m north of Pizza Hut, Paseo Colón ☎ 222-2022 🖷 255-4513 ⊕ www.horizontes.com. **Rain Forest Aerial Tram** ✉ Avda. 7, between Cs. 5 and 7, Barrio Amón ☎ 257-5961 ⊕ www.rainforestram.com. **Ríos Tropicales** ✉ 45 m south of Centro Colón, Paseo Colón ☎ 233-6455 🖷 255-4354 ⊕ www. riostropicales.com. **Tren Tico** ☎ 226-1346. **Tropical Bungee** ✉ Sabana Sur, 90 m west and 45 m south of Contraloría, Sabana Sur ☎ 232-3956.

TRAVEL AGENCIES

🗹 Local Agent Referrals **Galaxy** ✉ C. 3, between Avdas. 5 and 7, Barrio Amón ☎ 233-3240. **Intertur** ✉ 45 m west of KFC, Avda. Central, between Cs. 31 and 33, Barrio Francisco Peralta ☎ 253-7503.

VISITOR INFORMATION

The Instituto Costarricense de Turismo (ICT) staffs the city's most conveniently located branch of the tourist information office in the Correos. Pick up free maps, bus schedules, and brochures weekdays 8–4. The main ICT office is in the inconveniently located CINDE building on the highway to the airport. The ubiquitous TOURIST INFORMATION signs you see around downtown are really private travel agencies looking to sell you tours rather than provide unbiased information.

🗹 Tourist Information **Instituto Costarricense de Turismo (ICT)** ✉ Edificio CINDE, Autopista General Cañas, Barrio La Uruca ✉ C. 2, between Avdas. 1 and 3, Barrio La Merced ☎ 222-1090

CENTRAL COSTA RICA

2

Updated by
David
Dudenhoefer

COUNTRY ROADS WIND UP THE HILLS of the Meseta Central, or Central Valley, past coffee farms, patches of forest, bright green pastures, and colorful villages. Scattered between them are some of the country's most charming hotels and restaurants, and when skies are clear, several of these have sweeping views of the valley below.

The valley floor is more than 3,000 feet above sea level, and occupies Costa Rica's approximate geographic center. It is sandwiched between hulking mountain chains—the foothills of the Cordillera de Talamanca define the valley's southern edge, and the Cordillera Central sweeps across its northern border. Three volcanoes along this chain are within easy reach: Volcán Irazú, Costa Rica's highest, towers to the east of San José; Poás, whose active crater often spews a plume of sulfuric smoke, stands to the northwest; and the older, dormant Volcán Barva looms between the two. Dramatic craters and thick cloud forests at their summits are protected within national parks, and the slopes are covered with coffee plantations and quaint agricultural hamlets.

Though most of the region's colonial architecture has been destroyed by earthquakes and the ravages of time, several smaller cities preserve a bit more history than you'll find in San José. The central squares of Alajuela, Escazú, and Heredia, for example, are surrounded by architectural mixtures of old and new. Cartago, the country's first capital, has scattered historical structures and the impressive Basílica de Nuestra Señora de Los Angeles. Beyond these small cities lie dozens of tiny farming communities, where lovely churches and adobe farmhouses look out onto coffee fields. You can easily tackle the Central Valley's attractions on a series of half- or full-day excursions from San José, but the abundance of excellent food and lodging in the valley's other towns invites you to base yourself here, and make your visits to the capital day trips.

Exploring Central Costa Rica

The region has an extensive network of paved roads, many of which are in relatively good shape. The Pan-American Highway runs east–west through the valley (through the center of San José) and turns south at Cartago. Dozens of roads head off this well-marked highway, but if you stray from the main travelers' routes, you may find a lack of road signs. If you do, don't despair—locals are always happy to point you in the right direction.

About the Restaurants

Restaurants in Central Costa Rica range from rustic mountain lodges, where hearty meals are enhanced by the beauty of the natural surroundings, to the exceptional eateries in the hills above Escazú. Even if you keep your base in San José, consider venturing to this bedroom community for a meal or two.

About the Hotels

In Central Costa Rica, you can stay in rustic *cabinas* (cottages), sprawling coffee plantations, nature lodges, and hilltop villas with expansive views of the immediate rural landscape and the city beyond. Many lodges have unique, sometimes whimsical designs that take advantage of exceptional countryside locations. For getting away from it all and still being close to the country's primary transportation hub, the lodges around San José are ideal.

	WHAT IT COSTS				
	$$$$	**$$$**	**$$**	**$**	**¢**
RESTAURANTS	over $25	$20–$25	$10–$20	$5–$10	under $5
HOTELS	over $200	$125–$200	$75–$125	$35–$75	under $35

Restaurant prices are per-person for a main course at dinner. Hotel prices are for two people in a standard double room in high season, excluding service and tax (16.4%).

Timing

From January to May it tends to be sunny and breezy here. On the upper slopes of the volcanoes, January and February nights can get quite cold. Afternoon downpours are common starting mid-May, dropping off a bit between July and September. From mid-September to December, precipitation picks up again. But don't rule out travel to Costa Rica during the rainy season (May to December)—some days are spared rain, and when it does rain, it's usually during what you might call the siesta hours. Because few travelers visit in the rainy season, you probably won't need reservations. The valley is swathed in green after the rains, but come January the sun begins to beat down, and by April the countryside is parched. Costa Ricans generally take their vacations during Holy Week (the week before Easter) and the last two weeks of the year, so it's essential to reserve cars and hotel rooms in advance for these periods.

AROUND SAN JOSÉ

As you drive north or west out of San José, the city's suburbs and industrial zones quickly give way to arable land, most of which is occupied by coffee farms. Coffee has come to symbolize the prosperity of both the Central Valley and the nation as a whole; as such, this all-important cash crop has inspired a fair bit of folklore. Costa Rican artists, for example, have long venerated coffee workers, and the painted oxcart, once used to transport coffee to the coast, has become a national symbol.

Within Costa Rica's coffee heartland are plenty of tranquil agricultural towns and two provincial capitals, Alajuela and Heredia. Both cities owe their relative prosperity to the coffee beans cultivated on the fertile lower slopes of the Poás and Barva volcanoes. The upper slopes, too cold for coffee crops, are dedicated to dairy cattle, strawberries, ferns, and flowers, making for markedly different and thoroughly enchanting landscapes along the periphery of the national parks. Since the hills above these quaint valley towns have some excellent restaurants and lodgings, rural overnights are an excellent alternative to staying in San José, and a wonderful way to stretch out your exploration, before, after, or instead of a trip to the coast.

Most Central Costa Rica towns stand in the shadows of volcanoes. To reach Volcán Poás, for example, you have to drive through Alajuela; Heredia lies on the road to Volcán Barva, and Cartago sits at the foot of Irazú. From Irazú you can take the serpentine roads eastward to Volcán Turrialba, Turrialba, and Guayabo National Monument, Costa Rica's most important archaeological site. Paraíso, just southeast of Cartago, is the gateway to the Valle de Orosi (Orosi Valley), southeast of San José.

Numbers in the text correspond to numbers in the margin and on the Central Costa Rica map.

2

If you have
2 days

Drive up 🎦 **Volcán Poás** ⑧ ⌐, where you can also visit nearby La Paz Waterfall Gardens, and then settle in for a night near the summit or just have a good lunch before returning to warmer **Alajuela** ⑦, **San Antonio de Belén** ③, or **Escazú** ①. The next day, explore the Orosi Valley, stopping at the fascinating Jardín Lankester on the way, and lunching in **Cachí** ⑯.

If you have
5 days

Head to 🎦 **Heredia** ⑤ ⌐ and the adjacent coffee communities, continuing up the slopes of **Volcán Barva** ⑥ for lunch, or a picnic in the cool mountain air. The energetic can hike through the cloud forest near the volcano's peak, or take a horseback ride or a canopy tour before retiring in the hills for the night. The next day, continue exploring the western Central Valley, spending the morning at either La Paz Waterfall Gardens or 🎦 **Volcán Poás** ⑧. In the afternoon, visit the towns of **Alajuela** ⑦, 🎦 **Grecia** ⑨, and **Sarchí** ⑩. On your third day, head east to the summit of **Volcán Irazú** ⑬ stopping in **Cartago** ⑫ and Jardín Lankester in the afternoon, and spending the night in the Orosi Valley. Spend the next morning in **Tapantí National Park** ⑱, then drive east to 🎦 **Turrialba** ⑲, and visit **Guayabo National Monument** ⑳ in the afternoon. Devote your final day to a white-water rafting trip on the Pacuare River.

Escazú

① *5 km (3 mi) southwest of San José.*

A 15-minute drive west of San José takes you to Escazú, a traditional coffee-farming town and now a bedroom community at the foot of a small mountain range called the Cordillera de Escazú. Narrow roads wind their way up the steep slopes of that range past coffee fields and well-tended farmhouses with tidy gardens and the occasional oxcart parked in the yard—precisely the kind of scene that captured the attention of many a Costa Rican painter in the early 20th century. There are also plenty of fancy homes between the humble farmhouses, especially in the San Antonio and San Rafael neighborhoods. Escazú's ancient church faces a small plaza, surrounded in part by weathered adobe homes. Several blocks downhill from the town center is the busy road to Santa Ana, which is lined with a growing selection of restaurants, bars, and shops. Those businesses serve this once sleepy town's burgeoning population, as well as visitors from San José and other nearby towns.

During colonial days, Escazú was dubbed the City of Good Witches because many native healers lived in the area. Locals say that Escazú is still home to witches who will tell your fortune or concoct a love potion for a small fee, but you'd be hard-pressed to spot them in the town's busy commercial district.

High in the hills above Escazú stands the tiny community of **San Antonio de Escazú,** famous for its annual oxcart festival held the second Sunday of March. The view from here—of nearby San José and distant volcanoes—is impressive by both day and night. If you head higher than San Antonio de Escazú, brace yourself for virtually vertical roads that wind up into the mountains toward **Pico Blanco,** the highest point in the Escazú Cordillera, which is a half-day hike to ascend.

Where to Stay & Eat

$$–$$$$ ✕ **Le Monastère.** This former monastery turned formal restaurant high in the San Rafael hills has a great view of the Central Valley. The dining room is dressed up in antiques, with tables set for a five-course meal; waiters don friar robes. The Belgian owner prepares outstanding classic French dishes and some original Costa Rican items. La Cava, the bar beneath the dining room, has live music Monday through Saturday and is open into the wee hours. ⊠ *San Rafael de Escazú; take old road to Santa Ana, turn left at the Paco Shopping Center, and follow signs* ☎ *289–4404* ▭ *AE, DC, MC, V* ⊘ *Closed Sun. No lunch.*

$$–$$$$ ✕ **Restaurante Cerutti.** The diva of San José's Italian eateries, this little restaurant occupies a lovely century-old adobe house near a busy intersection called El Cruce (The Cross). Whitewashed walls are adorned with antique prints. The menu is extensive, ranging from octopus and asparagus in pesto, to ravioli with mushrooms in a truffle sauce, to the more traditional *cordero al horno* (rack of lamb roasted with vegetables). ⊠ *Cruce de San Rafael de Escazú* ☎ *228–4511* ▭ *AE, DC, MC, V* ⊘ *Closed Tues.*

★ $–$$$$ ✕ **El Invernadero.** The name translates as "The Greenhouse," which could refer to the ferns hanging from the ceiling of the main dining room, or the orchids that decorate the tables. At night, the low lighting and candles make this an especially cozy spot. The menu is a mix of French and Italian, with a few Costa Rican touches, such as the heart of palm salad and salmon with a *pejibaye* (peach palm) sauce. Choose from the likes of risotto de *mariscos* (seafood), mushroom ravioli in a four-cheese sauce, and corvina *al invernadero* (sea bass in a creamy asparagus and shrimp sauce). ⊠ *San Rafael de Escazú, 800 m south and 75 m west of El Cruce* ☎ *228–0216* ▭ *AE, DC, MC, V* ⊘ *Closed Sun.*

$–$$ ✕ **Barbecue Los Anonos.** Established in 1960, Los Anonos expanded from its original rustic dining area—a collection of deep booths with wooden benches—in the late 1990s, adding a more elegant room decorated with historic photos and tropical paintings. It is a popular spot with Costa Rican families, who pack it on weekend nights, and businesspeople, who head there during the week for economical three-course lunches. The best bet is the grilled meat, and there is plenty to choose from, including imported U.S. beef and less expensive Tico cuts. Despite the name, barbecue sauce is not used. Fresh fish, shrimp, and

Cloud Forests

Monteverde may be Costa Rica's most famous cloud forest, but Central Costa Rica has more than a dozen spots where you can explore that exuberant highland ecosystem that is home to colorful tanagers, trogons, toucanets, and hundreds of other species. Volcán Poás, Braulio Carrillo, and Tapantí national parks hold vast expanses of cloud forest, as do various private reserves, such as La Paz Waterfall Gardens on the eastern side of Poás National Park, and Valle Escondido, north of San Ramón.

Horseback Riding

This region is less commonly associated with horseback riding than the country's northwest, but the mountain climate here is actually more conducive to equestrian exploration. Rides through the cloud forest reserves of Villa Blanca, Poás Volcano Lodge, and Canopy Adventure, above Barva, double as bird-watching expeditions; Casa Turrire and Valle Escondido are more agricultural settings; and at the Albergue Volcán Turrialba, you can trot past unforgettable views.

River Rafting

Costa Rica's most popular rafting rivers flow out of the eastern Central Valley into the Atlantic lowlands, and a trip down one of those churning waterways is one of the country's great adventures. The Río Reventazón is a Class III river that is popular with beginners, but it flows through a largely agricultural region. Costa Rica's best rafting option is the Class III–IV Río Pacuare, which passes virgin rain forest, steep cliffs, and various waterfalls— some of the most spectacular scenery in the country. It can be navigated in one long day, but two-day trips with Aventuras Naturales or Ríos Tropicales (Sports & the Outdoors *in* Smart Travel Tips A to Z) are highly recommended.

Volcanoes

Some of Costa Rica's most accessible volcanoes stand on the northern edge of the Central Valley, and paved roads run right to the summits of two, Poás and Irazú. Volcán Poás is very popular, because it has an active crater, a luxuriant forest, and a jewel-like blue-green lake. Volcán Irazú, Costa Rica's highest volcano, is topped by a desolate landscape (the result of violent eruptions in the early 1960s), but on a clear day the view from the summit is unparalleled. Barva, in the southern section of Braulio Carrillo National Park, north of Heredia, is cloaked in cloud forest that resounds with the songs of birds such as the Emerald Toucanet and Resplendent Quetzal. You can visit all three of these volcanoes on day trips from San José, or any of the Central Valley's hotels; Poás and Irazú require only a morning, but to reach the summit of Barva, you'll need a full day. The ascent of Volcán Turrialba, on the other hand, is an adventure that requires overnights at a rustic lodge named after that peak.

---

half a dozen salads are other choices, along with good local desserts, and original cocktails. ⊠ *400 m west of Los Anonos Bridge* ☎ *228–0180* 🖃 *AE, DC, MC, V* ⊘ *Closed Mon.*

$$$ ✕🖾 **Tara Resort Hotel.** Modeled after the famous fictitious mansion from *Gone With the Wind* and decorated in antebellum style, this luxurious little inn is near the top of Pico Blanco. Hardwood floors through-

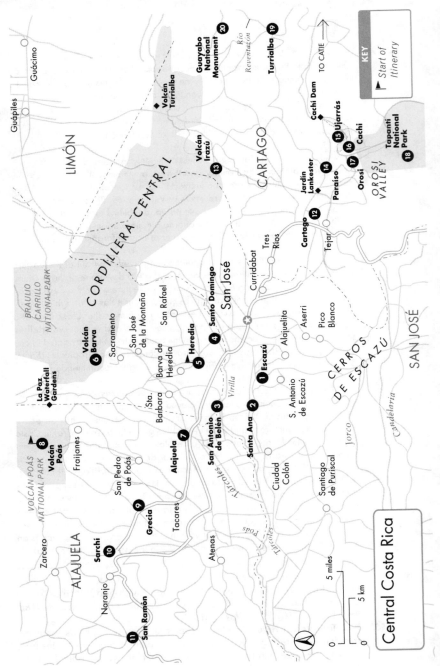

Central Costa Rica

KEY

▲ Start of Itinerary

ALAJUELA

LIMÓN

CARTAGO

SAN JOSÉ

CORDILLERA CENTRAL

BRAULIO CARRILLO NATIONAL PARK

VOLCÁN POÁS NATIONAL PARK

CERROS DE ESCAZÚ

OROSI VALLEY

Tapantí National Park

Guácimo
Guápiles
Volcán Turrialba
Guayabo National Monument ⑳
Río Reventazón
Turrialba ⑲
Volcán Irazú ⑬
Cachi Dam
Ujarrás ⑮
Cachi ⑯
Orosi ⑰
Tapantí National Park ⑱
Jardín Lankester ⑭
Paraíso
Cartago ⑫
Tejar
Tres Ríos
Curridabat
Sacramento
San José de la Montaña
San Rafael
Volcán Barva ⑥
La Paz Waterfall Gardens
Sta. Barbara
Barva de Heredia
Heredia ⑤
Santo Domingo ④
San José ★
Alajuelita
Aserrí
Pico Blanco
Escazú ①
S. Antonio de Escazú
Santa Ana ②
San Antonio de Belén ③
Virilla
Alajuela ⑦
Fraijanes
San Pedro de Poás
Volcán Poás ⑧
Tacares
Grecia ⑨
Sarchí ⑩
Zarcero
Naranjo
San Ramón ⑪
Atenas
Ciudad Colón
Santiago de Puriscal
Río Grande de Tárcoles
Jorco
Candelaria
TO CATIE

0   5 miles
0   5 km

out the three-story white-and-green building are covered with patterned area rugs. French doors in rooms open onto the public veranda. The Atlanta Dining Gallery ($$–$$$) has an eclectic mix of entrées that includes beef tenderloin in a mushroom-peppercorn sauce, chicken with a shrimp curry sauce, or corvina *del chef* (sea bass in a shrimp and mussel cream sauce). ✉ *½ km (¼ mi) south of the cemetery of San Antonio de Escazú* ☎ *Interlink 345, Box 02–5635, Miami, FL 33102* ☎ *228–6992* 🖷 *228–9651* ⊕ *www.tararesort.com* ⇱ *5 rooms, 8 suites, 1 bungalow* ⚶ *Restaurant, fans, in-room safes, cable TV, pool, hot tub, massage, spa; no a/c* ☰ *AE, MC, V* ⑩ *CP.*

$–$$ 🏠 **Posada El Quijote.** Perched on a hill in the Bello Horizonte neighborhood (on the San José side of Escazú), this homey bed-and-breakfast has a great view of the city. The best vantage point is on the sundeck, just off the spacious living room, which has a couch, a fireplace, and lots of modern art. The two "Deluxe" rooms and apartments have comparable views. Smaller "Standard" rooms overlook the surrounding gardens, and aren't nearly as nice. The inn is pet-friendly and the staff is extremely helpful, but it's a bit hard to find, so you may want to take a taxi there, or call for directions. ✉ *Bello Horizonte de Escazú, first street west of Anonos Bridge, 1 km (½ mi) up hill* ☎ *Dept. 239–SJO, Box 025216, Miami, FL 33102-5216* ☎ *289–8401* 🖷 *289–8729* ⊕ *www.quijote.co.cr* ⇱ *8 rooms, 2 apartments* ⚶ *Fans, cable TV, travel services, some pets allowed; no a/c* ☰ *AE, DC, MC, V* ⑩ *BP.*

$ 🏠 **Costa Verde Inn.** Rooms at this large B&B on the outskirts of Escazú make nice use of local hardwoods, and their white walls display traditional Peruvian art. South American art also adorns the main building, where a large sitting area has comfortable chairs and a fireplace. The inn is surrounded by gardens, and at night you can see the lights of San José twinkling to the east, but it is a bit isolated, making it less than ideal if you don't have a car. ✉ *From southeast corner of second cemetery, 200 m west and 100 m north* ☎ *SJO 1313, Box 025216, Miami, FL 33102-5216* ☎ *228–4080* 🖷 *289–8591* ⊕ *www.costaverdeinn.com* ⇱ *15 rooms* ⚶ *Fans, cable TV, tennis court, pool, hot tub; no a/c, no room phones* ☰ *AE, MC, V* ⑩ *CP.*

Nightlife & the Arts

Escazú is the Central Valley's hot spot for nightlife—many Josefinos head here for the restaurants, bars, and dance clubs that cater to a young, cell phone–toting crowd. The highest concentration of nightspots is in the **Trejos Montealegre shopping center** (✉ Next to the highway between San José and Ciudad Colón), which has several bars and dance clubs.

One of the more popular watering holes with the younger set is **Harry's Beach Bar** (✉ Plaza San Rafael, 2nd fl. ☎ 289–6250), which features Caribbean music and a coastal decor, with beach paintings and surfboards. **Q'Tal** (✉ San Rafael, 100 m east of El Cruce ☎ 228–4091) has live Latin music performed by the house band Requete on Fridays and cabaret shows on Saturdays. **Orale** (✉ San Rafael, 120 m east of El Cruce ☎ 228–6436) has live Latin music Fridays and Saturdays. **Sambuka** (✉ Centro Comercial La Rambla ☎ 289–7506) is a lively discotheque with Latino and pop rhythms catering to a twentysomething crowd.

★ An English-language company, the **Little Theatre Group** (✉ Blanche Brown Theatre, Bello Horizonte, Escazú ☎ 289–3910), has been performing several plays a year since 1949; check the *Tico Times* for the latest.

Shopping

★ You can watch local craftsmen ply their trade at **Biesanz Woodworks** (✉ Bello Horizonte, first entrance west of Anonos Bridge; follow signs ☎ 289–4337), where expat artist Barry Biesanz creates unique items from Costa Rican hardwoods, which are carved on-site. **El Sabor Tico** (✉ Behind Plaza Colonial ☎ 289–5270) sells a hodgepodge of woodworked souvenirs.

Santa Ana

❷ *12 km (7 mi) southwest of San José.*

This once tranquil agricultural community on the opposite side of the *cordillera* (mountain range) from Escazú is in the midst of a boom, and shopping malls and housing developments are popping up along its periphery. But the town center, with its rugged stone church surrounded by homes and businesses, has changed little in the past decade. The church, which was built between 1870 and 1880, has a Spanish-tile roof, carved wooden doors, and two pre-Columbian "Diquís" stone spheres flanking its entrance. Its rustic interior—bare wooden pillars and beams and black iron lamps—seems appropriate for an area with a tradition of ranching. Because it is warmer and drier than the towns to the east, Santa Ana is one of the few Central Valley towns that doesn't have a good climate for coffee, and is consequently surrounded by pastures and patches of forest. It isn't unusual to see men on horseback here, and on a quiet night, you may hear coyotes howling at the edge of town.

Where to Stay & Eat

$–$$ ✕ **Tex Mex.** The name is accurate enough; this place serves a fairly standard Mexican menu—tacos, burritos, quesadillas, and so on—plus a few grilled meat items, such as the Argentinian *churrasco* (a thick tenderloin cut), complete with *salsa chimichuri* (diced garlic and parsley in olive oil). There are about two dozen *bocas* (appetizers, or snacks), which are mostly smaller versions of entrée items. The enchiladas may not be as good as what you find in Denver or San Antonio, but the setting is pleasant, next to an old house with a yard shaded by massive trees. Seating is on a covered brick patio or in an adjacent dining area enclosed by windows, for those cool nights. A few simple, inexpensive rooms are available for rent. ✉ *Northeast of Catholic church* ☎ *282–6342* ▭ *MC, V* ☺ *Closed Mon.*

★ **$$$** ✕▦ **Alta.** The view from this Iberian-style hotel perched on a hillside above Santa Ana is impressive, but then, so is the hotel. The sloping stairway entrance lined with tall columns and palms is reminiscent of a narrow street in southern Spain, an effect reinforced by the barrel-tile roof and ocher-stuccoed walls. Guest rooms are hardly spacious, but are nicely done in earth tones, with colonial-style furniture and bathrooms with hand-painted tiles. The restaurant, La Luz ($$), has a hardwood floor, beamed ceiling, and plenty of windows for admiring the distant hills and the pool and gardens below. The eclectic and unusual menu includes veal with dolmas, shrimp tempura, marinated lamb chops, and Moroccan chicken. ⊠ *Old road between Santa Ana and Escazú* ⌖ *Interlink 964, Box 02–5635, Miami, FL 33102* ☎ *282–4160, 888/388–2582 in U.S.* 🖷 *282–4162* ⊕ *www.thealtahotel.com* ⬎ *18 rooms, 5 suites* ⌂ *Restaurant, in-room safes, minibars, cable TV, pool, gym, hot tub, sauna, laundry service, Internet* ⊟ *AE, DC, MC, V.*

Shopping

★ You can watch local craftsmen ply their trade at **Cerámica Las Palomas** (⊠ Old road to Santa Ana, opposite Alta Hotel ☎ 282–7001). Large, glazed pots with ornate decorations that range from traditional patterns to modern motifs are the specialties here.

San Antonio de Belén

❸ *17 km (10 mi) northwest of San José.*

San Antonio de Belén has little to offer visitors but its rural charm and proximity to the international airport. The latter led developers to build several of the San José area's biggest hotels here. The town also lies on the route of entry for Alajuela's Butterfly Garden. The Pan-American Highway skirts the northern edge of town, placing San Antonio a mere 20 minutes from San José and 10 minutes from the airport, and making it a convenient departure point for trips to the western Central Valley, Pacific coast, and northern region.

The town's only attraction is the **Ojo de Agua** (Spring), where refreshing springwater flows through a series of swimming pools surrounded by green areas. Costa Rican families mob Ojo de Agua on weekends and holidays, but it tends to be quiet during the week. ⊠ *1½ km (1 mi) northwest of Parque Central* ☎ *441–2808* 💲 *$2* ⊙ *Daily 8–4.*

Where to Stay & Eat

$ ✕⌂ **El Rodeo.** Amid the farms south of town, this quiet hotel has spacious rooms with polished hardwood floors, high ceilings, and narrow balconies overlooking small gardens and rooms in the adjacent building. An open-air lounge on the second floor has a pool table and wicker furniture. Breakfast is served on a porch overlooking the pool, which gets very little use, since most of the guests are business travelers. The large wooden restaurant ($–$$) in front of the hotel is quite popular with Ticos, who pack it on weekends. Decorated with saddles, steer skulls, and other ranching paraphernalia, the restaurant serves an array of grilled meats, from the Argentinean churrascos to T-bones, as well as several fish and shrimp dishes. ⊠ *Road to Santa Ana, 2 km (1 mi) east of Parque Central* ☎ *293–3909* 🖷 *293–3464* ⬎ *20 rooms, 9 suites* ⌂ *Restaurant, in-room safes, minibars, cable TV, 2 tennis courts, pool, sauna, laundry service, Internet, travel services* ⊟ *AE, DC, MC, V* ⍾⦿ *BP.*

★ $$$–$$$$ ⌂ **Marriott Costa Rica Hotel.** Towering over a coffee plantation west of San José, the stately Marriott evokes an unusual colonial splendor. The building's thick columns, wide arches, and central courtyard are straight out of the 17th century, and hand-painted tiles and abundant antiques complete the historic appearance. Guest rooms are more contemporary, but they're elegant enough, with hardwood furniture and sliding glass doors that open onto tiny balconies. ✉ ¾ km (½ mi) west of Firestone, off Autopista General Cañas, San Antonio de Belén ☎ 298–0000, 800/ 228–9290 in U.S. 🖶 298–0011 ⊕ www.marriott.com 🖳 248 rooms, 7 suites ♨ 4 restaurants, café, in-room data ports, in-room safes, driving range, putting green, 3 tennis courts, 2 pools, gym, health club, hair salon, sauna, lobby lounge, shop, baby-sitting, dry cleaning, laundry service, concierge, business services, meeting rooms, airport shuttle, car rental, travel services, free parking 🖭 AE, DC, MC, V.

$$$ 🏨 **Meliá Cariari.** The low-rise Meliá Cariari was San José's original luxury hotel, and it remains popular for its excellent service and out-of-town location. Just off the busy General Cañas Highway, about halfway between San José and the international airport, the Cariari is surrounded by thick vegetation that buffers it from traffic noise. Spacious, carpeted guest rooms in back overlook the pool area. The relaxed poolside bar, with cane chairs and colorful tablecloths, and nearby casino are popular spots. ✉ Autopista General Cañas, ½ km (¼ mi) east of intersection for San Antonio de Belén, Cariari 🕮 Apdo. 737–1007, San José ☎ 239–0022, 800/227–4274 in U.S. 🖶 239–2803 ⊕ www.solmelia.com 🖳 196 rooms, 24 suites ♨ 3 restaurants, some in-room data ports, in-room safes, minibars, cable TV, 18-hole golf course, golf privileges, 12 tennis courts, pool, gym, hot tub, 2 bars, casino, shops, laundry service, Internet, business services, meeting rooms, airport shuttle, free parking 🖭 AE, DC, MC, V.

Santo Domingo

➍ 18 km (11 mi) northeast of Escazú, 7 km (4 mi) northwest of San José.

Between Heredia and San José, the town of Santo Domingo de Heredia has plenty of traditional architecture and a level of tranquility that belies its proximity to the capital, which is a mere 15-minute drive away. Established in the early 19th century, Santo Domingo is surrounded by coffee farms and several smaller, even quieter communities. It has two Catholic churches, including one of the country's only two basilicas. The Iglesia del Rosario, which faces the town's sparsely planted Parque Central, was built in the 1840s and is open for mass every morning from 8 to 10. The larger Basilica de Santo Domingo, which stands across from a soccer field on the north end of town, is open for evening mass, from 4 to 6, and occasionally serves as a venue for classical music concerts during the July to August International Music Festival.

Santo Domingo's main attraction is **INBioparque,** an educational center that offers an excellent introduction to three of the country's ecosystems before you head out to see them for real. After watching short videos, wander trails through climate-controlled wetlands and out to tropical dry forest. Along the way, stop at the butterfly farm, snake and insect exhibits, and bromeliad garden. English-speaking guides end the tour with a discussion on biodiversity and the work of INBio (the National Biodiversity Institute). A pleasant restaurant serves typical Costa Rican fare, and the gift shop has an extensive selection of books on natural history and eco-friendly souvenirs. ✉ Road between Santo Domingo

and Heredia, 400 m north and 300 m west of Shell gas station
☎ *507–8107* 🎫 *$12* ⏰ *Daily 7:30–4.*

Heredia

▶ *4 km (3 mi) north of Santo Domingo, 11 km (6 mi) northwest of San José.*

With a population of around 30,000, Heredia is the capital of one of Costa Rica's most important coffee provinces, which has some of the country's best-preserved colonial towns. Founded in 1706, the city bears witness to how difficult preservation can be in an earthquake-prone country, since most of its colonial structures have been destroyed by the tremors and tropical climate. Still, the city and neighboring towns retain a certain historic feel, with old adobe buildings scattered amid the predominant concrete structures. You'll find more colonial and adobe buildings in the nearby villages of Barva and Santo Domingo de Heredia, and the roads that wind through the hills above those towns pass through charming scenery and rural enclaves, making them excellent routes for exploration.

Heredia proper is centered around a tree-studded **Parque Central,** which is surrounded by a few historic buildings. The park has a cast-iron fountain imported from England in 1897 and a simple kiosk where the municipal band sometimes holds Sunday-morning concerts. At the eastern end of the park stands the impressive **Iglesia de la Inmaculada Concepción,** a whitewashed, stone church built between 1797 and 1804 to replace an adobe temple dating from the early 1700s. Its thick, stone walls, small windows, and squat buttresses have kept it intact through two centuries of quakes and tremors. It has a pale interior with marble floors and stained-glass windows, and is flanked by tidy gardens. ✉ *C. Central and Avda. Central* ☎ *237–0779* ⏰ *Daily 6–6.*

To the north of the Iglesia is a handsome, barrel-tile house built in 1843, which was once the home of former president Alfredo González Flores. It is now the **Casa de la Cultura,** or cultural center, and thus hosts occasional art exhibits and performances. ✉ *C. Central and Avda. Central* ☎ *261–4485* 🎫 *Free* ⏰ *Weekdays 8–4.*

To the north of the Parque Central stands a strange, decorative tower called the **Fortín** (Little Fort), which was built in the 1880s by the local oligarch Fadrique Gutiérrez. Once used as a prison, it now serves as a symbol of the province. The old brick building next to the Fortín is the Palacio Municipal (Town Hall). ✉ *C. Central and Avda. Central.* ☎ *No phone* 🎫 *Free* ⏰ *Weekdays 8–4.*

Two blocks south of the Parque Central is Heredia's **Mercado Viejo** (Old Market), which has fewer souvenirs for sale than San José's Mercado Central, but is less cramped, brighter, and safer. On the next block to the southeast is the Mercado Nuevo (New Market), which holds dozens of *sodas* (simple restaurants). ✉ *C. Central and Avda. 6.* ⏰ *Mon.–Sat., 7–6.*

At the edge of a middle-class neighborhood between Heredia and Barva is the **Museo de Cultura Popular** (Museum of Popular Culture), which preserves an early-20th-century farmhouse built with an adobelike technique called *bahareque*. Run by the National University, the museum is furnished with antiques and surrounded by a small garden and coffee fields. An adjacent, open-air restaurant serves inexpensive Costa Rican lunches on weekends. ⊠ *Between Heredia and Barva; follow signs* ☎ *260–1619* ☜ *$1* ☉ *Museum daily 9–4, restaurant weekends 11–2.*

Fodor'sChoice
★
The producer of Costa Rica's most popular export-quality coffee, **Café Britt** offers a lively tour of its working coffee plantation that highlights Costa Rica's history of coffee cultivation through a theatrical presentation. (You have to see it to believe it.) Take a short walk through the coffee farm and processing plant, and learn how professional coffee tasters distinguish a fine cup of java from a not-so-nice one. ⊠ *West of road between Heredia and Barva; follow signs* ☎ *260–2748* ⊕ *www.cafebritt.com* ☜ *$19, $26 with transportation, $30 with transportation and lunch* ☉ *Tours Dec.–May daily at 9, 11, and 3, and June–Nov. daily at 11.*

★
At the center of **Barva de Heredia**, a small community about 3 km (2 mi) north of Heredia proper, is the Parque Central, surrounded by old adobe houses with Spanish tile roofs on three sides and a white stucco church to the east. Flanked by royal palms, the stout, handsome church dates from the late 18th century; behind it is a lovely little garden shrine to the Virgin Mary. On a clear day you can see verdant Volcán Barva towering to the north, and if you follow the road that runs in front of the church, and veer left at the Y, you will wind your way up the slopes of that volcano to Vara Blanca, where you can either drive north to the Waterfall Gardens, or continue straight to Poás Volcano National Park. If you veer right at the Y and drive up the steep, narrow road, you'll pass through San José de la Montaña and Paso Llano to reach Sacramento, where the road turns into a rough dirt track leading to the Barva sector of Braulio Carrillo National Park. If you turn left when you reach Barva's central plaza, you'll head to San Pedro and Santa Barbara, from where roads head south to Alajuela and north to Vara Blanca.

Where to Stay

★ **$$** ✕🏨 **Hotel Bougainvillea.** You might forget that you're only 15 minutes from San José on the Bougainvillea's extensive grounds amid the coffee farms east of Santo Domingo de Heredia. The spacious, carpeted guest rooms are furnished with local hardwoods and have large balconies; be sure to get one with a view of the gardens behind the hotel, which are shaded by large trees and hold an extensive bromeliad collection. Pre-Columbian pottery and paintings by Costa Rican artists decorate the lobby and restaurant ($–$$), which serves a small but excellent selection of Continental cuisine. An hourly shuttle takes you to the Hotel Villa Tournón in San José. ⊠ *Santo Tomas, 2 km (1 mi) east of Santo Domingo de Heredia* ✑ *Apdo. 69–2120, San José* ☎ *244–1414* ☐ *244–1313* ⊕ *www.bougainvillea.co.cr* ☜ *77 rooms, 4 suites* ☖ *Restaurant, fans, cable TV, tennis court, pool, sauna, bar, shop, laundry services, Internet, travel services; no a/c* ☐ *AE, DC, MC, V.*

$$$–$$$$
Fodor'sChoice
★
🏨 **Finca Rosa Blanca Country Inn.** There's nothing common about this luxurious little B&B overlooking coffee farms; you need only step through the front door of the Gaudíesque main building to marvel at its soaring ceiling, white-stucco arches, and polished wood. Each guest room is dif-

COFFEE, THE GOLDEN BEAN

WHEN COSTA RICA'S FIRST ELECTED PRESIDENT, Juan Mora Fernandez, began encouraging his compatriots to cultivate coffee back in 1830, he could hardly have imagined how profound an impact the crop would have on his country. Over the last 100 years, coffee has transformed Costa Rica from a colonial backwater into a relatively affluent and cosmopolitan republic.

It was the "golden bean" that financed the construction of most of the nation's landmarks. Founding families owned the largest plantations, creating a coffee oligarchy that has produced the majority of Costa Rican presidents. Lured by plantation jobs, tens of thousands of immigrant families from Europe and elsewhere in the Americas moved to Costa Rica in the 1800s and early 1900s, and were given land in exchange for cutting down the forest and planting coffee. They formed the backbone of a middle-class majority that has long distinguished Costa Rica from most of the rest of Latin America.

Thanks to its altitude and mineral-rich volcanic soil, the Central Valley is ideal for growing coffee, and the crop covers nearly every arable acre of this region. But coffee is not actually native to Costa Rica: biologists claim the plant evolved in the mountains of Ethiopia. Arab nations were sipping the aromatic beverage as early as the 7th century—its scientific name is Coffea arabica—but it didn't catch on in Europe until the 1600s. Coffee plants first arrived in Costa Rica from the Caribbean, probably in the early 1820s.

The coffee-growing cycle begins in May, when the arrival of annual rains makes the dark-green bushes explode into a flurry of white blossoms. By November, the fruit starts to ripen, turning from green to red, and the busy harvest begins as farmers race to get picked "cherries" to beneficios, processing plants where the beans—two per fruit—are removed, washed, dried by machine, and packed in burlap sacks for export. Costa Rica's crop is consistently among the world's best, and most of the high-grade exports wind up in Europe and the United States.

Traditionally, coffee bushes are grown in the shade of trees, such as citrus or the nitrogen-fixing members of the bean family. Recently, however, many farmers have switched to sun-resistant varieties, cutting down shade trees to pack more coffee bushes into each acre. Shade farms provide habitats for migratory birds and other animals, so the shadeless farms are practically biological deserts. Environmentalists are promoting a return to the old system by labeling shade coffee ECO-OK, and more and more farmers are returning to the old system. Not only does the coffee taste better, but the planations look more vibrant, with trees dotting the redundant rows of coffee. Coffee prices have declined sharply since 2000, leading many coffee farmers to explore different crop options, such as tomato farming or cattle ranching. But coffee still remains king in the Central Valley.

Ticos are fueled by an inordinate amount of coffee. They generally filter it through cloth bags, a method that makes for a stronger cup of java than your average American brew. The mean bean is even used in a favorite local dish: chicken roasted with coffee wood. Sadly, many Ticos drink the low-grade stuff, often mixed with molasses, peanuts, or corn for bulk. If you're buying, reliable brands are Café Rey's Tarrazú, Café Britt, Américo, Volio, and Montaña.

ferent, but all have original art, local hardwoods, and colorful fabrics. The spacious, two-story suite is out of a fairy tale, with a spiral staircase leading up to a window-lined tower bedroom. On the grounds, which are planted with tropical flowers and shaded by massive fig trees, are two two-bedroom villas. Four-course dinners are available. ⊠ *Barrio Jesus; 1 km (½ mi) east and 800 m north of Santa Barbara de Heredia* ⏏ *SJO 3475, Box 025369, Miami, FL 33102-5216* ☎ *269–9392* 🖷 *269–9555* ⊕ *www.fincarosablanca.com* ↩ *7 rooms, 2 villas* ♨ *Dining room, fans, in-room safes, pool, hot tub, horseback riding, airport shuttle, travel services; no a/c, no room TVs* ▤ *AE, MC, V* ⦿ *BP.*

¢ 🏨 **Hotel Ceos.** Occupying an old wooden home a block north of the Parque Central, the Hotel Ceos has basic accommodations for travelers on a tight budget. Historic photos decorate the ground floor, and the rooms are painted bright colors, but are small and time-worn. The nicest spot in the place is the large balcony on the second floor, furnished with a sofa and chairs. The restaurant serves inexpensive breakfasts and light meals. ⊠ *Avda. 1 and C. Central* ☎ *262–2628* 🖷 *262–2639* ↩ *10 rooms* ♨ *Restaurant, fans, cable TV, laundry services; no a/c, no room phones* ▤ *AE, MC, V.*

Volcán Barva

❻ *20 km (12 mi) north of Heredia, 30 km (19 mi) northwest of San José.*

North of Barva de Heredia, the road grows narrow and steep as it winds its way up the verdant slopes of **Barva Volcano,** whose 9,500-foot summit is the highest point in **Braulio Carrillo National Park.** To the east of Heredia, a similar road climbs the volcano from San Rafael de Heredia to the **Monte de la Cruz,** a ridge bordering the national park that is topped with a cross. Dormant for 300 years now, Barva is massive: its lower slopes are almost completely planted with coffee fields and hold more than a dozen small towns, nearly all of which are named after saints. On the upper slopes are pastures lined with exotic pines and the occasional native oak or cedar, giving way to the botanical diversity of the cloud forest near the top. The air is usually cool near the summit, which combines with the pines and pastures to evoke the European or North American countryside.

Any vehicle can make the trip up to Vara Blanca, or above San Rafael de Heredia to the Monte de la Cruz, and even buses follow the loop above Barva via **San José de la Montaña,** but it's rough going up the mountain from San José de la Montaña to the entrance to Braulio Carrillo National Park. In the dry months, you can take a four-wheel-drive vehicle over the extremely rocky road to the park entrance; alternatively, leave your car and hike up on foot, a four-hour trip to the crater lakes on the summit.

Barva's misty, luxuriant summit is the only part of Braulio Carrillo where camping is allowed, and it's a good place to see the rare Resplendent Quetzal if you're here early in the morning. Because it's somewhat hard to reach, Barva receives a mere fraction of the crowds that flock to the summits of Poás and Irazú. A 30-minute hike in from the ranger station takes you to the main crater, which is about 540 feet in diameter. Its almost vertical sides are covered in poor man's umbrellas, a plant that thrives in the highlands, and oak trees laden with epiphytes (non-parasitic plants that grow on other plants). The crater is filled with an otherworldly, black lake. Farther down the track into the forest lies a smaller crater lake. Bring rain gear, boots, and a warm shirt, and stick to the trails—even experienced hikers who know the area have lost their way up here. ☎ 283–5906, 192 in Costa Rica ☞ $7 ☉ Tues.–Sun. 7–4.

San Rafael de Heredia (✉ 2 km [1 mi] northeast of Heredia) is a quiet, mildly affluent coffee town with a large church notable for its stained-glass windows and bright interior. The road north from the church winds its way up Volcán Barva to the hotels Chalet Tirol and La Condesa, ending atop the Monte de la Cruz lookout point.

Where to Stay

$$–$$$ 🏨 **Hotel La Condesa.** The stone fireplace surrounded by armchairs and a small bar in the La Condesa lobby is one of the many facets of the hotel that suggest a lodge you'd expect to find in a more northern latitude. In the central courtyard, topped by a giant skylight, is one of the hotel's three restaurants. A tropical garden is similarly enclosed in the pool area. Guest rooms are carpeted and tastefully furnished, and each has a picture window. Suites have bedroom lofts, sitting areas, and the hotel's best views. The log-cabin villas with full kitchens are ideal for families. ✉ Next to Castillo Country Club, 10 km (6 mi) north of San Rafael de Heredia ☎ 267–6001 🖷 267–6016 ⊕ www.condesahotel.com ☞ 61 rooms, 31 suites, 4 villas ⚿ 3 restaurants, in-room safes, some kitchens, minibars, cable TV, indoor pool, hot tub, horseback riding, squash, 2 bars, laundry service, meeting room, car rental, travel services; no a/c ⊟ AE, DC, MC, V.

$ 🏨 **Las Ardillas.** Surrounded by old pines on a country road, these unpretentious log cabins are inviting retreats for those looking to lock themselves up in front of a fireplace and tune out the world. The small on-site spa is a good reason to venture from the comfortable, romantic rooms. The restaurant specializes in meats roasted over a wood fire and has a nice selection of Spanish wines. All rooms have modest wood furniture and queen-size beds. ✉ Main road, Guacalillo de San José de la Montaña 🖅 Apdo. 44–309, Barva ☎ 260–2172 🖷 266–0251 ☞ 15 cabins ⚿ Restaurant, kitchenettes, hot tub, massage, sauna, spa, hiking, bar; no a/c, no room phones ⊟ AE, MC, V ⧈ BP.

$ 🏨 **Hotel Chalet Tirol.** The Chalet Tirol's Austrian design doesn't seem out of place amid the pines, pastures, and cool air of Volcán Barva's upper slopes. The replica of a cobbled Tirolean town square—complete with fountain and church—may be a bit much, but the cozy, bright two-story wooden chalets are charming, as is the restaurant, with its ivy, wooden ceiling, and elegant murals. High-quality French cuisine makes this a popular weekend destination for Costa Ricans. The suites have fireplaces and are more private than the chalets. ✉ Main road, 10 km (6 mi) north of San Rafael de Heredia 🖅 Apdo. 7812–1000, San José ☎ 267–6222 🖷 267–6373 ☞ 13 suites, 10 chalets ⚿ Restaurant, cable TV, tennis court, bar, laundry service; no a/c ⊟ AE, DC, MC, V ⧈ CP.

Nightlife

La Lluna de Valencia (✉ 100 m north of Pulpería La Máquina, San Pedro de Barva ☎ 269–6665) has live music on the weekends, and great paellas and other Valencian specialties by day. It is open from Thursday through Sunday.

The Outdoors

CANOPY TOUR The cloud forest has the lushest, most diverse canopy of any tropical forest, and what better way to appreciate that diversity than by gliding through the treetops? **Canopy Adventure** (✉ Passo Llano, 7 km [4 mi] north of Barva de Heredia ☎ 266–0782), in the mountains above San Jose de la Montaña, runs two-hour canopy tours in a private reserve that involve sliding along cables strung between platforms perched high in massive tropical trees.

HIKING The upper slopes of **Volcán Barva** have excellent hiking conditions: cool air, vistas, and plentiful birds. The crater lakes topping the volcano can be reached only on foot, and if you haven't got a four-wheel-drive vehicle, you'll also have to trek from Sacramento up to the entrance of Braulio Carrillo National Park.

HORSEBACK RIDING Horseback-riding tours along the upper slopes of Volcán Barva combine views of the Central Valley with close exposure to the cloud forest and resident bird life. **Canopy Adventure** (✉ Passo Llano, 7 km [4 mi] north of Barva de Heredia ☎ 266–0782), above San José de la Montaña, runs horseback tours in its private cloud-forest reserve that can be combined with a canopy tour and lunch. **Hotel Condessa** (☎ 267–6001) offers horseback tours with local guides.

Alajuela

❼ *20 km (13 mi) northwest of San José.*

Because of its proximity to the international airport (5–10 minutes away) many travelers spend their first or last night in Alajuela, but the beauty of the surrounding countryside persuades some to stay here longer. Alajuela is Costa Rica's second-largest city (population 50,000), and a mere 30-minute bus ride from the capital, but it has a decidedly provincial air. Architecturally it differs little from the bulk of Costa Rican towns: it's a grid of low-rise structures painted in primary colors.

Royal palms and massive mango trees fill the **Parque Central,** which also has a lovely fountain imported from Glasgow and concrete benches where locals gather to chat. Surrounding the plaza is an odd mix of charming old buildings and sterile concrete boxes. ✉ *C. Central, between Avdas. 1 and Central.*

The large, neoclassic **Catedral** has interesting capitals decorated with local agricultural motifs and a striking red metal dome. The interior is spacious but rather plain, except for the ornate cupola above the altar. ✉ *C. Central, between Avdas. 1 and Central* ☎ 441–0769 ☉ *Daily 8–6.*

To the north of the park stands the **old jail,** which now houses the local offices of the Ministry of Education—an appropriate metaphor for a country that claims to have more teachers than police. ⊠ *C. Central, between Avdas. 1 and Central.*

Alajuela was the birthplace of Juan Santamaría, the national hero who lost his life in a battle against the mercenary army of U.S. adventurer William Walker (1824–60) when the latter invaded Costa Rica in 1856. The **Parque Juan Santamaría** has a statue of the youthful Santamaría. ⊠ *C. 2 and Avda. 3.*

Juan Santamaría's heroic deeds are celebrated in the **Museo Juan Santamaría,** one block north of Parque Central. The museum contains maps, compasses, weapons, and paintings, including an image of Walker's men filing past to lay down their weapons. The colonial building that houses the museum is as interesting as the displays, as is the orchid collection. ⊠ *C. 2 and Avda. 3* ☎ *441–4775* ⊠ *Free* ☉ *Tues.–Sun. 10–6.*

☸ Spread over the lush grounds of **Zoo Ave** (Bird Zoo) is a collection of large cages holding macaws, toucans, hawks, and parrots, not to mention crocodiles, turtles, monkeys, pumas, and other interesting critters. The zoo runs a breeding project for rare and endangered birds, all of which are destined for eventual release. It has a total of 120 bird species, including such rare animals as the quetzal, Fiery-billed Aracari, and several types of eagles. An impressive mural at the back of the facility shows Costa Rica's 850 bird species painted to scale. To get here, head west from the center of Alajuela past the cemetery and turn left after the stone church in Barrio San José, or head west of the Inter-American Highway to the Atenas exit, then turn right. ⊠ *La Garita de Alajuela* ☎ *433–8989* ⊠ *$9* ☉ *Daily 9–5.*

☸ The **Finca de Mariposas** (Butterfly Farm), in the suburb of La Guácima, offers a regular lecture on the ecology of these delicate insects and gives you a chance to observe and photograph them up close. In addition to an apiary exhibit, the farm's several microclimates keep comfortable some 40 rare species of butterflies. Try to come here when it's sunny, as that's when butterflies are most active. ⊠ *From San José, turn south (left) at the intersection just past Real Cariari Mall, turn right at church of San Antonio de Belén, then left at the corner, then follow the butterfly signs* ☎ *438–0115* ⊕ *www.butterflyfarm.co.cr* ⊠ *$15, $25 with transportation from San José* ☉ *Daily 8:30–5.*

Considering the amount of coffee you'll drive past in the Central Valley, you might want to dedicate 90 minutes of your vacation to learning about the crop's production. **Doka Estate,** a working coffee plantation with more than 70 years in the business, offers a comprehensive tour that takes you through the fields, shows you how the fruit is processed and the beans are dried, and lets you sample the local brew. Though it's offered year-round, the best time to take this tour is during the November to March picking season. ⊠ *San Luis de Sabanilla; 9 km (5½ mi) north of Alajuela's Tribunales de Justicia, turn left at San Isidro and follow signs* ☎ *449–5152* 🖷 *449–6427* ⊕ *www.dokaestate.com* ⊠ *$15, $30 with transportation from San José, Alajuela, Heredia, Escazu, or San Antonio* ☉ *Tours Sun.–Fri. at 9:30 and 1:30, Sat. at 9:30.*

en route

If you head straight through Alajuela, with the Parque Central on your right, you'll be on the road to Poás Volcano; you should pass the *Tribunales de Justicia* (the county courthouse) on your right as you leave town. If you turn left upon reaching the Parque Central, and pass the town cemetery on your right, you'll be on the old road to Grecia. About 3 km (2 mi) northwest of town on that road, you'll come upon an old concrete church on the right, which marks your arrival in *Barrio San José*, a satellite community of Alajuela. A left turn after the church will take you to a lovely rural area called **La Garita** (the Guardhouse), from where the road continues west to Atenas and the Central Pacific beaches. La Garita is a popular weekend destination for Tico families, who head there for the warm climate and abundant restaurants.

Where to Stay & Eat

$–$$ ✕ **Bar y Restaurante El Mirador.** Perched on a ridge several miles north of town, El Mirador has a sweeping view of the Central Valley that is impressive by day, but more beautiful at dusk and night when the basin is filled with twinkling lights. Get a window table in the dining room, or one on the adjacent porch if it isn't too cool; reservations are recommended on weekends. The food, though tasty, is less of a draw than the view. Choose from *lomito* (tenderloin) and corvina served with various sauces, and several shrimp or chicken dishes. You could just stop in for the sunset and sample from the good wine list and decent appetizer selection. You can arrange to be picked up from most Alajuela hotels free of charge. ⊠ *Road to Poás, 5 km (3 mi) north of Tribunales de Justicia* ☎ 441–9347 ▭ *AE, DC, MC, V.*

¢–$ ✕ **Delicias de Mi Tierra.** The name translates as "Delicacies of my Land," and the menu is strictly Costa Rican. Tico favorites are served here: arroz con pollo, *pozol* (corn and pork soup), *casado campesino* (stewed beef with rice, beans, corn, potatoes, and plantains), and *chorreada con natilla* (a corn-bread pancake with sour cream). Long wooden tables and benches are surrounded by cane walls, decorative oxcart wheels, dried gourds, and tropical plants. Ordering a few *entraditas* (appetizers) is a good way to sample dishes, as is the *tablita mi tierra,* a platter with grilled chicken, beef, pork, rice, beans, fried plantains, and salad, or the larger *fiesta de gallos,* a mixed platter of corn tortillas with various fillings. Since it's primarily a lunch spot, this place closes at 7 PM weekdays and 8 PM on weekends. ⊠ *1½ km (1 mi) west of Barrio San José* ☎ 282–6342 ▭ *AE, DC, MC, V.*

¢–$ ✕ **La Princesa Marina.** This large open-air eatery at the intersection of the old Alajuela-Grecia road and the road to La Garita is popular with Ticos, who pack it on weekends to feast on inexpensive seafood. The selection is vast, with 10 types of *ceviche* (fish, shrimp, or octopus marinated in lime juice), fish fillets served with various sauces, three sizes of shrimp prepared a dozen ways, whole fried fish, lobster tails, and several *mariscadas* (mixed seafood plates). Pastas, rice dishes, beef, and chicken are some other choices, but the seafood is your best bet here. The decor is utilitarian—bare tables, ceiling fans, and dividers full of potted plants separating the various sections. ⊠ *Barrio San José, across from church* ☎ 433–7117 ▭ *AE, DC, MC, V.*

$–$$ ✕🖫 **Orquídeas Inn.** The colorful, Spanish-style main building of this friendly hotel holds an excellent restaurant, a suite just steps away from the pool, and a bar dedicated to Marilyn Monroe. The surrounding tropical gardens are populated by caged birds and their wild cousins. Deluxe rooms, on a hill with a view of three volcanoes, are spacious, with pastel walls and bamboo furniture. Smaller standard rooms have terra-cotta tile floors and Guatemalan fabrics; those on the garden side are quieter, and worth the extra $10. This place's proximity to a busy road is its only shortcoming. The restaurant ($–$$) offers an eclectic selection ranging from Costa Rican *casados* (plates of rice, beans, fried plantains, salad, and meat, chicken, or fish) to chateaubriand, and including such unusual dishes as talapia in a shrimp and corn sauce. A sumptuous breakfast buffet is served on the bar's patio. ✉ *5 km (3 mi) west of cemetery* ✆ *29 rooms, 4 suites* ☎ *433–9346* 🖶 *433–9740* ⊕ *www.orquideasinn.com* ♨ *Restaurant, fans, cable TV, pool, massage, bar, shop, laundry service, meeting room, travel services; no room phones* ▭ *AE, DC, MC, V* ⍣ *BP.*

$$$–$$$$ 🖫 **Xandari Resort Hotel & Spa.** The tranquil and colorful Xandari is a
FodorśChoice strikingly original inn. Its bold design is the brainchild of a talented cou-
★ ple—he's an architect, she's an artist. Contemporary pueblo-esque villas along a ridge overlooking Alajuela and San José are spacious, with plenty of windows, colorful paintings, large terraces, and secluded lanais (sunbathing patios). Some villas stand alone and some share a building, but nearly all of them have spectacular views. So does the restaurant, which serves tasty, low-fat food. A trail through the hotel's forest reserve winds past five waterfalls. ✉ *6 km (3 mi) north of Tribunales de Justicia, turn left after small bridge, follow signs, Apdo. 1485–4050* ☎ *443–2020, 800/686–7879 in U.S.* 🖶 *442–4847* ⊕ *www.xandari.com* ✆ *20 villas* ♨ *Restaurant, fans, in-room safes, minibars, 2 pools, hot tub, spa, bar, shop, laundry service, Internet, airport shuttle, travel services, no-smoking rooms; no a/c, no room TVs* ▭ *AE, DC, MC, V.* ⍣ *CP.*

$$$ 🖫 **Pura Vida Yoga Retreat & Spa.** Yoga workshops are an integral part of your stay here. The weekly rate includes two daily yoga classes, tours, transfers, three healthful meals per day, and one massage. Rooms have large windows and bamboo furniture, and more creature comforts than the luxury tents surrounded by tropical gardens. Staying in the carpeted tents (with nightstands and a small wood desk) is meant to strengthen your connection with the outdoors, which means you're up with the sun to practice yoga. Packages are booked by the week only and can be booked only in the United States. ✉ *½ km (¼ mi) south of Bar Lobo Azul, Pavas de Carrizal, Apdo. 1112, 4050* ☍ *R&R Resorts, Box 1496, Conyers, GA 30012* ☎ *392–8099, 888/767–7375 in U.S.* 🖶 *483–0041* ⊕ *www.puravidaspa.com* ✆ *30 rooms, 12 tent bungalows, 3 suites, 1 villa* ♨ *Dining room, spa, airport shuttle, travel services; no a/c, no room phones, no room TVs* ▭ *AE, MC, V* ⍣ *FAP.*

$$ 🖫 **Buena Vista Hotel.** Perched high above Alajuela, this hotel does have the "good view" it is named for, but few of its rooms share in that vista, which is best appreciated from the back lawn. Three balcony rooms on the second floor in back have decent views of the Central Valley, but even better are the views of Poás Volcano from the three rooms above the lobby. Most rooms, however, overlook the lawns, or pool area. They are carpeted and sparsely decorated, with small baths and TVs. The restaurant behind the lobby serves international dishes and grilled items. ⊠ 7 *km (4 mi) north of Alajuela's Tribunales de Justicia on road to Poás* ☎ *442–8595, 800/506–2304 in U.S.* 🖨 *442–8701* ⊕ *www.arweb.com/ buenavista* ⇨ *21 rooms, 4 junior suites* ⟋ *Restaurant, cable TV, pool, shop, airport shuttle, travel services, no-smoking rooms; no a/c, no room phones* ⊟ *AE, DC, MC, V* ⟊ *CP.*

★ **$–$$** 🖭 **Pura Vida Hotel.** Thanks to its location on a ridge north of town, several of this hotel's rooms have views of Poás Volcano, and all of them offer tranquility and abundant birdsong. The two rooms in the main house have the best views, but *casitas* (little houses), scattered around the garden offer more privacy. Some of these bright bungalows have separate bedrooms, and most of them have small terraces with chairs. Continental breakfasts, light lunches, and delicious dinners are served on a covered terrace behind the house. The helpful owners and proximity to the airport (15 minutes) make this a good place to begin and end a trip. ⊠ *Tuetal, 2 km (1 mi) north of Tribunales de Justicia, veer left at Y* ☎🖨 *441–1157* ⊕ *www.puravidahotel.com* ⇨ *2 rooms, 6 bungalows* ⟋ *Restaurant, airport shuttle, travel services, no-smoking rooms; no a/c, no room phones, no room TVs* ⊟ *AE, DC, MC, V* ⟊ *CP.*

¢ 🖭 **Hotel Alajuela.** Perfect for travelers on tight budgets, this three-story concrete hotel across from the Parque Central's southwest corner has basic rooms with tile floors, ceiling fans, and tiny bathrooms. There's a large lounge on the ground floor and plenty of restaurants within walking distance. More important, it's a 10-minute taxi ride from the airport, and just a few blocks from the bus stops for La Garita, Poás, and most destinations in central and northwest Costa Rica. ⊠ *C. 2 and Avenida Central, southwest corner of Parque Central* ☎ *441–1241* 🖨 *441–7912* ⇨ *28 rooms* ⟋ *Fans; no a/c, no room phones, no room TVs* ⊟ *MC, V.*

Volcán Poás

▶ ❽ *37 km (23 mi) north of Alajuela, 57 km (35 mi) north of San José.*

Towering to the north of Alajuela, the verdant mass of Volcán Poás is covered with a quilt of farms and topped by a dark green shawl of cloud forest. A paved road leads all the way from Alajuela to its 8,800-foot summit, winding past coffee fields, patches of forest, pastures, fern farms, and increasingly spectacular views of the Central Valley. Most of the volcano's southern slope is covered with coffee, but the higher altitudes, which are too cold for that crop, hold screened-in fern and flower farms, neat rows of strawberries, and the light green pastures of dairy farms. Only the volcano's upper slopes and summit are still covered with cloud forest, which stretches northward toward Cerro Congo and east toward Volcán Barva. The road bifurcates at Poasito, not far from the summit, where the route to the left leads to the national park, and the one to the right heads toward the intersection of Vara Blanca. At Vara Blanca, you can turn left for the Waterfall Gardens and Northern Zone, or continue straight to wind your way down the slopes of Volcán Barva to Heredia.

Fodor'sChoice   The 57-square-km (22-square-mi) **Volcán Poás National Park** protects epi-
★   phyte-laden cloud and elfin (small-tree) forest near the summit as well as
a blue-green crater lake and the volcano's massive active crater. The main
crater, nearly 1½ km (1 mi) across and 1,000 feet deep, is one of the largest
active craters in the world. The sight of this vast, multicolored pit with
smoking fumaroles and a gurgling, gray-turquoise sulfurous lake, is captivating. All sense of scale is absent here, as the crater is devoid of vegetation. No one is allowed to venture onto the crater, or walk along its edge.

The peak is frequently enshrouded in mist, and many who come here
see little beyond the lip of the crater. If you're faced with pea soup, wait
a while, especially if some wind is blowing—the clouds can disappear
quickly. The earlier in the day you go, the better your chance of a clear
view. If you're lucky, you'll see the famous geyser in action, spewing a
column of gray mud high into the air. Poás last had a major eruption
in 1953 and is thought to be approaching another active phase; at any
sign of danger, the park is closed to visitors. It can be very cold and wet
up top, so dress accordingly. If you come ill equipped, you can duck under
a *sombrilla de pobre* (poor man's umbrella) plant, the leaves of which
grow to diameters of 4 to 5 feet.

The park has a paved road that leads from the visitor center to the edge
of the active crater, from which two trails head into the forest. The second trail, on the right just before the crater, winds through a thick mesh
of shrubs and dwarf trees to the eerie but beautiful **Laguna Botos** (Botos
Lake), which occupies an extinct crater. It takes 30 minutes to walk there
and back. **Sendero Escalonia,** a tree common to the area, runs through
a taller stretch of forest between the picnic area and the parking lot; boards
along the way bear sentimental eco-poetry (in Spanish). Mammals are
rare on Poás, but you should see various birds on either of these trails,
including several kinds of hummingbirds and large, black Sooty Robins.
Quetzals live in the park, but they rarely venture near the trails and crater.
Note that Volcán Poás is a popular spot and gets quite crowded, especially on Sunday. It's not the place to go to commune with nature in
solitude, but it is definitely worth seeing. The large visitor center has a
scale model of the park, a display on volcanology, a modest gift shop,
and a cafeteria that serves hot coffee—perfect for those chilly afternoons.
✉ *37 km (23 mi) north of Alajuela; from San José, take Inter-American Hwy. to Alajuela, drive straight through town, and follow signs.*
☎ *482–2424, 192 in Costa Rica* ✆ *$7* ⊙ *Daily 8:30–3:30.*

★   Five magnificent waterfalls are the main attractions at **La Paz Waterfall
Gardens,** on the eastern edge of Volcán Poás National Park, but they
are complemented by the beauty of the surrounding cloud forest, an abundance of hummingbirds and other avian species, and the country's
biggest butterfly garden. A concrete trail leads down from the visitor
center to the multilevel, screened butterfly observatory and continues
to gardens where hummingbird feeders attract swarms of those multicolored creatures. The trail then enters the cloud forest, where it leads
to a series of metal stairways that let you descend into a steep gorge to
viewing platforms near each of the waterfalls. A free shuttle will transport you from the trail exit back to the main building, if you prefer to

avoid the hike uphill. Several alternative paths lead from the main trail through the cloud forest, and along the river's quieter upper stretch, providing options for hours of exploration—it takes about 1½ hours to hike down the waterfall trail. The visitor center has a gift shop and open-air cafeteria with a great view. The gardens are 20 km (12 mi) northeast of Alajuela. ⊠ *6 km (3 mi) north of Vara Blanca* ☎ *482–2720* ⊕ *www. waterfallgardens.com* ⬚ *$21, $31 with lunch* ☉ *Daily 8–3:45.*

Where to Stay & Eat

$ ✕ **Chubascos.** Amid tall pines and colorful flowers on the upper slopes
Fodor's Choice of Poás Volcano, this popular restaurant has a small menu of traditional
★ Tico dishes and delicious daily specials. Choose from the full selection of casados and platters of *gallos* (homemade tortillas with meat, cheese, or potato fillings). The *refrescos* (fresh fruit drinks) are top-drawer, especially the ones made from locally grown *fresas* (strawberries) and *moras* (blackberries), blended with milk. ⊠ *1 km (½ mi) north of Fraijanes* ☎ *482–2280* ▭ *AE, MC, V.*

$ ✕ **Jaulares.** Named after the Jaul, a tree common in the nearby cloud forest, this spacious restaurant specializes in grilled meat, though there are also several fish dishes and *chicharrones* (deep-fried meaty pork rinds). All the cooking is done with wood, which adds to the rustic ambience of terra-cotta floors, bare wooden beams, and sylvan surroundings. The house specialty, *lomito Jaulares* (Jaulares tenderloin), is a strip of grilled meat served with *gallo pinto* (rice and beans) and a mild *salsa criollo* (creole sauce). Though primarily a lunch spot, Jaulares stays open until midnight on weekends for concerts—Latin music on Friday nights and rock on Saturday nights. Four basic cabinas in back are an inexpensive overnight option, though you'll need to reserve them early for concert nights. ⊠ *2 km (1 mi) north of Fraijanes* ☎ *482–2155* ▭ *AE, DC, MC, V.*

★ **$$$–$$$$** ▦ **Peace Lodge.** These rooms overlooking the misty forest of La Paz Waterfall Gardens seem like something out of the *Lord of the Rings*, with their curved, clay-stucco walls, hardwood floors, stone fireplaces (gas), and four-poster beds made of varnished logs, complete with mosquito-net canopy. They are proper abodes for elfin kings, especially the spacious, grottolike bathrooms with two showers, a hot tub, tropical gardens, and private waterfall. Most hotels settle for a room with a bath. Peace Lodge gives you a bath with a room. And as if that weren't enough, you can soak in your second hot tub, on a porch with a cloud-forest view. Being able to explore the waterfall gardens before they open is another perk. The cuisine here is a couple of notches below the accommodations. ⊠ *3 km (2 mi) north of Vara Blanca* ☎ *482–2720* ☏ *482–2722* ⊕ *www.waterfallgardens.com* ⇗ *18 rooms* ♦ *Restaurant, fans, in-room hot tubs, minibars, cable TV, shop; no a/c, no room phones* ▭ *AE, DC, MC, V* ⦿ *BP.*

$–$$ ▦ **Poás Volcano Lodge.** The rustic architecture of this former dairy farmhouse, with rough stone walls and pitched beam roof, fits perfectly into the rolling pastures and forests that surround it. The interior mixes Persian rugs with textiles from Latin America, and Guaitil Indian pottery with North American pieces. The oversize sunken fireplace may be the lodge's most alluring feature. All rooms are different, so if possible, look at a few before you decide: one has an exquisite stone bathtub. A small dairy farm and garden supply the kitchen with ingredients for the hearty breakfasts. ✉ *6 km (4 mi) east of Chubascos restaurant, on road to Vara Blanca* 🏤 *Apdo. 5723–1000, San José* ☎ *482–2194* 🖷 *482–2513* 🌐 *www.poasvolcanolodge.com* 🛏 *9 rooms, 7 with bath* ⚒ *Dining room, billiards, Ping-Pong, laundry service, Internet; no a/c, no room phones, no room TVs* ▭ *AE, DC, MC, V* ❙❍❙ *BP.*

$ 🏨 **Siempreverde B&B.** A night at this isolated B&B in the heart of a coffee plantation might be as close as you'll ever come to being a coffee farmer. The attractive wooden house has four nicely decorated rooms upstairs, with hardwood floors and small windows; the room downstairs is a bit dark. There's also a living room, kitchen, lounge, and terrace in back where breakfast is served. Photos of the coffee harvest decorate the walls, and just beyond the yard and manicured gardens that surround the house, neat rows of coffee stretch off into the distance. ✉ *12 km (5 mi) northwest of Tribunales de Justicia de Alajuela, turn left at colegio (high school)* 🏤🏤 *449–5134* 🛏 *4 rooms with bath* ⚒ *Dining room; no a/c, no room phones, no room TVs* ▭ *AE, DC, MC, V* ❙❍❙ *BP.*

The Outdoors

HORSEBACK RIDING
Poás Volcano Lodge (✉ 2 km [1 mi] west of Vara Blanca ☎ 482–2194) leads guided horseback tours in the cloud forest of Finca Legua, a private reserve 5 km (3 mi) north of the lodge. The tours usually start at dawn or in the late afternoon, the best hours for bird-watching, since the reserve is home to a wealth of avian life.

Shopping

The **Neotrópica Foundation** sells nature-theme T-shirts, cards, and posters in the national park's visitor center and devotes a portion of the profits to conservation projects. A number of **roadside stands** on the way up Poás sell strawberry jam, *cajeta* (a pale fudge), and corn crackers called *biscochos.*

WEST OF ALAJUELA

The rolling countryside west of Alajuela holds a mix of coffee, sugarcane, and pasture, with tropical forest filling steep river valleys and ravines. The Inter-American Highway makes a steady descent to the Pacific Coast through this region, which is also traversed by older roads that wind their way between tidy agricultural towns and past small farms and pastoral scenery. West of San Ramón, the valley becomes narrow and precipitous as the topography slopes down to the Pacific lowlands. An even narrower valley snakes northward from San Ramón to the northern lowlands, past luxuriant cloud forests that can be explored from nature lodges.

Grecia

9 *26 km (16 mi) northwest of Alajuela, 46 km (29 mi) northwest of San José.*

Founded in 1838, the quiet farming community of Grecia is reputed to be Costa Rica's cleanest town, but the reason most people stop there is to admire its unusual church. The brick-red, prefabricated iron **Iglesia** (Church) overlooks a small, sparsely shaded **Parque Central.** The church was one of two buildings in the country made from steel frames imported from Belgium in the 1890s (the other is the metal schoolhouse next to San José's Parque Morazán), when some prominent Costa Ricans decided that metal structures would better withstand the periodic earthquakes that had taken their toll on so much of the country's architecture. The pieces of metal were shipped from Antwerp to Limón, then transported by train to Alajuela—from which point the church was carried, appropriately, by oxcarts. ⊠ *Avda. 1, between Cs. 1 and 3* ☉ *Daily 8–4.*

On a small farm outside Grecia, the **Mundo de las Serpientes** (World of Serpents) is a good place to see some of the snakes that you are unlikely—and probably don't want—to spot in the wild. Sequestered in the safety of cages here are some 50 varieties of serpents, as well as crocodiles, iguanas, Poison Dart Frogs, and various other cold-blooded creatures. Admission includes a 90-minute tour, and if you want your guide to take something out of its cage for petting or photographing, just ask. ⊠ *2 km (1 mi) east of Grecia, on road to Alajuela* ☎ *494–3700* 🖃 *$11* ☉ *Daily 8–4.*

Where to Stay

★ **$$–$$$** 🏨 **Vista del Valle Plantation Inn.** Honeymooners frequent this B&B on an orange and coffee plantation outside Grecia overlooking the canyon of the Río Grande. Cottages are decorated in minimalist style with simple wooden furniture and sliding French doors that open onto small porches. Each has its own personality; the Nido, removed from the rest and with the nicest decor, is the most romantic. The hotel's forest reserve has an hour-long trail leading down to a waterfall. Breakfast is served by the pool or in the main house, where you can relax in a spacious living room. The food is quite good, and special dietary requests are accommodated with advance notice. It's a mere 20-minute drive from the airport. ⊠ *On highway, 1 km (½ mi) west of Rafael Iglesia Bridge; follow signs* 🕭 *c/o M. Bresnan, SJO–1994, Box 025216 Miami, FL 33102-5216* ☎ *450–0800* 🖷 *451–1165* ⊕ *www.vistadelvalle.com* 🛏 *2 rooms, 10 cottages* 🍴 *Restaurant, fans, pool, hot tub, hiking, horseback riding, travel services; no a/c, no room phones, no room TVs* 🖃 *AE, MC, V* ⟐ *BP.*

The Outdoors

BUNGEE JUMPING Just west of the turnoff for Grecia on the Inter-American Highway, down a dirt road on the right, an old metal bridge spans a forested gorge over the Río Colorado. It is here that **Tropical Bungee** (⊠ *2 km (1 mi) west of Grecia exit on Inter-American Highway* ☎ *290–5629* ☉ *Daily 8–4*) offers the adrenaline rush of bungee jumping in a tranquil, tropical setting. Even if you aren't up for the plunge, it's worth stopping to watch a few mad souls do it.

Sarchí

❿ *8 km (5 mi) west of Grecia, 53 km (33 mi) northwest of San José.*

Tranquil little Sarchí is spread over a collection of hills surrounded by coffee plantations. Though many of its inhabitants are farmers, Sarchí is also one of Costa Rica's centers for crafts and carpentry. People drive here from all over Central Costa Rica to shop for furniture, and caravans of tour buses regularly descend upon the souvenir shops outside town. Local artisans work native hardwoods into bowls, boxes, toys, platters, and even jewelry, but the area's most famous products are its brightly colored oxcarts—replicas of those traditionally used to transport coffee. Trucks and tractors have largely replaced oxcarts on Costa Rican farms, but the little wagons retain their place in local folklore and can be spotted everywhere from small-town parades to postcards.

The **church** dates only from the 1950s and is not particularly elaborate, but it is a colorful structure with several statues of angels on its facade and a simple interior with some nice woodwork. Flanked by small gardens, the church faces a multilevel park in which a brightly decorated oxcart is displayed under its own roof. ⊠ *Center of town, across from the park.*

The town's only real oxcart factory, **Taller Eloy Alfaro e Hijos** (Eloy Alfaro and Sons Workshop), was founded in 1923, and its carpentry methods have changed little since then. The two-story wooden building housing the wood shop is surrounded by trees and flowers—usually orchids—and all the machinery on the ground floor is powered by a waterwheel at the back of the shop. Carts are painted in back, and although the factory's main product is a genuine oxcart—which sells for about $2,000—there are also some smaller mementos that can easily be shipped home. ⊠ *200 m north of soccer field* ☎ *No phone* 🖂 *Donations accepted* ☉ *Weekdays 8–4.*

Shopping

Sarchí is the best place in Costa Rica to buy miniature oxcarts, the larger of which are designed to serve as patio bars and can be broken down for easy transport or shipped to your home. Another popular item is a locally produced rocking chair with a leather seat and back. There's one store just north of town, and several larger complexes to the south. The nicest is the **Chaverri Factory** (⊠ Main road, about 2 km [1 mi] south of Sarchí ☎ 454–4944), and you can wander through its workshops (in back) to see the artisans in action. Chaverri is a good place to buy wooden crafts; nonwood products are cheaper in San José. Chaverri also runs a restaurant next door, **Las Carretas,** which serves international meals all day and has a good lunch buffet. The street behind the Taller Eloy factory comes alive on Friday for the local **farmers' market.**

San Ramón

⓫ *23 km (14 mi) west of Sarchí, 59 km (36 mi) northwest of San José.*

Having produced a number of minor bards, San Ramón is known locally as the City of Poets, and you may well be tempted to wax lyrical yourself as you gaze at the facade of its church or stroll through its tidy Parque Central. As pleasant a little town as it may be, however, San Ramón hides its real attractions in the countryside to the north, on the road to

La Fortuna, where comfortable nature lodges offer access to private nature preserves.

Aside from the poets, the massive **Iglesia de San Ramón,** built in a mixture of the Romanesque and Gothic styles, is the city's claim to fame. In 1924 an earthquake destroyed the smaller adobe church that once stood here, and the city lost no time in creating a replacement—this great gray concrete structure took a quarter of a century to complete, from 1925 to 1954. To ensure that the second church would be earthquake-proof, workers poured the concrete around a steel frame that was designed and forged in Germany (by Krupp). Step past the formidable facade and you'll discover a bright, elegant interior. ⊠ *Across from Parque Central* ☎ *445-5592* ☉ *Daily 6–11:30* AM *and 1:30–7* PM.

Where to Stay & Eat

$–$$ ✕ **La Colina.** This roadside diner, with its requisite lime-green plastic chairs, offers an eclectic menu with some typical and some not-so-typical entrées. Start your meal with a delicious ceviche, moving on to the famous rice and chicken or, for the brave at heart, *lengua en salsa* (tongue in tomato sauce). Meals begin with complimentary chips and pickled vegetables. ⊠ *2 km (1 mi) west of San Ramón, Carretera a Puntarenas* ☎ *445–4956* ═ *AE, DC, MC, V.*

$$ ✕⌂ **Valle Escondido.** "Hidden Valley" lies within an ornamental plant farm at the edge of a 250-acre forest preserve. You could spend days exploring the 20 km (12 mi) of trails, which wind through primary forest past waterfalls and giant trees, or going on horseback rides and canopy tours. The rooms lack personality, but are spacious and have covered porches with wonderful views of a forested mountainside. Two restaurants ($–$$$), one by the road and one near the rooms, serve high-quality international fare, especially the Italian dishes such as fettuccine *a lo Marco* (with a shrimp cream sauce). You're welcome to hike in the preserve even if you just stop for lunch, which is a good option if you're traveling to or from Arenal. ⊠ *Road between San Ramón and La Fortuna, 32 km (19 mi) north of San Ramón* ⌂ *Apdo. 452–1150, La Uruca* ☎ *231–0906 or 475–1082* ⊟ *232–9591* ⊕ *www. hotelvalleescondido.net* ⇆ *33 rooms* ⌂ *Restaurant, fans, pool, hot tub, hiking, horseback riding, laundry service; no a/c, no room TVs* ═ *AE, MC, V* ⍓ *CP.*

★ $$ ⌂ **Villablanca.** Built by former Costa Rican president Rodrigo Carazo, this charming hotel is on a working dairy and coffee farm. The farm-house contains the reception desk, bar, and restaurant; down the hill are lovely casitas, which are tiny replicas of traditional adobe farmhouses complete with whitewashed walls, tile floors, cane ceilings, and fireplaces. Resident guides lead nature walks through the adjacent cloud-forest reserve, which is excellent bird-watching territory. Horses are available for exploring the rest of the farm. ⊠ *20 km (12 mi) north of San Ramón on road to La Fortuna* ⌂ *Apdo. 247–1250, Escazú* ☎ *228–4603 or 461–0301* ⊟ *228–4004* ⊕ *www.villablanca-costarica.com* ⇆ *43 casitas* ⌂ *Restaurant, hiking, horseback riding, bar, shop; no a/c, no room phones, no room TVs* ═ *AE, DC, MC, V* ⍓ *BP.*

THE EASTERN CENTRAL VALLEY

East of San José are Costa Rica's highest volcano and the remains of both the country's most important archaeological site and its oldest church. The region's ecological attractions include a botanical garden, a protected cloud forest, and a spectacular white-water river. Cartago, due east of San José, was the country's first capital, and thus has scattered historical structures and the impressive Basílica de Los Angeles. To the north of Cartago towers massive Irazú Volcano, which is covered with farmland and topped by an impressive crater; to the east is the tamed and labeled jungle of Lankester Botanical Garden.

Cartago

⑫ *22 km (14 mi) southeast of San José.*

Although it's a small city, Cartago was the country's first capital and held that title for almost three centuries. It's much older than San José, but earthquakes have destroyed most of its colonial structures, leaving just a few interesting buildings among the concrete boxes. Cartago became Costa Rica's second most prominent city in 1823, when the seat of government was moved to the emerging economic center of San José. You'll see some attractive old buildings as you move through town, most of them erected after the 1910 quake. The majority of the architecture in tiny Cartago is bland, with one impressive exception: the gaudy Basílica de Nuestra Señora de Los Angeles.

The devastating earthquake of 1910 prevented completion of the central Romanesque cathedral. **Las Ruinas** (the ruins) of this unfinished house of worship now stand in a pleasant central park planted with tall pines and bright bougainvillea. ✉ *C. 1 and Avda. 2.*

The **Basílica de Nuestra Señora de los Angeles** (Our Lady of the Angels Basilica), 10 blocks east of the central square, is a hodgepodge of architectural styles from Baroque to Byzantine, with a dash of Gothic. The interior is even more striking, with a colorful tile floor, intricately decorated wood columns, and lots of stained glass. It's also the focus of an amazing annual pilgrimage: the night of August 1 and well into the early morning hours of the second, the road from San José clogs with worshippers, some of whom have traveled from as far away as Nicaragua, on their way to celebrate the 1635 appearance of La Negrita (the Black Virgin), Costa Rica's patron saint. At a spring behind the church, people fill bottles with water believed to have curative properties. Miraculous healing powers are attributed to the saint herself, and devotees have placed thousands of tiny symbolic crutches, ears, eyes, and legs next to her diminutive statue in recognition of her gifts. The constant arrival of tour buses and school groups, along with shops selling candles and bottles of holy water in the shape of La Negrita, makes the scene a bit of a circus. The statue has twice been stolen, most recently in 1950 by José León Sánchez, now one of Costa Rica's best-known novelists, who spent 20 years on the prison island of San Lucas for having purloined the Madonna. ✉ *C. 16, between Avdas. 2 and 4* ☎ *551–0465* ⊙ *Daily 6 AM–7 PM.*

Volcán Irazú

★ ⑬   *31 km (19 mi) northeast of Cartago, 50 km (31 mi) east of San José.*

Volcán Irazú is Costa Rica's highest volcano, at 11,260 feet, and its summit has long been protected as a national park. The mountain looms to the north of Cartago, and its eruptions have dumped considerable ash on the city over the centuries. The most recent eruptive period lasted from 1963 to 1965, beginning the day John F. Kennedy arrived in Costa Rica for a presidential visit. Boulders and mud rained down on the countryside, damming rivers and causing serious floods. Although farmers who cultivate Irazú's slopes live in fear of the next eruption, they're also grateful for the soil's richness, a result of the volcanic deposits.

The road to the summit climbs past vegetable fields, pastures, and native oak forests. You'll pass through the villages of Potrero Cerrado and San Juan de Chicoá before reaching the summit's bleak but beautiful **crater.** Irazú is currently dormant, but the gases and steam that billow from fumaroles on the northwestern slope are sometimes visible from the peak above the crater lookouts. Head up as early in the morning as possible—before the summit is enveloped in clouds—to see the chartreuse crater lake and, if you're lucky, views of nearby mountains and either the Pacific or Caribbean in the distance. There are no trails at the summit, but a paved road leads all the way to the top, where a small coffee shop offers hot beverages to warm up intrepid visitors. Here you can also find a tiny visitor's kiosk, which is open only on occasion. Before reaching the park's main entrance, about 1 km (½ mi) from the village of Potrero Cerrado, Volcán Irazú's **Area Recreativa de Prusia** (Prusia Recreation Area) has hiking trails through oak and pine forest and picnic areas in case you've packed your own supplies. Admission at either entrance allows entry to both sectors of Volcán Irazú. Bring warm, waterproof clothing for your time on the summit. ✉ *Carretera a Irazú; signs from Cartago lead you to the park* ☎ *551–9398, 192 in Costa Rica* ✑ *$7* ⊙ *Daily 8–3:30.*

Where to Eat

¢–$ ✕ **Restaurant 1910.** Decorated with vintage photos of turn-of-the-20th-century buildings and landscapes, this restaurant documents the disastrous 1910 earthquake that rocked this area and all but destroyed the colonial capital of Cartago. The menu is predominantly Costa Rican, with such traditional specialties as pozol and arroz con pollo, but they also have some less common dishes, such as a corvina fillet with béarnaise sauce. ✉ *Road to Parque Nacional Volcán Irazú; 300 m north of Cot–Pacayas turnoff* ☎ *536–6063* ▭ *AE, MC, V.*

Paraíso

⑭   *8 km (5 mi) east of Cartago.*

Many a visitor has wondered, upon first seeing this dreary town of concrete-block buildings and crowded roads, how it ever ended up with so prodigious a name as "Paradise." But you need merely drive a couple of kilometers south from the central park and gaze down at the vast Orosi Valley to understand what inspired the town's founders. For travelers, Paraíso is on the map for only two reasons: it is the gateway to Orosi, and it has one of the country's best botanical gardens.

If you're into plants, especially orchids, be sure to visit the **Jardín Lankester** (Lankester Botanical Garden). Created in the 1950s by British naturalist Charles Lankester to help preserve the local flora, it's now maintained by the University of Costa Rica. The lush garden and greenhouses contain one of the largest orchid collections in the world—more than 800 native and introduced species. Orchids are mostly epiphytes, meaning they use other plants for support without damaging them in the process. Bromeliads, heliconias, and aroids also abound, along with 80 species of trees, including rare palms, bamboo, torch ginger, and other ornamentals. The diversity of plant life attracts many birds. The best time to come here is January through April, when the most orchids are in bloom. To reach the gardens, drive through the center of Cartago, turn right at the Basílica, then left on the busy road to Paraíso and Orosi. After 6 km (4 mi), an orange sign on the right marks the garden's short dirt road. ⊠ *About 300 m off the road from Cartago to Paraíso, to the right, Dulce Nombre; 6 km (4 mi) east of Cartago, 2 km (1 mi) west of Paraíso* ☎ *552–3247* ✆ *$5* ☉ *Daily 8:30–4:30.*

Where to Eat

$–$$ ✕ **Sanchiri Mirador.** On a hillside high above the Orosi Valley, this rustic restaurant's greatest asset is its amazing view. The large, open-air dining room, half of which is semi-enclosed with windows, has simple wooden chairs and flowery tablecloths, but your gaze is bound to be fixed on the vista. The menu is dominated by such Costa Rican standards as *olla de carne* (beef and tuber stew) and arroz con pollo, but they also offer some original dishes, such as *chuleta en salsa tamarindo* (pork chop with a tamarind sauce) and corvina *tucurrique* (in a pejibaye sauce). On the premises are a small butterfly farm and 10 wooden cabinas for rent, three of which share the restaurant's valley view. ⊠ *2 km (1 mi) south of Parque Central* ☎ *574–5454* ⊟ *AE, DC, MC, V* ☉ *No dinner.*

Shopping

The **gift shop** (☎ 552–3247) in Jardín Lankester is one of the few places in Costa Rica where you can buy orchids that you can take home legally: along with the endangered plants comes a CITES certificate—a sort of orchid passport—that lets you ferry them across international borders without any customs problems. These orchids come in small bottles and don't flower for four years, so you'll need some serious patience.

en route To get to the Orosi Valley, turn right when you reach Paraíso's shady Parque Central. If you turn left at the *bomberos* (fire station), which houses some splendid old-style fire engines, you'll be on your way to Ujarrás; if you go straight, you'll wind your way down a steep slope to the town of Orosi, beyond which is Tapantí National Park. Whichever route you choose, you'll eventually end up back at the same intersection, since the two roads join in a loop. As you approach the valley, keep your eyes open for a *mirador,* or lookout point, with covered picnic tables perched on top of the canyon.

THE OROSI VALLEY

2 km (1 mi) south of Paraíso; 8 km (4 mi) southeast of Cartago; 30 km (19 mi) southeast of San José.

This area of breathtaking views and verdant landscapes holds remnants of both the colonial era and the tropical forest that covered the country when the Spanish first arrived. The valley was one of the earliest parts of Costa Rica to be settled by Spanish colonists—in the 17th century, as ruins and a colonial church attest. Rich soil and proximity to San José have combined to make this an important agricultural area, with extensive plantations of coffee, chayote, and other vegetables. The valley is fed in the west by the confluence of the Navarro and Orosi rivers and drained in the east by the ferocious Reventazón. A dam built in the 1970s to create one of the country's first hydroelectric projects formed the Lago de Cachí, or Cachí Reservoir. The two roads that descend into the Orosi Valley come together at the dam that forms the Cachí Reservoir. The two roads that descend into the Orosi Valley come together at the dam that forms the Cachí Reservoir, thus creating a loop through the valley that passes dozens of coffee plantations and several small towns before meeting at the Represa de Cachi(Cachí Dam).

Ujarrás

⑮ *10 km (6 mi) southeast of Paraíso, 18 km (11 mi) southeast of Cartago.*

The ruins of Costa Rica's oldest church, **Iglesia de Ujarrás,** stand in a small park at the site of the former town of Ujarrás, on the floor of the Orosi Valley, just down the hill from Paraíso. Built between 1681 and 1693 in honor of the Virgin of Ujarrás, the church, together with the surrounding village, was abandoned in 1833 after a series of earthquakes and floods. An unlikely Spanish victory in 1666 over a superior force of invading British pirates was attributed to a prayer stop here. Today it's a pleasant monument surrounded by well-kept gardens and large trees, which often attract flocks of parakeets and parrots. ⊠ *From Cartago, follow signs on Hwy. 224 to Paraíso and Cachí; ruins are 1 km (¼ mi) from Restaurante Típico Ujarrás* ⊙ *Daily 8–5.*

Cachí

⑯ *9 km (5 mi) southeast of Paraíso, 6 km (3 mi) east of Ujarrás, 10 km (6 mi) east of Orosi.*

Amid coffee farms on the eastern end of the Orosi Valley, the village of Cachí survives on two industries: coffee and electricity. In the 1960s, the national power company, ICE, dammed the Reventazón River near Cahcí to create a reservoir for what was once the country's biggest hydroelectric project. The Represa de Cachí (Cachí Dam) is the closest thing the town has to a tourist attraction, and is worth stopping at for the view of the reservoir and narrow Reventazón Valley, but most people stop here to eat at the Casona del Cafetal, just north of town.

Where to Eat

★ **$–$$** ✕ **La Casona del Cafetal.** The valley's best lunch stop is on a coffee plantation overlooking the Cachí Reservoir. Its name translates as "The Big House of the Coffee Field." The spacious brick building has a high, barrel-tile roof, with tables indoors and on a tiled portico on the lake side. The menu is predominantly Costa Rican, with such staples as the casado, but inventive dishes are also available, such as *arroz tucurrique* (baked rice with cheese and heart of palm) and corvina *jacaranda* (stuffed with shrimp). A gift shop sells local coffee, wood sculptures, and other souvenirs. ⊠ *2 km (1 mi) south of Cachí Dam; 6 km (4 mi) east of Ujarrás* ☎ *577–1414* ▭ *AE, MC, V* ☉ *No dinner.*

Shopping

The unique **Casa del Soñador** (House of the Dreamer; ⊠ 1 km [½ mi] south of the Cachí Dam on the main road through the valley ☎ 533–3297) was built by local wood sculptor Macedonio Quesada. Though Macedonio died years ago, his son and a former apprentice are still here, carving interesting, often comical little statues out of coffee wood. The **Casona del Cafetal** (⊠ 2 km [1 mi] south of Cachí Dam ☎ 577–1414) sells similar sculptures to those fashioned at Casa del Soñador that have been carved from coffee roots by yet another apprentice of Macedonio Quesada. His name is José Luís Sojo, and he also carves the huge totem poles depicting coffee harvesting that are displayed at the restaurant.

Orosi

🔟 *7 km (4½ mi) south of Paraíso, 35 km (22 mi) southeast of San José.*

The town of Orosi, in the heart of the valley, has but one major attraction: a beautifully restored **colonial church.** Built in 1743, the structure has a low-slung whitewashed facade; the roof is made of cane overlaid with terra-cotta barrel tiles. Inside are an antique wooden altar and ancient paintings of the stations of the cross and the Virgin of Guadalupe, all brought to Costa Rica from Mexico. The **museum** in the cloister annex has a small collection of old religious regalia, polychrome wood carvings, and colonial furniture. ⊠ *Across from soccer field* ☎ *No phone* ▧ *Church free; museum 50¢* ☉ *Church daily 9–5; museum hrs vary (ask around for someone to open it).*

The **Balneario** (Thermal Baths), fed by a hot spring, are open to the public for a nominal fee. ⊠ *South of Orosi on road to Orosi Lodge* ▧ *Less than $1* ☉ *Wed.–Mon. 10–6.*

Where to Stay

$ 🛏 **Orosi Lodge.** Run by a German couple who have built a warm rapport with the community, the little lodge blends in with Orosi's pretty, old-town architecture with its whitewashed walls trimmed in blue, high ceilings, and lovely use of natural wood. Local artisans provided some of the furnishings, such as the clay lamps in each room. The lodge's bright, airy coffee shop looks out onto the town's main square, and Latin music usually plays from an authentic 1960s jukebox in the foyer. The simple rooms have wood floors and wicker headboards, but common areas are colorful, with lots of painting and sculpture by local artisans. Rooms on the second floor have views of the Orosi Valley and Volcán Irazú. ⊠ *50 m east of the Balneario* ⵠ *Apdo. 1122–7050, Cartago* 🏠 *533–3578* ⊕ *www.orosilodge.com* 🛏 *6 rooms* ⌂ *Dining room, fans, kitchenettes, minibars, mountain bikes, travel services; no a/c, no room phones, no room TVs* ▭ *AE, MC, V.*

Tapantí National Park

★ **⑱** *14 km (8 mi) south of Orosi, 30 km (18 mi) southeast of Cartago.*

Stretching from the southern corner of the Orosi Valley up into the Talamanca Mountains, Parque Nacional Tapantí encompasses a 47-square-km (18-square-mi) preserve, the bulk of which is pristine, remote wilderness. The 14-km (8-mi) rugged track that runs from Orosi to Tapantí follows the course of the Río Grande de Orosi past coffee plantations, elegant *fincas* (farmhouses), and seasonal barracks for coffee pickers before it's hemmed in by the steep slopes of thick jungle. That luxuriant cloud forest provides refuge for more than 350 bird species, including the Emerald Toucanet, Violaceous Trogon, most of the country's hummingbirds, and the spectacular Resplendent Quetzal. Quetzals are most readily visible in the dry season (mid-December to April), when they mate; ask the park rangers where to look for them.

The rangers' office and visitor center are on the right just after the park entrance. You can leave your vehicle 1½ km (1 mi) up the road, at a parking area where trails head off into the woods on both sides. The Sendero Oropéndola trail leads to two loops. The first loop passes a picnic area and several swimming holes with brisk but inviting emerald waters. The trail on the other side of the parking lot forms a loop along a forested hillside. Farther up from the parking area, about 2½ km (1½ mi), is an entrance to the La Pava Trail on the right. This trail leads down a steep hill to the riverbank. Several miles farther up the road from La Pava is a lovely view of a long, slender cascade on the far right of the valley.

Since the park clouds up in the afternoon, it's best to get an early start. Staying at the nearby lodge or in Orosi are your best options. Taxis that carry as many as five people can be hired for the trip at Orosi's soccer field. Camping is permitted. ☎ *551–2970, 192 in Costa Rica* 🎫 *$7* ⊘ *Weekdays 8–4, weekends 7–5.*

¢ 🏨 **Kiri Mountain Lodge.** This small, family-run hotel not only offers easy access to the park, but also has its own 123-acre private reserve that is home to most of the same wildlife seen at the park. A 3-km trail into the reserve passes two waterfalls. The number of bird species in the lodge's gardens is impressive, especially the abundant hummingbirds. The rooms are small and simple, with tile floors and tiny bathrooms, but they open onto porches with views of a steep, jungle-laden hillside. The restaurant serves complimentary breakfasts and a small selection of Costa Rican food; fresh trout, raised in nearby ponds, is the best option. ⊠ *12 km*

(7 mi) southeast of Orosi, 2 km (1 mi) south of Tapantí entrance ☎ *533–2272* 🖷 *257–8065* 🛏 *8 rooms* ⚒ *Restaurant, hiking, laundry service; no a/c, no room phones, no room TVs.* ▭ *MC, V* ⑩ *BP.*

Turrialba & the Guayabo Ruins

The agricultural center of Turrialba and the nearby Guayabo ruins lie considerably lower than the Central Valley, so they enjoy a more tropical climate. There are two ways to reach this area from San José, both of which pass spectacular scenery. The more direct route, accessible by heading east through both Cartago and Paraíso, winds through coffee and sugar plantations before descending abruptly into Turrialba. For the second route, turn off the road between Cartago and the summit of Irazú near the town of Cot. That narrow route twists along the slopes of Irazú and Turrialba volcanoes past some stunning scenery—stately pollarded trees lining the road, riotous patches of tropical flowers, and white-girder bridges across crashing streams. From Santa Cruz, a hiking trail leads up to the 10,900-foot summit of Volcán Turrialba. As you begin the descent to Turrialba town, the temperature rises and neat rows of coffee bushes blanket the slopes.

Turrialba

⑲ *58 km (36 mi) east of San José.*

The relatively well-to-do agricultural center of Turrialba (population 30,000) suffered when the main San José–Puerto Limón route was diverted through Guápiles in the late 1970s. The demise of the famous Jungle Train that connected these two cities was an additional blow. But today, because of the beautiful scenery and a handful of upscale nature lodges, ecotourism is beginning to make inroads and has begun to revamp the stagnant economy. Though pleasant enough, Turrialba doesn't have much to offer, but the surrounding countryside hides some spectacular scenery and patches of rain forest. Turrialba is also near two of Costa Rica's best white-water rivers—the Pacuare and Reventazón—which explains why kayakers and rafters flock here. Serious water enthusiasts, including the white-water Olympic kayaking teams from a handful of countries, stay all winter.

off the beaten path

CENTRO AGRONÓMICO TROPICAL DE INVESTIGACIÓN Y ENSEÑANZA (Center for Tropical Agricultural Research and Education) – Known by its acronym, CATIE is one of the leading tropical research centers in the world, drawing students and experts from all over the Americas. The 8-square-km (3-square-mi) property includes modern labs and offices, landscaped grounds, seed-conservation chambers, greenhouses, orchards, experimental agricultural projects, a large swath of rain forest, and lodging for students and teachers. A muddy trail leads down into the forest behind the administration building, where you can see some of the biggest rapids on the Reventazón River. CATIE is also a good place to bird-watch; you might even catch sight of the Yellow-winged Northern

Jacana or the Purple Gallinule in the lagoon near the main building. Call ahead to reserve a free tour. ⊠ *Just outside Turrialba, on the road to Siquirres* ☎ 556–6431 🖷 556–1533 ☞ *Free* ⊙ *Daily 7–4.*

Where to Stay

$$$$ 🏨 **Rancho Naturalista.** Customized guided horseback and bird-watching tours within a 125-acre private nature reserve are the reasons to stay here. Three hundred species of birds and thousands of different kinds of moths and butterflies live on the reserve, and a resident ornithologist helps you see and learn as much as you want. The two-story lodge is upscale modern with rustic touches, as are its two separate cabins. Good home cooking is served in the indoor and outdoor dining rooms, both of which have beautiful views of Volcán Irazú and Turrialba Valley. Rates include guided tours. ⊠ *20 km southeast of Turrialba, 1½ km (1 mi) along a semipaved road from Tuís* 🖹 *SBO 840, Box 025292, Miami, FL 33102* ☎ *433–8278, 888/246–8513 in U.S.* 🖷 *433–4925* ⊕ *www.ranchonaturalista.com* ⮎ *14 rooms, 11 with bath* ⚭ *Dining room, horseback riding, Internet; no smoking, no a/c, no room phones, no room TVs* 🖃 *No credit cards* ⦿ *FAP.*

★ **$$** 🏨 **Casa Turire.** Backed by a sugar plantation and overlooking an artificial lake, this timeless hotel looks like a manor house that has survived mysteriously intact from the turn of the 20th century. In fact, it's the product of more recent imaginations. From the royal palms that line the driveway to the tall columns and tile floors, Casa Turire is an exercise in elegance and attention to detail. High-ceilinged guest rooms have hardwood floors and furniture, small balconies, and bright bathrooms with tubs. The central courtyard is a civilized spot in which to relax after a day's adventure. ⊠ *12 km (7 mi) north on Carretera a la Suiza from Turrialba, Apdo. 303–7150* ☎ *531–1111* 🖷 *531–1075* ⊕ *www.hotelcasaturire.com* ⮎ *12 rooms, 4 suites* ⚭ *Restaurant, fans, in-room safes, cable TV, pool, hot tub, massage, boating, horseback riding, bar, shop, laundry service, Internet, travel services; no a/c in some rooms* 🖃 *AE, MC, V* ⦿ *BP.*

$ 🏨 **Albergue Volcán Turrialba.** In the slope of the volcano, accessible only by four-wheel-drive vehicle (which the lodge will arrange for a fee), the Albergue has simple but comfortable rooms. You'll eat well, too: the proprietors serve healthful Costa Rican food cooked on a wood-burning stove. Even more compelling are the tours, one of which goes deep into the Turrialba crater, and another of which visits the fumaroles and thermal waters of Volcán Irazú. Mountain-biking and horseback-riding trips can be arranged, as well as a 10-hour trek from the Volcán Turrialba to Guápiles via Braulio Carrillo National Park. ⊠ *20 km (12 mi) east of Cot, turn right at Pacayas on the road to Volcán Turrialba, 4 km (2½ mi) on dirt road* 🖹 *Apdo. 1632–2050, San José* 🖷 *273–4335* 🖷 *273–0703* ⊕ *www.volcanturrialbalodge.com* ⮎ *22 rooms* ⚭ *Dining room, bar; no a/c, no room phones, no room TVs* 🖃 *AE, DC, MC, V* ⦿ *FAP.*

$ 🏨 **Turrialtico.** Dramatically positioned on a hill overlooking the valley east of Turrialba, this hotel has impressive views of the surrounding countryside. An open-sided restaurant occupies the ground floor, above which are handsome rooms with hardwood floors and colorful

Guatemalan fabrics. Ask for one on the west side—these have dazzling views of Turrialba and, if there are no clouds, Volcán Irazú. The restaurant serves a small selection of authentic Costa Rican dishes cooked on a woodstove. The only problem is that Turrialtico is a breakfast stop for rafting tours. ⊠ *8 km (5 mi) east of Turrialba on road to Siquirres, Apdo. 121–7150* ☎ *538–1111* 🖷 *538–1575* ⊕ *www.turrialtico.com* ↪ *14 rooms* ⚭ *Restaurant, fans, shop, laundry service; no a/c, no room phones, no room TVs* ⊟ *AE, MC, V* ⚭⦿ *BP.*

The Outdoors

RAFTING &
KAYAKING
It's no coincidence that half a dozen Olympic kayaking teams use Turrialba as their winter training ground: it lies conveniently close to two excellent white-water rivers, the Reventazón and the Pacuare. And despite their appeal to the experts, these rivers can also be sampled by neophytes. The **Río Reventazón** flows right past Turrialba and has several navigable stretches; the most popular stretch has unfortunately been cut short by the construction of a dam (the Tucurrique section, Class III). The Florida section (Class III), above Turrialba, is a rip-roaring alternative for inexperienced rafters.

Fodor'sChoice
★
Just southeast of Turrialba is the **Río Pacuare**, Costa Rica's most spectacular white-water route, which provides rafters with an unforgettable, exhilarating, adrenaline-pumping experience. The 32-km (20-mi) Pacuare run includes a series of Class III and IV rapids with evocative nicknames such as Double Drop, Burial Grounds, and Magnetic Rock. The astoundingly beautiful scenery includes lush canyons where waterfalls plummet into the river and vast expanses of rain forest. Stretches of the Pacuare stood in for Africa in the otherwise forgettable 1995 film *Congo.* That riverine landscape is inhabited by toucans, kingfishers, oropéndolas, and other birds—along with Blue Morpho butterflies, the odd river otter, and other interesting critters. The rafting outfitters Aventuras Naturales and Ríos Tropicales have their own lodges on the river, making them the best options for two- and three-day trips that include jungle hikes.

For details on rafting or kayaking both the Pacuare and Reventazón rivers, contact **Aventuras Naturales** (☎ 225–3939 or 224–0505 🖷 253–6934 ⊕ www.toenjoynature.com). White-water adventures on the Pacuare and Reventazón are also available through the San José–based **Costa Rica Whitewater** (☎ 257–0766 🖷 255–4354 ⊕ www.costaricaexpeditions.com). The Turrialba-based **Rainforest World** (☎ 556–2678 ⊕ www.rforestw. com) specializes in white-knuckle trips on the Pacuare and Reventazón rivers. **Ríos Tropicales** (☎ 233–6455 🖷 255–4354 ⊕ www.riostropicales. com) is a San José–based operator with day tours and multiple-day rafting adventures on the Pacuare and Reventazón.

Guayabo National Monument

★ ❷⓪ *19 km (12 mi) north of Turrialba, 72 km (45 mi) east of San José.*

On the slopes of Volcán Turrialba is Monumento Nacional Guayabo, Costa Rica's most significant archaeological site. In 1968 a local landowner was out walking her dogs when she discovered what she thought was a tomb. A friend, archaeologist Carlos Piedra, began excavating the site and unearthed the base wall of a chief's house in what eventually turned out to be the ruins of a large community (around 20,000 inhabitants) covering 49 acres. The city was abandoned in AD 1400, probably because of disease or starvation. A guided tour in Spanish takes you through the rain forest to a mirador from which you can see the layout of the excavated circular buildings. Only the raised foundations survive, since the conical houses themselves were built of wood. As you descend into the ruins, notice the well-engineered surface and covered aqueducts leading to a trough of drinking water that still functions today. Next you'll pass the end of an 8-km (5-mi) paved walkway used to transport the massive building stones—abstract patterns carved on the stones continue to baffle archaeologists, but some clearly depict jaguars, which were revered by Indians as deities. The hillside jungle is captivating, and the trip is further enhanced by bird-watching possibilities: sacklike nests of oropéndolas hang from many of the trees. The last few miles of the road are in such bad shape that you'll need a four-wheel-drive vehicle to get here. Camping is allowed near the ranger station. ☎ 556–9507, 192 in Costa Rica ⌷ $7 ☉ Daily 8–3:30.

CENTRAL COSTA RICA A TO Z

To research prices, get advice from other travelers, and book travel arrangements, visit www.fodors.com.

AIRPORTS & TRANSFERS

The Aeropuerto Internacional Juan Santamaría is 16 km (10 mi) northwest of downtown San José, just outside Alajuela.

🔢 Airport Information **Aeropuerto Internacional Juan Santamaría** ✉ 16 km (10 mi) northwest of downtown San José just outside Alajuela ☎ 443–2942.

AIRPORT TRANSFERS You can get taxis from the airport to any point in Central Costa Rica for $8 to $50, though most rides should cost $12 to $15. Immediately upon departing the airport, you'll see a booth where you can hire a taxi to anywhere in the country. Some hotels can arrange a pickup for you when you reserve your room. Buses leave the airport for Alajuela several times an hour; from Alajuela you can catch buses to Grecia, Sarchí, and San Ramón. Less frequent buses (one to three per hour) serve Heredia. To travel between the airport and Escazú, Cartago, or Turrialba, you have to change buses in San José.

BUS TRAVEL

AROUND SAN JOSÉ Buses leave for Escazú from San José (Avda. 6, between Cs. 12 and 14) every 20 minutes, and can be caught at the western end of Paseo Colón. Buses to Santa Ana depart from the Terminal Coca-Cola (⇨ Bus Travel *in* San José A to Z, Chapter 1) every 20 minutes, and can also be caught at the western end of Paseo Colón. Buses begin the 30-minute trip to Heredia, from C. 1, between Avdas. 7 and 9, and from Avda. 2, between Cs. 10 and 12, every 10–15 minutes.

Departures for Alajuela, a 20-minute ride, are from Avda. 2, between Cs. 12 and 14, with TUASA bus lines, which depart daily every 10 minutes 6 AM–7 PM, and every 40 minutes 7 PM–10:30 PM. Buses travel between Alajuela's and Heredia's main bus stations every half hour. To reach Zoo Ave, take the bus to La Garita, which departs every hour from the Terminal de Buses in Alajuela.

For a 20-minute trip to Volcán Barva, take the Paso Llano bus from Heredia with the Rapidos Heredianos bus line, and get off at Sacramento crossroads; the first bus is at 6:30 AM. Note: some Paso Llano buses go only as far as San José de la Montaña, adding an hour to the hike; ask the driver to make sure you're on the right bus. TUASA also has an excursion bus for Volcán Poás that departs San José daily at 8:30 AM from C. 12, between Avdas. 2 and 4 (a 90-minute ride), and returns at 2:30 PM.

WEST OF ALAJUELA Departures for the 40-minute trip to Grecia leave every 30 minutes on the TUAN bus line from the Terminal Coca-Cola. Direct buses to Sarchí on TUAN take 1½ hours and leave from the Terminal Coca-Cola at 12:15 and 5:30. To get to Sarchí (or Grecia), it is more convenient to take a TUAN bus first to Naranjo—these buses depart from the Coca-Cola station every 30 minutes—and then transfer to a Sarchí bus, which departs every hour from Naranjo.

Buses for the one-hour ride to San Ramón with Empresarios Unidos leave from the Terminal de Puntarenas (⇨ Bus Travel *in* San José A to Z, Chapter 1) every hour 6 AM to 7 PM. Direct buses to Sarchí depart from Alajuela (C. 8, between Avdas. 1 and 3) every 30 minutes 6 AM–9 PM; the ride takes 90 minutes. Buses traveling between San José and Grecia or San Ramón pick up passengers on the southern edge of Alajuela (C. 4 at Avda. 10). Departures for Grecia and Sarchí leave from Naranjo, from Naranjo's Terminal de Buses, hourly 6 AM–7 PM. Both trips are a 15-minute hop.

THE EASTERN CENTRAL VALLEY SACSA buses leave San José for the 45-minute trip to Cartago from C. 5 and Avda. 18 every 10 minutes daily; going from Cartago to Orosi Valley, Autotransportes Mata buses leave hourly, weekdays 8 AM–2 PM, and weekends 2 PM–7 PM, from the southern side of Las Ruinas in Cartago. An excursion bus, run by Metropoli, departs San José for the two-hour ride to Volcán Irazú every Saturday and Sunday at 8 AM from Avda. 2, between Cs. 1 and 3, across from the Gran Hotel Costa Rica; this bus returns at 1 PM. To visit Jardín Lankester, take the Paraíso bus, which leaves the south side of Cartago's Parque Central every 15 minutes daily.

THE OROSI VALLEY Hourly Autotransportes Mata buses depart from Cartago's southern side of Las Ruinas for a loop around the Orosi Valley, stopping at Orosi, Chachí, and Ujarrás. To reach Tapantí, you'll have to hire a taxi in Orosi.

TURRIALBA & THE GUAYABO RUINS TRANSTUSA buses leave for Turrialba, a two-hour trip, from C. 13, between Avdas. 6 and 8, hourly 8–8. The bus to Guayabo National Monument, a 50-minute ride, leaves once a day from one block south of the bus station in Turrialba, Monday to Saturday at 11 AM and Sunday at 9:30 AM.

🚌 **Bus Companies Autotransportes Mata** ☎ 391-8268. **Empresarios Unidos** ✉ C. 16 at Avda. 12 ☎ 222-0064. **Metropoli** ☎ 272-0651. **Rapidos Heredianos** ✉ C. 1, between Avdas. 7 and 9 ☎ 233-8392. **SACSA** ☎ 233-5350. **TRANSTUSA** ☎ 556-0073. **TUAN** ☎ 494-2139. **TUASA** ☎ 222-5325.

🚌 Bus Terminal **Terminal de Buses** ✉ C. 8, between Avdas. 1 and 3, Alajuela ☎ No phone.

CAR RENTAL

Most of the car-rental agencies in San José (⇨ Car Rental *in* San José A to Z, Chapter 1) have offices in Alajuela, near the airport. They will deliver vehicles and contracts to any of the hotels listed in this chapter, except those in Turrialba, the Orosi Valley, or San Ramón.

CAR TRAVEL

Nearly all points in the western Central Valley can be reached by car. To drive to Escazú from San José, turn left at the western end of Paseo Colón, which ends at the Parque La Sabana. Take the first right, and get off the highway at the first exit. Turn right at the traffic light for San Rafael addresses, and right again at the bottom of the hill for the old road to Santa Ana. A quicker way to reach Santa Ana is to stay on the highway to the third exit.

To reach Heredia, San Antonio de Belén, Alajuela, and points beyond from San José, turn right at the west end of Paseo Colón onto the Inter-American Highway (also called the Carretera General Cañas). For Heredia, turn right off the highway just before it heads onto an overpass, just after the Hotel Irazú (on the right). To get to the center of Heredia, follow that road for several miles, then turn left at the Universidad Nacional; continue straight on this road to reach the Britt Coffee Tour, Museo de Cultura Popular, Sacramento, Barva, and points beyond. At Sacramento the paved road turns to dirt, growing worse as it nears the ranger station. A four-wheel-drive vehicle can make it all the way to the ranger station in the dry season.

The exit for San Antonio de Belén is at an overpass several miles west of the exit for Heredia, by the Cariari Real Mall. For Alajuela, continue west on the highway from the San Antonio turnoff to the airport and turn right. You can reach Grecia by continuing west on the highway past the airport—the turnoff is on the right—or by heading into Alajuela and turning left just before the Alajuela cemetery. For Sarchí, take the highway well past the airport to the turnoff for Naranjo; then veer right just as you enter Naranjo. San Ramón is on the Pan-American Highway west of Grecia; head straight through San Ramón and follow the signs to reach the hotels to the north.

All the attractions in the eastern Central Valley are accessible from San José by driving east on Avenida 2 through San Pedro, then following signs from the intersection to Cartago. Shortly before Cartago, a traffic light marks the beginning of the road up Irazú, with traffic to Cartago veering right. For the Jardín Lankester head straight through Cartago, turning right at the Basílica and left after two blocks; the entrance to the gardens is on the right.

To get to the Orosi Valley, head straight through Cartago, turn right at the Basílica de Los Angeles, and follow the signs to Paraíso. To get to

Ujarrás, Orosi, or Tapantí, turn right at Paraíso's central plaza. A few blocks east, at the fire station, you can either turn left for the Loop Road East to Ujarrás or continue straight to the Loop Road South to Orosi and Tapantí National Park and the route that loops around to Cachí and back to Ujarrás.

The road through Cartago and Paraíso continues east to Turrialba, where you pick up another road a few blocks east of that town's central plaza. Marked by signs, this road leads north to Guayabo National Monument.

EMERGENCIES

In case of any emergency, dial 911, or one of the numbers listed below.

🚩 Emergency Services **Ambulance** ☎ 128. **Fire** ☎ 118. **Police** ☎ 117. **Traffic Police** ☎ 222-9330.

🚩 Hospitals **HospitalCIMA** ✉ next to PriceSmart, Escazú ☎ 208-1000.

🚩 Late-Night Pharmacies **Fischel Pharmacy** ✉ 300 m west of Basílica de Los Angeles, Cartago ☎ 552-2430 ✉ Old highway to Santa Ana, Guachipelían, Escazú ☎ 289-7212 ✉ Mall International, Alajuela ☎ 442-1343 ✉ 25 m south of Parque Central, Heredia ☎ 260-5765.

MAIL & SHIPPING

Every town in Costa Rica has a post office, which is usually facing or near the central plaza, but letters mailed from them tend to take a good bit longer than if they were posted from San José. If you won't be heading through San José, ask the receptionist at your hotel whether mail will be sent to the city soon. Internet cafés are fairly common in Central Costa Rica towns, and tend to charge the equivalent of $1 per hour. Many hotels offer Internet access, but some of them charge as much as $3–$6 per hour.

🚩 Internet Cafés **Cybercafe San Ramón** ✉ 100 m east of Banco Central, San Ramón ☎ 447-9007. **Cyber Izkafe** ✉ Behind Pali supermarket, next to La Taverna bar, Escazú ☎ 289-0082. **Internet Belén** ✉ West of the church, San Antonio de Belén ☎ 293-5572. **Internet Punto Com** ✉ C. Central, Santa Ana ☎ 282-8612.

🚩 Post Offices **Correos de Costa Rica** ✉ Across from Parque Central, Alajuela ☎ 441-8107 ✉ Across from Las Ruinas, Cartago ☎ 552-4595 ✉ Across from Parque Central, Heredia ☎ 260-0461.

MONEY MATTERS

ATMS There are ATMs in just about every one of the Central Valley's towns, and most of them accept both Visa and MasterCard, but some accept only one of the two. ATMs tend to be attached to banks, but shopping centers and some gas stations also have them. Ask your hotel receptionist where the nearest one is. In the unlikely event that it's out of order, you should be able to find another one nearby, in any but the smallest towns.

CURRENCY EXCHANGE Bank branches in all but the tiniest Central Costa Rica towns will exchange U.S. dollars, though it's quicker to get Costa Rican currency from an ATM. Most hotels, restaurants, tour operators, taxi drivers, gift shops, and supermarkets accept or change U.S. dollars, though at slightly less than the bank rate. All non-U.S. currency must be exchanged in banks;

Australian and New Zealand dollars cannot be exchanged anywhere, even in banks.

🏦 Banks **Banex** ✉ 50 m south of Parque Central, Alajuela ☎ 442-5555 ✉ 100 m north and 25 m west of Correos, Heredia ☎ 261-4133 ✉ North side of Colegio San Luis Gonzaga Cartago ☎ 552-8330.

TAXIS

All the Central Valley's towns have taxis, which usually wait for fares along their central parks. Taxis at the central parks of Alajuela, Cartago, and Heredia can take you up to Poás, Irazú, and Barva volcanoes, respectively, but the trips are quite expensive (about $50) unless you can assemble a group. If you don't have a car, the only way to get to Tapantí National Park is to take a cab from Orosi ($15 to $20). Taxis parked near San Ramón's central plaza can take you to the nature lodges north of town. Consult with your hotel's front desk manager, who can sometimes recommend private drivers who charge less, and be sure to always arrange the fee ahead of time.

TOURS

Most San José tour offices can also set you up with guided tours to the Poás and Irazú volcanoes or the Orosi Valley. Swiss Travel is one of the oldest operators in the country. Horizontes offers expertly guided adventure and natural-history tours in Central Costa Rica and beyond. The popular coffee tour run by Café Britt, in Heredia, presents the history of coffee harvesting and drinking via skits, a coffee-farm tour, and a tasting.

🚐 Tour Operators **Café Britt** ✉ 1 km (½ mi) north and 350 m west of Comandancia, Barva de Heredia, Heredia ☎ 260-2748 🖷 260-1456 ⊕ www.cafebritt.com. **Horizontes** ✉ Paseo Colón, 130 m north of Pizza Hut, San José ☎ 222-2022. **Swiss Travel** ✉ Meliá Corobicí hotel lobby, C. 42, between Avdas. 5 and 7, San José ☎ 231-4055.

VISITOR INFORMATION

Visitor Information services are based in San José (⇨ San José A to Z *in* Chapter 1), although hotels are often good local sources of information.

THE NORTHERN ZONE

3

HIGH-STRUNG FUN
The Original Canopy Tour ⇨*p.100, 116*

MOST TEMPESTUOUS VOLCANO
Volcán Arenal ⇨*p.103*

BEST WAY TO HORSE AROUND
On a Lake Arenal trail ride ⇨*p.101*

HOTTEST PLACE TO CHILL
Tabacón Springs and Resort ⇨*p.95, 97*

DAIRY DIVERSION
La Lechería Quaker cheese factory ⇨*p.110*

ATTACK OF THE GIANT TREES
Monteverde Cloud Forest ⇨*p.111*

BEST HOME ON THE RANGE
Los Inocentes Lodge, a working ranch ⇨*p.126*

Updated by
Jeffrey Van
Fleet

THERE AREN'T MANY PLACES ON THE GLOBE WITH CLOUD FORESTS, miles of sun-drenched beaches, and active volcanoes. But here in the northwest, what Costa Ricans call the Zona Norte (Northern Zone), all are within proximity of one another. Beyond the myriad ecosystems of the dry coastal plain are the lush cloud and rain forests of Monteverde; waterfalls, hot springs, and estuaries bursting with life; and the volcanoes and peaks of the Cordillera de Guanacaste, the Cordillera de Tilarán, and sections of the Cordillera Central. From the wetlands of Caño Negro National Wildlife Refuge in the far north to the green farmlands and foothills around La Fortuna and San Carlos, east of Volcán Arenal, this prosperous part of the country has a magnificent landscape and array of things to do in it.

The province of Guanacaste is bordered by Nicaragua and the Pacific Ocean. It derives its name from the broad ear-pod trees that shade the lounging white Brahman cattle so prevalent in the region. An independent province of Spain's colonial empire until 1787, when it was ceded to Nicaragua, Guanacaste became part of Costa Rica in 1814. After their independence in 1821, both Nicaragua and Costa Rica claimed Guanacaste for their own. The Guanacastecos themselves were divided: the provincial capital, Liberia, wanted to return to Nicaragua, whereas rival city Nicoya favored Costa Rica. Nicoya got its way, helped by the fact that at the time the vote was taken, Nicaragua was embroiled in a civil war.

Guanacaste's far-northwestern coastline, still for the most part unblemished, offers everything the Nicoya Peninsula does and more: the dry forests and pristine sands of Santa Rosa National Park, the bird sanctuary of Isla Bolaños, the endless beaches of the Gulf of Santa Elena, and breezy Bahía Salinas. A pair of beachfront resort hotels has set up camp on this part of the coast, but the high-rise tourist-driven development common farther south on the Nicoya has yet to materialize up here.

East of the Carretera Interamericana (Pan-American Highway), Guanacaste's dry plains and forests slope upward into volcano country and the northern sector of the province of Alajuela. Marching northwest to southeast in a rough, formidable line, the volcanoes of the Cordillera de Guanacaste include Orosi, Tenorio, Rincón de la Vieja and its nearby sister Santa María, and Arenal, which looms over the southeast end of man-made Lake Arenal. The northernmost peak in the Cordillera de Tilarán, Arenal ranks as one of the world's most active volcanoes. Coughs that sound like thunder, tufts of smoke, lava flow, and mini-avalanches are perceptible to those who come within 32 km (20 mi) of the place—and many do. Below and between these active and not-so-active craters and calderas, the terrain ranges from dry forest to impassable jungle, from agricultural plain to roadless swamp.

Parks in the province of Guanacaste protect some of the last remnants of the Mesoamerican tropical dry forest that once covered the Pacific lowlands from Costa Rica to the Mexican state of Chiapas. A few of the parks and destinations in this area are relatively accessible from San José, even for day trips. Others require grueling hours of driving over pothole-scarred roads. As you contemplate spending time in this region—

As you plan your travels in this region, know that a fair amount of your time will be spent on the road. That is simply the reality of travel in Costa Rica, and particularly in these spread-out parts.

Numbers in the text correspond to numbers in the margin and on the Northern Zone map.

If you have 3 days

Head northeast out of San José and through the mountains around **Zarcero ❶ ➤**, en route to ☒ **La Fortuna ❸**. The next day, hike to the La Fortuna waterfall; drive to ☒ **Volcán Arenal ❺**, checking out the Tabacón Resort's hot springs; or take a rafting trip on the Río Sarapiquí or the Río Toro. Arrange one of the taxi-boat-taxi connections across the lake for an early trip to Monteverde. Spend the afternoon taking in the unique area attractions—the frog pond, the butterfly garden, a canopy tour—and devote the next morning to exploring the cloud-forest reserve, the earlier the better.

If you have 5 days: parks

Start from San José with a predawn drive to the ☒ **Monteverde Cloud Forest Biological Reserve ➤** and spend a day hiking in the cloud forest. The compelling but smaller Santa Elena Reserve is just down the road (north). Another crack-of-dawn drive will take you to ☒ **Tilarán ❼** by way of the mountain track (four-wheel-drive vehicle only), or via the Pan-American Highway, for an active day on Laguna de Arenal. Stay in Tilarán or in one of the lodges at the lake's north-westerly end. An alternative to a direct trip to Tilarán is a taxi-boat-taxi connection from Monteverde to La Fortuna, where you can arrange a day tour of the **Caño Negro National Wildlife Refuge ❹**. Early the next day return to the highway and drive north and then inland again for a day hike in ☒ **Rincón de la Vieja National Park ❿**. Stay at the mountain lodge, or return to the highway and head north to Hacienda Los Inocentes, the 100-year-old lodge on the northern border of ☒ **Guanacaste National Park ⓭**. Stay a second night in the lodge, or late in the day head down to **Santa Rosa National Park ⓫**. For a break from parks, your four-wheel-drive vehicle will safely deliver you to Playa Naranjo for a day at the beach.

If you have 5 days: parks & beach

After a pass through **Zarcero ❶ ➤**, spend a day and night in the Laguna de Arenal area—☒ **La Fortuna ❸**, ☒ **Nuevo Arenal ❻**, or ☒ **Tilarán ❼**—and see the volcano, lake, Tabacón Resort, and/or the La Fortuna waterfall. From La Fortuna, head north to spend a day touring the **Caño Negro National Wildlife Refuge ❹**. Then take the road northwest that leads through the San Rafael de Guatuso area and continues around the Volcán Orosi. Stop for a mind-expanding look at Lago de Nicaragua from the *mirador* (lookout) at La Virgen, near Santa Cecilia, and then continue down the west slope of the mountains. Spend a night at Hacienda Los Inocentes, near ☒ **Guanacaste National Park ⓭**, then a day hiking or horseback riding before continuing on to ☒ **La Cruz ⓮** and the resorts on the south shore of the ☒ **Bahía Salinas ⓯**. After a night (or two) here, work your way down to **Santa Rosa National Park ⓫** for a day at the beach or take a day hike in **Rincón de la Vieja National Park ❿**. Camp in the park or, more comfortably, tuck yourself into one of the nearby lodges or hotels.

or anywhere in Costa Rica, for that matter—be sure to allow plenty of time for excruciatingly slow driving. That brief hop from the smooth pavement of the Pan-American Highway up to the famous cloud forests of Monteverde, for example, looks like 30 minutes behind the wheel when measured on the map. In reality, it's two hours of bone-jarring road, although stretches of it are being repaved.

Exploring the Northern Zone

Northern Guanacaste and Alajuela encompass the volcanic mountains of the Cordillera de Guanacaste, the northern section of the Cordillera de Tilarán, and the plains stretching west to the sea and north to Nicaragua. Most destinations on the west side of the mountains, including the coastal beaches, national parks, and the northwestern end of Laguna de Arenal, lie within easy reach of the Pan-American Highway. To reach La Fortuna, Tabacón, Volcán Arenal, the east end of Laguna de Arenal, and points farther east—including Caño Negro and Upala—the easiest drive is by way of Zarcero and San Carlos (Ciudad Quesada). Several roads pass through the mountains, linking these two distinct zones. Though they're mostly paved, these roads—one follows the northern shore of Laguna de Arenal and the other skirts the volcanoes along the nation's northern edge—still have poorly surfaced stretches and are subject to washouts and other difficulties. Always get a report on road conditions before setting out on long trips.

About the Restaurants

Filling, prix-fixe lunches are standard features at most restaurants in northern Costa Rica. You have your choice of meat, with salad, beans, fruit beverage, and dessert, served *casado*-style ("married"-style, meaning that the components are joined together on the plate). Dinner begins about 6 and is a more leisurely, à la carte affair. In this largely rural, early-to-bed, early-to-rise section of the country, most restaurants stop serving about 9.

About the Hotels

East and west of the mountains, Costa Rica's far northern zone offers a good mix of high-quality hotels, nature lodges, working ranches, and basic *cabinas* (cottages). In the areas of Monteverde and La Fortuna, a range of low- and mid-price hotels, cabinas, and resorts fills the demand generated by visitors to Volcán Arenal and the cloud forest. Book ahead if you're headed to the coast during the dry season (December–April), especially for weekends—and absolutely for Christmas and Easter weeks—when Ticos flock to the beach.

WHAT IT COSTS					
	$$$$	**$$$**	**$$**	**$**	**¢**
RESTAURANTS	over $25	$20–$25	$10–$20	$5–$10	under $5
HOTELS	over $200	$125–$200	$75–$125	$35–$75	under $35

Restaurant prices are per-person for a main course at dinner. Hotel prices are for two people in a standard double room in high season, excluding service and tax (16.4%).

3

Cloud Forests & Wildlife Refuges

The far north encompasses high- and low-altitude—wetland and dry forest conservation—areas. The lowland rain-forest Caño Negro National Wildlife Refuge abounds with waterfowl, crocodiles, and caimans. Contrast that with Santa Rosa National Park's dry forest, crawling with ocelots, armadillos, various species of small monkeys, and the Olive Ridley Sea Turtle, which comes to nest on the park's beaches August–November. World renowned, the Monteverde Cloud Forest Biological Reserve is one of Costa Rica's top tourist draws. Expect to see an incredible variety of mammalian and avian life within its confines. If you're lucky, you'll catch a glimpse of that bird-watcher's Holy Grail, the Resplendent Quetzal. Monteverde also affords you the opportunity to make like a bird and view the cloud forest via a canopy tour. With the aid of cables, secure harnesses, and platform landings, you can glide through the air with the greatest of ease.

Hot Springs & Waterfalls

After a day of heavy-duty sightseeing, pamper yourself and soak those tired muscles in one of the region's three hot-springs complexes. The famed Tabacón Resort complex and the smaller Baldi Termae and Eco-Termales Fortuna, both near La Fortuna, as well as the Hotel Occidental El Tucano and Termales del Bosque, outside San Carlos, all offer chances to take the waters. You're in for a more invigorating experience with a moderately strenuous hike to the *cataratas* (waterfalls) of La Fortuna.

Volcanoes

The sheer mass and power of Volcán Arenal, often ringed with an ominous haze, dominates Lake Arenal. The volcano reiterates its presence at night, when you can sometimes see red-hot molten lava oozing from the cone, a flirtatious dance with disaster. Closest looks can be had from the Arenal Observatory Lodge, which, according to those who monitor the volcano, is also out of the path of danger. You may have to spend more than one day here, as the cone may be covered by clouds, especially during the rainy season. Farther northwest, experienced hikers can trek to the lip of the steaming Rincón de la Vieja crater on trails through the namesake national park; or you can check out Las Pailas, a cluster of miniature volcanoes, fumaroles, and mud pots encircled by a relatively easy trail. Among the other (inactive) volcanoes are Orosi, in Guanacaste National Park, and Tenorio, which shares its name with yet another national park. Guanacaste National Park is minimally developed for tourism, and Tenorio, though protected, as yet has no infrastructure.

Windsurfing

World-champion windsurfers have called Lake Arenal "one of the world's top five windsurfing spots." From December through April, Caribbean trade winds sneak through a pass in the Cordillera Central, crank up to 80 kph (50 mph) or more, and blow from the east toward the northwest end of the lake, creating perfect conditions for high-wind freshwater sailing. On the far northwest Pacific coast, Bahía Salinas gives Lake Arenal a run for its money in windsurfing circles. The winds aren't quite as strong, but the November–August season makes Costa Rica close to a year-round windsurfing destination. Kitesurfing is still novel enough here that you'll draw throngs of spectators if you decide to try it.

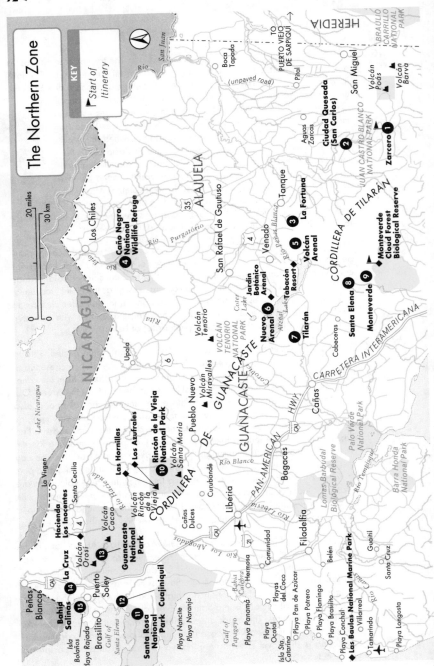

The Northern Zone

KEY

▶ Start of Itinerary

20 miles
30 km

NICARAGUA

Lake Nicaragua

San Juan

Río

Río San Juan

Boca Tapada

(unpaved road)

TO PUERTO VIEJO DE SARPIQUÍ →

Pital

HEREDIA

BRAULIO CARRILLO NATIONAL PARK

San Miguel

Volcán Poás ▲

Volcán Barva ▲

JUAN CASTRO BLANCO NATIONAL PARK

Zarcero ❶

Aguas Zarcas

Ciudad Quesada (San Carlos) ❷

ALAJUELA

Caño Negro National Wildlife Refuge ❹

Los Chiles

Río Frío

Río Purgatório

35

San Rafael de Guatuso

Tanque

La Fortuna ❸

Venado

4

Río Peñas Blancas

Volcán Arenal ❺

CORDILLERA DE TILARÁN

Monteverde Cloud Forest Biological Reserve

Upala

Río

Río

Volcán Tenorio

VOLCÁN TENORIO NATIONAL PARK

Corte

Lake Arenal

Jardín Botánico Arenal ❻

Tabacón Resort ◆

Nuevo Arenal ❼

Tilarán ❼

Santa Elena ❽

Monteverde ❾

Cordillera

Coter Lake

Aizinal

GUANACASTE

CORDILLERA

DE

GUANACASTE

Pueblo Nuevo

Volcán Miravalles ▲

Cabeceras

CARRETERA INTERAMERICANA

Cañas

CAL HWY

Corobici

Bagaces

PAN-AMERICAN

Río Blanco

Curubandé

Las Hornillas ◆

Los Azufrales ◆

Rincón de la Vieja National Park ❿

Volcán Rincón de la Vieja ▲

Volcán Santa María ▲

CORDILLERA

Volcán Cacao ▲

Hacienda Los Inocentes

Santa Cecilia

La Virgen

Río Hacienda

4

Volcán Orosí ▲

Guanacaste National Park ⓭

Cuajiniquil ⓬

Santa Rosa National Park ⓫

La Cruz ⓮

Puerto Soley

Peñas Blancas

Bahía Salinas ⓯

Brasilito

Isla Bolaños

Playa Rajada

Gulf of Santa Elena

CAL

Cañas Dulces

Liberia

Comunidad

Filadelfia

Belén

Guaitil

Santa Cruz

Río Los Ahogados

Bahía Culebra

Playa Hermosa

Playa Panamá

Gulf of Papagayo

Playa Pan de Azúcar

Playa Ocotal

Playas del Coco

Isla Sta. Catarina

Playa Potrero

Playa Flamingo

Playa Brasilito

Playa Conchal

Villarreal

Tamarindo

Playa Longosta

Las Baulas National Marine Park ◆

Río

Palo Verde National Park

Lomas Barbudal Biological Reserve

Río Tempisque

Barra Honda National Park

Playa Nancite

Playa Naranjo

PRISAGO

20

CAL

Timing

Consider an off-season or edge-of-season trip to avoid the crowds, especially around Volcán Arenal and Monteverde. In terms of weather, the areas west of the Cordillera de Guanacaste are best toured in the dry season (December–April). However, during the wet season (May–November), rain generally falls for just an hour or two each day, so beyond the effect on the roads, problems with traveling are minimal. But beware September and October, when it can get extremely wet. (Rainfall is about 65 inches per year here, the lowest in the country.) Farther inland, the northern uplands and lowlands offer a mixed climatic bag— the more easterly lowlands share the humid Caribbean weather of the east coast, and less distinct rainy and dry seasons, and the uplands partake of the drier, cooler mountain clime.

THE CORDILLERA DE TILARÁN

Dense green cloud forests cloak the rugged mountains and rolling hills of the Cordillera de Tilarán extending northwest from San José. Great swaths of primary forest and jungle, including a marvelous cluster of reserves, straddle the continental divide at Monteverde. Farther north and west, Laguna de Arenal and the green hills around it pay homage to the dark heart of this region—fiery, magnificent Volcán Arenal.

Laguna de Arenal has two distinct personalities. The northwest end is windsurf central; a row of power-generating windmills, with blades awhirl on the ridge above the Hotel Tilawa, signals another use for the relentless, powerful wind. The more sheltered southeast end, closer to the dam, is popular for other water sports, especially fishing for *guapote* (it looks like a rainbow bass). The southeast is also a marvelous place from which to view the volcano. If you took away the volcanoes, you might mistake the green, hilly countryside for the English Lake District.

Numbers in the text correspond to numbers in the margin and on the Northern Zone and the Monteverde & Santa Elena maps.

Zarcero

▶ ❶ *70 km (43 mi) northwest of San José.*

Ninety minutes from San José, the small town of Zarcero looks like it was designed by Dr. Seuss. Evangelisto Blanco, a local landscape artist, modeled cypress topiaries in fanciful animal shapes—motorcycle-riding monkeys, a lightbulb-eyed elephant—that enliven the park in front of the town church. The church interior is covered with elaborate pastel stencils and detailed religious paintings by the late Misael Solís, a well-known local artist.

Passing through Sarchí and Naranjo on your way here, you wind upward through miles of coffee plantations, with spectacular views of the mountains. There are some hair-raising roadside chasms, particularly on the east slopes, and the highway gets foggy by late afternoon, but the road is paved all the way. Fog frequently clouds the mountainous route between Zarcero and Ciudad Quesada by afternoon. Try to get an early start and negotiate this section of the highway before then.

Juan Castro Blanco National Park. East of Zarcero, where foothills mark the transition from the coastal lowland to the central mountains, lies this park, which spans 142 square km (55 square mi). It was created to protect large tracts of virgin forest around the headwaters of the Plantar, Toro, Aguas Zarcas, Tres Amigos, and La Vieja rivers. Unfortunately, the park has no facilities of any kind at present, though it's possible to explore some of its southern trails on foot or with a four-wheel-drive vehicle. ☒ *10 km (6 mi) northeast of Zarcero* ☎ *192 in Costa Rica.*

Where to Stay

¢ 🏨 **Hotel Don Beto.** Flory Salazar, one of the country's most gracious hotel owners, opens her home on the central park to guests. The immaculate hotel is tastefully decorated with the mementos she has picked up in her travels. Rooms vary in size, and all are decorated with bright, pastel drapes and bedspreads. Consummate traveler though Flory is, she's an expert on the home front, too, and is happy to advise. ☒ *Northeast corner of Central Park* ☎ *463–3137* 🛏 *8 rooms, 4 with bath* 🛬 *Airport shuttle, travel services; no a/c, no room phones, no room TVs* 🍽 *No credit cards.*

Shopping

Zarcero is renowned for its peach preserves and mild white cheese, both of which are sold in stores around town and along the highway. Stop at **El Tiesto Souvenir Shop,** across from the park, and talk politics with owner Rafael, a native Tico who lived in New Jersey for a while. He knows everything about the area and can arrange day trips to nearby waterfalls. At the tiny café-store **Super Dos** on the main street opposite the church in Zarcero, you can get a coffee and empanada *de piña* (of pineapple) while you mull over jars of excellent local peach preserves.

Ciudad Quesada (San Carlos)

❷ *45 km (28 mi) northwest of Zarcero.*

Highway signs point you to Ciudad Quesada, but it's simply "San Carlos" in local parlance. This lively, if not particularly picturesque, mountain market town serves a fertile dairy region and is worth a stop for a soak in the soothing thermal waters. Choose from a variety of sources. Hotel Occidental El Tucano is a private resort marketed to travelers on tours. A day pass (weekdays only) is $12. Just west of El Tucano's grounds but served by the same hot springs, **Termales del Bosque** lets you soak those tired muscles for $4 per day. At the hot springs is a branch of the **Original Canopy Tour** (☎ 291–4465 ⊕ www.canopytour.com), which takes you gliding through the air from tree to tree, via five platforms connected by zip lines. ☒ *Hwy. 140, 7 km (4½ mi) east of Ciudad Quesada* ☎ *460–1356.*

Where to Stay

$$ 🏨 **Hotel Occidental El Tucano.** The reason to come to El Tucano is the waters: the hotel abuts a river of hot, healing, marvelously invigorating

natural springs. Two large outdoor hot tubs, the Olympic-size pool, and the natural sauna are all fed by the Río Aguas Caliente, the cascading river that flows through the property. The hotel itself is somewhat overscale, and its public spaces suffer from too much concrete and the impersonality of any hotel subject to tour-group bookings. The food is ordinary at best, and air-conditioning and in-room safes cost extra. Spa treatments, including mud wraps, are brusque. ⊠ *Hwy. 140, 8 km (5 mi) east of Ciudad Quesada* ☎ *460–6000, 221–9095 in San José* 🖴 *460–1692* 🕮 *Apdo. 434–1150, San José* ⊕ *www.occidental-hoteles. com* 🛏 *87 rooms* ⋄ *Restaurant, in-room safes, cable TV, miniature golf, 2 tennis courts, pool, gym, sauna, spa, horseback riding, 2 bars, shop, laundry service, meeting rooms* ☰ *AE, MC, V* ⭐ *BP.*

★ $ 🏨 **Laguna del Lagarto Lodge.** One of Costa Rica's smaller eco-lodges is a hideaway in a 1,250-acre rain forest near the Nicaraguan border. Most of the rustic cabin rooms come with single beds. Some 380 bird species and counting have been logged here, including the endangered Great Green Macaw. Buffet-style meals are served on a patio with splendid river and forest views. Rates include one guided walk and use of canoes. Recommended extras include horseback riding and a boat trip up to the border on the San Carlos River. ⊠ *7 km (4 mi) north of Boca Tapada* ☎ *289–8163* 🖴 *289–5295* ⊕ *www.lagarto-lodge-costa-rica.com* 🛏 *20 rooms, 18 with bath* ⋄ *Dining room, horseback riding, bar, laundry service; no a/c, no room phones, no room TVs* ☰ *MC, V.*

La Fortuna

③ *17 km (11 mi) east of Volcán Arenal, 50 km (30 mi) northwest of Ciudad Quesada.*

At the foot of towering, overpowering Volcán Arenal, the small farming community of La Fortuna de San Carlos (commonly called La Fortuna) attracts visitors from around the world. The town overflows with restaurants, hotels, and tour operators. Volcano-viewing can be hit-and-miss during the May–November rainy season. One minute, Arenal looms menacingly over the village; the next minute, clouds shroud its cone. (Early morning is always the best time to catch a longer gaze.) La Fortuna is also the best place to arrange trips to the popular Caño Negro National Wildlife Refuge. Tours vary in price and quality, so ask around, but all provide an easier alternative than busing up north to Los Chiles and hiring a boat to take you down through the rain forest on Río Frío.

The town's squat, pale, concrete **Church of San Juan Bosco,** unremarkable on its own, wins Costa Rica's most-photographed-house-of-worship award. The view of the church from across the central park, with the volcano in the background, a juxtaposition of serene and menacing, makes a great photo. This is also one of the few Catholic churches that doesn't follow the typical Costa Rican convention of facing west. Its entrance is on the east side of the building. ⊠ *Central Park* ☎ *No phone.*

Fodor's Choice **Tabacón Hot Springs.** Besides access to a multitude of outdoor adventures,
★ La Fortuna also provides the opportunity for some serious soaking and pampering. Where else can you lounge in a natural hot-springs water-

fall with a volcano spitting fireballs overhead? Kick back at the Tabacón Resort, a busy day spa and hotel, with gorgeous gardens, waterfalls, mineral-water soaking streams (average 39°C [102°F]) complete with subtle ladders and railings, plus swimming pools, swim-up bars, and dining facilities, which mingle in a florid Latin interpretation of grand European baths. If you aren't a guest of the hotel, you can purchase a day pass. The best deal is to sign up for a zip-through-the-trees canopy tour ($45), the price of which includes access to the waters. If you're seeking a treatment at the Iskandria Spa, make an appointment a day in advance. The resort operates every-two-hour van shuttle service from noon until evening from the office of Sunset Tours in La Fortuna. ⊠ *Hwy. toward Nuevo Arenal, 13 km (8 mi) northwest of La Fortuna* ☎ *460–2020, 256–1500 in San José* 🖷 *460–5724, 221–3075 in San José* ⊕ *www.tabacon.com* ✉ *$29; package with lunch and dinner $45; 45-min massage $55* ⊘ *Daily noon–10.*

need a break? A couple of trendy cafés are the perfect place to wrap your hands around a warm cup of coffee on a chilly afternoon. The semi-open-air **Café Rainforest** (⊠ 30 m south of central park ☎ 365–6370) serves high-altitude-grown gourmet Café Monteverde, and sells souvenir packages of the same coffee brand. **Lo Nuestro** (⊠ 50 m north of gas station ☎ 479–9489) brews hot gourmet coffee drinks with pastries as accompaniment.

Baldi Termae. If Tabacón is full or if you want a less expensive spa alternative, head to Baldi Termae. The complex's 10 hot-springs-fed pools vary in temperature but share views of Volcán Arenal. There's also a swim-up snack bar. ⊠ *4 km (2½ mi) west of La Fortuna* ☎ *479–9651* ✉ *$12* ⊘ *Daily 10–10.*

Eco-Termales Fortuna. Another alternative to Tabacón is this small family-run complex with four hot-springs-fed pools and a trail through a primary forest. To keep things uncrowded and small scale, the owners require advance reservations. ⊠ *4 km (2½ mi) west of La Fortuna* ☎ *479–8484* ✉ *$14* ⊘ *Daily 10–10.*

off the beaten path **VENADO CAVERNS** – In 1945 a farmer in the mountain hamlet of Venado fell in a hole, and thus were discovered the Cavernas de Venado (Venado Caverns). The limestone caves, 45 minutes north of La Fortuna and 20 minutes southeast of San Rafael, contain a series of eight chambers with an assortment of stalactites, stalagmites, underground streams, and other subterranean formations. Sunset Tours and Bobo Adventures (➪ Tours *in* The Northern Zone A to Z) run trips from La Fortuna. The excursion is not advisable if you suffer from claustrophobia. ☎ *479–9415* ✉ *$35* ⊘ *Daily 7 AM–8 PM.*

Where to Eat

$–$$ ✕ **Las Brasitas.** Chicken turns over wood on a rotisserie in a brick oven at this pleasant restaurant on the road heading out of town toward the volcano. Try the succulent chicken when it ends up in the tangy fajitas or any of the other amply sized Mexican dishes. You have your choice of three open-air dining areas arranged around a garden. Two are se-cluded and intimate; the third less so, being closer to the road. ⌧ *150 m west of church* ☎ *479–9819* ▭ *MC, V.*

¢–$ ✕ **La Choza de Laurel.** The tantalizing rotisserie chicken and the cloves of garlic and bunches of onions dangling from the roof always draw in passersby to this open-air Costa Rican–style restaurant near the center of town. These folks open early; it's a great place to grab a hearty breakfast on your way to the volcano. ⌧ *100 m northwest of church* ☎ *479–9231* ▭ *MC, V.*

¢–$ ✕ **Rancho la Cascada.** You can't miss its tall, palm-thatch roof in the cen-ter of town. The festive upstairs contains a bar, whose large TV, neon signs, and flashing lights give it the appropriate ambience. Downstairs, the spacious dining room—decorated with foreign flags—serves basic, midpriced Costa Rican fare as well as hearty, American-style breakfasts. ⌧ *Across from northeast corner of Parque Central* ☎ *479–9145* ▭ *AE, DC, MC, V.*

¢–$ ✕ **La Vaca Muca.** The food is good and the servings are generous at this small café just outside of town. The exterior is draped with foliage, and the interior has turquoise paneling, glass tables, and bamboo and can-dles aplenty. Go for the steak, or if you're in the mood for something more basic, try the casado heaped with chicken, beef, or fish; rice; beans; fried egg; fried banana; and cabbage salad. Stroll through the small orchid and butterfly garden next door after you're through. ⌧ *2 km (1 mi) west of La Fortuna* ☎ *479–9186* ▭ *AE, DC, MC, V.*

¢ ✕ **Soda La Parada.** It's busy 24 hours a day but never crazy. Grab an open-air seat alongside the locals, under the canvas tarp (from which hangs a huge color TV), and devour fresh carrot-and-orange juice, a beef or chicken empanada, or one of the tasty casados. You and your wal-let leave full. ⌧ *Across from town church and regional bus stop* ☎ *479–9547* ▭ *No credit cards.*

Where to Stay

$$$ ▦ **Arenal Observatory Lodge.** You're as close as anyone should be to an active volcano at the end of the winding road leading to the lodge—a mere 1¾ km (1 mi) away. The isolated lodge was founded by Smithso-nian researchers in 1987. It's fairly rustic, emphasizing that outdoor ac-tivities are what it's all about. Rooms are comfortable and simply furnished (comforters on beds are a cozy touch), and most have stellar views. After a hike, take a dip in the infinity-edge pool or 12-person hot tub, which face tall pines on one side and the volcano on the other. The dining room, which serves tasty and hearty food, has great views of the volcano and lake. ⌧ *3 km (2 mi) east of dam on Laguna de Arenal; from La Fortuna, drive to Tabacón Resort and continue 4 km (2½ mi) past resort to turnoff at base of volcano; turn and continue for 9 km (5½ mi)* ☏ *Apdo. 13411–1000, San José* ☎ *692–2070, 290–7011 in San José* 🖷 *692–2074, 290–8427 in San José* ⊕ *www.arenal-observatory. co.cr* ⇩ *35 rooms, 2 suites* ⌂ *Restaurant, pool, outdoor hot tub, horse-back riding, bar, laundry service; no a/c, no room phones, no room TVs* ▭ *AE, MC, V* |◎| *BP.*

★ $$$ ▦ **Tabacón Resort.** Without question, Tabacón, with its impeccably land-scaped gardens and hot-springs rivers at the base of Volcán Arenal, is one of Central America's most compelling resorts. The hot springs and small but lovely spa customarily draw visitors inland from the ocean with no regrets. All rooms have tile floors, a terrace or patio, and big bathrooms. Some have volcano views; others overlook the manicured gardens. The suites are some of the country's finest lodgings, with tile floors, plants, beautiful mahogany armoires and beds, and two-person whirlpool baths. The hotel's intimacy is somewhat compromised by its scale and its popularity with day-trippers, but it has some private areas—including a dining room and pool—for overnight guests only. ⊠ *13 km (8 mi) northwest of La Fortuna on highway toward Nuevo Arenal* 🕾 *460–2020, 256–1500 in San José* 🖷 *460–5724, 221–3075 in San José* ✆ *Apdo. 181–1007, San José* ⊕ *www.tabacon.com* ⇗ *73 rooms, 9 suites* ♨ *2 restaurants, dining room, cable TV, 9 pools, outdoor hot tub, spa, 3 bars, business services, meeting rooms, airport shuttle, travel services* ▭ *MC, V* ⦿❙ *BP.*

$$ ⊞ **Arenal Country Inn.** It doesn't quite approximate an English country inn, although it is charming. Each brightly furnished modern room has two queen-size beds and a private patio. The lush grounds have great views of the Arenal volcano. A big breakfast is served in the restaurant, an open-air converted cattle corral. You can take lunch and dinner there as well. ⊠ *1 km (½ mi) south of church of La Fortuna, south end of town* 🕾 *479–9670* 🖷 *479–9433* ⊕ *www.arenalcountryinn.com* ⇗ *20 rooms* ♨ *Dining room, in-room safes, minibars, pool, bar, laundry service, meeting room, travel services; no room TVs* ▭ *AE, DC, MC, V* ⦿❙ *BP.*

$$ ⊞ **Chachagua Rain Forest Hotel.** At this working ranch, intersected by a sweetly babbling brook, you can see *caballeros* (horsemen) at work, take a horseback ride into the rain forest, and look for toucans from the open-air restaurant, which serves beef, milk, and cheese produced on the premises. Each cabina has a pair of double beds and a deck with a picnic table. Large, reflective windows enclosing each cabina's shower serve a marvelous purpose: birds gather outside your window to watch their own reflections while you bathe and watch them. The lodge is 3 km (2 mi) up a rough track—four-wheel drive is recommended in rainy season—on the road headed south from La Fortuna to La Tigra. ⊠ *12 km (7 mi) south of La Fortuna* ✆ *Apdo. 476–4005, Ciudad Cariari* 🕾 *239–6464* 🖷 *290–6506* ⊕ *www.chachaguarainforesthotel.com* ⇗ *27 cabinas* ♨ *Restaurant, tennis court, pool, massage, bar, meeting rooms; no room phones, no room TVs* ▭ *AE, MC, V.*

$$ ⊞ **Montaña de Fuego.** On a manicured grassy roadside knoll, this highly recommended collection of cabins affords utterly spectacular views of Volcán Arenal. The spacious, well-made hardwood structures have large porches, and rooms have rustic decor. The friendly management can arrange tours of the area. ⊠ *8 km (5 mi) west of La Fortuna* 🕾 *460–1220* 🖷 *460–1455* ⊕ *www.montanadefuego.com* ⇗ *48 cabinas* ♨ *Restaurant, fans, cable TV, 2 pools, hot tub, spa, horseback riding, shop, laundry service, travel services* ▭ *AE, DC, MC, V* ⦿❙ *BP.*

FodorśChoice
★

$$ ⊞ **Tilajari Hotel Resort.** As a comfortable base from which to have outdoor or adventure tours, this 35-acre resort with a butterfly garden and orchard is a good choice. The hotel organizes horseback tours through its own rain-forest preserve, kayak tours in the river that nudges up against the property, and other area tours. "Papaya on a stick" feeders hang outside the open-air dining room, attracting an array of raucous toucans and parrots to entertain you while you sip your morning coffee. The modest guest quarters have river-view balconies; family suites have lofts. Tilajari is a half hour outside of town, and there's no shuttle service. ⊠ *San Carlos Valley, just outside Muelle (follow signs), about 25 km (15 mi) east of La Fortuna* ⌖ *Apdo. 81, San Carlos, Alajuela* ☎ *469–9091, 291–4081 in San José* 🖷 *469–9095* ⊕ *www.tilajari.com* 🛏 *60 rooms, 16 suites* ⚅ *Restaurant, snack bar, in-room safes, cable TV, 6 tennis courts, 2 pools, outdoor hot tub, sauna, basketball, horseback riding, Ping-Pong, racquetball, bar, laundry service, meeting rooms* ⏐⊙⏐ *BP* ▤ *AE, DC, MC, V.*

$ ⊞ **Cabinas Los Guayabos.** A great budget alternative to the more expensive lodgings lining the road to the volcano is this group of basic but spotlessly clean cabins managed by a friendly family. The units have all the standard budget-lodging furnishings, but each comes with its own porch facing Arenal, ideal for viewing the evening spectacle. ⊠ *9 km (5½ mi) west of La Fortuna* ☎ *460–6644* 🛏 *5 cabins* ⚅ *No a/c, no room phones, no room TVs* ▤ *No credit cards.*

★ $ ⊞ **Hotel San Bosco.** Covered in blue-tile mosaics, this two-story hotel is certainly the most attractive and comfortable in the main part of town. Two kitchen-equipped cabinas (which sleep 8 or 14 people) are a good deal for families. The spotlessly clean, white rooms have polished wood furniture and firm beds and are linked by a long veranda lined with benches and potted plants. ⊠ *220 m north of La Fortuna's gas station* ☎ *479–9050* 🖷 *479–9109* ⊕ *www.arenal-volcano.com* 🛏 *34 rooms, 2 cabinas* ⚅ *Pool, hot tub; no room phones* ▤ *AE, DC, MC, V.*

$ ⊞ **Lomas del Volcán.** You'd think you were right on top of the volcano, but Arenal is really a reassuring 6 km (4 mi) away. You need a four-wheel-drive vehicle to get here, but once you do, you can luxuriate in the splendid isolation. The simple cabins have hot water and come with two beds and throw rugs. Each has a volcano-viewing porch. ⊠ *Road entrance 1½ km (1 mi) west of La Fortuna* ☎ *479–9000* 🖷 *479–9836* ⊕ *www.lomasdelvolcan.com* 🛏 *15 cabins* ⚅ *Restaurant, fans, refrigerators, hot tub, horseback riding; no a/c, no room phones* ▤ *AE, MC, V* ⏐⊙⏐ *BP.*

$ ⊞ **Luigi's Lodge.** Every one of this hotel's rooms fronts a stunning view of the volcano: it's the only lodging in the center of town able to make that claim. Rooms also have high wooden ceilings and stenciled animal drawings. The green-and-white-tiled bathrooms have bathtubs, a rarity in Costa Rica. The adjoining restaurant serves pizza. ⊠ *200 m west of town church* ☎ *479–9636* 🖷 *479–9898* ⊕ *www.luigislodge.com* 🛏 *21 rooms* ⚅ *Restaurant, cable TV in some rooms, pool, gym, hot tub, billiards, bar, casino, meeting room; no TV in some rooms* ▤ *V* ⏐⊙⏐ *BP.*

¢ ⊞ **Don Manuel Inn.** The folks at Sunset Tours operate this basic but good-value budget lodging near the center of town. The tile-floor rooms are simple. All contain one double and one single bed. Opt for one of the rooms with private bath. They're more secluded and a bit more removed from the commotion of the common areas. ⊠ *Across from south side of church* ☎🖷 *479–9069* 🛏 *8 rooms, 4 with bath* ⚅ *Fans, Internet; no a/c, no room phones, no room TVs* ▤ *AE, DC, MC, V* ⏐⊙⏐ *CP.*

¢ 🏨 **La Pradera.** "The Prairie" is a simple roadside hotel with comfortable guest rooms that have high ceilings, spacious bathrooms, and verandas. Two rooms have whirlpool tubs. Beef eaters should try the thatch-roof restaurant next door. The steak with jalapeño sauce is a fine, spicy dish. ✉ *About 2 km (1 mi) west of La Fortuna* 🕾 479–9597 🖨 479–9167 ➲ *20 rooms* ⚒ *Restaurant, pool, hot tubs, bar; no a/c in some rooms* ▤ *AE, DC, MC, V* ⚄ *BP.*

Shopping

Lunática (✉ 350 m east of town church 🕾 479–8255) exhibits and sells vibrant, colorful works by artists, local and from across the country, established and emerging, and has become a focal point for La Fortuna's small but growing art community. Charming owner Francesa Maschi knows the area's arts, from the works of the nearby indigenous Maleku groups to those from a cooperative made up of women from local villages.

Nightlife

A soak at Tabacón or a gaze at the volcano makes up most of La Fortuna's nightlife. **Volcán Look** (✉ 5 km [3 mi] west of La Fortuna 🕾 479–9616), which bills itself as the largest Costa Rican disco outside San José, erupts with dancing and music on weekends. Pizzeria **Vagbundo** (✉ 3 km [2 mi] west of La Fortuna 🕾 479–9565) turns into a lively bar in the evening with foosball and billiards in the backroom.

Sports & the Outdoors

CANOEING If you're looking for the intimacy you don't get in a big group or on a rafting trip, **Canoa Aventura** (🕾 479–8200 ⊕ www.canoaaventura.cr.gs) is just the ticket, with two half-day tours and ample wildlife-viewing on the Río Peñas Blancas. Departures are at 5 and 8 AM, and include breakfast or lunch served on the turned-over canoe used as a table. There's also a daylong canoe tour of the Caño Blanco Wildlife Refuge. Tours are appropriate for beginners, and instruction is provided, but the folks here can tailor excursions if you're more experienced.

CANOPY TOURS Want a bird's-eye view of the trees? Let the professionals at the **Origi-**
FodorsChoice **nal Canopy Tour** (✉ Tabacón Resort, 13 km [8 mi] northwest of La For-
★ tuna on highway toward Nuevo Arenal 🕾 460–2020 or 256–1500 🖨 221–3075 ⊕ www.canopytour.com) show you the canopy from a new perspective. You're securely strapped into a rock-climbing harness and attached to a pulley and horizontal zip line. Well-trained guides then send you whizzing between trees that stand about 328 feet over the streams of Tabacón. (If it's a small tour, they may even be able to snap a picture of you.) The tour requires a certain amount of fearlessness, but it's not rigorous, and it's certainly exhilarating and unique. Tours are at 7:30 AM, 10 AM, 1:30, and 4. The price of a tour ($45) includes admission to Tabacón Hot Springs for the day.

Down at ground level, the 15 **Arenal Hanging Bridges** (✉ 4 km [2½ mi] west of Tabacón at Arenal Dam 🕾 479–9686, 253–5080 in San José ⊕ www.hangingbridges.com) scatter over 3 km (2 mi) paved-block interpretive trails on a 250-acre private reserve, with great bird-watching and volcano-viewing. A cafeteria and souvenir shop await at the end of the route. The complex is open daily 7–4:30, and reopens 5:30–7 for a guided evening walk. Admission during the day is $20; the $30 evening ticket readmits you the next day. The folks here can provide shuttle service from La Fortuna.

In line with the "bigger is better" phenomenon overtaking tourist activities in this region, the Sky Trek–Sky Walk folks in Monteverde have opened the **Arenal Rain Forest Reserve** (⊠ 12 km [7 mi] west of La Fortuna, El Castillo ☎ 479–9944 ⊕ www.arenalreserve.com), a second canopy tour–bridge walk complex near La Fortuna. Alpine-style gondolas transport you to the site, from where you can descend via a zipline canopy tour or hike through the cloudforest along a series of suspended bridges. Or, if you don't feel so adventurous, take the gondola back down. The reserve is open daily 7–4; admission is $60.

FISHING The eastern side of **Laguna de Arenal** has the best freshwater fishing in Costa Rica, with guapote aplenty, although it is difficult to fish from the shore. **Arenal Observatory Lodge** (☎ 695–5033) is one of many hotels and tour companies in the area offering boats and guides.

HIKING A pleasant but steep 6-km (4-mi) day hike takes you from La Fortuna to the 177-foot **Cataratas de la Fortuna.** Look for the yellow entrance sign off the main road toward the volcano. After walking 1½ km (1 mi) and passing two bridges, turn right and continue straight ahead until you reach the river turnoff. Then walk 10 or 15 minutes down a steep but very well-constructed trail that has a few vertiginous spots along the way. Swimming in the pool under the waterfall is fairly safe. You can work your way around into the cavelike area behind the cataract for an unusual rear view, but you have to swim in turbulent waters and/ or hike over slippery rocks. A $6 fee is collected at the head of the trail, which is open daily 8–4. If you don't want to walk, several operators in La Fortuna can take you to the falls by car or on horseback.

Ecocentro Danaus (⊠ 4 km [2½ mi] east of La Fortuna ☎ 393–8437 or 460–8005), a small ecotourism project outside of town, exhibits 300 species of tropical plants, abundant animal life—including sloths and caimans—and butterfly and orchid gardens, and is open daily 8–4. It's also a great place to see Costa Rica's famed red venomous dart frogs up close. Admission is $5. A guided evening tour ($12) should be reserved in advance.

HORSEBACK RIDING If you're interested in getting up to Monteverde from the Arenal–La Fortuna area without taking the grinding four-hour drive, there's an alternative: the ever-ingenious Suresh Krishnan, a transplant from California, has a wonderful adventure out of his tour agency, **Desafío Adventures** (⊠ Behind church ☎ 479–9464 ⊕ www.desafiocostarica.com). The 4½-hour guided horseback trip takes you around the southern shore of Lake Arenal along a flat, well-maintained trail. The trip involves taxi service from La Fortuna to the southern shore of Lake Arenal, and from that trail's end to Monteverde, circumventing the steep, muddy, poorly maintained trails at both ends. A boat ride across Laguna de Arenal is included. You can also take the trip in reverse, from Monteverde to La Fortuna. Desafío transports your luggage for $65 per person and will transport your rental car (while you travel on horseback) for an extra charge and enough advance notice to get the driver included on your rental contract. You leave La Fortuna at 7:30 AM and arrive in Monteverde around 2:30 PM. Many other agencies in La Fortuna and Monteverde lead horseback tours but don't provide taxi service to avoid the treacherous trails, and some riders have returned with stories of terrified horses barely able to navigate the way. Stick with Desafío.

RAFTING Several La Fortuna operators offer Class III and IV white-water trips on the Río Toro. The narrow shape of this river requires the use of special, streamlined, U.S.-made boats that seat just four and go very fast. The easier Ríos Balsa and San Carlos have Class II and III rapids and are close enough to town that they can be worked into half-day excursions. **Desafío Adventures** (✉ Behind church, ☎ 479–9464 ⊕ www. desafiocostarica.com) has trips on the Toro, San Carlos, and Balsa rivers for $45–$65 per person.

RAPPELLING Rappel down four waterfalls ranging in height from 60 to 150 feet with **Pure Trek Canyoning** (✉ La Fortuna ☎ 479–9940, 800/452–3195 in U.S. ⊕ www.puretrek.com). Two guides lead small groups—10 is the maximum size—on the four-hour tour with plenty of wildlife-viewing opportunities to a private farm near La Fortuna. The $80 price includes transportation, all gear, breakfast, and a light lunch.

Caño Negro National Wildlife Refuge

❹ *91 km (57 mi) northwest of La Fortuna.*

A lowland rain-forest reserve in the far northern reaches of Alajuela, Refugio Nacional de Vida Silvestre Caño Negro covers 98 square km (38 square mi). Caño Negro has suffered severe deforestation over the years, but most of the Río Frío is still lined with trees, and the park's vast lake is an excellent place to watch such waterfowl as Jabiru, Anhinga, and the Roseate Spoonbill, as well as a host of resident exotic animals. In the dry season, you can ride horses, but the visit here chiefly entails a wildlife-spotting boat tour. Caño Negro can be reached from the Nuevo Arenal–La Fortuna area, or you can approach via Upala (a bus from here takes 45 minutes). Visiting with a tour company is the best way to see the park. Camping is permitted, or you can stay in a couple of surprisingly nice lodgings in Caño Negro village—ones you'd never expect to find in such a far-flung corner of the country. ▨ $6 ☉ *Daily 7–4.*

Sunset Tours (☎ 479–9415), in La Fortuna, runs top-notch, informative daylong tours, among the best in the country, down the Río Frío to Caño Negro for $45. Bring your jungle juice: the mosquitoes are voracious.

Where to Stay

$$ ▣ **Caño Negro Natural Lodge.** That such an upscale property exists in this remote place might amaze you, but this Italian-designed, family-operated resort on the east side of the reserve is never pretentious. Rooms have high ceilings, colorful drapes and bedspreads, and huge showers; some rooms have bunk beds. There are two- and three-day packages available for fishers or nonfishers alike. The lodge offers a variety of meal options; most guests opt for taking all meals here, since there are

few other restaurants in town. ☒ *Caño Negro village* ☎ *471–1428, 265–2560 in San José* 🖶 *265–4561* ⊕ *www.canonegrolodge.com* ⮑ *10 rooms* ᗡ *Restaurant, in-room safes, miniature golf, pool, hot tub, fishing, badminton, croquet, Ping-Pong, volleyball, laundry service, meeting room; no room phones, no room TVs* ▤ *AE, MC, V* ˡ◎ˡ *CP.*

$ 🏠**Fishing Club Caño Negro.** Despite the name, all are welcome here, though the lodge is best known for its tours, and equipment and boat rental for the tarpon and bass fishing to be found in the lake. Four white bungalows of high-quality wood each contain two bright, sparkling rooms with terra-cotta tile floors, and are arranged around the wooded property. The produce from the lodge's citrus orchard ends up on your breakfast plate. ☒ *Caño Negro village* ☎ *471–1012* 🖶 *656–0260* ⊕ *www. canonegro.com* ⮑ *8 rooms* ᗡ *Restaurant, fans, fishing, bar; no a/c, no room phones, no room TVs* ▤ *AE, MC, V* ˡ◎ˡ *CP.*

Los Chiles

12 km (7 mi) north of Caño Negro National Wildlife Refuge.

Costa Rica and Nicaragua share a border crossing just north of Los Chiles. Few tourists use it because of the difficulty of access to the rest of Nicaragua from here. There are virtually no roads on the other side, making a boat crossing via the Río San Juan your only option. Twice-weekly public boat service travels up the river to Lake Nicaragua and stops at the Solentiname Islands, Ometepe and Granada, a total trip of 11 hours. Opt for the easier approach via Peñas Blancas (⇨ below) instead.

Volcán Arenal

❺ *17 km (11 mi) west of La Fortuna, 128 km (80 mi) northwest of San*
Fodor'sChoice *José.*
★

If you've never seen an active volcano, Arenal, whose perfect conical profile dominates the southern end of Lake Arenal, makes a spectacular first. Night is the best time to observe it, as you can clearly see rocks spewing skyward and red-hot molten lava enveloping the top of the cone. Phases of inactivity do occur, however, so it's wise to check ahead. The volcano is also frequently hidden in cloud cover, so you may have to stay more than one day to get in a good volcano-viewing session.

Arenal lay dormant for 400 years until 1968. On July 29 of that year an earthquake shook the area, and 12 hours later Arenal blew. Pueblo Nuevo to the west bore the brunt of the shock waves, poisonous gases, and falling rocks; 87 people perished. Since then, Arenal has been in a constant state of activity—eruptions, accompanied by thunderous grumbling sounds, are sometimes as frequent as one per hour. An enormous eruption in 1998 put the fear back into the local community and led to the closure of Route 42 and the evacuation of several nearby hotels. This earthshaking event reminded everyone what it really means to coexist with an active volcano.

Though folks here still do it, hiking is not recommended on the volcano's lower slopes; in 1988 two people were killed by fast-flowing lava when they attempted to climb it. History repeated itself in 2000 with the death of an American traveler and her guide who were hiking on the lower slopes in a supposedly safe area. The conventional wisdom in these parts is that it's still safe to approach from the south and west, within the national park. It's really best to enjoy the spectacle from no closer than any of the lodges themselves.

> **en route** Despite years of government promises to upgrade the major tourist route from Volcán Arenal to Nuevo Arenal, the highway around the north shore of Lake Arenal remains one of Costa Rica's most potholed. Expect smooth sailing west of the Tabacón Resort as far as the Arenal Dam, after which sections of the road deteriorate badly until you arrive in Nuevo Arenal. Beware of deep, tire-wrecking washouts at all times. This stretch adds a bone-jarring hour to an otherwise lovely drive with spectacular lake and volcano views all the way. In addition to dodging the potholes, watch out for the raccoonlike coatimundis (*pizotes* in Spanish) that scurry along the road. If you get out of your car to take pictures—one large colony just west of the dam causes occasional traffic jams as tourists do exactly that—the animals will approach you looking for a handout. Longtime human feeding has diminished their ability to search for food on their own, and the cookies and potato chips they frequently get make matters worse.

Nuevo Arenal

❻ *40 km (25 mi) west of La Fortuna.*

There's little reason to stop in Nuevo Arenal itself. Off the main road, the pleasant, if nondescript, *nuevo* town was created in 1973 to replace the original Arenal, flooded when the lake was created. If you're staying overnight in the area, make sure you find a hotel with a view of the volcano or the lake.

Jardín Botánico Arenal. More than 2,000 plant species from around the world are exhibited at the elegantly organized Arenal Botanical Gardens. Countless orchids, bromeliads, heliconias, and roses; varieties of ferns; and a Japanese garden with a waterfall are among the many floral splendors laid out along well-marked trails. An accompanying brochure describes everything in delightful detail; well-placed benches and a fruit-and-juice stand provide resting places along the paths. The complex also includes a serpentarium and butterfly garden. ⊠ *5 km (3 mi) east of Nuevo Arenal* ☎ *694–4305* 🖰 *$8* ☉ *Nov.–Apr., daily 9–5; May–Oct., Mon.–Sat. 9–5.*

Where to Stay

$$–$$$ 🏨 **Arenal Lodge.** Surrounded by macadamia trees and rain forest, this modern white bungalow is high above the dam, midway between La Fortuna and Nuevo Arenal. You need four-wheel drive to negotiate the steep 2-km (1-mi) road, but the hotel can ferry you from the bottom. Bedroom suites, some in a newer annex, are pleasantly furnished, with pretty green-tile baths; there are also cheaper, smaller, darker rooms without volcano views. Interiors are finished in natural wood, with walls of louvered windows. Hilltop chalets have floor-to-ceiling windows and kitchenettes. Perks include a small snooker table and a free hour of horse-back riding. ⊠ *18½ km (11½ mi) west of La Fortuna, past Arenal Dam, then 2 km (1 mi) north* ☎ *383–3957, 228–3189 in Escazú* ⊟ *289–6798* ⑆ *Apdo. 1139–1250, Escazú* ⊕ *www.arenallodge.com* ⇆ *6 rooms, 18 suites, 10 chalets* ⌂ *Dining room, some kitchenettes, hot tub, fishing, bicycles, hiking, horseback riding, bar, library, shop, laundry service, Internet, meeting room; no a/c, no room phones, no room TVs* ⊟ *AE, MC, V* ⑩ *BP.*

$$

\$\$ ⊡ **Villa Decary.** There's everything to recommend at this hillside lodg-
Fodor'sChoice ing overlooking Lake Arenal, but it all goes back to owners Jeff and Bill
★ and their attentive service. Rooms have large picture windows and pri-vate balconies—great places to take in the ample bird-watching op-portunities—and bright yellow-and-blue spreads and drapes. Higher up the hill, spacious bungalows afford an even better view. Rates include a filling breakfast of eggs, pancakes, fruits, and juices. ⊠ *2 km (1½ mi) east of Nuevo Arenal* ☎ *383–3012* ⊟ *694–4330* ⊕ *www.villadecary. com* ⇆ *5 rooms, 3 bungalows* ⌂ *Dining room; no a/c, no room phones, no room TVs* ⊟ *AE, DC, MC, V* ⑩ *BP.*

\$ ⊡ **Chalet Nicholas.** John and Cathy Nicholas (and their resident Great
Fodor'sChoice Danes) have converted their hillside home into a charming bed-and-break-
★ fast with stunning views of the lake and volcano. The two rosewood rooms downstairs have tile floors. Up a spiral staircase lies the L-shape, all-wood double loft with three beds and a back porch that overlooks the large garden. All rooms have volcano views. Bird-watching abounds: 100 species have been cataloged on the grounds. Chat about your plans for the day with your fellow guests during one of Cathy's ample break-fasts. ⊠ *2 km (1½ mi) west of Nuevo Arenal* ☎☎ *694–4041* ⊕ *www. chaletnicholas.com* ⇆ *3 rooms* ⌂ *Dining room, shop; no a/c, no room phones, no room TVs, no smoking* ⊟ *No credit cards* ⑩ *BP.*

\$ ⊡ **Hotel Joya Sureña.** In the midst of a working coffee plantation, this Canadian-owned property with variously sized suites occupies a rather imposing three-story hacienda-style building surrounded by tropical gardens. It's fairly luxurious for up-country Costa Rica. Extensive trails in and around the place bring a rich diversity of plant, animal, and bird life to view. ⊠ *1½ km (1 mi) down a rocky road that leads east from Nuevo Arenal* ☎ *694–4057* ⊟ *694–4059* ⇆ *28 rooms* ⌂ *Restaurant, fans, in-room safes, pool, health club, hot tub, massage, sauna, boat-ing, fishing, hiking, horseback riding, laundry service; no a/c, no room TVs* ⊟ *AE, MC, V.*

\$ ⊡ **Lake Coter Eco-Lodge.** This ruggedly handsome mountain hideaway tucked into cloud forest offers lots to do, thanks to the setting. The lodge has canopy tours on-site, hikes on 29 km (18 mi) of trails, kayaking and sailing on Laguna de Arenal, and an extensive stable of horses for trail rides through the cloud forest. Stay in comfortable ridge-top cabinas, if they're available. Clean, basic rooms are attached to the main brick-and-hardwood reception building, which has a friendly bar and a fire-place. ⊠ *3 km (2 mi) up a rough track off north shore of Laguna de Arenal* ☎ *694–4470 or 440–6768* ⊟ *694–4460 or 440–6725* ⊕ *www.*

ecolodgecostarica.com ⤳ *21 rooms, 25 cabinas* ☖ *Dining room, boating, billiards, hiking, horseback riding, bar, laundry service, meeting room; no a/c, no room phones, no room TVs* ▭ *AE, MC, V.*

Shopping

Toad Hall (✉ Road between Nuevo Arenal and La Fortuna ☏ 692–8020), open daily from 7:30 to 5, sells everything from indigenous art to maps to recycled paper. The owners can give you the lowdown on every tour and tour operator in the area; they also run a deli-café with light Mexican food and stunning alfresco views of the lake and volcano.

Tilarán

❼ *22 km (14 mi) southwest of Nuevo Arenal, 62 km (38 mi) west of La Fortuna.*

Heading west around Laguna de Arenal, you pass a couple of small villages and several charming hotels ranging from the Cretan-inspired fantasy Hotel Tilawa to the rustic Rock River Lodge. The quiet white-washed town of Tilarán, on the southwest side of Laguna de Arenal—a windmill farm in the hills high above the town attests to this being the windiest place in the country—is used as a base by bronzed wind-surfers. For those days when windsurfers get "skunked" (the wind fails to blow), there's horseback riding and mountain biking to keep you busy.

Where to Stay & Eat

$ ⊞ **Hotel Tilawa.** This knockoff of the Palace of Knossos on Crete has neoclassic murals, columns, and plant-draped arches that somehow don't seem dramatically out of place, even on the west of Laguna de Arenal. The large rooms have two queen-size beds with Guatemalan bed-spreads and natural wood ceilings; the bathrooms are especially spacious. Sailing tours in a 39-foot catamaran, the windsurfing and kitesurfing school and shop, and the skateboarding park make this a practical place to base yourself if you want an active vacation. Packages include the use of windsurfing gear. The open-air patio restaurant dishes up steaks and seafood. ✉ *8 km (5 mi) north of Tilarán* ☏ *695–5050* 🖷 *695–5766* ⊕ *www.hotel-tilawa.com* 🕮 *Apdo. 92–5710, Tilarán* ⤳ *20 rooms* ☖ *Restaurant, pool, windsurfing, boating, mountain bikes, hiking, horseback riding, bar, laundry service; no a/c, no room TVs* ▭ *MC, V.*

$ ⊞ **Rock River Lodge.** A long, handsome building on a grassy hill above the road leading from Tilarán to Nuevo Arenal houses rustic wooden cabinas. They share a shaded front porch with views of the volcano. Santa Fe–style cabinas are farther up the hill. The restaurant, bar, and lobby occupy another building closer to the road, with plenty of porch space and lounging sofas, an open kitchen, and a welcoming fireplace. The hotel rents windsurfing gear; its launching site is across the lake from that of the Hotel Tilawa. The restaurant serves well-prepared food at reasonable prices. ✉ *19 km (11 mi) northeast of Tilarán* 🕮 *Apdo. 95–5710* 🖷 *692–1180* ⊕ *www.rockriverlodge.com* ⤳ *6 rooms, 8 cabinas* ☖ *Restaurant, windsurfing, fishing, mountain bikes, horseback riding, bar, laundry service; no a/c, no room phones, no room TVs* ▭ *MC, V.*

¢ ▦ **Hotel Naralit.** Spell Tilarán backward and you get the name of a great budget option in the center of town. It's very basic but comfortable, run by friendly folks, and spotlessly clean. A large glass door fronts a porch in each pleasantly furnished room, letting in lots of light. The Naralit manages a small restaurant next door. ⊠ *Opposite south side of cathedral* 🕾 *695–5393* 🖷 *695–6767* 🛏 *25 rooms* ⚴ *Fans, some refrigerators; no a/c, no room phones* ▤ *MC, V.*

Sports & the Outdoors

HORSEBACK RIDING
Uncounted miles of good horse trails cover a marvelous mix of terrain. **Hotel Tilawa** (🕾 695–5050) and nearly every other reputable hotel can make arrangements for guided and unguided horseback treks. Tilawa charges $20 per hour; $40 for a half-day tour. Most trails are appropriate for beginners.

WINDSURFING & KITESURFING
Rock River Lodge (⊠ 19 km [11 mi]) northeast of Tilarán 🕾 692–1180) is one of several hotels that rent windsurfing equipment. Expect to pay $40 per day. The best selection of wind- and kitesurfing equipment for rent or purchase can be found at **Tilawa Wind Surf** (⊠ 8 km [5 mi]) north of Tilarán 🕾 695–5050), the lakefront shop associated with the Hotel Tilawa and the only outfitter here open year-round. You'll pay $50 a day for windsurfing equipment; $120 a day if you want to partake of kitesurfing.

en route
If your bones can take it, a very rough track leads from Tilarán via Cabeceras to Santa Elena, near the Monteverde Cloud Forest Biological Reserve, doing away with the need to cut across to the Pan-American Highway. You may well need a four-wheel-drive vehicle—inquire locally about the current condition of the road—but the views of Nicoya Peninsula, Lake Arenal, and Volcán Arenal reward those willing to bump around a bit. Note, too, that you don't really save much time—on a good day, it takes about 2½ hours as opposed to the 3 required via Cañas and Río Lagarto on the highway.

MONTEVERDE & SANTA ELENA

❽ ❾ *Monteverde is 167 km (104 mi) northwest of San José. Santa Elena is 6 km (4 mi) north of Monteverde and 35 km (22 mi) southeast of Tilarán.*

The area's first residents were a handful of Costa Rican families fleeing the rough-and-ready life of nearby gold-mining fields during the 1940s. They were joined in the 1950s by Quakers, conscientious objectors from Alabama drawn by this country that had just a few years earlier abolished its army, and who came in search of peace, tranquility, and good grazing. But the cloud forest that lay above their dairy farms was soon to attract the attention of ecologists. Educators and artisans followed, giving Monteverde and its "metropolis," the village of Santa Elena, a mystique all their own. Monteverde's Quakers, or, more officially, the Society of Friends, no longer constitute the majority these days, but their imprint on the community remains strong.

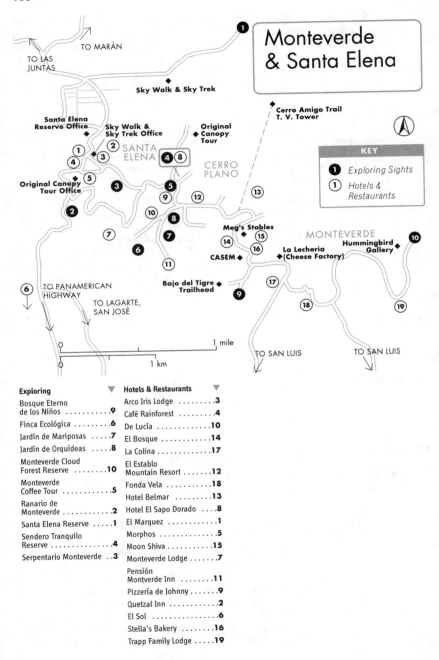

Monteverde & Santa Elena

TO MARÁN

TO LAS JUNTAS

Sky Walk & Sky Trek

Santa Elena Reserve Office

Sky Walk & Sky Trek Office

SANTA ELENA

Original Canopy Tour

Cerro Amigo Trail T. V. Tower

CERRO PLANO

Original Canopy Tour Office

TO PANAMERICAN HIGHWAY

TO LAGARTE, SAN JOSÉ

Meg's Stables

CASEM

Bajo del Tigre Trailhead

MONTEVERDE

La Lecheria (Cheese Factory)

Hummingbird Gallery

TO SAN LUIS

TO SAN LUIS

1 mile

1 km

KEY

❶ *Exploring Sights*

① *Hotels & Restaurants*

Getting here means negotiating some of the country's legendarily rough roads, but don't let that deter you from a visit. Years of promises to pave the way up here have collided with politics and scarce funds, but many residents remain just as happy to keep Monteverde out of the reach of tour buses and day-trippers. Your own vehicle gives you the greatest flexibility, but a burgeoning number of shuttle-van services connect Monteverde with San José and other tourist destinations around the country. And once you're here, if without wheels, the community's rugged taxis can get you from hotel to restaurant to reserve. "Monteverde" refers generally to the entire area, but officially it's the original Quaker settlement that congregates around its dairy-processing plant down the mountain from the reserve entrance. (Road signs designate it that way.) Houses and hotels amorphously flank the 6-km (4-mi) road between Santa Elena and the reserve.

The only way to really see the area's reserves, including the Monteverde Cloud Forest, is to hike them. ⇨ For information on trails, *see* Hiking in Sports & the Outdoors, *below.*

Several conservation areas that have sprung up near Monteverde make attractive day trips, particularly if the Monteverde Reserve is too busy. The **Santa Elena Reserve** just west of Monteverde is a project of the Santa Elena high school and has a series of trails that can be walked alone or with a guide. The **Camino Verde Information Center** (✉ Main street in town) operates a shuttle service to the reserve with fixed departures and returns. Reservations are required, and the cost is $2 each way. ✉ *6 km (4 mi) north of Santa Elena* ☎ *645–5390* ⊕ *www.monteverdeinfo. com/reserve* ✄ *$9* ⊙ *Daily 7–4.*

Only in Monteverde would visitors groove to the nightlife at an exhibition of 20 species of frogs, toads, and other amphibians. Bilingual biologist-guides take you through a 45-minute tour of the terrariums in ★ ☾ the **Ranario de Monteverde**, just outside Santa Elena. For the best show, come around dusk and stay well into the evening, when the critters become more active and much more vocal. There's a small frog-and-toad-theme gift shop. ✉ *½ km (¼ mi) southeast of Supermercado La Esperanza, Santa Elena* ☎ *645–6320* ✄ *$8* ⊙ *Daily 9–8:30.*

☾ At the **Serpentario Monteverde**, greet 40 species of live Costa Rican reptiles and amphibians with glass safely between you and them. Guided tours in English or Spanish are included in your admission price. ✉ *Just outside Santa Elena on road to Monteverde* ☎ *645–6002* ⊕ *www. snaketour.com* ✄ *$7* ⊙ *Daily 9–8.*

The 200-acre **Sendero Tranquilo Reserve** is bordered by the Monteverde Cloud Forest Biological Reserve and the Guacimal River. Narrow trails are designed to have as little impact on the forest as possible (only groups of two to six are allowed). A guide leads you through primary and secondary forest and a deforested area. Because of the emphasis on minimal environmental impact, animals here tend to be more timid than at some other reserves. ✉ *3 km (2 mi) north of Monteverde park entrance, Cerro Plano* ☎ *645–5010* ✄ *$20* ⊙ *Tours depart daily at 7:30 AM and 1 PM; reservations required.*

Bite your tongue before requesting Costa Rica's ubiquitous Café Britt up here. Export-quality Café Monteverde is the locally grown product. ★ The **Monteverde Coffee Tour** lets you see the process up close from start to finish, from shade growing on the area's Finca La Bella plantation; transport to the *beneficio*, the processing mill where the beans are washed and dried; and finally to the roaster. Reservations are required. ⊠ *Cerro Plano, at start of road to Jardín de Mariposas* ☎ *645–7090* ⊕ *www.crstudytours.com* ✉ *$15* ⊙ *Tours at 8 AM and 1 PM.*

Finca Ecológica is a private wildlife refuge with four trails on its 75-acre Ecological Farm, plus abundant bird life, sloths, agoutis, coatimundis, two waterfalls, and a coffee plantation. If you can't make it all the way up to the Monteverde Reserve for the evening hike, there's a top-notch guided, two-hour twilight walk that begins each evening at 5:30. Reservations are required. ⊠ *Turnoff to Jardín Mariposas, off main road between Santa Elena and Monteverde* ☎ *645–5554* ⊕ *www.fincaecologicamonteverde.com* ✉ *$7, twilight walk $14* ⊙ *Daily 7–5.*

Forty species of tropical butterflies flit about in four enclosed botanical gardens at the **Jardín de Mariposas** (Butterfly Garden), all of which have stunning views of the Golfo de Nicoya. You'll see more activity during a morning visit; the butterflies are less active when it clouds over in the afternoon. A guided tour helps you understand the stages of a butterfly's life. Do stop and watch the passing parade on the leaf-cutter ant trail. A small theater presents an informational video in English, Spanish, French, Dutch, or German. ⊠ *Near Pensión Monteverde Inn; take right-hand turnoff 4 km (2½ mi) past Santa Elena on road to Monteverde, continue for 2 km (1 mi)* ☎ *645–5512* ✉ *$8* ⊙ *Daily 9:30–4.*

The **Jardín de Orquídeas** (Orchid Garden) showcases more than 400 species of orchids, including two unnamed, one of which is the world's smallest. The Monteverde Orchid Investigation Project manages the gardens. ⊠ *1½ km (1 mi) southeast of Santa Elena on road to Monteverde Reserve* ☎ *645–5510* ✉ *$5* ⊙ *Daily 8–5.*

The 54,000-acre **Bosque Eterno de los Niños** (Children's Eternal Rain Forest) dwarfs the Monteverde and Santa Elena reserves. Much of it is not open to the public, but for those seeking a rugged experience, the Monteverde Conservation League offers stays at San Gerardo and Poco Sol, two remote field stations within the forest. The $34 packages include dormitory accommodation and meals. Hiking tours of the forest are available (⇨ Hiking, *below*). ⊠ *100 m south of CASEM* ☎ *645–5305* ✉ *Forest $5; transportation from area hotels $2* ⊙ *Daily 8–4:30.*

need a break? Long before tourists flocked up here, dairy farming was the sole foundation of Monteverde's economy. Quakers still operate what is locally referred to as the Cheese Factory, or **La Lechería** (⊠ ½ km [¼ mi] south of CASEM, halfway between Santa Elena and Monteverde Reserve ☎ 645–2850, 645–7090 tours). It's a much grander milk-processing plant today than the original settlers ever envisioned. The factory store scoops up some of the best ice cream around. Stop in for a dish or a cone when you pass by. It's open Monday–Saturday 8–4 and Sunday 10–4; it's closed Sunday April–November. If you have more time, take a two-hour tour of the operation Monday–Saturday at 9 or 2. Tours are $8 and wind up with a cheese-sampling session. Reserve in advance.

★ ▶ In close proximity to several fine hotels, the private **Monteverde Cloud Forest Biological Reserve** (Reserva Biológica Bosque Nuboso Monteverde) is one of Costa Rica's best-kept reserves, with well-marked trails, lush vegetation, and a cool climate. The collision of moist winds with the continental divide here creates a constant mist whose particles provide nutrients for plants growing at the upper layers of the forest. Giant trees are enshrouded in a cascade of orchids, bromeliads, mosses, and ferns, and, in those patches where sunlight penetrates, brilliantly colored flowers flourish. The sheer size of everything, especially the leaves of the trees, is striking. No less astounding is the variety: 2,500 plant species, 400 species of birds, 500 types of butterflies, and more than 100 different mammals have so far been cataloged at Monteverde. A damp and exotic mixture of shades, smells, and sounds, the cloud forest is also famous for its population of quetzals, which can be spotted feeding on the *aguacatillo* (like an avocado) trees; best viewing times are early mornings from January until September, and especially during the mating season of April and May. Other forest-dwelling inhabitants include hummingbirds and multicolor frogs.

For those who don't have a lucky eye, a short-stay aquarium is in the field station; captive amphibians stay here just a week before being released back into the wild. Although the reserve limits visitors to 160 people at a time, Monteverde is one of the country's most popular destinations and gets very busy, so come early and allow a generous slice of time for leisurely hiking to see the forest's flora and fauna; longer hikes are made possible by some strategically placed overnight refuges along the way. At the entrance to the reserve you can buy self-guide pamphlets and rent rubber boots; a map is provided when you pay the entrance fee. A two-hour guided night tour starts each evening at 7:15, and the reserve provides transport from area hotels for an extra $2. ✉ *35 km (22 mi) southeast of Tilarán, 167 km (104 mi) northwest of San José* ☎ *645–5122* ⊕ *www.cct.or.cr* ✒ *$12, guide $15; night tour $13* ☉ *Daily 7–4.*

Where to Stay & Eat

$–$$ ✕ **De Lucía.** Cordial Chilean owner José Belmar is the walking, talking (in five languages) menu at this elegant restaurant, always on hand to explain with enthusiasm such masterfully prepared dishes as sea bass with garlic sauce and orange chicken. All entrées are served with an impressive assortment of grilled vegetables and fried plantains. The handsome wooden restaurant with red mahogany tables is given a distinct South American flavor by an array of Andean tapestries and ceramics. An excellent dessert choice is *tres leches* (a rich cake of condensed and evaporated milk and sugar) with decaf coffee—a novelty in Costa Rica.

CloseUp

COSTA RICAN BIRDS 101

IF YOU VISIT A COSTA RICAN CLOUD FOREST, you'll probably have your eyes peeled for the Emerald Toucanet or the Three-wattled Bellbird, but if you're here between October and April, you'll be just as likely to see a Kentucky Warbler. Experienced birders won't be surprised to see that some of their feathered friends from home made similar vacation plans. When northern birds fly south for the winter, they don't all head to Miami.

Seasonal visitors are just part (about a quarter) of the amazing avian panorama in Costa Rica. Nearly 850 bird species have been identified here, more than the United States and Canada have combined, and all in an area about half the size of Kentucky. The country is consequently a mecca for amateur ornithologists, who flock here by the thousands. Though the big attractions tend to be such spectacular species as the Keel-billed Toucan and Resplendent Quetzal, it is the diversity of shape, size, coloration, and behavior that makes bird-watching in Costa Rica so fascinating.

The country's avian inhabitants range in size from the Scintillant Hummingbird, standing a mere 2½ inches tall and weighing just over 2 grams, to the Jabiru, a long-legged stork that reaches a height of more than 4 feet and a weight of 14 pounds. The diversity of form and color varies from such striking creatures as the showy Scarlet Macaw and the quirky Purple Gallinule to the relatively inconspicuous, and seemingly ubiquitous, Clay-colored Robin, which is, surprisingly enough, Costa Rica's national bird. These robins may look a bit plain, but their song is a melodious one, and since the males sing almost constantly toward the end of the dry season—the beginning of their mating season—local legend has it that they call the rains, which play a vital role in a nation so dependent on agriculture.

Birds associated with the tropics—parrots, parakeets, and macaws; toucans and toucanets; and the elusive but legendary quetzal—are a thrill for those of us who don't see them every day. But there are many other, equally impressive species to see, such as the motmots, with their distinctive racket tails; oropéndolas, which build remarkable hanging nests; and an amazing array of hawks, kites, and falcons.

On the color scale, tanagers, euphonias, manakins, cotingas, and trogons are some of the country's loveliest plumed creatures, but none of them match the iridescence of the hummingbirds. Costa Rica hosts 51 members of the hummingbird family, compared with just one species for all of the United States east of the Rocky Mountains. Time spent near a hummingbird feeder will treat you to an unforgettable display of accelerated aerial antics and general pugnacity.

You just might find that the more you observe Costa Rica's birds, the more interesting they get. Bird-watching can be done everywhere in the country—all you need is a pair of binoculars and a copy of A Guide to the Birds of Costa Rica, the excellent field guide by Gary Stiles and Alexander Skutch. Wake up early, get out into the woods or the garden, focus those binoculars, and you'll quickly be enchanted by the beauty on the wing. For more information about Costa Rican birds, see the Wildlife Glossary in the Understanding Costa Rica chapter.

⊠ *Turnoff to Jardín de Mariposas, off main road between Santa Elena and Monteverde* ☎ 645–5337 ⊟ *AE, MC, V.*

$–$$ ✕ **Pizzería de Johnny.** Everyone makes it to this stylish but informal place with candles and white tablecloths during a visit. The Monteverde pizza, with the works, is the most popular dish, and pastas, sandwiches, and a fine wine selection round out the menu. ⊠ *1½ km (1 mi) southeast of Santa Elena on road to Monteverde Reserve* ☎ 645–5066 ⊟ *MC, V.*

$ ✕ **El Márquez.** You don't expect seafood up here in the mountains, but the owner gets fresh shipments up from Puntarenas several times weekly. The place is nothing fancy; expect plastic tables and chairs, with lots of local flavor. Portions are big, but prices aren't. You'll have trouble finishing the generous mixed seafood platter with shrimp, crab, and octopus in a white-wine sauce, or the jumbo shrimp with a sauce of mushrooms and heart of palm. ⊠ *Diagonal from Banco Nacional, next to Suárez veterinary clinic, Santa Elena* ☎ 645–5918 ⊟ *MC, V* ⊙ *Closed Sun.*

★ $ ✕ **Moon Shiva.** Costa Rican tropics meet the sands of the Middle East at this breezy, casual place with large glass windows overlooking a forested garden. Falafel, pita, tahini, and baba ghanouj figure prominently on the menu, but the build-your-own *gallos* (tortillas that you fill yourself) might include standard Tico black-bean paste or hummus. Many of the dishes include the house sauce mixed from pineapple, curry, and coconut. Top off your meal with ice cream with fried bananas in rum and cinnamon. ⊠ *100 m east of CASEM* ☎ 645–6270 ⊟ *AE, MC, V* ⊙ *No lunch Sun.*

$ ✕ **Morphos.** This is about as upscale as Santa Elena dining gets, but Morphos is still pretty casual. It serves up a mix of meat, with quite a few vegetarian options on the menu—a rarity up here. Inside this second-floor restaurant are stone walls, log-hewn chairs, artwork, and huge wooden light fixtures in the shape of the famed blue butterfly from which the restaurant takes its name. A large glass window lets you survey all that goes on in town. ⊠ *Across from La Esperanza Supermarket, Santa Elena* ☎ 645–5607 ⊟ *MC, V.*

¢–$ ✕ **Café Rainforest.** Here's a great, trendy place to warm up with a cup of coffee on a chilly evening, and there are plenty of those up here. Gourmet Café Monteverde, the region's pride and joy, is used in the beverages and sold in souvenir packages but under this establishment's own label. Natural fruit drinks, plus sandwiches, pastries, and desserts round out the fare. If it's not too cold, an open-air second-floor balcony lets you survey the goings-on in the street below. ⊠ *Across from AyA, Santa Elena* ☎ 645–5841 ⊟ *No credit cards.*

¢–$ ✕ **Stella's Bakery.** An old standby that dishes up fast food, Monteverde-style, Stella's is one of the few spots that open at 6 AM, and it is a great place to get an early morning fix before heading to the reserve. Luscious pastries, rolls, muffins, natural juices, and coffee are standard breakfast fare. Take them with you if you're running short of time. Lunch consists of light sandwiches, soups, and pastas. All are prepared with organic ingredients grown right here on the property. ⊠ *Across from CASEM, Monteverde* ☎ 645–5560 ⊟ *V* ⊙ *No dinner.*

$$ ×⊞ **Fonda Vela.** Owned by the Smith brothers, whose family was among
Fodor'sChoice the first American arrivals in the 1950s, these steep-roof chalets have
★ large bedrooms with white-stucco walls, wood floors, and huge windows. Some have markedly better views of the wooded grounds, so specify when booking. The most innovatively designed of Monteverde's hotels is also one of the closest to the reserve entrance. Local and international recipes, prepared with flair, are served in the restaurant or on the veranda. ⊠ *1½ km (1 mi) northwest of Monteverde park entrance, Monteverde* ☎ *645–5125, 257–1413 in San José* 🖷 *645–5119, 257–1416 in San José* ⊕ *www.fondavela.com* 🕮 *Apdo. 70060–1000, San José* ⇆ *40 rooms* ⟡ *2 restaurants, minibars, refrigerators, horseback riding, bar, laundry service, Internet, meeting room; no a/c, no TV in some rooms* ▭ *AE, DC, MC, V.*

$$ ×⊞ **Hotel El Sapo Dorado.** After beginning its life as a nightclub, the "Golden Toad" became a popular restaurant and then graduated into a very pleasant hotel. Geovanny Arguedas's family arrived here to farm 10 years before the Quakers did, and he and his wife, Hannah Lowther, have built secluded hillside cabins with polished paneling, tables, fireplaces, and rocking chairs. The restaurant is renowned for its pasta, pizza, vegetarian dishes, and sailfish from Puntarenas. ⊠ *6 km (4 mi) northwest of Monteverde park entrance, Monteverde* ☎ *645–5010* 🖷 *645–5180* ⊕ *www.sapodorado.com* 🕮 *Apdo. 9–5655, Monteverde* ⇆ *30 rooms* ⟡ *Restaurant, massage, bar, laundry service; no a/c, no room phones, no room TVs* ▭ *V.*

$–$$ ×⊞ **Hotel Belmar.** Built into the hillside, Hotel Belmar resembles two tall Swiss chalets and commands extensive views of the Golfo de Nicoya and the hilly peninsula. The amiable Chilean owners have designed both elegant and rustic rooms, paneled with polished wood; half the rooms have balconies. In the dining room, you can count on adventurous and delicious *platos del día* (daily specials) of Costa Rican and international fare. ⊠ *4 km (2½ mi) north of Monteverde* ☎ *645–5201* 🖷 *645–5135* ⊕ *www.hotelbelmar.com* 🕮 *Apdo. 17–5655, Monteverde Puntarenas* ⇆ *34 rooms* ⟡ *Restaurant, hot tub, basketball, billiards, bar, laundry service, travel services; no a/c, no phones in some rooms, no room TVs* ▭ *DC, V.*

$$ ⊞ **Monteverde Lodge.** The venerable Costa Rica Expeditions operates this
Fodor'sChoice old standby close to Santa Elena. Rooms have vaulted ceilings and bath-
★ tubs—an amenity rarely seen here—and great views. A coffee table abuts the angled bay window overlooking the 15 acres of grounds, a perfect place to have a cup of coffee and bird-watch from indoors. The restaurant and bar congregate around an enormous but cozy lobby fireplace. Relax in the hot tub in the enormous solarium, a perfect place to unwind after a day of tromping through the reserves. Or take in the evening slide presentation, showcasing cloud-forest life. ⊠ *200 m south of Ranario de Monteverde, Santa Elena* 🕮 *Apdo. 6941–1000, San José* ☎ *257–0766 in San José* 🖷 *257–1165 in San José* ⊕ *www.costaricaexpeditions.com* ⇆ *27 rooms* ⟡ *Restaurant, hot tub, bar, shop, Internet, meeting room, travel services; no a/c, no room TVs* ▭ *AE, DC, MC, V.*

$–$$ ⊞ **El Establo Mountain Resort.** Mixing old and new, "The Stable" began life as just that, a stable near the road, remodeled and apportioned into comfortable rooms with basic furnishings. A newer pink building perches on the hill above with large suites with wood-and-stone walls. Some contain lofts; all come with amenities rarely seen up here, such as bathtubs, phones, and enormous windows with views of the Golfo de Nicoya. The newest building, even higher on the hill, has rooms with hot tubs, private balconies, and even more commanding views. ⊠ *3½ km (2 mi) northwest of Monteverde* ☎ *645–5110* 🖷 *645–5041* ⊕ *www.hotelelestablo.com* ☞ *63 rooms* ⚐ *Restaurant, snack bar, cable TV, pool, hot tub, massage, bar, travel services; no a/c, no TV in some rooms* ▤ *AE, DC, MC, V* ❢❂❢ *BP.*

$–$$
Fodor's Choice
★ 🖾 **El Sol.** A charming family, natives of the Canary Islands, tends to guests at one of those quintessential get-away-from-it-all places just 10 minutes down the mountain from—and a noticeable few degrees warmer than—Santa Elena. Two fully furnished *ojoche*-wood cabins perch on the mountainside on the 25-acre farm. Every vantage point in the cabins—the living area, the bed, the desk, the shower, and even the toilet—possesses stupendous views. The property has 3 km (2 mi) of trails, a stone-walled pool, and a Finnish sauna. Gourmet cuisine is a mix of Spanish and German; meals can be taken in the main house or brought to your cabin. ⊠ *4 km (2½ mi southwest of Santa Elena* ☎ *645–5838* 🖷 *645–5042* ⊕ *www.elsolnuestro.com* ☞ *2 cabins* ⚐ *Dining room, pool, sauna; no a/c, no room phones, no room TVs* ▤ *No credit cards.*

$ 🖾 **La Colina.** This Colorado ranch–style place is a longtime Monteverde standby. Rust colors and earth tones prevail in the rooms, which are accentuated with the occasional wagon wheel and Old West–style trunk. A hearty American-style breakfast keeps you going until your evening dinner. The friendly management gives discounts for extended stays, and has camping facilities for $5 per person in addition to the rooms. ⊠ *290 m south of Cheese Factory* ☎ *645–5009* 🖷 *645–5580* ⊕ *www. lacolinalodge.com* ☞ *10 rooms, 7 with bath* ⚐ *Dining room; no a/c, no room phones, no room TVs* ▤ *MC, V* ❢❂❢ *BP.*

$ 🖾 **Trapp Family Lodge.** Take a whiff in this cozy lodge and you can imagine yourself in a lumberyard. The enormous rooms, with wood paneling and ceilings, have lovely furniture marvelously crafted from—you guessed it—wood. The architectural style is appropriate, as the lodge is surrounded by trees, just a 10-minute walk from the park entrance, making it the closest lodge to the reserve. The friendly Chilean owners are always around to provide personalized service. ⊠ *Main road from Monteverde Reserve, Monteverde* ☎ *645–5858* 🖷 *645–5990* ⊕ *www. trappfam.com* 🖃 *Apdo. 70–5655, Monteverde* ☞ *22 rooms* ⚐ *Restaurant, bar, laundry service; no a/c, no room TVs, no smoking* ▤ *MC, V.*

★ **¢–$** 🖾 **Arco Iris Lodge.** You can't tell that you're in the center of town at this tranquil spot, with its cozy cabins among 4 acres of birding trails. Cabin decor ranges from rustic to more plush, but all lodgings come with porches. Start your day with a delicious breakfast buffet, including homemade bread, granola, and marmalades. A commitment to environmental sustainability is reflected throughout the lodge; many of the kitchen's ingredients come from its own organic garden. The laid-back German management can provide good advice about how to spend your time in the area. ⊠ *70 m south of Banco Nacional, Santa Elena* ☎ *645–5067* 🖷 *645–5022* ⊕ *www.arcoirislodge.com* ☞ *12* *cabins ᕯ Horseback riding, laundry service; no a/c, no room phones, no room TVs* ⊟ *AE, MC, V.*

¢–$ ⊡ **El Bosque.** Convenient to the Bajo del Tigre nature trail and Meg's Stables, El Bosque's quiet, simple rooms are grouped around a central camping area. A bridge crosses a stream and leads to the hotel. Brick-oven pizzas are served on the veranda. ⊠ *2½ km (1½ mi) southeast of Santa Elena on road to Monteverde Reserve* ☎ *645–5221* ᕲ *645–5129* ⬙ *el-bosque@racsa.co.cr* ✆ *Apdo. 5655, Santa Elena* ⤵ *29 rooms* ᕯ *Restaurant, bar, laundry service; no a/c, no room TVs* ⊟ *AE, MC, V.*

¢ ⊡ **Pensión Monteverde Inn.** One of the cheapest Monteverde inns is quite far from the park entrance, on a 28-acre private preserve. The bedrooms are basic, but they have stunning views of the Golfo de Nicoya and have hardwood floors, firm beds, and powerful, hot showers. Home cooking is served by the chatty David and María Savage and family. ⊠ *5 km (3 mi) past Butterfly Garden on turnoff road, Monteverde* ☎ᕲ *645–5156* ⤵ *10 rooms* ᕯ *Dining room; no a/c, no room phones, no room TVs* ⊟ *No credit cards.*

¢ ⊡ **Quetzal Inn.** Three buildings ascend a hill at three levels, both in price and elevation, at this inn near the center of Santa Elena. Opt for the rooms in cedar-and-guanacaste–wood cabins with balconies, in the lower-level building: they're the nicest. The lowest-priced rooms with shared bath sit overhead the main building. Highest on the hill are more spartan wood-and-plaster cabins, the medium-range rooms here. All are pleasantly furnished. This is a real budget find. ⊠ *75 m south of Banco Nacional, Santa Elena* ☎ *645–6076* ᕲ *645–5358* ⤵ *15 rooms, 11 with bath* ᕯ *Restaurant; no a/c, no room phones, no room TVs* ⊟ *No credit cards.*

Sports & the Outdoors

CANOPY TOURS One of the most unique ways to explore the rain-forest canopy is on a canopy tour. Though billed as a way to get up close with nature, the tours more resemble a ride—they're great fun, but don't plan on seeing the Resplendent Quetzal as you zip from platform to platform. (Your shouts of exhilaration will probably scare them all away.) Canopy tours have sprung up all over Costa Rica, and are even making forays into other countries, but they got their start here, in amongst the trees of the cloud forest, which gives more scenic views than you get over the flat terrain of a beach. Don't hesitate to ask questions about the safety of all canopy tour companies, and be prepared to walk away if the trip doesn't look professionally handled.

You can visit the Monteverde cloud-forest treetops courtesy of the **Original Canopy Tour** (⊠ Across from La Esperanza Supermarket, Santa Elena ☎ 645–5243, 291–4465 in San José ⊕ www.canopytour.com), which has 10 platforms in the canopy—the company's longest tour. You arrive at most of the platforms using a cable-and-harness traversing system and climb 42 feet inside a strangler fig tree to reach one. Several knockoff tours, with uneven reputations, have sprung up around Costa Rica, also calling themselves "canopy tours." This one, which calls itself "the original," is top-notch. The tours last 2½ hours and are held at 7:30 AM, 10:30 AM, and 2:30 PM. The cost is $45, a price that includes transport from area hotels.

Sky Walk (✉ Across from Banco Nacional, Santa Elena ☎ 645–5238 ⊕ www.skywalk.co.cr) lets you walk between treetops, up to a height of 138 feet, by way of five hanging bridges connected from tree to tree. Imposing towers are also used as support, although they somewhat mar the landscape. The hour-long walk can be done anytime between 7 and 4 daily and costs $15. Tours with an English-speaking guide ($27) leave at 8 and 1; be sure to make reservations (between 7 AM and 9 PM). At the same facility is the more adventurous **Sky Trek** (⊕ www.skytrek.com), which uses rock-climbing gear and zip lines and has 11 cables, longer than those of the Original Canopy Tour—the most extensive tops out at more than 2,500 feet. Note that the lines here extend between towers above the canopy, rather than among trees as do the cables on the area's other three tours, and you'll more likely notice the effects of the wind on this one. Tours cost $40 and leave at 7:15, 9, 11:15, and 1:15. The company provides transport to and from hotels for $2 extra when called a few hours in advance.

You can find it all—canopy tour, bridge walks, butterfly and hummingbird gardens—at **Selvatura** (✉ Across from church, Santa Elena ☎ 645–5929 ⊕ www.selvatura.com), a complex just outside the Santa Elena Reserve. Selvatura's 18-line, 20-platform canopy tour ($35) is the only such operation built entirely inside the cloud forest. If zipping from tree to tree isn't quite your thing, the operation's **Tree Top Walkways** ($15) takes you on 3 km (2 mi) of very stable bridges through the same canopy terrain. Quite frankly, if viewing nature is what you're after, the bridge walk is a more realistic way to do it. A 100-bird hummingbird garden and an enormous enclosed 25-species *mariposario* (butterfly garden) sit near the visitor center. Transportation from area hotels is included in the price. You can choose from numerous mix-and-match combinations, depending on which activities interest you, or take it all in, with lunch included, for $78.

The newest in the ever-expanding number of zip-line operations is the **Aventura Canopy** (✉ Across from bus terminal, Santa Elena ☎ 645–6901) on the road to the Santa Elena Reserve. Tours depart at 7:30 and 10:30 AM and 12:30 and 2:30 PM and last 2½ hours. They take you over 16 cables—some extending 2,000 feet—one rappel, and one Tarzan swing. Rates are $45 and include transportation from area hotels.

A more sedate variation on the canopy tours is the **Natural Wonders Tram** (✉ Off main road between Santa Elena and Monteverde, on turnoff to Jardín de Mariposas ☎ 645–5960), in which two-person carriages on an elevated track take you on an hour-long ride through the rain-forest canopy. You control the speed of your carriage. Alternatively, a 1½-km (1-mi) walk gives you a different ground-level perspective. The site opens for night visits with advance reservations.

HIKING Hike trails guided or unguided at the **Santa Elena Reserve** (✉ 6 km [4 mi]) north of Santa Elena, just west of Monteverde ☎ 645–5390 ⊕ www.monteverdeinfo.com/reserve). The 1.4-km Youth Challenge Trail takes about 45 minutes to negotiate and contains an observation platform with views as far away as the Arenal volcano, that is, if the clouds clear. If you're feeling hardy, try the 5-km (3 mi) Caño Negro Trail, clocking in at four hours. Admission to the reserve, which is open daily 7–4, is $9.

The 75-acre private wildlife refuge **Finca Ecológica** (✉ Turnoff to Jardín Mariposas, off main road between Santa Elena and Monteverde ☎ 645–5554 ⊕ www.fincaecologicamonteverde.com) has four trails ranging from 1 to 3 km and a two-hour guided twilight walk ($14) each evening at 5:30. Reservations are required. Admission to the refuge is $7, and it's open daily 7–5.

The Monteverde Conservation League's (MCL's) **Bajo del Tigre trail** (✉ Bosque Eterno de los Niños, 100 m south of CASEM ☎ 645–5305) makes for a gentle, self-guided 1½-km (1-mi) hike through secondary forest. Along the trail are 27 points of interpretation, many with lessons geared toward kids. A separate guided twilight walk ($15) begins at 5:30 PM and lasts two hours—reservations are required—affording the chance to see the nocturnal side of the cloud forest. The trail is open daily 8 to 4:30; admission to the forest is $5, and transportation from area hotels is $2.

Hike 200 acres through four different stages of cloud forest at the **Sendero Tranquilo Reserve** (✉ 3 km [2 mi] north of Monteverde park entrance, Cerro Plano ☎ 645–5010 in El Sapo Dorado), including one area illustrating the results of cloud-forest devastation. Tours are arranged through the El Sapo Dorado hotel and require a two-person minimum and six-person limit. Admission to the reserve is $20.

HORSEBACK RIDING Long-established **Desafío Adventures** (✉ Across from La Esperanza supermarket, Santa Elena ☎ 645–5874 ⊕ www.monteverdetours.com) leads tours on horseback, two hours each way, to the San Luis Waterfall, an area not often taken in by Monteverde visitors, as well as shorter excursions on farms around Santa Elena. Desafío should be your only choice for getting to La Fortuna by horse. The operator combines car and boat with a three-hour horseback ride on a flat trail along Lake Arenal, with farms for resting the animals at each end. It's infinitely more humane for the horses (and you) than the muddy, treacherous mountain trails used by dozens of other individuals who'll offer to take you to Arenal.

Meg's Stables (✉ Main road, halfway between Santa Elena and Monteverde ☎ 645–5419) leads horseback-riding trips for everyone from toddlers to seasoned experts. Guided rides through the Monteverde area cost $15 an hour; prices drop for longer rides. Reservations are a good idea in high season, and essential if you want an English-speaking guide. A $50 tour to the San Luis waterfalls is geared toward experienced riders. Just outside of Santa Elena, family-operated **El Palomino** (☎ 645–5479) gives escorted half-day horseback-riding tours ($40) on farm areas around Santa Elena. El Palomino provides transportation from your hotel to the tour location. The **Caballeriza El Rodeo** (✉ West entrance of Santa Elena, at tollbooth ☎ 645–5764) operates escorted half-day horseback-riding tours on a private farm near the tollbooth near the entrance to Santa Elena. Excursions are for everyone from beginner to experienced rider. A two-hour sunset tour begins at 4 PM and runs $25. All that glitters was gold around here in the early 20th century, and the **Gold Tour** (✉ 150 m northeast of Cerro Plano school ☎ 645–6914) takes you on a three-hour trip on horseback—no riding experience necessary—to visit a mine opened in the 1920s. The excursion ($40) includes a demonstration of the panning methods used during those heady days, and on the trip back, a visit to a *trapiche*, a traditional sugarcane mill.

RAPPELLING **Desafío Adventures** (✉ Across from Supermercado La Esperanza ☎ 645–5874 ⊕ www.monteverdetours.com) takes you rappelling on its Canyoneering Tour at the private El Mirador Reserve and Lodge 30 minutes outside Santa Elena. The excursion begins with a half-hour hike to the first of four waterfalls—the falls range in height from 50 to 100 feet, and you lower yourself with the aid of a guide and very secure harnesses. Tours begin at 7:30 with a return by early afternoon. The $45 price includes transportation and gear, and is appropriate for any level of experience. (The walk back uphill at the end might tax you more than the rappelling did.) An optional lunch at the lodge is extra.

Shopping

Part gallery, part workshop, **Art House** (✉ 1½ km [1 mi] southeast of Santa Elena on road to Monteverde Reserve ☎ 645–5275) has five rooms of colorful, locally made carvings, masks, wall hangings, and hammocks. **Atmosphera** (✉ Turnoff to Jardín de Mariposas, Cerro Plano ☎ 645–6555) specializes in locally made primitivist wood carvings and has a small café. **Art of the Forest** (✉ Next to Supermercado La Esperanza ☎ 645–5881) sells art made from the large, native jícara bean—they look fragile, but really aren't—that artist Mitch Lantz turns into lamps and candleholders.

Bromelia's (✉ 100 m east of CASEM, Monteverde ☎ 645–6272) bills itself as a bookstore with a good selection of nature books and music, but sells colorful batiks, masks, and jewelry, too. **Chorotega** (✉ Next to gas station, Cerro Plano ☎ 645–6919) sells ceramics made by the indigenous Chorotega from the artisan community of Guaitil in northwest Costa Rica as well as Nicaraguan woodwork. In Monteverde, the 150-member **Coooperativa de Artesanía de Santa Elena y Monteverde** (CASEM; ☎ 645–5190), an artisans' cooperative next to the El Bosque hotel-restaurant, sells locally made crafts, mostly by women, and English-language books. **Coopesanta Elena** (✉ Next to CASEM ☎ 645–5901) is the area's distributor for packages of the area's gourmet Café Monteverde coffee and accoutrements.

A project of the Monteverde Institute, the **Community Art Center** (✉ 50 m southwest of Cheese Factory ☎ 645–6121) exhibits and sells the works of local artists and artisans with a minimum of overhead and fuss in one of the half-century-old original Quaker houses. Local artist and art instructor Marco Tulio Brenes exhibits and sells his wood reliefs and turning, painting, and ceramics works at **Galería Extasis** (✉ 100 m west of CASEM, Monteverde ☎ 645–5548). Artists from around the country exhibit at Extasis, too.

The **Hummingbird Gallery** (✉ Just outside entrance to Monteverde Reserve ☎ 645–5030) sells books, gifts, T-shirts, great Costa Rican coffee, prints, and slides by nature specialists Michael and Patricia Fogden, as well as watercolors by nature artist Sarah Dowell. **Librería Chunches** (⊠ 25 m south of Banco Nacional, Santa Elena ☎ 645–5147) has books in English, as well as a good selection of Spanish-language literature and CDs from Costa Rican artists.

Nightlife & the Arts

NIGHTLIFE "Wild night" takes on its own meaning here. You can still get up close with nature after the sun has gone down. Several of the reserves hold guided evening walks—advance reservations and separate admission are required—and the Ranario and Serpentario keep evening hours. Restaurant **Moon Shiva** (⊠ 100 m east of CASEM ☎ 645–6270) holds a movie night each Monday and Wednesday at 8 PM, showing a recent film on DVD. You can show off your talents at the monthly open mike. Noted area biologist Richard LaVal presents a slide show called **Sounds and Scenes of the Cloud Forest** (⊠ Monteverde Lodge conference room ☎ $5) nightly at 6:15. Advance reservations are required.

THE ARTS The hills are alive with the sound of music at various venues for six weekends each March and April during the **Monteverde Music Festival** (☎ 645–5053 ⊕ www.mvinstitute.org), sponsored by the Monteverde Institute. Schedules vary, depending on when Holy Week falls.

FAR NORTHERN GUANACASTE

The mountains, plains, and Pacific coastline north of Liberia up to the border of Nicaragua are encompassed in Far Northern Guanacaste. The capital of Guanacaste is Liberia, which is home to Costa Rica's second-largest airport. You'll most likely pass through it on your way to the beaches west of the city and on the Nicoya Peninsula or up north to the national parks of Guanacaste, Santa Rosa, or Rincón de la Vieja. Volcán Rincón de la Vieja, an active volcano that last erupted in 1991, is pocked with eerie sites such as boiling creeks, bubbling mud pools, and vapor-emitting streams—look, but don't touch!

West of Rincón de la Vieja, on the coast, Santa Rosa National Park is a former cattle ranch where Costa Ricans defeated the invading mercenary army of American William Walker in 1856. Santa Rosa is also home to Playas Naranjo and Nancite, where hundreds of thousands of Olive Ridley Sea Turtles lay their eggs between August and November. Closer still to the Nicaraguan border are Guanacaste National Park and the town of La Cruz, overlooking the pristine beaches and a pair of resorts on the lovely Golfo de Santa Elena and Bahía Salinas.

Rincón de la Vieja National Park

❿ *27 km (17 mi) northeast of Liberia.*

Parque Nacional Rincón de la Vieja is Costa Rica's Yellowstone, with volcanic hot springs and boiling, bubbling mud ponds. The park protects more than 177 square km (54 square mi) of Volcán Rincón de la Vieja's upper slopes, much of which is covered by dry forest. The wildlife here is diverse: 200 species of birds, including Keel-billed Toucans and

Blue-crowned Motmots, plus mammals such as brocket deer, tapirs, coatis, jaguars, sloths, and armadillos.

The mass of Volcán Rincón de la Vieja, often enveloped in a mixture of sulfurous gases and cloud, dominates the scenery to the right of the Pan-American Highway as you head north. The volcano has two peaks: **Santa María** (6,868 feet) and **Rincón de la Vieja** (6,806 feet). The latter, which is barren and has two craters, is thought unlikely to erupt violently because of the profusion of fumaroles through which it constantly lets off steam. (The last violent eruptions were between 1966 and 1970, but vulcanologists were alarmed by a temporary increase in activity in 1995.) **Las Hornillas** (The Kitchen Stoves), on the southern slope of the Rincón de la Vieja crater, is a 124-acre medley of mud cones, hot-water pools, bubbling mud pots, and vent holes most active during the rainy season. Don't get too close to the mud pots—their edges are brittle, and several people have slipped in and been severely burned. To the east, **Los Azufrales** are hot sulfur springs in which you can bathe; be careful not to get sulfur in your eyes.

Bosque Encantado, where the Río Zopilote cascades into the forest to form an enticing pool, is a 2-km (1-mi) hike from Santa María. Three kilometers (2 mi) farther are Los Azufrales, and 4 km (2½ mi) beyond that are the boiling mud pots and fumaroles of Las Hornillas, near the Las Pailas entrance to the park.

The trail to the summit heads into the forest above Las Pailas, but it's a trip for serious hikers, best done in dry season with preparation for cold weather at the top. A less strenuous option is the 3-km (2-mi) loop through the park, along which you'll see fumaroles, a *volcáncito* (baby volcano), Las Pailas, and many animals, including semidomesticated, raccoonlike coatis, looking for handouts (a plea you should ignore: a cardinal rule of wildlife encounters is don't feed the animals).

Trail maps and hiking information are available at the park stations by both entrance gates. If you want to explore the slopes of the volcano, go with a guide; the abundant hot springs and geysers have given unsuspecting visitors some very nasty burns. In addition, the upper slopes often receive fierce and potentially dangerous winds—before your ascent, check at either ranger station for conditions. Alternatively, head to **Rincón de la Vieja Mountain Lodge** (☎ 661–8156), which has guides for hiking or horseback riding; call ahead to check availability.

From Liberia, access to Rincón de la Vieja National Park is on 27 km (17 mi) of unpaved road. The road begins 6 km (4 mi) north of Liberia off the Pan-American Highway (follow signs for Albergue Guachipelín) or 25 km (15 mi) along the Colonia Blanca route northeast from Liberia, which follows the course of the Río Liberia to the Santa María park headquarters. A four-wheel-drive vehicle is recommended, though not essential, for either of these bone-rattling 1- to 1½-hour rides. ⊠ *Entrances at Hacienda Santa María on road leading northeast from Liberia, and at Las Pailas, via mostly unpaved road through Curubandé* ☎ 661–8139 ⚏ *$6* ☉ *Daily 7–4.*

CloseUp

GOING FISHING?

COSTA RICA TEEMS with a constant supply of pescado (fish), some of which might seem unique to North Americans. Below are some local catches and where you'll find them.

Gaspar (alligator gar), found in Barra del Colorado river and Lake Arenal, look like a holdover from prehistoric times and have a long narrow snout full of sharp teeth; they make great sport on light tackle. Gar meat is firm and sweet (some people say it tastes like shrimp), but the fish's eggs are toxic to humans.

Guapote (rainbow bass) make their home in Lake Arenal, a man-made and beautiful 35-km-long (22-mi-long) lake with views of the Arenal volcano. It's a hard-hitting catch, though; 5- to 6-pounders are common. Taxonomically, guapote are not related to bass, but are caught similarly, by casting or flipping plugs or spinner bait. It's difficult to fish from the shore at Lake Arenal; area hotels and tour operators can arrange boats. Alternatively, lodges offering trout fishing are near the Cerro de la Muerte, off the Pan-American Highway leading south from San José. The streams are stocked, and the fish tend to be small. However, the scenery in this area makes a day spent here worthwhile.

Marlin and sailfish migrate northward through the year, beginning about November when they are plentiful in the Golfito region. From December into April they spread north to Quepos, which has some of the country's best deep-sea fishing, and are present in large numbers along Nicoya Peninsula at Carrillo and Sámara from February to April, and near Tamarindo and Flamingo, from May to September. Pacific Ocean sailfish average over 45 kilos (100 pounds), and are usually fought on a 15-pound line or less. Costa Rican laws require that all sails, except record catches, are released. Sportfishing operators run full-service charters out of the towns mentioned above, and all of the country's travel agencies and larger hotels can arrange fishing trips.

Tarpon and snook fishing is big on the Caribbean coast, centered at the mouth of the Barra del Colorado River, which hosts several world-renowned fishing lodges. The acrobatic tarpon, which averages about 85 pounds here, is able to swim freely between saltwater and freshwater and is considered by many to be the most exciting catch on earth. Tarpon sometimes strike like a rocket, hurtling 5 m (16 ft) into the air, flipping, and twisting left and right. Anglers say the success rate of experts is to land about one out of every 10 tarpon hooked. In the Colorado, schools of up to 100 tarpon following and feeding on schools of small, sardinelike fish called titi travel for more than 160 km (100 mi) to Lake Nicaragua. Tarpon are in greatest abundance just outside the river mouth, but are also present on the river itself, and in its backwaters and lagoons. Snook also make the long swim up the Barra del Colorado River following the titi. The long-standing International Game Fishing Association all-tackle record was taken in this area.

Where to Stay

$ ▦ **Rincón de la Vieja Lodge.** On the slopes of Rincón de la Vieja are the lodge's paneled cabins, small doubles, and comfy dormitory-style rooms. The sitting room has a TV with a VCR and a few movies. Meat, fish, and vegetarian (made with homegrown produce) entrées are good, though on the pricey side. The affable staff can take you to explore the park and volcano on foot or on horseback through the woods. Trails lead to a hot-water, sulfur bathing pool and a blue lake and waterfall. The lodge provides transport up from Liberia for up to six people. ✉ *2 km (1 mi) northeast of park entrance* ☎ *661–8198 or 200–5133* ⊕ *www.rincondelaviejalodge.com* ⊡ *Apdo. 114–5000, Liberia* ↪ *38 rooms* ♿ *Dining room, fans, pool, horseback riding, bar, travel services; no a/c, no room phones, no room TVs* ▭ *No credit cards* ⦿ *FAP.*

Sports & the Outdoors

Treetop Trails (☎ 661–8156) runs four-hour canopy tours ($50) from the Rincón de la Vieja Mountain Lodge, which include a forest-floor hike and canopy observation from 16 cable-linked treetop platforms. A more elaborate seven-hour tour ($79) also includes horseback riding to the park's blue lake and waterfall.

Santa Rosa National Park

❶ *35 km (22 mi) north of Liberia.*

With the largest swath of tropical dry forest in Central America, Parque Nacional Santa Rosa is one of Costa Rica's most impressive parks. Because of its less luxuriant, low-density foliage, the park is a good one for viewing wildlife, especially if you station yourself next to water holes during the dry season. The park might also be the country's most beloved of protected areas because of its historic significance as the sight of the 1856 triumph over American invader William Walker in the famous Battle of Santa Rosa. Santa Rosa is also the country's first national park, so it has become a model for community involvement in preservation and conservation. As you approach the entrance from the Pan-American Highway, you can see the forested slopes of Volcán Orosi, protected within Guanacaste National Park. A few miles after you enter Santa Rosa, a scenic overlook on the right grants your first good view of the park's dry forest.

Typical dry-forest vegetation includes oak, wild cherry, mahogany, calabash, bullhorn acacia, hibiscus, and gumbo-limbo, with its distinctive reddish-brown bark. Inhabitants include Spider, White-faced Capuchin, and Howler monkeys, as well as deer, armadillos, coyotes, tapirs, coatis, and ocelots. Ocelots, commonly known as *manigordos* (literally, "fat hands") on account of their large feet, are wildcats that have been brought back from the brink of extinction by the park's conservation methods. These wildlands also define the southernmost distribution of many North American species such as the Virginia Opossum and the cantil, a pit viper snake. From the ecology perspective, Santa Rosa is important because it protects and regenerates 520 square km (200 square mi) of forest land, both moist, basal-belt transition and deciduous, tropical dry forests.

Arsonists burned the park's centerpiece, the **Hacienda La Casona,** to the ground in 2001. The rambling colonial-style farmstead was the site of a famous 1856 battle in which a ragged force of ill-equipped Costa Ricans routed the superior army of the notorious William Walker. Fundraising and reconstruction, in true Costa Rican style, were slated to take several years. But awash in patriotism for the beloved monument, one of the few military historic sites in this army-less country, Costa Ricans raised funds and rebuilt La Casona in record time.

From the entrance gate, 7 km (4½ mi) of paved road leads to the **park headquarters.** A small nature trail loops through the woods, and there's a large camping area nearby. Note that Santa Rosa's **campgrounds,** which can sleep 150 people, sometimes fill up during the dry season, especially in the first week of January and during Easter week. Throughout the park it's wise to carry your own water, since water holes are none too clean.

White-sand **Playa Naranjo** (⊠ 13 km [8 mi] west of the administrative area; a two- to three-hour hike or one-hour trek with a four-wheel-drive vehicle) is popular for beachcombing thanks to its abundance of shells and for surfing because of its near-perfect break. The campsite here has washing facilities, but bring your own drinking water. The lookout at the northern tip of the beach has views over the entire park. ⊠ *Km 269, Pan-American Hwy., 13 km (8 mi) northwest of Porterillos* ☎ *666–5020* ⊠ *$6* ☉ *Daily 7–5.*

Playa Nancite. A two-hour walk north from Playa Naranjo—and also accessible by four-wheel-drive vehicle—this beach is a premier place to watch turtle *arribadas* (mass nestings). It is estimated that 200,000 turtles nest here each year. Backed by dense hibiscus and button mangroves, the gray-sand beach is penned in by steep, tawny, brush-covered hills. Previously a difficult point to get to, it's now the world's only totally protected **Olive Ridley Turtle arribada.** Olive Ridleys are the smallest of the sea turtles (average carapace, or hardback shell, is 21–29 inches) and the least shy. The majority arrive at night, plowing the sand as they move up the beach and sniffing for the high-tide line, beyond which they use their hind flippers to dig the holes into which they lay their eggs. They spend an average of one hour on the beach before scurrying back to the sea. Hatching also takes place at night. Because the brightest light is that of the shimmering ocean, the phototropic baby turtles naturally know to head for the sea, which is vital for their continued survival. Many of the nests are churned up during subsequent arribadas, and predators such as coatis, ghost crabs, raccoons, and coyotes lie in wait; hence just 0.2% of the eggs laid result in young turtles reaching the sea. Their nesting season is August to November, peaking in September and October. You need a permit to stay at Nancite; ask at the park's headquarters. ⊠ *7 km (4 mi) northwest of Playa Naranjo* ☎ *666–5020* ⊠ *$6* ☉ *Daily 8–4.*

Camping

¢ ⛺ **La Casona.** Santa Rosa National Park has a rugged terrain and an isolated feel. The campsite, near the Hacienda La Casona, overhung by giant strangler figs, has no set sites—you choose where to set up—and provides washing facilities, rustic bathrooms, and picnic tables. Be careful of snakes. Between Playas Naranjo and Nancite, another campground at Estero Real is available with tables only. ☒ *Santa Rosa National Park* ☎ *666–5051* ♿ *Picnic areas; no a/c, no room phones, no room TVs* ☰ *No credit cards.*

Cuajiniquil

⑫ *10 km (6 mi) north of Santa Rosa National Park.*

North from Santa Rosa on the Pan-American Highway is the left turn to Cuajiniquil, famous for its waterfalls. If you have time and a four-wheel-drive vehicle, Cuajiniquil has lovely views. The Golfo de Santa Elena is renowned for its calm waters, which is why it's now threatened by tourist development. Playa Blanca in the extreme west has smooth white sand, as its name implies. The rough track here passes through a valley of uneven width caused, according to geologists, by the diverse granulation of the sediments formerly deposited here. To the south rise the rocky Santa Elena hills (2,548 feet), bare except for a few *chigua* and *nancite* shrubs.

Guanacaste National Park

⑬ *32 km (20 mi) north of Liberia.*

The 325-square km (125-square mi) Parque Nacional Guanacaste was created in 1989 to preserve rain forests around **Volcán Cacao** (5,950 feet) and **Volcán Orosi** (5,330 feet), which are seasonally inhabited by migrant wildlife from Santa Rosa. The park is a mosaic of interdependent protected areas, parks, and refuges; the goal is eventually to create a single Guanacaste megapark to accommodate the natural migratory patterns of myriad creatures, from jaguars to tapirs. Much of the park's territory is cattle pasture, which, it is hoped, will regenerate into forest. Currently, there are 300 different birds and more than 5,000 species of butterflies here. Camping is possible at each of the park's biological stations. Call the park headquarters in advance to arrange accommodations.

The **Mengo Biological Station** (☎ No phone) lies on the slopes of Volcán Cacao at an altitude of 3,946 feet. Accommodation is in rustic wood dormitories; bedding is provided but towels are not. From the Mengo Biological Station, one trail leads up Volcán Cacao, and another heads 9 km (5½ mi) north to the **Maritza Station** (☎ No phone), about a three-hour hike away at the base of Orosi, with lodging. There are meals and electricity here; conditions are a bit more luxurious than at Mengo. You can also reach Maritza by four-wheel-drive vehicle, a minimum half-hour drive from Mengo. From the Maritza Station you can trek about two hours, a 4-km (2½-mi) jaunt, to **Llano de los Indios** (Plain of the Indians), a cattle pasture dotted with volcanic petroglyphs. North and a little east of Llano de los Indios is **Pitilla Station** (☎ 661–8150). The station has basic lodging with electricity and very basic meals. Despite its lower elevation than other stations in the park, it has views of the coast and Lago de Nicaragua across the border. Advance reservations are essential to stay at any of the park's field stations.

✉ *From Liberia, head 32 km (20 mi) north on Pan-American Hwy. to Po-
terillos, then 18 km (11 mi) northwest* ☎ *666–5051* 🖃 *$6* ◷ *Daily 7–5.*

Where to Stay

★ **$$** 🖭 **Los Inocentes Lodge.** Built more than 100 years ago, this handsome,
exquisitely maintained hardwood hacienda is in a private reserve along
the northern border of Guanacaste National Park. A 14-km (8½-mi) drive
on a smoothly paved road east from the Pan-American Highway to Santa
Cecilia takes you to the entrance of the working ranch, with horses, cat-
tle, and numerous birds. The hardwood-finished rooms are rustic but
comfortable, with hot showers in bathrooms (some shared by two
rooms) across the halls. Meals are included in most packages. Experi-
enced ranch-hand guides, friendly horses, and miles of trails get you into
the forests. ✉ *15 km (9 mi) west of La Cruz* ☎ *679–9190, 265–5484,
888/613–2532 in U.S.* ☎ *679–9224 or 265–4385* ⊕ *www.
losinocenteslodge.com* ✉ *Apdo. 228–3000, Heredia* ↩ *11 rooms, 12
cabins* ⚘ *Dining room, fans, pool, horseback riding, bar; no a/c, no room
phones, no room TVs* ▭ *AE, MC, V* ◎ *FAP.*

La Cruz

14 *56 km (35 mi) north of Liberia, 12 km (7 mi) south of the Nicaraguan
border.*

Farther north on the west side of the highway is a turnoff to La Cruz,
noteworthy for the stunning views of Bahía Salinas from its bluff. It also
serves as a gateway to the two resorts and beaches on the south shore
of Bahía Salinas, the hamlet of Puerto Soley, and the Golfo de Santa Elena.

The Nicaraguan border lies just north of La Cruz at Peñas Blancas. All
travelers are stopped at two preborder checkpoints south of La Cruz
for passport and cursory vehicle inspection. You will notice heightened
police vigilance in the region.

Where to Stay & Eat

$ ✕🖭 **Colinas del Norte.** On the Pan-American Highway halfway between
La Cruz and the Nicaraguan border, 20 km (12 mi) north of Peñas Blan-
cas, this rugged, two-story hardwood hotel bills itself as a touring base
for the surrounding dry tropical forest, but its most appealing feature is
its large pool, surrounded by shady palms. At the outdoor disco you can
dance 'til you drop, then hop into the pool. The indoor-outdoor restau-
rant ($–$$) specializes in pizza and Italian food. Modest but comfortable
upstairs rooms have private terraces. ✉ *Pan-American Hwy., about 6 km
(4 mi) north of La Cruz* ✉ *Apdo. 10493–1000, San José* ☎ *679–9132*
↩ *24 rooms* ⚘ *Restaurant, miniature golf, tennis court, pool, horseback
riding, bar, dance club, laundry service; no a/c in some rooms, no room
TVs* ▭ *AE, MC, V.*

¢ 🖭 **Amalia's Inn.** The late U.S. artist Lester Bounds and his Costa Rican
wife, Amalia, created this breezy little inn on the cliff overlooking Bahía
Salinas. Amalia now runs the inn. Bounds is also survived by his art—
colorful modern paintings and prints that decorate the place and rooms.
The inn has spacious rooms with private baths and balconies. Amalia's
is a fine budget alternative to the two pricier resorts on the bay's south

shore. ⊠ *East of central park, on left (south) side of road heading into town* 🏠🏠 *679–9181* 🛏 *7 rooms* ⚴ *Pool, laundry service; no a/c, no room phones, no room TVs* 🗐 *AE, MC, V.*

Bahía Salinas

⑮ *7 km (4½ mi) west of La Cruz.*

Several dirt and rock roads dead-end on different beaches along Bahía Salinas, the pretty little half-moon bay that lies at the very top of Costa Rica's Pacific coast. Just turn right off the "main" road to the resorts, and you'll probably end up on or near the beach, or in the hamlet of Puerto Soley, a tiny town tucked in off the bay—look for the salt flats to find the town, which is roughly 5–6 very slow-going km (3–4 mi) from La Cruz. There's public beach access along the bay.

The wind usually blows year-round, except in September and October, the height of the rainy season, so windsurfing here is supreme. Winds are generally not as powerful as those at Laguna de Arenal, but they're strong enough to make this a viable alternative (stay on the south side for stronger winds), or accompaniment, to the Arenal experience.

Ranking among the most beautiful beaches in all of Costa Rica are a couple of secluded, wind-sheltered strands, including the gorgeous, pristine **Playa Rajada,** with fine swimming and snorkeling. Just offshore is **Isla Bolaños,** a bird refuge and nesting site for thousands of endangered frigate birds as well as brown pelicans.

Where to Stay

$$ 🏨 **Ecoplaya Beach Resort.** Although it's on the same stretch of Bahía Salinas as the Bolaños Bay Resort, about 1 km (½ mi) to the west, Ecoplaya has plenty of luxury amenities unusual for the area. Every room has a small but fully equipped kitchen, hot water, and custom hardwood furniture. The nearly 1-km-long (½-mi-long) beach fronting the hotel is flanked by bird- and wildlife-filled estuaries. Be warned, nonsailors: the wind blows hard here much of the time. ⊠ *La Coyotera Beach* 🏠🏠 *679–9380 or 289–8920 in San José* 🏢 *Plaza Colonial, Escazú, No. 4, San José* 🏢 *289–4536 in San José* ⊕ *www.ecoplaya.com* 🛏 *36 suites* ⚴ *Restaurant, in-room safes, kitchens, pool, beach, windsurfing, horseback riding, bar, laundry service* 🗐 *AE, MC, V.*

Sports & the Outdoors

WATER SPORTS **Kite Centre 2000** (☎ 826-5221 ⊕ www.suntoursandfun.com) on Copal Beach offers 10 hours of kitesurfing lessons (including equipment use) for $225. **Tico Wind** (☎ 679–9380 ⊕ www.ticowind.com) at Ecoplaya Resort will fix you up for all your windsurfing needs. Equipment rental runs $65 a day.

Peñas Blancas

12 km (7 mi) north of La Cruz.

Costa Rica and Nicaragua share a busy border crossing at Peñas Blancas. Rental vehicles may not leave Costa Rica, so crossing into Nicaragua is an option only if you've come this far on public transportation. Disembark from the bus and head into the immigration building, where Costa Rican officials place an exit stamp in your passport. The bus then continues to the Nicaraguan side, where you purchase a $7 tourist card to enter the country, and will be levied a $2 surcharge if you cross during the busy noon–2 pm period or on weekends. U.S. and U.K. visitors may stay in Nicaragua up to 90 days; Canadian, Australian, and New Zealand tourists, 30 days. Nicaraguan officials strictly enforce a requirement that your passport have at least six months' remaining validity beyond your intended departure from the country. If you are not traveling on one of the international bus routes (Tica Bus or Transnica), you can negotiate the border crossing on foot and will find taxis waiting on the Nicaraguan side to take you to Rivas, the first city of any size you'll encounter, about 30 km (18 mi) inside the country. Returning to Costa Rica means the same process in reverse, but the bus driver collects passports and presents them en masse to Nicaraguan officials upon leaving. You are charged a $4 exit tax to leave Nicaragua by land, and will get your passport back when you reboard the bus. Coming and going, plan to spend about an hour with border formalities on each side if you're traveling through by bus. The Nicaraguan side of the border has a few duty-free shops for departing visitors, but prices are no lower than anything you can find elsewhere in the country. Peñas Blancas is not really a town, so there is no place to stay here, but you can grab a bite in the cafeteria in the immigration building on the Costa Rican side.

The crossing is open daily 6 AM–8 PM. Banks on both sides of the border change their own currency and U.S. dollars, but not Costa Rican colónes or Nicaraguan córdobas directly. No one in Nicaragua will accept or exchange colónes. And upon leaving Nicaragua, there's nothing you can do with your leftover córdobas except save them for your next trip. Try to gauge your currency needs accordingly.

THE NORTHERN ZONE A TO Z

To research prices, get advice from other travelers, and book travel arrangements, visit www.fodors.com.

AIR TRAVEL

The closest airport is Aeropuerto Internacional Daniel Oduber in Liberia. For airline information to Liberia *see* the Nicoya Peninsula A to Z *in* Chapter 4.

🛪 Airport **Aeropuerto Internacional Daniel Oduber** ⊠ Hwy. 21, 5 km (3 mi) west of Liberia ☎ 668–1032 or 668–1010.

BOAT TRAVEL

Desafío Adventures in La Fortuna and Monteverde provides a fast, popular three-hour transfer between the communities. The taxi-boat-taxi service costs $21 one-way.

🚤 Boat Information **Desafío Adventures** ⊠ Behind church, La Fortuna ☎ 479–9464 ⊕ www.desafiocostarica.com ⊠ Across from Supermercado La Esperanza ☎ 645–5874 ⊕ www.monteverdetours.com.

BUS TRAVEL

Buses in this region are typically large, clean, and comfortable but often crowded Friday through Sunday. Don't expect air-conditioning, and even supposedly express buses marked *directo* often make some stops. Bus schedules are constantly changing. If your plans aren't flexible, go to the station the day before you depart to check the schedule.

THE CORDILLERA TILARÁN

Auto Transportes San José–San Carlos buses leave San José for the three-hour trip to Ciudad Quesada from C. 12, between Avdas. 7 and 9, daily every hour 5 AM–7 PM. The company runs three buses daily from this same station in San José to La Fortuna, near Arenal, at 6:15, 8:40, and 11:30 AM. From Ciudad Quesada you can connect to Arenal and Tilarán. The company also has buses for Los Chiles (Caño Negro), which depart from C. 12 at Avda. 9, daily at 5:30 AM and 3:30 PM; the trip takes five hours.

Transportes La Cañera has service to Cañas, and the turnoff for Tilarán and Arenal, daily at 8:30 AM, 10:20 AM, 12:20 PM, 1:20 PM, and 2:30 PM from C. 16, between Avdas. 3 and 5 in San José. The trip to Cañas takes 3½ hours. Transportes Tilarán sends buses on the four-hour trip to Tilarán daily from C. 12, between Avdas. 7 and 9 in San José, at 7:30 AM, 9:30 AM, 12:45 PM, 3:45 PM, and 6:30 PM. From Tilarán you can continue to Nuevo Arenal and Volcán Arenal.

MONTEVERDE & SANTA ELENA

Transmonteverde makes the five-hour trip to Monteverde, departing weekdays at 6:30 AM and 2:30 PM. This route is notorious for theft; watch your bags.

FAR NORTHERN GUANACASTE

Transportes Deldu goes to La Cruz and the Nicaraguan border at Peñas Blancas, normally a six-hour trip that passes through Liberia; daily departures are at 5 AM, 1:20 PM, and 4:10 PM. Express buses cut the trip to 4½ hours; they leave from C. 20 and Avda. 1 in San José, at 4:30 AM and 7 AM. The slower buses pass the entrance to Santa Rosa National Park after about five hours. Buses don't serve Rincón de la Vieja and Guanacaste National Parks.

Tica Bus provides international bus service three times daily from its terminal in San José to the Nicaraguan border and beyond to Managua. Vehicles also stop at Granada and Rivas in southern Nicaragua with advance reservations. Transnica buses bound for Managua leave twice daily from the Transnica terminal in San José, stopping at the Hotel Guanacaste in Liberia. Travel time for both companies is nine hours between San José and Managua, including border formalities.

SHUTTLE VANS

If you prefer a more private form of travel, consider taking a shuttle. Fantasy Bus has daily service between San José and Arenal and Monteverde. Comfortable, air-conditioned vans leave various San José hotels early in the morning and return midafternoon. Tickets cost $25 to Arenal and $38 to Monteverde and must be reserved a day in advance. Service is also provided from Arenal and Monteverde to several Pacific-coast beaches. In similar fashion, Interbus connects San Jose with La Fortuna ($25) and Monteverde ($38), with connections from there to a few of the north Pacific-coast beaches.

🚌 Bus Companies **Auto Transportes San José–San Carlos** ☎ 256-8914 or 460-5032. **Pulmitan Liberia** ☎ 256-9552. **Tica Bus** ✉ C. 9 and Avda. 4, San José ☎ 221-8954.

Transmonteverde ☎ 222-3854. Transnica ✉ C. 22, between Avdas. 3 and 5, San José ☎ 223-4242 ✉ Hotel Guanacaste, Liberia ☎ 666-0085. **Transportes Deldu** ☎ 256-9072. **Transportes La Cañera** ☎ 222-3006. **Transportes Tilarán** ☎ 222-3854. 🚌 Shuttle Van Services **Gray Line Tourist Bus** ☎ 232-3681 or 220-2126 ⊕ www. graylinecostarica.com. **Interbus** ☎ 283-5573 ⊕ www.interbusonline.com.

CAR RENTAL

Car rental in San José is the easiest option for traveling in this region, but you'll find a few branch offices up here as well. Alamo has an office in La Fortuna and near Liberia's Daniel Oduber International Airport. Budget maintains a branch near Liberia's airport. Local firm Sol Rentacar has an office across from the Hotel Bramadero in Liberia. Costa Rican rental agency Poás Rentacar has a branch in the center of La Fortuna.

🚌 Major Agencies **Alamo** ✉ 100 m west of church, La Fortuna ☎ 479-9090 ✉ 2 km (1 mi) north of Daniel Oduber Airport, Liberia ☎ 668-1111. **Budget** ✉ 6 km (4 mi) southwest of Daniel Oduber Airport, Liberia ☎ 668-1024.

🚌 Local Agencies **Poás Rentacar** ✉ 50 m south of church, La Fortuna ☎ 479-8418. **Sol Rentacar** ✉ Pan-American Hwy., across from Hotel Bramadero, Liberia ☎ 666-2222.

CAR TRAVEL

Road access to the northwest is by way of the paved two-lane Pan-American Highway (Carretera Interamericana, or CA1), which starts from the west end of Paseo Colón in San José and runs northwest through Cañas and Liberia and to Peñas Blancas (Nicaraguan border). The drive to Liberia takes about three to four hours. Turnoffs to Monteverde, Arenal, and other destinations are often poorly marked—drivers must keep their eyes open. The Monteverde (Santa Elena) turnoff is at Río Lagarto, about 125 km (78 mi) northwest of San José. From here, an unpaved 30-km (19-mi) track snakes dramatically up through hilly farming country; it takes 1½ to 2 hours to negotiate it, less by four-wheel-drive vehicle. At the junction for Santa Elena, bear right for the reserve.

The turnoff for Tilarán and the northwestern end of Laguna de Arenal lies in the town of Cañas. At Liberia, Highway 21 west leads to the beaches of the northern Nicoya Peninsula. To reach San Carlos, La Fortuna, and Caño Negro from San José, a scenic drive (Highway 35) takes you up through the coffee plantations and over the Cordillera Central by way of Sarchí and Zarcero.

On the Pan-American Highway (CA1) north of Liberia, the first turn for Rincón de la Vieja is easy to miss. Look for the Guardia Rural station on the right around 5 km (3 mi) north of town; turn inland and head for Curubandé. Turnoffs for Santa Rosa National Park and La Cruz on CA1 are well marked. Because of the nearness of the border, you need to stop at two police checkpoints on the Pan-American Highway south of La Cruz.

From the easterly zone of Arenal and the Cordillera de Tilarán (La Fortuna), you can head west by way of the road, badly potholed in sections, around Laguna de Arenal. For the paved road (Highway 4) that parallels the Nicaraguan border and loops west all the way to La Cruz, follow the signs out of Tanque (east of La Fortuna) northwest to San Rafael de Guatuso, Upala, and Santa Cecilia.

You cannot drive a rental car across the border into Nicaragua.

ROAD
CONDITIONS

Four-wheel-drive vehicles are recommended, but not essential, at least not in the dry season, for most roads. If you don't rent a four-wheel-drive vehicle, at least rent a car with high clearance—you'll be glad you did. Many rental agencies insist you take a four-wheel-drive vehicle if you mention Monteverde as part of your itinerary. The most important thing to know is that short drives can take a long time when the road is potholed or torn up. Plan accordingly. Most minor roads are unpaved and either muddy in rainy season or dusty in dry season—the pavement holds out only so far, and then dirt, dust, mud, potholes, and other impediments interfere with driving conditions and prolong hours spent behind the wheel. Watch for numerous one-lane bridges once you get off the Pan-American Highway. If the triangular CEDA EL PASO sign faces you, yield to oncoming traffic before you proceed across the bridge.

The Pan-American Highway (CA1) and other paved roads run to the Nicaraguan border; paved roads run west to small towns such as Filadelfia and La Cruz. The roads into Rincón de la Vieja are unpaved and very slow; figure on an hour from the highway, and be prepared to park your vehicle and walk the last 1 km (½ mi) to the Las Pailas entrance. The road into Santa Rosa National Park is smooth going as far as the ruins of La Casona. Beyond that, it gets dicey and very steep in places. The National Park Service encourages you to walk, rather than drive, to the beach. A couple of dirt roads lead into various sections of Guanacaste National Park.

EMERGENCIES

In case of any emergency, dial 911, or one of the numbers below.

🔳 Emergency Services **Fire** ☎ 118. **Police** ☎ 911. **Traffic Police** ☎ 227-8030.
🔳 Hospitals **Hospital de Los Chiles** ✉ Hwy. 35, Los Chiles ☎ 471-1045. **Hospital de San Carlos** ✉ 2 km (1 mi) north of Central Park, Ciudad Quesada ☎ 460-1176. **Hospital Dr. Enrique Baltodano** ✉ Across from stadium, Liberia ☎ 666-0011.

MAIL & SHIPPING

Privatized Correos de Costa Rica provides reasonable postal service from this region, though you're better off waiting to post those cards and letters from San José. Public Internet access is not widespread in this part of the country. Expect to pay about $2 per hour of access time. Dial-up services are less zippy than connections in San José. A few travel agencies in La Fortuna give one free hour of Internet access for every tour booked with them.

🔳 Internet Cafés **Destiny Internet** ✉ 50 m north of Banco Nacional, La Fortuna ☎ 479-9850. **Historias Internet Café** ✉ 75 m down road to Jardín de Mariposas from Pizzería de Johnny, Cerro Plano, Monteverde ☎ 645-6914. **Internet Café** ✉ 150 m north of park, Ciudad Quesada ☎ 460-3653. **Internet Taberna** ✉ Next to Serpentario, Santa Elena ☎ 645-5825. **Tom's Pan** ✉ 300 m south of gas station, Nuevo Arenal ☎ 694-4547. **Tranquilo Comunicaciones** ✉ 150 m downhill from La Esperanza Supermarket, Santa Elena ☎ 645-6782.

🔳 Post Offices **Correos de Costa Rica** ✉ Across from CoopeCompro, Cañas ✉ Across from Escuela Chávez, Ciudad Quesada ✉ Central park La Cruz ✉ 45 m north of police station, La Fortuna ✉ Across from Tribunales, Los Chiles ✉ Next to Guardia Rural, Nuevo Arenal ✉ 45 m downhill from La Esperanza Supermarket, Santa Elena ✉ 115 m west of municipal stadium, Tilarán ✉ Northwest corner of park, Zarcero.

MONEY MATTERS

Most larger tourist establishments are prepared to handle credit cards. Changing U.S. dollars or traveler's checks is possible at the few offices of Banco Nacional scattered throughout the region, but lines are long. You'll find a small but growing number of ATMs (*cajeros automáticos*) out here: Banco Nacional offices in La Fortuna and Santa Elena, as well as Banex in Ciudad Quesada and CooTilarán in Tilarán, are affiliated with the ATH (A Todas Horas) network, and accept Cirrus- and Plus-linked cards.

🏦 Banks **Banco Nacional** ✉ Across from cathedral, Ciudad Quesada ☎ 460-0290 ✉ Pan-American Highway, La Cruz ☎ 679-9296 ✉ Central Plaza, La Fortuna ☎ 479-9022 ✉ 50 m north of bus station, Santa Elena ☎ 645-5027 ✉ Central Plaza, Tilarán ☎ 695-5255 ✉ 100 m north of church, Zarcero ☎ 463-3838. **Banex** ✉ 500 m north of Mercado Municipal, Ciudad Quesada ☎ 460-5801. **CooTilarán** ✉ 150 m north of cathedral, Tilarán ☎ 695-5282.

TAXIS

Official red taxis hang out at designated taxi stands in La Fortuna, Ciudad Quesada, La Cruz, and Tilarán. Monteverde's rugged vehicles always manage to navigate the rough roads. Catch one on the main street in Santa Elena. Elsewhere, taxi service is much less official, with private individuals providing rides. To be on the safe side, ask your hotel or restaurant to call one for you.

TOURS

Sunset Tours specializes in all Arenal-area tours, and in excursions to the Caño Negro Wildlife Refuge. La Fortuna's Bobo Adventures specializes in excursions to the Venado Caverns and the Caño Negro Wildlife Refuge. Fourtrax ATV Tours leads guided ATV tours in the countryside around La Fortuna and the Arenal volcano.

With branches in Monteverde and La Fortuna—and offering transportation between the two—Desafío Adventures will take you rafting, horseback riding, hiking, and rappelling. Monteverde's Costa Rica Study Tours can fix you up with all manner of area excursions. Horizontes customizes natural-history and adventure trips with expert guides to any Costa Rican itinerary.

🎫 Tour Operators **Bobo Adventures** ✉ La Fortuna ☎ 479-9390. **Costa Rica Study Tours** ✉ Cerro Plano, Monteverde ☎ 645-7090 ⊕ www.crstudytours.com. **Desafío Adventures** ✉ Behind the church, La Fortuna ☎ 479-9464 ⊕ www.desafiocostarica. com ✉ Across from Supermercado La Esperanza, Santa Elena ☎ 645-5874 ⊕ www. monteverdetours.com. **Fourtrax ATV Tours** ✉ La Fortuna ☎ 479-8444 ⊕ www. fourtraxadventure.com. **Horizontes** ✉ 130 m north of Pizza Hut, Paseo Colón, San José ☎ 222-2022 ⊕ www.horizontes.com. **Sunset Tours** ✉ 50 m north of Banco Nacional, La Fortuna ☎ 479-9800 ⊕ www.sunsettourcr.com.

VISITOR INFORMATION

The ubiquitous TOURIST INFORMATION signs around La Fortuna and Monteverde are really storefront travel agencies hoping to sell you tours rather than provide unbiased sources of information.

The tourist office in San José has information covering the northwest, including maps, bus schedules, and brochures. It's on the first floor of the main post office, and is open weekdays 8–4. In Santa Elena, the local chamber of commerce operates a Monteverde tourist office called CETAM, across from the hardware store, open daily 9–6.

🔁 Tourist Information **CETAM** ✉ 150 m downhill from La Esperanza Supermarket, Santa Elena ☎ 645-5771. **Instituto Costarricense de Turismo** (ICT) ✉ C. 2, between Avdas. 1 and 3, Barrio La Merced, San José ☎ 222-1090.

THE NICOYA PENINSULA

4

LEAST LIVELY NIGHTLIFE
After-dark turtle tours at Hotel Las Tortugas ⇨*p.156*

BEST "HUMP-DAY" COMBO
Fish tacos and karaoke at Cantina Las Brisas ⇨*p.147*

WET AND WILD
Ríos Tropicales sea-kayaking trips ⇨*p.173*

MOST PAINFUL HOTEL PERK
In-house tattoo artist at Arco Iris ⇨*p.156*

PUKKA WITH POLISH
Elegant Villa del Sueño Restaurant ⇨*p.142*

TOO COOL FOR SCHOOL
Nosara surf courses ⇨*p.165*

BATHING BEAUTY
Carrillo Beach ⇨*p.167*

Updated by
Dorothy
MacKinnon

FAMOUS FOR ITS MILES OF SURFING BEACHES that gained world renown in the *Endless Summer* surfer movies, Nicoya is also ecologically rich with limestone caverns, river deltas filled with flocks of wading birds, and small tracts of wet and dry forest. As you watch surfers master the Pacific's white-and-blue waves or glimpse huge leatherback turtles laying their eggs at Playa Grande on a midnight tour, you'll know why you're in Nicoya.

Many of the traditions now referred to as typically Costa Rican were started by the Guanacastecos, descendants of both the Chorotegan Indians and early Spanish settlers. One Chorotegan leader, Chief Nicoya, welcomed the conquistadores in 1523, and his name lives on in the town and peninsula. Centuries later, the dry forest was cleared to create vast cattle ranges, lending a *sabanero* (cowboy) flavor to the landscape and culture. A strong folkloric character is still evident here. As you travel down the peninsula, you might encounter traditional costumes, folk dancing, and music during seasonal fiestas and rodeos, as well as meals made from recipes handed down from colonial times.

Nicoya—especially the coastal areas—attracts earthy ecotourists and their younger backpack- and surfboard-toting cousins in search of environmental enlightenment or good waves. But it also attracts sun- and golf-seekers, lured by azure pools and manicured putting greens bathed in tropical sun. Sportfishermen congregate in Flamingo Beach, where there is a large charter-fishing fleet. Most anglers are after large billfish, which they catch and release. Tamarindo is becoming famous for its restaurant and bar scene. But there are still plenty of almost-deserted beaches where you can feel alone.

Much of the interior of the peninsula is windswept, sun-baked cattle pasture, thanks to a government initiative in the 1950s to cut down forests and build a beef industry. As a result, today much of the landscape is brown and parched in the dry season.

The area has received huge amounts of investment and is under immense development pressure. A Four Seasons hotel with a golf course opened in January of 2004 in the huge Papagayo Peninsula resort area. The endless miles of untracked beaches are increasingly interspersed with sprawling, all-inclusive resort behemoths.

Exploring the Nicoya Peninsula

Separated from the mainland by the Gulf of Nicoya, the peninsula is a roughly thumb-shape spit of land in the southwestern section of Guanacaste province. The peninsula's southern end, which includes Playa Naranjo, Tambor, and Montezuma, is part of Puntarenas province. Bear in mind that aside from the Carretera Interamericana (Pan-American Highway, or CA1), many of the roads in this region are of the pitted, pocked rock-and-dirt variety, with the occasional river rushing across. Covering seemingly short distances can require long hours behind the wheel, and four-wheel drive is often essential. If you can swing it, fly instead; some beach resorts, such as Tamarindo, Carrillo, and Tambor, have nearby airstrips. Many northern beach resorts are most easily reached from the international airport at Liberia.

About the Restaurants

New restaurants with international flavors are sprouting up around the Pacific beach resorts. Dining prices are approaching North American heights, but so is the quality of food and service. Seafood is abundant, but be sure to ask the market price for lobster and shrimp, which can be surprisingly expensive. *Pargo* (red snapper) and corvina are tasty, inexpensive, and almost always available.

About the Hotels

Nicoya has a good mix of high-quality hotels, nature lodges, and more basic *cabinas* (cottages), many of which include breakfast in the rate. It's wise to reserve ahead for the dry season (December–April), especially weekends, when Ticos can fill beach hotels to bursting. A number of luxury hotels line the coast, catering to an upscale clientele.

WHAT IT COSTS					
	$$$$	$$$	$$	$	¢
RESTAURANTS	over $25	$20–$25	$10–$20	$5–$10	under $5
HOTELS	over $200	$125–$200	$75–$125	$35–$75	under $35

Restaurant prices are per-person for a main course at dinner. Hotel prices are for two people in a standard double room in high season, excluding service and tax (16.4%).

Timing

Averaging just 65 inches of rain per year, the Nicoya Peninsula and much of Guanacaste constitute Costa Rica's driest zone. The dry season, from December to April, is generally the best time to visit Costa Rica's Pacific coast, but the northwest, especially the Nicoya Peninsula, is most appealing in the rainy season (barring only the *really* wet months of September and October, when the roads become quagmires of mud and potholes). The Guanacastecos call the rainy season the "green" season, and that it is: the countryside—tending toward brown and arid the rest of the year—blooms lush and green from a few hours of rain each day. It's warm and sunny before and after the rain. The roads may be muddy, but there are far fewer tourists in the rainy season, and prices are lower everywhere. If you're bent on turtle-watching, you have to come during the dry season, but for most other activities any time of year will do. If you travel around the edges of the dry season in November, April, or May, you get the benefits of the rain (lush greenery) without the violent downpours that happen at the height of the rainy season.

THE NICOYA COAST

Strung along the coast of the Nicoya Peninsula are sparkling sand beaches lined with laid-back fishing communities, along with hotels and resorts in every price category. Don't be in a rush to get anywhere; take things one hour at a time and you'll soon be as mellow as the locals.

The ideal Nicoya Peninsula trip is comfortably divided between lazy days on the beach, swims in the surf, and hikes and leisurely exploration of natural sights—caverns, forests, rivers, and estuaries. The beach towns and resorts can be clustered into three loose geographical groups: those on the south end of the peninsula, accessible by ferry from Puntarenas or by plane to Tambor; areas in the central peninsula, accessible by plane to Punta Islita, Carrillo, and Nosara or by car via the new Río Tempisque Bridge or via the roads through Carmona, Curime, and Nicoya; and towns on the northern part of the peninsula, accessible by plane to Tamarindo or Liberia or by car through Liberia and Comunidad.

4

Numbers in the text correspond to numbers in the margin and on the Nicoya Peninsula and the Playa Tamarindo & Playa Langosta maps.

**If you have
3 days**

Fly to 🏖 **Tamarindo** ❾, 🏖 **Nosara** ⓮, **Tambor** ⓴, 🏖 **Punta Islita** ⓱, *or* **Playa Carrillo** ⓰ for a three-night stay at a beach resort. If you stay in Tambor or 🏖 **Montezuma** ㉑, a short drive takes you to Cabo Blanco, where you can hike through the **Cabo Blanco Strict Nature Reserve** to deserted Playa Cabo Blanco, a diving and frolicking ground for hundreds of pelicans. You can also visit the 🏖 **Curú National Wildlife Refuge.** If you surf and are staying at the Florblanca Resort, hit the waves at **Malpaís** ㉒, just north of Cabo Blanco, reputed home of the largest surfing waves in Costa Rica.

Alternatively, spend three to five nights at a beach between 🏖 **Playa Hermosa** ❷ and 🏖 **Tamarindo** ❾. In season, you can also watch the Leatherback turtles arrive by night at **Las Baulas Marine National Park.** For dedicated surfers, 🏖 **Playa Negra** ⓬ and **Playa Avellanas** ⓫ offer great access to excellent waves and plenty of other recreational pastimes. You can also shop for pottery in the nearby artisan towns of Guaitil and Santa Cruz.

**If you have
5 days**

Extend one of the three-day itineraries above into five days. Book a three-day sea-kayaking adventure that leaves from **Curú National Wildlife Refuge,** or just settle into a hotel in **Tambor** ⓴ for a couple of extra days of luxurious R&R.

**If you have
7 days**

Begin with some bird-watching in **Palo Verde National Park** ㉓ ↦; then continue on through **Nicoya** ㉕ and Santa Cruz and overnight in 🏖 **Tamarindo** ❾ or at one of the beach resorts. Spend several days relaxing on the beach or exploring the Tamarindo and Río San Francisco estuaries north and south of Tamarindo, with nights watching turtles (in season) at **Las Baulas Marine National Park.** Fly to 🏖 **Tambor** ⓴, spending your nights here or in 🏖 **Montezuma** ㉑. Here you can hike to a seaside waterfall, bird- and animal-watch; swim in the lazy, sheltered waters of the southern Nicoya Peninsula; and book a sea-kayaking tour that leaves from **Curú National Wildlife Refuge.** Spend three days exploring the ruggedly beautiful islands in the gulf before flying back to San José.

Tourism is still relatively new here. Only 20 years ago, fishing and cattle ranching were the area's mainstays. Development is picking up speed, bringing with it the advantages of sophisticated restaurants, hotels, and shops selling international surf gear and beachwear. But roads are only starting to catch up, so you'll find the interesting anomaly of a fabulous restaurant or hotel plunked at the end of a tortuous dirt road. Open-air bars, beach barbecue parties, and some traditional marimba folk music can be found at night, as well as sports bars with satellite TVs offering *Monday Night Football*. But after watching one of Nicoya's magnificent sunsets, most visitors head to bed early to catch the early morning waves, fishing boats, and wildlife walks.

Numbers in the text correspond to numbers in the margin and on the Nicoya Peninsula and the Playa Tamarindo & Playa Langosta maps.

Liberia

❶ *234 km (145 mi) northwest of San José.*

North of San José on the Pan-American Highway, Liberia is a low-rise, grid-plan cattle-market town with a huge central square dominated by a not-so-pretty modern church. As the capital of Guanacaste province, it's the gateway to several spectacular and biologically important national parks and turtle-nesting sites on the Pacific coast. More importantly, it is a gateway for the coastal beaches. The jet runway at Liberia's Daniel Oduber International Airport serves both national and international flights, with direct flights and charters from American and Canadian cities, making it the arrival point of choice for many travelers. Buses also stop here before traveling on to Nicoya's Pacific beaches. Liberia is a good place to make a bank stop and do some shopping at the MegaSuper. Or, if you need a dose of American culture, you can drop in at the huge Burger King food court or catch a movie at the multiplex cinema, the only movie theater in Guanacaste.

Where to Stay & Eat

¢–$ ✕ **Café Europa/The German Bakery.** Just south of the Liberia airport is this rustic café shaded by trees where you can sample hearty German breads baked in a wood-fired oven, or strudels, bundt cakes, and flaky fruit pastries. Breakfast is served, along with robust bratwurst-and-sauerkraut lunches. ✉ *2 km (1 mi) south of Liberia Airport* ☎ *668–1081* ▤ *AE, D, MC, V.*

¢–$ ✕ **El Café Liberia.** A touch of sophistication in the center of Liberia, this handsome, air-conditioned café serves quiche, cakes, and imported French cheeses and pâtés sandwiched between layers of homemade breads. There are a polished wood bar and tables where you can sip imported wines, single malt Scotches, and sherries. Coffee is freshly roasted and there's a used-book exchange. The café is open from 10 AM to 7 PM. ✉ *Liberia's main street, 75 m south of Banco de Credito Agricola* ☎ *665–1660* ▤ *No credit cards* ⊘ *Closed weekends.*

¢–$ ✕ **La Cocina de José.** Locals gather at this simple restaurant with an outdoor patio, gingham tablecloths, and upscale Tico fare. Fish is a specialty, with fresh tilapia served six different ways. A signature dish is

4

Beaches

Each beach along Nicoya's coast, most of which are lined with palms and tamarind trees, has its distinct merits. Playa Brasilito, for example, gives you a taste of life in a Costa Rican fishing village. Turtles nest at Playa Grande. Tamarindo, a long, white strand, shelters sailing fleets and has good beachfront bars. Playa Negra has some of Costa Rica's best surfing waves. Playa Santa Teresa has miles of tidal pools. Hemmed in by rocks, Playa Pelada is a gem, and a great spot for snorkeling. Nosara has a long beach backed by rich jungle, with tendrils of sea grape reaching to the water's edge. The long, clean Playa Guiones has a coral reef suitable for snorkeling. Perhaps the most beautiful beach in the country, Playa Carrillo fronts an idyllic half-moon bay. The peninsula's great advantage is its climate, which in the rainy season (May–December) is far drier than that of other areas. Beware of riptides while swimming in surfing waters.

Spelunking

The caves in Barra Honda National Park beckon you toward a serious plunge into the underworld. Terciopelo Cave, in particular, contains a vast assortment of oddly shaped rock formations, and some stretches of the cave system are reputedly unexplored to this day.

Surfing

Costa Rica was "discovered" in the 1960s surf-film classic *The Endless Summer* and revisited in the sequel. But with its miles of coastline marked by innumerable points, rock reefs, river-mouth sandbars, and other wave-shaping geological configurations, the Nicoya Peninsula would have emerged as a surfer's paradise in any case. Tamarindo is a good base for decent sandbar and rock-reef breaks, a superb low-tide river-mouth break, and the consistently good Playa Grande beach break. Sámara, Guiones, and Nosara all have decent beach breaks. Avellanas's surf spots range from beach breaks to rock-reef breaks to river-mouth sandbar breaks. Witches Rock, in Santa Rosa National Park, and Playa Langosta both have right river mouths. Ollie's Point offers excellent right point-break waves. Playa Negra's right rock-reef break was showcased in *The Endless Summer II*. Malpaís, just above Cabo Blanco, is hit by some of the largest waves in Costa Rica. In all these places, beware of riptides.

Turtle-Watching

The Nicoya Peninsula provides ace opportunities to watch the nesting rituals of sea turtles. Olive Ridley sea turtles nest year-round, but the peak season runs July to October. Leatherbacks arrive between October and April, though nesting is largely over by mid-February. Occasionally you can see Pacific Green Sea Turtles. Playa Nancite in Santa Rosa National Park and the Ostional National Wildlife Refuge are prime areas for watching the mass *arribadas*, or nestings, of thousands of Olive Ridleys. More accessible are Playas Langosta and Grande, which used to teem with Leatherbacks. Sadly, numbers have dwindled in recent years. Word of mouth has it that locals at Junquillal and Langosta are still stealing turtle eggs as if there were an endless supply. To watch the turtles, go with a legitimate guide and follow the rules to ensure the turtles' safety. Playa Grande's turtle tours are very well organized.

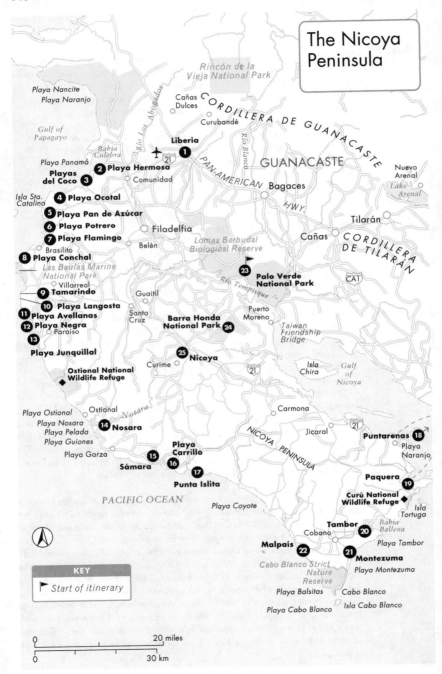

The Nicoya Peninsula

Rincón de la Vieja National Park

Playa Nancite
Playa Naranjo

Gulf of Papagayo

Cañas Dulces

Curubandé

CORDILLERA DE GUANACASTE

1 Liberia

Bahía Culebra

Playa Panamá

2 Playa Hermosa

Playas del Coco 3

Comunidad

GUANACASTE

Río Blanco

PAN-AMERICAN

Bagaces

HWY.

Nuevo Arenal

Lake Arenal

Isla Sta. Catalina

4 Playa Ocotal

5 Playa Pan de Azúcar

6 Playa Potrero

7 Playa Flamingo

Filadelfia

Belén

Lomas Barbudal Biological Reserve

Tilarán

Cañas

CORDILLERA DE TILARÁN

8 Playa Conchal

Brasilito

Las Baulas Marine National Park

Villarreal

9 Tamarindo

10 Playa Langosta

11 Playa Avellanas

12 Playa Negra

Paraíso

13

Playa Junquillal

Guaitil

Santa Cruz

Barra Honda National Park 24

23 Palo Verde National Park

Río Tempisque

CA1

Puerto Moreno

Taiwan Friendship Bridge

Ostional National Wildlife Refuge ◆

25 Nicoya

Curime

Isla Chira

Gulf of Nicoya

Playa Ostional

Ostional

Nosara

Carmona

Playa Nosara
Playa Pelada
Playa Guiones

14 Nosara

Playa Garza

15

Sámara

16

Playa Carrillo

Jicaral

NICOYA PENINSULA

Puntarenas **18**

Playa Naranjo

17

Punta Islita

PACIFIC OCEAN

Playa Coyote

Paquera **19**

Curú National Wildlife Refuge ◆

Isla Tortuga

Tambor

20

Bahía Ballena

Playa Tambor

Malpaís 22

Cobano

21

Montezuma

Cabo Blanco Strict Nature Reserve

Playa Montezuma

Playa Balsitas

Cabo Blanco

Playa Cabo Blanco

Isla Cabo Blanco

KEY

▶ *Start of itinerary*

0 — 20 miles

0 — 30 km

sirloin steak tips in a spicy jalapeño sauce, unusual for Tico cuisine, which is generally mild. There's also tasty *comida rapida* (fast food), such as tacos, chalupas, and hamburgers. ⊠ *C. 4, 100 m south and 25 m west of Farmacia Lux* ☎ 666–1202 ⊟ *AE, D, MC, V.*

¢–$ ✕ **Pizza Pronto.** This pizzeria in a white-adobe colonial house on a quiet side street has 23 different pizzas and takes you 100 years back in time. From the outdoor courtyard tables you can watch the pizza bakers push your pie on long-handled wooden shovels into the stone ovens. Wooden booths are inside. You can also get pasta, roasted chicken, and sandwiches. ⊠ *Avda. 4 and C. 1* ☎ 666–2098 ⊟ *AE, MC, V.*

$ ⊞ **Best Western Las Espuelas.** Smaller scale and with more personal attention than the business-oriented Best Western on the other side of town, this 44-room hotel is shaded by a majestic Guanacaste tree. Rooms face a landscaped courtyard and a large, sunny lap-size pool. The modern, fresh rooms have private terraces. The restaurant is off a cool, shady lobby with a fountain. ⊠ *2 km (1 mi) south of Liberia* ☎ 666–0144 ⊟ *666–2441* ✉ *espuelas@racsa.co.cr* ⇆ *44 rooms* ⟁ *Restaurant, cable TV, pool, outdoor hot tub, bar, meeting rooms* ⊟ *AE, D, MC, V* ⦿| *BP.*

$ ⊞ **Best Western Hotel El Sitio.** Spacious, modern rooms and extensive facilities, including an Italian restaurant, a casino, two pools shaded by stately Guanacaste trees, and a car-rental agency, are the reasons to consider Hotel El Sitio. It's basically a nondescript roadside motel, but the conveniences and free breakfast redeem it. ⊠ *South of Burger King complex on road heading west toward airport and beaches* ☎ 666–1211 ⊟ *666–2059* ⊕ *www.bestwestern.co.cr* Ⓓ *Apdo. 134–5000, Liberia* ⇆ *52 rooms* ⟁ *Restaurant, cable TV, 2 pools, spa, horseback riding, volleyball, casino, laundry service, meeting room, car rental* ⊟ *AE, MC, V* ⦿| *BP.*

¢ ⊞ **Hotel Aserradero.** A cheaper alternative to the roadside business hotels, this small hotel just off the highway has simple high-ceilinged rooms, all with air-conditioning and fans. Rows of wooden rocking chairs and polished tree stumps in the open-air corridors are reminders of the sawmill that used to stand on this site. The stylish Jardín Cervecero La Jarra next door serves innovative dinners. ⊠ *200 m north of the traffic lights at Liberia's main intersection* ☎ 666–1939 ⊟ *666–0475* ✉ *abalto@racsa.co.cr* ⇆ *18 rooms* ⟁ *Fans; no room phones, no room TVs* ⊟ *MC, V.*

Playa Hermosa

❷ *35 km (22 mi) southwest of Liberia, 25 km (16 mi) southwest of airport.*

Playa Hermosa, not to be confused with the mainland beach of the same name south of Jacó, has a relaxed village atmosphere that recalls a Mexican beach town. Rows of sunny villas are springing up and filling with American and Canadian expatriates, giving Hermosa a residential feel. The full length of the beach has long been occupied by hotels, restaurants, and homes, so the newer hotel behemoths and other developments have been forced to set up shop off the beach or on other beaches in the area. Playa Hermosa's crescent of grayish sand fronts a line of trees—

a welcome respite from the heat of the sun. At the beach's north end, low tide creates wide, rock-lined tidal pools. Playa Panama, just to the north, is a dark-sand beach that is rapidly being developed with large all-inclusive resorts and luxury condominiums.

Where to Stay & Eat

$ ✕ **Aqua Sport.** Tuck into a fish fillet stuffed with shrimp, one of the many fresh seafood dishes served at this casual beachfront restaurant. The grilled mixed-seafood platter is a good choice for big appetites. ⊠ *Beach road; heading south, take second entrance to Playa Hermosa and follow signs* ☎ *672–0050* ☐ *AE, MC, V.*

$–$$ ✕▦ **Villa del Sueño Hotel and Restaurant.** The handsome garden restaurant ($–$$$) is the main attraction at this elegant 14-room hotel. The food is formal and the service very polished, but the atmosphere is comfortable. Filet mignon with a brandy-and-peppercorn sauce, perfectly cooked mahimahi in shrimp sauce, and garlicky butterfly shrimp are always on the menu. Bread is homemade, country French, inspired by the owners' Quebec roots. There's mellow, live music most weekends to accompany dinner or drinks at the poolside bar. Superior rooms are spacious and comfortable with bamboo furniture in sitting areas and two double beds; smaller standard rooms look out onto the pool. Apartments for longer stays are available in the villa development across the street. ⊠ *First entrance to Playa Hermosa, 350 m west of main highway* ▦▦ *672–0026* ⊕ *www.villadelsueno.com* ↘ *14 rooms, 12 apartments* ⚒ *Restaurant, bar, fans, some kitchens, pool, shop, Internet; no a/c in some rooms, no room phones, no room TVs.* ☐ *AE, MC, V.*

$$ ▦ **Resort de Playa Villa Acacia.** Spacious rooms and private octagonal villas with hardwood details reside in a tranquil garden with brick paths and a round pool at this luxury hotel. Particularly impressive are the large, tiled baths with tubs and bidets, and the vanity sinks that are sensibly separated from the bathrooms. Each room has a private terrace. At the Internet café you can sip espresso made in Italian machines. The beach is a short walk away. ⊠ *Beach road; heading south, take second entrance to Playa Hermosa* ☎*672–1000* ▦*672–0272* ⊕*www.villacacia. com* ↘ *8 rooms, 8 villas* ⚒ *Restaurant, café, refrigerators, cable TV, pool, Internet, meeting rooms, no-smoking rooms; no room phones* ☐*AE, MC, V* ❍*| CP.*

★ $ ▦ **Hotel El Velero.** Spacious, attractive white rooms at this two-story beachfront hotel have arched doorways, terra-cotta tiles, bamboo furniture, and large windows. A satellite TV room keeps you in touch with the world, and the hotel runs daily snorkeling cruises on a handsome 38-foot sailboat. In the restaurant, sample the jumbo shrimp with rice and vegetables or the always-fresh mahimahi. Or come for Wednesday or Saturday barbecue nights, when live music is performed. ⊠ *100 m north of Aqua Sport* ☎ *672–0036* ▦ *672–0016* ⊕ *www.costaricahotel. net* ↘ *22 rooms* ⚒ *Restaurant, in-room safes, pool, snorkeling, boating, jet skiing, volleyball, bar, laundry service; no room phones, no room TVs* ☐ *AE, MC, V.*

$ ▦ **Playa Hermosa Inn.** Run by the family who owns Aqua Sport, this friendly bed-and-breakfast has gardens and spacious rooms in a two-story stucco building. There are two very cheap cold-water cabinas for rent and one large apartment with a kitchen. The inn is a little bare-bones in the decor department, but the beach is right at your doorstep. ⊠ *Heading south, take second entrance to Playa Hermosa* ☎ 672–0063 🖷 672–0060 ⊕ *www.costarica-beach-hotel.com* ⤶ *8 rooms, 2 cabins, 1 apartment* ⟁ *Fans, some kitchens, some refrigerators, pool; no a/c in some rooms, no room phones, no room TVs* ▤ *AE, MC, V* ⧦ *BP.*

Nightlife

Hotel El Velero (⊠ 100 m north of Aqua Sport ☎ 672–0036) hosts beach barbecues, with live music, on Wednesday and Saturday nights in high season. Weekend nights at **Villa del Sueño** (⊠ First entrance to Playa Hermosa, 350 m west of main highway ☎☎ 672–0026) there's live mellow jazz, as well as some classic rock. For a sunset cruise, set sail on **Spanish Dancer** (☎ 841–5604 or 672–0012), a 36-foot MacGregor racing catamaran, which runs December through May. The three-hour voyage includes appetizers and open bar and a chance to see dolphins, whales, and turtles. Tickets are $50 and cruises depart at 3 PM in front of Hotel El Velero.

Sports & the Outdoors

Diving Safaris (⊠ Second entrance road to Playa Hermosa, across from Villa Huetares Hotel ☎ 672–0012, 877/853–0538 in U.S. 🖷 672–0231, 954/453–5044 in U.S. ⊕ www.costaricadiving.net) runs a complete range of scuba activities, from beginner training to open-water PADI (Professional Association of Diving Instructors) certification courses. Multitank dives are organized at more than 30 tantalizing sites off the Guanacaste coast. Guides and trainers here know underwater Guanacaste—alive with rays, sharks, fish, and turtles—and their safety standards have the DAN (Divers Alert Network) seal of approval. Prices range from $50 for a one-tank afternoon dive to $375 and up for PADI open-water and Dive Master certification courses.

At the general store–cum–restaurant **Aqua Sport** (⊠ Beach road; heading south, take second entrance to Playa Hermosa and follow signs ☎ 672–0050), you can rent water-sports equipment or organize a fishing or surfing trip. At the north end of the beach, below Hotel Condovac, an independent **kiosk** rents Boogie boards, plastic kayaks, Jet Skis, and other water toys.

Shopping

You can shop for a beach picnic at the **Aqua Sport** (⊠ Beach road; heading south, take second entrance to Playa Hermosa and follow signs ☎ 672–0050) minimarket and liquor store and buy souvenirs in the gift shop. **Kaltak Art and Craft Market** (⊠ South of airport ☎ 668–1048) has five rooms of high-quality crafts and gifts. **La Gran Nicoya** (⊠ Just north of the small bridge over Río Tempisque ☎ 667–0062) has an excellent jewelry selection plus an international shipping service and tourist information and maps. Kaltak and La Gran Nicoya, both on the road between Liberia airport and the turnoff for Playa Hermosa, have nearly any souvenir you could want.

Playas del Coco

❸ *35 km (22 mi) southwest of Liberia.*

Playas del Coco has a reputation as a slightly seedy beachfront town. But if you like your resorts to have some local color, Coco's scruffy pier, slightly down-at-the-heels appearance, and trinket and souvenir stands can be appealing. It's one of the most accessible beaches in Guanacaste, so it serves as a playground for Costa Rica's college kids. Christmas and Semana Santa in March are impossibly crowded. But the quieter, north part of the beach has some lovely grown-up restaurants and hotels. For surfers, this is the only point of departure for boat trips to famed Ollie's Point and Witch's Rock.

Where to Stay & Eat

$–$$ ✕ **Louisiana Bar & Grill.** This second-story restaurant is cool and breezy, but the Cajun cuisine is hot, with authentic jambalaya and gumbo chockablock with shrimp, crab, and sausage. Fish is fresh, thanks to one of the owner's fleet of fishing boats, and it's served any way you like it, with a choice of 10 intriguing sauces, including macadamia pesto or orange chipotle sauce. ☒ *Main road through town, across street from Hotel Coco Verde* ☎ *670–0882* ▭ *AE, MC, V.*

★ $ ✕ **El Sol y La Luna.** Finding haute-Italian cuisine in a romantic alfresco restaurant in Playas del Coco is a surprise. Host Alessandro Tolo has brought his design ideas and superb jazz CD collection from Rome, and his wife, Silvia Casu, has brought culinary skills from her native Sardinia. Both food and service are memorable, with homemade pasta and homegrown basil lending authentic Italian flavor. Other distinctively Italian tastes include a wide selection of Italian wines, sparkling San Pellegrino mineral water, and aromatic sambuca liqueur. Memorable home-baked desserts include Arenal, a volcano-shaped chocolate cake with chocolate sauce flowing down the sides. ☒ *La Puerta del Sol hotel, 180 m to right off main road to Playas del Coco* ☎ *670–0195* ▭ *AE, MC, V.*

$ ✕ **Tequila Bar and Grill.** This popular gringo hangout with a concrete floor and old wooden tables is created in the image of a humble, almost grubby Mexican restaurant. The meals are authentic and tasty, especially the fajitas, which come with chicken, beef, shrimp, or *pulpo* (octopus). Locally, this place is famous for its excellent margaritas and its cool jazz and blues recordings. ☒ *Main strip, 130 m east of (away from) beach* ☎ *670–0741* ▭ *No credit cards* ☉ *Closed Wed.*

$$ ✕⬚ **La Puerta del Sol.** A tranquil enclosure of stylish suites overlooks a formal garden with sculpted shrubs and a lovely pool. The modern, airy Mediterranean-style guest rooms have aqua-and-tangerine color schemes and filmy fabrics. King-size beds roost atop adobe platforms, and gleaming white bathrooms have high ceilings. El Sol y La Luna, the wonderful Italian restaurant in the garden, serves homemade pasta and Italian wines with a Sardinian flair. ☒ *180 m to right (north) off main road to Playas del Coco* ☎ *670–0195* ⎙ *670–0650* ⊕ *www.lapuertadelsol. com* ➪ *10 suites* ♦ *Restaurant, in-room safes, cable TV, pool, gym, Ping-Pong* ▭ *AE, MC, V* ⦿ *BP.*

$ ⬚ **Villa del Sol.** The French-Canadian owners of this B&B offer quiet, spacious, light-filled rooms in a contemporary building with a lovely pool out front. There are also open-plan studios, each with kitchen, a queen-size bed, and a pull-out trundle bed that sleeps two. Well away from Coco's main drag, Villa del Sol is just 100 m from the quiet part of the beach. Views of the lush tropical garden and the ocean are best from the upstairs balconies. ⊠ *1 km (½ mi) north of Villa Flores* 🕿 *670–0085* ⊕ *www.villadelsol.com* ⌧ *Apdo. 052–5019, Playas del Coco* ⏎ *7 rooms, 5 with bath; 6 studios* ⌂ *Some kitchens, pool, laundry service; no a/c in some rooms, no room phones, no room TVs* ▤ *AE, MC, V* ⊺◯⊺ *BP.*

$ ▦ **Villa Flores.** The American owners have prettied up this nine-room B&B with floral motifs inside and out. The high-ceilinged upstairs suites are spacious, whereas the downstairs rooms are cozier, with smallish bathrooms. The gardens have been replanted with flowering shrubs and the pool is inviting, as are the hammocks slung between tall palm trees. A tiled terrace restaurant serves breakfast and, in high season, dinner, too. ⊠ *180 m east of main road* 🕿 *670–0269* 🕾 *670–0787* ⌧ *Apdo. 2, Playas del Coco* ⊕ *www.hotel-villa-flores.com* ⏎ *7 rooms, 2 suites* ⌂ *Restaurant, fans, pool, gym, hot tub, laundry service; no a/c in some rooms, no room phones, no TV in some rooms* ▤ *V* ⊺◯⊺ *BP.*

Nightlife

Banana Surf (⊠ Across street from casino), a second-floor disco-restaurant, has dancing until 2 AM. There's happy hour and gambling every night at the **Hotel Coco Verde** (⊠ Main road through town). Occasionally, there are dances down by the dock when a live band comes to town; dancing doesn't get under way until after 10 PM.

Sports & the Outdoors

Witch's Rock and Ollie's Point, a 1½-hour boat ride away from Playas del Coco off the coast of Santa Rosa National Park, are favorite surfing spots, but overcrowding has led the park authorities to limit the number of daily surfers to 25. You can sign up for a surfing trip with any beach-town tour operator, but all excursions leave from the main dock at Playas del Coco in boats owned by local fishermen.

Playa Ocotal

❹ *3 km (2 mi) west of Playas del Coco.*

Despite its proximity to student-thronged Coco, Playa Ocotal is a serene spot, with a lilliputian crescent of beach sheltered by rocks. Right at the entrance to the Gulf of Papagayo, it's a good place for sportfishing enthusiasts to hole up between excursions. There's good diving at Las Corridas, just 1 km (½ mi) away, as well as excellent snorkeling in nearby coves and islands.

Where to Stay

$$$ ▦ **El Ocotal Beach Resort.** High above secluded Ocotal Bay, this luxury hotel has a sportfishing fleet and a day spa. Rooms have huge French windows and unsurpassed views of verdant coast looking north to the Peninsula Santa Elena. The freestanding triangular bungalows down the hill are larger, with polished wood floors and private pools. ⊠ *3 km (2 mi) south of Playas del Coco, down newly paved road* 🕿 *670–0321*

🕾 670–0083 ⊕ www.ocotalresort.com ⎙ Apdo. 1, Playas del Coco
⟳ 59 rooms, 5 suites, 12 bungalows ⚹ Restaurant, fans, in-room
safes, cable TV, tennis court, 3 pools, spa, dive shop, boating, horseback riding, bar, laundry service, Internet ⊟ AE, MC, V ⏀ BP.

★ $$ 🗔 **Hotel Villa Casa Blanca.** Secluded and romantic, and surely one of the
finest B&Bs in Costa Rica, the Casa Blanca occupies a hillside Mediter-
ranean-style building buried in a bower of tropical plantings. The inti-
mate, junglelike setting attracts numerous colorful birds (and talkative
pet parrots are attracted by breakfast). Victorian-influenced rooms com-
fort you with pleasant wood details and artwork, canopy beds, and enor-
mous bathrooms with mirrored walls. The pool is small but pretty, with
a bridge and a sundeck. There's a condo with a kitchen for longer stays.
⊠ Just inside gated entrance to El Ocotal Beach Resort 🕾 670–0518
🖷 670–0448 ⊕ www.informationcostarica.com ⎙ Apdo. 176–5019,
Playa Ocotal ⟳ 10 rooms, 5 suites, 1 condo ⚹ Pool, outdoor hot tub;
no room phones, no room TVs, no smoking ⊟ AE, MC, V ⏀ BP.

Nightlife

At sunset on the beach below El Ocotal, you can enjoy a quiet margarita
with a view at **Father Rooster Sports Bar & Grill** (⊠ El Ocotal Beach Re-
sort, 3 km [2 mi] south of Playas del Coco 🕾 670–0321). The action
heats up later in the evening with big-screen TV, music, pool, beach vol-
leyball, and Tex-Mex bar food. During peak holiday weeks, huge crowds
of partyers descend on the bar to dance by torchlight.

Playa Pan de Azúcar

❺ 8 km (5 mi) north of Playa Flamingo.

Playa Pan de Azúcar (Sugar Bread Beach) has a quality that can be hard
to come by in this area: privacy. There are good islands for snorkeling
just offshore.

Where to Stay

$$–$$$ 🗔 **Hotel Sugar Beach.** Picture a thin, curving white-sand beach and a se-
cluded hotel and shimmering pool shaded by trees. Most of the rooms have
idyllic ocean views, and each room's wooden door has a hand-carved image
of a local bird or animal. Bright yellow-and-blue fabrics along with wa-
termelon, aqua, and yellow walls make rooms festive and fresh. The open-
air rotunda restaurant serves good seafood dishes. The hotel organizes surfing
tours to Witch's Rock and leatherback turtle–watching tours at Playa
Grande. Several golf courses are nearby. ⊠ 8 km (5 mi) north of Playa
Flamingo 🕾 654–4242 🖷 654–4239 ⊕ www.sugar-beach.com ⎙ Apdo.
90, Santa Cruz ⟳ 22 rooms, 3 suites, 1 apartment, 2 houses ⚹ Restau-
rant, in-room safes, minibars, some kitchens, cable TV, pool, snorkeling,
boating, horseback riding, bar, laundry service ⊟ AE, D, MC, V.

Playa Potrero

❻ 3 km (2 mi) south of Playa Pan de Azucar.

With more development than Azúcar, and less than Flamingo, Playa
Potrero, between the two, is a wide, white-sand stretch. The road from

Flamingo is dusty and bumpy, so this beach tends to be less crowded. You can rent boats from area hotels to go snorkeling.

There's excellent swimming as well as diving around **Isla Santa Catalina,** 10 km (6 mi) offshore from Playa Potrero. You can rent a boat from local hotels to make the trip. The island is also a bird-watching destination: it's one of the few places in Costa Rica where the Bridled Tern nests (March–September).

Where to Stay & Eat

¢–$ ✕ **Cantina Las Brisas.** The perfect beach bar, Las Brisas looks like a shack with a view. The Texan owner serves excellent Mexican-inspired food and seafood. The fish tacos are outstanding—breaded strips of fish smothered in lettuce, tomato, and refried beans and encased in both a crisp taco and a soft tortilla shell. Wednesday is ladies' night and karaoke, and the joint really jumps. As advertised in the name, there are always cooling breezes wafting through the place, which is decorated with old surfboards, rusty U.S. license plates, and wall murals. ✉ *Beside the supermarket* ☎ *654–4047* ☰ *No credit cards.*

$$–$$$ ▢ **Club Bahía Potrero.** This new luxury hotel has a splendid swimming pool and a flower-bordered path to the beach, which is just a few steps away. The design is modern, with elegant Costa Rica–made wood furniture and ceramic floors with interesting tile patterns. Ask for one of the three rooms that has outdoor showers and hot tubs in private patio gardens. Uniformed waiters serve seafood and international dishes in the handsome *rancho* restaurant (open-sided, with a conical thatch roof) with ocean views. ✉ *South end of Potrero Beach, across from Hotel Monte Carlo* ☎ *654–4671* 🖷 *654–5182* ⊕ *www.potrerobay.com* ⟿ *25 rooms, 14 suites* ♧ *Restaurant, fans, cable TV, pool, some in-room hot tubs, beach, bar* ☰ *MC, V.*

$ ▢ **Hotel Monte Carlo.** Hidden behind a sunny orange-and-yellow wall, this small Italian-owned hotel fronts the south end of Potrero Beach. There's a gorgeous beachside *ranchito* (a small rancho) for sipping sunset cocktails. The houses, set back in a garden, are connected to the beach via white gravel paths. Each house has a kitchen, a lovely terrace, a huge, tiled bathroom, and a room that sleeps four. The open-air Italian-French restaurant is open all day and serves afternoon tea. ✉ *South end of Potrero Beach* 🖷🖷 *654–5048* ⊕ *www.montecarlobeachresort.com* ⟿ *5 houses* ♧ *Restaurant, fans, kitchens, pool, beach, bar; no room phones, no room TVs* ☰ *No credit cards.*

Playa Flamingo

❼ *35 km (22 mi) west of Belén, 3 km (2 mi) south of Playa Potrero.*

Flamingo was one of the first of the northern Nicoya beaches to experience the wonders of overscale resort development, a fact immortalized in the huge concrete towers that dominate the landscape. The beach, however, is still a welcome oasis, and a fleet of sportfishing boats is moored in the busy marina. To get to Playa Flamingo from Playa Ocotal, you drive northeast to Playas Coco, then east on the main road, south to Belén, and then west. If you have four-wheel drive and an excellent sense of direction, you can attempt to drive (dry season only) the 16-km (11-mi) Monkey Trail, which cuts through the mountains from Coco to Flamingo. But even some Ticos get lost on this route.

Where to Stay & Eat

★ **$–$$** ✕ **Marie's Restaurant.** At the north end of the beach, look for this veranda restaurant furnished with sliced-tree-trunk tables painted with sea creatures. Here you can settle back at lunch or dinner for generous helpings of fresh seafood at reasonable prices. There's delightful ceviche and a delicious *plato de mariscos* (shrimp, lobster, and fish fillets served with garlic butter, potatoes, and salad). Save room for the dark and delicious banana-chocolate bread pudding. Breakfasts feature unusual papaya pancakes and French toast made with cream cheese and jam. ⊠ *Main road, near north end of beach* ☎ *654–4136* ☰ *V.*

$$–$$$$ ▥ **Flamingo Marina Resort.** This resort, made up of hillside pink buildings with brightly colored tile roofs, has more personality than most other large resorts in the area. The fashionably decorated rooms, color washed in a mango hue, have terra-cotta lamps, hand-carved wooden furniture, and shell-shape sinks. The luxurious condos have full modern kitchens and spacious sitting areas with leather couches. Nearly all rooms and condos have large verandas with excellent views of the sea below. One suite has a private hot tub. ⊠ *Hill above Flamingo Bay* ☎ *654–4141, 290–1858 in San José* ☒ *654–4035, 231–1858 in San José* ⊕ *www.flamingomarina.com* ✆ *Apdo. 321–1002, San José* ⇆ *72 condos, 22 rooms, 8 suites* ⚹ *Restaurant, in-room safes, some kitchens, minibars, cable TV, tennis court, 4 pools, wading pool, outdoor hot tub, dive shop, 2 bars, laundry service, meeting room* ☰ *AE, DC, MC, V* ꙴ *BP.*

★ **$$$** ▥ **Colores del Pacífico.** From high atop a commanding cliff, this small, exquisite, family-run hotel presides over Potrero Bay. It looks like a page out of *Architectural Digest* with a very modern, minimalist design that incorporates terra-cotta walls, Mexican-tile floors, sculptural cactus plantings, and indirect lighting. Each room has a dramatic bed "treatment" by the Belgian interior designer–owner. Fresh flowers and fruit greet you in your room, each with a private terrace and hammock. Breakfast and lunch, along with sunset cocktails and canapés, are served in a thatch-roof restaurant with a sweeping ocean view. Aqua exercise sessions in the infinity-edge pool and yoga sessions are offered every day. The minimum stay is three nights. ⊠ *At intersection of roads leading out of Flamingo and to Playa Potrero* ☎ *654–4769* ☒ *654–4976* ⊕ *www.coloresdelpacifico.com* ⇆ *6 rooms, 1 suite* ⚹ *Dining room, minibars, pool, fitness classes, snorkeling, waterskiing, fishing, bar; no TV in some rooms, no kids under 12* ☰ *AE, MC, V* ꙴ *BP.*

$ ▥ **Hotel Guanacaste Lodge.** On the outskirts of Flamingo, this quiet, new, Tico-run lodge has 10 rooms in five houses on manicured grounds with tall trees. Rooms are large with high beamed ceilings, and are comfortably furnished with wood furniture and walk-in closets. Bathrooms are tiled and spacious. Each room has a picture window looking out onto the pool and a cascading fountain. The attached Rancho Grande Restaurant/Bar serves Tico, Mexican, and Spanish dishes in a huge, open rancho with handmade wooden furniture. ⊠ *200 m south of the Potrero-Flamingo crossroads,* ☎ *654–4494* ☒ *654–4495* ✆ *por-*

tolsa@racsa.co.cr ⌨ *10 rooms* ☁ *Restaurant, fans, in-room safes, cable TV, pool, bar, laundry service* ▤ *MC, V.*

Playa Conchal

❽ *35 km (22 mi) west of Belén; 1 km (½ mi) south of Playa Brasilito and 8 km (5 mi) south of Flamingo.*

Playa Conchal, one of Guanacaste's finest and most secluded beaches, is aptly named—it's sprinkled with shells. The sprawling Paradisus Playa Conchal resort looms large here, and the road leading to it is sprinkled with trendy new restaurants, shops, and small hotels.

A small fishing village just 1 km (½ mi) north of Conchal, **Brasilito** has a ramshackle row of houses that huddle around its main square, which doubles as the soccer field. Before high tide, boats line up just off a white-sand beach that is the equal of Flamingo minus the megahotels.

Where to Stay & Eat

$-$$ ✕ **El Camarón Dorado.** This bougainvillea-drenched bar-restaurant de-
Fodor'sChoice rives much of its appeal from its shaded location on Brasilito's beauti-
★ ful beach. Some tables are right on the beach, with the surf lapping just yards away, and a small-vessel fishing fleet anchored offshore assures you of the freshness of the bountiful portions of seafood on the menu. Thanks to its spectacular sunset views, this is a popular place for early evening drinks. If you have a reservation, a van can pick you up from Flamingo or Tamarindo hotels. ✉ *200 m north of Brasilito Plaza, Brasilito* ☎ *654–4028* ▤ *AE, DC, MC, V.*

¢-$$ ✕ **Il Forno Restaurant.** For a break from seafood, try lunch or dinner at this Italian garden restaurant. There are 15 versions of thin-crust piz-zas, plus fine, homemade pastas, veal marsala, and risotto. Vegetarians can indulge in eggplant lasagna and interesting salad choices. At din-ner, fairy lights and candles glimmer all through the garden, and some tables are romantically set apart under thatched roofs. Spanish and Italian wines are available by the glass or bottle to further enhance the mood. ✉ *Main road, 200 m south of the bridge in Brasilito* ☎ *654–4125* ▤ *No credit cards* ☉ *Closed Mon.*

$$$$ ⊡ **Paradisus Playa Conchal Beach & Golf Resort.** The former Meliá Playa Conchal is now a deluxe all-inclusive Paradisus resort, one of only six in the world. From the enormous, open-air, marble-floored lobby, you can survey the massive grounds, encompassing almost 4 square km (1½ square mi) of manicured golf course, bungalows, tennis courts, the largest pool in Central America, and a distant beach. Suites, in low-slung, colonial-style houses, are large and luxurious. The per-person rate is $200 per night. The restaurants serve a range of à la carte international fare. ✉ *Entrance less than 1 km (½ mi) south of Brasilito* ☎ *654–4123* 🖷 *654–4181* ⊕ *www.solmelia.com* ⌨ *292 suites* ☁ *5 restaurants, in-room safes, minibars, cable TV, 18-hole golf course, 4 tennis courts, pool, gym, hair salon, beach, jet skiing, bicycles, casino, dance club, laundry service, Internet, meeting room* ▤ *AE, DC, MC, V* ℠ *AI.*

¢-$ ⊡ **Hotel Brasilito.** Fronting the sea, this hotel made of aged wood has an open-air restaurant that catches the breeze. Tables and chairs are arrayed beneath lazily turning ceiling fans; a collection of old saddles straddles wooden beams. The sparely furnished but comfortable rooms occupy both floors of an old but freshly painted two-story wooden building behind the restaurant. Ask for one of the two larger rooms above the restaurant; they share a veranda with unobstructed sea views. ⊠ *Next to the square and soccer field, Brasilito* ☎ *654–4237* 📠 *654–4247* ⊕ *www. brasilito.com* 🡒 *15 rooms* ⚒ *Restaurant, fans, snorkeling, horseback riding, laundry service, Internet; no a/c, no room phones, no room TVs* ▭ *MC, V.*

Tamarindo

❾ *37 km (23 mi) west of Belén.*

Tamarindo is a vibrant beach community with a dazzling variety of restaurants, cabins, bars, and hotels at all price levels. Surfing is the main attraction for both the young crowd that parties hard at beachfront bars after a day riding the waves, and for the gray-haired veterans who combine surfing with golfing at nearby golf courses, including Hacienda Pinilla, an 18-hole championship course with ocean views. The older nonsurfing crowd is attracted by the upscale beachfront hotels away from the bustling town center. Developmental hustle is everywhere, evidenced by the presence of condo projects and mini–strip malls. Still, Tamarindo's beaches are great for snorkeling, boating, kayaking, diving, surfing, and just plain swimming; there are estuaries north and south of town for bird- and animal-watching; and there are two turtle-nesting beaches nearby—Playa Langosta to the south, and Playa Grande to the north. With an airstrip just outside town, Tamarindo is also a convenient base for exploring all of Guanacaste. Except for some sections through the middle of town, roads are very dusty and potholed, but there are plans afoot to pave the road to Playa Langosta.

To learn about the life cycle of the Giant Leatherback turtles and the threats they face, visit the creative **El Mundo de la Tortuga** museum in Playa Grande. Audio tours (in English, Spanish, German, or French) through the interactive exhibits last 20 minutes. The museum also conducts excellent turtle tours, which often occur late at night, sometimes until 3 AM, depending on turtle sightings. ⊠ *Road to Hotel Las Tortugas* ☎ *653–0471* 🖂 *$5* ⊘ *Turtle tours usually Oct. 20.–Feb. 15 nightly, depending on high tide; returning not earlier than 11 PM. Museum 4 PM until tours return. Closed May–Oct.*

North of Tamarindo, across an estuary, the **Las Baulas Marine National Park** (Parque Nacional Marino Las Baulas) protects the long **Playa Grande.** This beach hosts the world's largest visitation of nesting Giant Leatherback turtles (nesting season is October through April). Playa Grande is also a great surf spot. Environmental activist Lewis Wilson, also the owner of the Hotel Las Tortugas, struggled for a decade to get Las Baulas established and has a true understanding of the importance of balancing the oft-conflicting needs of locals, turtles, and tourists. An evening spent discussing ecotourism and ecopolitics with him is a real education. The adjacent **Tamarindo Wildlife Refuge,** a mangrove estuary with some excellent

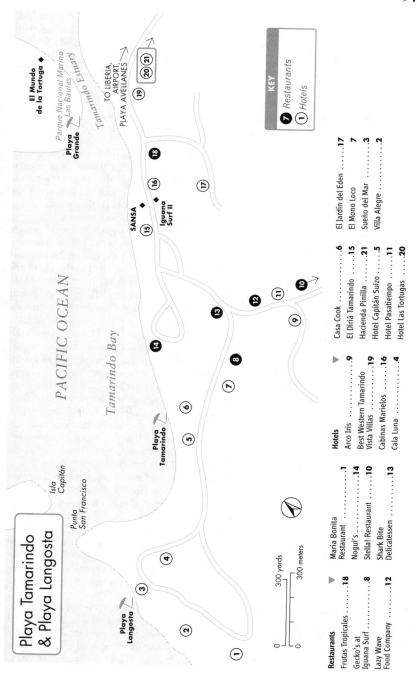

Playa Tamarindo & Playa Langosta

Isla Capitán

Punta San Francisco

Playa Langosta

Playa Tamarindo

PACIFIC OCEAN

Tamarindo Bay

0 300 yards
0 300 meters

El Mundo de la Tortuga ◆

Parque Nacional Marino Las Baulas

Playa Grande

Tamarindo Estuary

TO LIBERIA, AIRPORT, PLAYA AVELLANES →

SANSA ◆

Iguana Surf II ◆

KEY
7 *Restaurants*
1 *Hotels*

Restaurants

Frutas Tropicales **1**
Gecko's at Iguana Surf **8**
Lazy Wave Food Company **12**
María Bonita Restaurant **14**
Nogui's **10**
Stella! Restaurant **13**
Shark Bite Delicatessen **13**

Hotels

Arco Iris **9**
Best Western Tamarindo Vista Villas **19**
Cabinas Marielos **16**
Cala Luna **4**
Casa Cook **6**
El Diriá Tamarindo **15**
Hacienda Pinilla **21**
Hotel Capitán Suizo **5**
Hotel Pasatiempo **11**
Hotel Las Tortugas **20**
El Jardín del Eden **17**
El Mono Loco **7**
Sueño del Mar **3**
Villa Alegre **2**

bird-watching, has been under some developmental pressure of late. Just south of Tamarindo, accessible by dirt road, is the **Río San Francisco,** with an estuary system that's also rich in bird life. Unlike Tamarindo, it's free of motorboats. ⊠ *Playa Grande is 33 km (20 mi) north of Tamarindo by rough road; most tours go by motorboat, a short ride across the estuary* ☎ *653–0470.*

Where to Eat

$-$$ ✕ **Gecko's at Iguana Surf.** This rustic, thatch-roof restaurant brimming with trickling fountains is attached to a surf shop and is very popular with local American families. Chef John Szilasi bakes his own bread and bread sticks studded with spicy seeds. His ambitious dinner menus revolve around fresh local ingredients such as tuna, plump calamari, and lobster. The chocolate cake is famous and sells out quickly. By day, the restaurant becomes Gil's Place, serving Mexican-style breakfasts and lunches, 8 AM to 3 PM Monday through Saturday. ⊠ *Beside Iguana Surf, on road to Playa Langosta* ☎ *653–0334* ▱ *No credit cards* ☺ *Closed Mon.*

$-$$ ✕ **Nogui's.** Also known as the Sunrise Café, Nogui's is considered by local aficionados to have Tamarindo's freshest seafood. The place has a reputation for reasonable prices, but is getting expensive. Nogui's alfresco plastic tables and chairs are practically on the beach. There are salads and shrimp tacos for lunch; the full seafood menu is available only at dinner. The langostino is highly recommended, but be prepared to pay about $20 for one. ⊠ *South of Hotel Zullymar, on Tamarindo Circle* ☎ *653–0029* ▱ *AE, MC, V* ☺ *Closed Wed. and 2 wks in Oct.*

$-$$ ✕ **Stella! Restaurant.** For a romantic night out, head to this elegant alfresco rancho restaurant. The kitchen doesn't always live up to the great service and atmosphere, but the menu is ambitious and always interesting. Sure bets are the wood-oven pizzas, excellent fresh fish served with any of seven sauces, and classic Wiener schnitzel, a holdover from the former German owner. A chocolate cake made with Cafe Rico liqueur is worth saving room for. Along with Italian and Chilean wines, there's a selection of European and Japanese beers. You can take advantage of complimentary shuttle service when you make a reservation. Pizza and meals can be delivered to your hotel. ⊠ *90 m east of Hotel Pasatiempo* ☎ *653–0127* ☺ *Closed Sat.* ▱ *AE, DC, MC, V.*

$ ✕ **Lazy Wave Food Company.** For serious food at laughable prices, visit
Fodor'sChoice this casual, open-air restaurant built around a giant dead tree. The
★ eclectic dinner menu, using fresh local ingredients, changes daily. There may be chunks of seared tuna with a dab of wasabi and a heap of Furlani's signature crispy, hand-cut shoestring fries and blanched green beans swirled in sesame oil. Or there might be a salad of warm conch or whatever the local fishermen caught that morning. Desserts are standouts, too. The recorded music can get a little loud for more sedate diners, and the atmosphere is always high-energy. ⊠ *Beside Hotel Pasatiempo, behind storefronts* ☎ *653–0737* ☺ *Closed Sun.* ▱ *V.*

$ ✕ **Shark Bite Delicatessen & Carnicería.** The young American owners deliver hearty sandwiches piled high on crusty French or sourdough bread. You can build your own from a wide selection of meats, cheeses, and roasted, marinated vegetables or try one of the special combinations. The bottomless cup of coffee, fudge brownies, Internet access, and used-

TICO TURTLES

ANNUAL TURTLE VISITATIONS to beaches on both the Pacific and the Atlantic-Caribbean coasts are renowned among devoted ecotourists. Nesting turtles come ashore at night to beaches that have been set aside for their protection. They plow an uneven furrow with their flippers to propel themselves past the high-tide line, then use their hind flippers to scoop out a hole in which to lay their eggs. A few months later, hatchlings struggle out of the nests and make their perilous journey back to the sea.

That's where you come in. Turtle preservation organizations rely on volunteers to shepherd the tiny animals on their journey from the nest to the sea. This help from humans prevents predatory frigate birds from scooping up hatchlings for their breakfast. Don't pick up the babies, because females return to the beach where they were born to lay their eggs, and scientists believe it's this first journey from nest to sea that imprints them.

In spite of this protection and their "endangered" classifications, turtle populations remain seriously threatened. Poachers have for generations harvested the eggs—a rumored aphrodisiac—and the meat and shells. Beachfront development, with its bright lights, can disorient the turtles; and fishermen's lines entangle and drown them.

Four species of turtles nest at Tortuguero National Park: the Green Turtle, Hawksbill, Loggerhead, and Giant Leatherback. Green Turtles reproduce in large groups from July to October. They lay eggs every two to three years and produce two or three clutches each time. Smaller Hawksbill turtles are threatened because of their transparent brown shells, sought after for jewelry making. Loggerheads have oversize heads and shorter flippers and make rare appearances at Tortuguero. Giant Leatherbacks are the largest of all turtles— they grow up to 6½ feet long and can weigh up to 1,000 pounds—and have a tough outer skin rather than a shell. From mid-February through April, they nest mainly in southern Tortuguero. Olive Ridleys are the smallest sea turtles—the average carapace is 21–29 inches long. This species is also the least shy. During mass nestings, or arribadas, thousands of Olive Ridley turtles take to the Pacific shores at night. An estimated 200,000 of the 500,000 turtles that nest in Costa Rica each year choose Playa Nancite, a gray-sand beach in Guanacaste's Santa Rosa National Park, the world's only totally protected Olive Ridley arribada.

Easier to reach is the Ostional National Wildlife Refuge, near Nosara. Locals harvest the eggs in the early stages of the arribada—turtle visits run August–December and peak in September and October—because later waves of mother turtles destroy the earlier nests. Another accessible spot is Playa Grande, November–April stomping ground of the Leatherback turtles. Las Baulas National Marine Park was created specifically to protect the Leatherbacks, who also show up in smaller numbers at Playas Langosta and Junquillal. Nicoya Peninsula turtle-watching crowds are dense between Christmas and New Year's Day.

To help save these gentle giants, you can volunteer with such organizations as the **Caribbean Conservation Corporation** (CCC; ☎ 709–8011 Tortuguero, 224–9215 San José, 352/373–6441 or 800/678–7853 in U.S. ⊕ www.cccturtle.org), based on the northern Caribbean coast. The **National Association for Indigenous Affairs** (ANAI; ☎ 224–3570 ⊕ www.anaicr.org) works to protect the turtles in the Gandoca-Manzanillo Wildlife Refuge.

book exchange are good excuses to hang out inside the deli or outside at a picnic table or at the bar. ⊠ *Across street and south of Lazy Wave, next to Amnet office* ☎ *653–0441* ▭ *No credit cards.*

¢–$ ✕ **Frutas Tropicales.** The plastic tables and chairs here stay full for a reason—the restaurant dishes out Costa Rican food at Costa Rican prices. The food is nothing fancy, but the *casados* (plates of rice, beans, fried plantains, cabbage salad, tomatoes, noodles, and fish, chicken, or meat) and breakfasts are tasty and substantial. The menu includes hamburgers and fries and great *frutas tropicales* (tropical fruit drinks). ⊠ *Main road, north end of town* ☎ *653–0041* ▭ *AE, MC, V.*

Where to Stay

$$ ✕▣ **El Jardín del Edén.** The only drawback to the "Garden of Eden" (this one, anyway) is that it's not right on the beach. Instead, the two-tier, Mediterranean-style, pink building resides amid lush hillside gardens. Rooms, some on the small side, are being renovated by new French owners with a penchant for crisp blue-and-white Moroccan decor. All rooms have ocean views, and two beautiful pools provide the missing water element. One two-bedroom apartment has its own kitchen. The thatch-roof restaurant ($$), candlelit at dinner, prepares outstanding fresh seafood, pastas, and steaks with French flair. Breakfast is excellent, with perhaps the best coffee in town. ⊠ *From Hotel El Milagro on main road, turn left, go 180 m, then right for 180 m uphill* ⌂ *Apdo. 1094–2050, San Pedro* ☎ *653–0137* 🖷 *653–0111* ⊕ *www.jardindeleden. com* ⤳ *19 rooms, 1 apartment* ⌂ *Restaurant, fans, in-room safes, minibars, refrigerators, cable TV, 2 pools, hot tub, 2 bars, laundry service, Internet* ▭ *AE, MC, V* ⵘ *BP.*

$$$ ▣ **Casa Cook.** The one-bedroom, hardwood-detailed cabinas right on Tamarindo's beach are owned by an amiable retired American couple. Each comfortable cabina has a full kitchen, its own water heater, a queen-size sofa bed in the living room, a queen bed in the bedroom, and screened doors and windows. The honeymoon cabina—a 550-square-foot, one-bedroom apartment—has a private bath, kitchen, living room, and outside eating area. Air-conditioning is $10 extra per night. ⊠ *On road to Playa Langosta, north of the Hotel Capitán Suizo* ☎ *653–0125* 🖷 *653–0753* ⊕ *www.tamarindo.com/cook* ⤳ *3 cabinas, 1 casita* ⌂ *Fans, in-room safes, kitchens, cable TV, pool, beach; no smoking* ▭ *AE, MC, V.*

$$$ ▣ **El Diriá Tamarindo.** A shady tropical garden right next to the beach eliminates the need to stray far from Tamarindo's first luxury hotel. Rooms in the contemporary three-story building have been updated with pre-Columbian design motifs, tile floors, and modern furniture, and each has a spacious balcony. Try to avoid the rooms facing the noisy main road; rooms facing the beach—called sunset-view rooms—deliver spectacular sunsets, as promised. The thatched rotunda bar and restaurant overlook a large rectangular pool. A newer pool in the residential condo development across the street is also made available to hotel guests. ⊠ *¾ km (½ mi) before Tamarindo center* ☎ *653–0031, 291–2881 in San José* 🖷 *653–0208* ⊕ *www.eldiria.com* ⌂ *Apdo. 476–1007, San José* ⤳ *123 rooms* ⌂ *Restaurant, in-room safes, minibars, cable TV, driving range, tennis court, 2 pools, bar, casino, laundry service, meeting rooms* ▭ *AE, MC, V* ⵘ *BP.*

$$$ ☆ **Hotel Capitán Suizo.** On a relatively quiet stretch of Tamarindo's gorgeous beach, elegant balconied rooms and luxurious bungalows surround a large, shaded pool set in a mature garden. The stunning, three-story rooms have high, angled ceilings and amusing flourishes of original art on the walls. The two-level bungalows have sybaritic bathrooms with sunken tubs, beautiful tile work, and outdoor garden showers. The four-bedroom apartment has a kitchen and hot tub. A beautifully decorated and subtly lighted restaurant serves contemporary cuisine and hosts lively beach barbecues. Service is friendly and polished. Diving and kayaking trips can be arranged. ⊠ *Right side of road toward Playa Langosta (veer left before circle)* ☎ *653–0075 or 653–0353* 🖷 *653–0292* ⊕ *www.hotelcapitansuizo.com* ⇋ *22 rooms, 8 bungalows, 1 apartment* ⟁ *Restaurant, in-room safes, refrigerators, pool, boating, fishing, bicycles, horseback riding, shop, laundry service; no a/c in some rooms, no room TVs* ▭ *AE, MC, V* ⦿*BP.*

FodorsChoice ★

$$–$$$ ☆ **Best Western Tamarindo Vista Villas.** A mecca for surfers, the comfortable rooms and equipped suites in this sparkling-white garden resort overlook some of Tamarindo's best surf breaks. There's an on-site surf shop named for Robert August, a veteran surfer of *Endless Summer* movie fame, a surf school, and lots of surfing talk during happy hour at the Monkey Bar. A pool with a waterfall and a swim-up bar gives guests a chance to get wet without battling the waves. The hotel also leads diving trips. ⊠ *On main road entering Tamarindo* ☎ *653–0114, 800/536–3241 in U.S.* 🖷 *653–0115* ⊕ *www.tamarindovistavillas.com* ⇋ *12 rooms, 17 suites* ⟁ *Restaurant, minibars, cable TV with movies, pool, snorkeling, fishing, bar* ▭ *AE, MC, V* ⦿*CP.*

$$–$$$ ☆ **Hacienda Pinilla.** Golfers drive from miles around to play the beautiful par-72 championship course at this complex on the 4,500-acre grounds of a former ranch. At Hacienda Pinilla's colonial-style hotel, the Posada del Sol, even the standard rooms are luxurious, with soft indirect lighting, expensive fabrics, and spacious bathrooms. Villas are scattered around a garden and share a pretty pool and upscale outdoor restaurant-bar. Hacienda Pinilla also has a castlelike house by the 18th hole with eight suites and its own pool, as well as three rustic, secluded beach houses. Horseback riding is the main activity here after a round of golf. ⊠ *10 km (6 mi) south of Tamarindo via Villa Real* ☎ *680–7062* 🖷 *680–7063* ⊕ *www.haciendapinilla.com* ⇋ *22 rooms, 8 suites, 3 houses* ⟁ *Restaurant, fans, minibars, cable TV, golf, pool, beach, snorkeling, fishing, mountain bikes, hiking, bar* ▭ *AE, MC, V* ⦿*CP.*

$ ☆ **Cabinas Marielos.** In high season Tamarindo presents few decent bargain rooms; among the best are these cabinas, which are decorated with painted floral motifs in the style of the famous artisan town of Sarchí. They're in two wings, flanking a colorful flower garden well back from the noise and dust of the road. Guests sometimes share their meals in the well-equipped common kitchen. The atmosphere is surprisingly serene. Note that there is no hot water except in the three newest air-conditioned rooms. ⊠ *Across main dirt road from beach, north of town center (follow signs)* ☎🖷 *653–0141* ✐ *cabinasmarielos@hotmail.com* ⇋ *20 rooms* ⟁ *Fans, some refrigerators; no a/c in some rooms, no room phones, no room TVs* ▭ *AE, MC, V.*

$ ▦ **Hotel Pasatiempo.** One of the better bargains in Tamarindo, Pasatiempo is a friendly, laid-back hotel with updated cabinas, each named after a Guanacaste beach. They're scattered around the nicely landscaped grounds and the pool; each has a patio with a hammock and a unique hand-painted mural. Suites have one bedroom and daybeds in the living room. Tuesday is open-mike night at the bar with local musicians. A wide-screen satellite TV provides sports fans with their periodic fix in the popular bar and restaurant, now open for breakfast, too, and serving the best eggs Benedict in town. Water sports, a sailing cruise, and other activities are easily arranged by the fun-loving American owners. ⊠ *Off dirt road to Playa Langosta, 180 m from beach behind Tamarindo Circle* ☎ *653–0096* 🖷 *653–0275* ⊕ *www.hotelpasatiempo.com* ⇆ *15 cabinas, 2 suites* ⚘ *Restaurant, fans, pool, bar, laundry service; no room TVs* ▤ *AE, MC, V.*

$ ▦ **Hotel Las Tortugas.** On a turtle-nesting beach, this hotel was built with turtles in mind. Room windows do not overlook the nesting beaches, since light interferes with the turtles' nighttime rituals. Rooms are quiet, with good beds, stone floors, and stucco walls. Long-term rentals are available in apartments with kitchenettes, as is basic housing for turtle volunteers. The surf is good, but it sometimes has dangerous rip currents, at which times you can retreat to the pool with a turtle mosaic bottom. Local guides lead turtle tours at night, and the hotel also has canoe trips in the nearby Tamarindo Wildlife Refuge. ⊠ *Las Baulas Marine National Park, 33 km (20 mi) north of Tamarindo, in Playa Grande* ☎ *653–0423* ⊕ *www.cool.co.cr/usr/turtles* ✉ *Apdo. 164, Santa Cruz de Guanacaste* ⇆ *11 rooms, 7 apartments* ⚘ *Restaurant, some kitchenettes, refrigerators, pool, boating, bar, laundry service; no room phones, no room TVs* ▤ *MC, V.*

$ ▦ **El Mono Loco.** Behind a sunny yellow wall you'll find eight fresh rooms arranged around a small swimming pool and pretty garden in this hotel close to the beach. All rooms have fans and air-conditioning, brand-new beds on tree-trunk frames, and new ceramic bathrooms. As many as six can fit into one room, making it a surfer-beachgoer's bargain. There's no restaurant, but there is a thatched picnic hut and communal kitchen. ⊠ *On road to Langosta, between Iguana Surf and Casa Cook* ☎🖷 *653–0238* ⇆ *8 rooms* ⚘ *Fans, pool; no room phones, no room TVs* ▤ *No credit cards.*

¢–$ ▦ **Arco Iris.** This arty, alternative hotel is on the hill above the road to Playa Langosta. The four cheery, wildly imaginative cabinas are painted in primary colors and decorated with distinct themes by the creative Italian owners. Aerobics, stretching, kickboxing, dance classes, and yoga sessions are taught on-site, and in case it all gets too strenuous, there's also a massage therapist and a tattoo artist. You can use the communal kitchen. ⊠ *Follow signs past Hotel Pasatiempo and go up hill to right* ☎ *653–0330* ⇆ *4 cabinas* ⚘ *Some kitchenettes, refrigerators, fitness classes, massage; no a/c, no room phones, no room TVs* ▤ *No credit cards* ⎺⎺⎺ *BP.*

Nightlife

Saturday night there is usually a big, noisy beach party thrown by **Big Bazar** (⊠ Entrance just across from Iguana Surf ☎ 653–0307) with music, sometimes live, and a barbecue and bonfire on the beach. Wednesday night, the action is all at **Cantina Las Olas** (⊠ On road to Playa Langosta ☎ No phone) near Iguana Surf, thanks to ladies' night, with free drinks for the ladies in town. For a more sedate evening, try barbecue on the beach at the **Capitán Suizo Hotel** (⊠ Right side of road toward Playa Langosta; veer left before circle ☎ 653–0075 or 653–0353), starting at 6:30 with a welcome cocktail, lavish barbecue buffet, and live folk music and dancing ($25, reserve in advance). During the week, you'll find musical entertainment at Tuesday open-mike sessions at **Hotel Pasatiempo** (⊠ Off dirt road to Playa Langosta, 180 m from beach behind Tamarindo Circle ☎ 653–0096). Sail off into the sunset aboard a 50-foot traditional schooner with cruise company **Mandingo** (☎ 653–0623). Soft drinks, beer and wine, and *bocas* (snacks) are included on the three-hour cruise. The boat leaves at 3 PM from the white tower on the beach ($50 per person). Thursday night there's live music, both acoustic and amplified, at **The Monkey Bar** in the Tamarindo Vista Villas.

Sports & the Outdoors

BOATING & SURFING Inquire about surfing conditions at Iguana Surf or the Robert August Surf Shop. At Playa Grande, the best waves usually break just south of the Hotel Las Tortugas.

Iguana Surf (⊠ On road to Playa Langosta ☎☎ 653–0148 ⊕ www.iguanasurf.net) has information for surfers and visitors, as well as guided kayaking tours of the San Francisco Estuary. **Iguana Surf 2** (⊠ At beach near Frutas Tropicales) rents surfboards, Boogie boards, and snorkeling equipment and gives motorboat-driven snorkeling tours. **Maresias Surf Shop** (⊠ Next to Banco Nacional ☎ 653–0224) has equipment, lessons, and lots of local knowledge. Check out the **Robert August Surf Shop** (⊠ Tamarindo Vista Villas ☎ 653–0114) for boards to buy or rent, wax, surfing gear, swimsuits, and plenty of sunblock. **High Tide Surf Shop** (⊠ Tamarindo Aventuras ☎ 653–0108) has high-end surfing equipment and clothing and a large selection of beachwear; it also organizes kayaking, ATV tours, and surf lessons.

GOLF Mike Young, who has designed some of the best courses in the southern United States, designed the par-72 championship course at **Hacienda Pinilla** (⊠ 10 km [6 mi] south of Tamarindo via Villa Real ☎ 680–7062 ⊕ www.haciendapinilla.com). It has ocean views and breezes, and plenty of birds populate the surrounding trees.

SPORTFISHING A number of fishing charters in Tamarindo cater to saltwater anglers. The best among them is probably **Tamarindo Sportfishing** (☎ 653–0090 ☎ 653–0161 ⊕ www.tamarindosportfishing.com), run by Randy Wilson, who has led the way in developing catch-and-release techniques that are easy on the fish. Wilson has roamed and fished the Guanacaste waters since the 1970s, and he knows where the big ones lurk. His boat, the *Talking Fish,* is equipped with a marlin chair and a cabin with a shower. For up to six people, full days run $975, half days $575.

Shopping

Most stores in the strip malls lining the main road sell similar souvenirs and beachwear. It's hard to leave without at least one sarong in your
★ suitcase. The most original clothing and jewelry are at **Azul Profundo**

(⊠ Centro Comercial ☎ 653–0395), designed by a talented young Argentine woman. All her jewelry is made with real and semiprecious stones. **Bobatik** (⊠ Next to Costa Rica Tropical, Tamarindo Circle ☎ 653–0521) is an outpost of the elegant San José store and has wood carvings and upscale women's clothing. **Souvenirs Guanacaste** (⊠ Centro Comercial Aster, 50 m south of Super Tamarindo at crossroads of main road into town and road up to Hotel Pasatiempo ☎ 653–0868) stands out from the sarong-and-souvenir shops in this shopping center for its delicate wood carvings and handsome silver jewelry studded with polished stones, made by a local Italian artist. Try **Costa Rica Tropical** (⊠ Tamarindo Circle ☎ No phone) for interesting, out-of-the-ordinary natural handicrafts and Costa Rican–made cotton dresses. **Papagayo Excursions** (⊠ Next to Banco Nacional ☎ 653–0254) has a range of Rainforest-brand natural candles, soaps, and lotions, as well as whimsical hand-painted T-shirt dresses and tops for women and kids. For a great selection of swimsuits and cotton sarongs made in Costa Rica, check out **Tienda Bambora** (⊠ On beach, south side of Tamarindo Circle), the swimsuit shop attached to Nogui's Restaurant.

Playa Langosta

🔟 *2 km (1 mi) south of Tamarindo.*

Playa Langosta, once a quiet, leatherback-turtle nesting beach, is fast becoming an upscale, gentrified extension of Tamarindo, separated by a rocky headland at high tide. Expensive, private villas are beginning to crowd out the refined B&Bs, and the sound of hammers and drills now competes with the calls of seabirds. But the beach is still quiet in the early morning, perfect for bird-watching and solitary walks. Big, well-shaped river-mouth waves near the north end of the beach also make it popular with surfers.

Where to Stay & Eat

¢–$ ✕ **Maria Bonita Restaurant.** The only nonhotel restaurant in town, Maria Bonita has a fresh and interesting mix of Latin and Caribbean dishes such as seafood cakes in orange-chipotle sauce and Cuban-style garlicky pork tenderloin. Owners Tom and Adela Peter have years of hotel and restaurant experience in Cuba and throughout the Caribbean and they live above the restaurant, so they are literally on top of everything. Adela's specialty is dessert; save room for her bread pudding with chocolate sauce. There are just three tables in the pretty patio garden and four tables inside the restaurant, which is strikingly decorated in sapphire blue, so come early or make reservations. ⊠ *Beside the Playa Langosta supermarket* ☎ *653–0933* ▭ *No credit cards* ☾ *Closed Mon. and Oct. No lunch.*

$$$ ✕▦ **Cala Luna.** A labyrinth of hibiscus hedges leads to large, luxurious, ocher-color rooms with king-size beds and alcoves softly lighted with half-moon–shape sconces. Oversize bathrooms have dolphins cavorting on walls around curved bathtubs for two. Each private villa has its own small pool. One large, glorious pool is for shared use and is overlooked by the pretty Cala Moresca restaurant ($$). The chef leans toward Mediterranean cuisine, and the exotic fruit plate (part of the Continental breakfast) is a work of art. Dinner prices can climb high if you

order lobster or shrimp. ⊠ *Across from Sueño del Mar* ☎ *653–0214* 🖨 *653–0213* ⊕ *www.calaluna.com* ⇔ *20 rooms, 21 villas* ♂ *Restaurant, in-room safes, cable TV, pool, massage, snorkeling, fishing, bicycles, bar* ☰ *AE, MC, V* ⧈ *CP.*

$$$
FodorsChoice
★

🏠 **Sueño del Mar.** A garden gate opens into a dreamy world of intimate gardens and patios adorned with frescoes and antique tiles. Seashells are embedded in window frames and strung together in mobiles. The adobe-style house, which descends a stepped passageway, has three double rooms with high, queen-size beds, and Balinese showers open to the sky. The two casitas have kitchens, and there's a breezy, romantic honeymoon suite upstairs. A lavish breakfast is served on the patio looking onto a tiny garden pool. Or you can take your morning coffee a few steps away on the beach, which, with few people and driftwood furniture, feels a bit like being on a desert island. ⊠ *130 m south of Capitán Suizo, turn right for 45 m, then right again for about 90 m to entrance gate, across from back of Cala Luna Hotel* ☎🖨 *653–0284* ⊕ *www.tamarindo.com/sdmar* ⇔ *3 rooms, 1 suite, 2 casitas* ♂ *Dining room, some kitchens, pool, beach, snorkeling, boating, fishing, bicycles, horseback riding, laundry service, Internet; no room phones, no room TVs* ☰ *MC, V* ⧈ *BP.*

★ **$$–$$$**

🏠 **Villa Alegre.** Owned by congenial and helpful Californians Barry and Suzye Lawson, this homey but very sophisticated Spanish-style B&B has a lovely location, close to a stand of trees and a somewhat rocky but swimmable beach. The pool provides swimming and sunning with a beach view. Rooms are furnished with souvenirs from the Lawsons' travels to Japan, Russia, Guatemala, and other lands. Each well-appointed room has a private patio, and the lavish gourmet breakfast is included in the price. The hotel often plans and hosts weddings; ceremonies take place at a huge boulder on the beach dubbed Marriage Rock. ⊠ *Playa Langosta, south of Sueño del Mar* ☎ *653–0270* 🖨 *653–0287* ⊕ *www.villaalegrecostarica.com* ⇔ *4 rooms, 2 villas, 1 casita* ♂ *Fans, pool, beach, snorkeling, fishing, no-smoking rooms; no room phones, no room TVs* ☰ *AE, MC, V* ⧈ *BP.*

Playa Avellanas

⓫ *17 km (10½ mi) south of Tamarindo.*

Geographically and atmospherically separate from Langosta, this beach is a beautiful 1-km (½-mi) stretch of pale-gold sand with rocky outcroppings, a river mouth, and a mangrove swamp estuary. You have to drive inland from Tamarindo to Villareal and then 13 km (8 mi) down a very bumpy road to travel between Langosta to Avellanas. Locals claim there are eight surf spots when the swell is strong. There's a funky seasonal beach café called Lola's on the Beach (complete with a beach-loving pet pig named Lola) where you can hang out at driftwood tables and stools and exchange surfing stories while sipping fruit smoothies.

Where to Stay

$
🏠 **Cabinas Las Olas.** Frequented mainly by surfers, the hotel's five spacious glass-and-stone cabinas, divided into two units each, are scattered in a forest behind Playa Avellanas and its renowned surfing waves. But

with monkeys and other critters lurking in and around the extensive grounds, the hotel also appeals to bird-watchers, animal lovers, and naturalists. An elevated boardwalk leads from the cabinas to the beach through a protected mangrove estuary. The restaurant, which has an adjacent outdoor video bar, serves reasonably priced breakfasts, lunches, and dinners. ⊠ *Road to Avellanas; follow signs to Cabinas Las Olas* ☎ *233–4455 or 658–8315* 🖷 *658–8331* ⊕ *www.cabinaslasolas.co.cr* ✉ *Apdo. 1404–1250, Escazú* ☞ *10 rooms* ⚭ *Restaurant, dive shop, boating, bicycles, bar, laundry service; no a/c, no room phones, no room TVs* ▭ *AE, MC, V* ⊗ *Closed Oct.*

Playa Negra

⓬ *3 km (2 mi) south of Playa Avellanas, 4 km (2½ mi) northwest of Paraíso.*

Americans—surfers at least—got their first look at Playa Negra in *The Endless Summer II,* which featured some dynamite sessions at this spectacular rock-reef point break. Surfing cognoscenti will dig the waves, which are almost all rights and often beautifully shaped. Surfer culture is also apparent in the wave of casual restaurants, health-food bakeries, Internet cafés, and bikini shops springing up along the road. A roadside tent bazaar sells sarongs and crafts.

Where to Stay

★ **$** 🏨 **Hotel Playa Negra.** Facing the ocean, this collection of round, brilliantly colored thatch-roof cabinas has sunny lawns strewn with lush plantings. The cabinas have built-in sofas and beautiful tile bathrooms. The ocean is good for swimming and snorkeling, with tidal pools, swimming holes, and rock reefs providing shelter. This is paradise found for surfers, with a good swell running. There are also surfing lessons and Boogie-board classes. The restaurant serves deftly prepared Latin and European dishes. ⊠ *4 km (2½ mi) northwest of Paraíso on dirt road (watch signs for Playa Negra), then follow signs carefully at forks in road* ☎ *658–8034* 🖷 *658–8035* ⊕ *www.playanegra.com* ☞ *10 cabinas* ⚭ *Restaurant, fans, in-room safes, pool, beach, horseback riding, volleyball, bar, laundry service; no a/c, no room phones, no room TVs* ▭ *AE, MC, V.*

$ 🏨 **Mono Congo Lodge.** Mono Congo translates as "Howler Monkey," and those noisy but endearing creatures are plentiful here. New owners of the formerly casual, communal B&B are expanding and creating a more sophisticated hotel but retaining the eco-tourism orientation. There's a new restaurant and bar, and a pool and hideaway cabins in the forest are planned for 2004 or early 2005. The four existing guest rooms have orthopedic mattresses, Indian cotton sheets, and feather pillows. Decent waves, boards for rent, an animal-rich estuary, and rustic, comfortable accommodations make this a good surfing and naturalist holiday spot. ⊠ *450 m north of La Plaza soccer field in Los Pargos* ☎ *382–6926* ✉ *Apdo. 177–5150, Santa Cruz* ⊕ *www.monocongolodge.com* ☞ *4 rooms with shared bath* ⚭ *Restaurant, fans, tennis court, bar, laundry service; no a/c, no room phones, no room TVs* ▭ *MC, V.*

Playa Junquillal

⑬ *4 km (2½ mi) south of Paraíso, along a rough road; 34 km (21¼ mi) south of Santa Cruz on partially paved road.*

Junquillal (pronounced hoon-key-*yall*), to the south of Playa Negra, is a long swath of uninterrupted beach stretching about 3 km (2 mi), with calm surf and only one hotel. This is one of the quieter beaches in Guanacaste and a real find for seekers of tranquility. New restaurants—Peruvian, German, Italian, Swiss—are adding an international flavor, and away from the beach, Junquillal is definitely getting livelier. In rainy season, the beach road from Playa Negra to Playa Junquillal is not passable, and even in dry season and with a four-wheel-drive vehicle, it's challenging. Ask around about local conditions before attempting to take this route.

Where to Stay & Eat

★ $$–$$$ ✕ **La Puesta del Sol.** Food aficionado Alessandro Zangari and his wife, Silvana, have created what he modestly calls "a little restaurant in my home." But regulars drive all the way from San José to sit at one of the four tables and enjoy the haute-Italian menu. Alessandro spares no expense or effort to secure the best ingredients, and each fall he travels to Italy to buy truffles in season. The softly lighted patio restaurant, tinted in tangerine and deep blue, evokes a Moroccan courtyard. All the pasta is made from scratch, of course; the ravioli *boscaiolo* contains a woodsy trio of cremini, porcini, and Portobello mushrooms. ⊠ *Just north of Playa Junquillal* ☎ *658–8442* ⌕ *Reservations essential* ▤ *No credit cards* ☉ *Closed May, June, Sept., and Oct.*

$$ ⌂ **Hotel Iguanazul.** Two miles of beach stretch south from this isolated resort on a bluff. Rooms are simply furnished, with two double beds. The hotel itself is looking a little tired, but the fabulous surf of Playa Negra is 10 minutes away, and there's often decent surfing in front of the hotel. Satellite TV is available in a recreation room. The open-air restaurant, which serves unexciting standard Costa Rican fare, and open-air bar are usually filled with a young surfing crowd. ⊠ *North end of Playa Junquillal* ☎ *658–8124* 🖷 *658–8123* ⊕ *www. hoteliguanazul.com* ✆ *Apdo. 130–5150, Santa Cruz* ↜ *24 rooms* ⌂ *Restaurant, fans, in-room safes, pool, beach, Ping-Pong, volleyball, bar, recreation room, laundry service; no a/c in some rooms, no room phones, no room TVs* ▤ *AE, MC, V* ⦿⊙⦿ *BP.*

$–$$ ⌂ **Land Ho! at Hotel Villa Serena.** Cape Cod comes to Costa Rica. American owners Olive and John Murphy have created a tropical version of New England, with shell-motif quilts and wall stencils, and hooked rugs with palm trees. Rooms are spacious and comfortable; for the ultimate in romance, ask for No. 10, a round room with an ocean view. The lovely landscaped garden has a large pool, and there's a full-service day spa on the property. To reach the terrace restaurant overlooking the beach, you pass a collection of Costa Rican student art, some of it for sale. Coffee is delivered each morning to your room, but breakfast is à la carte. ⊠ *Across the dirt road from Playa Junquillal* ☎ *658–8430* 🖷 *658–8091* ⊕ *www.land-ho.com* ↜ *12 rooms* ⌂ *Restaurant, tennis court, pool, spa,* *snorkeling, boating, fishing, horseback riding, bar; no a/c in some rooms, no room phones, no room TVs* ⊟ *AE, MC, V* ☺ *Closed Oct. and Nov.*

$ ⊞ **Guacamaya Lodge.** Secluded Guacamaya, on a breezy hill, has expansive views of surrounding rolling countryside and a river estuary below, so it's ideal for bird-watching. Swiss siblings Berni and Alice Iten have a delightful compound, where flocks of parrots visit each morning and cranes rise up from the estuary. The landscaping around the pool is exceptional, with chenille plants trailing velvety pink tails and tall gingers blazing vibrant red torches. The three-meal restaurant serves excellent, reasonably priced food. The spacious cabinas have lovely fabric curtains and bedspreads. Cabinas are air-conditioned but there are lots of windows to let in the cooling evening breezes. There's also an airy, modern house with a full kitchen. ⊠ *275 m off Playa Junquillal* ☎ *658–8431* 🖷 *658–8164* ⊕ *www.guacamayalodge.com* ⌂ *Apdo. 6, Santa Cruz* ⇆ *6 cabinas, 1 house* ⌂ *Restaurant, some kitchens, pool, volleyball, bar, shop, playground, laundry service, Internet; no room phones, no room TVs* ⊟ *AE, MC, V.*

Nosara

🄯 *23 km (14 mi) south of Paraíso along rough roads in dry season; 32 km (20 mi) south of Nicoya, with 22 km (14 mi) of bad road.*

Set a bit inland, Nosara itself is a minor and not very exciting town. The Nosara that people come to visit is more a state of mind—one of the last remote havens for people who want to get away from it all. The attractions here are the surfing waves and wild stretches of neighboring beaches Playas Pelada and Guiones, as well as the nearby Ostional National Wildlife Refuge, a haven for nesting turtles. The Nosara Yoga Institute, which focuses on teacher certification but also offers daily yoga classes to the public, is increasingly a draw for holistic-minded people who are creating a demand for health food and spa treatments. This whole area of Guanacaste is being subdivided and settled by Europeans and Americans at a fairly rapid pace, with a strong Swiss contingent. So far, Nosara has escaped really large-scale development, largely owing to the abysmal state of the roads. Private houses, however, are springing up on every available piece of property. Local businesses have banded together to place wooden signs along the main road to help tourists find their way among the sometimes confusing side roads.

To approach from the north, you have to ford the Río Nosara, often impossible in the wet season; it's better to take the slightly longer but safer route from the Dulce Nombre turnoff of the Nicoya–Samara road, 10 km (6 mi) south of Nicoya. There's a sometimes passable 23-km (14-mi) beach road that connects Junquillal and Nosara during the dry season. Whichever way you go, the roads into Nosara are in really bad shape, and a four-wheel-drive vehicle is necessary.

With some of the best surf breaks around, **Playa Guiones** attracts a lot of surfboard-toting visitors. But the breezy beach, with tendrils of sea grape curling almost down to the high-tide mark, is also a haven for shell-seekers and sun lovers. There isn't a building in sight anywhere on this beach.

Playa Guiones segues seamlessly into **Playa Pelada,** to the north, where the water is a little calmer for swimming. There are also tide pools to explore and a blowhole that sends water shooting up at high tide. This beach is the locals' favorite vantage point for watching sunsets. For a cool beer, there's Olga's Bar, a ramshackle Tico beach bar. Or sip a sunset cocktail at the funky La Luna Bar & Grill, Olga's nearby neighbor.

Apart from sun and sand, the main reason to come to the central Nicoya is to visit the **Ostional National Wildlife Refuge** (Refugio Nacional de Fauna Silvestre Ostional), with its top-notch turtle-watching. During the rainy season you'll probably need a four-wheel-drive vehicle to cross the river just north of Nosara; a track then leads through shrubs to the reserve, which protects one of Costa Rica's major breeding grounds for Olive Ridley turtles. Locals have formed an association to run the reserve on a cooperative basis, and during the first 36 hours of the *arribadas* (nesting) they are allowed to harvest the eggs, on the premise that eggs laid during this time would likely be destroyed by subsequent waves of mother turtles. These eggs, believed by some to be powerful aphrodisiacs, are sold to be eaten raw in bars. Members of the cooperative take turns guarding the beach from poachers and give guided tours for $2.50 per person. Turtle arrivals at this and most other nesting sites depend on the moon and tides as well as the time of year; nesting peaks between October and April. Before you go to the refuge, try to get a sense from the locals of when, if ever (some years they come in very small numbers), the turtles will arrive. ⊠ *7 km (4½ mi) north of Nosara* ☎ *682–0470.*

Where to Stay & Eat

$ ✕ **Pizzería Giardino Tropical.** Famous for its crispy-crusted, wood-oven pizzas loaded with toppings and homemade chili-pepper sauce, this restaurant casts a wider net to include excellent fresh seafood and fish—the carpaccio of sea bass is a sure bet. Service is always fast and friendly. In the lush gardens surrounding the thatch-roof, two-story restaurant, three new luxury cabinas and a swimming pool are being built, to be completed in 2005. Seven smaller cabins have already been renovated and have solar-heated hot water, ceiling fans, and new roofed-over patios. ⊠ *Main street, past entrance to Playa Guiones* ☎ *682–0258* ▭ *No credit cards.*

¢-$ ✕ **La Mariposa Panadería Café-Bar.** Swiss bakers Karin Lang and Roland Locher started out selling their baked goods door to door. Now they sell their multigrain breads, baguettes, carrot cake, and brownies from a garden café a stone's throw from Playa Pelada. Savory empanadas, quiches, sandwiches, daily hot specials, and a chicken salad plate that is an edible work of art are other menu items. You can get takeout or counter service or enjoy a healthful meal at candlelit cedar tables under the sloping roof. ⊠ *Across from Los Condominios las Flores, Playa Pelada* ☎ *682–0545* ▭ *No credit cards.*

$$ ✕⊞ **Harbor Reef Lodge.** Lose yourself in five acres of jungly garden centered on a small pool presided over by a concrete crocodile. Your wake-up call is given by a resident howler monkey. The rooms and suites cater to surfers of every age, with plenty of room for both boards and fami-

lies inside the large but sparely furnished rooms. Spacious houses are rented by the night or by the week. The surf breaks at Playa Guiones are a 300-m walk away, and a surf school operates out of the hotel. The rancho restaurant is noteworthy for its generous portions of fresh fish and local specialties, plus—a rarity in Costa Rica—tasty low-cholesterol options. Another rarity is the shop that sells women's swimsuits that are larger than dishcloths; you can find North American sizes up to 10 or 12 here. The small grocery store comes in handy if you've rented a house. ⊠ *Follow signs from Café de Paris turnoff, Playa Guiones* ☎ *682–0059* 🖷 *682–0060* ⊕ *www.harborreef.com* 🛏 *9 rooms, 7 suites, 6 houses* ⚘ *Restaurant, some kitchens, refrigerators, pool, fishing, bar; no a/c in 1 house and some rooms, no room phones, no room TVs* 🖃 *AE, DC, MC, V.*

$–$$ ✕🏠 **Café de Paris.** High-spirited French-Swiss owners set a tone of *joie de vivre* at this restaurant and hotel. Fresh-baked French pastries and desserts are the main draw at the restaurant-bakery ($). Sweet and savory croissants are excellent, as is the chocolate tart. Each year the menu becomes more sophisticated. As well as the tried-and-true wood-oven pizza, nachos, casados, huge salads, and hearty sandwiches, you can order snails in garlic butter and duck in peanut sauce. Low-fat vegetarian dishes, such as tofu in curry sauce, cater to the health-conscious. If you're too full to move, you can bed down in a cabin room, surrounded by tropical gardens, or rent a villa with an ocean view. The Internet café has high-speed satellite connection. ⊠ *Main road at Playa Guiones entrance* ☎ *682–0087* 🖷 *682–0089* ⊕ *www.cafedeparis.net* 🛏 *14 rooms, 3 villas* ⚘ *Restaurant, fans, some kitchens, some refrigerators, pool, billiards, bar, Internet; no a/c in some rooms, no room phones, no room TVs* 🖃 *AE, MC, V.*

$–$$$ 🏠 **Hotel Villa Taype.** Bordering long, lovely Playa Guiones and its good surf breaks, this well-maintained, high-ceilinged hotel has standard rooms in a low-rise building that forms a U shape around a pair of swimming pools. More private and luxurious bungalows are down palm-lined paths. At the other end of the scale, there are seven simple, cheap rooms with no air-conditioning or TV. The hotel rents surfboards, Boogie boards, and snorkeling gear, as well as tennis rackets for the lighted tennis court. All local tours can be arranged through the hotel. ⊠ *Down entrance road to Playa Guiones, 250 m west of Café de Paris, Playa Guiones* 🖃 *Apdo. 8–5233, Nosara* ☎ *682–0333* 🖷 *682–0187* ⊕ *www.villataype.com* 🛏 *19 rooms, 13 bungalows, 2 suites* ⚘ *Restaurant, fans, some refrigerators, cable TV, tennis court, 2 pools, beach, bicycles, Ping-Pong, 2 bars, laundry service; no a/c in some rooms* 🖃 *AE, MC, V* 🍽 *BP.*

$–$$ 🏠 **Casa Romántica.** The name ("romantic house") says it all: the Spanish colonial–style house has a veranda upstairs and a graceful arcade below. Six older rooms under the shady arcade are a little dark, but they have views of a glorious garden and a large pool with a huge, thatched cabana. An upstairs suite is brighter and can accommodate large families. The real finds here are in the terra-cotta Casita Romántica, a house with three exquisite suites with kitchens and a shared pool. Each suite has a wonderful wall mural, loads of light, and stylish furnishings.

An alfresco restaurant beside the main pool serves excellent breakfasts. The short path to the beach is lined with aloe, cactus, and costus (a type of flowering ginger) and filled with birds. ⊠ *Turn down road at Il Giardino Pizzería, Playa Guiones* ☏ *682–0019* ⊕ *www. hotelcasaromantica.com* ⇆ *7 rooms, 4 suites* ⌂ *Dining room, some kitchens, 2 pools, massage, beach; no a/c in some rooms, no room phones, no room TVs* ▤ *V* ❚◎❚ *BP.*

$ ▥ **Lagarta Lodge.** This magnificent property on a promontory has the best views of Ostional National Wildlife Refuge and recently garnered a Sustainable Tourism Certificate, the coveted badge of ecolodges given by the National Tourism Institute. The private Nosara Biological Reserve, directly below the lodge, is laced with trails running through mangroves. A 10-minute steep walk down takes you through a monkey-filled forest to beautiful Playa Guiones and surfing waves. The eagle's-nest lobby-restaurant is famous for its views and Sunday barbecues. Each of the comfortable rooms has a balcony and a view of Ostional. At meals, served at a communal table, birders and naturalists share sightings with the friendly Swiss host Marcel Schaerer. ⊠ *Top of hill at the north end of Nosara* ☏ *682–0035* ⎙ *682–0135* ⊕ *www.lagarta.com* ✆ *Apdo. 18–5233, Nosara* ⇆ *7 rooms* ⌂ *Restaurant, pool, boating, hiking, laundry service, Internet; no a/c, no room phones, no room TVs* ▤ *MC, V.*

Nightlife

There's always plenty of surfing talk at **Blew Dog's Surf Club** (⊠ Playa Guiones ☏ 682–0080). Friday nights, **Café de Paris** (⊠ Entrance to Playa Guiones ☏ 682–0207) shows DVD movies on a big outdoor screen. **The Gilded Iguana** (⊠ Playa Guiones ☏ 682–0259) is a popular surfer's hangout and sports bar with big-screen TV. Sip a margarita and watch the sun set at tony **La Luna Bar&Grill** (⊠ Playa Pelada, 200 m north of Olga's ☏ 682–0122). Sunset is the main evening event on the Nosara beaches, and people gather on the beach at Playa Pelada to down a local beer at **Olga's Bar** (⊠ Playa Pelada ☏ No phone), a ramshackle beach bar.

Sports & the Outdoors

SURFING If you ever wanted to learn to surf, Nosara is the place. Try **Corky Carroll's Surf School** (⊠ Across from Café de Paris, at entrance to Playa Guiones ☏ 682–0385 ⊕ www.surfschool.net). The **Safari Surf School** (⊠ Ask for directions at Nosara Surf Shop, on road to Playa Guiones ☏ 682–0573 ⊕ www.safarisurfschool.com) is run by two surfing brothers from Hawaii. It's closed September and October.

HORSEBACK **Boca Nosara Tours** (⊠ 150 m below Lagarta Lodge, at the mouth of the
RIDING Nosara River ☏ 682–0610) takes small groups of two to four people on horseback nature tours through the jungle and along the beach. The price is $40 per person for a 2½-hour ride. The experienced equestrian owner also gives introductory riding lessons and bird-watching and fishing tours in a catamaran along the Río Nosara ($60 for two people, $25 per person for more than three people). To get here, follow the signs with a yellow fish with a red head all the way to the mouth of the Nosara River.

Sámara

⓯ *36 km (23 mi) south of Nicoya by paved road, 26 km (16½ mi) south of Nosara by rough road in dry season.*

The drive to Sámara from Nicoya may be one of the most scenic in Costa Rica, and it is now one of the most comfortable, thanks to paving that extends all the way to Playa Carillo. Sámara's clean, white sweep of beach is framed by two forest-covered hills jutting out on either side. This giant protected cove is ideal for swimming, and a coral reef 1½ km (1 mi) from the shore is the site of many diving and snorkeling excursions. Long a favorite with Ticos, many of whom built summer houses on the beach, Sámara is flourishing and attracting a lot of improvement-bent Europeans—the town even has a sidewalk. A new branch of the language school **Intercultura** (☎ 656–0127) is also attracting students of all ages. Sámara has a distinctively Italian flavor, but with a school, soccer field, and church right in the center of town, Tico spirit predominates.

Where to Stay & Eat

$ ✕ **El Dorado di Dolcetti.** After one visit to Costa Rica, Andrea Dolcetti and his wife, Luigina Sivieri, sold their restaurant in Ferrara, Italy, and opened one here. Their open-air *palenque* (wood-and-thatch building) specializes in seafood, pasta, and, at dinner, wood oven–baked pizzas. Andrea brings home the fish and Luigina supervises the kitchen. Pasta is made from scratch, and real Parmesan cheese and salami are imported to help create authentic Italian flavors. The spaghetti *al mare* is an inspired marriage of local shellfish and Italian cooking. For dessert, there are fruit *crostatas* (tarts) and chocolate "salami." ⊠ *West off main road, just past church in Sámara* ☎ 656–0145 ▭ *V.*

$ ✕ **Restaurante Las Brasas.** Seafood and meat grilled over hot *brasas* (coals) are the specialties at this Spanish restaurant, along with paella, gazpacho, and a variety of *tortillas* (hearty omelets). Avocado stuffed with shrimp salad makes an excellent shared starter or a light lunch. An upstairs balcony is perfect for sipping Spanish wines. Downstairs, enormous green elephant-ear leaves frame the rustic wooden-railed restaurant, decorated with oxen horns and yokes. Hungry groups can feast on an entire roast suckling pig with a one-day advance reservation. ⊠ *Main road to beach, beside soccer field* ☎ 656–0546 ▭ *V.*

¢ ✕ **Soda Ananas.** Fruit rules at this garden-gazebo café on the hill leading into town. Pure-fruit *naturales* (fruit smoothies) are made with water or milk and tropical fruit salad, and fruity sundaes are made with homemade ice cream. The *ananas* (pineapple) sundae comes in a scooped-out pineapple. Breakfast is served Tico-style, with rice and beans, or health food–style, with granola and fruit. Baguette sandwiches and salads make a light lunch. Home-baked cakes and specialty coffees are available all day. ⊠ *Main road leading into Sámara* ☎ 656–0491 ▭ *No credit cards* ⊗ *Closed Tues.*

★ $ ✕▥ **Hotel Giada.** Giada, which means "jade," is truly a gem of a hotel. The artistic Italian owners have used washes in watermelon, terra-cotta, and yellow to give the walls an antique Mediterranean look. In contrast, thatch roofs overhang private terraces, which overlook a tropical garden and curvaceous blue pool. The large rooms have elegant bamboo furniture, and whimsical sea creatures are hand-painted on the bathroom tiles. Other arty and clever details make this affordable hotel a delight to visit. Another irresistible attraction is the Pizza & Pasta Go-Go restaurant (¢), which serves excellent Italian food and a tiramisu that transcends the tropics and delivers your taste buds to Italy. ⊠ *Main strip, 150 m from beach* ☎ *656–0132* 🖷 *656–0131* ⊕ *www.hotelgiada.net* 🖃 *Apdo. 5235–67, Sámara* 🛏 *13 rooms* 🖧 *Restaurant, pizzeria, cable TV, snorkeling, boating, fishing, horseback riding, laundry service; no room phones* 🖃 *AE, MC, V.*

$$$ 🏨 **Villas Playa Sámara.** A long stretch of beach is the dreamy location of these white-stucco villas. The water is shallow and safe enough for swimming, though there's also a large pool. Families abound, with a regular clientele of Ticos, Europeans, and North Americans. The one-, two-, and three-bedroom villas are comfortable and pretty; air-conditioning is in the bedrooms only. The restaurant food is not terrific; it's best to cook for yourself or dine in Sámara. ⊠ *Off main road, 2 km (1¼ mi) south of Playa Sámara* ☎🖷 *656–0372 or 256–8228 in San José* 🖂 *htlvilla@racsa.co.cr* 🛏 *58 villas* 🖧 *Restaurant, fans, kitchens, pool, beach, boating, fishing, bicycles, horseback riding, Ping-Pong, volleyball, bar; no room phones, no room TVs* 🖃 *AE, MC, V.*

$–$$ 🏨 **Las Brisas del Pacífico.** At one of the few beachfront hotels in Sámara, white Spanish-style bungalows climb a steep, landscaped hill. The best of the well-maintained bungalows face a gorgeous pool and thatch-roof restaurant. "Sky rooms," in a two-story building at the top of the hill, have ocean-view balconies and a pool topside, as well as a separate parking lot, so you have to climb up and down the hill only for meals and beach walks. The hotel can arrange diving trips. ⊠ *South end of beach, Sámara* ☎ *656–0250* 🖷 *656–0076* ⊕ *www.brisas.net* 🛏 *22 bungalows, 16 rooms* 🖧 *Two restaurants, in-room safes, 2 pools, 2 outdoor hot tubs, massage, beach, snorkeling, bar; no a/c in some rooms, no room phones, no TV in some rooms* 🖃 *AE, D, MC, V* ℺ *BP.*

$ 🏨 **Casa del Mar.** Less than a block from the beach on a small property, this well-tended hotel has simple, tidy rooms with dark-wood furniture, white walls, and ceramic floors. The hotel has a giant cold-water whirlpool in a small garden. ⊠ *Main strip, 45 m east of school* ☎ *656–0264* 🖷 *656–0129* ⊕ *www.casadelmarsamara.com* 🛏 *17 rooms, 11 with bath* 🖧 *Dining room, fans, some refrigerators, bar; no a/c in some rooms, no room phones, no room TVs* 🖃 *AE, MC, V* ℺ *CP.*

Sports & the Outdoors

Darrell Harrelson at **Bike Costa Rica** (☎ 656–0120 ⊕ www.latitude10. com) organizes mountain bike tours for cyclists, including a bird-watching tour that takes in nearby marshes to view wading birds. Drop into his office behind the Casa del Mar Hotel to book an adventure tour in the area, or to log on in the Internet Café.

Playa Carrillo

16 *7 km (4 mi) south of Sámara.*

Fodor'sChoice
★

With its long, reef-protected beach backed by an elegant line of swaying palms and sheltering cliffs, Playa Carrillo is a candidate for the most picturesque beach in Costa Rica. Totally unmarred by even a single building, it's ideal for swimming, snorkeling, walking, and lounging—just remember not to sit under a loaded coconut palm. You can fly in and land at the airstrip, or head south on the paved road from Sámara.

Where to Stay & Eat

$–$$ ✕ **El Mirador.** A fabulous view of fishing boats moored in Carrillo Bay makes the fresh seafood taste even better at this open-air restaurant perched on a cliff. There is no decor to speak of, just the view and the natural air-conditioning of the breeze off the bay. The whole, fried pargo is moist and crispy and comes with a salad and fries. Specialties include lobster (a good value here), jumbo shrimp, and mahimahi. ⊠ *Beachfront, at bend in main road* 🕾 656–0307 🚍 *AE, MC, V.*

$ 🏠 **Hotel Esperanza.** A young couple from Montréal designed and now run this attractive bed-and-breakfast hotel. They have given it an eclectic Mediterranean look, with columns seemingly from classical Greece and an arcade resembling one from Renaissance Italy. Rooms are stylishly simple with high ceilings, striking blue-and-yellow-tiled bathrooms, and handsome locally made *pochote* (Costa Rican hardwood) headboards and furniture. A huge breakfast is served in a beautiful small garden, and fresh fish dinners can be ordered. ⊠ *90 m west of Hotel Guanamar* 🕾🕾 *656–0564* ⊕ *www.hotelesperanza.com* ⟳ *7 rooms* ♨ *Fans; no a/c in some rooms, no room phones, no room TVs* 🚍 *MC, V* ﷼ *BP.*

$ 🏠 **Puerto Carrillo Sunset Luxury B&B.** High on a hill, these rooms can't be beat for spectacular views of distant Sámara and nearby Carrillo Beach. Each sunny and spacious room is decorated in yellow, blue, and white fabrics and upholstery. Large bathrooms have solar-heated hot water. Breakfast is served poolside in an open rancho facing the view. Surrounded by secondary forest, the hotel's garden has specially planted flowers to lure hummingbirds and butterflies. ⊠ *500 m up steep road to left of public parking area in Playa Carrillo* 🕾 *656–0011* 🖻 *656–0009* ⟳ *puertocarillosunset@yahoo.com* ⟳ *6 rooms* ♨ *Fans, pool; no a/c in some rooms, no room TVs, no room phones* 🚍 *No credit cards* ﷼ *BP.*

Sports & the Outdoors

PoPo's Adventures (⊠ Off main Carrillo road, just south of Hotel Esperanza 🕾 656–0086) arranges river kayaking trips and float trips—where you sit atop a kayak and float with the current. For serious sportfishermen, **VIP Sportfishing** (⊠ Main Carrillo road, near Restaurant El Mirador, just before Hotel Guanamar 🕾 654–4808 ⊕ www.vipsportfishing.com) has two state-of-the-art fishing boats loaded with tournament-quality tackle.

Punta Islita

⑰ *12 km (7 mi) south of Carrillo when Río Oro is passable or 50 km (31 mi) by overland route on rough roads.*

Punta Islita is named for a tiny tuft of land that becomes an island at high tide. The curved beach is rather rocky but good for walking, especially at low tide when tidal pools form in the volcanic rock. Another interesting stroll is through the small village, which has become a work of art in progress, thanks to a community art project, led by renowned

ECO-FRIENDLY BEACHES

T HE WORLD GIVES HIGH MARKS *to Costa Rica for its environmental awareness, but a visit here shows that the accolades don't always match the reality. Deforestation occurs at an alarming rate, and the country has major trash-disposal issues. Recognizing that three-quarters of visitors to Costa Rica make a beach excursion, the national water utility, Aqueductos y Alcantarillados, in conjunction with the Instituto Costarricense de Turismo, began evaluating and ranking water and environmental quality in coastal communities in 1996. Those that achieved a 90 percent score were awarded a Bandera Azul Ecológica (ecological blue flag) to fly as a symbol of excellence.*

The program, modeled on one begun in Spain in 1986 and now used in the European Union, awards flags to communities, rather than to individual hotels. Participating areas are required to form a Blue Flag committee, a move that brings together diverse sectors of an area's population, many of which otherwise fiercely compete for tourist dollars. In true developing-country fashion, Costa Rica's wealth concentrates in the capital and the Central Valley. But the Blue Flag program has prompted less-affluent lowland and coastal communities to put resources into improving environmental quality of life for themselves and for their guests.

Only 10 beaches won a Blue Flag that first year, a fact that Costa Rica sheepishly decided not to publicize, not wanting to call attention to the high number of communities that didn't make the cut. When 19 succeeded the following year, the results went public. Officials inspect heavily visited beaches once a month. More isolated communities get an every-other-month assessment of water quality—both ocean and drinking water—trash cleanup, waste management, security, signage, and environmental education. In 2002, the competition was opened to inland communities. Out of 92 that applied, 65 communities—56 beaches and nine inland towns—won flags at the 2004 ceremonies.

Blue Flags fly proudly in the following communities covered in this guide:

Central Costa Rica: *San Rafael de Heredia.*

The Northern Zone: *La Fortuna.*

The Nicoya Peninsula: *Playa Hermosa, Playa Ocotal, Playa Flamingo, Playa Pan de Azúcar, Playa Conchal, Tamarindo, Playa Langosta, Playa Junquillal, Ostional, Nosara (Playa Guiones), Playa Carrillo, Punta Islita, Malpaís, Santa Teresa.*

The Central Pacific: *Atenas, Puntarenas, Manuel Antonio (Playa Manuel Antonio, Playa Espadilla Sur, Puerto Escondido, Playa Gemelas), Isla Tortuga, Punta Leona (Playa Blanca, Playa Limoncito).*

The Southern Pacific: *San Gerardo de Rivas, Dominical, Playa Zancudo, Ballena National Marine Park (Playa La Colina, Playa Piñuela, Playa Ballena).*

The Caribbean: *Cahuita (Puerto Vargas, Playa Blanca), Puerto Viejo de Talamanca (Playa Negra, Playa Chiquita, Playa Cocles, Punta Uva), Gandoca-Manzanillo National Wildlife Refuge.*

Costa Rican artists, that uses town buildings as their canvas. The main draw here is the one and only hotel, a luxury destination perched high above the secluded beach. In rainy season, it's often impossible to cross the Río Oro, south of Carrillo, so you have to make a 50-km (31-mi) detour along dirt roads with spectacular mountain views but lots of potholes, too. Most people fly into the hotel's private airstrip.

Where to Stay

$$$$ ⊞ **Hotel Punta Islita.** Overlooking the Pacific from a forested ridge, this
Fodor'sChoice   exquisite, secluded hotel is luxury incarnate. Hidden around the hill-
★   side are villas, casitas, suites, and spacious rooms, all with private porches and a hammock. If the ocean view doesn't keep you mesmerized, some rooms also have VCRs and CD players. Beds have rough-hewn wooden bedposts, and bathrooms are tiled, with deep tubs. Casitas have their own private plunge pools or outdoor whirlpools and private gardens, one of the main attractions for the myriad honeymooners here. A massive thatched dome covers the restaurant and opens onto an infinity-edge pool with a sea view and a swim-up bar. If you overdo with the many activities here—including swinging a golf club at their driving range or zipping along a canopy tour (it's shorter and lower to the ground than most canopy tours)—stop by the spa for unique massage treatments using local herbs. ⊠ *South of Playa Carrillo* ☎ *661–3322, 231–6122 in San José* 🖷 *656–0473, 231–0715 in San José* ⊕ *www. hotelpuntaislita.com* ⊕ *Apdo. 242–1225, San José* ⮐ *15 bungalows, 13 casitas, 6 suites, 5 villas* ⚒ *2 restaurants, minibars, cable TV, some in-room VCRs, driving range, 2 tennis courts, 2 pools, gym, spa, beach, boating, fishing, mountain bikes, horseback riding, hiking, 2 bars, laundry service, Internet, airstrip, helipad* ▤ *AE, DC, MC, V* ⦿⧵ *CP.*

THE SOUTHERN TIP
PUNTARENAS TO MALPAÍS

Catch a ferry from Puntarenas to the southern tip of the Nicoya Peninsula and you'll be just a bumpy bus hop away from gorgeous beaches with waterfalls and tidal pools. Within the region are two quiet, well-preserved national parks where you can explore caves and pristine forests or travel by boat or sea kayak to remote islands and wildlife preserves for bird-watching, snorkeling, diving, and even camping. Not too remote, and thus at times overcrowded, is Isla Tortuga, ringed by some of Costa Rica's most beautiful beaches. If you like to mix nightlife with your outdoor adventures, the town of Montezuma and its nearby beaches are often jammed with an international cast of surfers, ecotourists, and misfits of all sorts, from practitioners of alternative lifestyles to expatriate American massage therapists living out their dreams.

Puntarenas

 110 km (69 mi) west of San José.

The main reason to visit Puntarenas is to catch a ferry to the eastern coast of the Nicoya Peninsula and its beaches. But a millennial beautification campaign, plus a modern bus station and a major marine-life museum, make it worth an afternoon visit or a one-night stop before taking the ferry. This bustling commercial fishing center and docking point for international cruise ships sits on a narrow spit of sand—*punta de arenas* (literally, "point of sand")—protruding into the Gulf of Nicoya, with splendid views across to the peninsula, especially at sunset. The locals, called Porteños, and the tourist police scoot around on bicycles, enjoying what must be the smoothest stretch of paved road in Costa Rica, the Paseo de Los Turistas.

Sidewalk lamps, concrete benches, and a modern cruise-ship dock enliven this wide beachfront promenade. On days when cruise ships arrive, local artisans sell their wares at a market near the dock. The town's clean, tree-lined beach beckons to strollers and swimmers. Seafood restaurants, cafés, ice cream parlors, casinos, and an Internet café in an old restored building provide lots of diversions and places to people-watch.

Art exhibitions are shown in the grand entrance hall of the **Casa de la Cultura**, a former port headquarters. The **Museo Regional-Histórico Marino** (☎ 661–5036) shares the same august building. The free exhibits focus on the history of Puntarenas as Costa Rica's main coffee-shipping port. The museum is open Tuesday–Sunday 9 to noon and 1 to 5. ✉ *Three blocks from Parque Central* ☎ *661–1394.*

Ambitious **Parque Marino del Pacífico** is the new jewel in Puntarenas's slightly tarnished crown. The town fell on hard times once Limón took over as Costa Rica's major port. The aquarium, full of Gulf of Nicoya sea life, is a government effort to bring visitors back to Puntarenas. ✉ *300 m east of cruise-ship dock* ☎ *661–5272* ✉ *$7* ☉ *Tues.–Sun. 9–5.*

off the beaten path

ISLA TORTUGA – Soft bleached sand and casually leaning palms fringe Isla Tortuga, an island of tropical dry forest that makes a perfect day trip from Puntarenas, Montezuma, and other beach towns. Though state owned, the island is leased and inhabited by a Costa Rican family who funded efforts to reintroduce such species as deer and wild pig to the island some years ago and now leads tours to the island from nearby Curú Wildlife Refuge in Paquera. A 40-minute hiking trail wanders past monkey ladders, strangler figs, bromeliads, orchids, and the fruit-bearing *guanabana* (soursop) and *marañón* (cashew) trees up to a lookout point with tantalizing vistas. You can take a short canopy tour on the beach. Transportation to the island and tours are arranged by tour operators in both Puntarenas and from San José, including **Calypso Tours** (✉ C. 36 between Avdas. 5 and 7, San José ☎ 256–2727 🖷 256–6767 ⊕ www.calypsocruises. com) for $99 per person in high season only, including transportation from San José. ✉ *90 mins by boat from Puntarenas* ✉ *Hike $5, canopy tour $10.*

Where to Stay & Eat

$–$$$ ✕ **La Caravelle.** The interior, dark blue walls adorned with antique musical instruments, is unexpectedly elegant—but then so is a French restaurant across the street from the ocean. True to the French manner, the service is somewhat insouciant and offhand. The cooking concentrates on sauces: try the corvina *ostendaise* (with a lemon and white-wine cream sauce, smothered in tiny shrimp) or beef fillet *con salsa oporto y hongos* (with a port-and-mushroom sauce). The wine selection is decent. ⊠ *Paseo de los Turistas, between Cs. 21 and 23* ☎ *661–2262* ⊟ *AE, MC, V* ☺ *Closed Mon. No lunch Tues.–Thurs.*

$–$$ ✕ **Restaurante La Yunta.** For a taste of old Costa Rica, sit yourself down at this Puntarenas landmark, presided over by an eponymous mounted ox head (*la yunta* means a yoked pair of oxen) and shaded by beach almond trees. The old-fashioned veranda restaurant has delicately spindled, pink-and-cream railings and a view of the ocean and of passersby strolling down the Paseo. It's open all day and seafood is the specialty, with ceviche to start, followed by octopus, jumbo shrimp, lobster, and whole fish. Try the interesting Corvina Tropical, a large portion of corvina smothered in a tropical fruit sauce. Service is polished, and crisp table linens add a courtly touch of times past, when San Joséfinos used to take the train to Puntarenas just to dine on fresh seafood. ⊠ *West end of Paseo de los Turistas, 100 m east of Hotel Tioga* ☎ *661–3216* ⊟ *AE, MC, V.*

$–$$ ▦ **Hotel Tioga.** The pastel green-and-yellow courtyard in this stately 40-year-old establishment has the look of an ocean liner. Your best bets are the seven "executive" guest rooms upstairs, with balconies overlooking the gulf. They're handsomely decorated with colorful, tropical prints and heavy varnished dark-wood furniture. The courtyard centers on a tiny pool with a *guachepelín* tree growing from the islet in its center. The pleasant second-floor restaurant is open to cool breezes off the gulf. ⊠ *Paseo de los Turistas, Apdo. 96–5400* ☎ *661–0271* 🖷 *661–0127* ⊕ *www.hoteltioga.com* ➥ *52 rooms* ♨ *Restaurant, cable TV, pool, bar, casino, laundry service* ⊟ *AE, MC, V* ⦿ *BP.*

$ ▦ **Hotel Las Brisas.** This white, two-story motel-style building wraps around its pool, where the views of the sun setting over the Nicoya Peninsula are terrific. The hotel is across the street from the beach and a stone's throw from the ferry docks. Three of the simple rooms have balconies with views of the ocean. The hotel has a secured parking lot. The restaurant serves Greek-influenced seafood and meat and some Mexican dishes. ⊠ *West end of Paseo de los Turistas* ☎ *661–4040* 🖷 *661–2120* ✍ *brisas@racsa.co.cr* ➥ *19 rooms* ♨ *Restaurant, fans, cable TV, pool, laundry service, Internet; no room phones* ⊟ *AE, DC, MC, V* ⦿ *BP.*

Paquera

⑲ *1½ to 2 hrs southwest of Puntarenas by ferry.*

Most travelers heading south to the beach towns of Montezuma and Malpaís arrive in Paquera by car ferry or *lancha* (small passenger launch) from Puntarenas. Paquera itself is a growing small community about 5 km (3 mi) south of the ferry dock. You can pick up beach supplies at the many stores, supermarkets, and gas stations here. Since the roads are rough on cars, it's better to fly into the Tambor airstrip and take a taxi or bus to your destination. The trip overland by car from Nicoya via Playa Naranjo is grueling.

Curú National Wildlife Refuge (Refugio Nacional de Vida Silvestre Curú), established by former farmer and logger turned conservationist Federico Schutt in 1933, was given the indigenous name for the pochote trees that flourish here. Trails lead through the forest and high-salinity mangroves where you see hordes of phantom crabs on the beach, Howler and White-faced Capuchin monkeys in the trees, and plenty of hummingbirds, kingfishers, woodpeckers, trogons, and manakins (including the coveted Long-tailed Manakin). The refuge is working to reintroduce Spider Monkeys and Scarlet Macaws into the wild. Some very basic accommodations, originally designed for students and researchers, are available by the beach ($25 per person, including three meals and park admission); call ahead to arrange for lodging, guides, and early morning bird-watching walks. Luis Schutt, son of the owner, arranges year-round **motorboat or kayak excursions** (⊠ Main road, across from Esso station in Paquera ☎ 641–0673 ✉ turismocuru@hotmail. com) to Isla Tortuga for $15; snorkeling equipment is $5 extra. Or you can take a horseback tour of the *finca* (property) or ride to a sparkling white beach. A canopy tour is $15 per person. From Paquera, you can catch a bus to the refuge. ⊠ *7 km (4½ mi) south of Paquera* ☎ *710–8236 or 641–0014* 🖷 *641–0004* 🕾 *Schutt family, Apdo. 14–5357, Paquera* 🖾 *$6* ⊙ *Daily 7–4.*

Sports & the Outdoors

San José–based adventure tour operator **Ríos Tropicales** (☎ 233–6455 ⊕ www.riostropicales.com) has three- and four-day sea-kayaking trips for a minimum of six people, which start from Curú National Wildlife Refuge and take you along the coast and among the barely inhabited islands in the Gulf of Nicoya. The professionally run camping and kayaking trips give kayakers at every level the opportunity to explore wild islands, wildlife reserves, and more. Expert natural guides explain the natural history of the region and teach kayak surfing.

Tambor

⑳ *20 km (12 mi) south of Curú National Wildlife Refuge, 27 km (17 mi) south of Paquera.*

Tucked into large half-moon Bahía Ballena, Tambor has undergone a land-sale frenzy similar to that at Tamarindo—you can see a golf course and housing development from the road, and signs of further development all around them. The area's luxe resort hotels arrange plenty of activities, but you could break out on your own. The hike from Tambor around the Piedra Amarilla point to Tango Mar Resort is about 8 km (5 mi), and the trees along the way resound with the throaty utterings of male Howler Monkeys. You can fly directly to Tambor from San José on SANSA and NatureAir.

Along the dusty road through the low-key town are interesting souvenir shops, a supermarket, a SANSA office, and an adventure-tour office, as well as restaurants and hotels. **Cóbano,** 12 km (7½ mi) to the west of Tambor, is a bustling crossroads with supermarkets, a bank, restaurants, shops, a gas station, and even an ice cream parlor.

Where to Stay

$$$$ 🏨 **Barceló Tambor Beach.** This Spanish-owned megacomplex was one of Costa Rica's first all-inclusive resorts. You can partake of lots of activities around the resort's grassy grounds and an almost endless buffet beside the lovely beach. But be prepared to share with as many as 1,200 other guests during high season. The airy though fairly standard rooms have spacious bathrooms. ✉ *Main road, south of Tambor village* ☎ *683–0303* 🖷 *683–0304* ⊕ *www.barcelo.com* 🛏 *402 rooms* ⚐ *2 restaurants, snack bar, cable TV, 3 tennis courts, pool, fitness classes, hair salon, massage, windsurfing, boating, basketball, 3 bars, casino, dance club, laundry service, Internet, travel services* ☰ *AE, MC, V* ⍟ *AI.*

★ **$$$–$$$$** 🏨 **Tango Mar Resort.** This resort lives up to most people's idea of a tropical paradise. Thatch-roof tiki suites on stilts look rustic on the outside but are pure luxury inside. Rooms in the main hotel are luxurious, too, with private balconies right on the beach. The breezy Cristóbal restaurant serves international cuisine with an ocean view, while a more casual, poolside restaurant serves lighter fare. On the grounds are a lushly landscaped, spring-fed, two-tiered pool as well as a new pool by the beach; a spectacular beachfront waterfall; and an immaculate 9-hole golf course. ✉ *3 km (2 mi) west of Tambor* ☎ *683–0001* 🖷 *683–0003* ⊕ *www.tangomar.com* 🛏 *4 villas, 18 rooms, 17 suites* ⚐ *2 restaurants, in-room safes, some in-room hot tubs, some kitchenettes, refrigerators, cable TV, 9-hole golf course, 2 tennis courts, 2 pools, massage, beach, boating, fishing, hiking, horseback riding, 2 bars, Internet* ☰ *AE, DC, MC, V* ⍟ *BP.*

$$$ 🏨 **Tambor Tropical.** You may have seen this collection of five duplex cabinas, which surround a pool in the palm trees off Playa Tambor in Bahía Ballena, when it was featured on the TV series *Temptation Island.* The 1,000-square-foot cabinas are made from strips of local hardwoods arranged in attractive diagonal patterns. Each cabina has an upper and lower suite, and each suite has its own living room, bedroom, and fully equipped kitchen. The brown-sand beach is not all that picturesque, but the water here is shallow and calm enough for safe swimming. Friendly staff members go out of their way to be helpful. ✉ *Follow main street of Tambor toward water (hotel fronts beach)* ☎ *683–0011* 🖷 *683–0013* ⊕ *www.tambortropical.com* 🛏 *10 suites* ⚐ *Restaurant, fans, kitchens, pool, hot tub, beach, horseback riding, bar; no a/c, no room phones, no room TVs* ☰ *AE, MC, V* ⍟ *BP.*

Montezuma

㉑ *7 km (4½ mi) southeast of Cóbano, 45 km (28 mi) south of Paquera, 18 km (11 mi) south of Tambor.*

Beautifully positioned on a sandy bay, Montezuma is hemmed in by a precipitous wooded shoreline. There are two routes into town, both bumpy and unpaved; the more direct route has had problems with the road subsiding at the top of the hill into town, so watch for possible detour signs via the alternate Las Delicias route. At the bottom of the hill, the funky town center is a pastel cluster of new-age health-food cafés, trendy beachwear shops, and jaunty tour kiosks mixed with older Tico *sodas* (casual eateries) and noisy open-air bars. Montezuma has been on the international vagabond circuit for years, attracting surfers and alternative-lifestyle types, and some unsavory characters as well. But the community, like its pioneers, is growing up, with Internet cafés and more sophisticated hotels and restaurants. Today you are as likely to meet older, outdoorsy European tourists as dreadlocked surfers. The main attraction for everybody is the beach that stretches across one national park and two nature preserves to the north, leading to a spectacular beachfront waterfall, a popular destination for hikers and horseback tours.

Just over a bridge, 10 minutes south of town, a slippery path patrolled by howler monkeys leads upstream to two waterfalls, the second one an impressive 108 feet high with a thrilling **swimming hole.** Do not jump or dive from the waterfalls. Despite signs posting the danger, some young people are still jumping to their deaths or serious injury.

Where to Stay & Eat

★ $-$$ ✕ **Playa de los Artistas.** This creative open-air Italian restaurant with driftwood tables scattered along the beach specializes in modern, Mediterranean-style fresh seafood. Flickering lanterns combine with crashing surf to create a *muy romantica* atmosphere at dinner. Portions are plentiful and dramatically presented on huge platters. Try the carpaccio *de atun,* a raw tuna appetizer seasoned with oregano and garlic, and soak up the marinade with freshly baked, savory focaccia. The lunch menu emphasizes homemade pasta. ✉ *275 m south of town, just past Los Mangos Hotel* ☎ *No phone* ▭ *No credit cards* ☉ *Closed Sun. and Oct.*

¢ ✕ **Cafe Iguana.** This funky café, subtitled La Esquina Dulce (The Sweet Corner), serves up real Italian espresso, fresh fruit juices, and baked goods from 6 AM on. Check out the impressive selection of huge muffins and dessert breads, including such exotic flavors as mango and pineapple. The overstuffed sandwiches, made on fresh, crusty home-baked bread, are big enough for two. Wooden stools on a terrace make perfect perches for watching the passing parade of *todo el mundo* Montezuma. ✉ *Town center* ☎ *No phone* ▭ *No credit cards.*

★ $ ✕▣ **El Sano Banano Restaurant and B&B.** Fish and hormone-free chicken are included on the healthful but delicious menu at Montezuma's original natural-food restaurant (¢–$). A terrace café provides excellent people-watching, as well as tall glasses of sinfully delicious Mocha Chiller, made with frozen yogurt. A battalion of ceiling fans keeps the air moving in the spacious, adobe-style restaurant. It's open for breakfast from 7 AM; if you come for dinner around 7:30 PM, you can take in a nightly free movie. Attached to the restaurant is an Internet café, and above is a B&B annex. The comfortable rooms have air-conditioning, a rare treat in Montezuma, and they're decorated in Mexican style. They are amazingly quiet for being in the center of town. ✉ *Main road* ☎ *642–0638* 🖷 *642–0631* ⊕ *www.elbanano.com* ⟿ *12 rooms* ♢ *Restaurant, cable TV, Internet; no room phones* ▭ *AE, MC, V* ⦿*l BP.*

★ $$ ▣ **Cabinas El Sano Banano.** This colony of eight tropical cabins is a fantasy island, huddled in the woods north of town close to the beach. Each geodesic-dome bungalow is a luxurious, cozy cave for two, perfect for honeymooners. A two-story building has three comfortable suites, with

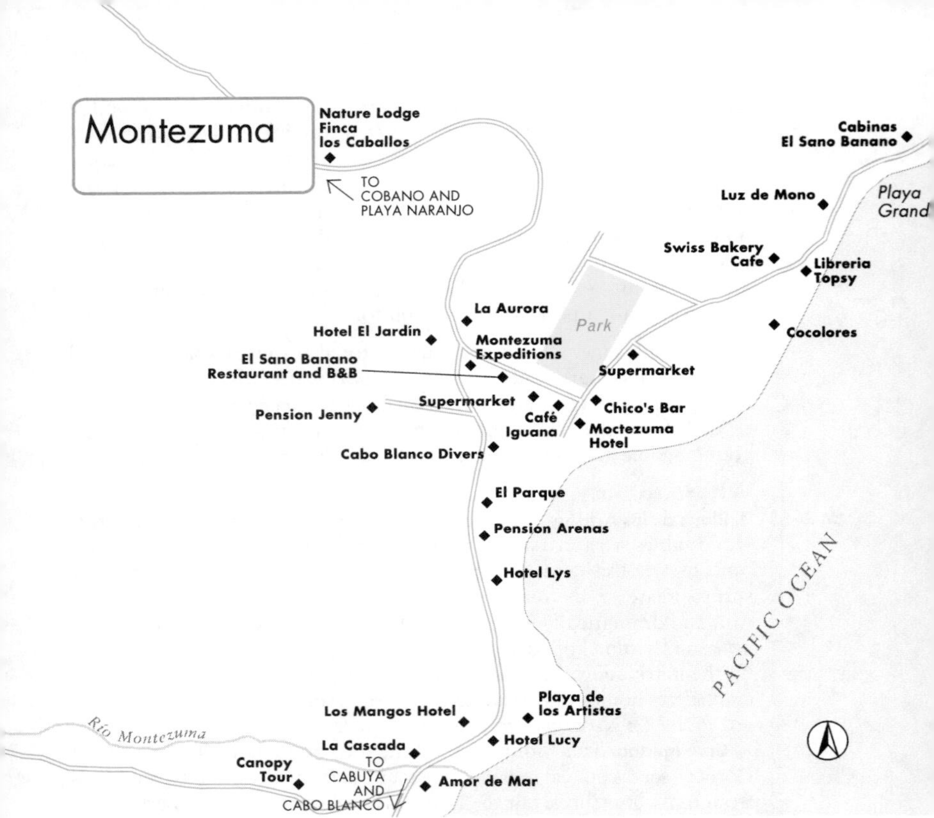
Montezuma
Nature Lodge
Finca
los Caballos
TO
COBANO AND
PLAYA NARANJO
Cabinas
El Sano Banano
Playa
Grand
Luz de Mono
Swiss Bakery
Cafe
Libreria
Topsy
La Aurora
Park
Hotel El Jardín
Montezuma
Expeditions
Cocolores
El Sano Banano
Restaurant and B&B
Supermarket
Supermarket
Chico's Bar
Pension Jenny
Café
Iguana
Moctezuma
Hotel
Cabo Blanco Divers
El Parque
Pension Arenas
Hotel Lys
PACIFIC OCEAN
Playa de
los Artistas
Los Mangos Hotel
Río Montezuma
Hotel Lucy
La Cascada
Canopy
Tour
TO
CABUYA
AND
CABO BLANCO
Amor de Mar

kitchenettes above, and three double rooms below. They're decorated with original watercolors of local birds. Adding to the romance is a garden-fringed pool with a waterfall. The reception desk—and the complimentary breakfast—are at the El Sano Banano Restaurant in town. ✉ *Main road, on beach, 700 m north of school in Montezuma* ☎ *642–0638* 🖷 *642–0631* 🌐 *www.elbanano.com* *3 rooms, 3 suites, 8 bungalows* *Some kitchenettes, refrigerators, pool, beach, hiking, laundry service; no a/c in some rooms, no room phones, no room TVs* 💳 *AE, MC, V* *BP.*

$ **Hotel Amor de Mar.** Take the time to walk the ½ km (¼ mi) south of town to find this ruggedly handsome, two-story wooden hotel surrounded by trees. A grassy lawn stretches to the rocky seashore, where you can cool off in a natural tidal pool. Great breakfasts and immediate access to the waterfall hike across the main road make this one of the finest small hotels in Montezuma. The breezy, wood-paneled rooms are rustic but comfortable; two of the rooms share a bathroom. The dining room serves breakfast and light lunches only. There's also a two-story, equipped oceanfront house with four bedrooms for rent. ✉ *Beach road, just past bridge south of town* ☎🖷 *642–0262* 🌐 *www.amordemar.com* *11 rooms, 9 with bath; 1 house* *Dining room, fans, beach, laundry service; no a/c, no room phones, no room TVs* 💳 *V.*

$ Hotel El Jardín. Climbing the hill above town, this Italian-owned hotel has panoramic ocean views. True to its name, the cabins are scattered around a garden lush with flowering gingers and populated by indigenous stone-sculpture people. Teak paneling and furniture, stained-glass pictorial panels, and terraces with hammocks give this hotel style as well as comfort. There's no formal breakfast, but fresh fruit and coffee are laid out in the reception area each morning. ✉ *Main road, just inside town limits from the north* ☎ *642–0548* 🖷 *642–0074* ⊕ *www.hoteleljardin.com* ⬅ *15 rooms* ⚭ *Fans, some kitchens, refrigerators, pool, outdoor hot tub; no a/c in some rooms, no room phones, no room TVs* ➠ *AE, MC, V.*

$ Nature Lodge Finca los Caballos. At this charming small hotel high on a hill, the open-air restaurant and lounge both have bird's-eye views of ocean and valley below. Besides gazing at the view, the main activities here are horseback riding and bird-watching. Designed with a southwestern U.S. motif, the comfortable rooms have pastel walls decorated with stencils of lizards and frogs. A two-bedroom bungalow, formerly the owner's house, is set apart from the hotel and accommodates up to four. The restaurant serves dinner to nonguests by reservation. ✉ *3 km (2 mi) north of Montezuma on main road* ☎ *642–0124* ⊕ *www.naturelodge.net* ✒ *Apdo. 22, Cóbano de Puntarenas* ⬅ *7 rooms, 1 bungalow* ⚭ *Restaurant, fans, pool, horseback riding; no a/c, no room phones, no room TVs* ➠ *V* ☉ *Closed Sept. and Oct.*

¢–$ Los Mangos Hotel. Looking for affordable accommodation within sight and sound of the sea? Here it is: octagonal wood cabins and a rose-colored two-story wooden building with verandas and rocking chairs, all in a shady mango grove. The secluded, scenic pool has ocean views. Yoga classes are given in an open-air pavilion. For an inexpensive breakfast, lunch, or dinner, just walk across the road to Lucy's Restaurant, a pleasant Tico soda with tables on a terrace overlooking the ocean. ✉ *Just before entrance to Cascada Trail, ¼ mi south of town* ☎ *642–0076* 🖷 *642–0259* ⊕ *www.hotellosmangos.com* ⬅ *10 rooms, 6 with bath; 10 cabins* ⚭ *Pool, outdoor hot tub, horseback riding; no a/c, no room phones, no room TVs* ➠ *MC, V.*

Sports & the Outdoors

☾ Surfing, diving, snorkeling, fishing, and horseback tours to the **El Choro Beach Waterfall** are the most popular excursions. All the outfitters in town, including Aventuras en Montezuma, organize these tours. **Aventuras en Montezuma** (✉ Main road, at center of town ☎ 642–0050) offers snorkeling, rafting, fishing, diving, and horseback tours.

Shopping

Beachwear and surfing gear abound in colorful shops that change owners with the seasons, and souvenirs and leather-and-seed jewelry are sold on streetside tables. For some intellectual stimulation at the beach, visit **Librería Topsy** (☎ 642–0576), where you can buy, exchange, or rent a book—one whole room is devoted to a lending library; you pay a deposit on each book you rent. Some foreign newspapers are also available, and you can leave your postcards and letters here to be mailed. There's a great selection of natural-history books. The shop is open weekdays 8 AM to 4 PM and weekends 8 AM to noon.

Malpaís

 12 km (7½ mi) southwest of Cóbano, 52 km (33 mi) south of Paquera.

Once considered a remote preserve, Malpaís was frequented only by die-hard surfers in search of some of the country's largest waves and by naturalists en route to the nearby Cabo Blanco Nature Preserve. Since the town and its miles of beach were accessible only down a steep gravel road, it was likely that this reputation might have remained the case. However, as in much of this coastal area, hotels and restaurants are now springing up at both ends of the populated part of the beach, despite the bad roads.

Surfing is best at Playa Santa Teresa, the sandy north end of this long stretch of beach. The more southerly Malpaís end of the beach is rockier but interesting for its tidal pools and beachcombing. The crowds at both beaches are fairly young, with tanned-and-buff surfers walking or bicycling their boards to wherever the surf is up. But increasingly, older, more upscale visitors are drawn to the tranquility of luxury retreats that cater to mind and body.

Conquistadores named this area Cabo Blanco on account of its white earth and cliffs, but it was a more benevolent pair of foreigners—Nils Olof Wessberg and his wife, Karen, arriving here from Sweden in 1950—who made it the **Cabo Blanco Strict Nature Preserve** (Reserva Natural Absoluta Cabo Blanco). Appalled by the first clear-cut in the Cabo Blanco area in 1960, the couple launched a pioneering and international appeal to save the forest. In time, their efforts led not only to the creation of the 12-square-km (4½-square-mi) reserve but also to the founding of Costa Rica's national park service, the National Conservation Areas System (SINAC). Nils Olof Wessberg was murdered on the Osa Peninsula in 1975 while researching the area's potential as a national park. A reserve just outside Montezuma was named in his honor. A reserve has been created to honor his wife, who dedicated her life to conservation after her husband's death. The **Karen Mogensen Fischer Museum** (⊠ Internet Café, El Sano Banano Restaurant ☎ 650–0607) details her life and contributions.

The tropical moist forest in Cabo Blanco has a combination of evergreen species and lush greenery. New signs with informative natural-history captions dot the trails. Look for the sapodilla trees, which produce a white latex used to make gum; you can often see V-shape scars where the trees have been cut to allow the latex to run into containers placed at the base. Olof Wessberg cataloged a full array of animals here: porcupine, Hog-nosed Skunk, Spotted Skunk, Gray Fox, anteater, cougar, and jaguar. Resident birds include Brown Pelicans, White-throated Magpies, toucans, Cattle Egrets, Green Herons, parrots, and Turquoise-browed Motmots. A fairly strenuous 4-km (2½-mi) hike, which takes about two hours in each direction, follows a trail from the reserve entrance to **Playa Cabo Blanco**. The beach is magnificent, with hundreds of pelicans flying in formation and paddling in the calm waters offshore—you can wade right in and join them. Off the tip of the cape is the 7,511-square-foot **Isla Cabo Blanco**, with pelicans, frigate birds, Brown

Boobies, and an abandoned lighthouse. As a strict reserve, Cabo Blanco has bathrooms and a visitor center but no other tourist facilities. Rangers and volunteers act as guides. Roads to the reserve are usually passable only in dry season. ⊠ *10 km (6 mi) southwest of Montezuma, about 11 km (7 mi) south of Malpaís* ☎ *642–0093* ⊠ *$8* ☉ *Wed.–Sun. 8–4.*

Where to Stay & Eat

¢–$ ✕ **Piedra Mar.** With all the new restaurants popping up along the beach road, the favorite standby is still this old shack down on the beach, part *pulpería* (grocery–juice bar), part restaurant. Plastic tables are set up under a corrugated tin roof and the only decor is the rocky seascape, about 10 feet away. Your lobster (for less than $10) or grilled shrimp comes flavored with garlic and—on windy days—the sea spray crashing against the rocks. Sunset is popular with locals in the know, so come early. Or come for breakfast at 7 and watch the early morning sun lighting up the ocean. ⊠ *275 m south of Blue Jay Lodge* ☎ *No phone* ⊟ *No credit cards.*

★ $$$$ ✕⌂ **Resort Florblanca.** Named for the white flowers of the frangipani trees that shade the beachfront property, this collection of simply luxurious villas ministers to body and soul. Each handsome villa has an outdoor Balinese-inspired bathroom and a sunken tub. There's a dojo for karate and yoga, a massage therapist, a music room, cable TV in a comfortable lounge, and an art and pottery studio. Two pools flow into each other in front of Nectar, the excellent alfresco restaurant ($$–$$$), which serves four-course dinners with inventive menus. Multicourse breakfasts are lavish. Resident biologist guides lead horseback tours and nature walks into Cabo Blanco and snorkeling excursions in its surrounding waters. Only the bedrooms are air-conditioned. ⊠ *2 km (1 mi) north of Santa Teresa* ☎☎ *640–0232* ⊕ *www.florblanca.com* ⇨ *10 villas* ⌂ *Restaurant, in-room safes, refrigerators, 2 pools, gym, massage, spa, beach, snorkeling, fishing, hiking, mountain bikes, horseback riding, shop, laundry service, Internet; no room TVs* ⊟ *AE, DC, MC, V* ❍| *BP.*

★ $$ ✕⌂ **Milarepa.** Created by two Parisians searching for a tropical Shangri-la, Milarepa is a perfect place for renewal, whether romantic or spiritual. The four bamboo houses are spaced apart to ensure privacy and are furnished in ascetic but exquisite taste, with carved Indonesian wooden beds draped with mosquito netting, and bamboo armoires. Bathrooms are open to the sky, with alcoves for Buddhist deities. Each cottage has a veranda looking out onto the carefully raked white beach, shaded by a grove of palms. The restaurant is *très français*; try the salade niçoise. ⊠ *Playa Santa Teresa, beside Resort Florblanca* ☎ *640–0023* ☎ *640–0168* ⊕ *www. milarepahotel.com* ⌂ *Apdo. 49–5361, Cóbano, Puntarenas* ⇨ *4 cottages* ⌂ *Restaurant, fans, pool, snorkeling, fishing, hiking, horseback riding; no a/c, no room phones, no room TVs* ⊟ *MC, V.*

☾ $ ⌂ **Blue Jay Lodge.** Here's your chance to live in a tree house. The wooden cabins, with only screens for walls on three sides (the bathroom wall is on the fourth side), are built on stilts. Steep stairs lead up the forested mountainside to the rustic aeries with hot-water showers, open to nature on one side. Ceiling fans keep the air moving, but warm blankets are on hand for cool, breezy nights. Breakfast is in the wooden-terrace restaurant at ground level. The beach is 200 m away, or you can climb the mountain to look for birds and Howler Monkeys. ⊠ *Turn left at* *main Malpaís crossroads at end of road from Cóbano ☎ 640–0089 or 640–0342 🖨 640–0141 ⊕ www.bluejaylodgecostarica.com ➯ 7 cabins ⚿ Restaurant, fans, pool, bar, laundry service; no a/c, no room phones, no room TVs ⊟ AE, D, MC, V ⊚ BP.*

THE TEMPISQUE RIVER BASIN

This northeastern section of the peninsula encompasses the parks in and around the Río Tempisque—prime places to watch birds and other wildlife—and Nicoya, the commercial and political hub of the northern Nicoya Peninsula. By road, Nicoya provides the best access to Sámara, Nosara, and points south and north and is also linked by a smooth, well-paved road to the artisan community of Guaitil and the northern Nicoya beach towns.

A $26.9 million bridge, built with funds from the Taiwanese government, was completed in 2003. The Taiwan Friendship Bridge, more commonly referred to as the Río Tempisque Bridge, crosses the Río Tempisque just north of the old ferry crossing at Puerto Moreno and has eliminated the long wait for the ferry, speeding travelers to points west and south. The toll is 400 colónes (about $1) per car. For the bridge, head north from San José on the Pan-American Highway, turn left about 48 km (30 mi) north of the Puntarenas turnoff, and drive 27 km (17 mi) west.

Palo Verde National Park & Lomas Barbudal Reserve

▶ ㉓ *Palo Verde is 28 km (17 mi) southwest of Bagaces, which is 24 km (15 mi) south of Liberia; Lomas Barbudal is 20 km (12 mi) southwest of Bagaces.*

Bordered on the west by the Río Tempisque, these wildlife preserves protect a significant amount of deciduous dry forest. Palo Verde extends over 95 square km (37 square mi) of mainly flat terrain, and its main attraction is bird-watching. Its swampland is a temporary home for thousands of migratory birds toward the end of the rainy season. From December through March a raised platform near the ranger station, about 8 km (5 mi) past the park entrance, helps you to see dozens of species of aquatic birds, including herons, ducks, Wood Storks, and elegant Roseate Spoonbills.

Camping, rustic dormitory facilities ($7), and meals ($2.50 for lunch or dinner) can be arranged through the park headquarters. Or you can book a tour through the **Organization for Tropical Studies** (✉ ½ km [¼ mi] west of Lincoln School in Moravia, San José ☎ 240–6696 ⊕ www.ots.ac.cr), which has double rooms with shared baths for $50 per person, including three meals, taxes, and a guided walk. Most people visit on a tour. The park headquarters is 8 km (5 mi) beyond the park entrance. ✉ *Pan-American Hwy.; drive 42 km (26 mi) north of Puntarenas turnoff to gas station in Bagaces, which is about 15 km (9 mi) north of Cañas, look for Palo Verde sign and drive 28 km (17 mi) left along rough road to park ☎ 200–0125 ⚋ $6 ☉ Daily 7–4; last admission at 1 PM.*

Sports & the Outdoors

BOATING **CATA Tours** (✉ 200 m west, then 25 m north of the Teletica Canal 7 TV station on west side of Sabana Park ☎ 674–0126, 296–2133 in San José ⊕ www.catatours.com) runs wildlife and bird-watching boating adventures down the Río Bebedero into Palo Verde from a starting point on the Pan-American Highway north of Cañas. Calm adventure trips are led by **Safaris Corobicí** (☎☎ 669–6191 ⊕ www.nicoya.com) with guides rowing rafts down the Río Corobicí, covering some of the same wildlife-rich territory not far from Palo Verde and Lomas Barbudal. Follow signs from the highway to Km 193.

Barra Honda National Park

24 *23 km (14 mi) west of new Friendship Bridge across the Río Tempisque.*

The limestone ridge rising from the surrounding savanna was once thought to be a volcano but was later found to contain an intricate network of caves, formed as a result of erosion once the ridge had emerged from the sea. Some caves on the almost 23-square-km (14-square-mi) park remain unexplored, and they're home to abundant animal life, including bats, birds, blindfish, salamanders, and snails.

Every day from 8 AM to 1 PM, local guides take groups down a 67-foot flexible aluminum ladder to the **Terciopelo Cave,** which shelters unusual formations shaped like fried eggs, popcorn, and shark's teeth, as well as sonorous columns collectively known as "the organ." You must wear a harness with a rope attached for safety. The tour costs $12 for equipment rental, plus $17 per person for a guide; park admission is not included. Don't attempt to visit the caves without a guide who is authorized by the local community development association.

You can climb 1,184-foot **Barra Honda peak** from the northwest (the southern wall is almost vertical), following the 3-km (2-mi) Los Laureles trail. From the summit you have fantastic views sweeping across the islet-filled Gulf of Nicoya. The surface is pocked with orifices and white rocks eroded into odd shapes, and some of the ground feels dangerously hollow. Surface wildlife includes howler monkeys, skunks, coatis, deer, parakeets, and iguanas. The relatively open, deciduous-forest vegetation makes viewing the fauna easy. Hikers must be accompanied by local guides. The park has camping facilities; a community tourism association provides guides and runs a simple, inexpensive restaurant and lodge by the park entrance. A park office in Nicoya, across from the colonial church, provides information and maps of the park. If you need food or lodging in the park, make reservations before the weekend. ☎ 686–6760 ⌷ $6 ⊙ *Park daily 8–4; Nicoya office weekdays 8–4.*

Nicoya

25 *30 km (19 mi) west of Puerto Moreno, 11 km (7 mi) southwest of Barra Honda National Park.*

Often referred to as Guanacaste's colonial capital, Nicoya is a prosperous provincial town, with a pleasant, shady central park where you can get a taste of everyday small-town life, including Sunday-night band concerts. With the promise of increased traffic from the Río Tempisque Bridge, the town has spruced up old buildings and added new ones, including three Internet cafés and an ATM that takes international cards.

The Chorotegan chief Nicoya greeted the Spanish conquistadores upon their arrival here in 1523, and many of his people were converted to Catholicism. A Chinese population, descendants of 19th-century railroad workers, gives the place a certain cosmopolitan air, manifested in part by numerous Chinese restaurants. If you're heading to Tamarindo, consider a stop in Santa Cruz, a small town known for its annual Fiesta de Santa Cruz, a folklore festival in January, or in Guaitil for pottery shopping (⇨ Shopping, *below*).

Church of San Blas, Nicoya's only colonial landmark, is a mission-style church steeped in history. Originally built in 1644, the current church was reconstructed after an 1831 earthquake. The spare interior is made grand by seven pairs of soaring, carved-wood columns. Folk-art wood carvings of the stations of the cross are arrayed around the stark white walls, imbuing the space with an aura of spirituality. Three arched doorways bring in light and frame verdant views of park greenery and distant mountains. There's a small collection of huge, 18th-century bronze mission bells and some antique wooden statues of saints. ⊠ *North side of central park* ☎ *No phone* 🖾 *Donations accepted* ☉ *Daily dawn–dusk; closed during evening mass.*

Where to Stay & Eat

¢–$ ✗ **Restaurante Nicoya.** There are many Chinese restaurants from which to choose in Nicoya. This one is the most elegant, with hanging lanterns, a colorful collection of international flags, and an enormous menu with 85 Asian dishes, such as stir-fried beef with vegetables, along with some familiar favorites, such as fried chicken. The fresh sea bass sautéed with fresh pineapple, chayote, and red peppers is excellent. ⊠ *Main road, 70 m south of Coopmani building* ☎ *685–5113* ▭ *No credit cards.*

¢–$ ✗ **Un Dulce Momento.** Pizza, pasta, and pastry star at this Italian restaurant-café in a formerly derelict art deco movie house. There are 40 pizzas to choose from, along with homemade lasagna and ravioli. Sip a cappuccino in the vast expanse of this theatrical space, now decorated with whimsical sun and moon stencils and Ferrari racing-car banners. ⊠ *East side of central park* ☎ *686–4585* ▭ *No credit cards.*

¢ ✗ **Café Daniela.** For baked goods and light lunches, including hamburgers and sandwiches, try this small, casual restaurant–art gallery, decorated in blue and yellow, with interesting local artwork on the walls. The pizzas are Costa Rican–style, with very little tomato sauce, and there are typical Tico desserts, such as coconut flan and *tres leches* (three milks) cake. The television is usually tuned to a soccer game. ⊠ *Main road, 70 m south of Coopmani building* ☎ *686–6148* ▭ *No credit cards.*

$ 🏨 **Best Western Hotel Curime.** This hotel's tranquil, tree-shaded setting beside a stream is hard to improve upon. The large, comfortable rooms are in citrus-color adobe-style buildings arranged around a mango-bordered soccer field, a great place for kids to let off steam. The huge swimming pool allows for serious laps. The open-air restaurant is a little spare, but the view of the pool and the mature gardens makes up for it. ✉ *Road to Sámara, ½ km (¼ mi) south of town* ☎ *685–5238* 🖶 *685–5530* 🛏 *26 rooms* ⚐ *Restaurant, in-room safes, some refrigerators, cable TV, pool, playground, meeting room; no room phones* ▤ V ⚑ CP.

$ 🖼 **Cabinas Río Tempisque de Lujo.** Rooms here, with high wooden ceilings and big picture windows, are luxurious by any standards, but on the road to Santa Cruz they are a marvel. The owner is in the hardware business, and the hotel has high-quality materials inside and out, including palatial iron gates at the entrance. Huge, white-tiled bathrooms have mirrored closets and showers big enough for two. The gardens and pool area are beautifully landscaped. There is no restaurant, but room fridges are stocked with juice and soft drinks. ✉ *Highway north to Santa Cruz, just outside Nicoya* ☎ *686–6650* 🛏 *30 rooms* ⚐ *Refrigerators, cable TV, pool; no room phones* ▤ AE, MC, V.

¢ 🖼 **Las Tinajas.** This simple and clean bare-bones budget hotel near the bus station has a friendly staff and basic rooms with cold water. The decor consists of lots of large clay pots called *tinajas*. An outdoor café in back, from which you can watch strutting chickens in the neighbor's yard, serves a simple, cheap breakfast. ✉ *50 m east of Supercrompro* 🖶 *685–5081* 🛏 *28 rooms* ⚐ *Fans; no a/c in some rooms, no room phones, no TV in some rooms* ▤ V.

Shopping

Nicoya has many trendy new stores, along with old-fashioned general stores that are fascinating to browse through. **Casa del Sol y La Luna** (✉ Just west of the main road, around the corner from Café Daniel ☎ 686–4646) is noteworthy for its locally made crafts and gifts.

At **Coope-Tortillas** (✉ Santa Cruz, 8 km west of Guaitil ☎ 680–0688) watch tortillas being cooked the old-fashioned way over an open fire by friendly women in blue uniforms, members of a local women's cooperative in the town of Santa Cruz. Family-style meals featuring traditional *Guanacasteco* foods are served at picnic tables in a high-ceilinged, corrugated-metal building that once housed generators. Try the delicious *arroz de maiz,* a corn stew. In Santa Cruz, go straight through the business district, past the plaza, and look for the peaked-roof metal structure. The restaurant is open 4 AM to 6 PM.

In the country village of **Guaitil** (✉ 24 km [15 mi] north of Nicoya) artists—most of them women—have revived a vanishing tradition by producing clay pottery handmade in the manner of pre-Columbian Chorotegans. The town square is a soccer field, and almost every house facing it has a pottery shop out front and a round, wood-fired kiln in back. Pottery designs range from imitation Mexican to inspired Cubist abstractions. Every artisan's style is different, so take the time to wander from shop to shop. Prices are very reasonable, and although the pieces are rumored to crack rather too easily, they make wonderful keepsakes and gifts if you can get them home in one piece.

THE NICOYA PENINSULA A TO Z

To research prices, get advice from other travelers, and book travel arrangements, visit www.fodors.com.

AIR TRAVEL

Liberia is a good gateway town to the coast with its international airport, Aeropuerto Internacional Daniel Oduber (LIR). Tamarindo, Playa Nosara, Playa Carrillo, Punta Islita, and Tambor also have airstrips. Flying in from San José to these airports is the best way to get here if you are already in the country. If your primary destination lies in Guanacaste and/or Nicoya, make sure your travel agent investigates the possibility of flying into Liberia instead of San José, which saves some serious hours on the road.

CARRIERS   Delta Airlines connects Atlanta with Liberia's airport six times weekly. American Airlines flies from Miami to Liberia three times weekly. Continental Airlines connects Houston and Liberia with three flights each week. Various charters serve the airport on changing schedules as well. For information on international carriers and San José airports, *see* Air Travel and Airports *in* Smart Travel Tips A to Z at the front of this book.

Costa Rican domestic airline SANSA flies to Liberia from San José's Juan Santamaría Airport. Domestic carrier NatureAir flies from San José's Tobías Bolaños Airport to Liberia with continuing service to Granada, Nicaragua. SANSA flies daily from Juan Santamaría International Airport in San José to Tamarindo, Tambor, Playa Carrillo, Punta Islita, and Nosara. NatureAir flies from Aeropuerto Internacional Tobías Bolaños in Pavas, a northern suburb of San José, to Liberia, Tamarindo, Playa Carrillo, Punta Islita, and Tambor.

🚹 Airlines & Contacts **Aeropuerto Internacional Daniel Oduber** ☎ 668–1032 or 668–1010. **NatureAir** ☎ 220–3054 🖷 220–0413 ⊕ www.natureair.com. **SANSA** ☎ 668–1047 Liberia, 656–0131 Sámara, 682–0168 Nosara, 653–0012 Tamarindo, 683–0015 Tambor 🖷 666–1017 ⊕ www.flysansa.com.

BOAT & FERRY TRAVEL

Car ferries run by Naviera Tambor and the Asociación de Desarrollo Integral Paquera (some boats still have the old name, Ferry Peninsula, painted on) connect Puntarenas with Paquera, with continuing bus service to Montezuma. The trip takes 1¼ hours, and the car ferries leave six to eight times daily, depending on the season, between 4:30 AM and 8:30 PM, with an equal number of return trips. The Puntarenas–Playa Naranjo car ferry, run by Cooantramar, takes 1½ hours, departing daily at 6 and 10 AM and 2:20 and 7 PM.

A passenger-only *lancha* (launch), run by the Asociación de Desarrollo Integral de Paquera, leaves Puntarenas for Paquera twice daily at 11:30 AM and 4 PM from a hard-to-find small dock just west of the Banco Nacional near the market. On the Paquera side, launches leave for Puntarenas at 7:30 AM and 2 PM. Bus links and cabs are available at the Nicoya end of the ferry lines.

These schedules are subject to change from weekdays to weekends, high to low season, and during holidays. Expect long waits on all car ferries in high season and on weekends. Avoid Sunday crossings from Paquera at any time of the year. To avoid a longer-than-necessary wait and to get current schedules, always call ahead.

🛈 Boat & Ferry Information **Asociación de Desarrollo Integral de Paquera** 🕾641-0118 or 641-0515. **Coonatramar** 🕾 661-1069. **Naviera Tambor** 🕾 661-2084.

BUS TRAVEL

Bus service connects the larger cities to each other and to the more popular beaches, but forget about catching a bus from beach to beach; you'll generally have to backtrack to the inland hubs of Nicoya and Liberia unless you take a minibus, which may take just as long as a bus, although they're usually more comfortable. Bus companies rarely answer their phones and the schedules are always changing, so if accurate information is important to you, it's best to ask at the stations in San José. Your hotel front desk should be able to confirm which station specific buses and lines depart from.

Buses range from plush coaches to dirty old rattletraps, and there is no way of knowing which will be your fate until you get on the bus. During busy times, the worst buses are added to the fleet. Only some buses have air-conditioning.

With the new bridge across the Río Tempisque, bus routes and schedules to some Nicoya beach destinations have changed slightly and become more efficient. Get a list of bus schedules from the main ICT tourist office beneath the Plaza de la Cultura in San José.

Bus schedules listed below are accurate at this writing, but departure times change frequently. To get up-to-date schedules, go to the bus station a day before your departure.

LIBERIA & NORTH COAST
Pulmitan buses run from San José (C. 24 between Avdas. 5 and 7) to Liberia and Playasa del Coco daily. Liberia buses leave every hour 6–6 and then a last bus at 8 PM; the trip is four hours. Playas del Coco buses depart at 8 AM, 2 PM, and 4 PM for the five-hour trip. Empresa Esquivel buses from Liberia leave daily for Playa Hermosa and Panamá at 4:45, 7:30, and 11:30 AM and 1, 3:30, and 5:30 PM. Tralapa buses make the five-hour trip from San José (C. 20 between Avdas. 3 and 5) to Brasilito and Playa Flamingo daily at 8 and 10:30 AM and at 3 PM. For Tamarindo, a five-hour trip from San José, buses run by Empresa Alfaro leave from C. 14 at Avda. 5 daily at 11 AM and 3:30 PM.

CENTRAL & SOUTH COAST
Empresa Alfaro buses run from San José (C. 14 between Avdas. 3 and 5) to Nicoya daily, via Liberia, at 6:30 AM, 10 AM, 1:30 PM, 3 PM, and 5 PM, a five-hour trip; to Nosara daily via the Tempisque Bridge at 6 AM, a six-hour trip; and to Sámara daily at 12:30 and 6:30 PM, a five-hour trip.

The Castillos company (🕾 No phone) runs a bus to Junquillal from the central market in Santa Cruz, leaving at 10:15 AM, 2:30, and 5:30 PM; the trip takes about an hour. Buses leave Junquillal for Santa Cruz from the Pulperia at 5:30 AM, noon, and 4 PM. Tralapa buses to Santa

Cruz leave hourly from San José (Avda. 5, between Cs. 20 and 22) from 7 to 10 AM and then at 10:30 AM, noon, and 1, 4, and 6 PM; the trip is five hours.

Empresa Rojas buses leave Nicoya from a stop near the Hotel Las Tinajas (50 m east of Supercrompro) for Nosara and Guiones weekdays at 5 and 10 AM, noon, and 2 and 3 PM. The same line runs from Nicoya to Sámara and Carrillo weekdays starting at 5 AM, then at 6, 7:45, and 10 AM, noon, and every hour on the half hour from 1:30 to 5:30 PM; weekends, buses leave Nicoya at 10 AM and 3 PM for Nosara and Sámara.

Empresarios Unidos buses leave for the 2½-hour trip from San José (C. 16 between Avdas. 10 and 12) to Puntarenas daily every 40 minutes, from 6 AM to 7 PM. From Puntarenas, take a ferry to Paquera. Buses run to Montezuma and Tambor from the ferry landing in Paquera, via Cóbano, six times daily between 6:15 AM and 6:15 PM, returning six times between 5:30 AM and 4:30 PM; but inquire about the latest schedule for this route before you set off. Buses to Malpaís run from Cóbano four times a day, connecting directly from Paquera.

SHUTTLE VANS   You can ride in a comfortable, air-conditioned minibus with Gray Line Tourist Bus, connecting San José, Liberia, Playa Flamingo, Playa Hermosa, Tamarindo, and other destinations in Guanacaste. Fares range from $25 to $58, depending on destination. The Gray Line Tourist Bus from San José to Tamarindo and Liberia begins picking up passengers from hotels daily around 6 AM. The return bus leaves Tamarindo around 2 PM and passes through Liberia around 3:30 PM. Gray Line also has a weekly pass that lets you ride all over Costa Rica for $63. Interbus has door-to-door minivan shuttle service from San José hotels to all the major beach destinations (Papagayo, Panama, Hermosa, Flamingo, Tamarindo, Hermosa, Cocos, and Ocotal in Nicoya), for $25 per person. You can also buy a monthly Flexipass with 4 to 10 transfers within the country for $110 to $200. Reserve at least one day in advance.

🔳 Bus Companies **Empresa Alfaro** ☎ 222–2666, 685–5032 in Nicoya. **Empresa Esquivel** ☎ 666–0042. **Empresa Rojas** ☎ 685–5352. **Empresarios Unidos** ☎ 222–1867. **Pulmitan** ☎ 222–1650. **Tralapa** ☎ 223–5859 or 680–0392.

🔳 Shuttle Van Services **Gray Line Tourist Bus** ☎ 232–3681 or 220–2126 ⊕ www.graylinecostarica.com. **Interbus** ☎ 283–5573 ⊕ www.interbusonline.com.

CAR RENTAL

It's best to stick with the main rental offices in San José, because they have more cars available and you're more likely to reach an English-speaking agent on the phone; some have local satellite offices. Alamo has pickup and car delivery in Liberia. Budget has branches in San José and also 6 km (4 mi) west of Liberia's airport. Economy, Alamo, and Elegante rent cars in Tamarindo; Economy has a good supply of automatic four-wheel-drive vehicles.

🔳 Major Agencies **Alamo** ✉ 2 km (1 mi) north of Liberia airport, Liberia ☎ 668–1111, 800/462–5266 in U.S. ✉ Hotel Diría, main road, Tamarindo ☎ 653–0727. **Budget** ✉ 6 km (4 mi) southwest of Liberia airport, Liberia ☎ 668–1024 or 668–1126 ✉ Hotel Zullymar, main road just past Hotel Diría, Tamarindo ☎ 653–0756. **Economy** ✉ 3½ km

(2 mi) south of Liberia airport, Liberia ☎ 666-2816 or 666-7560 ✉ Main road entering Tamarindo, next to Restaurant Coconut, Tamarindo ☎ 653-0728.
🖪 Local Agencies **Elegante** ✉ 5 km (3 mi) south of Liberia Airport, Liberia ☎ 667-0511 ✉ Pueblo Dorado Hotel, main road as you enter town from north, Tamarindo ☎ 653-0015. **Sol Rentacar** ✉ In front of Hotel El Bramadero, across from Burger King at intersection of Pan-American Highway and entrance to town, Liberia ☎ 666-2222 ✉ Second entrance to Playa Hermosa, beside Aqua Sport ☎ 356-9872.

CAR TRAVEL

The northwest is accessed via the paved two-lane Pan-American Highway (CA1), which begins at the top of Paseo Colón in San José. The bridge across the Río Tempisque, opened in 2003, has cut down travel time considerably to the Pacific beaches south of Liberia and, so far, is not heavily traveled. Ferries continue to run from Puntarenas to Paquera and Playa Naranjo for access to destinations on the Gulf of Nicoya side of the peninsula.

Paved roads run down the spine of the Nicoya Peninsula all the way to Playa Naranjo, with many unpaved and potholed stretches. Once you get off the main highway, the pavement holds out only so far, and then dirt, dust, mud, potholes, and other factors come into play. The roads to Playa Sámara, Playas del Coco, and Ocotal are paved all the way; every other destination requires some dirt-road maneuvering. If you're headed down to the coast via unpaved roads, be sure to get advance information on road conditions. Take a four-wheel-drive vehicle if possible.

If you want to drive around the Nicoya Peninsula, be prepared to spend some serious time in the car. The road to Nicoya's southern tip is partly paved and partly just gravel, and it winds up and down and around various bays. Some roads leading from Liberia to the coast are intermittently paved. As you work your way toward the coast, pay close attention to the assorted hotel signs at intersections—they may be the only indicators of which roads to take to your lodging.

EMERGENCIES

In case of any emergency, dial 911 or one of the numbers below.
🖪 Emergency Services **Fire** ☎ 118. **Police** ☎ 118. **Red Cross Ambulance** ☎ 128.

MAIL & SHIPPING

Surfing the Internet is as popular for tourists here as surfing the waves, so there are plenty of Internet cafés in beach towns. Provincial towns also have cafés catering to locals. Prices range from just over $1 an hour for standard telephone access to $5 an hour for fast satellite connections. The town of Nicoya may be the most wired small town in the country; there are Internet cafés around every corner. In Puntarenas, surf in air-conditioned comfort at Millennium Cyber Café. In Tamarindo, try Internet Café. In Playa Hermosa, sip espresso and surf the Web at Villa Acacia Beach Resort. There's a Café Internet on the main road into Playas del Coco. In Montezuma, be cool in the air-conditioned Surf the Banana Internet Café. In Sámara, check out the Internet and local tours at Tropical Latitude Internet Café. In Nosara, Café de Paris has satellite-connected computer service, plus French pastries, less than 1 km from the waves at Playa Guiones.

Finding a post office in beach towns is almost impossible since most beach areas are not incorporated towns. Post offices are to be found only in Tico communities, but some hotels and businesses in beach towns provide a mail drop-off service. Your best bet is to wait until your return to San José. Cóbano, Liberia, Nicoya, Nosara, Playas del Coco, Puntarenas, Sámara, and Santa Cruz all have post offices; just ask at any business and they will give you directions. In Tamarindo, you can drop off posted mail at Super Tamarindo. In Montezuma, Librería Topsy sells stamps and provides postal drop-off.

🔢 Internet Cafés **Café Internet** ✉ Main road into town, beside Hotel Sol y Mar, Playas del Coco. **Café de Paris** ✉ Entrance to Playa Guiones, Nosara. **Internet Café** ✉ Road to Hotel Pasatiempo, next door to ABC Realty, Tamarindo. **Millennium Cyber Café** ✉ Paseo de Los Turistas, just east of Hotel Tioga, Puntarenas. **Surf the Banana Internet Café** ✉ Main road, next door to El Sano Banano Restaurant, Montezuma. **Tropical Latitude Internet Café** ✉ Behind the Casa del Mar Hotel, Sámara. **Villa Acacia Beach Resort** ✉ Second entrance road to beach, Playa Hermosa.

🔢 Post Offices **Librería Topsy** ✉ Across from school, Montezuma. **Super Tamarindo** ✉ Main road, across from Hotel Diría, Tamarindo.

MONEY MATTERS

ATMS ATMs that accept international bank cards are few and far between in Guanacaste. ATH (A Todas Horas) machines are the most reliable, although even they may be out of cash during peak holiday times. Banco Nacional branches display the Plus logo but aren't always connected to the international system. You can get a cash advance on a Visa card at a bank, but be prepared for a long wait and be sure you have your passport (not a copy) with you. Your best bets for ready cash are the Burger King ATH near Liberia, the Mutual Alajuela ATH in Puntarenas, and the Coopmani ATH in Nicoya.

Branches of Banco Nacional and Banco de Costa Rica can be found in Filadelfia, Liberia, Nicoya, Puntarenas, and Santa Cruz. Banco Nacional also has branches in Cóbano, Playas del Coco, and Jicaral. Banco de Costa Rica is in Playa Flamingo and at the Liberia airport.

🔢 ATM Information **Burger King ATH** ✉ Inter-American Hwy., at entrance to Liberia. **Coopmani ATH** ✉ Main street, beside Fuji Film store, Nicoya. **Mutual Alajuela ATH** ✉ Across from the Ferretería Tung Sing, near central market, Puntarenas.

CURRENCY The best exchange rate is via ATMs, when you can find them. Exchange
EXCHANGE rates at national banks vary daily, and central banking offices in San José are the most efficient. Small-town banks are very busy places, where tellers tend to chat at length with local customers and transactions are slow and paper-intensive. So be prepared for a lengthy wait.

TOURS

In addition to the following major agencies, most hotels can organize guided tours for you. Ríos Tropicales, a high-quality adventure tour company, runs excellent multiday sea-kayaking trips that leave from Curú National Wildlife Refuge and meander among the islands of the Gulf of Nicoya. The company also leads river-rafting trips throughout the country and a float trip in a slow-moving inflatable raft for bird-watchers down Guanacaste's Río Corobicí. Day trips to the idyllic Isla Tortuga in the Gulf of Nicoya are popular, and Calypso Tours has been leading them longer than anyone else. The excellent Horizontes specializes in more independent tours, with as few as eight people, that include four-wheel-drive transport, naturalist guides, and guest lecturers.

A boat service shuttles surfers between Montezuma and Jacó. These tours can easily be arranged by your hotel or by any one of the tour agencies in town. Cocozuma organizes a boat shuttle service to Jacó and has some tours of the area.

⚑ Tour Operators **Calypso Tours** ⊠ C. 36, between Avdas. 5 and 7, San José ☎ 256-2727 🖷 256-6767 ⊕ www.calypsotours.com. **Cocozuma** ⊠ Next to El Sano Banano Restaurant and B&B, Montezuma ☎ 642-0911 ⊕ www.cocozuma.com. **Horizontes** ⊠ 150 m north of Pizza Hut Paseo Colón, San José ☎ 222-2022 🖷 255-4513 ⊕ www.horizontes. com. **Ríos Tropicales** ⊠ 45 m south of Centro Colón on C. 38, San José ☎ 233-6455 🖷 255-4354 ⊕ www.riostropicales.com.

VISITOR INFORMATION

The tourist office in San José has information on Guanacaste and the peninsula. Puntarenas has two tourist offices: La Camera de Turismo is open weekdays 8–noon and 2–5, and weekends when cruise ships are in port; La Oficina de Información Turistica, near the Puntarenas car ferry terminal, provides information daily 8–5.

⚑ Tourist Information **La Camera de Turismo** ⊠ Plaza de las Artesanias, in front of Muelle de Cruceros, Puntarenas ☎ 661-2980. **La Oficina de Información Turistica** ⊠ Near car ferry terminal, Puntarenas ☎ 661-9011.

THE CENTRAL PACIFIC

5

Revised by
David
Dudenhoefer

MUCH OF WHAT DRAWS PEOPLE TO COSTA RICA is encompassed in the Central Pacific region, with its lush tropical forests, palm-lined beaches, and excellent conditions for an array of outdoor activities—all within hours of San José. It's easy to understand why the area has become so popular: its verdant hills, vibrant sea, and soft-sand beaches provide a veritable cornucopia of vacation opportunities.

The region—Carara National Park in particular—is a transition zone between the tropical dry forests of the northwest and the wet forests of the Pacific coast farther to the south. But because most of its woodlands were cut decades ago, the Central Pacific landscape is dominated by steep coffee farms, vast oil-palm plantations, and bright green pastures populated by cows and Cattle Egrets. Manuel Antonio National Park, together with the private reserves of nearby hotels, protects one of the last patches of coastal rain forest in the region, as well as several idyllic, white-sand beaches.

Despite the fact that the region's protected areas are among the smallest in the country, they are rich habitats with an amazing variety of flora and fauna, including such endangered species as the Scarlet Macaw and the Central American Squirrel Monkey. Outside the national parks, there is plenty of forest and wildlife in private reserves, and even on the grounds of many hotels. You can explore that wilderness on guided hikes, horseback tours, or canopy adventures, or you can relax on your balcony, or by the pool at one of more than a dozen hotels in the rain forest, and wait for the birds and monkeys to come to you.

The Central Pacific's forested mountains hold spectacular waterfalls, and several of the rivers flowing out of them are exciting white-water rafting routes. The meandering, muddy Río Tarcoles and Damas Estuary can be explored on boat trips that bring you eye to eye with crocodiles and other wild things. The ocean here is equally diverse, which you can confirm by snorkeling in Manuel Antonio or Punta Leona or by sportfishing off Playa Herradura, Jacó, or Quepos. Area beaches have excellent surfing, and sea-kayaking is a great way to appreciate the rocky coastline between strands.

Exploring Central Pacific Costa Rica

Attractions lie conveniently close to each other, making it easy to combine beach time with forest exploration or marine diversions. Every destination in this chapter is between two and three hours from San José by road. A winding mountain road passes through Atenas on the way to Orotina, from where the Costanera, or coastal road, heads southeast to Tárcoles, Punta Leona, Herradura, Jacó, Hermosa, Esterillos, and Quepos. A narrower, serpentine route connects Quepos to the beaches and national park of Manuel Antonio. The 30-minute flight from San José to Quepos is an excellent option if you have little time or don't want to drive.

About the Restaurants

Restaurants in Manuel Antonio and Jacó serve some of Costa Rica's best meals, from upscale Pacific Rim flavors to traditional Tico fare. Thanks to top-notch fishing, seafood—from fresh-caught dorado and yellowfin tuna to spiny lobster—is the forte of the area's best chefs. In Manuel Antonio, the ambience is often as exotic as the food, with tables set amid tropical foliage, overlooking the sea, or on the beach itself.

The restaurants (all of which are indicated by a ✕) that we list are the cream of the crop in each price category. Properties indicated by a ✕🏨 are lodging establishments whose restaurant warrants a special trip.

About the Hotels

This region has some of the priciest lodgings in the country—upward of $200 for a double during high season—but it is not without its deals. Travelers on a budget can find plenty of doubles for less than $100 and a few decent rooms for less than $50. As a rule, prices drop 20%–30% during the low season (May–mid-December). Though Playas Jacó and Hermosa have plenty of accommodations on the beach, most of Manuel Antonio's hotels are on a hill, a short drive from the beach, where they enjoy splendid views of the coast and jungle.

WHAT IT COSTS				
$$$$	**$$$**	**$$**	**$**	**¢**
RESTAURANTS over $25	$20–$25	$10–$20	$5–$10	under $5
HOTELS over $200	$125–$200	$75–$125	$35–$75	under $35

Restaurant prices are per-person for a main course at dinner. Hotel prices are for two people in a standard double room in high season, excluding service and tax (16.4%).

Timing

The weather in the central Pacific region follows the same dry- and rainy-season weather patterns common to the rest of the Pacific slope, which means lots of sun from December to May and frequent rain from September to November. Since you'll have to share the area with other travelers in the dry season, consider touring the region at another time. The weather tends to be perfect in July and August, with lots of sunny days and occasional light rain.

THE HINTERLANDS

Beaches may be this region's biggest draw, but the countryside holds some splendid scenery, from the steep coffee farms around Atenas to the tropical forests of the lowlands. In the wilderness of Carara National Park and surroundings, you might encounter anything from White-faced Capuchin Monkeys to Collared Aracaris to crocodiles lounging on a riverbank. Because it's an ecological transition zone, the region is extremely diverse biologically, making it a boon for bird-watchers and other wildlife enthusiasts.

Numbers in the text correspond to numbers in the margin and on the Central Pacific Costa Rica and the Quepos & Manual Antonio maps.

Numbers in the text correspond to numbers in the margin and on the Central Pacific Costa Rica map.

If you have 3 days

Head straight for ▣ **Quepos** ❽ ► and hit the beach at ▣ **Manuel Antonio** ❾. If you're driving from San José, be sure to stop at **Carara National Park** ❷ on your way to Manuel Antonio. Rise early the next day to spend the morning exploring **Manuel Antonio National Park** ❿, and enjoy the afternoon horseback riding or relaxing on the beach. Dedicate the third morning to white-water rafting, sea-kayaking, skin diving, surfing, or exploring a private reserve, then catch an afternoon flight back to San José.

If you have 6 days

Spend your first night at one of the lodges near the ▣ **Carara National Park** ❷ ► or ▣ **Tárcoles** ❸. Enjoy some bird-watching, hike to a waterfall, or take a canopy tour. On the second morning, visit the national park; then head to either ▣ **Jacó** ❻ or ▣ **Playa Hermosa** ❼ to get your beach fix. You may want to spend another night here to get into the rhythm of relaxation. On Day 3 or 4, go south to ▣ **Manuel Antonio** ❾ and spend the afternoon horseback riding, sea-kayaking, fishing, or lounging on the beach. Visit **Manuel Antonio National Park** ❿ early on Day 5; then drive back into the mountains to spend your last night in **Atenas** ❶, just 40 minutes from the international airport. Alternately, since Quepos and Manuel Antonio have so much to offer, fly straight there and stay put—you won't get bored.

Atenas

❶ *42 km (26 mi) west of San José.*

National Geographic once listed Atenas as having one of the 12 best climates in the world, and that's pretty much this little town's only claim to fame. In addition to having lovely weather, Atenas is a pleasantly quiet, traditional community that few foreigners visit, despite the fact that it's en route to the Central Pacific beaches. Some well-kept wooden and adobe houses are scattered around the town's pink concrete church and central plaza dominated by royal palms. The hilly countryside that surrounds Atenas is even more attractive, with a mix of coffee farms, cattle ranches, and patches of forest. Just west of town, the road to the coast winds its way down the mountains past spectacular views of coffee farms clinging to steep slopes, with the Pacific in the distance.

Where to Stay & Eat

★ ¢–$ ✕ **Mirador del Cafetal.** An obligatory stop even if you aren't hungry, this open-air restaurant perched next to the road between Atenas and Jacó is a great spot to enjoy the view of steep hillsides covered with coffee plants. The best view is from the bars with tall stools that line the edge of the building, but the wooden tables and chairs might be more comfortable. A mix of Costa Rican and Mexican cuisine is served, including a dozen *bocas* (snacks) such as miniature tamales, black bean purée, and *patacones* (fried, squashed plantain slices). If you're hungry for more, try chicken in a tomato-and-onion sauce or *sopa azteca* (spicy fish soup). Cappuccinos and other coffee drinks are available. The restaurant's own brand of coffee is sold by the pound. ☒ *Road to Jacó, 6 km (3 mi) west of Atenas* ☎ *446–7361* ⚴ *Reservations not accepted.*

¢–$ ✗ **Provence.** As the name suggests, the owner of this little restaurant in an old wooden house near the center of town is from the south of France. She prepares a small selection of nightly specials—no menu—which usually includes a beef, a chicken, and a seafood dish, as well as a few desserts. Seating is available in a tiny garden patio, on the porch, or in rooms decorated with paintings done by the owner, Jaqueline Carcagno. Since this place is basically a one-woman show, the service can be slow when it's crowded, but the food is worth the wait. ☒ *100 m south of Coopeatenas* ☎ *446–8239* ⚴ *Reservations recommended* ➤ *No credit cards* ◷ *Closed Mon. and Tues. No lunch.*

¢ ✗ **C@fé K–puchinos.** On a corner across from the town's palm-shaded central park is this Internet café in an attractive old adobe house. The Spanish owners serve a good selection of breakfasts, sandwiches, and salads, as well as a few full meals such as *camarones a la plancha* (sautéed shrimp) and *salmón en salsa de vino* (salmon in a wine sauce). The owners' nationality is reflected by such menu items as sangria and *tortilla española* (an egg-and-potato dish). ☒ *Across from northwestern corner of central park* ☎ *446–4784* ➤ *No credit cards* ◷ *Closes at 8 PM Apr.–Dec.*

$$ ⌂ **El Cafetal Inn.** A friendly Salvadorean–Colombian couple owns this bed-and-breakfast; they go out of their way to make you comfortable and help with your travel plans. On a hilltop coffee farm, the two-story concrete lodge has comfortable accommodations. The superior tower rooms are larger and have curved windows for panoramic views. Breakfast, which includes home-grown and -roasted coffee, is served on the back patio. It's a 30-minute drive to the airport, which makes this a good, quiet option for a first or last night in the country. ☒ *8 km (5 mi) north of Atenas, Santa Eulalia de Atenas; heading west from San José on highway to Puntarenas, turn left (south) just before bridge 5 km (3 mi) west of Grecia, then follow signs* ✆ *Apdo. 105, Atenas* ☎ *446–5785* 📠 *446–7028* ⊕ *www.cafetal.com* ➥ *12 rooms* ⚴ *Restaurant, fans, pool, bar, laundry service, travel services, no-smoking rooms; no a/c, no room phones, no room TVs* ➤ *AE, MC, V* ⊙⍓ *BP.*

$ ⌂ **Ana's Place.** Trees and flowers fill the large property of Ana's Place, in town. The nicest rooms are in the house, with parquet floors and big windows, but most of these rooms share bathrooms. Smaller cabinas in a concrete building in the backyard are pretty basic, but have private baths, as do the two larger "apartments." There are a small pool and a communal kitchen–dining area under a thatched roof. ☒ *200 m east of AyA (Acuaductos y Acantarrillados, the national water company), behind church* ✆ *Apdo. 105, Atenas* ☎ *446–5785* 📠 *446–7028* ➥ *4 rooms, 4 cabinas, 2 apartments* ⚴ *Fans, pool, laundry service; no a/c, no room phones, no room TVs* ➤ *No credit cards* ⊙⍓ *BP.*

$ ⌂ **Villas de la Colina.** A colorful archway of bougainvillea guides you to rustic quarters at this hilltop retreat in the countryside north of town.

5

Fishing

The sportfishing off Herradura, Jacó, and Quepos is among the best in the world. Year-round billfish makes Quepos a favorite fly-fishing spot. But marlin, sailfish, dorado, black and yellowfin tuna, mackerel, wahoo, snook, and several kinds of snapper and jack can all be found in Central Pacific waters. Marlin fishing is best in October and November. Most species can be found year-round. Tuna are most abundant from May to September. Not a few world records have been broken off the Central Pacific coast. A number of hotels have excellent fishing packages.

Rain Forests

Ecologically, the Central Pacific is in a transition zone between the tropical dry forests of northwest Costa Rica and the rain forests of the southwest. This brings a great diversity of plants and animals, especially birds. Carara National Parks and surroundings is one of the few areas in Costa Rica where you can see the spectacular Scarlet Macaw in the wild, whereas Manuel Antonio is one of only two spots where you're likely to see the rare Central American Squirrel Monkey. The region's wilderness is also home to toucans, parrots, iguanas, vine snakes, coatis, and agoutis. The forests themselves are gorgeous, with massive mahogany, kapok, and tropical cedar trees towering over palms, heliconias, and an array of other plants. Those forests can be explored in the region's two national parks, or any of half a dozen private preserves, such as Punta Leona and Rainmaker. You can hike through those jungles on narrow trails, explore them on horseback tours, or glide through their treetops like the toucans do on one of various canopy tours.

Nightlife

This region may be known for its macaws and monkeys, but the Central Pacific beaches also hold plentiful habitat for lounge lizards and dance-floor felines. Jacó and Manuel Antonio have some of the best nightlife outside of the capital, especially on weekends, when Josefinos (residents of San José) head there in significant numbers. At either beach, the options range from a sunset cocktail to an all-night dance-athon, and include such diversions as casinos, live music, and intimate spots ideal for a romantic meal. And if you can't be bothered to wake up early for bird-watching, you can always party until the birds start to sing.

Water Sports

The beaches of Jacó and Hermosa are synonymous with surfing, and Manuel Antonio gets some decent swells, too, but this region's aquatic diversions don't end there. When the ocean is calm, it holds good snorkeling around Punta Leona, off Playa Escondida, near Jacó, and in front of Playas Manuel Antonio and Biesanz. Certified divers can scuba dive near Manuel Antonio's islands, which can also be explored on a kayak tour. And if you prefer your water flowing, there are two white-water rivers near Quepos—Ríos Naranjo and Savegre—that provide exciting Class II, III, and IV rafting during the rainy months.

Central Pacific
Costa Rica

La Garita

Atenas **1**

Heredia

Puntarenas

San José

Cartago

San Mateo

Orotina

Caldera

27

CA1

CA2

SAN JOSÉ

Paquera

CURÚ
NATIONAL
WILDLIFE
REFUGE

Carara
National
Park

2

Tárcoles **3**

Punta Leona **4**

Playa Herradura **5**

San Marcos

Santa
María

Jacó **6**

CABO BLANCO
STRICT
NATURE
RESERVE

Playa
Hermosa **7**

Cabo Blanco

Quepos **8**

Manuel
Antonio
National
Park

Manuel Antonio **9** **10**

Playa Palo Seco

PACIFIC OCEAN

Playa Espadilla
Punta Catedral
Playa Manuel Antonio
Playa Escondido

Isla Mogote

0   30 miles

0   45 km

Sweeping views of the surrounding countryside and an ample pool—also with a view—are the lodge's best assets, making it a good overnight stop on the way to the beach. The rooms, in two-story structures, are simple but comfortable. The upper rooms cost $10 more but are brighter and have private balconies with hammocks. ⊠ *4 km (2 mi) west and 2 km (1 mi) north of Coopeatenas* ⬭ *Apdo. 165, Atenas* ☎ *446–5015* 🖷 *446–8545* 📠 *6 cabinas* ⛄ *Fans, kitchenettes, pool, horseback riding, laundry service; no a/c, no room phones, no room TVs* ⊟ *No credit cards* ⭐ *BP.*

Carara National Park

❷ *85 km (51 mi) southwest of San José, 43 km (25 mi) southwest of Atenas.*

On the east side of the road between Puntarenas and Playa Jacó, Parque Nacional Carara protects one of the last remnants of an ecological transition zone between Costa Rica's drier northwest and the more humid southwest. It consequently holds a tremendous collection of plants and animals. Much of the 47-square-km (18-square-mi) park is covered with primary forest on steep slopes, where the massive trees are laden with vines and epiphytes. The sparse undergrowth makes wildlife easier to see here than in many other parks, but nothing is guaranteed. If you're lucky, you may glimpse armadillos, basilisk lizards, Blue-crowned Motmots, Chestnut-mandibled Toucans, trogons, coatis, and any of several monkey species. Carara is one of the few places in Costa Rica where you might see Scarlet Macaws.

The first trail on the left shortly after the bridge that spans the Río Tárcoles (a good place to spot crocodiles) leads to a horseshoe-shape lagoon, called *laguna meandrica* (oxbow lake). The small lagoon covered with water hyacinths is home to turtles, crocodiles, and waterfowl such as the northern jacana, roseate spoonbill, and boat-billed heron. It is a two- to four-hour hike from the trailhead to the lagoon. Cars parked at the trailhead have been broken into, so ask at the main ranger station (several miles south of the trailhead) if there is a ranger on duty at the *sendero laguna meandrica* lagoon. If there isn't, you may be able to leave your belongings at the main ranger station, where you can also buy drinks and souvenirs and use the rest room.

Two trails lead into the forest from the parking lot. One short stretch is wheelchair-accessible. A longer trail connects with the Quebrada Bonita loop, which takes two to three hours to hike. The latter can be quite muddy during the rainy months, when you may want rubber boots. Carara's proximity to San José and Jacó means that tour buses arrive regularly in high season, scaring some animals deeper into the forest. Come very early or late in the day to avoid crowds. Bird-watchers can call the day before to arrange admission before the park opens. Camping is not permitted in Carara. ⊠ *Turn left off CA1 for Atenas and follow signs for Jacó; reserve is on left after you cross Río Tárcoles* ☎ *383–9953* 🎫 *$8* 🕐 *Daily 7–4.*

Tárcoles

❸ *90 km (54 mi) southwest of San José.*

The town of Tárcoles doesn't warrant a stop, but it's the departure point for crocodile-watching boat tours up the Río Tárcoles, and is near a spectacular waterfall in a private reserve. Bird-watchers have plenty to focus their binoculars on, because the combination of the transitional forest and adjacent river results in an inordinate diversity of birds within a small area.

If you pull over just after crossing the Río Tárcoles bridge, you can walk back onto it and admire the massive crocodiles usually lounging on the banks (bring binoculars). Be sure to lock your car—vehicles have been broken into here. The entrance to the town of Tárcoles is on the west side of the road, just south of Carara National Park; across the highway is a dirt road that leads to the Hotel Villa Lapas and the waterfall reserve.

Shortly after the entrance to town, the Costanera passes a small beach called **Playa La Pita,** which will provide your first glimpse of the Pacific if you're coming down from the Central Valley. The beach is rocky, and its proximity to the Tárcoles River makes the water murky and unfit for swimming, but it's a nice spot to stop and admire the ocean. La Pita lies within a cove, which means the water is always calm, so local fishermen anchor their boats off its southern end. There are often pelicans diving into the water here, and in the distance, you should be able to discern the southern tip of the Nicoya Peninsula. ⊠ *Costanera, 1 km (½ mi) south of Tarcoles turnoff.*

Manantial de Agua Viva, a 656-foot waterfall on a private reserve next to Carara National Park, flows into 10 natural pools, any of them perfect for a refreshing dip after the hike into the reserve. The forest surrounding the waterfall is home to parrots, monkeys, Scarlet Macaws, and most of the other animals found in the nearby park. A tough 2½-km (1½-mi) trail makes a loop through the woods, passing the waterfall and pools; it takes between 40 minutes and 2 hours to hike, depending on how much bird-watching you do; good physical condition and hiking shoes are needed. ⊠ *Entrance 9 km (5 mi) from the coastal highway, up dirt road that leads to the Hotel Villa Lapas* 🎟 *$10* ⊗ *Daily 8–5.*

Where to Stay & Eat

¢–$$ ✕ **Steve n' Lisa's.** A convenient location, an ocean view, and good food make this roadside restaurant overlooking Playa La Pita a popular pit stop for those traveling between San José and the Central Pacific beaches. Sit on the covered porch, or at one of the concrete tables on the adjacent patio, and enjoy the view of the Gulf of Nicoya through the palm fronds. Choose from a full breakfast menu, or a selection of lunch and dinner entrées that ranges from the humble *casado* (plate of rice, beans, fried plantains, cabbage salad, and fish, chicken, or meat) to a pricy surf and turf. They also have a salad bar and an eclectic list of bocas that includes a chicken quesadilla, three types of *ceviche* (fish, shrimp, or octopus marinated in lime juice), onion rings, and deep-fried cauliflower. ⊠ *Costanera, 1 km (½ mi) south of Tarcoles turnoff* 🕾 *637–0594.*

$$ 📷 **Hotel Villa Lapas.** Tall trees and a stream flowing by make Villa Lapas a great place for nature lovers, as does the series of suspension bridges that wend through the canopy of the hotel's protected forest. Kids enjoy the ample lawns and games. For the adventurous, there is a canopy tour on the property. Rooms are in low concrete buildings with porches and barrel-tile roofs. Though nothing special, they are pleasant enough, with terra-cotta floors, hardwood ceilings, and large baths. ⊠ *Off Costanera, 4 km (2½ mi) after bridge over Tárcoles River* 🏠 *Apdo. 419–4005, Heredia* ☎ *637–0232* 🖷 *637–0227* 🌐 *www.villalapas.com* 💭 *47 rooms* ⚭ *Restaurant, fans, in-room safes, miniature golf, pool, bar, recreation room, shop, laundry service, meeting room; no room TVs* 🖃 *AE, DC, MC, V* 🍴 *FAP.*

Sports & the Outdoors

BOAT TRIPS One of the most popular activities in the area is the river trip up the muddy **Río Tárcoles,** home to massive crocodiles and colorful waterfowl. **Jungle Crocodile Safaris** (☎ 637–0338) runs a boat tour that guarantees close encounters of the crocodilian kind. On the **Crocodile Man Tour** (☎ 637–0426) boat trip you watch your guide feed the crocs.

HIKING Trails in this area can keep you afoot for a couple of days. **Carara National Park** (⊠ Left off CA1 for Atenas and follow signs for Jacó; reserve is on left across Río Tárcoles ☎ 383–9953) has four trails through its rain forest. Admission to the park, which is open daily 7–4, is $8. The **Manantial de Agua Viva** has a steep trail that leads to one of the country's highest waterfalls. You can also visit the Agua Viva waterfall on a horseback tour run by **Complejo Ecológico la Catarata** (⊠ 9 km [5½ mi] up the dirt road to Hotel Villa Lapas ☎ 661–8263).

THE COAST

Along this short stretch of Costa Rica's Pacific Coast from Tarcoles to Manuel Antonio are patches of undeveloped jungle, the popular Manuel Antonio National Park, and some of the country's most accessible beaches. The proximity of these strands to San José leads Costa Ricans and foreigners alike to pop down for quick beach vacations. Surfers have good reason to head for Playas Jacó and Hermosa, because of the consistency of the waves, and anglers and golfers should consider Playa Herradura's links and ocean access. Other travelers may find most of these beaches overrated, or overdeveloped. Manuel Antonio could be accused of the latter, but nobody can deny its spectacular natural beauty.

Punta Leona

❹ *10 km (6 mi) south of Tárcoles, 100 km (60 mi) southwest of San José.*

The 300-hectare (740-acre) private reserve and resort community that surrounds Punta Leona (Lion's Point) is an odd mix of nature, residential development, and vacation spot. Punta Leona's attractions include three beaches and some 500 acres of tropical forest, which is home to much of the same wildlife found in nearby Carara National Park, including the endangered Scarlet Macaw. A series of trails traverse sections of the reserve, which can also be explored on a canopy tour, bird-watching hikes (there's a complimentary hike each morning), and occasional night tours.

Development of this formerly forested cattle ranching area began in the 1980s, when roads were built and the first lots for vacation homes were sold. In 1991, much of the Ridley Scott film *1492: Conquest of Paradise* was shot here, and a hotel was built to accommodate the film's cast and crew. The lush rain forest and unblemished coastline provided a convincing facsimile of the pristine islands of Columbus's Caribbean landfall, and though the area around two of the beaches seen in the movie has since been significantly developed, most of the Punta Leona is as wild as ever, and the beaches remain quite lovely. The only problem is that on weekends in the dry season, the beaches are invaded by crowds of sun worshipers that Columbus couldn't have imagined in his most feverish dreams.

Just behind Playa Mantas is the height of the development, with two restaurants, two bars, several swimming pools, shops, offices, a church, and wide lawns shaded by tropical trees. In addition to a 120-room hotel, Punta Leona has hundreds of homes and a time-share club with more than 2,000 members. This means the beaches can get crowded on weekends. For much of the year, though, they're relatively quiet, and even during the busiest holidays, the forest is empty compared with this region's national parks. One of the refreshing things about Punta Leona is that it has been marketed predominantly to Costa Ricans, which means you can expect to have more interaction with Ticos here than at most of the country's beach resorts.

Playa Blanca is Punta Leona's nicest beach—an ivory crescent lined by Indian almond trees and cropped by rocks—in fact, it's one of the country's most beautiful beaches. To the north of it is the point for which the area is named, on the other side of which is the longer Playa Mantas. In the shade of the coconut palms and Indian almond trees, you'll find dozens of concrete tables and chairs, which fill up with families on weekends, and a snack bar. The rocky points at either end of the beach are good snorkeling areas. ⊠ *2 km (1 mi) south of Hotel Punta Leona reception; 100 m south of Playa Mantas, 2 km (1 mi) by road.*

☺ **Playa Mantas** has grayish sand, but is longer than Playa Blanca—nearly a kilometer (½ mile) long. It is lined by tropical foliage, and though not as calm as Playa Blanca, is usually a safe place to swim. ⊠ *Behind Club Punta Leona, 100 m north of Playa Blanca.*

Narrow **Playa Limoncito** is completely covered with water at high tide. It is Punta Leona's least-visited beach, because there is no road access to it, and it can be reached only at low tide. It is backed by jungle where you might see monkeys, iguanas, or Scarlet Macaws. ⊠ *200 m north of Playa Mantas.*

Where to Stay & Eat

$$$–$$$$
FodorśChoice
★

✕🏨 **Villa Caletas.** Perched on a promontory south of Punta Leona, this collection of elegant rooms sequestered in the jungle has amazing views of the surrounding foliage and sea below. Freestanding suites and villas are gorgeous, but rooms in the main building are far inferior; if you can't afford a suite, at least get a deluxe room. French and Caribbean motifs are combined throughout, with tile floors, framed prints, and cane chairs. France is the predominant influence in the open-air restaurant ($$), which has a spectacular view at sunset, and serves some excellent seafood and beef entrées. The infinity-edge pool is lovely, but tiny, as is the distant, private beach. ☒ *Off coastal highway, 3 km (1½ mi) south of Punta Leona* ☎ *637–0606* 🖷 *637–0404* ⊕ *www.hotelvillacaletas. com* 🖉 *Apdo. 12358–1000, San José* 🖙 *15 rooms, 12 suites, 10 villas* ♻ *Restaurant, fans, in-room safes, minibars, cable TV, pool, exercise equipment, spa, beach, bar, shop, laundry service, concierge, no-smoking rooms* ▤ *AE, DC, MC, V.*

★ **$$** ✕▥ **Hotel Punta Leona.** This collection of concrete bungalows surrounded by rain forest is ½ km (¼ mi) from Playa Mantas, where most of Punta Leona's facilities are located. The bungalows are colorful, with faux-antique furniture, two double beds, and covered porches with views of exuberant tropical gardens. There is a small tile pool and an open-air restaurant nestled in the jungle nearby, where buffet breakfasts and dinners are served. Restaurants near the beach serve lunch and dinner. An hourly shuttle travels between the rooms, restaurants, and beaches. The 2-km (1-mi) jungle hike to Playa Blanca is recommended if you want to see wildlife. ☒ *½ km (¼ mi) east of Clube Punta Leona* ☎ *231–3131 or 661–2414* 🖷 *232–0791* ⊕ *www.hotelpuntaleona.com* 🖉 *Apdo. 8592–1000, San José* 🖙 *108 bungalows, 12 suites* ♻ *3 restaurants, 2 snack bars, in-room safes, refrigerators, cable TV, 4 pools, beach, snorkeling, boating, hiking, volleyball, 3 bars, shops, laundry service, Internet* ▤ *AE, DC, MC, V.*

Playa Herradura

❺ *12 km (7 mi) south of Punta Leona.*

Dark brown, rocky Playa Herradura is one of Costa Rica's least attractive beaches, but its calm ocean and proximity to San José have made it quite popular. Its name, Spanish for "horseshoe," refers to the shape of the deep bay it lies in, which is responsible for its tranquil waters, making it considerably safer for swimming than most of the beaches to its south. The bay, defined by mountainous points, is a pleasant enough sight, though less impressive than the views of Manuel Antonio or Punta Leona. More than a decade of development has resulted in a bit of a dichotomy at Playa Herradura. The southern half of the beach is lined with a mix of restaurants, bars, and humble homes. The northern end, on the other hand, is dominated by the multimillion-dollar Los Sueños Resort, with its stately Spanish-style hotel, Ted Robinson golf course, modern marina, and expanding supply of condos, which make it as much a real estate development as a tourist destination. If sportfishing and golf are your priorities, this is a good option. If you're looking for nature, seclusion, a beautiful beach, or a bargain, it definitely is not.

Where to Stay & Eat

$–$$$$ ✕ **Restaurante El Pelicano.** It may not look like much at first glance, but this open-air restaurant across the street from the beach serves some dishes you'd be hard-pressed to find on other Costa Rican menus. The decor is limited to green-tile floors and yellow tablecloths under a corrugated metal roof, but the street-side tables have decent ocean views. You can start with fish croquettes in a lemon sauce, green pepper stuffed with shrimp and mushrooms, or clams au gratin; then delve into grilled tuna in a mango sauce, corvina in a heart-of-palm sauce, or one of several surf-and-turf options. ⊠ *Playa Herradura* ☎ *637–8910* 🍽 *AE, DC, MC, V.*

$$$$ ✕🏨 **Marriott Los Sueños Beach and Golf Resort.** This palatial, colonial-style building combines modern amenities with Nicaraguan barrel-tile roofing, Guatemalan textiles, and Costa Rican hand-painted tiles. Its rooms, though attractive and some of the country's most expensive, are nothing special compared with those at other hotels in this price range. Rooms have marble baths, watercolors of historic Costa Rica, and tiny balconies. Be sure to get a room with an ocean view, or you'll be contemplating condominiums. The hotel has a gorgeous lobby, an enormous pool with islands and swim-up bars, a golf course, a marina, and various diversions. The restaurant ($–$$$$) selection ranges from Italian to "Nuevo Latino," with delicacies such as saffron shrimp and plantain-crusted red snapper. ⊠ *Playa Herradura* ☎ *630–9000, 800/228-9290 in U.S.* 🖷 *630–9090* ⊕ *www.marriott.com* ⤺ *191 rooms, 10 suites* ☐ *4 restaurants, café, in-room safes, minibars, cable TV, 18-hole golf course, pool, gym, massage, beach, boating, fishing, 2 bars, casino, shops, children's programs (ages 5–15), laundry service, concierge, business services, meeting rooms, travel services, no-smoking rooms* 🍽 *AE, DC, MC, V.*

Jacó

❻ *2 km (1 mi) south of Playa Herradura, 114 km (68 mi) southwest of San José.*

Jacó is primarily the destination of American surfers, Europeans on package tours, and Costa Ricans who flock here on weekends and major holidays. Its proximity to San José and its wide, sandy bay resulted in Jacó's development as one of Costa Rica's first beach resorts several decades ago. More than 50 hotels and cabinas back its long, gray-sand beach, and the mix of restaurants, shops, and hotels lining Avenida Pastor Díaz, the town's main drag, gives it a rather cluttered appearance. From the water, however, the development is mostly hidden behind the coconut palms that line the beach, and forest-covered hills rise in the distance. In addition to sunbathing and surfing, you can take a kayak or canopy tour, go horseback riding or deep-sea fishing, hike through the nearby Carara National Park, or boat up the crocodile-infested Río Tárcoles.

Long, palm-lined **Playa Jacó** is a pleasant enough spot in the morning, but it can burn the soles of your feet on a sunny afternoon. Though the gray sand makes it less attractive than most other Costa Rican beaches, it's a good place to enjoy a sunset. Playa Jacó is popular with surfers for the consistency of its waves. Riptides can make the sea hazardous for swimmers, so don't go in deeper than your waist if the sea is rough. ⊠ *Just east of town.*

Where to Stay & Eat

★ $-$$$ ✕ **Marisquería El Hicaco.** Not many restaurants in Jacó have an ocean view. This one does, along with tables on the beach (in dry season) and some of the best seafood in town. In fact, they serve little else. Tuna, mahimahi, squid, prawns, lobster, and other marine edibles are prepared half a dozen ways, with everything from garlic butter to a shrimp sauce. On Wednesdays, a dinner buffet offers all of the above cooked to order, plus side dishes, beer, wine, and an impressive dessert selection. ⊠ *100 m south and 90 m west of Más x Menos supermarket* ☎ *643–3226* ▭ *AE, DC, MC, V.*

$-$$ ✕ **BBQ Tangeri.** Seafood is the most popular fare at the beach, but when a carnivorous urge hits, this is the place to go in Jacó. The grilled meat selection ranges from pork ribs to *churrasco,* a thick tenderloin cut popular in Argentina—Americans shouldn't expect the kinds of sauce used at BBQs back home; churrasco has none. A number of seafood dishes are served, though marlin is the only fish that's grilled; everything else is sautéed. It's a pleasant enough spot, with high ceilings and lush gardens around the dining areas. ⊠ *Avda. Pastor Diaz, in front of Hotel Tangeri* ☎ *643–3669* ▭ *AE, DC, MC, V* ۞ *Closed Tues. Apr.–Dec.*

★ $-$$ ✕ **El Chalan.** This open-air Peruvian eatery across the street from the beach distinguishes itself from the bulk of Jacó's restaurants with its ocean view and its seafood, whose preparation is more interesting than that of most Costa Rican restaurants, because of Peru's richer culinary tradition. The menu is long on seafood, from the signature ceviche to *picante de camarones* (shrimp in a spicy cream sauce), but it includes some good meat dishes. One caveat: the hot sauce is volcanic. ⊠ *Hotel Balcon del Mar* ☎ *643–2223* ▭ *AE, DC, MC, V.*

$-$$ ✕ **Hotel Poseidon Restaurant.** One of Jacó's best restaurants is in front of the lobby at tiny Hotel Poseidon. They have patio seating, friendly service, good music, and a small selection of inventive dishes that changes every few days. The half-dozen meat and seafood dishes are usually Pacific Rim innovations, such as mahimahi topped with toasted pecans, filet mignon with a balsamic demi-glace, or Thai-style prawns. ⊠ *C. Bohío, 25 m west of main road* ☎ *643–1642* ▭ *AE, MC, V.*

¢-$ ✕ **Rioasis.** With an eclectic menu of Tex-Mex, pastas, and salads, this large place on the main drag is popular with locals and surfers, who head here for cheap eats. Pizza is the best bet: more than two dozen kinds are baked in a wood-burning oven. You can eat on the front patio or under a high roof hung with ceiling fans. There's a long bar in back, a pool table, and a dartboard for after-dinner entertainment. ⊠ *Avda. Pastor Diaz, north of Banco Nacional* ☎ *643–3354* ▭ *AE, MC, V* ۞ *Closed Tues.*

$$$-$$$$ ✕▦ **Club del Mar.** Amid massive trees and gardens at the southern extreme of the beach, this friendly place has some of Costa Rica's best accommodations. A dozen two-story buildings hold *casitas*: spacious one- and two-bedroom apartments with abundant windows that take advantage of the ocean breeze and views of sea and foliage. Green-tile floors, carved hardwoods, and framed prints complement the natural surroundings, and the open design makes air-conditioning optional. Tasteful standard-size rooms with sea-view balconies are perched over the airy bar and restaurant ($-$$), which serves some of Jacó's best din-

Fodor's Choice
★

ners—from chateaubriand to lobster thermidor. ✉ *Costanera, 275 m south of gas station* ⏪ *Apdo. 107–4023* 📠 *643–3194* ⊕ *www.clubdelmarcostarica.com* 🛏 *8 rooms, 22 casitas* ⚬ *Restaurant, fans, in-room safes, kitchens, cable TV, pool, spa, bar, shop, laundry facilities, laundry service, travel services* ⊟ *AE, MC, V.*

$$ 🏨 **Hotel Canciones del Mar.** In addition to one of the most poetic names in Jacó—"Songs of the Sea Hotel"—this hotel has rooms that are among the closest to the ocean in question. Rooms are in a two-story concrete building, with well-equipped kitchenettes and sofas that can be separated from the bedroom with a sliding wooden door. Each room has a small porch overlooking lush gardens and the blue-tile pool. The chalets are slightly larger, and have ocean views. Breakfast and drinks can be enjoyed under a thatched roof next to the beach, or in the shade of palms on the beach itself. ✉ *End of dirt road north of Hotel Tangeri* 🕾 *643–3273* 📠 *643–3296* ⊕ *www.cancionesdelmar.com* ⏪ *Apdo. 86–4023, Garabito* 🛏 *14 rooms, 3 chalets* ⚬ *Restaurant, fans, in-room safes, kitchenettes, pool; no room phones, no room TVs,* ⊟ *AE, MC, V* ⦿ *BP.*

★ $–$$ 🏨 **Hotel Tangeri.** Spread over a verdant lot on the beach, the Tangeri has various lodging options. Of the bright, spacious rooms in two-story concrete buildings, six have ocean views (those with numbers ending in 1, 2, or 3); the rest overlook the palm-shaded lawn. All have white-tile floors and two double beds. Families and small groups can rent chalets, which have kitchenettes and either one bedroom and a sofa bed or three bedrooms. Rates increase slightly on weekends. ✉ *Avda. Pastor Diaz, north of Copey River* 🕾 *643–3001* 📠 *643–3636* ⊕ *www.hoteltangeri.com* ⏪ *Apdo. 622–4050, Alajuela* 🛏 *14 rooms, 13 chalets* ⚬ *2 restaurants, fans, in-room safes, refrigerators, cable TV, 3 pools, volleyball, playground; no a/c in some rooms, no room phones* ⊟ *AE, MC, V* ⦿ *BP.*

★ $ 🏨 **Aparthotel Flamboyant.** This small oceanfront hotel is a good deal, especially if you take advantage of the cooking facilities. Most rooms have kitchenettes, though four on the second floor have cable TV, air-conditioning, and a refrigerator instead. Tiny terraces with chairs overlook a lush garden and pool area, where there's a grill for your use. It's all just a few steps from the beach, and a block east of Jacó's busy main strip. ✉ *100 m east of Centro Comercial Il Galeon* 🕾 *643–3146* 📠 *643–1068* ✆ *flamboya@racsa.co.cr* ⏪ *Apdo. 018–4023, Puntarenas* 🛏 *13 rooms* ⚬ *Fans, in-room safes, some kitchenettes, some refrigerators, pool; no a/c in some rooms, no TV in some rooms* ⊟ *AE, MC, V.*

$ 🏨 **Mar de Luz.** It may be a few blocks from the beach, and it doesn't look like much from the street, but Mar de Luz is a surprisingly pleasant, quiet place. The Dutch owner is dedicated to cleanliness and providing extra amenities, such as the poolside grill, plentiful public areas, and inexpensive tours. Older, pastel-hue rooms have two queen-size beds and small porches; the newer, split-level rooms are a bit larger, with stone walls. ✉ *45 m east of Avda. Pastor Diaz, behind Onyx bar* 📠 *643–3259* ⊕ *www.mardeluz.com* 🛏 *29 rooms, 2 suites* ⚬ *Fans, in-room safes, kitchenettes, cable TV, pool, Ping-Pong, laundry service; no room phones* ⊟ *V.*

¢–$ ▥ **Hotel El Jardín.** Near the northern end of the beach away from Jacó's busy center, El Jardín is just half a block from the sand and surf. Rooms surround a large pool and are shaded by coconut palms. They are simple but clean, with wooden ceilings, small baths, and tiny TVs. They open onto a portico with benches overlooking the pool and gardens. An open-air restaurant in front specializes in grilled items and some Italian dishes. The rates increase 20 percent on weekends. ⊠ *Calle Jardín, 50 m west of Cabinas Antonio* 📠 *643–3050* ➦ *10 rooms* ⚒ *Restaurant, fans, cable TV, pool, laundry service, travel services; no a/c in some rooms, no room phones* 🗖 *AE, DC, MC, V.*

¢ ▥ **La Cometa.** If you want clean, convenient rooms without expensive frills, this place delivers. Across the street from Jacó's strip of souvenir shops and restaurants, La Cometa fills with budget travelers who can usually be found reading or lazing on the long patio that overlooks a parking lot camouflaged by a simple tropical garden. Most rooms have ceiling fans, but air-conditioning costs just a few dollars more. ⊠ *Avda. Pastor Diaz, across from Restaurante Colonial* 📠 *643–3615* ⌖ *Apdo. 116–4023* ➦ *10 rooms, 6 with bath* ⚒ *Fans; no a/c in some rooms, no room phones, no room TVs* 🗖 *No credit cards.*

Nightlife & the Arts

After-dinner spots in Jacó range from restaurants perfect for a quiet drink to loud bars with pool tables to a dance club or a casino. A mix of classic rock and sports on big-screen TVs makes the **Beatles Bar** (⊠ Avda. Pastor Diaz, north of town center 📞 643–2211) a popular hangout for U.S. expats, but its claim to fame is as the pickup spot for Jacó's thriving prostitution scene. The dance club **La Central** (⊠ On the beach, end of the street across from Más x Menos 📞 643–3076) plays a mix of Latin and pop music, and is the only place with air-conditioning. No one arrives before 11 PM, and it stays open until 5 AM. The large **Club Olé** (⊠ Avda. Pastor Diaz, north of the Beatles Bar 📞 643–3226) has a dance floor, pool tables, darts, and other diversions, but rarely gets busy. For a quiet drink, head to **Colonial** (⊠ Avda. Pastor Diaz, across from Il Galeon shopping center 📞 643–3326), a restaurant with a large bar and lots of wicker chairs surrounded by potted plants. The open-air **Filthy McNasty's Bar** (⊠ Avda. Pastor Diaz, 100 m north of Onyx 📞 643–1442) has loud music and frozen fruit drinks. Jacó's only casino is in the **Hotel Amapola** (⊠ 130 m east of the Municipalidad government building 📞 643–2255), on the south end of town. One of the most popular spots with the young set is the second-floor **Onyx** (⊠ Avda. Pastor Diaz, across from Hotel Tangeri 📞 643–3911), which has five pool tables, darts, and a large bar.

Sports & the Outdoors

CANOPY TOURS **Canopy Adventure Jacó** (📞643–3271) takes you sliding along cables strung between 12 platforms high in trees in the hills southeast of Jacó, some of which have views of the coast. In a private reserve east of Jacó, the **Waterfalls Canopy Tour** (📞 643–3322) allows you to glide between platforms in tropical trees while enjoying a monkey's-eye view of the rain forest and waterfalls.

HANG GLIDING — For a pelican's-eye view of the Pacific coastline, you can take a tandem hang-gliding flight, or fly in a three-seat ultralight with **Hang Glide Costa Rica** (☎ 643–1569), which has an airstrip south of Playa Hermosa.

HORSEBACK RIDING — **Horse Tours at Hacienda Agujas** (☎ 643–2218 or 838–7940) runs late afternoon horseback tours on a cattle ranch north of Jacó that include a trail ride through the rain forest and down a beach.

KAYAKING — **Kayak Jacó** (☎ 643–1233) runs sea-kayaking tours for novices and seasoned adventurers. Owner Neil Kahn also arranges half-day outrigger-canoe trips to secluded Jacó area beaches.

SURFING — Jacó has several beach breaks, all of which are best around high tide. The waves are even better at nearby Playa Escondida, which is accessible only by boat. Surfboard-toting tourists abound in Jacó, but you don't need to be a bona fide surfer dude to enjoy the waves—there are several places that rent boards, a surfing school gives lessons, and the swell is often small enough for beginners. If you plan to spend more than a week surfing, but don't have a board, it might be cheaper to buy a used board and sell it before you leave. However, if you don't have much experience, don't go out when the waves are really big—Jacó sometimes gets very powerful swells, which result in dangerous rip currents.

Surfing lessons for all ages available through the **Academia de Surfing** (☎ 643–1948) include board rental, transportation, and lunch. **Mother of Fear** (✉ Avda. Pastor Diaz, south of Hotel Tangeri ☎ 643–2001) has the best selection of used surfboards in the country. **Surf Shop Walter** (✉ Avda. Pastor Diaz, south of the bridge ☎ 643–1056) sells boards and repairs dings.

SWIMMING — It's no coincidence that Jacó is so popular with surfers; this beach often has big waves, and big waves mean dangerous rip currents. If the ocean is really rough, stay on the beach—dozens of swimmers have drowned at Jacó over the years. If the waves are small, this can be a good place for body surfing, but only if you're a strong swimmer. If you do get caught in a rip current, don't panic, and don't try to swim against it—swim parallel to shore, and once you feel that you've left the current safely behind you, swim back to the beach. The important thing to do in such a situation is avoid fighting the current and, if a wave is about to break on top of you, dive deep underneath it.

When the ocean is calm, you can swim just about anywhere along Jacó Beach. You will, however, want to avoid its northern and southern extremes, and the areas around any of several small rivers that flow into the ocean, since the beach and ocean bottom are littered with rocks there.

Shopping

Souvenir shops are crowded along the main street at the center of town along with jewelry vendors who set up shop wherever they can find a spot. Most of the goods are similar to what you'll find in San José shops, at slightly elevated prices. **Cocobolo** (✉ Avda. Pastor Diaz, next to Banana Café ☎ 643–3486) sells woodwork, jewelry, T-shirts, bags, books, hammocks, and other souvenirs. The spacious **El Cofre** (✉ Avda. Pastor Diaz, across from Más x Menos ☎ 643–1912) mostly sells furniture,

LONG WAVES, SWELL BREAKS

N THE MID-1970S, an article in Surfing magazine spread the word about Costa Rican surfing, divulging a well-kept surfer secret. American and European surfers started arriving soon after, and the flood has increased every year. With two coasts to surf, you are guaranteed year-round waves that, although not the size of Hawaiian waves, are consistently long and nicely shaped. Riptides are a frequent problem, so be wary. And with the exception of the beaches at Jacó and Manuel Antonio, lifeguards are rarely found.

The beaches between Quepos and Manuel Antonio have steady waves—a good choice for intermediate surfers. Manuel Antonio also has surf rental shops. Playa Naranjo in Santa Rosa National Park on the Pacific Coast has one of the best breaks around and draws surfers eager to experience long tubes at Witch Rock. Farther south in Playa Tamarindo

and Junquillal, the biggest waves break April through October. On the Nicoya Peninsula, Boca de Barranca and Playa Dona Ana have excellent facilities for the surfers who flock there May through December. Playas Jacó and Hermosa host an annual international surfing competition in August, and Hermosa has a strong beach break for the pros.

If you plan to travel with your board, check out airline policies before you depart. SANSA will not allow boards longer than 7 feet on domestic flights. A number of carriers, including United, Delta, and Continental, enforce "excess baggage embargoes" during some peak travel periods (normally November 15–January 15, Easter, and parts of the summer) when they disallow surfboards as checked luggage.

but has some Guatemalan masks and other interesting decorative items. Both locations of **Guacamole** (✉ Il Galeon shopping center, Avda. Pastor Diaz ✉ Across the street from Restaurante Pancho Villa ☎ 643-3297) have lovely locally produced batik clothing. **Padang** (✉ Avda. Pastor Diaz, near Banana Café ☎ 643-3486) sells everything from jewelry and wood crafts to beachwear and surfboards.

Playa Hermosa

❼ 5 km (3 mi) south of Jacó, 113 km (70 mi) southwest of San José.

Just over the rocky ridge that forms the southern edge of Jacó is Playa Hermosa, a swath of gray sand stretching southeast as far as the eye can see. Unlike its *tranquilo* northern neighbor of the same name, this southern belle has jaw-dropping surf breaks and caters to a much younger crowd. The beach's northern end is very popular with surfers. Because of its angle, it often has waves when Jacó and other spots are flat. If you're not a surfer, Hermosa's beach holds little charm: its gray sand is scorchingly hot in the afternoon, and frequent rip currents make it unsafe to swim when the waves are big. It does, however, have several nice hotels, and outdoor options for nonsurfers, such as horseback and canopy tours in the nearby forested hills, or ultralight and hang-gliding flights along the coast. From August to December, Olive Ridley Turtles nest on the beach, on nights when the moon is small.

Where to Stay & Eat

¢–$ ✕ **Jungle Surf Cafe.** This humble eatery next to the Costanera serves some of Hermosa's best food. Seating is on a patio shaded by tropical trees, with a view of the road and soccer field. Breakfasts are hearty, and the eclectic lunch selection ranges from shish kebabs to fish sandwiches. The dinner menu changes nightly, but usually includes fresh tuna and mahimahi, and beef and chicken prepared with inventive sauces or glazes. The appetizer and dessert menus are short but fresh, and the prices are quite palatable. It's a BYOB establishment, but you can carry drinks down from a nearby bar. ⊠ *Costanera, north of soccer field* ☎ *643–1945* ▭ *No credit cards.*

★ $$ ✕▭ **The Backyard.** Surfers are the main clientele at this two-story concrete hotel on the beach. Rooms have high ceilings, tile floors, and sliding-glass doors that open onto balconies and terraces, most of which have good views of Playa Hermosa. Second-floor rooms have better views, as do the two corner suites with separate bedrooms and large balconies—they're a good deal for small groups. The open-air bar and restaurant next door serves burgers, Tex-Mex treats, fresh fish, and a few other dinner entrées. It's a popular nightspot, especially on Wednesday and Friday—"ladies night." ⊠ *Costanera, southern end of town* ✆ *Apdo. 132–4023, Jacó* ☎🖷 *643–1311* ⊕ *www.backyardhotel.com* ☞ *6 rooms, 2 suites* ⚭ *Restaurant, fans, in-room safes, cable TV, minibars, pool, bar, massage, laundry service, travel services; no room phones* ▭ *AE, DC, MC, V.*

$–$$ ▭ **Hotel Fuego del Sol.** Most rooms in this two-story white stucco building just behind the beach overlook a lawn shaded by palms and other foliage, and a large blue-tile pool with a swim-up bar, but the four closest to the beach have ocean views. They all have tile floors, wall paintings, small balconies, and one single and one queen-size bed. The open-air restaurant is right next to the beach, where hammocks and concrete tables are shaded by Indian almond trees. ⊠ *100 m north of soccer field's northwest corner* ☎ *643–3737* 🖷 *643–3736* ⊕ *www. fuegodelsolhotel.com* ☞ *18 rooms, 3 apartments* ⚭ *Restaurant, cable TV, pool, bar, laundry service, business services, meeting room, travel services* ▭ *AE, DC, MC, V* ◉ *BP.*

★ $ ▭ **Casa Pura Vida.** Small, elegant, and friendly, Casa Pura Vida isn't exclusive; rather it offers enough privacy to please a millionaire at a working man's rates. The two-story, Spanish-style building has just three apartments, each with two bedrooms and a kitchenette. The second-floor apartment has an ocean view, whereas the two downstairs open onto a large patio with a green-tile pool and tables and chairs under a barrel-tile roof. The beach is just across the lawn. Perks such as filtered water, a fully equipped communal kitchen, and a charming owner make this one of Costa Rica's great deals. ⊠ *Costanera, 100 m south of soccer field* ☎🖷 *643–2039* ⊕ *www.casapuravida.com* ☞ *3 apartments* ⚭ *Fans, room safes, kitchenettes, cable TV, pool, massage, playground, laundry service, travel services* ▭ *AE, MC, V.*

¢-$ 🏨 **Vista Hermosa.** This older hotel on the beach is popular with Costa Rican families, who pack its larger rooms, which sleep six to eight, though it has a variety of accommodations. The rooms and restaurant surround two pools shaded by large tropical trees a stone's throw from the surf. Most rooms are in a two-story building that is a bit dog-eared, but there are two smaller, inexpensive rooms (with shared toilet and shower) in a separate building just below it. ✉ *Costanera, 150 m south of soccer field* 📞 *643–3422* ⊕ *www.olabonita.com* 🛏 *12 rooms* 🛎 *Restaurant, fans, kitchenettes, cable TV, 2 pools, billiards, Ping-Pong, laundry service, travel services; no room phones* ▭ *AE, MC, V* ◎| *BP.*

Sports & the Outdoors

CANOPY TOUR **Chiclets Tree Tour** (✉ West of Costanera, ½ km [¼ mi] north of Hermosa 📞 643–1880) has four guided tours daily that take you through the rainforest canopy on cables strung between platforms perched high in a dozen trees, where you have views of tropical foliage, wildlife, and the nearby coast.

HANG GLIDING & ULTRALIGHT FLIGHTS **Hang Glide Costa Rica** (✉ A few miles south of town 📞 643–1569) leads tandem hang-gliding tours and flights along the coast in a three-seat, ultralight plane.

HORSEBACK RIDING If you tire of surf and sand, consider a horseback tour with **Discovery Horseback** (📞 643–7550), which leads tours through the nearby mountains and on the beach. **Horse Tours at Hacienda Agujas** (📞 643–2218, 838–7940) runs late afternoon rides on a cattle ranch north of Jacó that head through a forest good for bird-watching and down a nearby beach.

SURFING Most people who bed down at Playa Hermosa are here for the same reason—the waves that break just a shell's toss away. One of the country's most consistent surf spots, Hermosa often has waves when other beaches are flat. There are half a dozen beach breaks scattered along the beach, but the surf is always best around high tide. Because it is a beach break, though, the waves here often close out, especially when the surf is big. If you don't have much experience, don't go out when the waves are really big—Hermosa sometimes gets very powerful swells, which result in dangerous rip currents. You can rent, repair, and purchase boards in nearby Jacó.

Quepos

▶ ❽ *23 km (14 mi) south of Parrita, 174 km (108 mi) southwest of San José.*

With a population of about 15,000, Quepos is the largest, most important town in this corner of Costa Rica. It owes its name to the tribe that inhabited the area when the first visiting Spaniard, Juan Vásquez de Coronado, rode through the region in the mid-1500s. It's not certain whether those Indians were called Quepos or Quepoa, but we do know that they lived by a combination of farming, hunting, and fishing until the violence and disease that accompanied the Spanish conquest wiped them out.

For centuries after the conquest, the town of Quepos barely existed, but in the 1930s, the United Fruit Company put it on the map by building a banana port and populating the area with workers from other parts of Central America. The town thrived for nearly two decades, until Panama disease decimated the banana plantations in the late 1940s. The fruit company then switched to (less lucrative) oil palms, and the area slipped into a prolonged depression. Only since the 1980s have tourism revenues lifted the town out of its slump, a renaissance owed to natural causes: the beauty of the nearby beaches and Manuel Antonio National Park. The town today, though still a bit seedy because of the vestiges of its banana-port past, draws a number of expats for its world-famous sportfishing, laid-back pace, 24-hour bars, and party atmosphere.

The forests immediately to the north and east of Quepos were destroyed half a century ago, and that landscape is now dominated by oil palm plantations. But the rain forests of Manuel Antonio begin just south of town, and some 10 km (6 mi) to the east is the massive Talamanca Mountain Range, which holds one of the largest expanses of wilderness in Central America.

Spread over Fila Chota, a lower ridge of the Talamanca Range 22 km (13 mi) northeast of Quepos, is the private nature reserve of **Rainmaker,** which protects more than 1,500 acres of lush and precipitous forest. The lower part of the reserve can be visited on guided tours from Manuel Antonio, or as a stop on your way to or from Quepos. Tours begin at 8:30 and 12:30, and can include lunch. There are two tours available: a walk up the valley of the Río Seco, which includes a dip in a pool at the foot of a waterfall; or a hike into the hills above the waterfall and over a series of suspension bridges strung between giant tropical trees. The reserve is home to most of the species found in Costa Rica, and you may spot birds here that you won't find in Manuel Antonio. It isn't as good a place to see animals as the national park, but Rainmaker's forest is different from the park's—more lush and precipitous—and the view from its bridges is impressive. It's best to visit Rainmaker in the morning, since—true to its name—it often rains there in the afternoon. ⊠ *15 km (9 mi) north and 7 km (4 mi) east of Quepos* ☏ *777–3565* 🖳 *$35* ⊙ *Mon–Sat, 8–4.*

Where to Stay & Eat

★ **$–$$$** ✕ **El Gran Escape.** A favorite with sportfishermen ("You hook 'em, we cook 'em"), the Great Escape is the best place for seafood in this area. The menu is dominated by marine entrées, from shrimp scampi to blackened tuna, but you can also get hearty burgers and a small selection of Mexican food. Seating is scattered between an old wooden building and a large annex. Next door is a small bar that draws young crowds late into the night. ⊠ *Kitty-corner from Banco Nacional* ☏ *777–0650* ▭ *AE, MC, V, DC* ⊙ *Closed 2 wks in June.*

$–$$ ✕ **La Lanterna.** One of the best Italian restaurants outside of the San José area, La Lanterna has a healthy selection of pastas, seafood, and meat dishes, as well as 18 types of pizza, baked in a wood oven out front. In addition to many Italian standards, the menu includes such treats as *penne mari e monti* (with shrimp and Gorgonzola) and *filetto pomodoro e olive* (mahimahi with tomato and olives). Tables covered with white cloths are distributed along the sidewalk of this quiet corner, and beneath the ceiling fans inside, where there's usually Italian pop music playing. ⊠ *Southwest corner of Quepos waterfront* ☎ 777–0395 ⊟ *AE, MC, V, DC.*

¢–$ ⊞ **Hotel Malinche.** The older rooms on the second floor of this centrally located wooden building are cooled by ceiling fans and have small baths. They are also cheaper than the bulk of Manuel Antonio's rooms. A concrete annex holds larger, newer, more expensive rooms with white-tile floors, air-conditioning, and cable TV. Since there are comparable rooms in Manuel Antonio for the same price, but close to the beach, this place is recommended only when those hotels are full. ⊠ *½ block west of Quepos bus station* ☎☎ *777–0093* ✎ *hotelmalinche@racsa. co.cr* ⤴ *29 rooms* ⌂ *Fans, laundry service; no a/c in some rooms, no TV in some rooms* ⊟ *No credit cards.*

Nightlife

The place for dancing is **El Arco Iris** (⊠ Over the estuary north of the bridge ☎ 777–0449), which gets packed after midnight on weekends and holidays. The music is a mix of salsa, merengue, reggae, and pop. **Basarno Bar** (⊠ Second floor of a corner building one block north of El Gran Escape restaurant ☎ 849–3314) is a popular spot with locals, offering live music most nights. American expats often congregate at centrally located **Dos Locos** (⊠ Avda. Central at C. Central ☎ 777–0400) to listen to live music or people-watch. There is a small casino on the ground floor of the **Hotel Kamuk** (⊠ Across the street from the waterfront ☎ 777–0811). The hot spot with younger tourists is **Sargento Garcia** (⊠ Southern end of Calle Central ☎ 777–2960), where DJs spin reggae, Latin rock, and other popular sounds.

Sports & the Outdoors

HIKING A complement to exploring the forests of Manuel Antonio is the half-day tour to the 1,500-acre private reserve of **Rainmaker** (⊠ Office across from Banco Nacional, Quepos ☎ 777–3565), in the mountains 22 km (13 mi) south of Quepos. The guided hike takes you through pristine rain forest and past waterfalls on well-maintained trails and narrow suspension bridges high in the forest canopy.

HORSEBACK **Finca Valmy Tours** (⊠ Villa Nueva ☎ 779–1118) runs half-day horseback
RIDING tours through the forested mountains above Villa Nueva, east of Manuel Antonio, which include swimming in a pool below a waterfall and lunch.

Manuel Antonio

❾ *3 km (2 mi) south of Quepos, 179 km (111 mi) southwest of San José.*

You need merely reach the top of the forested ridge that Manuel Antonio's hotels are perched upon to understand why it is one of Costa Rica's most popular destinations. The first glimpse of that sweeping view—beaches, jungle, and shimmering Pacific dotted with rocky islets—confirms its reputation. The unassuming town of Manuel Antonio is spread over the back of the ridge that separates Quepos from Manuel Antonio National Park, and the road to the south of town is lined with restaurants and hotels that capitalize on their proximity to paradise. The best hotels are near the top of the hill, or on its southern slope, which af-

Quepos &
Manuel
Antonio

KEY
❶ *Restaurants*
③ *Hotels*

fords them amazing views of the rain forest, beaches, and offshore islands. The only problem with staying in one of those hotels is that you'll
need to drive, or take public transportation to and from the beach and
national park, a mere 10 minutes away. There are also a few good hotels at the bottom of the hill, which lack the view, but are a short walk
from the beach.

Nearly the entire ridge is covered with thick foliage, and there is more
rain forest on private land here than in Manuel Antonio National Park.
This means you are likely to see many of the animals the park is famous
for around the area's hotels and restaurants, perhaps even from the balcony of your room or from your breakfast table. It also means that local
landowners play an important role in conserving the area's flora and
fauna, especially the rare Central American Squirrel Monkey, or *mono
tití,* which is found only here, on the Osa Peninsula, and in a couple of
isolated spots in Panama. Though the construction of hotels and other
buildings has altered the natural landscape, the forest surrounding those
structures has largely been left intact, and the wildlife seems to have grown
used to the development. The greatest danger most animals face is the
traffic that flows between Quepos and Manuel Antonio, which is why
local conservationists have strung ropes over the road between large trees,

so that monkeys can cross the street without risking their simian necks. The conservation group **ASCOMOTI** (⊕ www.ascomoti.org) is working with local landowners to protect the titís by preserving forest corridors between the area's remaining islands of wilderness.

One private preserve that you can visit is **Fincas Naturales,** which stretches east from the road over the ridge near the Hotel Sí Como No. A footpath winds through part of this reserve's 30-acre rain forest, and naturalist guides will identify birds and explain some of the forest's myriad ecological relationships. The reserve is home to three kinds of monkeys, plus iguanas, motmots, toucans, tanagers, and large rodents called agoutis. Fincas Naturales also has a butterfly garden and a small botanical garden, and offers a variety of guided walks, the first of which starts at 6:30 AM for bird-watching, and the last of which is a nighttime jungle trek that begins at 5:30 PM. ⊠ *Entrance across street from Sí Como No Hotel* ☎ *777–0850* ☑ *$15–$35, depending on the tour* ☉ *Daily 6:30–5:30.*

As the road approaches the national park, it skirts the lovely, forest-lined beach of **Playa Espadilla,** which stretches for more than a mile north from the rocky crag that marks the park's border to the base of the ridge. One of the most popular beaches in Costa Rica, Playa Espadilla fills up with sunbathers, surfers, volleyball players, strand strollers, and sand-castle architects on dry-season weekends and holidays, but for most of the year, it is surprisingly quiet. Even during the busiest days, it is long enough so that you can escape the crowd, which tends to gather around the restaurants and lounge chairs near its southern end. Though it is often safe for swimming, beware of rough seas, which create deadly rip currents.

Where to Stay & Eat

$–$$ ✕ **Barba Roja.** Near the top of the hill, with a sweeping view of the sea and jungle, Barba Roja is one of this town's oldest and most popular restaurants. Hardwoods furnish the open-air dining room and the view compensates for the sparse decoration. It's a great spot for breakfast, and the lunch options include a fish burger and various tasty sandwiches. The best dinner options are tuna, mahimahi, or one of the daily seafood specials. The view is most impressive at sunset, when the bar fills up for a happy hour lighted by crepuscular colors. There's often live jazz on Sundays. ⊠ *Main road, top of hill* ☎ *777–0331* ☰ *AE, MC, V* ☉ *No lunch Mon.*

$–$$ ✕ **Karolas.** In the forest just below Barba Roja, with tables on several
Fodor's Choice patios surrounded by candles and greenery, Karolas is easily Manuel An-
★ tonio's most intimate dinner spot. At breakfast and lunch, it compensates for the lack of an ocean view with high-quality cuisine and close contact with nature. The most popular dishes are fresh tuna and mahimahi, but the tenderloin, ribs, Caribbean chicken, and Tex-Mex items are also top-notch, as are the desserts—leave room for a slice of macadamia pie. ⊠ *Down steep driveway south of Barba Roja* ☎ *777–1557* ☰ *AE, MC, V.*

$–$$ ✕ **Mirador Mi Lugar.** This open-air restaurant on a narrow ridge west of town is a popular spot for a sunset cocktail, especially from Thursday through Saturday, when traditional marimba music is performed. A number of bocas are available to accompany your drinks, such as *pinchos* (sticks of grilled chicken or beef, served with barbecue sauce), and there's a small dinner menu that includes fresh fish prepared to order, filet mignon, and a shrimp brochette. ⊠ *Down dirt road 1 km (½ mi) west of main road from Amigos del Río* ☎ *777–5120* ▤ *AE, DC, MC, V.*

$–$$ ✕ **Restaurante Mar Luna.** It's just a simple wooden restaurant propped on the hillside, but Mar Luna is packed on most nights. The decor is limited to illuminated plastic fish, ceramic mobiles, and colorful tablecloths, but it's the fresh seafood that draws the crowd. Starters range from sashimi to seafood soup, and the most popular entrées are grilled fish with peppers and onions, shrimp scampi, lobster, and a *mariscada* (seafood platter) that could easily feed two. ⊠ *130 m north of Manuel Antonio Elementary School* ☎ *777–5107* ▤ *AE, DC, MC, V.*

¢–$$ ✕ **Mar y Sombra.** You haven't been to Manuel Antonio unless you've contemplated the sea from one of the circular concrete tables in the sand at Mar y Sombra. The food may not win any awards, but it's hard to top the view of Playa Espadilla and the island-studded sea and the decor, a roof of Indian almond trees and thick lianas draped with moss, ferns, and orchids. You can get *gallo pinto* (rice with black beans) at breakfast and casados for lunch, but the best bet is the fresh dorado and other seafood. Even if you don't eat, be sure to have a drink here, preferably at sunset. ⊠ *Playa Espadilla* ☎ *777–0003* ▤ *AE, MC, V.*

¢–$$ ✕ **Marlin Restaurant.** This two-story concrete restaurant on a corner across the street from the beach makes up for its obstructed ocean view by serving high-quality food at reasonable prices. It's a convenient place to grab breakfast after an early morning hike through the park—be it banana pancakes or a *típico,* with eggs and gallo pinto. The lunch and dinner menu ranges from the ubiquitous arroz con pollo to sashimi, fried shrimp, and grilled mahimahi. The best place to sit is at the picnic tables with umbrellas in the front garden, which is nicely lighted at night. ⊠ *On corner across from bus stop* ☎ *777–1134* ▤ *AE, DC, MC, V.*

¢–$ ✕ **Café Milagro.** The only place in town that serves fresh-roasted coffee, Café Milagro doubles as a souvenir shop and meeting place. Aside from the Latin music, the atmosphere is decidedly North American, as is the menu of bagels, breakfast burritos, and banana bread. The consistently good breakfasts are available all day, but an inventive selection of sandwiches is also served. Tables on the front porch overlook the road, but there's also seating in the back garden. They have a sister locale in Quepos, just south of the bridge. ⊠ *Top of hill, across from road to Hotel Parador* ☎ *777–0794* ▤ *AE, MC, V.*

$$$$ ✕▦ **Makanda by the Sea.** Ocean breezes waft through the spacious villas of this secluded rain forest retreat. Villa rooms, which are among the country's best (and most expensive), have stone floors, colorful fabrics that complement the natural surroundings, and hypnotic views of the jungle-framed Pacific. Smaller studios below have inferior views; the same money will get you a better view at another hotel. Breakfast is delivered to your room, and the open-air restaurant ($–$$$), next to a multicolored, infinity-edge pool, serves inventive lunches and dinners. Such treats as shrimp in a ginger sauce and seafood fettuccine make this a good dinner option even if you stay elsewhere. ⊠ *1 km (½ mi) west of La Mariposa* ☎ *777–0442* ▤ *777–1032* ⊕ *www.makanda.com* ⇆ 6

Fodor's Choice
★

villas, 5 studios △ Restaurant, fans, in-room safes, kitchenettes, mini-bars, pool, spa, beach, laundry service, concierge; no a/c in one studio, no kids under 15 ⊟ *AE, MC, V* ⊖| *BP.*

★ ¢–$ ✕▦ **Hotel Vela Bar.** Abutting the jungle a mere 100 yards from Playa Espadilla, this low-key hotel has rooms of varying size and amenities at competitive rates. Though small, the rooms are attractive, with terra-cotta floors, white-stucco walls decorated with Guatemalan fabrics, and covered porches overlooking the hotel's gardens. The casita sleeps four. The restaurant ($), beneath a conical, thatched roof, is popular for its ample selection of entrées that are rare on Manuel Antonio menus, such as chicken marsala, fish fillet in caper sauce, and various vegetarian dishes. ⊠ *Up side road from Soda Marlin* ☎ *777–0413* 🖷 *777–1071* ⊕ *www.velabar.com* 🛏 *8 rooms, 1 casita, 2 apartments* △ *Restaurant, fans, in-room safes, bar, laundry service, Internet, travel services; no a/c in some rooms, no room phones, no room TVs* ⊟ *AE, MC, V.*

$$$–$$$$ ▦ **La Mariposa.** The sweeping panorama of verdant hills, the aquama-
Fodor'sChoice rine Pacific, and offshore islands at La Mariposa is the best view in town.
★ Accommodations range from standard rooms overlooking the rain forest to bright suites with large balconies and gorgeous views. All rooms are spacious, with pale, hand-carved furniture and large baths. Suites, villas, and deluxe rooms are in a series of buildings between the jungle and gardens ablaze with bougainvillea. A four-story tower above the lobby and restaurant holds long junior suites with semiprivate balconies. Those on the top (4th) floor have vertiginous views, but at this writing, there is no elevator. ⊠ *Top of hill, on right* ⊕ *www.hotelmariposa. com* ☎ *777–0355, 800/416–2747 in U.S.* 🖷 *777–0050* 🛏 *40 rooms, 18 suites, 3 apartments* △ *Restaurant, some in-room safes, some kitch-enettes, pool, 2 bars, shop, laundry service, concierge, Internet; no room TVs* ⊟ *AE, DC, MC, V* ⊖| *BP.*

$$$ ▦ **Hotel Sí Como No.** Designed to do as little damage to the forest as pos-sible, this eco-friendly place uses partial solar power, energy-efficient air-conditioning, and very little hardwood. Concrete painted to resemble bamboo and palm trees may evoke Disneyland, but the forest and ocean views are 100 percent Costa Rica. Rooms are in two-story concrete build-ings of varying sizes; all have tile floors, colorful fabrics, wicker furni-ture, and balconies. Request a room away from the road, and ask for a deluxe room for a sea view. Two pools—one for adults only—have cascades, swim-up bars, and adjacent restaurants. A free shuttle heads to the beach and park hourly. ⊠ *Top of hill, just south of Villas Nicolás* ☎ *777–0777* 🖷 *777–1093* ⊕ *www.sicomono.com* 🛏 *42 rooms, 18 suites* △ *2 restaurants, fans, in-room safes, some kitchenettes, minibars, 2 pools, hot tub, spa, bar, cinema, shop, laundry service, concierge, Internet, meet-ing rooms; no room TVs* ⊟ *AE, MC, V* ⊖| *BP.*

★ $$–$$$ ▦ **Costa Verde.** You're likely to see monkeys, iguanas, and all kinds of birds in the forest surrounding this extensive hotel's buildings, which are scattered over the hillside up the road from the beach. Studios in Building A are spacious, with large balconies and screened walls that let the breeze through. Those in the other buildings are smaller, but can be closed and air-conditioned. Splurge for a "plus," which means you'll have an ocean view. Cheaper efficiencies are a mixed lot—only those in

Building D, in the jungle overlooking the sea, are recommended. The Anaconda Restaurant, which has a great view, is quite good. ⊠ *South slope of hill, on left* ☎ *777–0584* 🖷 *777–0560* ⊕ *www.hotelcostaverde. com* ↔ *56 rooms* ⚭ *2 restaurants, fans, kitchenettes, cable TV in some rooms, 3 pools, 2 bars, laundry service, Internet; no a/c in some rooms, no room phones, no TV in some rooms* 🖃 *AE, DC, MC, V.*

$$–$$$ 🎞 **Villas Nicolás.** There's a certain serenity to the rooms in these Mediterranean-style villas. Narrow walkways between whitewashed, garden-lined villas lead to attractive split-level rooms built on a hillside. Rooms on the upper levels have Pacific views, lower-level rooms have jungle views, and those in the lower left corner overlook the hotel next door. Though each unit is decorated differently, all have terra-cotta floors and balconies, some of which are large enough to hold a table, chairs, and hammock. The small restaurant by the pool serves breakfast and dinner. ⊠ *Top of hill, after La Mariposa* ☎ *777–0481* 🖷 *777–0451* ⊕ *www.villasnicolas.com* ↔ *18 rooms* ⚭ *Restaurant, fans, in-room safes, some kitchenettes, pool, laundry service, travel services; no a/c in some rooms, no room TVs* 🖃 *AE, DC, MC, V.*

$–$$ 🎞 **Hotel and Cabinas Playa Espadilla.** The simple but spacious rooms in the hotel have big windows and are across the lawn from a blue-tile pool, adjacent bar, and large restaurant with a tennis court behind. The grounds are bordered by the rain forest of the national park, into which the hotel has a private trail. Across the street are the smaller cabinas, which lack TVs and phones, but are considerably cheaper. Those rooms open onto porches overlooking a wide lawn shaded by hammock-strung palm trees, near which is another pool. Hotel rooms are considerably more expensive, but include breakfast. ⊠ *1 block east of beach* ☎🖷 *777–0903* ⊕ *www.espadilla.com* 🖭 *Apdo. 195, Quepos* ↔ *16 rooms, 16 cabinas* ⚭ *Restaurant, fans, in-room safes, some kitchenettes, some cable TV, tennis court, 2 pools, bar, laundry service, travel services; no a/c in some rooms, no phones in some rooms, no TV in some rooms* 🖃 *AE, MC, V* ⑩ *BP.*

$–$$ 🎞 **Hotel Verde Mar.** Also known as La Casa del Sol, this whimsical little hotel is in the rain forest just a few steps from the beach. The rooms are in a long concrete building, and though a bit small, they have colorfully artistic interiors and large windows with views of the ubiquitous tropical foliage. There's a small pool in back, from which a wooden catwalk leads through the woods to the nearby beach. ⊠ *½ km (¼ mi) north of park* 🖭 *Apdo. 348–6350* ☎ *777–1805* 🖷 *777–1311* ⊕ *www.verdemar. com* ↔ *20 rooms* ⚭ *Fans, kitchenettes, pool, laundry service, travel services, no-smoking rooms; no room phones, no room TVs* 🖃 *AE, MC, V.*

¢–$ 🎞 **Cabinas Piscis.** Shaded by tall trees, a short walk through the woods from the beach, this older hotel has some of Manuel Antonio's cheapest rooms. Most of them are in a concrete building with a wide porch; they are simple but spacious, with small bathrooms and lots of windows. The tiny, lower-price rooms that share a separate bathhouse are geared toward backpackers. A small restaurant nearby serves breakfast and light lunches. ⊠ *Bottom of hill, on right after Hotel Karahe* ☎🖷 *777–0046* ↔ *15 rooms, 1 casita, 1 apartment* ⚭ *Restaurant, fans, laundry service; no a/c, no room phones, no room TVs* 🖃 *No credit cards.*

★ ¢–$ 🏨 **Hotel Manuel Antonio.** One of Manuel Antonio's original hotels, this place offers two lodging options—four rustic rooms above an open-air restaurant, which are a good option for budget travelers, and larger, newer rooms in a two-story concrete building next door, which have such amenities as cable TV and air-conditioning. Though nothing special, the new rooms have pastel drapes and bedspreads, and large balconies; be sure to get one with an ocean view, preferably on the second floor. This hotel's greatest assets are its low rates and its location, just steps away from the national park and beach. ✉ *End of road, across from beach* ☎ *777–1237* 🖶 *777–5172* 🛏 *26 rooms* 🍴 *Restaurant, fans, in-room safes, cable TV, laundry service; no a/c in some rooms, no room phones, no TV in some rooms* ☰ *AE, DC, MC, V.*

Nightlife & the Arts

Barba Roja (✉ Main road, top of hill ☎ 777–0331) has a popular sunset happy hour. It's primarily a restaurant, but the bar sometimes stays busy until 10 or 11. The **Billfish Bar** (✉ Byblos Hotel, across from Barba Roja ☎ 777–0411) is a sports bar with a casino next door. **Casino las Palmas** (✉ Hotel Divisamar, across from Barba Roja ☎ 777–0371) is one of Manuel Antonio's two gambling spots. **Cockatoo** (✉ 200 m north of Barba Roja ☎ No phone) plays danceable music in a gorgeous Spanish-style building. It has a gay bar on the second floor. **La Cantina** (✉ Across from the Costa Verde Hotel ☎ 777–0548) has live reggae or Latin music nightly, and serves dinner until 10. **Mar y Sombra** (✉ Next to Cabinas Ramirez ☎ 777–0003), the most popular restaurant on the beach, becomes an open-air dance club Thursday through Saturday nights. The **Tutu** (✉ Above Gato Negro, Casitas Eclipse ☎ No phone) is Manuel Antonio's late-night gay bar.

Sports & the Outdoors

In addition to the surf, sand, and jungle, there are plenty of activities available in and around Manuel Antonio. Kayak tours can take you out to the rocky islands offshore, or into the murky maze of a nearby mangrove estuary, whereas the riches of the open ocean please skin divers and sportfishermen alike. The forest that rises up behind the beach can be explored on foot, horseback, or a canopy tour, and as impressive as the coastal jungle are the forests of the mountains to the east, which can be explored on half-day horseback or hiking tours.

CANOPY TOUR **Canopy Safari** (☎ 777–0100) takes you sliding along cables strung between platforms high in trees in the rain forest near Manuel Antonio. The **Tití Canopy Tours** (☎ 777–1020), named after the locally abundant squirrel monkey, gives you a monkey's-eye view of the rain forest as you glide between the treetops on cables.

HORSEBACK **Equus** (☎ 777–0001) gives trail rides through the surrounding forest.
RIDING **Marlboro Stables** (✉ 200 m north of Hotel Verde Mar ☎ 777–1108) has horseback riding tours on the beach and in the nearby forest. **Finca Valmy Tours** (✉ Villa Nueva ☎ 779–1118) runs half-day horseback tours through the forested mountains above Villa Nueva, east of Manuel Antonio, that include lunch and swimming in a pool below a waterfall.

ROCK CLIMBING **Canyoning Tours** (☎ 777–1924) leads tours into the mountains near Manuel Antonio where you can climb up and rappel down waterfalls.

SEA-KAYAKING **Iguana Tours** (☎ 777–1262) runs sea-kayaking trips to the islands of Manuel Antonio National Park—which requires some experience when the seas are high—and a mellower paddle through the mangrove estuary of Isla Damas, where you might see monkeys, crocodiles, and various birds.

SCUBA DIVING **Costa Rica Adventure** (☎ 777–0234) offers scuba diving for experienced divers around the islands in the national park, as well as certification courses. **Playa Biesanz,** near the Hotel Parador and ½ km (¼ mi) south of Makanda by the Sea, is in a protected cove full of rocks that provide habitat for marine life. **Playa Manuel Antonio,** inside the national park, is a good snorkeling spot thanks to calm waters and the varied marine life on and around submerged rocks.

SPORTFISHING The southwest has some of Costa Rica's finest deep-sea fishing, and Quepos is one of the best points of departure. Fewer boats troll these waters than off Guanacaste, and they usually catch plenty of sailfish, marlin, wahoo, mahimahi, roosterfish, and yellowfin tuna. The fishing is better during the dry season, especially for sailfish and marlin. **Blue Fin Sportfishing** (☎ 777–2222) offers fly and heavy tackle charters from Quepos on any of three boats. **Costa Rica Dreams** (☎ 777–0593) has several boats and has been operating out of Quepos for years. **Luna Tours Sportfishing** (☎ 777–0725) offers custom fishing charters on either a 27- or a 32-foot boat. **Lynch Travel** (✉ Behind bus station ☎ 777–1170) arranges sportfishing excursions with various captains.

SWIMMING When the surf is up, rip currents are a dangerous problem on long **Playa Espadilla** (✉ North of the park). Riptides are characterized by a strong current running out to sea; the important thing to remember if you get caught in one of these currents is not to struggle against it but instead to swim parallel to shore. If you can't swim out of it, the current will simply take you out just past the breakers, where its power dissipates. If you conserve your strength, you can then swim parallel to shore a bit, then back into the beach. Needless to say the best policy is not to go in deeper than your waist when the waves loom large. Manuel Antonio's safest swimming area is sheltered **Playa Manuel Antonio** (✉ Manuel Antonio National Park, south of Playa Espadilla), which is also good for snorkeling.

ULTRALIGHT
FLIGHTS **Sky Riders** (✉ Quepos airstrip ☎ 777–4101) gives ultralight plane tours over Manuel Antonio and the surrounding area.

WHITE-WATER
RAFTING The three white-water rivers in this area have limited seasons. The Savegre, which flows past patches of rain forest, has two navigable stretches: the lower section (Class II–III), which is a mellow trip perfect for neophytes, and the more rambunctious upper section (Class III–IV). It is usually navigable from June to March. The Naranjo (Class III–IV) offers a short but exciting run that requires some experience and can be done only from June to December. The Parrita (Class II–III) is a relatively mellow white-water route, and in the dry season it can be navigated only in two-person, inflatable duckies. **Amigos del Río** (☎ 777–0082), Manuel Antonio's original rafting outfitter, leads trips down the Save-

gre and Naranjo. **Rios Tropicales** (📠 777–4092), the biggest outfitter in the country, offers kayaking excursions, and rafting trips on the Savegre and Naranjo.

Shopping

You'll find little in the way of local handicrafts here. Goods are similar to those in San José but slightly more expensive. **La Buena Nota** (✉ On the right at the bottom of the hill 📞 777–1002) has an extensive selection of beachwear, souvenirs, sunscreen, hats, postcards, used books, international newspapers, and magazines. **Regalame** (✉ Sí Como No shopping center 📞 777–0777) is primarily an art gallery, with paintings and drawings by dozens of artists, but it also sells wood handicrafts and other souvenirs.

Manuel Antonio National Park

10 *5 km (3 mi) south of Quepos, 181 km (112 mi) southwest of San José.*

Parque Nacional Manuel Antonio, though small (6½ square km [2½ square mi]), is one of the most popular protected areas in Costa Rica. This is no doubt because it holds such an impressive collection of natural attractions: three beaches, lush rain forest, mangrove swamps, marshland, and rocky coves that are home to abundant marine life. The park's forest is dominated by massive ficus, cow, kapok, and gumbo-limbo trees, and is home to two- and three-toed sloths, Green and Black Iguanas, White-faced Capuchin Monkeys, agoutis, and nearly 200 species of birds. It is also one of the two places in Costa Rica where you can see Squirrel Monkeys.

The park entrance is at the southern end of Playa Espadilla, across a shallow estuary that drops to a stream at low tide, but is deep enough at high tide that you have to pay a boatman to ferry across it. The boatmen wait next to a booth at the end of the road that belongs to the local guides association. They may have maps of the park, and you can hire a guide ($20 per person) for a two- to three-hour nature walk. Hiring a guide is highly recommended if you want to learn about the local flora and fauna; they wait for groups to form in the early morning.

To the south of the estuary is the ranger station where you pay your admission fee. From there, a trail leads through the rain forest behind **Playa Espadilla Sur,** the park's longest beach. It's also the least crowded because the water can be rough. At its southern end is a tombolo (an isthmus formed from sedimentation and accumulated debris) that connects a former island to the coast. The rocky hill draped with lush jungle is called **Punta Catedral,** and the steep path that makes a loop over it provides a wonderful perspective of the rain forest. The path also passes a lookout point from which you can gaze over the blue Pacific at some of the park's 12 islands.

The lovely strand of white sand east of the tombolo is **Playa Manuel Antonio,** a small, safe swimming beach tucked into a deep cove. At low tide you can see the remains of a Quepos Indian turtle trap on the right—the Quepos stuck poles in the semicircular rock formation, which trapped turtles as the tide receded. The bay, with coral formations on submerged volcanic rocks, is good for snorkeling. Walk even farther east, and you'll come to the rockier, more secluded **Playa Escondido.**

Beware of *manzanillo* trees (indicated by warning signs)—their leaves, bark, and applelike fruit secrete a gooey substance that irritates the skin. And don't feed or touch the monkeys, who have seen so many tourists that they might walk right up to you. They have been known to bite overly friendly visitors, and some of them are kleptomaniacs, so you'll want to keep your backpack tightly zipped. Because Manuel Antonio is so popular, you should come as early as possible, especially on weekends, when it can get packed. Remember that it's closed Mondays. ☎ 777–0654 ✉ $7 ◷ *Tues.–Sun. 7–4.*

CENTRAL PACIFIC A TO Z

To research prices, get advice from other travelers, and book travel arrangements, visit www.fodors.com.

AIR TRAVEL
The flight between San José and Quepos is 30 minutes and is more convenient than the 3½-hour drive or bus trip, which involves a steep mountain road.

CARRIERS SANSA flies six times daily between San José and Quepos in the high season, four in the low season. NatureAir also has six daily flights between San José and Quepos year-round and once daily between Quepos and Palmar Sur, the gateway to Drake Bay.
🖪 Airlines & Contacts **NatureAir** ☎ 777–1170 Quepos, 220–3054 San José ⊕ www.natureair.com. **SANSA** ☎ 777–0683 Quepos, 221–9414 San José ⊕ www.flysansa.com.

BUS TRAVEL
From San José, Coopetransatenas buses leave for Atenas from the Terminal Coca-Cola bus station (⇨ Bus Travel *in* San José A to Z, Chapter 1) every 30 minutes from 6 AM to 10 PM. From Atenas, buses depart from the Banco Nacional. The trip to Jacó from San José takes about three hours. Transporte Jacó buses to Jacó leave San José's Terminal Coca-Cola daily at 7:30 and 10:30 AM, and 1, 3:30, and 6:30 PM, returning from the Jacó bus terminal at 5 AM, 7:30 AM, 11 AM, 3 PM, and 5 PM. A more comfortable and quicker way to reach Jacó is on the hotel-to-hotel shuttle service offered by Interbus, which picks you up from San José hotels, beginning at 9 AM and 1 PM, or the slightly more expensive Gray Line Tourist Bus, which picks you up beginning at 8:30. Buses to Jacó can drop you off at the Carara National Park.

The trip to Quepos from San José takes about 3½ hours. Transportes Delio Morales runs express buses to Quepos and Manuel Antonio that depart San José's Terminal Coca-Cola daily at 6 AM, noon, and 6 PM, returning at 6 AM, noon, and 5 PM. The buses drop off and pick up at the Quepos bus station and at strategic points on the Manuel Antonio-Quepos road (ask where the bus stops). More comfortable shuttle service to Manuel Antonio hotels is offered by Interbus, with 8 AM and 1 PM departures from San José, and Gray Line, which departs at 8:30 and is slightly cheaper. Direct buses to Quepos and Manuel Antonio can drop you off in front of Playa Hermosa's hotels. All buses heading *toward* San José can drop you off at the airport, but you need to ask the driver when you board, and then remind him again as you draw near to the stop.

Buses make the short trip from Quepos to Manuel Antonio every half hour daily from dawn to dusk, then hourly until 10 PM. Buses leave Puntarenas for the three-hour trip to Quepos daily at 5 AM and 2:30 PM, returning at 10:30 AM and 3 PM, stopping at Playa Hermosa and on the outskirts of Jacó. For those moving on to the southern Pacific region, buses leave Quepos for Dominical (a 2½-hour trip) daily at 9 AM, 1:30 PM, 4:30 PM, and 6:30 PM, returning at 6 AM, 2 PM, and 2:45 PM.
🚍 Bus Companies **Coopetransatenas** ☎ 446-5767. **Transporte Jacó** ☎ 223-1109. **Transportes Delio Morales** ☎ 223-5567.
🚍 Shuttle Van Services **Gray Line/Fantasy Tours** ☎ 223-4650, 643-3231 Jacó. **Interbus** ☎ 283-5573.

Gray Line Tourist Bus and Interbus follow fixed daily schedules and pick you up from various San José hotels for fares starting at $25. Reserve at least one day in advance.

CAR RENTAL
There are several car-rental agencies to choose from in Jacó and Quepos/Manuel Antonio.
🚗 Major Agencies **Alamo** ✉ Quepos ☎ 777-3344. **Budget** ✉ Avda. Pastor Diaz, Jacó ☎ 643-2665. **Economy** ✉ Avda Pastor Diaz, Jacó ☎ 643-1098 ✉ next to Banca Proamerica, Manuel Antonio ☎ 777-5353. **National** ✉ Jacó ☎ 643-1752.
🚗 Local Agency **Elegante/Payless** ☎ 643-3224 Jacó, 777-0115 Quepos.

CAR TRAVEL
The quickest way to get to this region from San José is to take the Carretera Inter-Americana (Pan-American Highway, CA1) west to the exit for Atenas, where you turn left (south). Once you leave the highway, the road is one lane in each direction for the rest of the route, and between Atenas and Orotina it is steep and full of curves. If you don't have experience in mountain driving, you're better off taking a bus or flight to the coast. The coastal highway, or Costanera, heads southeast from Orotina to Tárcoles, Jacó, Hermosa, and Quepos. It is well marked and, except for a few stretches near bridges, well paved. An asphalt road winds its way over the hill between Quepos and Manuel Antonio National Park. Driving times from San José are about 1 hour to Atenas, 2½ hours to Jacó, 3 hours to Quepos, and 3½ hours to Manuel Antonio.

EMERGENCIES
In an emergency, dial 911 or one of the numbers below.
🚨 Emergency Services **Ambulance** ☎ 777-0116. **Fire** ☎ 118. **Police** ☎ 117 in towns, 127 in rural areas. **Traffic Police** ☎ 222-9245.

MAIL & SHIPPING
Atenas, Jacó, and Quepos all have a post office, but letters mailed from them tend to take a good bit longer than if they were posted from San José. If you won't be heading through San José within a week, ask the

receptionist at your hotel whether they will be sending mail to the city soon. There are plenty of Internet cafés in Jacó and the Quepos/Manuel Antonio area, and at least one each in Atenas and Hermosa. They charge the equivalent of $1–$3 per hour.

🚹 Internet Cafés **C@fé K-puchinos** ⊠ Northwest corner of Parque Central, Atenas ☏ 289-0082. **Cantina Internet** ⊠ Across from Costa Verde, Manuel Antonio ☏ 777-0548. **Centro de Computación** ⊠ Avda. Pastor Diaz, center of town Jacó ☏ 643-2713. **Goola Café and Internet** ⊠ Costanera, north of soccer field, Playa Hermosa ☏ 643-3469. **Quepos Internet Café** ⊠ C. 2, Quepos ☏ 777-2183.

🚹 Post Offices **Correos de Costa Rica** ⊠ Avda. Pastor Diaz, Jacó ☏ 643-2175 ⊠ C. Central, Quepos ☏ 777-1471.

MONEY MATTERS

ATMS There are various ATMs in Jacó and Quepos that accept either Visa or MasterCard, or both. Ask the receptionist at your hotel where the nearest one is. In the unlikely event that you come upon an ATM that's out of order, you should be able to find another one nearby.

CURRENCY EXCHANGE Banks in Jacó and Quepos will exchange U.S. dollars, though it's quicker to get Costa Rican currency from an ATM. Most hotels, restaurants, tour operators, taxi drivers, gift shops, and supermarkets will accept or change U.S. dollars, though at slightly less than the bank rate. Canadian, Australian, and New Zealand dollars and English pounds must be exchanged in banks.

🚹 Banks **BAC San José** ⊠ Il Galeon shopping center, Jacó ☏ 295-9595 ⊠ Avda. Central, Quepos ☏ 295-9595. **Banco Nacional** ⊠ Avda. Pastor Diaz, Jacó ☏ 213-3498 ⊠ 50 m west and 100 m north of bus station, Quepos ☏ 212-3498. **Banca Proamerica** ⊠ next to Economy Rent A Car, Manuel Antonio ☏ 296-4848.

TOURS

The *Okeanos Aggressor* makes all-inclusive 9- and 10-day guided dive trips to Cocos Island, one of the best dive spots in the world. Transfers to and from San José are provided from Puntarenas. Cruceros del Sur offers a seven-day natural-history cruise through Costa Rica's central and south Pacific regions and some islands off Panama aboard the *Temptress*, a 63-passenger ship. The *Undersea Hunter* also leads 10-day dive trips to Cocos Island.

A number of agencies can help you arrange land-bound tours. Costa Rica Expeditions and Horizontes, the country's two premier nature-tour operators, have expert guides and can arrange tours that visit Carara, Manuel Antonio, or both. Costa Tropical Expeditions is a small Jacó tour operator that specializes in trips to Carara but can arrange all kinds of personalized excursions. Book tours by phone or at Villa Caletas in Tárcoles or Club del Mar in Jacó. Fantasy Tours is the biggest operator in Jacó, but it deals primarily with large groups.

In Quepos, Lynch Travel offers a wildlife-watching boat trip to the Isla Damas Estuary, guided tours of the national park, horseback and sport-fishing trips, and more. Costa Rica Temptations has an office in Manuel Antonio from which it runs tours of the national park and other attractions. Iguana Tours specializes in sea-kayaking and river rafting, but it also runs trips on dry land. Fincas Naturales, in Manuel Antonio, runs hourly tours, Monday through Saturday, of its butterfly garden, private wildlife refuge, or both. Rainmaker leads daily hikes through a private reserve in the mountains south of Quepos that has canopy bridges through the treetops and waterfalls with swimming holes. Villas de la Colina, a hotel in Atenas, leads three eight- to nine-day motorcycle tours that include a trip from Volcán Arenal to the Monteverde Cloud Forest.

◪ Tour Operators **Costa Rica Expeditions** ✉ Avda. 3 and C. Central, San José ☎ 222-0333 🖷 257-1665. **Costa Rica Temptations** ✉ Manuel Antonio ☎ 777-5130. **Costa Tropical Expeditions** ☎ 393-6622. **Cruceros del Sur** ✉ Across from Colegio Los Angeles, Sabana Norte, San José ☎ 232-6672 🖷 220-2103. **Fantasy Tours** ✉ Best Western Jacó Beach Resort, Playa Jacó ☎ 643-3032. **Fincas Naturales** ✉ Across from Hotel Sí Como No, Manuel Antonio ☎ 777-0850. **Horizontes** ✉ 130 m north of Pizza Hut, Paseo Colón ☎ 222-2022 🖷 255-4513. **Iguana Tours** ✉ Across from soccer field, Quepos ☎ 777-1262. **Lynch Travel** ✉ Behind bus station, Quepos ☎ 777-1170. *Okeanos Aggressor* ✉ 1-17 Plaza Colonial, Escazú ☎ 556-8317, 877/506-9738 in U.S. 🖷 556-2825. **Rainmaker** ✉ Quepos ☎ 777-0850. *Undersea Hunter* ✉ San Rafael de Escazú, ½ km (¼ mi) north and 45 m west of Rosti Pollos ☎ 228-6535 🖷 289-7334. **Villas de la Colina** ✉ 6 km (4 mi) west of Coopeatenas on road to Orotina ✆ Apdo. 165, Atenas ☎ 446-5015 🖷 446-8545 ⊕ www.motoscostarica.com.

VISITOR INFORMATION

The Instituto Costarricense de Turismo (ICT) office in San José has information on the central Pacific region and is open weekdays 9–12:30 and 1:30–5. Lynch Travel in Quepos can give general advice.

◪ Tourist Information **Instituto Costarricense de Turismo (ICT)** ✉ C. 5 between Advas. Central and 2, Barrio La Catedral San José ✉ C. 2 between Avdas. 1 and 3, Barrio La Merced San José ☎ 222-1090. **Lynch Travel** ✉ Behind bus station, Quepos ☎ 777-1170.

THE SOUTHERN PACIFIC

6

Updated by
Dorothy
MacKinnon

COSTA RICA'S WILDEST COUNTRY IS FOUND IN THE SOUTHERN PACIFIC, which makes it well worth the extra effort it takes to visit this remote area. A trip here reveals what most of the country looked like decades, or even centuries, ago. Because it was the last part of the country to be settled—a road into the region from San José wasn't completed until the 1950s—the southern Pacific zone retains a disproportionate percentage of its wilderness. Much of that nature lies within several of Costa Rica's largest national parks, and other patches are protected as private reserves. From the exhilarating highland scenery of the Cordillera de Talamanca, Costa Rica's highest mountain range, to the pristine beaches and coastal rain forest of the Osa Peninsula, the southern Pacific has some of the country's most dramatic scenery and wildlife.

Costa Rica's highest mountain, Cerro Chirripó, is in Chirripó National Park, where the landscape ranges from rugged forest to glacial lakes. On the Osa Peninsula, the creation of Corcovado National Park put a halt to the furious logging and gold mining that threatened the rain forest; the park now houses most of the country's endangered species in a wide range of habitats, including large areas of swamp, deserted beach, cloud forest, and luxuriant lowland rain forest.

Some of Costa Rica's best surfing breaks and diving areas are in the southern Pacific. Anglers can fish the renowned Pacific waters. Rafters can take on the rambunctious Río General. Trekkers can climb Cerro Chirripó. Bird-watchers who go to the right places are almost guaranteed glimpses of the country's two most spectacular birds: the Resplendent Quetzal and Scarlet Macaw. Botany lovers, too, will find their jaws dropping here, especially at the Wilson Botanical Garden near San Vito, with its spectacular displays of canopy plant life brought down to earth.

Timing

In the rainy season, it rains considerably more here than in the northwest, but in July and August you may catch a week without any serious precipitation. The Osa Peninsula and Talamanca highlands are especially susceptible to downpours, making this region the last place you want to visit during the October–November deluge, when many lodges are closed.

Exploring the Southern Pacific Coast

This area includes four very different landscapes: the clear rivers and cool forests of the central highlands of the Cordillera de Talamanca; the hot, agricultural lowlands of the Valle de El General; the miles of uncrowded beaches running south from Dominical; and the wild, impenetrable—except on foot—Osa Peninsula with its two very different coastlines, the rugged Pacific and the gentler Golfo Dulce.

It's a lot of territory to cover on the ground. Although the driving is scenic, especially over the spectacular mountains of the Cordillera de Talamanca, it's tiring, especially if you are heading all the way down to the Osa and to Corcovado National Park. If you are Osa-bound, there are few drivable roads except on the Golfo Dulce side. It often makes more sense to fly into Puerto Jiménez, Golfito, or Drake Bay. If you fly into Palmar Norte, you can take a taxi to Sierpe and then a motorboat to destinations on the Pacific side of the Osa Peninsula.

If you're traveling by car, there are two routes into the region: the paved, heavily traveled Carretera Interamericana (Pan-American Highway, CA2), with lots of slow-moving trucks and impatient bus drivers, and the Costanera (Route 34), or coastal highway, which is not paved between Quepos and Dominical. Heading south from San José, the two-lane Pan-American Highway climbs up through the perennial fog at the top of Cerro de la Muerte, where you pass the turnoffs for La Ruta de los Santos and San Gerardo de Dota. The road then descends to San Isidro in the Valle de El General, and, eventually, to the South Pacific beaches and the Osa Peninsula and Panama.

About the Restaurants

Since the sun sets between 5 and 6 PM year-round, dinner is served relatively early down south, except in the Dominical area, where surfers keep restaurants and bars busy into the night. In the Osa Peninsula, don't count on finding many restaurants outside hotels, except in Puerto Jiménez.

About the Hotels

Nature lodges may be less expensive than they initially appear, as the price of a room usually includes three hearty meals a day, as well as tours and transportation to remote areas.

WHAT IT COSTS					
	$$$$	**$$$**	**$$**	**$**	**¢**
RESTAURANTS	over $25	$20–$25	$10–$20	$5–$10	under $5
HOTELS	over $200	$125–$200	$75–$125	$35–$75	under $35

Restaurant prices are per-person for a main course at dinner. Hotel prices are for two people in a standard double room in high season, excluding service and tax (16.4%).

THE CENTRAL HIGHLANDS

Less than an hour south of San José, the Pan-American Highway climbs up into the scenic Central Highlands of the Talamanca mountains, famous for mountain vistas, high-altitude coffee farms, cloud forest ecolodges, and challenging mountain hikes.

Zona de Los Santos

50 km (31 mi) southeast of San José.

Empalme, at Km 51 of the Pan-American Highway, marks the turnoff for Santa María de Dota, the first of the blessed coffee-growing towns, all named after saints, that dot this mountainous area, known as the Zona de Los Santos (Los Santos Zone). The scenic road that winds through the high-altitude valley from Empalme to San Pablo de León is appro-

Numbers in the text correspond to numbers in the margin and on The Southern Pacific Coast map.

6

If you have 3 days

Fly straight to the Golfo Dulce–Osa Peninsula area, where you can stay in a comfortable nature lodge in or near any of three pristine wilderness areas. You can fly direct to ▣ **Playa Pavones** ⑪ ⌐ on a charter arranged by the Tiskita Jungle Lodge, or fly to ▣ **Puerto Jiménez** ⑫, a short drive from the lodges of ▣ **Cabo Matapalo** ⑬. A third option is to fly a charter to **Carate** ⑭ and the Corcovado Lodge Tent Camp at the edge of ▣ **Corcovado National Park** ⑮. Alternatively, you can fly to Palmar Sur, where the taxi and spectacular boat trip—complete with guide who points out iguanas, crabs, and birds—depart for ▣ **Drake Bay** ⑯. Or you can fly directly to Drake on a daily scheduled flight.

If you have 5 days

In five days you can stretch out the three-day itinerary above or concentrate on inland areas. Drive south on the Pan-American Highway (CA2) into the cool mountain air and cloud forests of ▣ **San Gerardo de Dota** ① ⌐, a perfect place to hike and bird-watch. The next day explore the Dota Valley. On Day 3, head down out of the mountains to the coastal enclave of ▣ **Dominical** ⑦ or the nearby ▣ **Ballena Marine National Park** ⑧. Spend Day 4 and the morning of Day 5 enjoying the area's waterfalls, nature reserves, and beaches.

If you have 7 days

With seven days, you can spend two in ▣ **San Gerardo de Dota** ① ⌐, two around ▣ **Dominical** ⑦ and Playa Uvita, then go to Sierpe to take a boat to one of the ▣ **Drake Bay** ⑯ lodges for three days. Then visit either **Caño Island** ⑰ for snorkeling or diving, or **Corcovado National Park** ⑮. (Casa Corcovado has great three-day packages from Sierpe.) You can fly back to San José from Palmar Sur.

---

priately called La Ruta de Los Santos (Route of the Saints). It's well paved to facilitate shipping the coffee that's produced here, which is central to Costa Rica's economy. Along the length of the 45-minute (24-km [15-mi]) drive from Santa María de Dota to San Pablo de León Cortés, you'll see heavenly vistas of misty valleys ringed by precipitous mountain slopes terraced with lush, green coffee plants. The route also captures the essence of a traditional Tico way of life built around coffee growing. Stately churches center bustling towns full of prosperous, neat houses with pretty gardens and vintage, 1970s Toyota Landcruisers in a rainbow of colors parked in front.

Where to Eat

¢ ✕ **Café de Los Santos.** To sample the fruits of the area's coffee plants, stop in at pretty Café de Los Santos in San Marcos de Tarrazú. The café sign shows a chubby monk with a halo, pouring a cup of coffee. Run as a community project to showcase the region's coffee, the café serves

30 different kinds. The best bet, billed on the menu as "a celestial drink of the land of the saints," is high-altitude *arabica* Tarrazú coffee, for which this area is famous. The café has charming wooden tables and chairs, local art on the walls, and a selection of homemade sweet and savory pastries served by friendly waitresses. If you don't have time for the drive to San Marcos, there's a branch in Empalme. Breakfast is available Monday through Saturday at the San Marcos branch and Thursday through Sunday at the Empalme branch. ⊠ *50 m east of church, San Marcos de Tarrazú, 6 km west of Santa María de Dota* ☎ *No phone* 🗖 *No credit cards* ☉ *Closed Sun.* 🗎 *Pan-American Hwy., at entrance to Ruta de Los Santos, Empalme* ☎ *571–1118* 🗖 *No credit cards.*

Shopping

The best—and cheapest—place to buy local coffee is where the farmers themselves bring their raw coffee beans to be roasted and packed into jute bags, the **Coopedota Santa Maria** (⊠ Main road, just after the bridge, as you enter Santa María de Dota ☎ 541–2828). You can buy export-quality coffee here for less than $5 per kilo (2.2 pounds) *en grano* (whole bean) or *molido* (ground), and choose between light or dark roast. It's open Monday through Saturday 7–11:30 AM and weekdays 12:30–5 PM. You can also arrange for a tour of the coffee co-op by calling ahead.

San Gerardo de Dota

★ ▶ ❶ *89 km (55 mi) southeast of San José.*

Cloud forests, cool mountain air, pastoral imagery, and excellent birdwatching make San Gerardo de Dota one of Costa Rica's best-kept secrets. The village is in a narrow valley of the Río Savegre, 9 km (5½ mi) down a twisting, partially asphalted track that descends abruptly to the west from the Pan-American Highway. The peaceful surroundings look more like the Rocky Mountains than typical Central America, but hike down the waterfall trail and the vegetation quickly turns tropical again. Beyond hiking, activities include horseback riding and trout fishing, but you might well be content just to wander around the pastures and forests, marveling at the valley's avian inhabitants.

The damp, epiphyte-laden forest of giant oak trees is renowned for its high count of Resplendent Quetzals, for many the most beautiful bird in the Western world. Male quetzals are more spectacular than females, with metallic green feathers, bright crimson stomachs, helmetlike crests, and long tail streamers that look especially dramatic in flight. Quetzals commonly feed on *aguacatillos* (avocadolike fruits) in the tall trees scattered around the valley's forests and pastures. The staff in your hotel can usually point you in the direction of some quetzal hangouts; early morning is the best time to spot them. They are most easily seen here in their nesting season (March–May).

Where to Stay

$ 🏠 **Albergue Mirador de Quetzales.** Bird-watchers flock to this 8,530-foot-high perch with rustic A-frame cabins overlooking a misty valley. The main attraction is the Resplendent Quetzal, which swoops its famous tail feathers around the 106-acre cloud-forest reserve, also known as Finca

Bird-Watching

Birders from all over the world flock to this area in search of avifauna that are either unique or abundant enough to ensure reliable sightings. The dean of Central American ornithology, Alexander Skutch, still lives in the simple house south of San Isidro, where for more than 50 years he collected the data for the definitive *Guide to the Birds of Costa Rica*. Visitors can still walk the same trails Skutch blazed, although much of the surrounding forest has given way to farming. In the Central Highlands, the star of the bird show is the Resplendent Quetzal. Along the miles of mountain trails that crisscross the Albergue Montaña de Savegre, you are almost guaranteed a sighting of this magnificent, long-tailed bird. Scarlet Macaws and Red-breasted Baird's Trogons are the sought-after birds in the lowland rain forests of the Osa Peninsula. Even visitors with no previous interest in birds may find themselves drawn in by the excitement of spotting these colorful, distinctive creatures.

6

Fresh Fruit

Apples, peaches, and plums are grown in profusion in the upper reaches of the Cordillera de Talamanca, and the lowlands are the source of those thirst-quenching pineapples. If you're here between June and August, try rambutans, locally called *mamones chinos*; their red, spiky shells protect a succulent white fruit very similar to a lychee. Even in the remote Osa Peninsula, where supply lines are difficult, you can eat surprisingly well at health-minded eco-resorts that don't stint on just-picked produce and imaginative cuisine.

Outdoor Adventures

Outdoors enthusiasts may never want to leave these parts. This is hiking territory, with treks ranging from one-day jaunts through private reserves to more demanding multiday treks up Chirripó or into the Corcovado jungles. Simple horseback rides take you along spectacular beaches and forest trails. The lively water habitat surrounding Isla del Caño offers some of Costa Rica's best scuba diving, and there's prime sportfishing off the entire southern Pacific coast. The surf whips up into a half dozen breaks, and you can navigate the quieter waters of Golfo Dulce in a sea kayak.

Private Nature Preserves

In addition to celebrated national parks, this region has a growing number of private nature preserves, some of which run their own lodges. Dominical's Hacienda Barú, a 700-acre reserve, offers innovative ways to experience the rain forest, such as climbing up ropes to a treetop observation platform or spending the night in a tent in the forest. Lapa Ríos, near the southern tip of the Osa Peninsula, offers themed tours through its extensive protected rain forest that focus, for instance, on medicinal plants and their uses.

Eddie Serrano. The 4-km (2.5-mi) El Robledal trail wends past gnarly 1,500-year-old cypress trees, moss-enshrouded oaks, and 14-million-year-old marine fossils. The room rate includes a hearty breakfast, dinner, a guided tour, and a hot water bottle to take the chill off your bed at night, when the temperature can drop close to freezing. Day visitors

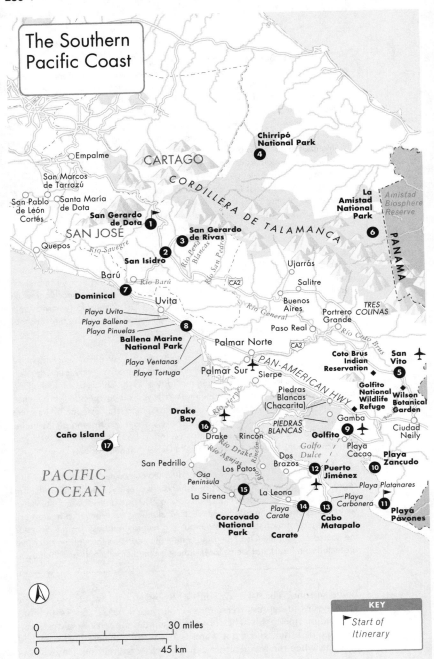

The Southern Pacific Coast

Empalme

San Marcos de Tarrazú

Santa María de Dota

San Pablo de León Cortés

San Gerardo de Dota ❶

SAN JOSÉ

Quepos

CARTAGO

CORDILLERA DE TALAMANCA

Chirripó National Park ❹

La Amistad National Park ❻

Amistad Biosphere Reserve

PANAMA

San Gerardo de Rivas ❸

❷

San Isidro

Río Savegre

Río Barú

Barú

Dominical ❼

Uvita

Playa Uvita
Playa Ballena
Playa Pinuelas

Ballena Marine National Park ❽

Playa Ventanas
Playa Tortuga

Río Peñas Blancas

Río San Pedro

CA2

Ujarrás

Salitre

Buenos Aires

Río General

Paso Real

Palmar Norte

CA2

Palmar Sur

Sierpe

PAN-AMERICAN HWY

Río Sierpe

Piedras Blancas (Chacarita)

Portrero Grande

TRES COLINAS

Río Coto Brus

Coto Brus Indian Reservation

San Vito ❺

Golfito National Wildlife Refuge

Wilson Botanical Garden

Ciudad Neily

Drake Bay ❶❻

Drake

Rincón

PIEDRAS BLANCAS

Gamba

Golfito ❾

Golfo Dulce

Playa Cacao

Caño Island ❶❼

PACIFIC OCEAN

San Pedrillo

Río Drake

Río Aguas

Río Rincón

San Pedrillo

Los Patos

Dos Brazos

Puerto Jiménez ❶❷

Playa Platanares

Playa Zancudo ❶❶

Osa Peninsula

La Sirena ❶❺

La Leona

Playa Carate

Corcovado National Park

❶❹

Carate

Cabo Matapalo ❶❸

Playa Carbonera

Playá Pávones ❶❶

0 ——— 30 miles

0 ——— 45 km

KEY

▶ *Start of Itinerary*

can pay $6 to walk the trail themselves. You can also camp here. ⊠ *At Km 70 of Pan-American Hwy.* 🖼🖼*381–8456* ⊕*www.exploringcostarica. com/mirador/quetzales.html* ⤵ *10 cabins* ⚲ *Restaurant, hiking; no a/c, no room phones, no room TVs* ☰ *No credit cards* |O| *MAP.*

★ $ 🏨 **Savegre Hotel de Montaña.** In the 1950s, Efrain Chacón bushwhacked through the mountains to homestead in San Gerardo. Today his eldest son leads quetzal-spotting tours on steep forest trails laced throughout the extensive family estate, which has become a model for conservation. Cozy cabinas have heaters and plenty of hot water; newer, spacious cabinas are screened by a butterfly garden, and there are two honeymoon suites with fireplaces and bathtubs. The main lodge has a fireplace and a veranda famous for its hummingbird feeders. Homegrown trout is the restaurant's specialty; an all-inclusive meal plan is available. You can get a lift to the hotel from the Km 80 turnoff on the Pan-American Highway ($10). On the hotel grounds, the **Quetzal Education Research Center** (QERC; ☎ 740–1010) hosts students and researchers; many take their meals at the hotel and are a great source for natural lore. ⊠ *Turn right at sign to San Gerardo de Dota on Pan-American Hwy., about 80 km (50 mi) southeast of San José, and travel 9 km (5½ mi) down a steep, gravel road with some paving* ☎ *740–1028* 🖼 *740–1027* 🖨 *Apdo. 482, Cartago* ⤵ *33 cabinas* ⚲ *Restaurant, fishing, hiking, horseback riding, bar, Internet; no a/c, no room phones, no room TVs* ☰*AE, MC, V* |O|*BP.*

$ 🏨 **Trogon Lodge.** A charming collection of green cabins nestled in a secluded garden in an enchanting valley, Trogon Lodge overlooks the cloud forest and boulder-strewn Río Savegre. Each cabin has two rooms with *almendro* (almond-wood) floors, big windows, white-tile baths with hot showers, and electric heaters and extra blankets for chilly mountain nights. Meals are served in a small dining hall. Quetzal-watching and waterfall tours are offered. ⊠ *Turn right at the sign to San Gerardo de Dota on the Pan-American Hwy., about 80 km (50 mi) southeast of San José, and follow signs; lodge is 7½ km (4½ mi) down a decent dirt road* ☎ *740–1051, 293–8181 in San José* 🖼 *229–8082 in San José* ⊕ *www. grupomawamba.com* 🖨 *Apdo. 10980–1000, San José* ⤵ *24 rooms* ⚲ *Restaurant, bicycles, hiking, horseback riding, bar; no a/c, no room phones, no room TVs* ☰ *AE, MC, V.*

Sports & the Outdoors

HIKING Some of the best hiking in the country is in this area. Expert birder Marino Chacón of Hotel de Savegre leads a daylong natural-history hike. You ★ drive up to the *páramo* (high altitude, shrubby ecosystem) near **Cerro de la Muerte**, and hike from a trail that begins near the cluster of communication towers, near Km 89, back down through the forest into the valley. Miles of trails wind through the forest reserve belonging to the Chacóns. The most challenging trail in the area is the one that begins ★ at the Hotel Savegre and follows the **Río Savegre** down to a waterfall. To get to the trailhead, follow the main road past Savegre Hotel to a fork, where you veer left, cross a bridge, and head over the hill to a pasture that narrows to a footpath. Although it is only 2 km (1¼ mi) each way, the hike is steep and vigorous, especially near the bottom, and takes about three hours each way. Above **Trogon Lodge** (⊠ Turn right at the sign to San Gerardo de Dota on the Pan-American Hwy., about 80 km

[50 mi] southeast of San José, and follow signs; lodge is 7½ km (4½ mi) down a decent dirt road), a short trail heads through the forest and ends in a pasture.

San Isidro

② *54 km (34 mi) south of San Gerardo de Dota, 205 km (127 mi) northwest of Golfito.*

Although San Isidro has no major attractions, it's a good place to have lunch and to get cash at the ATH cash machine (in the Coopealianza west of the church), which accepts North American debit and credit cards with a Visa/Plus logo. Buses to San Gerardo de Rivas, the starting point of the trail into Chirripó National Park, depart from San Isidro. The **National Parks Service** (⊠ Across from Camara de Cañeros ☎ 771–3155) office has information about Chirripó and can help you reserve lodging in the park's cabins. Buses to Dominical leave from a stop 100 m south and 200 m east of the cathedral, near the main highway.

off the beaten path

LAS QUEBRADAS BIOLOGICAL CENTER – In a lush valley 7 km (4½ mi) northeast of San Isidro, a community-managed nature reserve (*centro biológico*) protects 1,853 acres of dense forest in which elegant tree ferns grow in the shadows of massive trees and where colorful tanagers and euphonias flit about the foliage. A 3-km (2-mi) trail winds through the forest and along the Río Quebradas, which supplies water to San Isidro and surrounding communities. ⊠ *At the bottom of mountain as you approach San Isidro take sharp left off Pan-American Hwy. at sign for Las Quebradas and travel 7 km (4½ mi) northeast; center is 2 km (1 mi) north of town, along unpaved road* ☎ *771–4131* ⊘ *Apdo. 8000–30, Peréz Zeledón, San Isidro* 🖃 *$5* ⊙ *Tues.–Sun. 8–3.*

Where to Stay & Eat

¢–$ ✕ **El Trapiche de Nayo.** This restaurant with a panoramic valley view serves the kind of food Ticos eat at *turnos* (village fund-raising festivals), including hard-to-find *sopa de mondongo* (tripe soup) and a long menu of items, such as heart of palm and other root vegetables, to fill *gallos,* tortillas that you stuff yourself. Come on a Tuesday or a Saturday when raw sugarcane is pressed in an antique mill and boiled in huge iron cauldrons to make smooth *sobado,* a molasses-flavored fudge. ⊠ *Pan-American Hwy., 6 km (4 mi) north of San Isidro* ☎ *771–7267* 🖃 *AE, MC, V.*

$ 🏨 **Hotel Los Crestones.** Cheery flowers in window boxes give this pleasant, two-story motel-style building near the local stadium a homey feel. Affordable rooms are large and comfortable, and two have bathtubs. A small, informal grouping of tables in the reception area serves coffee and pastries and light breakfasts. ⊠ *Southwest side of stadium, on road to Dominical* ☎ *770–1200* 🖷 *771–6012* ⊕ *www.hotelloscrestones. com* 🖛 *16 rooms* ⟁ *Fans, cable TV, convention center, free parking; no a/c in some rooms, no room phones* 🖃 *V.*

$ 🏨 **Hotel del Sur Country Club & Casino.** An extensive and rambling complex with well-tended gardens, this hotel doubles as a local country club.

Weekday stays are tranquil, but the casino makes for lively weekends. Rooms are spacious, but sparsely furnished, and have large windows looking out onto a courtyard garden. Basic cabinas in back have kitchenettes, bunks, and separate bedrooms. ⊠ *Pan-American Hwy., 6 km (4 mi) south of town* ☎ *771–3033* 🖨 *771–0527* ⊕ *www.hoteldelsur. co.cr* 🕮 *Apdo. 4–8000, Peréz Zeledón, San Isidro* ➴ *48 rooms, 10 cabinas* ☖ *Restaurant, fans, some in-room safes, some kitchenettes, some minibars, cable TV, tennis court, pool, wading pool, basketball, bar, casino, playground; no a/c in some rooms, no TV in cabins* ⊟ *AE, MC, V* ⧖ *BP.*

$ 🖾 **Talari Mountain Lodge.** A 10-minute drive northeast from San Isidro on the road to San Gerardo de Rivas, this family-run lodge is on a small farm near the gurgling Río General. Rooms are very simple, with big windows, tile floors, and porches. The surrounding fruit trees and forest patches make for excellent bird-watching. A resident naturalist guide leads tours in high season and organizes trips to climb Chirripó. Meals are excellent; the dining room is closed Wednesday. ⊠ *Left off Pan-American Hwy. after second bridge south of San Isidro* 🖨🖨 *771–0341* ⊕ *www.talari.co.cr* 🕮 *Apdo. 517–8000, Peréz Zeledón, San Isidro* ➴ *8 rooms* ☖ *Dining room, pool; no a/c, no room phones, no room TVs* ⊟ *AE, MC, V* ⧖ *BP.*

Sports & the Outdoors

BIRD-WATCHING **Los Cusingos Neotropical Bird Sanctuary** (⊠ 15–20 km [8–12 mi] southeast of San Isidro, Quizarrá, near Santa Elena; phone for precise directions ☎ 253–3267 ⊕ www.cct.or.cr) is the home of Dr. Alexander Skutch, Central America's preeminent ornithologist/naturalist and the author of *A Guide to the Birds of Costa Rica,* the birders' bible. His 190-acre estate, an island of forest amid new farms and housing developments, is now run by the Tropical Science Center as a research facility. You can walk the trails and see the simple house where Dr. Skutch has lived since 1941. You may even catch a glimpse of the nonagenarian sitting on his porch. Bird species you might see include Fiery-billed Aracaris, colorful, small members of the toucan family, and mixed tanager flocks. Admission to the sanctuary is $8; it's open daily by appointment from 7 AM to sunset.

WHITE-WATER RAFTING Experience the country's longest white-water run via raft or kayak on the **Río General.** The white water flows through agricultural land and winds through a rocky canyon. Three-day camping and kayaking or rafting expeditions on the Class III–IV rapids of Río General are offered by San José–based **Ríos Tropicales** (☎ 233–6455 🖨 255–4354 ⊕ www. riostropicales.com) from July to December, for a minimum of six people per group. **Selva Mar** (☎ 771–4582 ⊕ www.exploringcostarica. com), in San Isidro, organizes hiking trips up Chirippó, bird-watching, and horseback tours.

San Gerardo de Rivas

❸ *20 km (12½ mi) northeast of San Isidro.*

Chirripó National Park is the main reason to venture to San Gerardo de Rivas, but if you aren't up for this physically challenging adventure, the town is still a great place to spend a day or two. Spread over steep terrain at the end of the narrow valley of the boulder-strewn Río Chirripó, San Gerardo de Rivas has a cool climate, good bird-watching, spectacular views reminiscent of Nepal, and an outdoor menu that includes hiking and horseback riding to waterfalls.

☙ The **Aguas Termales** (Hot Springs), on a farm above the road to Herradura, is a favorite tourist stop. To get here, you must cross a river on a rickety footbridge, then it's a steep climb on foot to a combination of natural rock and concrete pools in a forested area. It can be crowded with locals on weekends. In dry season only, the **Selva Mar travel agency** (🖀 771–4582) in San Isidro can arrange for a donkey or horse, as can local hotels. ⊠ *Above road to Herradura, about 1½ km (1 mi) past the ranger station, north of town* 🎟 *$2* 🕙 *Daily 7–6.*

Where to Stay

$ 🏨 **Río Chirripó Retreat.** Crystal mountain air, a rushing river, and a huge conical-roofed adobe temple hung with a monastery bell and Tibetan prayer flags make you feel as though you have suddenly arrived in the Himalayas. A popular place for yoga retreats, this bougainvillea-bedecked bed-and-breakfast is a great place for acclimatizing before climbing Chirripó or for clambering along the river, strewn with Druidic-looking stone seats and altars. The two-storied wooden cabins are cantilevered over a steep ravine, with porches made of twig railings. Inside, the comfortable rooms have large bathrooms and walls stenciled with runic symbols. There's a pool by the river and great bird-watching all around. ⊠ *Down a steep road (4-wheel drive required), just past cemetery* 🖀 *771–7065, 707/937–3775 in U.S.* ⊕ *www.riochirripo.com* 🛏 *8 rooms, 1 cabin* ⚭ *Dining room, pool, hiking, bar; no a/c, no room phones, no room TVs* ☰ *No credit cards* 🍽 *BP.*

¢ 🏨 **El Pelícano.** Perched on a ridge south of town, this wooden lodge is named for a chunk of wood that resembles a pelican—and that's not its only oddity. The restaurant, which has a gorgeous view of the valley below San Gerardo, is also an art gallery, with dozens of idiosyncratic wooden sculptures carved out of tree roots by owner Rafael Elizondo. Above the restaurant-gallery are economical small rooms. There's a more private wooden cabin near the pool. The owners can arrange everything for a climb up Chirripó, including a free lift to the park entrance. ⊠ *260 m south of National Parks Office* 🖀 *390–4194* 🖀 *770–3526* ✆ *Apdo. 942–8000, San Gerardo de Rivas* ⊕ *www. hotelelpelicano.net* 🛏 *10 rooms with shared bath, 1 cabin* ⚭ *Restaurant, tennis court, pool, horseback riding; no a/c, no room phones, no room TVs* ☰ *No credit cards.*

VALLE DE EL GENERAL

The Valle de El General (The General's Valley) is bounded to the north and west by the central highlands of the massive Cordillera de Talamanca and La Amistad International Park, above San Vito. The valley is named for the Río de El General, one of the many rivers that rise in the Talamancas and run down through the valley, making it ideal for farming. This area includes vast expanses of highland wilderness, on the upper slopes of the Cordillera de Talamanca and the high-altitude *páramo* (shrubby ecosystem) of Chirripó National Park, as well as prosperous agricultural communities amid vast, sun-baked fields of pineapple and sugarcane.

Chirripó National Park

❹ *12 km (7½ mi) east of San Gerardo de Rivas to park entrance.*

The highest mountain in Costa Rica is found in the **Parque Nacional de Chirripó.** The trail up to the park begins above the scenic agricultural community of San Gerardo de Rivas. Because it's so remote, there is no easy way in; hikers usually spend one night in San Gerardo de Rivas, which has several inexpensive lodges. It's a tough climb to the park—6 to 10 hours on the mountain road from town, depending on your physical condition—so try to head out of San Gerardo with the first light of day. You'll hike through pastures, then forests, and then the burned remains of forest fires. There is a modern but unheated (and chilly) hostel near the top. This will be your base for a night or two if you want to continue your hike up to the peaks, glacier lakes, and *páramo*—a highland ecosystem common to the Andes with flora that includes shrubs and herbaceous plants. Lodging at the hostel is $10 per night. Trails lead to the top of Chirripó—the highest point in Costa Rica—and the nearby peak of Terbi. The hostel has small rooms with four bunks each, bathrooms with cold water only, and a cooking area. You can rent camp stoves, blankets, and sleeping bags here, but you should bring your own good-quality sleeping bag, and you must bring food and water. Pack plenty of warm clothes as well. You are required to report to the park office in San Gerardo de Rivas the day before you start your climb. The office is open 6:30–4. ☎ *200–5348* 🖼 *$10* ☉ *July–Apr., daily dawn–dusk.*

San Vito

❺ *132 km (83 mi) southeast of San Isidro, 93 km (58 mi) northeast of Golfito.*

The bustling hilltop town of San Vito owes its 1952 founding to a government scheme whereby 200 Italian families were awarded grants to convert the rain forest into coffee, fruit, and cattle farms. Today this lively town retains a distinctive Italian flavor, with outdoor cafés serving ice cream and pastries, a Dante Alighieri Cultural Center, and lots of shoe stores. Because of its proximity to the Coto Brus Indian Reservation, San Vito is also one of the few towns in Costa Rica where you might see people from the Ngwobe or Guaymí tribes who are easy to recognize by the women's colorful dresses. If you're short of cash, the Coopealianza near the church has an ATM that accepts foreign cards.

★ Twenty-five hillside acres were converted from a coffee plantation in 1961 by U.S. landscapers Robert and Catherine Wilson to create the extensive and enchanting **Wilson Botanical Garden.** The Wilsons planted a huge collection of tropical species, including palms (an amazing 700 species), orchids, aroids, ferns, bromeliads, heliconias, and marantas, all linked by a series of neat grass paths; the gardens now hold around

3,000 native and 4,000 exotic species. The property was transferred to the Organization for Tropical Studies (OTS) in 1973, and in 1983 it became part of Amistad Biosphere Reserve. Wilson functions mainly as a research and educational center, but visitors and overnight guests are welcome, and there's a resident botanist to lead tours. Spending the night in the garden is a pleasure, though considerably more pricey than sleeping in San Vito. ⊠ *6 km (4 mi) south of San Vito on road to Ciudad Neily* ☏ *Apdo. 73–8257, San Vito* ☎ *773–4004* 🖷 *773–3665* ⊕ *www.ots.ac.cr* ⊠ *$6* ☉ *Daily 8–4.*

off the beaten path

CIUDAD NEILY – The 33-km (21-mi) road between San Vito and Ciudad Neily is twisting and spectacular, with views over the Coto Colorado plain to the Golfo Dulce and Osa Peninsula beyond. Much of this steep terrain is covered with tropical forest, making it an ideal route for bird-watching and picture-taking. The road from **San Vito to Paso Real** is equally scenic, traveling along a high ridge with sweeping valley views on either side. This road is relatively well paved, so even the driver can enjoy the scenery.

Where to Stay & Eat

$ ✕ **Pizzeria Liliana.** Treat yourself to real Italian pizza at this large, friendly, family-run restaurant with a garden terrace out back. Pizzas have crispy olive-oil crusts and come in three generous sizes: even the small easily serves two. Or dig into the macaroni *sanviteña*-style, with white sauce, ham, and mushrooms. The classics are here as well, and they're all homemade—lasagna, canneloni, and ravioli. The vinaigrette salad dressing is a welcome change from more acidic Tico dressings. ⊠ *150 m west of central square* ☎ *773–3080* 🖃 *V.*

★ $$ 🏨 **Wilson Botanical Garden.** A must-see paradise for gardeners and bird lovers, this pretty garden has cabins of modern glass, steel, and wood that blend into a forested ridge. Private balconies cantilevered over a ravine make bird-watching a snap even from your room. Each room is named after a plant growing at the doorway. Room rates include three excellent home-style meals and 24-hour access to the garden. Staying overnight is the easiest way to see the garden at dusk and dawn, a highly recommended experience. It's also the only way to get a chance to walk the Sendero Río Java, teeming with streams, birds, and monkeys. ⊠ *6 km (4 mi) south of San Vito on road to Ciudad Neily* ☏ *OTS, Apdo. 676–2050, San Pedro* ☎ *240–6696* 🖷 *240–6783* ⊕ *www.ots.ac.cr* 🛏 *12 cabinas* ⚒ *Restaurant, hiking; no a/c, no room phones, no room TVs* 🖃 *AE, MC, V* 🍴 *FAP.*

¢ 🏨 **Hotel El Ceibo.** Tucked in a quiet cul-de-sac behind Main Street, this well-maintained two-story hotel is reminiscent of Italy, with graceful arcades and white balconies. Rooms are compact but comfortable; many have views over a wooded ravine alive with birds. The restaurant serves homey Italian and Tico food at very reasonable prices. The curved 1950s-style wooden bar is a quaint spot to sit on a red stool and enjoy a drink. It's the best deal in town. ⊠ *140 m east of San Vito's central park, behind Municipalidad* ☎ *773–3025* 🖷 *773–5025* 🛏 *40 rooms* ⚒ *Restaurant, fans, cable TV, bar; no a/c, no room phones* 🖃 *V.*

Shopping

In an old farmhouse on the east side of the road between San Vito and the botanical garden, **Finca Cántaros** (✉ 3 km [2 mi] south of San Vito ☎ 773–3760) sells crafts by local indigenous artisans as well as colorful ceramics from San José artists featuring cavorting monkeys and tropical fruits and flowers. Rare animal carvings made from small tagua nuts, which resemble ivory in appearance and texture, are sold as well. Profits help support the adjacent children's library. A private park here has trails and lakeside picnicking spots.

La Amistad National Park

❻ *40 km (25 mi) northwest of San Vito.*

Covering more than 1,980 square km (765 square mi), Parque Nacional La Amistad is by far the largest park in Costa Rica, yet it's actually a mere portion of the vast **Reserva La Biósfera La Amistad**—a collection of protected areas stretching from southern Costa Rica into western Panama. The Costa Rican part of the park covers altitudes ranging from 1,000 m (3,280 feet) to 3,500 m (11,480 feet) and has an array of ecosystems that hold two-thirds of the country's vertebrate species. The park is difficult to access, but it's a worthwhile excursion for the adventurous. The easiest part to visit is **Altamira,** 35 km (23 mi) north of Paso Real. There's a ranger station there, as well as a biodiversity office, picnic area, rest rooms, potable water, and trails. The road winding its bumpy way up into the mountains is suitable only for four-wheel-drive vehicles. Camping is allowed for $5 per person at empty sites (bring your own tent). Reserve space about a week in advance at the regional office (✉ Buenos Aires ☎ 730–0846) or through the Altamira station (☎ 200–5355).

If you don't want to camp, San Vito is the most sensible place to base yourself when visiting La Amistad. The drive from San Vito to the park is about 31 km (20 mi). The last 20 km (13 mi) are uphill on a rough road, so the trip can take about an hour and a half. ☎ *730-0846 or 200–5355* ✍ *$5* ☉ *Daily 8–4.*

SOUTHERN PACIFIC BEACHES

After a 50-minute drive southwest of San Isidro, just over a scenic mountain ridge, you reach the southern Pacific coast with its miles of beaches for sunning, surfing, kayaking, and snorkeling. Ballena National Marine National Park alone encompasses almost 10 km (6 mi) of protected beaches. Scattered along the coast are small communities with increasing numbers of international residents and interesting restaurants and lodging options.

Dominical

❼ *34 km (21 mi) southwest of San Isidro.*

The small community of Dominical, once a sleepy fishing village, is now a slightly scruffy surfer town, with a smattering of interesting bars and restaurants that come and go with the waves of itinerant young people, though there are a few perennially popular places. Its real magic lies in the surrounding terrestrial and marine wonders: the rain forest grows right up to the beach in some places, and the sea offers world-class surfing. The beaches here are long, rarely crowded, and perfect for beachcombing among all the flotsam and jetsam that the surf washes up. Swimmers should beware of fatally dangerous rip currents. The local steep hillsides are covered with lush forest, much of it protected within private nature reserves. By leading hikes and horseback tours, several of these reserves are trying to finance preservation of the rain forest through ecotourism.

★ ☺ The **Hacienda Barú** nature reserve is a leader in both ecotourism and conservation, with a turtle protection project and nature education program in the local school. The bird-watching is spectacular, with excellent guides. You can stay at the hotel or just come for the day to walk the forest and mangrove trails, zip through the canopy on cables, or climb a tree to an observation platform. Tour prices range from $20 to $60 per person. ⊠ *2 km (1 mi) north of bridge into Dominical* ☎ *787–0003* ⊕ *www.haciendabaru.com* ⊠ *$6* ☺ *Daily dawn–dusk.*

Two reserves border the **Cataratas de Nauyaca** (Nauyaca Waterfalls), a massive double cascade that is one of the most spectacular sights in Costa Rica. The waterfalls—also known as Barú Falls—are on private property, so the only way to reach them is to take a hiking or horseback tour. **Don Lulo's tour** (☎771–3187) departs daily at 8 AM from the road to San Isidro, 10 km (6 mi) northeast of Dominical. The tour is $40 and includes breakfast and lunch at Don Lulo's family homestead near the falls. **Bella Vista tours** (☎388–0155) takes riders on a mountain, beach, and waterfall tour, morning or afternoon, depending on tides. The $45 tour includes breakfast before morning tours or sunset cocktails and snacks after the afternoon ride. The three- to four-hour tours start at the lodge, 5 km (3 mi) south of Dominical, then left up the steep, rough Escaleras road.

A considerably smaller waterfall than Cataratas de Nauyaca, **Pozo Azul** is in the jungle about 5 km (3 mi) south of town. Off the main highway, head up the road toward Bella Vista lodge and take the first road to the right, past the new school and through a stream; follow the road straight uphill for about 300 m to where the road widens. You can park here and climb down the steep trail to the river on the right, where there is a lovely swimming hole and waterfall.

Where to Stay & Eat

$–$$ ✕ **Fish Lips.** Restaurants come and go quickly in this town, but this cheery terrace with ocean-blue tables painted with lushly lipped fish waitresses looks like a keeper. Local fisherman Steve Sandusky ensures there's plenty of fresh mahimahi, tuna, snapper, and snook to grill, blacken, and marinate in teryaki sauce. Shrimp are main players, too: fried, breaded, or served with a Buffalo-style hot sauce. Desserts are homemade with tempting local twists such as coconut rum toppings and *mora* (blackberry) sauce. At night, lantern light creates a mellow atmosphere for sipping some out-of-the-ordinary French and South African wines. ⊠ *Main road, across from the San Clemente Grill* ☎ *787–0091* ▭ *No credit cards.*

¢–$$ ✕ **Restaurante El Rincón.** Savory meat and fish dishes are served with a sea view at this octagonal, alfresco restaurant run by an Argentine-Italian family. The tuna salad is unlike any other: chunks of succulent tuna sautéed in spicy oil and arranged over shredded lettuce, tomatoes, carrots, and mozzarella cheese. Beef and chicken empanadas make a light lunch, or you can go for broke with a T-bone or rib-eye steak grilled gaucho-style. Save room for a Latin version of a banana split, incorporating banana bread, bananas, ice cream, chocolate sauce, and walnuts. Sunsets are stunning here. ⊠ *Pueblo Comercial center at entrance to town* ☎ *787–0048* ⊟ *AE, MC, V* ☾ *Closed Wed.*

¢–$ ✕ **San Clemente Bar & Grill.** Signs you're in the local surfer hangout: dozens of broken surfboards affixed to the ceiling, photos of the sport's early years adorning the walls, and a big sound system and dance floor. Fresh seafood (grilled outdoors for dinner), sandwiches, and such Tex-Mex standards as burritos and nachos make up the menu. Owner Mike McGinnis is famous for making great hot sauces and for being a super source of information about the area. He also offers affordable accommodations at Cabinas San Clemente (¢–$) and a budget-price backpacker's hostel (¢), both right on the beach. ⊠ *Main road* ☎☎ *787–0055* ⊟ *AE, MC, V.*

$–$$$ 🏨 **The Necochea Inn.** The name sounds indigenous, but it's actually the Basque-origin last name of the young American owners, who have built a handsome B&B mountain retreat decorated with a sophisticated mix of safari-modern oversize furniture that is right at home in the huge rooms. Downstairs living and dining rooms face a wall of sliding glass doors looking onto a stone-decked pool with jungle and a slice of ocean for a view. Two streams run through the forested property, supplying a natural sound track. A curved stone stairway leads up to two luxurious, large rooms, which share a spacious bath, and two suites, each with private porch, decadent bathrooms with deep tubs or whirlpool tubs for two, antique armoires, and gleaming hardwood floors. ⊠ *Marina Vista Dr., off main highway; 4 km (2½ mi) south of Dominical, Dominicalito* ☎ *395–2984* ⊕ *www.thenecocheainn.com* ⤸ *2 rooms with shared bath, 2 suites* ♿ *Dining room, some in-room hot tubs, pool; no a/c, no room phones, no room TVs* ⊟ *MC, V* ⑩ *BP.*

$$ 🏨 **Roca Verde.** The sunny, stylish rooms of this beachfront hotel have stucco walls painted with swirling wall flowers, luxurious bathrooms, and cane-balustraded verandas looking onto a garden. There's no TV reception in the rooms, but you can request a VCR and a television. Surfing lessons are given. Late-night dances on Saturdays, sometimes with live music, draw *bailarinas* (dancers) from surrounding towns. ⊠ *1 km (½ mi) south of Dominical* ☎ *787–0036* ⊟ *787–0013* ⤸ *10 rooms* ♿ *Restaurant, pool, beach, fishing, laundry service; no room phones, no room TVs* ⊟ *AE, MC, V.*

$–$$ 🏨 **Hotel Diuwak.** An oasis of tranquility in slightly chaotic Dominical central, Diuwak—which means "people of the sun" in indigenous Bribri—has pleasant rooms in white stucco buildings nestled in mature gardens. High ceilings, tiled floors, clean bathrooms, and cheery rainbow-striped linens make these rooms very comfortable. You can enjoy the garden view from carved wooden benches on the verandas. A palm-lined avenue leads to a palatial pool with a theatrical waterfall. ✉ *South end of main road, near turnoff to beach* ☎ *787–0087* 🖷 *787–0089* ⊕ *www.diuwak.com* ⌁ *18 rooms* ♻ *Restaurant, grocery, fans, some kitchens, some refrigerators, pool, beach, Ping-Pong, bar, Internet; no a/c in some rooms, no TV in some rooms* ▭ *AE, MC, V.*

★ **$–$$** ▦ **Pacific Edge.** The forest grows right up to this stylishly rustic lodge high on a mountain ridge south of town with an unbeatable Pacific view. Private wood cabinas—one sleeps six—have newly tiled bathrooms, hammocks strung on wide porches, and comfortable orthopedic mattresses covered with colorful Guatemalan bedspreads. The lodge's bamboo-roofed, pagoda-style dining room serves great breakfasts and dinners on request. Two lookout towers at each end of the tiny pool catch the spectacular sunsets. The road up to this lofty perch definitely requires a four-wheel-drive vehicle, but a hotel shuttle can pick you up in town with advance notice. The reception desk closes at 6 PM. ✉ *Turn inland 4 km (2½ mi) south of Dominical on a rough road, follow road 2 km (1 mi)* ⊡ *Apdo. 531–8000, Dominical* ☎🖷 *787–8010* ✇ *pacificedge@pocketmail.com* ⌁ *4 cabinas* ♻ *Dining room, refrigerators, pool, bar; no a/c, no room phones, no room TVs* ▭ *AE, MC, V.*

$ ▦ **Cabinas Punta Dominical.** Picture a dream location: a high headland jutting out to sea with vistas up and down the Pacific coast. Add four simple wooden cabins on stilts, all facing the ocean, each with three walls of screened, floor-to-ceiling louvered windows to welcome in the constant breezes. Each cabin also has bamboo furniture, good reading lights, airy bathrooms, and a veranda with hammock. Throw in a breeze-swept restaurant, called La Parcela, which offers spectacular views despite none-too-exciting seaside cuisine. If you're just passing through Dominical, this is the best place for a tall glass of fruit juice or a cool beer with a view. ✉ *4 km (2½ mi) south of Dominical* ☎ *787–0016* 🖷 *787–0241* ⊕ *www.laparcela.net* ⌁ *4 cabins* ♻ *Restaurant, fans, hiking, bar, laundry service; no a/c, no room phones, no room TVs* ▭ *AE, MC, V* ⫶◉ *CP.*

$ ▦ **Hacienda Barú National Wildlife Refuge and Ecolodge.** Base yourself in these spacious but simple cabinas to explore the surrounding forests, mangroves, and beach. Tiled floors, sitting rooms with bamboo furniture, and two or three bedrooms make the cabins perfect for three or four people. Linger for an hour or two atop a lofty bird observation platform in the hotel's rain-forest canopy, zip along the canopy tour, climb a 114-foot-high tree with ropes, or stay overnight at a shelter in the heart of the forest. Excellent local guides interpret the miles of trails, or you can follow the self-guided trail with the help of a handbook. ✉ *2 km (1 mi) north of bridge into Dominical* ⊡ *Apdo. 215–8000, Pérez Zeledón* ☎ *787–0003* 🖷 *787–0004* ⊕ *www.haciendabaru.com* ⌁ *6 cabinas* ♻ *Restaurant, fans, kitchens, hiking; no a/c, no room phones, no room TVs* ▭ *AE, MC, V* ⫶◉ *CP.*

$ ▦ **Villas Río Mar.** The fanciest hotel in town is upriver from the beach on exquisitely landscaped grounds adrift in clouds of orchids. The 10 adobe-style cabinas—each with four separate rooms—feel like private cottages, with thatched roofs, cane ceilings, and clean white bathrooms. Each room has a private porch screened with mosquito netting and furnished with bamboo chairs and hammocks. Plants and elegant table settings fill the restaurant, which is covered by a giant thatched roof. There is a luxurious, large pool with a swim-up bar and handsome teak pool furniture. The hotel spa offers yoga. ⊠ *1 km (½ mi) west of Dominical on riverfront road* ☎ *787–0052* ⊠ *787–0054* ⊕ *www.villasriomar. com* ⅁ *Apdo. 1645–2050, San José* ⥽ *40 rooms* ⌂ *Restaurant, refrigerators, tennis court, pool, gym, hot tub, massage, spa, beach, bicycles, hiking, bar, convention center; no a/c, no room TVs* ⊟ *AE, MC, V* ⍾ *BP.*

¢ ⊞ **Posada del Sol.** Going no-frills? Here you'll find simple, clean accommodations in a tranquil atmosphere. Rooms are on the ground floor of a concrete building opening onto a narrow porch with chairs and tables and hammocks. In back is a little garden with a table and an area for washing clothes (by hand). Mattresses are firm and the hotel has its own freshwater well, so the water is safe to drink. The Costa Rican owners are friendly and helpful. ⊠ *Main road, just south of San Clemente Bar & Grill* ☎☎ *787–0085 or 787–0082* ⥽ *5 rooms* ⌂ *Fans; no a/c, no room TVs* ⊟ *No credit cards.*

Sports & the Outdoors

CANOPY TOURS **Hacienda Barú** (☎ 787–0003 ⊕ www.haciendabaru.com) is the best-organized ecotourism operation in Dominical. You can get hoisted to a platform in the crown of a giant tree on the rain-forest canopy tour ($35), spend a night in a shelter in the woods ($60), or take a zip-line tour ($35).

HORSEBACK RIDING You can travel to Nauyaca Falls via the private reserve of the **Bella Vista Lodge** (⊠ Halfway between Dominical and Dominicalito, up a steep road ☎ 388–0155) on a high ridge with a truly magnificent view. Bella Vista has 18 horses and gives a four-hour Mountains, Beach, and Waterfall Tour ($45, including homemade breakfast or cocktail snacks). One way to get to Nauyaca Waterfalls is with **Don Lulo's Horseback Tours** (⊠ Road to San Isidro, 12 km [8 mi] northeast of Dominical ☎ 787–0198). Lulo's trips to the falls ($40) include swimming in the natural pools below the cascades, a light breakfast, and a hearty Costa Rican lunch. Reserve a spot for Don Lulo's tour through your hotel or with **Dominical Adventures** (☎ 787–0191).

KAYAKING **Dominical Adventures** (⊠ San Clemente Bar & Grill, main road ☎ 787–0191) has a full range of watery adventures, including kayaking in mangroves and river tubing. **Southern Expeditions** (⊠ Entrance to town ☎ 787–0100) arranges kayaking, rafting, surfing, snorkeling, and diving trips. **Dominical Visitors Center** (⊠ Pueblo Comercial center, at entrance to town ☎ 787–0184) has information on everything available in and around town for body, mind, and spirit, including a night spent camping in a cave behind a waterfall and canyoneering tours.

SPORTFISHING Angling options range from expensive sportfishing charters to a trip in a small boat with a local fisherman to catch red snapper and snook. **Steve Sandusky** (☎ 787–0230) has been fishing local waters since 1996 aboard a high-powered 28-foot boat. You can fish for sport and take some of your catch home to eat. The Roca Verde hotel and Dominical Adventures at the San Clemente Bar & Grill can also arrange trips.

SURFING   Surfers have long flocked to Dominical for its consistent beach breaks. The **surf shop** near the San Clemente Cabinas and Surf Hostel on the beach rents, sells, and repairs surfboards.

Shopping

★ Shop in rare air-conditioned comfort at **Banana Bay Gallery & Gifts** (✉ Plaza Pacífica shopping center, highway just above Dominical ☎ 787–0106). It's open 9–5 daily, and it's stocked with an always intriguing and amusing mix of arts and crafts and unusual items, along with indigenous crafts such as Boruca masks and colorful woven-cotton hats and bags.

Ballena Marine National Park

❽ *20 km (12 mi) southeast of Dominical.*

One of Costa Rica's few marine parks, the Parque Nacional Marino Ballena (Whale Marine National Park) protects several beaches, a mangrove estuary, an important coral reef, and a vast swath of ocean with rocky isles and islets. There's some great snorkeling here. Humpback whales can be seen with their young from December to April, and frigate birds and Brown Boobies, a tropical seabird, nest on the park's rocky islands. With your less than $1 park admission, you'll receive a brochure and a plastic garbage bag to remind you to take your trash with you.

At the park's northern end, **Playa Uvita** stretches out into Punta Uvita, a long swath of sand, or *tombolo,* connecting a former island to the coast. At low tide, the sand bar resembles a whale's tail fanning out on either side of the point, hence the name of the bay: Bahía Ballena, or Whale Bay. **Playa Ballena,** 6 km (4 mi) to the south of Playa Uvita, is a lovely strand backed by lush vegetation. Tiny **Playa Piñuelas,** 3 km (2 mi) south of Playa Ballena, is in a deep cove that serves as the local port.

Playa Ventanas, just 1½ km (1 mi) south of Ballena Marine Park, is a beautiful beach that's popular for sea-kayaking. The mountains that rise up behind these beaches hold rain forests, waterfalls, and wildlife.

Where to Stay & Eat

$–$$ ✕ **Exotica Restaurant.** Nestled in the tiny French-Canadian enclave of Ojochal, you can feast on tropical fare with a French accent. For starters, there's a tangy refreshing avocado, pineapple, lime, and cilantro appetizer or an intriguing Tahitian fish carpaccio (with bananas!). Or try a hearty serving of fish in a spicy banana curry sauce. Presentation is artistic, with flourishes of flowers and sprigs of exotic greenery. Desserts, called "Sweet Moments," are all homemade and luscious. A clump of beach almond trees provides a canopy for the patio restaurant, which has only nine tables. ✉ *Main road into Ojochal, 15 km (9 mi) south of Uvita* 🚫 *No credit cards* 🕑 *Closed Sun.*

★ $ ✕ **Balcón de Uvita Restaurant.** Food and view vie for attention at this excellent balcony restaurant, with just six tables. The sunset view of Bahía Ballena is spectacular, but it's the authentic Indonesian cuisine that wins out. The rijstafel consists of seven exotic dishes that include sweetly spiced minced beef steamed in a banana leaf, succulent gin-

DIVING THE DEEP: COCOS ISLAND

RATED ONE OF THE TOP DIVING DESTINATIONS in the world, Isla del Coco is uninhabited and remote, and its waters are teeming with marine life. It is no place for beginners, but serious divers enjoy 100-foot visibility and the underwater equivalent of a big-game park: Scalloped Hammerheads, White-tipped Reef Sharks, Galápagos Sharks, Bottlenose Dolphins, Billfish, and Manta Rays mix with huge schools of brilliantly colored fish.

Encompassing about 22½ square km (14 square mi), Isla del Coco is the largest uninhabited island on earth. Its isolation has led to the evolution of dozens of endemic plant and animal species. The rocky topography is draped in rain forest and cloud forest and includes more than 200 waterfalls. Because of Isla del Coco's distance from shore (484 km [300 mi]) and its craggy topography, few visitors to Costa Rica—and even fewer Costa Ricans—have set foot on the island.

Costa Rica annexed Coco in 1869, and it became a national park in 1978. Today, only specialty-cruise ships, park rangers, scientists, and scuba divers visit the place Jacques Cousteau called "the most beautiful island in the world." The dry season (November–May) brings calmer seas and is the best time to see Silky Sharks. During the rainy season, large schools of Hammerheads can be seen, but the ocean is rougher.

Most dive cruises to Isla del Coco are about 10 days, and include three days of travel time on the open ocean. The **Okeanos Aggressor** (☏ 257–8686, 800/ 348–2628 in U.S. ⊕ www. okeanoscocosisland.com) and the **Undersea Hunter** (☏ 228–6613, 800/ 203–2120 in U.S. ⊕ www. underseahunter.com) run trips year-round at a cost of roughly $3,500.

---

gery chicken, and a toasted coconut–and-peanut condiment. ⊠ 1 km (½ mi) north of gas station (4-wheel-drive required), Uvita 🕿 743–8034 ⊗ Closed Mon.–Wed., except to guests of Balcón de Uvita hotel.

$–$$ ✕🏨 **Villas Gaia.** Spacious villas are spread around the jungle on a ridge here behind Playa Tortuga, overlooking forest ravines. The colorfully painted villas have handsome hardwood furnishings and balconies; the poolside villas catch the best breezes. A luxurious house has air-conditioning and satellite TV. The restaurant ($) is decorated with chandeliers made of mangrove roots and has cheerful banana stenciling on the walls, and serves an eclectic menu ranging from Greek salad to Thai-spiced fish, along with a tempting variety of banana desserts. There's a forest trail from the villas to the beach, where you can swim safely. Horseback, mangrove, and sea-kayaking tours can also be arranged through the hotel. ⊠ 15 km (9 mi) south of Uvita on coastal highway, Playa Tortuga 🕿 244–0316 in San José 🕿 363–3928 in Uvita ⊕ www.villasgaia.com ➷ 12 cabinas, 1 house ⟨ Restaurant, fans, pool, bar, laundry service; no a/c, no room phones, no room TVs ▭ AE, MC, V.

$$ ▦ **Rancho La Merced.** You can be a cowboy for a day at this 1235-acre hillside cattle ranch, milking, herding, and riding the range. Or you can hike mountain trails in search of wildlife and birds. Stay in a rambling original farmhouse made of wood shipped in from Puntarenas some 60 years ago and carried uphill on men's backs. The avocado-green hacienda has simple but comfortable rooms that share a modern bathroom extension and a homey eat-in kitchen. The cabin, great for families, sleeps up to seven. Resident guides can take you on foot or horseback into the forest. One guided tour of your choice is included in the rate. ⊠ *Mountain road, 100 m south of Villas Gaia, Uvita* ☎ *771–4582* 🖷 *771–8841* ⊕*www.wildlifecostarica.com* ⟿*10 rooms, 1 cabin* ⚥ *Fans, hiking, horseback riding; no a/c, no room phones, no room TVs* ▭ *AE, MC, V* ⏐◎⏐ *FAP.*

$ ▦ **Balcón de Uvita.** Three stylishly modern, comfortable casitas with large tiled bathrooms sleep four to six, and one has a full kitchen. They share the bay view, plus a lovely pool and garden in which to soak up the mountain tranquility. The restaurant (⇨ *above*) is highly recommended. ⊠ *1 km (½ mi) north of gas station (4-wheel-drive required), Uvita* ☎🖷 *743–8034* ⊕ *www.balcondeuvita.com* ⟿ *3 casitas* ⚥ *Restaurant, fans, some kitchens, pool, bar; no a/c, no room phones, no room TVs* ▭ *MC, V.*

Sports & the Outdoors

At **La Merced National Wildlife Refuge** (☎ 771–4582 ⊕ www. wildlifecostarica.com) you can ride the range on horseback, explore the forest on a nature hike, or go bird-watching with an excellent guide. Tours, which include transportation from your hotel and a guide, cost $25 for a half-day and $65 for a full day; the full day tour includes lunch.

ULTRALIGHT FLIGHTS   For a bird's-eye view of Bahía Ballena and the park, take off with aeronautical engineer Georg Kiechle in his ultralight flying machine for "the ultimate flying experience." Flights with **Skyline Fly Ultralight** (⊠ Road into Uvita ☎ 743–8037 ⊕ www.flyultralight.com) cost $65–$150 for 20 minutes to 1 hour.

WATER SPORTS   **Club Fred Adventure Tours** (☎ 307–0289 ⊕ www.clubfredcr.com) has kayaking tours on the Río Terraba as well as sea-kayaking tours exploring caves at Playa Piñuela. **Delfin Tours** (⊠ Playa Uvita ☎ 743–8169) organizes snorkeling trips to the nearby reef as well as sportfishing excursions to Caño Island.

THE GOLFO DULCE

At Chacarita, 33 km (20 mi) South of Palmar Sur, the southern coast assumes a multiple personality. Heading west, you reach the Osa Peninsula and, eventually, the Pacific Ocean. Continuing due south is the Golfo Dulce, a tropical fjord whose name means Sweet Gulf, connoting tranquil waters. This gulf creates two shorelines: a western shore that is accessible only by boat above Golfito, and an eastern shore, which is the western side of the Osa Peninsula. South of Golfito, the coast fronts the Pacific Ocean once again, with beaches that are a paradise for surfers and nature lovers.

Golfito

❾ *339 km (212 mi) southeast of San José.*

Overlooking a small gulf (hence its name) and hemmed in by a steep bank of forest, Golfito has a great location and little else—that is, unless you're an angler. Sport- and fly-fishing have taken off in this area, and many lodges here run these trips. The town was a thriving banana port for several decades—United Fruit arrived in 1938—with a dock that could handle 4,000 boxes of bananas per hour and elegant housing for its plantation managers. United Fruit pulled out in 1985 in response to labor disputes and rising export taxes, and Golfito promptly slipped into a state of poverty and neglect from which it has yet to recover completely. In an effort to inject some life into the town, the government declared it a duty-free port to attract Costa Rican shoppers, but the proposed Latin free-trade zone may mean its demise. The town itself consists of a pleasant older section and a long, ugly strip of newer buildings, dilapidated former workers' quarters, and abundant seedy bars. Visiting U.S. Navy ships dock here, and small cruise ships moor in the harbor. The Costa Rica Coast Guard headquarters is also here.

What to See

The northwestern end of town is the so-called **American Zone,** full of wooden houses on stilts, where the expatriate managers of United Fruit lived amid flowering trees imported from all over the world. These houses were purchased by Costa Ricans when the company departed, and some are now B&Bs.

Golfito doesn't have a beach of its own, but **Playa Cacao** is a mere five-minute boat ride across the bay from town. Hire a boat at the city dock or from a mooring opposite the larger cruise-ship dock, north of Golfito's center. Playa Cacao has a few restaurants and lodges, making it a cooler, quieter option when the heat in Golfito gets unbearable.

The hills behind Golfito are covered with the lush forest of the **Refugio Nacional de Vida Silvestre Golfito** (Golfito National Wildlife Refuge), known as Naranjal by the locals. At the entrance, just 500 m along a dirt road that runs parallel to the airport, you find the botanical legacy of the United Fruit Company's experimental farm, with flora from all over the world. The forest paths have been rehabilitated by the local tourism chamber and University of Costa Rica students, with signs leading you to waterfalls. ⊠ *500 m past the airport* ☎ *No phone* 🖅 *Free* 🕓 *24 hours.*

Parque Nacional Piedras Blancas (White Stones National Park), adjacent to the Golfito National Wildlife Refuge, has some great birding. The park is covered in verdant forest and is home to many species of endemic plants and animals. It's an important wildlife corridor because it connects to Corcovado National Park, and it's one of the few places in Costa Rica where jaguars still live. Follow the main road northwest through the old American Zone, past the airstrip and a housing project: the place where a dirt road heads into the rain forest is ground zero for bird-watchers.

If you have four-wheel drive, you can follow the dirt track through the heart of Piedras Blancas National Park to the community of La Gamba and the comfortable Esquinas Rain Forest Lodge. In the dry season when it's passable, this back route can cut miles off a trip to or from the north, and it passes through some gorgeous wilderness. ☒ *Adjacent to Golfito National Wildlife Refuge* ☎ *No phone* 🎫 *Free* ☉ *Daily dawn–dusk.*

★ A Garden of Eden with mass plantings of ornamental palms, bromeliads, heliconias, cycads, orchids, and flowering gingers, **Casa Orquideas** is accessible only by boat. It has been tended with care for more than 25 years by American owners Ron and Trudy MacAllister. The two-hour tour includes touching, tasting, and smelling, plus spotting toucans and hummingbirds. Tours require a minimum of four people. The water taxi from Golfito to the garden (about $50 for up to six people, including the return trip) is a tour in itself. ☒ *North of Golfito on the Golfo Dulce* ☎ *775–1614* 🎫 *$5* ☉ *Tours Sat.–Thurs. at 8:30* AM.

Where to Stay & Eat

$ ✕ **Restaurante Mar y Luna.** Strings of buoys, nets, and fishing rods give a nautical air to this terrace restaurant that juts out into Golfito Harbor. Even after the hottest day, there are cool evening breezes here and the restaurant's twinkling fairy lights frame a pleasant harbor view. The menu has a definite list toward seafood, including excellent shrimp and grilled whole fish, served with crisp, fried potatoes and refreshing salad. There are vegetarian choices, as well as chicken fillets smothered in a mushroom sauce. For atmosphere and above-average food, this is the best choice in Golfito. ☒ *South end of Golfito main street, just north of Hotel Las Gaviotas* ☎ *775–0192* 🖃 *AE, MC, V.*

$$$$ 🏨 **Golfito Sailfish Rancho.** Wedged between gulf and jungle, this comfortable, white-stucco lodge has all-inclusive, first-rate fishing packages ranging from $1,900 for three days to $2,900 for six days. Rates include taxi and boat transportation to the lodge, plus all meals, snacks, beer and wine, and fishing and snorkeling gear. Two wings of rooms with tiled verandas look onto a narrow strip of beach. The convivial restaurant serves buffet meals. Spacious rooms are meant for sharing and have racks for storing fishing rods. The Rancho's fleet includes 10 up-to-date fishing boats, where you spend the majority of your days. ☒ *15-min boat ride north of Golfito* ☎ *380–4262, 800/450–9908 in U.S.* 🖂 *5700 Memorial Hwy., Tampa, FL 33615* 📠 *813/889–9189* ⊕ *www.golfitosailfish. com* 🛏 *10 rooms* ♻ *Restaurant, fans, beach, bar; no a/c, no room phones, no room TVs, no kids under 12* 🖃 *AE, MC, V* ❒ *FAP.*

$$$ 🏨 **Esquinas Rainforest Lodge.** This well-managed ecolodge is run by an Austrian nonprofit group. A Teutonic sense of order prevails, with tidy gravel paths winding past five wooden cabins on manicured gardens surrounded by wild forest. Rooms have tile floors, good reading lamps, and airy bathrooms with plenty of hot water. A spring-fed pool is delightful, and the candlelit dining room serves excellent food. Fragrant white ginger and ylang-ylang encircle a pond with a resident caiman, well fed on pond trout. Wild and thrilling trails head to the waterfalls and primary forest of Piedras Blancas park. Local guides lead river walks and bird-watching tours. ☒ *Near La Gamba, 4 km (2½ mi) west of Villa Briceño turnoff* ☎ *775–0901* ⊕ *www.esquinaslodge.com* 🛏 *10 rooms* ♻ *Dining room, pool, hiking, horseback riding, bar; no a/c, no room phones, no room TVs* 🖃 *AE, MC, V* ❒ *AI.*

$$$ 🏨 **Playa Nicuesa Rainforest Lodge.** The newest addition to the Golfo Dulce lodging scene has set a new standard. The two-story main lodge is a palatial tree house, crafted from 15 kinds of wood. Luxurious, hexagon-shape wooden cabins with open-air showers are scattered around a lush garden that ensures privacy. A four-room stucco guesthouse is shaded by mango trees. Solar power means lots of hot water. The emphasis is on adventure. Out the front door of the lodge are beach, bay, and mangroves, with kayaks, snorkeling, fishing, sailing, and swimming; out the back door is a forested mountain with hiking trails, a waterfall, and plenty of wildlife. A resident naturalist interprets the trails. Imaginative meals are served in the second-story dining room–cum-lounge with an unbeatable tropical-garden view. ⌧ *Golfo Dulce, north of Golfito; accessible only by boat from Golfito or Puerto Jiménez,* ☎ *735–5237 (messages only)* ⊕ *www.nicuesalodge.com* ⇆ *5 cabins, 4 rooms* ⌂ *Restaurant, beach, snorkeling, fishing, boating, hiking, bar; no a/c, no room phones, no room TVs* ⊟ *MC, V* ☉ *Closed Oct.–Nov. 15* ⧖ *AI.*

$ 🏨 **Hotel Las Gaviotas.** Just south of town on the water's edge, this hotel has wonderful views over the inner gulf. Rooms have terra-cotta floors, teak furniture, and a veranda with chairs overlooking the well-tended tropical gardens and the shimmering gulf beyond. A pleasant open-air restaurant with fresh-tasting food looks onto the large pool, whose terrace is barely divided from the sea. The bar-restaurant has an extensive wine and cocktail list. The hotel books sportfishing trips. ⌧ *3 km (2 mi) south of Golfito town center* ⌂ *Apdo. 12–8201, Golfito* ☎ *775–0062* 🖷 *775–0544* ⊕ *www.resortlasgaviotas.com* ⇆ *18 rooms, 3 cabinas* ⌂ *Restaurant, fans, cable TV, pool, bar, shop* ⊟ *AE, MC, V.*

Sports & the Outdoors

SPORTFISHING Fishing is great in the waters off Golfito, either in the Golfo Dulce or out in the open ocean. The open ocean holds plenty of sailfish, marlin, and Roosterfish during the dry months, as well as mahimahi, tuna, and wahoo during the rainy season; there's excellent bottom fishing any time of year. Relatively low-cost tours given by **Froylan López** (☎ 824–6571) take you fishing the traditional Tico way, with rod and reel and a full ice chest. **Golfito Sailfish Rancho** (☎ 380–4262, 800/450–9908 in U.S.) runs the biggest fishing charter operation in Golfito. Its huge marina is right in town. **Hotel Las Gaviotas** (⌧ 3 km [2 mi] south of Golfito town center ☎ 775–0062) can arrange sportfishing trips. **Tierra Mar** (Land Sea Services; ⌧ Waterfront next to Banana Bay Marina ☎🖷 775–1614 ⊕ www.marinaservices-yachtdelivery.com) arranges day trips with independent captains in the area.

Shopping

Tierra Mar (⌧ Waterfront next to Banana Bay Marina) has an excellent selection of painted Boruca wood masks. It also has one-of-a-kind local crafts, such as woven straw hats, cotton purses, and painted gourds.

Playa Zancudo

❿ *51 km (32 mi) south of Golfito.*

Playa Zancudo, a 10-km (6-mi), palm-lined beach fronting the fishing village of Zancudo, is accessible by car or boat. You can hire a boat at the municipal dock in Golfito for the 25-minute ride ($25 for two). The rough road entails two hours of bone shaking and a short ride on a cable river ferry. There's a flurry of new construction here, with Canadians and Americans building substantial beachfront homes. Zancudo has a good surf break, but it's nothing compared with Playa Pavones a little to the south. There are some good swimming areas, and if you get tired of playing in the surf and sand, you can arrange a boat trip to the nearby mangrove estuary to see birds and crocodiles. Zancudo is also home to one of the area's best sportfishing operations, headquartered at Roy's Zancudo Lodge.

Where to Stay & Eat

$ ✕🍴 **Cabinas y Restaurante Sol y Mar.** As its name implies, Cabinas Sol y Mar has sun and sea, plus a beach fringed by coconut palms. Peach-colored cabinas with tiled porches and high ceilings look onto the gulf and have views of the Osa Peninsula. Each roomy cabina has a sunny bathroom with a pebble-paneled shower and sleeps four. The alfresco restaurant ($–$$) serves the consistently best food in town: excellent fish—try the mahimahi in coconut-ginger sauce—and elegant desserts. The popular U-shape bar is an easy place to meet new friends, including the friendly Canadian-American owners. A shop sells colorful sarongs and clothing from Thailand. ⊠ *Main road, south of Cabinas Los Cocos, Playa Zancudo* ☎ *776–0014* ⊕ *www.zancudo.com* 🛏 *5 cabinas, 1 house* ⟁ *Restaurant, fans, beach, volleyball, bar, shop; no a/c, no room phones, no room TVs* ▭ *V* ☉ *Closed Oct.*

$$$$ 🍴 **Roy's Zancudo Lodge.** Most people who stay here are anglers on all-inclusive sportfishing packages, taking advantage of Roy's 11 fishing boats. But the comfortable, modern hotel is a good choice even if you've never caught anything but a cold. It's right on the beach—the ample, verdant grounds surround an inviting pool and an open-air restaurant serves buffet meals. The nonfishing rate includes all meals and "national-brand" drinks (locally made brands of alcohol). The sea foam–green two-story hotel has huge rooms with hardwood floors, two firm double beds, and ocean views. Four suites are in cozy private cabinas, and three cheaper rooms don't have refrigerators. ⊠ *Main road, 1 km (½ mi) west of Cabinas Sol y Mar, Playa Zancudo* 🏠 *Apdo. 41, Zancudo* ☎ *776–0008* 🖨 *776–0011* ⊕ *www.royszancudolodge.com* 🛏 *15 rooms, 4 cabinas* ⟁ *Restaurant, fans, some refrigerators, cable TV, pool, hot tub, beach, fishing, bar* ▭ *AE, MC, V* ⊚ *FAP.*

$ 🍴 **Cabinas Los Cocos.** This little beachfront colony of four self-catering cabins is designed for people who want to kick back and enjoy the beach. Artist Susan England and her husband, Andrew Robertson, are Zancudo fixtures and can organize any activity, including river safaris and kayaking tours. There are two idyllic tropical cabins with thatched roof and hammock. The other two cabins are renovated 40-year-old banana company houses moved here from Palmar Norte. These charming white-and-green wooden cottages give visitors a rare chance to live a little bit of Costa Rican history. ⊠ *Beach road* ☎🖨 *776–0012* ⊕ *www.loscocos. com* 🛏 *4 cabins* ⟁ *Kitchens, beach; no a/c, no room phones, no room TVs* ▭ *No credit cards.*

Sports & the Outdoors

SPORTFISHING If you've got your own gear, you can do some good shore fishing from the beach or the mouth of the mangrove estuary, or hire one of the local boats to take you out into the gulf. **Arena Alta Sportfishing** (⊠ Town dock ☎ 776–0042) arranges daily fishing trips, serving some of the day's catch as sushi every night in its bar. It also provides boat taxis and rents golf carts for getting around Zancudo. **Roy Ventura** (⊠ Roy's Zancudo Lodge ☎ 776–0008) runs the best charter operation in the area, with 11 boats ranging in length from 22 feet to 32 feet. Packages include room, food, and drink, and you can arrange to be picked up in Golfito or Puerto Jiménez.

Playa Pavones

▶ **⑪** *53 km (33 mi) south of Golfito.*

On the southern edge of the mouth of Golfo Dulce stands Pavones, a windswept beach town at the end of a dirt road. Famous among surfers for having one of the longest waves in the world, the town also has pristine black-sand beaches and virgin rain forest in its favor. It's not close to anything in particular, but its seclusion makes it a worthwhile destination for adventurous types. Most surfers here are serious about their sport and bring their own boards, but you can rent surfboards, Boogie boards, and bicycles at Cabinas La Ponderosa.

Where to Stay

$$$$ **Tiskita Jungle Lodge.** Monkeys, coatis, birds, and other wildlife are lured by the hundreds of exotic fruit trees from all over the world that have been planted on the grounds by the lodge owner, a passionate farmer. Guides lead tours of the grounds and daylong dolphin-watching trips. Screened wooden cabins on stilts are surrounded by lush vegetation and have rustic furniture and open-air bathrooms. Trails invite you to explore the jungle and a cascading waterfall with freshwater pools. Simple, buffet-style meals are speedy. Cabins are spread out, but many are joined. If you want privacy, ask when booking. Most guests arrive by air taxi at the hotel's private airstrip. There's no phone at the lodge. ⊠ *6 km (4 mi) south of Pavones* ⊡ *Apdo. 13411–1000, San José* ☎ 296–8125 🖷 296–8133 ⊕ *www.tiskita-lodge.co.cr* ⇆ *16 rooms* ☪ *Dining room, fans, pool, beach, snorkeling, hiking, horseback riding, bicycles, bar, airstrip; no a/c, no room phones, no room TVs* ⊟ *AE, MC, V* ☉ *Closed Sept. 15–Oct. 15* ¶⊙¶ *AI.*

$$ **Cabinas La Ponderosa.** The world-famous Playa Pavones surfing break is on the doorstep of this surfer-owned hotel. It's a cut above the usual surfer place, with high-ceilinged rooms that sleep up to six and have hardwood furniture and walls. Screened porches overlook a lush garden, and nature trails wind through 14 acres. The house has two bedrooms and a screened balcony but no kitchen. You can rent surfboards, Boogie boards, or bicycles here. ⊠ *On beach* ☎ 824–4145 *for voice mail, 954/771–9166 in U.S.* ⊕ *www.cabinaslaponderosa.com* ⇆ *5 rooms, 1 house* ☪ *Dining room, fans, some refrigerators, beach, bicycles, Ping-Pong; no a/c in some rooms, no room phones, no room TVs* ⊟ *No credit cards* ¶⊙¶ *FAP.*

THE OSA PENINSULA

Some of Costa Rica's most breathtaking scenery and wildlife thrive on the Osa Peninsula, one-third of which is covered by Corcovado National Park. It's a paradise for backpackers and upscale vacationers alike, who can hike into the park on any of three routes. Corcovado also works for day trips from nearby luxurious nature lodges, most of which lie within private preserves that are home for much of the same wildlife you might see in the park. And to complement the peninsula's lush forests and pristine beaches, the sea around it offers great sportfishing and diving.

Most visitors fly to Puerto Jiménez, Drake, or Carate, but there's also a 90-minute water-taxi ride from Golfito. A rickety-looking launch leaves at 11:30 AM every day from the *muellecito* (small municipal dock) in Golfito. It returns the next morning from the concrete pier at Puerto Jiménez.

Puerto Jiménez

⑫ *127 km (79 mi) west of Golfito, 364 km (226 mi) southeast of San José.*

This sleepy and dusty town is the largest on the Osa Peninsula and is a convenient base for exploring some of the nearby wilderness. Main-street traffic consists mostly of bicycles and ancient pickup trucks. Be prepared for the humidity and mosquitoes—Jiménez has plenty of both. You won't find relief in the Golfo Dulce, which borders the town, as its water is quite warm. New restaurants, hotels, Internet cafés, and "green" newcomers are lending this town an interesting, funky edge.

Most people spend a night here before or after visiting Corcovado National Park, as Puerto Jiménez has the best access to the park's two main trailheads and is the base for the *collectivo* (public transport via pickup truck) to Carate (⇨ Bus Travel, The Southern Pacific A to Z).

The only place to change money in Puerto Jiménez is Banco Nacional on the main street, 500 m south of Super 96, directly across from the church. The bank has an ATM that accepts some foreign bank cards. You can get an advance using your MasterCard or Visa at the teller windows inside. Bank hours are weekdays 8:30–3:45. There are no phones in Cabo Matapalo or Carate, so take care of calls in Jiménez.

Check in at the **National Parks Service Headquarters** (⊠ Next to airstrip ☎ 735–5036 🖷 735–5276) to enter Corcovado or just to inquire about hiking routes and trail conditions. The Parks Service takes reservations for camping space, meals, or accommodations at **La Sirena ranger station** in Corcovado National Park.

Where to Stay & Eat

¢–$ ✕ **Juanita's Mexican Bar & Grill.** Swing open the saloon doors of this cantina, and you might think you're in another south-of-the-border frontier town. The popular bamboo bar dispenses signature margaritas to go along with the Tex-Mex menu of quesadillas, burritos, and taco salads. Brightly colored tablecloths and art enliven the eating experience, as do the antics of patrons on special-event nights with crab races and hula hoop contests. It's open for breakfast, too. ⊠ *Beside CafeNet El Sol, in center of town* ☎ 735–5056 ⊟ *No credit cards.*

¢ ✕ **Soda Marisquería Morales.** Miriam Torres, a dried-flower artist, has created a charming rustic nook here, with tree-trunk tables and chairs, where she serves delicious shellfish soups and fresh fish *ceviche* (fish, shrimp, or octopus marinated in lime juice). You'll also find local specialties such as cream of *ayote* (squash) soup and generous *casados* (plates of rice, beans, fried plantains, and salad), with fish, plus pasta dishes. The place is open daily 3–10. ⊠ *Across from north end of soccer field Puerto Jiménez* ☎ 735–5746 ⊟ *No credit cards.*

★ $$ ✕ ▥ **Parrot Bay Village.** A storybook collection of octagonal cottages in a tropical garden 20 minutes from town by foot, this hotel has caimans lurking in the nearby mangrove lagoon. Mahogany cabinas have four-poster beds, tile floors, hot-water showers, and intricately carved mahogany doors. They sleep up to eight; three cabinas have two stories. Some cabinas face the bar and restaurant, others face the gulf. The food at the attractive alfresco restaurant ($) is the best in town; the short dinner menu changes daily and full breakfasts are served. From the restaurant, you have a view of the beach, gulf, fishing boats, and the distant hills of Piedras Blancas. Order dinner at least an hour in advance. ⊠ *500 m southeast of airport, on beachfront* ☎ 735–5180 ☎ 735–5568 ⊕ *www.parrotbayvillage.com* ◿ *8 cabinas* ⚲ *Restaurant, in-room safes, beach, snorkeling, boating, fishing, volleyball, bar, laundry service; no room phones, no room TVs, no smoking* ⊟ *AE, D, MC, V* ⦿ *BP.*

¢ ✕ ▥ **Restaurante y Cabinas Carolina.** This simple alfresco restaurant in the heart of Puerto Jiménez serves decent *comida típica* (typical food) and reliably fresh seafood. It's also the central meeting place for every tourist and foreigner in town, ergo a good place to pick up information. The small guest rooms in back make it a good rest stop for backpackers entering or leaving Corcovado; rooms are basically concrete boxes with cold running water, but they're clean and convenient. Don't count on using a credit card, as phone lines are not always working. ⊠ *Center of town, 2 blocks south of soccer field* ☎ 735–5185 ◿ *7 rooms* ⚲ *No a/c in some rooms, no room phones, no room TVs* ⊟ *V.*

$$$ ▥ **Iguana Lodge.** Ideal for beach lovers, this comfortable, well-established lodge has breezy, screened-in cabins among mature trees fringing secluded Playa Platanares. The gentle Golfo Dulce waters are perfect for swimming, sea-kayaking, and Boogie boarding. Cabins are furnished elegantly in bamboo, with lots of thoughtful touches, including Egyptian cotton sheets and a raft of candles to light for romantic evenings. There's plenty of solar-heated hot water and excellent water pressure in the pebble-lined showers. Buffet-style dinners, with exotic foods reflecting the owners' worldwide travels, are served in a thatched-roof dining room with a huge horseshoe-shape table that can accommodate up to 24. There's also a communal kitchen, a yoga platform, and a Japanese soaking tub. Birds are plentiful in the Playa Preciosa Platanares Mixed Refuge, which borders the lodge. ⊠ *Playa Platanares, 5 km (3 mi) south of Puerto Jiménez airport,* ☎ 735–5205 ☎ 735–5436 ⊕ *www.iguanalodge.com* ◿ *8 rooms in 4 bungalows, 2 2-bedroom family cabins, 1 3-story house with 3 rooms* ⚲ *Restaurant, fans, kitchens, Japanese baths, beach, snorkeling, fishing, hiking, bar* ⊟ *MC, V* ⦿ *AI.*

$ 🏨 **La Choza de Manglar.** This former budget hotel just steps from the airport offers comfort with pizzazz. The huge restaurant area has spectacular hand-painted murals that create an indoor rain forest, and the bathrooms are immersed in a sea of painted underwater life. There's also an amazing amount of real wildlife in the surrounding mangrove forest. Rooms in the hotel are on the small side, with tile floors and colorful, hand-carved wooden furniture made in Nicaragua. The garden cabins are larger, with ceiling fans instead of air-conditioning, and hammocks on the porches. ⊠ *100 m west of airport* 🏠 *735–5002* 🖂 *info@manglares.com* 🛏 *6 rooms, 4 cabins* 🍴 *Restaurant, fans, bar; no a/c in some rooms, no room phones, no room TVs* 🖃 *No credit cards* 🍽 *BP.*

The Outdoors

BIRD-WATCHING For excellent bird-watching tours with expert English-speaking guides Liz Jones and Abraham Gallo, visit **Bosque del Río Tigre Lodge** (⊠ Dos Brazos del Tigre, 12 km (7½ mi) northwest of Puerto Jiménez 🕿 735–5725 🌐 www.osaadventures.com).

HIKING If you have four-wheel drive, it's just a 30-minute ride west to **Dos Brazos** and the Tigre sector of the park, which few hikers explore because of its more difficult access. You can take a taxi to Dos Brazos and hike from here or use rustic but comfortable Bosque del Río Tigre Lodge as a base. **Osa Aventura** (⊠ Central Puerto Jiménez 🕿 735–5670 🌐 www. osaaventura.com) specializes in multiday Corcovado hiking adventures, led by Mike Boston, an ebullient tropical biologist who sounds like Sean Connery and looks like Crocodile Dundee.

RAFTING & SEA-KAYAKING Puerto Jiménez is a good base for boat or sea-kayaking trips on the Golfo Dulce and the nearby mangrove rivers and estuaries. **Escondido Trex** (⊠ Restaurante Carolina, center of town, 200 m south of soccer field 🕿 735–5210 🖷 735–5196 🌐 www.escondidotrex.com) arranges sea-kayaking, charter-fishing, and small-boat outings for watching wildlife in addition to a number of land-based outings.

Cabo Matapalo

★ ⑬ *21 km (14 mi) south of Puerto Jiménez.*

The southern tip of the Osa Peninsula—where virgin rain forest meets the sea at a rocky point—retains the kind of natural beauty that people travel halfway across the world to experience. From its ridges you can look out on the blue Golfo Dulce and Pacific Ocean, sometimes spotting whales in the distance. The forest is tall and dense, with the highest and most diverse tree species in the country, usually draped with thick lianas. The name Cabo Matapalo means "cape strangler fig," a reference to the fig trees that germinate in the branches of other trees and extend their roots downward, eventually smothering the supporting tree by blocking the life-giving light with their roots and branches. Strangler figs are common in this area, as they are nearly everywhere else in the country, but Matapalo's greatest attractions are its rarer species, such as the *gallinazo* tree, which bursts into yellow blossom as the rainy season comes to a close. The brilliant Scarlet Macaw is another draw here.

A forested ridge extends east from Corcovado down to Matapalo, where the foliage clings to almost-vertical slopes and waves crash against the black rocks below. This continuous forest corridor is protected within a series of private preserves, which means that Cabo Matapalo has most of the same wildlife as the national park. Most of the point itself lies within the private reserves of the area's two main hotels, and that forest is crisscrossed by footpaths, some of which head to tranquil beaches or to waterfalls that pour into pools. Many of the lodges in this area do not have phones, only radio contact.

Where to Stay

$$$–$$$$
Fodor'sChoice
★

Bosque del Cabo. On a cliff at the tip of Cabo Matapalo, this lodge has unparalleled views of blue gulf waters meeting blue ocean. This is the ultimate in romantic seclusion, with hundreds of acres of animal-rich primary forest and luxuriously rustic, thatched-roof, very private cabinas with outdoor (hot-water!) garden showers. From your private porch you can gaze at the stars or take a siesta in a hammock. Two newer rustic cabins are set apart in a distant garden that has a bar topped by a wildlife-viewing platform. Appetizing meals are served in a small rancho overlooking a garden alive by day with hummingbirds. Dinners are lighted by lantern and accompanied by a chorus of frogs. Solar power provides enough light to read, and ocean breezes make air-conditioning superfluous. Resident guides are on hand to lead you along dense forest trails—on foot or along a canopy zip line—and down to the beach with its natural warm tidal whirlpools and river waterfalls. ⊠ *Road to Carate, 22 km (14 mi) south of Puerto Jiménez* ☎🖷 *735–5206* ⊕ *Puerto Jiménez* ⊕ *www.bosquedelcabo.com* ⇋ *12 cabinas, 2 houses* ⚑ *Restaurant, some kitchens, pool, beach, boating, fishing, hiking, horseback riding, bar; no a/c, no room phones, no room TVs* ⊟ *MC, V* |◯| *FAP.*

$$$$
Fodor'sChoice
★

Lapa Ríos. On a high, breezy jungle ridge within its own nature reserve teeming with wildlife Lapa Ríos is the most luxurious eco-resort in Costa Rica, winning awards worldwide for its mix of conservation and comfort. It is the only hotel in the country to have garnered five leaves: the tourism ministry's top ecotourism designation. You can explore the pristine wilderness and nearby beaches on foot or on horseback, accompanied by resident naturalist guides. The spacious, airy cabins, built of gleaming hardwood with high, thatched roofs, have four-poster beds, showers with one screened wall open to nature, and private garden terraces from which you can view passing wildlife. Inspired meals are served in a dramatic rancho with a spiral staircase leading up to a crow's-nest viewing platform. The sophisticated menus include lots of seafood, exotic local fruits and vegetables, and mouthwatering desserts. The service here is exceptional. ⊠ *20 km (12 mi) south of Puerto Jiménez* ⊕ *Apdo. 100, Puerto Jiménez, or Box 025216, SJO 706, Miami, FL 33102-5216* ☎ *735–5130* 🖷 *735–5179* ⊕ *www.laparios. com* ⇋ *16 cabinas* ⚑ *Restaurant, pool, beach, fishing, hiking, horseback riding, bar, laundry service; no a/c, no room phones, no room TVs* ⊟ *AE, MC, V* |◯| *FAP.*

$$$

El Remanso. Find tranquility and elegance at this retreat in a forest brimming with birds and wildlife, 400 feet above a beach studded with tide pools. Luxurious cabinas have louvered screened windows, large verandas, and showers behind curving Gaudí-like walls. A two-story, hot-pink stucco-and-cane cabina has two rooms that sleep four to six each. Excellent meals use local produce and are served on a shaded deck restaurant. The property reflects the owners' conservationist ideals; they met as Greenpeace volunteers. Waterfall rappelling, zip-line access to a canopy platform, and biologist-guided nature walks are the highlights, apart from soaking in the serenity. ⌂ *Road to Carate, a few meters south of the entrance to Bosque del Cabo* ☎ *735–5569* ⊕ *www. elremanso.com* ⌖ *2 rooms, 4 cabinas* ⌂ *Dining room, beach, hiking, bar; no a/c, no room phones, no room TVs* ▭ *MC, V* ⊙ *FAP.*

Sports & the Outdoors

Both Lapa Ríos and Bosque del Cabo can arrange horseback excursions, guided tours to Corcovado, or deep-sea fishing trips.

WATER SPORTS   On the eastern side of the point, waves break over a platform that creates a perfect right, drawing surfers from far and wide. This area also has excellent sea-kayaking.

Cabo Matapalo Sportfishing (☎ 735–5773 ⊕ www.cabo-matapalo. com), based in Puerto Jiménez, has excellent, experienced fishing captains and well-equipped boats, as well as surfing instruction.

Carate

❹ *60 km (37 mi) west of Puerto Jiménez.*

A stretch of beach with a tiny store, Carate is literally the end of the road. There are no phones here and few lodgings. You can fly via charter plane to Carate's small airstrip and from here head into Corcovado National Park. Public transportation is available from Puerto Jiménez, via a collectivo that leaves twice daily.

From Carate, the La Leona ranger station in Corcovado National Park is a four-hour hike and the La Sirena station is about an eight-hour hike. The walk to the Corcovado Lodge Tent Camp is 2 km (30–45 minutes) along the beach. Vehicles are not permitted on the beach, but if you're staying at the tent camp, a horse and cart can pick up your luggage from the store. If you're driving to Carate and venturing on to the park or to Corcovado Tent Camp, you can park at the store for $5 per day. Carate has no phones; the store and lodges have radio contact.

Where to Stay

$$$$ ⊡ **Luna Lodge.** Luna's charm lies in its remoteness and tranquility. On a mountain overlooking the Pacific and the rain forest, it's a true retreat, with a huge hardwood pavilion for practicing yoga or contemplating magnificent sunsets. Round cabinas, spaced apart for privacy, have thatched roofs, garden showers, and decks for bird-watching or relaxing in wood-and-leather rocking chairs. Or you can semi-rough it in a well-ventilated, comfortable tent. Guided hikes to nearby waterfalls and swimming holes are precipitous and thrilling. Healthful meals have an imaginative vegetarian flair, tempered with servings of fish and chicken spiced with herbs from a hilltop organic garden. Host Lana Wed-

more is a model of amiable helpfulness. ✉ *2 km (1 mi) up a steep, partially paved road from Carate* ☎ *380–5036, 358–5848, 888/409–8448 in U.S.* ⊕ *www.lunalodge.com* 🗋 *Box 025216–5216, Miami, FL 33102* 🛏 *8 cabinas, 7 tents* ⚶ *Restaurant, massage, boating, hiking, horseback riding, bar; no a/c, no room phones, no room TVs* ☰ *MC, V* 🍴 *FAP.*

$$$ 🏨 **Lookout Inn.** Living up to its roadside advertising, this is the only hotel on the beach in Carate. Pairs of Scarlet Macaws frequent the hotel's garden, shaded by beach almond trees that line the beach. The inn itself is perched on a hillside, up a steep concrete drive. Three luxurious rooms with huge ceramic bathrooms are in the three-story lodge. Two large, screened-in wooden cabins sit on stilts in the garden. There are lots of quirky, artistic touches here, such as a wooden handrail that terminates in a carved snake's head, and ceramic iguanas and frogs popping out of vases and walls. Inventive meals with lots of fresh fish are served on two breezy terraces with spectacular views of the coastline. There's also a spring-fed plunge pool and a steep stairway leading up to a prime bird-watching trail through primary forest. ✉ *300 m east of Carate landing strip* ☎☎ *735–5431 in Puerto Jiménez (satellite phone at inn for emergencies)* ⊕ *www.lookout-inn.com* 🛏 *3 rooms, 2 cabins* ⚶ *Dining room, fans, pool, beach, fishing, hiking, horseback riding, 2 bars, laundry service, some pets allowed; no a/c, no room phones, no room TVs* ☰ *MC, V* 🍴 *AI.*

$$ 🏨 **Corcovado Lodge Tent Camp.** Fall asleep to the surf pounding the

Fodor's Choice beach in tents on wooden platforms at this rustic lodge. Ecotourist pi-

★ oneer Costa Rica Expeditions owns the lodge and its 400 acres of forest reserve adjoining Corcovado National Park. Side by side facing the ocean, tents have two single beds, no electricity, and share eight showers and toilets. Vegetables are plentiful at family-style meals served in an open-air hut overlooking the ocean. The mango tree outside the hammock house is a good place to spot monkeys, as are the guided tours, one of which hoists you to a platform atop a 300-year-old tree; you can spend the night here, 90 feet off the ground. Bring a flashlight (there's no electricity after 9 PM), insect repellent, and sandals for river hikes. A package with all meals is a great deal, especially since there's nowhere to buy food nearby. Many packages include a charter flight to Carate, but you can also fly to Puerto Jiménez and take the collectivo (⇨ Puerto Jiménez, *above*). Before you leave San José or Puerto Jiménez, call to arrange for a horse and cart to pick up your luggage from the store in Carate. You can park at the store in Carate for $5 per day. ✉ *On beach 2 km (1 mi) north of Carate; 30–45 min by foot* ☎ *222–0333* 🗋 *Apdo. 6941–1000, San José* ☎ *257–1665, 800/886–2609 in U.S.* ⊕ *www. costaricaexpeditions.com* 🛏 *20 tents with shared bath* ⚶ *Dining room, beach, horseback riding, bar, laundry service; no a/c, no room phones, no room TVs* ☰ *AE, MC, V.*

Corcovado National Park

⑮ *2¼ km (1½ mi) north of Carate.*

Comprising 435 square km (168 square mi) and covering one-third of the Osa Peninsula, the Parque Nacional Corcovado is one of the largest and wildest protected areas in Costa Rica. Much of the park is covered with virgin rain forest, where massive *espavel* and *nazareno* trees tower over the trails, thick lianas hang from the branches, and animals such as toucans, Spider Monkeys, Scarlet Macaws, and poison dart frogs abound. Corcovado is also home to seldom-seen boa constrictors, jaguars, anteaters, and tapirs. In and around the park you will find some of Costa Rica's most luxurious jungle lodges and retreats.

The easiest way to visit remote Corcovado is on a day trip from one of the lodges in the nearby Drake Bay area, or from the Corcovado Tent Camp; but if you have a backpack and strong legs, you can spend days deep in its wilds. There are three entrances: La Leona (to the south), San Pedrillo (to the north), and Los Patos (to the east). The park has no roads, however, and the roads that approach it are dirt tracks that require four-wheel drive most of the year. A very limited number of bunks are available at the La Leona and (more remote) Sirena ranger stations—you'll need sheets and a good mosquito net. A limited number of meals can be arranged at the La Sirena station if you reserve in advance. Check with the National Parks Service office in Puerto Jiménez before you go into the park without food supplies.

During the dry season, the park takes reservations for bunks and camping on the first day of each month for the following month. You may be asked to deposit money into the Environment Ministry's account in the Banco Nacional to reserve space. Be sure to reconfirm your reservation a few days before you enter the park. Camping is allowed at the Sirena, La Leona, Los Patos, and San Pedrillo stations, but only 35 people are allowed to camp at any given station, so reservations with the National Parks Service (⇨ Puerto Jiménez, *above*) are essential in high season. ⊠ *La Leona, the southernmost entrance, is 43 km (27 mi) from Puerto Jiménez to Carate, then a 3-km (2-mi) hike. La Sirena entrance is another 13 km (8½ mi). Los Patos entrance is a 25-km (16-mi) drive from Puerto Jiménez to La Palma, then a 12-km (7-mi) hike. San Pedrillo entrance is accessible from Drake Bay by a 20-min boat ride or, in dry season only, via a 25-km (16-mi) hike along the Pacific-side beach.*

Sports & the Outdoors

HIKING There are three **hiking routes to Corcovado,** two beginning near Puerto Jiménez and the other beginning in Drake Bay, which follows the coast down to the San Pedrillo entrance to the park. You can hire a boat in Sierpe to take you to San Pedrillo or Drake Bay (from Drake it's a 25-km [16-mi] hike to San Pedrillo, but only in dry season). Alternatively, hire a taxi in Puerto Jiménez for the inland Los Patos trailhead, or at least to the first crossing of the Río Rincón (from which you hike a few miles upriver to the trailhead). The beach route, via La Leona, starts in Carate.

Hiking is always tough in the tropical heat, but the forest route (from Los Patos) is easier than the two beach hikes (from La Leona and San Pedrillo), and the latter are accessible only at low tide. The hike between any two stations takes all day, and the longest hike is between San Pedrillo and Sirena. (Note that this trail is passable only in the dry season, as the rivers get too high to cross in the rainy months.) The Sirena ranger station has great trails around it. There is potable water at every sta-

TOP WILDLIFE-VIEWING TIPS

I F YOU'RE ACCUSTOMED TO NATURE PROGRAMS ON TV, *with visions of wildebeest and zebra swarming across African savannah, your first visit to a tropical forest can be a bewildering experience. Where are all the animals!? If these forests are so diverse, why can't I see anything? Web sites, brochures, and books are plastered with lovely descriptions and close-up images of wildlife that give travelers high hopes. Reality is much different, but no less profound, so here are some tips to make your experience more enjoyable.*

First, expectations. It's extremely rare to spot a cat, especially a jaguar. Odds are similar for a Harpy Eagle or tapir. Monkeys can be the easiest animals to spot, but location is important. In some locations they are as reliable as the tides, but in others they are rare indeed. "Easy" sightings include agoutis, coatis, sloths, and innumerable bird species. Remember, though, that nearly all animals spend most of their time avoiding detection.

So how can you improve your chances? Be quiet! Nothing is more unsettling to a wary animal than 20 Homo sapiens conversing as they hike. It's best to treat the forest like a house of worship—quiet reverence is in order. Also, look and listen. Observe different levels of the forest. An enormous caterpillar or an exquisitely camouflaged moth may be only a few inches from your face, and the silhouettes in the tree 100 meters away may be Howler Monkeys. Scan trunks and branches where a sleeping sloth or anteater might curl up. A quick glance farther down the trail may reveal an agouti or peccary crossing your path. In any open area such as a clearing or river, use your binoculars and scan in the distance; Scarlet Macaws and toucans may be cruising above the treetops.

Listening closely is perhaps more difficult.

Many visitors are surprised when a flock of parrots overhead is pointed out to them, despite the incredible volume of noise they produce. That low-pitched growl you hear is a Howler Monkey call, which is obvious if nearby, but easily missed over the din of conversation. Try stopping for a moment and closing your eyes—there is always something to hear. It's also helpful to cultivate some level of interest in the less charismatic denizens of the forest—the plants, insects, and spiders. Together they make up the bulk of Costa Rica's diversity, and exhibit enough strange and wonderful adaptations to fascinate just about everyone. On a good day in the forest, you may see a Resplendent Quetzal or Spider Monkey, but should they fail to appear, focus on the rest of the forest. There are treasures everywhere you look— an intricate spiderweb, a column of marching army ants, mammal footprints in the mud, or colorful seeds and flowers fallen from high in the canopy. Charles Darwin, in his Voyage of the Beagle, *had this to say about his first day in a tropical forest: "To a person fond of natural history, such a day as this brings with it a deeper pleasure than he can ever hope to experience again."*

— Ryan Sarsfield

tion; don't drink stream water. Be sure to bring insect repellent, a sun hat and sunblock, and good boots.

Drake Bay

16 *10 km (6 mi) north of Corcovado, 40 km (25 mi) southwest of Palmar Sur.*

The rugged coast that stretches south from the mouth of the Río Sierpe to Corcovado probably doesn't look much different than it did in Sir Francis Drake's day (1540–96), when the British explorer anchored here. Small, picture-perfect beaches with surf crashing against dark, volcanic rocks are backed by steaming, thick jungle. Nature lodges scattered along the coast are hemmed in by the rain forest, which is home to troops of monkeys, serene sloths, striking Scarlet Macaws, and hundreds of other bird species.

This is *Castaway* country, a real tropical adventure, with plenty of hiking and some rough but thrilling boat rides. Most people reach this isolated area by boat via the sometimes treacherous mouth of the Río Sierpe, but direct flights to Drake are available. At the height of the dry season you can reach the town via a treacherous road that requires a four-wheel-drive vehicle.

Exceptionally fit backpackers can hike north out of Corcovado along a 25-km (16-mi) coastal path that follows the shoreline, cutting through shady forest when the coast gets too rocky. But it is impossible to walk during rainy season (September–December), when rivers flood and tides are too high. You can reach the Drake Bay area via small cruise ships sailing north from Panama or south from Jacó. The *Sea Voyager,* run by **Lindblad Expeditions** (☎ 212/765–7740, 800/397–5348 in U.S. ⊕ www. lindblad.com), makes landings in the Drake Bay area. The *Pacific Explorer,* operated by **Cruise West** (☎ 206/441–8687, 800/580–0072 in U.S. ⊕ www.cruisewest.com), brings passengers ashore for hikes, picnics, and horseback riding in Drake Bay and Corcovado.

The cheapest accommodations in the area can be found in the town of **Drake,** which is spread out along the bay. A trio of nature lodges—Drake Bay Wilderness Resort, Aguila de Osa Inn, and La Paloma Lodge—are also clumped near the Río Agujitas on the bay's southern end. They all offer comprehensive packages, including trips to Corcovado and Isla del Caño, as well as horseback tours, scuba diving, and deep-sea fishing. Lodges farther south, such as Punta Marenco Lodge and Casa Corcovado, run the same excursions from even wilder settings.

Where to Stay

$$$$ 🏨 **Aguila de Osa Inn.** The spacious rooms here have gorgeous hardwood interiors, huge bamboo beds, and luxurious tile bathrooms. Stained glass with tropical themes and hand-carved doors add artistic flair. Be prepared for a steep climb up a concrete path to your room with a view of Drake Bay. Morning coffee arrives outside your room before 6 AM, and the food is sophisticated and plentiful. The inn has two boats for sportfishing, its specialty. Scuba diving, snorkeling, and other excursions are easily arranged. ⊠ *South end of Drake, at mouth of Río Agujitas*

☎ *296–2190 in San José* 🖨 *232–7722* ⊕ *www.aguiladeosa.com* ✉ *Apdo. 10486–1000, San José* ⇥ *11 rooms* ⚐ *Restaurant, fans, massage, snorkeling, boating, fishing, horseback riding, bar, laundry service; no a/c, no room phones, no room TVs* ☰ *AE, MC, V* �🍽 *FAP.*

★ **$$$$** ▦ **Casa Corcovado.** This hilltop jungle lodge has it all: a prime location on the edge of Corcovado National Park, resident naturalist guides, luxury accommodations, and first-class service and food. A trail leads right into the park from here, so you can explore its forests hours before anyone else arrives. Spanish colonial–style cabinas are spread around a garden for maximum privacy. The guest rooms have elegant Chinese furniture, four-poster beds, and huge tile bathrooms with separate vanity, shower, and toilet areas. There's a sunset bar near the top of the very steep hill that climbs up from the beach where you make a thrilling, very wet landing: a tractor-towed cart transports guests and luggage. The restaurant serves four-course gourmet dinners. There's a two-night minimum stay, and the best way to go is on a three-night package that includes transportation from San José by plane, taxi, and boat, all meals, and a trip to Isla de Caño and Corcovado National Park. ✉ *Northern border of Corcovado* ☎ *No phone* ✉ *Apdo. 1482–1250, Escazú* ☎ *256–3181, 888/896–6097 in U.S.* 🖨 *256–7409* ⊕ *www. casacorcovado.com* ⇥ *14 rooms* ⚐ *Dining room, fans, pool, beach, snorkeling, boating, hiking, horseback riding, 2 bars; no a/c, no room phones, no room TVs* ☰ *AE, MC, V* ☺ *Closed Sept.–mid-Nov.* �🍽 *AI.*

★ **$$$$** ▦ **La Paloma Lodge.** Sweeping views and jungle seclusion make these deluxe cabinas the area's most romantic. Planted in a jungle garden on a high hill just south of Drake Bay, the elegant wooden villas have bedroom lofts and large porches with pretty green wicker furniture, huge wooden armoires, and hammocks. The tiled pool overlooks forest and ocean. The hotel runs a diving school and offers river kayaking, along with trips to Corcovado and Isla del Caño. The flower-filled restaurant serves delicious, fresh tropical fare. La Paloma is closest to Playa Cocolito, a gem of a beach just down the hill along the coastal path that eventually leads to Corcovado. There's a three-night minimum stay; packages are the best bet and include transportation from San José, all meals, and some tours. ✉ *Apdo. 97–4005, Heredia* ☎ *293–7502* 🖨 *239–0954* ⊕ *www. lapalomalodge.com* ⇥ *4 rooms, 7 cabinas* ⚐ *Restaurant, pool, beach, snorkeling, fishing, horseback riding; no a/c, no room phones, no room TVs* ☰ *AE, MC, V* ☺ *Closed Oct.* �🍽 *AI.*

$$$ ▦ **Drake Bay Wilderness Resort.** Spread over a grassy point between the Río Agujitas and the ocean, with the best views of Drake Bay, this resort has lots of open ground for kids to play and tidal pools to explore. The wooden cabins are camp-style with three to a building. But with hot-water, tiled bathrooms, wall murals, and carved animal bedposts supporting firm queen-size beds, this is very comfortable camping. Keep an eye out for the small troop of resident Squirrel Monkeys. Kayaks are at your disposal for paddles along the river. Most guests come here to see the rain forest, but you can also opt for scuba diving, sportfishing, and dolphin- and whale-watching tours. The minimum stay is three nights. ✉ *On peninsula at mouth of Río Agujitas, on southern end of bay* ☎🖨 *770–8012* ⊕ *www.drakebay.com* ✉ *Apdo. 30710–1000, San José* ☎ *561/371–3437 in U.S.* ⇥ *20 rooms* ⚐ *Restaurant, fans, salt-*

water pool, boating, fishing, horseback riding, bar, laundry facilities, Internet; no a/c, no room phones, no room TVs ▭ *AE, MC, V* ❄ *FAP.*

$$ 🏠 **Punta Marenco Lodge.** This small, rustic lodge has the best location on the Pacific side of the Osa, with idyllic, thatched-roof cabins along a ridge overlooking the sea. Private porches with two hammocks each are perfect for siestas, sunsets, and stargazing. Toucans and Scarlet Macaws are reliable visitors every morning. Trails lead down to the beach and coastal trail and deep into the Río Claro National Wildlife Refuge, and a resident guide is on hand to interpret the trails. The cozy rancho restaurant has a family feel, with communal tables and typical Tico food. There is electricity for only a few hours in the evening and no hot water. ✉ *Beachfront, directly east of Caño Island and north of Casa Corcovado* ☎ *234–1308 in San José, no phone at lodge* 🖷 *234–1227 in San José* 🏠 *Apdo. 462–2120, Calle Blancos, San José* ⊕ *www.corcovadozone. com* 🛏 *10 cabinas* 🛎 *Dining room, beach, hiking; no a/c, no room phones, no room TVs* ▭ *MC, V* ❄ *FAP.*

$ 🏠 **Eco-Manglares Sierpe Lodge.** For a taste of simple Tico-style river life, cross a narrow suspension bridge across the Río Sierpe to reach this eco-lodge. Five well-ventilated, thatched-roof cabins with screened windows line a flower-bordered stone path leading to the river. Bed frames made of mangrove wood, rustic furniture made of *caña blanca* (cane) and home-made curtains appliquéd with birds and flowers add a homey touch. Bathrooms are airy, and despite the rustic setting, there's plenty of hot water. The restaurant serves hearty portions of expertly cooked fish and is also renowned for its pizza. Kayaks and boat trips to explore the mangroves are the major activities, along with bird-watching. Rates include the use of kayaks. ✉ *14 km (8½ mi) southwest of Palmar Sur turnoff on Pan-American Highway, Sierpe* ☎ *786–7414* 🖷 *786–7441* ⊕ *www.costaricasur. co.cr* 🛏 *5 cabins* 🛎 *Restaurant, fans, boating; no a/c, no room phones, no room TVs* ▭ *No credit cards* ⊗ *Closed Sept. and Oct.* ❄ *BP.*

Sports & the Outdoors

Jinetes de Osa (☎ 236–5637 ⊕ www.drakebayhotel.com), right in Drake village, has diving and snorkeling and dolphin-watching tours, as well as a canopy tour with some interesting bridge, ladder, and rope transitions between platforms. It also has a restaurant and reasonably priced comfortable rooms to rent.

Nightlife

When you're in the Osa Peninsula, the wildest nightlife is outdoors. Join entomologist Tracie Stice, also known as the Bug Lady, on the **Night Tour** (☎ 382–1619 ⊕ www.thenighttour.com) of insects, bats, reptiles, and anything else moving around at night. Tracie is a wealth of bug lore, with riveting stories from around the world. Special night-vision optics and infrared flashlights help you see in the dark. Tours are $35 per person; Tracie will meet you at your hotel.

Caño Island

⑰ *19 km (12 mi) off Osa Peninsula, due west of Drake Bay.*

Most of uninhabited Isla del Caño (2½ square km [1 square mi]) and its biological reserve is covered in evergreen forest that includes fig, locust, and rubber trees. Coastal Indians used it as a burial ground, and the numerous bits and pieces unearthed here have prompted archaeologists to speculate about pre-Columbian long-distance maritime trade. Occasionally, mysterious stones that have been carved into perfect spheres of varying sizes are still found on the island. The uninhabited island's main attraction now is the ocean around it, which offers superb scuba diving and snorkeling. The snorkeling is excellent around the rocky points flanking the island's main beach; if you're a certified diver, you'll probably want to explore Bajo del Diablo and Paraíso, where you're guaranteed to encounter thousands of good-size fish. Lodges in Drake Bay run day trips here.

THE SOUTHERN PACIFIC A TO Z

To research prices, get advice from other travelers, and book travel arrangements, visit www.fodors.com.

AIR TRAVEL

Costa Rica's two domestic airlines offer regular flights from San José to Golfito, Palmar Sur, Puerto Jiménez, Coto 47 (near San Vito), and Drake Bay. Charter flights fly to more isolated spots. Because the drive from San José to this region takes six to eight hours, a one-hour flight is that much more attractive.

CARRIERS SANSA has several flights daily from San José to Golfito and some daily flights to Palmar Sur (for Drake Bay) and Puerto Jiménez. NatureAir has daily flights to Golfito, Palmar Sur, and Puerto Jiménez. Both airlines also have daily flights from Quepos to Palmar Sur. Costa Rica Expeditions runs several charter flights weekly to Carate. Both SANSA and NatureAir make daily scheduled flights to Drake Bay in small aircraft. Aerotaxi Alfa Romeo offers charter flights to Carate, Drake Bay, Puerto Jiménez, the Sirena ranger station in Corcovado National Park, the Tiskita Jungle Lodge in Playa Pavones, and anywhere else you want to go. You have to charter the whole plane, which is expensive, so it's best to fill it with the maximum capacity of five. The Osa Tropical travel agency (⇨ Travel Agencies) in Puerto Jiménez sells SANSA and NatureAir tickets. In other towns, buy your tickets at the airport or make arrangements through your hotel.

🗐 Airlines & Contacts **Aerotaxi Alfa Romeo** 🖩🖩 735-5178. **Costa Rica Expeditions** 🖩 222-0333 🖶 257-1665. **NatureAir** ✉ Aeropuerto Tobias Bolaños, Pavas, San José 🖩 220-3054 🖶 220-0413. **SANSA** ✉ In front of Restaurante Uno, Golfito 🖩🖩 775-0303 ✉ 150 m south and 100 m east of the Caja Costarricense del Seguro Social offices, Palmar Sur 🖩 786-6353 ✉ 75 m west of Catholic church, Puerto Jiménez 🖩 735-5017 🖶 735-5495.

BOAT & FERRY TRAVEL

Drake Bay is usually connected by boat from Sierpe, south of Palmar Norte. Boat reservations are often part of your hotel package; otherwise, ask around at a supermarket or bar in Sierpe. Boats pick you up from your hotel on the return trip. Many local boatmen use open motorboats, so bring sun protection. The mouth of the river can have dangerous waves at low tide or during storms; make sure your boat has life jackets. The crossing takes about an hour and a half. Travel between the Drake Bay lodges, Corcovado, and Isla del Caño is most commonly accomplished in small boats owned by the major lodges, or call Corcovado Expediciones in Drake Bay to arrange boat transportation.

A ferry crosses the Golfo Dulce, leaving Puerto Jiménez daily at 6 AM and returning from Golfito at 11:30 AM. Boat transportation to Zancudo or the more distant Pavones can be arranged through the Tierra Mar agency.

🚢 Boat & Ferry Information **Corcovado Expediciones** ✉ Beside the school, Drake Bay ☎ 396-7774. **Tierra Mar** ✉ Golfito ☎ 775-1614.

BUS TRAVEL
All Tracopa-Alfaro buses depart San José from C. 14 at Avda. 5.

CENTRAL HIGHLANDS, VALLE DE EL GENERAL & SOUTHERN PACIFIC BEACHES Musoc buses from San José to San Isidro, a three-hour trip, depart almost every hour between 5:30 AM and 6:30 PM, returning at the same times; they leave from C. Central, between Avdas. 22 and 24. Take a bus from San Isidro to San Gerardo de Rivas, the starting point of the trail into Chirripó National Park, at a stop on the west side of the park at 5:30 AM or from the terminal near the central market at 2 PM.

Tracopa-Alfaro buses depart from San José to San Vito, a seven-hour trip, daily at 5:45 AM, 8:15 AM, 11:30 AM, and 2:45 PM.

Buses run by Transportes Blanco (not to be confused with Transportes Blanco-Lobo in San José) leave San Isidro from 100 m south of the church for the one-hour trip to Dominical daily at 7 and 9 AM and 1:30 and 4 PM.

GOLFO DULCE & THE OSA PENINSULA Tracopa-Alfaro buses leave San José for the eight-hour trip to Golfito daily at 7 AM and 3 PM, returning at 5 AM and 1 PM. Tracopa-Alfaro buses from San José (C. 14 at Avda. 5) to Palmar Norte, a six-hour trip, depart daily at 5, 7, 8:30, and 10 AM and 1, 2:30, and 6 PM; buses to Golfito, Puerto Jiménez, and San Vito also stop in Palmar Norte. In Palmar Norte, you can hire a taxi to Sierpe, the river port for boats to Drake Bay.

Transportes Blanco-Lobo buses from San José to Puerto Jiménez, a nine-hour trip, leave from C. 14, between Avdas. 9 and 11 at noon and return at 5 AM. From San Isidro, Transportes Blanco buses make the five-hour trip to Puerto Jiménez at 6:30 AM and 3 PM. A truck for hikers leaves Puerto Jiménez daily at 6 AM and 1:30 PM for Carate, returning from Carate at 8:30 AM and 4 PM.

The collectivo from Puerto Jiménez to Carate from Autotransportes Blanco, 200 m west of the Super 96 in Puerto Jiménez, every day at 6 AM and 1:30 PM and returns from Carate at 8:30 AM and 4 PM. Reserve tickets ($6) in advance or at least show up early to get in line for the collectivo. If you're staying overnight in Puerto Jiménez, ask your hotel to reserve you a spot. The trip is 1½ hours along an extremely bumpy dirt road. Buses to San José and elsewhere also leave from Autotransportes Blanco.

🚌 Bus Companies **Musoc** ☎ 222-2422. **Tracopa-Alfaro** ☎ 222-2666. **Transportes Blanco** ☎ 771-4744 or 771-2550. **Transportes Blanco-Lobo** ☎ 257-4121.

CAR RENTAL

There are few area car-rental agencies in the south, which is quite appropriate given the condition of the roads and the lack of roads altogether. Brunca Rent-a-Car in San Isidro has manual-transmission *quatro por quatro* (four-wheel-drive vehicles) and some automatic sedans for rent. You can also rent in San José, or arrange to have a car delivered to or dropped off at a southern location for an extra fee. The Selva Mar travel agency in San Isidro can arrange for a rental car to be delivered to any location in San Isidro within three hours of when you place your order.

Puerto Jiménez also lies just 40 minutes by car from spectacular Cabo Matapalo. The trip costs $40 by taxi. Reserve through your hotel.

🚩 **Local Agencies Brunca Rent-a-Car** ⊠ Across from Hospital Escalante in northern part of town ☎ 770–4953. **Selva Mar** ⊠ 50 m south of cathedral ☎ 771–4582 ⊕ www.exploringcostarica.com.

CAR TRAVEL

The quickest way to reach the Costanera, or coastal highway, which leads past Jacó and Quepos to Dominical and the rest of the southern Pacific zone, is to take the Carretera Interamericana (Pan-American Highway, or CA2) west past the airport to the turnoff for Atenas, turn left, and drive through Atenas to Orotina, where you head south. Between Quepos and Dominical the highway is still not paved, but heading south of Dominical, the paved road offers relatively smooth sailing.

To reach the Southern Zone from the Central Valley via the Pan-American Highway, drive east out of San José and turn south before Cartago. Be sure to leave in the morning, because dense clouds and fog often reduce visibility in the mountains to zero in the afternoons during both dry and wet seasons. The Pan-American Highway runs into the Costanera at Palmar Norte, 33 km (21 mi) south of which is the turnoff for Puerto Jiménez. A faithful translation of the Spanish, "highway" is really a misnomer for these neglected two-lane roads.

EMERGENCIES

In an emergency, dial 911 or one of the numbers below.

🚩 Emergency Services **Ambulance** ☎ 128. **Fire** ☎ 118. **Police** ☎ 295–3311. **Traffic Police** ☎ 222–9330.

MAIL & SHIPPING

Internet cafés are popping up in all the major towns, but major portions of the South are still without phone service or even electricity. Internet service costs anywhere from $1 to $5 per hour, depending on the location and the type of connection. Post offices are few and far between. You are better off saving up your postcards and mailing them from the majestic Correos Central in downtown San José.

🚩 Internet Cafés **Brunc@Net** ⊠ Above Gallo Mas Gallo store, north side of park, San Isidro. **Café Colibrí** ⊠ Above San Clemente Bar & Grill, Dominical. **CaféNet El Sol** ⊠ Center of town, Puerto Jiménez. **Golfito On Line** ⊠ Main street, between city dock and gas station, next to Servicentro Pacifico Sur, Golfito ☎ 775–2424. **Internet Café** ⊠ Hotel

Chirripó, opposite side of park, San Isidro. **Internet café** ⊠ Main beach road, Playa Zancudo. **Super Diuwak** ⊠ Next to Hotel Diuwak, Dominical.

🔳 Post Offices **Correo de Costa Rica** ⊠ Across from soccer field; climb flight of stairs off the main road, just south of central park, Golfito ⊠ West side of soccer field, Puerto Jiménez ⊠ 200 m south of City Hall, south side of park, San Isidro.

MONEY MATTERS

ATMS · Cash machines and banks that accept foreign debit cards are few and far between. It's best to stock up in San José before heading south, or make a bank stop in San Isidro, Golfito, or San Vito, where you can get cash with a debit or credit card with a Visa/Plus logo at an ATH Coopealianza automatic cash machine.

CURRENCY EXCHANGE · U.S. dollars are happily accepted everywhere, but the exchange rate will probably not be as favorable as at the bank, or up-to-date. Change your money in San José before traveling south. Banking in local branches is very slow. Be sure to have your original passport with you, not a copy, if you want to get a cash advance from a bank using your credit card.

🔳 Banks **ATH Coopealianza** ⊠ Across from hospital, north end of town, Golfito ⊠ South side of central park, beside Hotel Chirripó, San Isidro ⊠ Center of town, San Vito.

TOURS

Horizontes designs customized tours led by naturalist guides to many remote jungle lodges. Costa Rica Expeditions, one of Costa Rica's oldest and best tour companies, runs guided tours to its Corcovado Tent Camp.

🔳 Tour Operators **Costa Rica Expeditions** ⊠ Avda. 3 at C. Central, San José ☎ 222-0333 📠 257-1665. **Horizontes** ⊠ 140 m north of Pizza Hut on Paseo Colón, San José ☎ 222-2022 📠 255-4513.

BOAT TOURS · Cruise West runs seven- and eight-day cruises on the 100-passenger, 185-foot *Pacific Explorer,* visiting Corcovado National Park, Drake Bay, Isla del Caño, and Manuel Antonio National Park. Participants are generally those drawn to "soft-adventure trips" and senior citizens. The trip, guided by a naturalist, begins at 6 AM with a hike through a privately owned patch of lush tropical jungle. The eco-adventure tour nudges right up to the pristine islands, funky towns, and rain forests of the Pacific coast, some too remote for roads. From the shore, excellent rain forest-hikes, horseback riding, bird-watching, snorkeling, sea-kayaking, and a visit to a luxuriant botanical garden are easily accessible. On the trails, friendly Tico guides point out fascinating organisms in the forest—a cavalcade of leaf-cutter ants, the coveted treasure of a cacao tree—and such critters as the Scarlet Macaw and White-faced Capuchin monkey. The day ends with drinks at sunset shared by tanned travelers and their guides, who tell stories as the ship glides to its next destination. The ship sails from Los Sueños near Jacó with transport to and from the airport in San José.

Lindblad Expeditions cruises the Pacific coast on nine-day trips aboard the *Sea Voyager,* which has 50 cabins. It sets sail from Los Sueños, and passengers can opt for extra days exploring by land on tours organized by Horizontes. For serious scuba divers in search of a thrill, there are 10-day scuba-diving expeditions to distant Cocos Island on the *Okeanos*

Aggressor. A smaller vessel, the *Undersea Hunter,* makes similar dive trips to Cocos Island.

From a sunset paddle to a one-week trip around the entire Golfo Dulce, Escondido Trex, in Puerto Jiménez, can arrange any type of sea-kayaking adventure. Other adventures include rappelling down waterfalls.

🛈 Operators **Cruise West** ✉ 2401 4th Ave., Ste. 700, Seattle WA 98121-1438 ☎ 206/441-8687, 800/580-0072 in U.S. ⊕ www.cruisewest.com. **Escondido Trex** ✉ Restaurante Carolina, Apdo. 9, Puerto Jiménez ☎ 735-5210. **Lindblad Expeditions** ✉ 720 5th Ave., New York, NY 10019 ☎ 212/765-7740, 800/397-3348 in U.S. ⊕ www.lindblad.com. **Okeanos Aggressor** ☏ 2011 N.W. 79th Ave., Miami, FL 33122 ☎ 257-8686, 800/348-2628 in U.S. 🖷 223-4176 ⊕ www.okeanoscocosisland.com. **Undersea Hunter** ☏ SJO 314, 1601 N.W. 97th St., Box 025216, Miami, FL 33102-5216 ☎ 228-6613, 800/203-2120 in U.S. 🖷 289-7334 ⊕ www.underseahunter.com.

HIKING TOURS Selva Mar leads hikes and nature tours to Chirripó and other areas. In Dominical, Hacienda Barú offers a number of guided hikes through the rain forest. Ecole Travel runs inexpensive guided hikes into Chirripó and Corcovado national parks. Osa Aventura specializes in multiday hikes into Corcovado.

🛈 Operators **Ecole Travel** ✉ C. 7, between Avdas. Central and 1, San José ☎ 223-2240 🖷 223-4128 ⊕ www.ecoletravel.com. **Hacienda Barú** ✉ 1 km (½ mi) north of Dominical ☎ 787-0003 ⊕ www.haciendabaru.com. **Osa Aventura** 🖷☎ 735-5670 ⊕ www. osaaventura.com. **Selva Mar** ☎ 771-4582 ⊕ www.exploringcostarica.com.

TRAVEL AGENCIES

In Puerto Jiménez, Osa Tropical has a visitor center, sells domestic airline tickets, offers varied tours, and makes reservations at lodges on the Osa Peninsula. Selva Mar, in San Isidro, can make hotel reservations throughout the country but specializes in working with remote jungle lodges and tour operators in the Southern Zone.

🛈 Local Agent Referrals **Osa Tropical** ✉ 50 m south of Catholic church, Puerto Jiménez ☎ 735-5062 🖷 735-5043 ⊙ Mon.-Sat. 8-5. **Selva Mar** ✉ 45 m south of central park, San Isidro ☎ 771-4582 ⊕ www.exploringcostarica.com.

VISITOR INFORMATION

Official tourist offices in San José have information on the southern Pacific coast. In San Isidro, CIPROTUR is a helpful visitor information center, with an Internet café. Also in San Isidro, the travel agency Selva Mar doubles as a visitor information center. In Dominical, Dominical Adventures in the San Clemente Restaurant provides visitor information and books tours. In Golfito, Land Sea Services offers traveler information. In Puerto Jiménez, Osa Natural is a tourist chamber of commerce and visitor center with lots of information and Internet access.

🛈 Tourist Information **CIPROTUR** ✉ 70 m south of Instituto Costarricense de Elect ricidad, San Isidro ☎ 771-6096. **Dominical Adventures** ✉ In San Clemente restau rant, near soccer field, Dominical ☎ 787-0191. **Land Sea Services** ✉ Next to Banar Bay Marina on left as you enter Golfito, Golfito ☎ 775-1614. **Osa Natural** ✉ Near p office, on north side of town ☎ 735-5440 ⊕ www.osanatural.com. **San José Tou Office** ✉ Central Post Office, Avda. 1 at C. 2 ☎ 258-8762. **Selva Mar** ✉ 45 m sc of central park, San Isidro ☎ 771-4582 ⊕ www.exploringcostarica.com.

THE CARIBBEAN

7

Updated by
Jeffrey Van
Fleet

CLOUD FORESTS, SPRAWLING BANANA PLANTATIONS, and thick tropical jungle characterize the Atlantic lowlands, in the provinces of Heredia and Limón on the Caribbean Sea. This expansive, largely untamed region stretches from the eastern slope of the Cordillera Central up to the Sarapiquí area northeast of San José (home to the private Rara Avis and La Selva reserves), east through banana-growing country, and down to the pristine beaches at Cahuita and Puerto Viejo de Talamanca on the southern Caribbean coast. The region also stretches north to the Nicaraguan border, encompassing the coastal jungles and canals of Tortuguero National Park and Barra del Colorado Wildlife Refuge, on whose beaches turtles arrive by the thousands to lay their eggs. The occasional caiman can be spotted here, sunning on a bank or drifting like a log down a jungle waterway; and farther north still, sportfishing fans find tarpon and snook to detain them off the shores of Barra del Colorado.

Roughly a third of the people in Limón province are Afro-Caribbeans, descendants of early-19th-century turtle fishermen and the West Indians who arrived in the late 19th century to build the Atlantic Railroad and remained to work on banana and cacao plantations. Some 4,000 Jamaicans are reputed to have died of yellow fever, malaria, and snakebites during construction of the first 40 km (25 mi) of railroad to San José. They were paid relatively well, however, and by the 1930s many Jamaicans had obtained their own small plots of land, and when the price of cacao rose in the 1950s, they emerged as comfortable landowners employing landless, migrant Hispanics. Until the Civil War of 1948, Afro-Caribbeans were forbidden from crossing into the Central Valley lest they upset the country's racial balance, and they were thus prevented from following work when United Fruit abandoned many of its northern Caribbean blight-ridden plantations in the 1930s for green-field sites on the Pacific plain. Although Jamaicans brought some aspects of British colonial culture with them, such as cricket and the maypole dance, these habits have long since given way to reggae, salsa, and soccer, much to the chagrin of the older generation. Many Atlantic-coast Ticos are bilingual, speaking fluent Spanish and Caribbean English, and around Puerto Viejo de Talamanca you may even hear some phrases derived from the language of the indigenous peoples, among them the Kekoldi, the Bribri, and the Cabécar.

With some justification, Caribbean residents bemoan the lack of attention their region gets from the government in San José and the tourism industry. Development has been slower to reach this part of the country. (Telephones and electricity are still newfangled inventions in some smaller communities here.) The Instituto Costarricense de Turismo (Costa Rican Tourism Institute; ICT), eager to tout Costa Rica to northerners as a fun-in-the-sun destination, devotes less space to the rainier Atlantic coast in its glossy tourist literature. The attention the region does get usually comes in the form of crime stories splashed across the front pages of San José newspapers. Many Ticos will advise you to avoid Limón province, but few have ever visited the area themselves. Communities are working hard to combat the problem with visibly beefed-up security, and crime is really no worse here than elsewhere in Costa Rica. If you stick to well-trodden tourist routes, you ought to be fine.

You will likely receive a warm welcome when you visit this "other" Costa Rica, a section of the country long ago discovered by European visitors but little known in North American circles. Venture here and you might be pleasantly surprised to discover the personalized attention and quality you get for your colónes. The flashy resorts so common on the Pacific are nowhere to be found here. Though they sometimes look with envy at their west-coast counterparts, most folks here on the Caribbean remain content to keep their tourism offerings smaller scale.

Exploring the Atlantic Lowlands & Caribbean Coast

Below the cloud- and rain-forested mountains and foothills of the Central and Talamanca ranges lie fertile plains and dense tracts of primary tropical jungle. Much of this land has been cleared and given over to farming and ranching, but vast expanses are still inaccessible by car. No roads lead to Barra del Colorado or Tortuguero; you have to fly from San José, take a jungle boat from Moín, or join one of the many organized tours from San José, an alluring prospect if it's solitude you crave. Coastal Talamanca, the region to the south, however, is accessible by car via the Carretera Guápiles (Guápiles Highway).

There are two towns called Puerto Viejo in this region. Puerto Viejo de Sarapiquí is a former river port in the northern, inland section of the lowlands; Puerto Viejo de Talamanca is on the southern coast not far from the Panamanian border. Keeping the two straight can be confusing, as locals often call both of them Puerto Viejo.

About the Restaurants

Dining is an informal, open-air affair, even at the nicest restaurants in the Caribbean region. Dinner is usually served from 7 to 10, and service is attentive but leisurely. Budget places serve their big meal of the day at noon and may not be open at all for dinner. Lunch comes Costa Rican *casado*-style—a "marriage" of rice, beans, fried plantains, salad, and meat, chicken, or fish, all on one plate—and is one of the best bargains around. Proprietors of restaurants serving international dishes—Italian cuisine is quite common in this part of the country—are fond of spicing their own menus with Caribbean flavors and ingredients in what many call "fusion style."

About the Hotels

The Atlantic lowlands have little in the way of luxury hotels, though a number of relatively upscale, self-proclaimed ecotourist lodges and some other, pricier accommodations exist along the highway south of Limón and (especially) on the beach road south of Puerto Viejo de Talamanca. The region's lower number of visitors compared with that of the Pacific coast means you can usually find vacancies at reasonable prices. The most basic places here do not accept credit cards; some smaller, family-run lodgings that do are always eager to avoid the high credit card service charges they are levied and will offer discounts if you pay with

7

You need at least a week to cover this territory, but three days are enough to sample its charms if you plan your time judiciously. In addition to keeping in mind the difficulties of getting around, remember that the Atlantic lowlands offer various activities requiring different levels of physical endurance and commitment, ranging from seaside lounging to rain-forest trekking. If your time, energy, and stomach for discomfort—mud, mosquitoes, and rain, for starters—are limited, you'll have to make choices. Another consideration is travel time. The Rara Avis preserve, for example, is a great place to visit, but because it's so hard to reach—via two- to four-hour tractor haul into the park—the lodge obliges you to stay for at least two nights.

Numbers in the text correspond to numbers in the margin and on the Caribbean map.

If you have 3 or 4 days: the beach

Hop on an early flight from San José to ✈ **Tortuguero** ❼ ► or ✈ **Barra del Colorado** ❽ for a jungle-boat tour, turtle-watching session, or fishing trip. The next morning take the boat down to **Moín** ❿ and then head to ✈ **Limón** ❾. Drive or take a bus south to ✈ **Cahuita** ⓫ and/or ✈ **Puerto Viejo de Talamanca** ⓭, where you can relax on the beach, play in the surf, snorkel, or hike in **Cahuita National Park** ⓬. Camp at Puerto Vargas or stay a couple of nights in Cahuita, Puerto Viejo de Talamanca, Punta Uva, or farther south along the beach road that terminates at the bird-filled jungles and deserted beaches of the **Gandoca-Manzanillo National Wildlife Refuge** ⓮.

If you have 3 or 4 days: beach & rain forest

Set out early from San José and drive or take a bus over the Guápiles Highway to hike in **Braulio Carrillo National Park** ❶ ► or ride the Rain Forest Aerial Tram. Drive to ✈ **La Selva Biological Station** ❸ and hike its trails in the afternoon. Spend a night here or in one of the lodges in the ✈ **Puerto Viejo de Sarapiquí** ❹ area. Drive south to ✈ **Cahuita** ⓫ and/or ✈ **Puerto Viejo de Talamanca** ⓭ and do some hiking, snorkeling, or other activities in **Cahuita National Park** ⓬. Stay a night or two in Cahuita, Puerto Viejo de Talamanca, Punta Uva, or farther south from Puerto Viejo on the beach road to the **Gandoca-Manzanillo National Wildlife Refuge** ⓮. Head back to San José, about a four-hour drive.

If you have 7 days

Throw in some variations on the above two themes: add an overnight rafting trip down the Río Pacuare, near Turrialba, or take a multiday fishing trip out of **Tortuguero** ❼ or **Barra del Colorado** ❽. Arrange to visit the Bribri, Cabécar, or Kekoldi indigenous reservation in the hills west of **Puerto Viejo de Talamanca** ⓭; hike into the remote Hitoy Cerere Biological Reserve.

cash. It's worth asking. Surprisingly few places on the coast have air-conditioning, but sea breezes and ceiling fans provide ventilation enough that you probably won't miss it. Most lodgings along the north Caribbean coast are rustic *cabinas* (cottages) or nature lodges. Often isolated in the jungle—accessible only by boat or strenuous hike—the lodges can be rough, no-frills places or can verge on the luxurious. Because it's hard to haul supplies to these places, indulgences such as hot showers and cold beers come with a hefty price tag.

	WHAT IT COSTS				
	$$$$	**$$$**	**$$**	**$**	**¢**
RESTAURANTS	over $25	$20–$25	$10–$20	$5–$10	under $5
HOTELS	over $200	$125–$200	$75–$125	$35–$75	under $35

Restaurant prices are per-person for a main course at dinner. Hotel prices are for two people in a standard double room in high season, excluding service and tax (16.4%).

Timing

This coastal area absorbs up to 240 inches of annual rainfall, so unless you want to watch turtles lay their eggs on the beach (each species has its own schedule), you should try to avoid the worst of it. Chances are you'll be rained on no matter when you go, but the Atlantic coast has two short "dry" seasons: September–October, which unfortunately does not correspond to the dry season in the rest of the country, and March–April, which does. During the rainy season, you pay lower prices and see fewer tourists in exchange for being waterlogged.

THE NORTHERN LOWLANDS

The immense Braulio Carrillo National Park, looming northeast of San José, protects virgin rain forest on either side of the highway to Guápiles. You can get a feel for it as you pass through on the highway, but inside it's another world: everywhere you look green things sprout, twist, and bloom. Bromeliads and orchids cling to arching trees while white-faced monkeys climb and swing and Blue Morpho butterflies dance and flutter. Adjacent to the park is a private reserve where you can explore the flora and fauna of the rain-forest canopy from a Rain Forest Aerial Tram.

After threading through Braulio Carrillo, the Guápiles Highway branches at Santa Clara, having completed its descent onto the Caribbean plain, and continues southeast to Limón and the Caribbean coast. If you turn left and head north, the smoothly paved road (Highway 4) leads through flat, deforested pasture and pockets of old-growth forest toward two private preserves, Rara Avis and La Selva. Just north are the old riverport town of Puerto Viejo de Sarapiquí and the forest-clad hills of the eastern slope of the Cordillera Central.

Continuing due east from Santa Clara, the well-maintained highway takes you through sultry lowlands to the growing community of Guápiles and the tropical agriculture research institution EARTH and, farther on, to Limón, the region's largest city.

7

Caribbean Flavors
Much of the cooking along the Caribbean has its roots in old West Indian recipes. *Rondón,* for example, is a traditional Jamaican meat or fish stew cooked in coconut milk, along with cabbage, tomatoes, onions, green peppers, and/or other vegetables that requires hours of preparation. Equally labor intensive, rice and beans—not at all the *gallo pinto* you've been eating elsewhere in Costa Rica—is flavored with coconut. Note that rondón and rice and beans might not be on the menu every day, or may need to be ordered in advance. Meat is fried with hot spices to make *paties* (pies); and fish or meat is boiled in coconut milk along with yams, plantains, breadfruit, peppers, and spices. Johnnycakes and *panbón* (a heavy, spicy dried-fruit bread) are popular baked goods. Seafood is, of course, readily available, as is a wide variety of fresh fruit. And though the translated name—"toad water"—could be more appetizing, don't pass up an *agua de sapo,* a delightful beverage concocted from lemon juice, ginger, and cane sugar.

Music
Latin salsa sounds and merengue moves give way to reggae rhythms in this part of the country. (This is the Caribbean, after all.) Partaking usually means hanging out at local bars and bopping to recorded music, but the fates might smile on you with an occasional live group, too. Puerto Viejo de Talamanca holds its annual Southern Caribbean Music Festival weekends each February–March or April before the fall of Holy Week.

Surfing
Some point breaks were badly affected by coastal uplift during the 1991 earthquake, but others were created—a left at Punta Cocles and a right at Punta Uva. You can still ride Puerto Viejo de Talamanca's famous and formidable Salsa Brava, but its spectacular waves are really only for the experienced and fearless surfer. Less hairy spots include Playa Negra, Cahuita, the beach break just south of Puerto Viejo, Playa Bonita north of Limón, and Isla Uvita, 20 minutes from Limón by boat. Beware of riptides. This coast is best surfed from December to March and June to August.

Turtle-Watching
Costa Rica's northern Caribbean shore is one of the few places in the world where the Green Sea Turtle nests: great groups of them descend on Tortuguero National Park from July to October each year. Three other turtle species—the Hawksbill, Loggerhead, and Giant Leatherback—also nest here. Leatherbacks nest on the beaches of the Gandoca-Manzanillo Wildlife Refuge on the southern Caribbean coast.

Braulio Carrillo National Park

➤ ❶ *30 km (19 mi) north of San José.*

In a country where deforestation is still rife, Parque Nacional Braulio Carrillo provides a rare opportunity to witness dense, primary tropical cloud forest. The park owes its foundation to the public outcry provoked

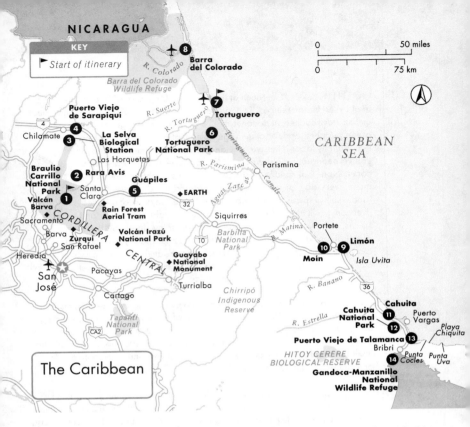

NICARAGUA

KEY

▶ Start of itinerary

8 **Barra del Colorado**

R. Colorado

*Barra del Colorado
Wildlife Refuge*

R. Suerte

7 **Tortuguero**

**Puerto Viejo
de Sarapiquí**

4

Chilamate

3

**La Selva
Biological
Station**

Las Horquetas

6 **Tortuguero
National Park**

R. Parismina

Parismina

*CARIBBEAN
SEA*

R. Tortuguero

**Braulio
Carrillo
National
Park**

2 **Rara Avis**

Guápiles

◆ **EARTH**

5

32

**Volcán
Barva**

1

Santa
Clara

Siquirres

Portete

10 9 **Limón**

Moín

Isla Uvita

Sacramento

◆ **Rain Forest
Aerial Tram**

CORDILLERA

Barva

Zurquí

San Rafael

**Volcán Irazú
National Park**

CENTRAL

*Barbilla
National
Park*

10

R. Matina

Heredia

✈

**San
José**

Pacayas

◆ **Guayabo
National
Monument**

Turrialba

*Chirripó
Indigenous
Reserve*

R. Banano

36

Cartago

*Tapantí
National
Park*

CA2

R. Estrella

Cahuita

**Cahuita
National
Park**

11

12

Cahuita

*Puerto
Vargas*

*Playa
Chiquita*

Puerto Viejo de Talamanca

13

Bribrí

*HITOY CERERE
BIOLOGICAL RESERVE*

14

**Punta
Cocles**

*Punta
Uva*

**Gandoca-Manzanillo
National
Wildlife Refuge**

The Caribbean

0 50 miles

0 75 km

by the construction of the highway of the same name through this region in the late 1970s—the government bowed to pressure from environmentalists, and, somewhat ironically, the park is the most accessible one from the capital thanks to the highway. Covering 443 square km (171 square mi), Braulio Carrillo's extremely diverse terrain ranges from 108 feet to more than 10,384 feet above sea level and extends from the central volcanic range down the Atlantic slope to La Selva research station near Puerto Viejo de Sarapiquí. The park protects a series of ecosystems ranging from the cloud forests on the upper slopes to the tropical wet forest of the Magsasay sector; it is home to 6,000 tree species, 500 bird species, and 135 mammal species.

The **Zurquí ranger station** is to the right of the highway, ½ km (¼ mi) before the Zurquí Tunnel. Here a short trail loops through the cloud forest. Hikes are steep; wear hiking boots to protect yourself from mud, slippage, and snakes. The main trail through primary forest, 1½ km (1 mi) long, culminates in a *mirador* (lookout point), but alas, the highway mars the view. Monkeys, tapirs, jaguars, kinkajous, sloths, raccoons, margays, and porcupines all live in this forest, and resident birds include the quetzal and the eagle. Orchids, bromeliads, heliconias, fungi, and mushrooms live closer to the floor. Another trail leads into the forest to the right, beginning about 17 km (11 mi) after the tunnel, where it follows the Quebrada González, a stream with a cascade and swimming hole. There are no campsites in this part of the park.

The **Carrillo ranger station**, 22 km (14 mi) northeast along the highway from Zurquí, marks the beginning of trails that are less steep. For access to the 10,384-foot **Volcán Barva**, start from Sacramento, north of Heredia. The walk through the cloud forest to the crater's two lakes takes two to three hours, but your efforts should be rewarded by great views (as long as you start early, preferably before 8 AM, to avoid the mist). You can camp at the **Barva ranger station**, which is far from any traffic. Stay on the trail when hiking anywhere in Braulio; it's easy to get lost in the cloud forest, and the rugged terrain makes wandering through the woods very dangerous. In addition, muggings of hikers have been reported in the park. Go with a ranger if possible. ☎ 283–8004 Sistemas de Areas de Conservación, 192 in Costa Rica ▦ $6 ☉ Daily 7–4.

Where to Stay

$ ▦ **CheTica Ranch.** A worldly Argentine and his Tica wife own this ranch, a good jumping-off point for those wanting to explore Braulio Carrillo National Park. Uniquely styled cabins follow an international theme: Old Tucson evokes the southwestern United States, and the two-storied Interlochen looks like a genuine Swiss chalet. Cabins have kitchens, living rooms, and a large collection of videos and books. During the day there are horseback trips into the park. The ranch also serves as a medical recovery center with all meals included for patients. ✉ Guápiles Hwy., ½ km (¼ mi) northeast of tollgate ☎▤ 268–6133 ☐ SJO 2989, Box 025216, Miami, FL 33102-5216 ⊕ www.cheticaranch.com ☞ 10 cabins ♨ Fans, some kitchens, cable TV, in-room VCRs, horseback riding, airport shuttle, no-smoking rooms; no a/c, no room phones ▤ AE, DC, MC, V ⑩ BP.

Rain Forest Aerial Tram

★ 15 km (9 mi) east of Braulio Carrillo National Park.

Just beyond the eastern boundary of Braulio Carrillo, a 4-square-km (2½-square-mi) preserve houses a privately owned and operated engineering marvel: a series of gondolas strung together in a modified ski-lift pulley system. (To lessen the impact on the jungle, the support pylons were lowered into place by helicopter.) The tram gives students, researchers, and travelers a way of seeing the rain-forest canopy and its spectacular array of epiphyte plant life and birds from just above, a feat you could otherwise accomplish only by climbing the trees yourself. The founder, Dr. Donald Perry, also developed a less elaborate system of canopy touring at nearby Rara Avis; of the two, this is more user-friendly. Though purists might complain that it treats the rain forest like an amusement park, it's an entertaining way to learn the value and beauty of rainforest ecology. The concept is expanding: in 2003, the company opened similar facilities one hour from the central Pacific town of Jacó and in the Caribbean-island nation of Dominica.

The 21 gondolas at the original site hold five people each, plus a bilingual biologist-guide equipped with a walkie-talkie to request brief stops for gaping or snapping pictures. The ride covers 2½ km (1½ mi) in 1½ hours. The price includes a biologist-guided walk through the area for ground-level orientation before or after the tram ride. You can arrange a personal pickup in San José for a fee; alternatively, there are public buses (on the Guápiles line) every half hour from the Gran Terminal del Caribe in San José (⇨ Bus Travel *in* The Caribbean A to Z). Drivers know the tram as the *teleférico*. Many San José tour operators make a daylong tour combining the tram with another half-day option; combos with the Britt Coffee Tour in Barva or INBioparque in Santo Domingo, both near Heredia, are especially popular (⇨ Chapter 2). Ten rustic (no a/c or TV) but cozy cabinas are available on-site for $80 per person. The facility operates the lodging only if at least two cabins are being rented at the same time. Electricity shuts off after 9 PM. Cabin rates include meals and tram tours. A café is open to all for breakfast and lunch. ⊠ *Reservations: Avda. 7 at C. 7 San José* ☎ *257–5961* 🖷 *257–6053* ⊕ *www.rainforestram.com* ✉ *$49.50; $78.50 includes round-trip transportation from San José hotels* 🖃 *AE, MC, V* ☺ *Tours Mon. 9–4, Tues.–Sun. 6:30–4. Call for reservations 6 AM–9:30 PM.*

Rara Avis

❷ *Las Horquetas is 17 km (11 mi) north of Santa Clara, 100 km (62 mi) north of San José.*

Toucans, sloths, Great Green Macaws, Howler and Spider Monkeys, Vested Anteaters, and tapirs may be on hand to greet you when you arrive at Rara Avis, one of Costa Rica's most popular private reserves and open only to overnight guests. Ecologist Amos Bien founded Rara Avis with the intent of combining research, tourism, and the sustainable extraction of forest products. Bilingual guides take you along the muddy trails—boots are provided—and canopy observation platforms and help point out wildlife. Or go on your own to the orchid house and butterfly garden. Bring a camera: the reserve's lacy double waterfall is one of Costa Rica's most photogenic sights.

The town of **Las Horquetas** is the jumping-off point for the 13-square-km (8-square-mi) private reserve. The 16-km (10-mi) trip from Las Horquetas to the reserve can be accomplished in three hours on horseback, two to three hours by tractor (leaves daily at 8:30 AM), or one hour by four-wheel-drive vehicle, plus a rough 3-km (2-mi) hike up to the lodge proper. The trails are steep and rugged, but the flora and fauna en route are remarkable. Note: there have been some complaints that, although the reserve itself is lovely, the guides and services are considerably less impressive. ⊠ *From Braulio Carrillo, turn left at signs for Puerto Viejo de Sarapiquí and go 17 km (11 mi) to Las Horquetas.*

Where to Stay

$$–$$$ 🖾 **Rara Avis.** Three lodging options exist here. The Waterfall Lodge, near a 197-foot waterfall, has hardwood-paneled rooms with chairs, firm beds, balconies, and hammocks. Despite the prices, accommodation is rustic, with minimal amenities and no electricity. More basic, Las Casitas are three two-room cabins with shared bath. On the high end, ideal for a rustic honeymoon, is the River Edge Cabin, a 10-minute walk through the forest (it's dark at night, but you're given a flashlight), with private bath and balcony and solar panel–generated electricity. Rates include guides and transport from Las Horquetas. It's time consuming to get here, so the recommended stay is two nights. ☒ *Las Horquetas* ☎ *764–3151* 📠 *764–4187* ⊕ *www.rara-avis.com* 🛏 *16 rooms, 10 with bath* ⌂ *Dining room; no a/c, no room phones, no room TVs* ▭ *AE, MC, V* ⧲ *AI.*

La Selva Biological Station

★ ❸ *14 km (9 mi) north of Rara Avis, 79 km (49 mi) northeast of San José.*

At the confluence of the Puerto Viejo and Sarapiquí rivers, La Selva is a biologist's paradise. Its 15 square km (6 square mi) pack about 420 bird species, 460 tree species, and 500 butterfly species. Spottings might include the spider monkey, poison dart frog, agouti, Collared Peccary, and dozens of other rare creatures. If you want to see wildlife without having to rough it, La Selva is much more agreeable than Rara Avis. Run by the **OTS (Organization for Tropical Studies)**, a consortium of 65 Latin and North American and Australian universities, the research station, one of three in Costa Rica, is designed for scientists but welcomes visitors in the daytime and offers basic lodging. Extensive, well-marked trails and swing bridges connect habitats as varied as tropical wet forest, swamps, creeks, rivers, secondary regenerating forest, and pasture. To see the place, take an informative 3½-hour morning or afternoon nature walk with one of La Selva's bilingual guides, who are some of the country's best. Walks start every day at 8 AM and 1:30 PM. Schedule a walk and lunch ($9; at noon, after the morning walk and before the afternoon walk) in advance. For a completely different view of the forest, set off on a guided dawn walk at 5:30 AM, or the night tour at 7 PM. Or get a group of at least five together and enroll in the Saturday-morning Bird-watching 101 course ($40 per person). Advance reservations are required for the dawn and night walks as well as for the Saturday-morning course. To get here, take a public bus to Puerto Viejo de Sarapiquí—La Selva is a $4 taxi ride from town. ☒ *6 km (3½ mi) south of Puerto Viejo de Sarapiquí; look for sign on west side of road* ☎ *766–6565 or 240–6696* 📠 *766–6535 or 240–6783* ⊕ *www.ots.ac.cr* ✇ *OTS, Apdo. 676–2050, San Pedro* ✉ *Nature walk $26, morning and afternoon walks $40, night walks $30* ☉ *Walks daily at 8 AM and 1:30 PM.*

Where to Stay

$$ 🏠 **La Selva.** Other lodges provide more comfort for the money, but none can match La Selva's tropical nature experience. The dorm-style rooms have large bunk beds, tile floors, and lots of screened windows. The restaurant, something like a school cafeteria, serves decent food but has a very limited schedule (reserve ahead). It's a good idea to pay the full-board fee, which includes a guided nature walk and three meals a day with your room rate, since there's nowhere else to eat. Priority is given to researchers, so advance reservations are essential. ☒ *6 km (3½*

mi) south of Puerto Viejo de Sarapiquí ☎ *766–6565, 240–6696 in San Pedro* ☏ *OTS, Apdo. 676–2050, San Pedro* 🖶 *240–6783* ☞ *60 bunk beds share 12 baths, 3 cabins* ♿ *Restaurant, fans, hiking, laundry facilities; no a/c, no room phones, no room TVs* 🖃 *AE, MC, V* ¶◎¶ *FAP.*

Puerto Viejo de Sarapiquí

❹ *6½ km (4 mi) north of La Selva.*

In the 19th century, Puerto Viejo de Sarapiquí was a thriving river port and the only link with the coastal lands straight east, now Barra del Colorado National Wildlife Refuge and Tortuguero National Park. Fortunes nose-dived with the construction of the coastal canal from the town of Moín, and today Puerto Viejo has a slightly run-down air. The activities of the Nicaraguan Contras made this a danger zone in the 1980s, but now that the political situation has improved, boats once again ply the old route up the Río Sarapiquí to the Río San Juan on the Nicaraguan frontier, from where you can travel downstream to Barra del Colorado or Tortuguero. Passports are required for the trip: the San Juan lies entirely within Nicaraguan territory.

A few tour companies, such as Costa Rica Expeditions, Ríos Tropicales, and Aventuras Naturales (⇨ The Caribbean A to Z), have Sarapiquí River tours with up to Class III rapids in the section between Chilamate and La Virgen and plenty of wildlife around. If you prefer to leave the driving to them, many of the lodges operate boat transport on the tamer sections of the river. If you don't have much time to spend in this region, **Ecoscape Nature Tours** (☎ 297–0664 ⊕ www.costaricasbesttour.com) has an excellent daylong Highlights Tour of the Sarapiquí loop for $79. In addition to a boat ride on the river, and a stop at a banana-processing plant, the day includes a visit to a coffee plantation and the Poás volcano. Or a Sunset Jungle Tour departs San José at 1 PM and takes in dinner and a night walk at the Selva Verde Lodge. A two-day option includes an overnight at the lodge and a white-water rafting excursion or rain-forest tour.

If you've gleaned your knowledge of bats entirely from Dracula legends and Batman movies, the **Tirimbina Rainforest Center** will set your views and fears straight with its **Bat Tour** at 7:30 PM nightly. (Bats are not blind, contrary to popular belief, and most have no interest in sucking your blood.) The nonprofit center, affiliated with the Milwaukee Public Museum, is dedicated to environmental research and education, and encompasses 750 acres of primary forest and 8 km (5 mi) of trails, portions of it via hanging bridges at canopy level. Tirimbina also conducts multiday classes and workshops with packages offering lodging at the Centro Neotrópico Sarapiquís next door. Advance reservations are required for all tours. ⊠ *La Virgen de Sarapiquí, 17 km (11 mi) southwest of Puerto Viejo* ☎ *761–1579* ⊕ *www.tirimbina.org* ⊗ *7–5* 🎟 *$14 day tour; $12 bat tour.*

Costa Rica's indigenous peoples don't get the visibility that nearby Guatemala's do, probably because they number only 40,000 out of a ★ population of 4 million. The **Museo de Culturas Indígenas Doctora María Eugenia Bozzoli** (Dr. María Eugenia Bozzoli Museum of Indigenous Cultures), part of the Centro Neotrópico Sarapiquís, provides a well-rounded all-under-one-roof introduction to the subject. That roof is thatched and covers a 1,000-square-meter stucco structure built to resemble an indigenous dwelling, and housing some 400 artifacts of the Boruca, Bribri, Cabécar, Guaymí, and Maleku peoples. But start off watching a 17-minute video introduction, *Man and Nature in Pre-Columbian Costa Rica,* in the adjoining amphitheater before moving on to the museum proper, named for one of Costa Rica's foremost anthropologists. The exhibits are especially strong in their display of masks, musical instruments, and shamanic healing sticks. A botanical garden next door cultivates medicinal plants still used by many traditional groups. In 1999, researchers discovered an archaeological site on the grounds that contains pre-Columbian tombs and petroglyphs dating from the 15th century. The site is still under study. ⊠ *La Virgen de Sarapiquí, 17 km (11 mi) southwest of Puerto Viejo* ☎ *761–1418* ⊕ *www.sarapiquis.org* ⊙ *Daily 9–5* ⊠ *$19.*

A working dairy farm and horse ranch, the **Hacienda Pozo Azul** offers riding excursions for all experience levels through the region around La Virgen. Or visit the ecologically sound 360-cattle dairy operation. Two levels of tour exist: a two-hour visit for experts, and a one-hour family tour for the lay public. ⊠ *La Virgen de Sarapiquí, 17 km (11 mi) southwest of Puerto Viejo* ☎*761–1360 or 438–2616* ⊕*www.haciendapozoazul. com* ⊠ *$10 dairy tour, $30 for two hrs of horseback riding.*

Heliconias abound at the aptly named **Heliconia Island** in the Sarapiquí River. Some 70 species of the flowering plant, a relative of the banana, are among the collections that populate five acres of botanical gardens here. Expect to see ample bird and butterfly life, too. ⊠ *La Chaves, 8 km (5 mi) south of Puerto Viejo de Sarapiquí* ☎ *766–6247* ⊠ *$7.50* ⊙ *Daily 9–5.*

Curious about the life and times of Costa Rica's most famous yellow fruit? The **Standard Fruit Company,** known as Dole in North America, has two-hour Banana Tours to guide you through the process from plantation to processing to packing. Visits are best arranged through several San José travel agencies, who will transport you to any of the three sites. Options include a plantation in Sarapiquí or sites in Siquirres or south of Limón. ☎ *768–8683 or 383–4596* ⊠ *$10* ⊙ *Tours daily at 10 AM.*

Where to Stay & Eat

$$ 🏨 **Centro Neotrópico Sarapiquís.** The center, operated by a Belgian non-profit organization, is environmental educational center, museum, gardens, and hotel all rolled into one, and overlooks the Sarapiquí River. Three indigenous-inspired circular palenque buildings with palm-thatched roofs house the amply sized rooms. All come with tile floor and pre-Columbian-style decor and private terrace. There's an extra cost to visit the CNS's numerous sightseeing attractions. ⊠ *La Virgen de Sarapiquí, 17 km (11 mi) southwest of Puerto Viejo* ☎*761–1004* 🖷*761–1415* ⊕ *www.sarapiquis.org* ⇌ *36 rooms* ⌂ *Restaurant, coffee shop, fans, bar, library, shop, laundry service, meeting room; no a/c, no room TVs, no smoking* ⊟ *AE, DC, MC, V.*

★ **$$** ⊞ **Selva Verde Lodge.** Built on stilts over the Río Sarapiquí, this expansive complex stands on the edge of a 2-square-km (1-square-mi) private reserve of tropical rain forest and caters primarily to natural-history tours. The buildings have wide verandas strung with hammocks, and the rooms come with polished wood paneling and mosquito blinds. Activities include guided walks, boat trips, canoeing, rafting, and mountain biking. Room prices include a bird-watching tour. Reserve a few weeks ahead, especially in high season; the place is very popular with tour groups. ⊠ *7 km (4 mi) west of Puerto Viejo de Sarapiquí* ☐ *Apdo. 55, Chilamate* ☎ *766–6800, 800/451–7111 in North America* 🖷 *766–6011* ⊕ *www.selvaverde.com* ⤶ *40 rooms, 5 bungalows* ♧ *Restaurant, fans, boating, hiking, horseback riding, library, laundry service, meeting room; no a/c, no room phones, no room TVs* ▭ *AE, MC, V* ⦿ *FAP.*

$ ⊞ **Hotel El Bambú.** Unlike the many isolated properties in this region, Bambú is in the heart of Puerto Viejo de Sarapiquí. The rooms are simple but comfortable. A dense cluster of tall bamboo stalks climbs like Jack's bean stalk out of the garden, lending shade for the bar and restaurant, the latter of which serves Costa Rican–influenced Chinese food at reasonable prices. ⊠ *Main street across from town square–soccer field* ☎ *766–6005* 🖷 *766–6132* ⊕ *www.elbambu.com* ☐ *Apdo. 1518–2100, Guadalupe* ⤶ *16 rooms* ♧ *Restaurant, pool, gym, bar, laundry service, travel services, no-smoking rooms* ▭ *AE, MC, V* ⦿ *BP.*

$ ⊞ **Hotel Gavilán Río Sarapiquí.** Beautiful gardens run down to the river, and colorful tanagers and three types of toucan feast in the citrus trees. Not bad for an erstwhile hub of a fruit and cattle farm. The two-story lodge has comfortable rooms with white walls, terra-cotta floors, and decorative crafts. The food, Costa Rican *comida típica* (typical fare), has earned its good reputation. Prime activities are horseback jungle treks and boat trips up the Río Sarapiquí. ⊠ *700 m north of Comando Atlántico (naval command)* ⊕ *www.gavilanlodge.com* ☐ *Apdo. 445–2010, San José* ☎ *766–6743, 234–9507 in San José* 🖷 *253–6556* ⤶ *13 rooms* ♧ *Restaurant, fans, hot tub, fishing, horseback riding; no a/c, no room phones, no room TVs* ▭ *AE, DC, MC, V* ⦿ *BP.*

Guápiles

❺ *60 km (38 mi) northeast of San José.*

You may not see any reason to stop in Guápiles, off the main road, other than weariness or the need for a fuel fix, automotive or gastronomic. But because this farm and forest area is a crossroads of a sort—more or less equidistant to the palm beaches of the Caribbean shore, the jungles to the north, and the rain-forested mountains looming in the west—it's not a bad place to linger for a day or two, day-tripping in any of three directions. The Guápiles area is home to several major biological-research facilities as well as commercial producers of tropical plants.

Curious how those tropical houseplants you have at home started out? Ornamental plant farm **Costa Flores** conducts one-and-a-half-hour English-language tours—advance reservations are required—through its gardens and facilities. (Riotously colored heliconias are a specialty here.) The tour ends at the packing house, where you see how plants are prepared for exportation. Then you get to create your own floral bouquet to take with you as a souvenir. ⊠ *3½ km (2 mi) north of Guácimo on road to Río Jiménez* ☎ *716–6457* ☜ *$15* ☉ *Daily 5:30 AM–3 PM.*

Where to Stay

$ ⊡ **Hotel Río Palmas.** Think of it as a hacienda motel. Proximate to EARTH, near the town of Guácimo, the Río Palmas has a red-tile-roof open-air restaurant that grabs your eye as you're speeding by on the Guápiles Highway. Behind an arched, whitewashed entry gate, one-story, tile-roof whitewashed cabinas wrap around a central courtyard with a fountain and plants. Exotic plantings abound (the hotel is actually on an ornamental-plant farm), and the staff can arrange hikes, farm and jungle tours, and horseback rides to private waterfalls. ⊠ *Guápiles Hwy., Pocora de Guácimo* ☎ *760–0330* ☐ *760–0296* ⊕ *www. hotelriopalmas.com* ⇌ *32 rooms* ⬙ *Restaurant, fans, pool, hiking, horseback riding, laundry service; no a/c in some rooms, no room phones, no room TVs* ▱ *AE, MC, V.*

Sports & the Outdoors

Tour company **Ríos Tropicales** (⊠ On the highway in Siquirres, 28 km [17 mi] east of Guápiles ☎ 233–6455 ⊕ www.riostropicales.com) offers Río Pacuare tours on a Class III–IV section of the river between Siquirres and San Martín. Not quite so wild, but still with Class III rapids, is the nearby Florida section of the Río Reventazón. Day excursions begin in San José, or at the company's operations center in Siquirres.

EARTH

15 km (9 mi) east of Guápiles on Guápiles Hwy.

The nonprofit institution of higher education EARTH (Escuela de Agricultura de la Región Tropical Húmeda, or Agricultural School of the Tropical Humid Region) researches the production of less pesticide-dependent bananas and other forms of sustainable tropical agriculture, as well as medicinal plants. The university graduates some 100 students from Latin America and Africa each year. EARTH's elegant stationery, calendars, and other paper products made from banana stems, coffee leaves and grounds, and tobacco leaves are sold at the on-site Oropéndola store and in many tourist shops around the country. The property encompasses a banana plantation and a forest reserve with nature trails. Tours are $5 and lunch is $4 for day visitors. Though priority is given to researchers and conference groups, you're welcome to stay in the school's 50-person lodging facility, with private bathrooms, hot water, and ceiling fans, for $55 a night, which includes the use of a swimming pool and exercise equipment. Advance reservations are required. ⬠ *Apdo. 4442–1000, San José* ☎ *713–0000* ☐ *713–0001* ⊕ *www.earth.ac.cr.*

| en route | If you're bypassing Limón entirely en route south to Cahuita and Puerto Viejo de Talamanca, a right turn via Moín, 3 km (2 mi) shy of Limón, will give you an alternate route—a smooth road that weaves through the hills. Look for the green road sign indicating a right turn to Sixaola (the Panamanian border) and other points south. |

THE NORTHERN CARIBBEAN COAST

Tortuguero means "turtle region," and, indeed, this northeastern sector remains one of the world's prime places to watch the life cycle of sea turtles. It also remains one of Costa Rica's most popular destinations despite its remoteness and difficult access. The tourism seasons here are defined not by the rains or lack thereof (it's wet here most of the year) but by the months of prime turtle hatching. The stretch of beach between the Colorado and Matina rivers was first mentioned as a nesting ground for sea turtles in a 1592 Dutch chronicle, and because the area is so isolated—there's no road here to this day—the turtles nested undisturbed for centuries. By the mid-1900s, however, the harvesting of eggs and catching of turtles had reached such a level that these creatures faced extinction. In 1963 an executive decree regulated the hunting of turtles and the gathering of eggs, and in 1970 the government established Tortuguero National Park. At the same time, a system of canals taking advantage of inland lagoons and rivers was constructed providing safer access for the region than the dangerous journey up the seacoast. You can continue up the canals that begin in Moín and run parallel to the coast, to the less visited Barra del Colorado Wildlife Refuge, an immense protected area that's connected to the park.

Tortuguero National Park

6 *50 km (31 mi) northwest of (3 hrs by boat from) Moín.*

Fodor'sChoice
★

The palm-lined beaches of Parque Nacional Tortuguero stretch off as far as the eye can see, and its additional ecosystems include lowland rain forest, estuaries, and swampy areas covered with *Jolillo* palms. You can wander the beach independently, but riptides make swimming dangerous, and shark rumors persist. At various times of the year, Green, Hawksbill, Loggerhead, and Giant Leatherback Turtles lumber up the 36 km (22 mi) of beach and deposit their eggs for safekeeping—a fascinating natural ritual. If you want to watch the *deshove* (the egg laying), contact your hotel or the parks office to hire a certified local guide. One must accompany you on turtle-watching excursions. Note that you won't be allowed to use a camera on the beach, and that only your guide is permitted to use a flashlight and it must be covered with red plastic, as lights can deter the turtles from nesting. As the signs around town admonish you regarding the turtles: "Don't become another predator."

Freshwater turtles inhabit Tortuguero's rivers, as do crocodiles—most populous in the Río Agua Frío—and the endangered *vacas marinas,* or manatees. Manatees consume huge quantities of aquatic plants and are endangered mainly because their lack of speed makes them easy prey. You might also glimpse tapirs (watch for these in Jolillo groves), jaguars, anteaters, ocelots, howler monkeys, Collared and White-lipped Peccaries, raccoons, otters, skunks, and coatis. Some 350 species of birds and countless butterflies, including the iridescent Blue Morpho, also call this area home. At a station deep in the Tortuguero jungle, volunteers from the Canadian Organization for Tropical Education and Rainforest Con-

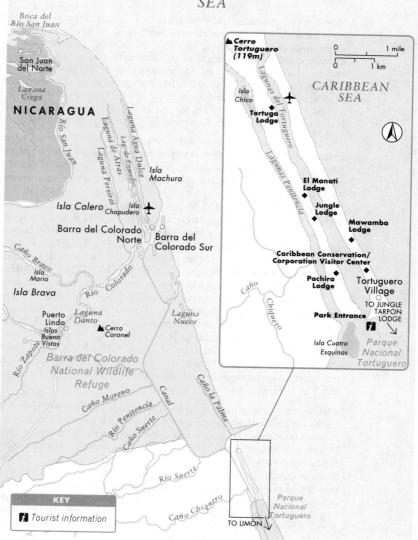

servation manage a butterfly farm, catalog plants and animals, and explore sustainable forest practices. ⊠ *Entrance at south end of Tortuguero Village* ⌑ *$7* ⊘ *Daily 6–6.*

Tortuguero

▶ ❼ *225 km (135 mi) northeast of San José. There are officially no roads to Tortuguero, though illegal attempts have been made to cut one through the jungle. Travel time is 30 mins by plane from San José, 3 hrs by boat from Moín.*

North of the national park, the hamlet of Tortuguero is a pleasant little place with 600 inhabitants, two churches, three bars, a handful of souvenir shops, and a growing selection of inexpensive accommodation alternatives to the big lodges. Pick up information on the park, turtles, and other wildlife at the kiosk in the town center. You can also take a stroll on the 32-km (20-mi) beach, but swimming is not recommended because of strong riptides and the presence of large numbers of bull sharks and barracuda (not threatening, say the locals). Visitors who have more than a week's time in Costa Rica typically spend a couple of nights here.

The logistics of getting to this roadless part of Costa Rica mean most visitors opt for an all-inclusive stay at one of the big lodges north of town, which includes transportation to and from Tortuguero. But it's entirely possible to stay in the village and arrange your own transport. Arriving on the early-morning NatureAir or SANSA flights from San José is the easiest option. SANSA agent Victor Barrantes meets both flights and offers boat transport into town for $3. Boat captains will transport passengers from the docks at Moín near Limón. **Alexis Soto and Sebastien Torres** (☎ 297–1010 beeper) partner to provide a reliable (virtually daily) boat service between Moín and Tortuguero for about $50 round-trip. Biologist **Daryl Loth** (⊠ Casa Marbella ☎ 833–0827 or 709–8011) is a wealth of information about the area and conducts boat excursions on the canals and responsible turtle-watching tours in season with advance notice. If you arrive in Moín in your own vehicle, JAPDEVA, Costa Rica's Atlantic port authority, operates a secure, guarded parking facility for your car while you are in Tortuguero. A direct bus departs from San José's Gran Terminal del Caribe to Cariari, north of Guápiles, at 9 AM. At Cariari, you disembark at the Geest Banana Plantation for boat transport to Tortuguero. Buses tend toward the crowded and uncomfortable, but this is how locals travel.

Tortuguero is one of those "everybody's a guide" places; the quality of guides varies, but most are quite knowledgeable. A few unscrupulous locals will offer to take you on a turtle-watching tour outside the allowed February–November turtle tour season, and will disturb sensitive nesting sites in the process. If it's not the season, there's no reason to go on a turtle excursion. If you stay at one of the lodges, guided tours are included in your package price. The **Caribbean Conservation Corporation** (☎709–8011) can recommend good local guides. **Victor Barrantes** (☎ 709–8055 or 838–6330) is a local SANSA agent who conducts hiking tours to Cerro Tortuguero and around the area when he's not meeting the early-morning flights. Daryl Loth (⇨ *above*) is another recommended local guide.

The **Caribbean Conservation Corporation** (CCC) runs a visitor center and a museum with excellent animal photos, a video narrating local history, and detailed discussions of the latest ecological goings-on and what you can do to help. There's a souvenir shop next door. For the committed eco-tourist, the **John H. Phipps Biological Field Station,** affiliated with the CCC, has camping areas as well as dorm-style quarters with a communal kitchen. If you want to get involved in the life of the turtles—using satellite technology, current research has tracked turtle migration as far as the Florida Keys—or help catalog the population of neotropical migrant birds, arrange a stay in advance through the center. ⊠ *From beach, walk north along path and watch for sign* ☎ *709–8011, 224–9215 in San José, 352/373–6441 or 800/678–7853 in U.S.* ⊕ *www.cccturtle.org* ⊕ *Apdo. 246–2050, San Pedro* ⊡ *$1* ⊗ *Mon.–Sat. 10–noon and 2–5, Sun. 2–5:30.*

off the beaten path

COASTAL CANALS – The jungle life that you see on a three-hour boat trip through the combination of natural and man-made canals between Tortuguero and Moín is awesome, providing a kind of real-life Indiana Jones adventure. Running parallel to the coast a couple of miles inland, the waterway provides a safer alternative to making the journey up the coast via the ocean. Most San José tour operators will not take you all the way to Moín to board canal boats but instead access them via the Parsimina or Aguas Zarcas River. As you swoop through the sinuous turns of the natural waterways, your captain-guide may spot monkeys, snakes, caimans, mud turtles, sloths, and dozens of bird species, including flocks of bright and noisy parrots, kingfishers, aracari toucans, and assorted herons. The densely layered greenery is highlighted by brilliantly colored flowers, and the visual impact is doubled by the jungle's reflection in the mirror-smooth surface of the water. Consider hiring a dugout canoe and a guide to explore some of the rivers flowing into the canal; these waterways bear less boat traffic and often have more wildlife.

Where to Stay & Eat

The big lodges here offer one- or two-night excursion packages. Rates are expensive, but prices include everything from guides, tours, meals, and snacks to minivan and boat transport, and in some cases air transport to and from San José. If you stop and calculate what you get, the price may not be as bad as it first seemed.

$ ✕ **Miss Junie.** Most Tortuguero travelers take meals at their lodges, but this restaurant is worth a special trip. Miss Junie, the village's most well-known cook, continues a tradition started by her mother more than a half century ago and serves cheap, filling, tasty food at an open-air restaurant adjoining her home. (Fidel Castro and Che Guevara were among the early diners here.) Selection is limited, and it's best to call ahead, but you can usually count on a chicken, beef, or fish platter with rice and beans simmered in coconut milk. Your meal includes a beverage and dessert. ⊠ *150 m north of Paraíso Tropical, Tortuguero village* ☎ *709–8102* ⊟ *No credit cards.*

¢–$ ✕ **La Casona.** You dine at long picnic tables here, the floor is sandy, and reggae plays in the background—it's nothing fancy—but grab a table and chat with your fellow diners about the day's sightseeing. Fish and vegetarian dishes are the staples here, and the banana pancakes for breakfast are a great way to fortify yourself before setting out for the day. ⊠ *North side of soccer field, Tortuguero Village* ☎ *709–8047* ▭ *No credit cards.*

$$$$ ⊡ **Jungle Lodge.** The Jungle Lodge experience begins with your hotel pickup in San José and continues via a minivan trip to the docks north of Siquirres, where you board the lodge's *Miss Caribe* or *Miss America* barges for the last leg of the canal trip. The luxuriously rustic hardwood cabins are well ventilated and have huge bathrooms. Everything is included, save for a few small tours. Rates begin at $170 per person. The restaurant serves buffet-style meals. ⊠ *1 km (½ mi) south of airstrip* ☎ *382–8965, 233–0133 in San José* 🖷 *233–0778* ⊕ *www. grupopapagayo.com* ⇆ *44 rooms* ⚲ *Dining room, fans, pool, hot tub, bar, shop, laundry service; no a/c, no room phones, no room TVs* ▭ *AE, MC, V* ꤷ *AI.*

$$$$ ⊡ **Jungle Tarpon Lodge.** On 100 acres, this intimate lodge specializes in sportfishing packages, but there's plenty to do here if you don't fish. Eco-adventure activities, turtle-watching, and custom tours are arranged here. Though small, the lodge is a deluxe affair, crafted in fine wood with large rooms, modern tiled bathrooms, and beamed ceilings. Savory local cuisine—heavy on fish, of course—is served in the dining room; some meals are enjoyed riverside. Transfers to San José, meals, and charters are included in the four- to nine-day packages. Packages begin at close to $1,500 per person. ⊠ *Parsimina River lagoon, southern end of Tortuguero National Park* ☎ *No phone* ⚲ *May–mid-Oct.: Great Alaska, 33881 Sterling Hwy., Sterling, AK 99672* ☎ *907/262–4515, 800/ 544–2261 in U.S., 360/697–6454 in WA* 🖷 *907/262–8797, 360/697– 7850 in WA* ⚲ *Mid-Oct.–Apr.: Great Alaska, Box 2670, Poulsbo, WA 98370* ⊕ *www.jungletarpon.com* ⇆ *4 rooms* ⚲ *Restaurant, dining room, fans, boating, fishing, hiking, bar; no a/c, no room phones, no room TVs* ▭ *AE, MC, V* ꤷ *AI.*

★ $$$$ ⊡ **Mawamba Lodge.** Nestled between the river and the ocean, Mawamba is the perfect place to kick back and relax. You're whisked from the put-in at the river town of Matina in a 2½-hour launch ride to stay in comfortable rustic cabinas with hot water and garden views and take meals in the spacious dining room, all on a 15-acre site. Meals, transfers, and guided tours of the jungle and canals are included; trips to turtle-heavy beaches cost $10 extra. Packages begin at about $210 per person. ⊠ *½ km (¼ mi) north of Tortuguero on ocean side of canal* ☎ *293–8181 in San José* ⊕ *www.grupomawamba.com* ⚲ *Apdo. 10980–1000, San José* 🖷 *239–7657* ⇆ *54 cabinas* ⚲ *Restaurant, dining room, fans, pool, hot tub, beach, billiards, volleyball, bar, shop, laundry service, meeting room; no a/c, no room phones, no room TVs* ▭ *AE, MC, V* ꤷ *AI.*

★ $$$$ ⊡ **Pachira Lodge.** Here is the prettiest and most luxurious of Tortuguero's lodges—although not the costliest. Each almond-wood cabina in the lush, well-manicured gardens contains four guest rooms with high ceilings, king-size beds, and bamboo furniture. The stunning pool is shaped like a giant sea turtle: the head is a hot tub, the left paw is a wading pool, and the right paw is equipped for swimmers with disabilities. The only drawback here is that you have few options at night, as there is no cross-river transportation into town. Package deals include transport from San José, a jungle tour, and all meals; rates begin at about $260 per person. ⊠ *Across river from Mawamba Lodge* ☎ *382–2239, 256–7080 San José* ⊕ *www.pachiralodge.com* 🖶 *Apdo. 1818–1002, San José* 🖶 *223–1119* ⥱ *44 rooms* ♿ *Restaurant, fans, pool, wading pool, bar, laundry service; no a/c, no room phones, no room TVs* ☰ *AE, MC, V* ⦿ *AI.*

$$$$ ⊞ **Tortuga Lodge.** Lush lawns, orchids, and tropical trees surround this thatched riverside lodge owned by Costa Rica Expeditions and renowned for its nature packages. Guest rooms are comfortable, with much-needed mosquito blinds—the mosquitoes can be voracious. Considering that most of the restaurant ingredients are flown in, the chefs do an excellent job of preparing hearty food. The lodge is across the river from the airstrip, 2 km (1 mi) from Tortuguero. Rates begin at around $230 per room, with double occupancy. An all-inclusive rate is available. ⊠ *20 mins north by boat from Tortuguero National Park or 35 mins by plane from San José* ☎ *710–8016, 222–0333, 257–0766 in San José* ⊕ *www.costaricaexpeditions.com* 🖶 *Apdo. 6941–1000, San José* 🖶 *257–1665* ⥱ *24 rooms* ♿ *Dining room, fans, pool, fishing, hiking, bar, laundry service; no a/c, no room phones, no room TVs* ☰ *AE, MC, V* ⦿ *FAP.*

★ $ ⊞ **Casa Marbella.** The best of the in-town accommodations is a real find and a great alternative to the big lodges north of the village. Canadian owner and biologist Daryl Loth is a respected authority on all things Tortuguero and can arrange for all your touring needs. If he's unable to take you out in his boat himself, he'll find someone who can. Immaculate rooms have tile floors and varnished wood finishing with vaulted ceilings and skylights in the bathrooms. Ample breakfasts are served on the covered back patio facing the lodging's own private canal dock. The terrace is also a relaxing place for a coffee break on a rainy afternoon. There's a small kitchenette. ⊠ *Across from Catholic church, Tortuguero Village* ☎ *833–0827 or 709–8011* ⊕ *casamarbella.tripod. com* ⥱ *4 rooms* ♿ *Fans, travel services; no a/c, no room phones, no room TVs* ☰ *No credit cards* ⦿ *BP.*

$ ⊞ **El Manatí.** Simple and reasonably priced, El Manatí is popular with budget travelers and researchers, some of whom study the lodge's namesake—the endangered manatee. The comfortable but slightly run-down rooms have firm beds and mosquito screens. The contiguous terraces look across a narrow lawn to the river, where you can kayak and canoe. Chestnut-beaked Toucans, poison dart frogs, and three types of monkey hang out in the surrounding jungle. ⊠ *Across river, about 1 km (½ mi) north of Tortuguero* ☎ *383–0330* ⊕ *www.fundacionmanati.org* ⥱ *8 cabins, 11 rooms* ♿ *Restaurant, fans, boating, Ping-Pong, bar; no a/c, no room phones, no room TVs* ☰ *No credit cards* ⦿ *BP.*

¢ ⊞ **Cabinas Miriam.** Nicaraguan owner Miriam fusses over her guests in a two-story building just a short walk from the beach. Rooms are simple, with tile floors and three beds each. Miriam whips up Caribbean food at her restaurant next door. ⊠ *300 m north of entrance to national park, Tortuguero Village* ☎ *709–8107* ⥱ *6 rooms* ♿ *Restaurant, fans; no a/c, no room phones, no room TVs* ☰ *No credit cards.*

¢ ⊞ **Cabinas Tortuguero.** The friendly, exuberant Italian proprietor makes this place a favorite among European backpackers. The two-story building is in a shady garden, with a small restaurant serving Caribbean and Italian food next door. Rooms have tile floors and bright drapes and spreads. ⊠ *200 m north of entrance to national park, Tortuguero Village* ☎ *839–1200 or 223–3030 in San José* ⇨ *7 rooms, 5 with bath* ⚱ *Restaurant, fans; no a/c, no room phones, no room TVs* ☱ *No credit cards.*

Shopping

Paraíso Tropical (⊠ West side of Tortuguero school ☎ 709–8095) has a large selection of wood carvings and sandals in addition to the standard T-shirt and postcard fare, and will cash traveler's checks for a small commission. **Souvenirs Pura Vida** (⊠ Across from police station ☎ 709–8037) has a nice variety of colorful T-shirts and wood carvings.

Barra del Colorado

❽ *25 km (16 mi) northwest of Tortuguero, 30 minutes by plane from San José.*

Farther up the coast from Tortuguero is the ramshackle hamlet of Barra del Colorado, a popular sportfishing hub characterized by plain stilted wooden houses, dirt paths, and a complete absence of motorized land vehicles (though some locals have added outboard motors to their hand-hewn canoes). Bordered to the north by the Río San Juan and the frontier with Nicaragua is the vast, 905-square-km (350-square-mi) **Refugio Nacional de Fauna Silvestre Barra del Colorado** (Barra del Colorado Wildlife Refuge; ☎ No phone), really the only local attraction for nonanglers. Most people approach by air or boat (via the canals) from San José or Tortuguero; you can also come from Puerto Viejo de Sarapiquí up the Sarapiquí and San Juan rivers. Transportation once you get here is almost exclusively waterborne, as there are virtually no paths in this swampy terrain. The list of species that you're likely to see from your boat is almost the same as that for Tortuguero; the main difference here is the feeling of being farther off the beaten track. The refuge is open at all hours, and admission is free.

Where to Stay

$$$$ ⊞ **Río Colorado Lodge.** This jungle lodge caters almost exclusively to sportfishing folk and tours, complete with a modern fleet of 10- and 26-foot sportfishing vessels. Guest rooms have twin beds with patterned bedspreads, paneled ceilings, white curtains, and basket lamp shades. The all-inclusive tours include airport pickup, all meals, and fishing trips; rates begin at about $1,500 per person. Alternatively, there are some fly-in, boat-out nature-tour packages that include Tortuguero National Park and are considerably cheaper. Given the logistics of getting here, it doesn't pay to stay only one night. ⊠ *35-min flight from San José via NatureAir* ☎ *No phone at lodge, 232–4063 San José, 800/243–9777 in U.S.* ☎ *231–5987, 813/933–3280 in U.S.* ⊕*www.riocoloradolodge.com* ⌂*Apdo. 5094–1000, San José* ⇨ *18 rooms* ⚱ *Restaurant, fans, fishing, bar, laundry service; no room phones, no room TVs* ☱ *AE, MC, V* ⧾*AI.*

The San Juan River to Nicaragua

40 km (24 mi) by boat north of Puerto Viejo de Sarapiquí, 18 km (11 mi) by boat north of Barra del Colorado.

Crossing into Nicaragua from northeastern Costa Rica is both difficult and easy. An 1858 treaty established the San Juan River as the eastern section of the border between the two countries, but granted Nicaragua complete sovereignty over the waterway. A boat trip from Puerto Viejo de Sarapiquí up the Río Sarapiquí takes you to the San Juan and lets you officially enter Nicaragua. Passports are required for the trip, but you won't acquire a Nicaraguan stamp as a souvenir if you remain on the river. Venturing any farther into Nicaragua on your own is difficult here; you run up against the largely forested eastern half of the country. It remains essentially roadless, much like Tortuguero and Barra del Colorado immediately to the south.

Spurred on by the California Gold Rush during the 1840s, the San Juan became an important 19th-century crossroads connecting the Atlantic and Pacific oceans some 70 years before the opening of the Panama Canal. Cornelius Vanderbilt financed the dredging of the waterway to allow passage of ships up the river to the large freshwater Lake Nicaragua. A short rail connection completed the journey from the lake's western shore to the Pacific Ocean, allowing miners to head west from New York to San Francisco and their gold to move back east. As the Panama Canal ages, there is again talk these days of resurrecting this "wet-dry" canal through this portion of the isthmus. So far, plans remain on the drawing board.

The river has become a thorny issue between the two countries in recent years with Nicaragua's insistence that Costa Rican border patrols ask permission to carry arms when navigating the San Juan, and Costa Rica's frequent refusal to abide by the request. Heated words are frequently exchanged. The San Juan issue is mixed in with larger problems, primarily the enormous influx of Nicaraguans heading south in search of work and a better life. (Estimates are that some 20 percent of Costa Rica's population today is Nicaraguan.) Relations remain mostly cordial, however, and when things do flare up, they merely take the form of the press publishing unflattering pictures of each other's leaders in both countries.

You can realistically get as far as the 640,000-acre Río Indio-Maiz Biological Reserve when crossing the border here, a continuation of the Barra del Colorado Wildlife Refuge, but in Nicaraguan territory. In the midst of it all, near the small village of San Juan del Norte, sits the **Río Indio Adventure Lodge,** Nicaragua's only true ecotourism lodge, with rustic luxury in 34 rooms for $325 per night. Packages include van transport from San José to Puerto Viejo de Sarapiquí, with continuation by boat another three hours up the Sarapiquí and San Juan rivers to the lodge. Or you can opt for air transport to Barra del Colorado with another hour's boat journey up the Río Colorado to the site. The lodge can handle the $10 immigration levied by Nicaraguan authorities. So tied is San Juan del Norte to Costa Rica that the lodge's information offices and telephone numbers are in Costa Rica rather than Nicaragua. E San Juan del Norte, Nicaragua P 381–1549 or 296–3338 San José, 866/593–3176 in North America w www.rioindiolodge.com.

COASTAL TALAMANCA

The quickest route from San José to the Atlantic coast runs through the magnificent cloud forest of Braulio Carrillo National Park on its way to the Caribbean Sea and the lively and sometimes dangerous port town of Limón. The 160-km (100-mi) trip along the Guápiles Highway to the coast takes about 2½ hours if all goes well; the highway is carved out of mountainous jungle and is susceptible to landslides. Make sure it's not blocked before you set off. (The alternate route is a long, painfully slow journey via Turrialba and Siquirres—it's doable, but best avoided.) As the highway descends and straightens toward Guápiles, you'll enter the province of Limón, where cloud forest gives way to banana plantations and partially deforested pastureland. (Note well that the highway gives way to potholes, some big enough to swallow an entire wheel and ruin your car's suspension.) Local farms produce cacao, exotic export plants, and macadamia nuts. After passing through villages with names such as Bristol, Stratford, and Liverpool, you arrive in the provincial capital, Limón.

Limón

❾ *130 km (81 mi) southeast of Braulio Carrillo National Park, 100 km (62 mi) southeast of Guápiles.*

Limón inherited its promontory setting, overlooking the Caribbean, from the ancient Indian village of Cariari, which lay close to Uvita Island, where Christopher Columbus dropped anchor on his final voyage in 1502. The colorful Afro-Caribbean flavor of Costa Rica's most important port (population 50,000) is the first sign of life for seafaring visitors to Costa Rica's east coast. Limón is a lively, if shabby, town with a 24-hour street life. The wooden houses are brightly painted, but the grid-plan streets look rather worn, largely because of the damage caused by a 1991 earthquake. Street crime, including pickpocketing and nighttime mugging, is not uncommon here. But *"Limón cambia,"* (Limón is changing), say residents. Long charged with neglecting the city, the national government has turned attention to Limón. New businesses are coming in, providing hopeful signs of urban renewal, and the town has beefed up security with a more visible police presence. There are several appealing hotels at Portete, just north of Limón town, with easy access to the docks at Moín.

Limón's newest incarnation is that of a port of call; the **Terminal de Cruceros** hosts 11 cruise ships per week during the December–April high season, though none the rest of the year. Some of the passengers scatter to the four winds on organized shore excursions around the Caribbean region—a few even venture as far away as the Rain Forest Aerial Tram or San José—but many remain in town to shop and explore. A legion of taxi drivers waits at the cruise-terminal exit to take you wherever your heart desires, and with a group, you can organize your own reasonably priced do-it-yourself excursion. And downtown shopkeepers are eagerly learning how to convert their colón prices to dollars. St. Thomas or Puerto Vallarta it is not—perhaps someday, residents hope—but Limón has a seasonal tourist vibe these days that the city has never before experienced.

Avenidas run east and west, and calles north and south, but Limón's street numbering system differs from that of other Costa Rican cities. "Number one" of each street begins at the water and numbers increase sequentially as you move inland, unlike the evens-on-one-side, odds-on-the-other scheme seen in San José. But the scarcity of street signs means everyone uses landmarks anyway. (This is Costa Rica, after all.)

On the left side of the highway as you enter Limón is a large **Chinese cemetery,** Chinese workers having made up a large part of the 1880s railroad-construction team that worked here. Thousands died of malaria and yellow fever.

From the Chinese cemetery, follow the railroad into town as far as the palm-lined promenade that runs around the city's central park, the **Parque Vargas.** From the promenade you can see the raised dead coral left stranded by the quake. Nine or so Hoffman's two-toed sloths live in the trees of Parque Vargas; ask a passerby to point them out, as spotting them requires a trained eye.

From Parque Vargas, find the lively enclosed **Mercado Central** (Central Market; ⊠ Pedestrian mall, Avda. 2, between Cs. 3 and 4), where you can buy fruit for the road ahead. If you prefer more familiar surroundings, stock up on food at the Más x Menos supermarket across from the northeast corner of the Mercado.

Where to Stay & Eat

$-$$ ✕ **Brisas del Caribe.** An old downtown-Limón standby, Brisas is a perpetually incongruous mix of businessmen in tropical guayabera shirts, locals hoping to get lucky on the video poker machines inside the door, and waiters dusting off their best English and adjusting the crooked umbrellas at the outdoor sidewalk tables to serve the cruise passengers who stop in for a break and a bite. Seafood and surprisingly decent hamburgers, a real rarity in Costa Rica, are the fare here. ⊠ *North side of Parque Vargas* ☎ *758–0138* ▤ *AE, DC, MC, V.*

¢-$ ✕ **Springfield.** Protected from the street by a leafy conservatory, this Caribbean kitchen whips up tasty rice-and-bean dishes. Decor consists of wood paneling, red tablecloths, and a white-tile floor. Bring your dancing shoes: the huge dance floor out back creaks to the beat of soca, salsa, and reggae on weekends. ⊠ *On road north from Limón to Portete, left opposite hospital* ☎ *758–1203* ▤ *AE, DC, MC, V.*

$$ ▥ **Hotel Maribú Caribe.** Perched on a cliff overlooking the Caribbean Sea between Limón and Portete, these white conical thatched huts have great views and hot water. The lovely grounds have green lawns, shrubs, palm trees, and a large, kidney-shape pool. The poolside bar discourages exertion. ⊠ *4 km (2½ mi) north on road to Portete, Apdo. 623–7300* ☎ *795–2543* 🖷 *795–3541* ✎ *maribu-caribe@hotmail.com*

📞 *52 rooms ⚬ Restaurant, snack bar, pool, bar, laundry service; no phones in some rooms* ☰ *AE, DC, MC, V* 🍴 *BP.*

$ 🏨 **Hotel Matama.** If you're coming from San José and planning to catch an early boat north out of Moín, this is a great place to get your first taste of the Caribbean. Across the street from the beach, the property has a pool and bar in close proximity, and the grounds are gorgeously landscaped with botanical trails exhibiting 50 tropical plant species. The open-air restaurant dishes up seafood and Caribbean cuisine and has lovely garden views. ✉ *4 km (2½ mi) west of Limón on road to Portete, Apdo. 606–7300* ☎ *795–1123 or 795–1490* 🖨 *795–3399* 🌐 *www.matama.com* 📞 *16 rooms ⚬ Restaurant, pool, bar, dance club, laundry service, meeting room; no room phones* ☰ *AE, MC, V* 🍴 *BP.*

$ 🏨 **Hotel Park.** The rooms are just a tad worn at the pastel-and-pink Park, but the prices can't be beat here at central Limón's business-class hotel. All rooms have modern furnishings and private balconies, so opt for one fronting the ocean. The air-conditioned dining room is a pleasant respite from the heat of the port city. ✉ *Avda. 3, between Cs. 2 and 3* ☎ *798–0555* 🖨 *758–4364* ✉ *irlyxie@racsa.co.cr* 📞 *32 rooms ⚬ Restaurant, meeting room; no room TVs* ☰ *AE, MC, V.*

Moín

🔟 *5 km (3 mi) north of Limón.*

The docks at Moín are a logical next stop after visiting neighboring Limón, especially if you want to take a boat north to explore the Caribbean coast. You'll probably be able to negotiate a waterway and national-park tour with a local guide, and if you call in advance, you can arrange a tour with the man considered the best guide on the Caribbean coast: **Modesto Watson** (☎ 226–0986), a local Miskito Indian guide. He's legendary for his bird- and animal-spotting skills as well as his howler-monkey imitations.

en route | The proximity of the Panamanian border means added police vigilance on the coastal highway. Expect a passport inspection and cursory vehicle search at a checkpoint just north of Cahuita. The border itself lies at Sixaola, 44 km (26 mi) south of the turnoff to Puerto Viejo de Talamanca.

Cahuita

⓫ *44 km (26 mi) southeast of Limón.*

The Caribbean character of the Atlantic lowlands becomes powerfully evident in the surf rolling shoreward as you head south from Limón to Cahuita, the hot, humid stir of the Caribbean trade winds, and the laid-back pace of the people you meet. This is tropical Central America, and it feels like another country, its slow, somewhat sultry atmosphere far removed from the business and bustle of San José.

Dusty Cahuita, its main dirt street flanked by wooden-slat cabins, is a backpackers' vacation town with something of a seedy reputation—a

Cahuita

CARIBBEAN
SEA

PUNTA CAHUITA

Miss Edith

Post Office

Police

School

Cabinas Smith

Cahuita Tours
& Rentals

Cha Cha Chá

Yoli's

Phones ◆ ◆ Turistica Cahuita

Restaurante Relax, ◆
Ricky's Bar

Puerto Viejo Bus

Bus
Terminal

0   100 yards

0   150 meters

TO
PLAYA
NEGRA

TO
PUERTO
VARGAS

TO RTE. 36
(LIMÓN & PUERTO VIEJO),
CAHUITA BUTTERFLY GARDEN,
AVIARIOS DEL CARIBE

Kelly Creek
Hotel–Restaurante

Kelly Creek Park Entrance Station ◆

Parque
Nacional
Cahuita

hippie hangout with a dash of Afro-Caribbean spice tossed in. Like Puerto Viejo de Talamanca, Cahuita has a few junkies, but the locals don't see them as a threat. And after years of negative crime-related publicity, Cahuita has beefed up security—this is one of the few places in the country where you will be conscious of a visible and reassuring, though not oppressive, police presence—and is making a small but well-deserved comeback on the tourist circuit. Tucked in among the backpackers' digs are a few surprisingly nice get-away-from-it-all lodgings and restaurants with some tasty cuisine at surprisingly decent prices.

☺ If you've visited other butterfly gardens around Costa Rica, you've probably gotten wet during the rainy season. (The mesh enclosures don't offer much protection from the moisture.) But that's not the case at the **Cahuita Butterfly Garden**. A bamboo roof covers the 1,100-square-meter facility. The friendly owners conduct tours in English, French, and Spanish. There's a souvenir shop and small café that serves refreshments. ⊠ *Coastal highway at the entrance to Cahuita* ☎ 755–0361 ⌑ $7 ☉ *Daily 9–4*.

Where to Stay & Eat

$–$$ ✕ **Blue Spirit.** The Caribbean-Italian couple who owns this small beach restaurant on Playa Negra has "married" their respective native cuisines.

You can opt for spaghetti *al pomodoro* (with tomato sauce), red snapper, or something in between. Try the *fruta del mar* pasta that mixes shrimp, lobster, and crab cuisine in a tangy barbecue sauce. There's live entertainment many evenings, and owner Tito makes amazing piña coladas. ⊠ *200 m west of police station on Playa Negra road* ☎ *755–0122* ⊟ *No credit cards* ⊘ *Closed Wed. No lunch.*

$–$$ ✕ **Cha Cha Chá.** You can order anything from Thai shrimp salad to Tex-
Fodor'sChoice Mex fajitas at this world-cuisine restaurant. A delectable specialty is *lan-
★ gosta cha cha chá*, lobster in a white-wine garlic sauce with fresh basil. Paintings by local artists hang on the light-blue walls of the candlelit outdoor dining area, separated from the street by miniature palm trees. ⊠ *Main street, 1 block north of Ricky's Bar* ☎ *394–4153* ⊟ *MC, V* ⊘ *Closed Mon. No lunch.*

$–$$ ✕ **Sobre las Olas.** The name means "over the waves," and this is one of the few seaside restaurants around, at the black-sand beach heading just out of town. Octopus is a specialty here, but if you're not that adventurous, a variety of other seafood and pasta dishes await. Lunch includes sandwiches and lighter fare. Or stop by for the delicious all-afternoon *bocas* (appetizers) when those 3 PM hunger pangs hit you. ⊠ *180 m west of police station at Playa Negra* ☎ *755–0109* ⊟ *AE, DC, MC, V* ⊘ *Closed Tues.*

$ ✕ **Miss Edith.** Miss Edith is revered for her flavorful Caribbean cooking, vegetarian meals, and herbal teas for whatever ails you. You won't be fed in a hurry—most dishes are made to order—but the *rondón* (stew of vegetables and beef or fish) and spicy jerk chicken are worth the wait. Back in the day, Miss Edith used to serve on her own front porch; she's since moved to more ample surroundings on an easy-to-miss side street at the north end of town. ⊠ *East of police station* ☎ *755–0248* ⊟ *No credit cards* ⊘ *Closed Sun.*

$ ✕ **Restaurante Relax.** From your vantage point at this open-air restaurant above Ricky's Bar, you can survey all that goes on in Cahuita's main intersection. Skewers of shrimp and chicken turn on the grill, but the Italian-Mexican owners also toss in pastas and fajitas to give their native cuisines sufficient representation. ⊠ *Above Ricky's Bar* ☎ *755–0322* ⊟ *No credit cards* ⊘ *Closed Tues. No lunch.*

¢–$ ✕ **Yoli's.** Chicken is the name of the game at this small, cozy, informal place on Cahuita's main street. It spins slowly and enticingly on a rotisserie *a la leña* (over firewood), and ends up as your main dish, with or without a tangy barbecue sauce, or in tacos or potato salad or with rice as arroz con pollo. If you don't have time to eat in, Yoli does a brisk carry-out business. ⊠ *Across from Turística Cahuita* ☎ *755–0157* ⊟ *No credit cards* ⊘ *Closed Sun.*

★ $$ ✕▦ **Magellan Inn.** Arguably Cahuita's most elegant lodging, this group of bungalows is graced with tile-floor terraces facing a pool and gardens growing on an ancient coral reef. Carpeted rooms have original paintings and custom-made wooden furniture. Feast on intensely flavored French and creole seafood specialties at the Casa Creole ($–$$) on the hotel's patio; don't miss the house pâté or the homemade ice cream. The open-air bar rocks to great blues and jazz recordings in the evenings and mellows with classical music at breakfast. ⊠ *2 km (1 mi) north of*

Cahuita at far end of Playa Negra ⌖ *Apdo. 1132–7300, Limón* 📠 *755–0035* ⊕*magellaninn.toposrealestate.org* ⤳*6 rooms* ⌂ *Restaurant, fans, pool, bar; no a/c in some rooms, no room phones, no room TVs* ⊟ *AE, MC, V* ⦾ *BP.*

$$ 🏨 **Aviarios del Caribe.** It's a lodge, sloth rescue center, and bird-watch-

FodorśChoice ing sanctuary all rolled into one. More than 310 bird species have been

★ spotted here, many with the help of the telescope on the wide second-floor deck. Buttercup, the resident three-toed sloth, oversees the proceedings in the upstairs open-air dining room. The spacious guest rooms have white walls, blue-tile floors, and fresh flowers. For $5 you can hike the adjoining wildlife refuge on a self-guided tour, and $30 will get you an unforgettable 3½-hour riverboat tour guided by the owner, Luis, himself. ⊠ *9 km (5 mi) north of Cahuita, follow hotel signs on Río Estrella delta* ⌖ *Apdo. 569–7300, Limón* 📠 *750–0775 or 200–5105* ⊕*www. ogphoto.com/aviarios* ⤳*7 rooms* ⌂ *Hiking, laundry service; no a/c, no room phones, no room TVs* ⊟ *AE, MC, V* ⦾ *BP.*

$–$$ 🏨 **El Encanto Bed & Breakfast.** Zen Buddhist owners have cultivated a

FodorśChoice serene and beautiful environment here, ideal for physical and spiritual

★ relaxation. Lodgings are in a garden with an extensive bromeliad collection and Buddha figures. Choose between comfortable rooms or bungalows, all decorated with art from all over the globe; some rooms have a double vaulted ceiling with strategically placed screens that keep the place wonderfully ventilated. Amenities include queen-size beds, hot water, and secure parking. Breakfast comes complete with homemade breads and cakes. The beach is across the street, and massage and yoga classes are available weekends. ⊠ *Playa Negra road, 200 m west of police station* 📠 *755–0113* ⊕ *www.2000.co.cr/elencanto* ⌖ *Apdo. 7–7302, Cahuita* ⤳*4 rooms, 3 bungalows* ⌂ *Fans, some kitchenettes; no a/c in some rooms, no room phones, no TV in some rooms* ⊟ *AE, MC, V* ⦾ *BP.*

$ 🏨 **Atlántida Lodge.** Attractively landscaped grounds, the beach across the road, and a large pool are Atlántida's main assets. You're welcomed to your room with a lovely assortment of fresh and dried flowers; the rooms themselves have tile floors and pretty terraces. ⊠ *Next to soccer field at Playa Negra* ☎ *755–0115* 📠 *755–0213* ⊕ *www.atlantida. co.cr* ⤳*30 rooms* ⌂ *Restaurant, fans, pool, gym, hot tub, massage, volleyball, shop, laundry service, meeting room; no a/c, no room phones, no room TVs* ⊟ *AE, MC, V.*

$ 🏨 **Bungalows Malú.** This is one of the rare places with air-conditioning on the coast, but it doesn't need it: the octagonal stone-and-wood bungalows scattered around the grounds get plenty of cool breezes from the beach across the road. Each unit has shuttered screened windows, hardwood floors, and a private porch with a hammock. ⊠ *Playa Negra road, 2 km (1 mi) north of Cahuita* ☎ *755–0006* 📠 *755–0114* ✎ *bungalowmalu@hotmail.com* ⤳*7 bungalows* ⌂ *Restaurant, fans, bar; no room phones, no room TVs* ⊟ *MC, V.*

$ 🏨 **Kelly Creek Hotel-Restaurante.** Owners from Madrid have created a wonderful budget option in this handsome wooden hotel on the creek bank across a short pedestrian bridge from the park entrance. Each of the four hardwood-finished guest rooms is big enough to sleep a small army and has two double beds. Señor de Alcalá barbecues meat and fresh fish on an open-air grill and also cooks paella and other Spanish specialties. Caiman come to the creek bank in search of snacks, and the monkeys, parrots, jungles, and beaches of the national park are just yards away, as is the lively center of Cahuita. ⊠ *Next to park entrance* ☎ *755–0007* ⊕ *www.hotelkellycreek.com* ⊅ *4 rooms* ♦ *Restaurant, fans, beach; no a/c, no room phones, no room TVs* ⊟ *AE, MC, V.*

¢ 🖭 **Alby Lodge.** You're right in town, but you'd never know it at this friendly lodging. Cabins with hardwood floors prop up on stilts and come complete with hot-water baths, log tables, mosquito nets, and a hammock on the front porch. Make use of the shared kitchen facilities and outdoor barbecue. The forested grounds and high thatched roof keep the temperature pleasantly bearable in otherwise balmy Cahuita. It's next to the park, so the howler monkeys are your morning alarm clock. ⊠ *180 m west of national park entrance* ☎☎ *755–0031* ⊘ *alby_lodge@racsa. co.cr* ⊅ *4 cabins* ♦ *Fans; no a/c, no room phones, no room TVs* ⊟ *No credit cards.*

¢ 🖭 **Cabinas Smith.** The nicest of Cahuita's rock-bottom lodgings sits on a quiet street and is owned by a friendly family who lives next door. Rooms are arranged along a long porch that faces a shady garden. They're basic, but this place is only about $5 more and a huge step up in value and quality from the typical Cahuita backpacker's digs. ⊠ *200 m north and 50 m east of Ricky's Bar* ☎ *755–0068* ⊅ *8 rooms* ♦ *Fans, refrigerators; no room phones, no room TVs* ⊟ *No credit cards.*

Sports & the Outdoors

At Cahuita Tours (⊠ 180 m north of Ricky's Bar ☎ 755–0232) the friendly folks can set you up with any of a variety of adventures, including tours of the canals, indigenous reserves (for a glimpse into traditional life), and mountains; river rafting and kayaking; and bike rentals. They can also reconfirm flights and make lodging reservations. **Turística Cahuita** (⊠ Across from Supermercado Safari ☎ 755–0071) arranges personalized tours to nearby rain forests and indigenous reserves and rents snorkeling equipment.

BICYCLING Bicycles are a popular means of utilitarian transport in Cahuita. Seemingly everyone rents basic touring bikes for $4–$8 per day, but quality varies widely. Count on **Caribbean Flavor** (⊠ Next to Coco's Bar ☎ 755–0017) for decent equipment.

Nightlife

Lively reggae, soca, and samba blast weekend evenings from the turquoise **Coco's Bar** on the main road, and the assemblage of dogs dozing on its veranda illustrates the rhythm of local life. On the opposite corner from the bus stop, **Ricky's Bar** (☎ 755–0228) is more subdued, quiet, and touristed than Coco's.

Cahuita National Park

⑫ *Puerto Vargas is 5 km (3 mi) south of Cahuita.*

The only Costa Rican park jointly administered by the National Parks Service and a community, Parque Nacional Cahuita starts at the south-

PACKING FOR ADVENTURE

YOU HAVE TO GET DOWN AND DIRTY—*well, more like wet and muddy—to see many of the country's natural wonders. This packing list is not comprehensive; instead, it's a guideline for some of the things you might not think to bring. See Packing in Smart Travel Tips for more information on what to pack. For your main piece of luggage, a sturdy internal-frame backpack is great, but a duffel bag works, too. You can get by with a rolling suitcase, but then bring a smaller backpack as well.*

Hiking shirts and socks (they dry more easily than cotton)

Hiking boots or shoes that can get muddy and wet (and stay wet!)

Waterproof sport sandals (especially in Osa, where most transportation is by boat, and often there are no docks)

Knee-high socks for rubber boots that are supplied at many lodges

A pair of lightweight pants (fire ants, mosquitoes, and other pests make covering yourself a necessity on deep-forest hikes)

Pants for horseback riding (if that's on your itinerary)

Waterproof, lightweight jacket, windbreaker, or poncho

Day pack for hikes

Sweater for cool nights and early mornings

Swimsuit

Insect repellant (with DEET, for forested areas and especially on the Caribbean coast, where there are pockets of malaria)

Flashlight with spare batteries

Sunscreen with a minimum of SPF 30 (waterproof sunscreens are best; even if

you're not swimming, you might be swimming in perspiration)

Large, portable water bottle

Hat and/or bandanas (not only do they provide shade, but they prevent perspiration from dripping down your face)

Binoculars (with carrying strap)

Camera (waterproof, or with a waterproof case or dry bag, sold in outdoor shops)

Film (film in Costa Rica can be old and is expensive)

Imodium and Pepto-Bismol (tablet form is best)

Swiss Army knife (and remember to pack it in your checked luggage, never your carry-on—even on domestic flights in Costa Rica)

Zip-lock bags (they always come in handy)

Travel alarm clock or watch with an alarm (don't count on wake-up calls)

Nonelectric shaving utensils

Toilet paper (you never know—but if you find out, you'll be glad you have it) ern edge of the town of Cahuita. The park's rain forest extends right to the edge of its curving, 3-km (2-mi) utterly undeveloped white-sand beach. Roughly parallel to the coastline, a 7-km (4-mi) trail passes through the forest to Cahuita Point, encircled by a 2½-square-km (1½-square-mi) coral reef. The hike takes only a few hours, but you have to ford several rivers on the way, so check conditions beforehand, as they can be prohibitive in the rainy season.

There's good snorkeling off Cahuita Point—watch for blue parrot fish and angelfish as they weave their way among equally colorful species of coral, sponges, and seaweeds. Sadly, the coral reef is slowly being killed by sediment, intensified by deforestation and the erosive effects of a 1991 earthquake. Use a local guide to find the best reefs (or to snorkel independently, swim out from the beach on the Puerto Vargas side), and don't snorkel for a few days after it rains, as the water is sure to be murky. You can take a ride in a glass-bottom boat from Cahuita (visibility is best in September and October). The road to the park headquarters at Puerto Vargas is 5 km (3 mi) south of Cahuita on the left. Here you find the ranger station as well as campsites that have been carved out of the jungle, scattered along the beachfront. ⊠ *Cahuita entrance at southern end of Cahuita's main street; Puerto Vargas entrance 5 km (3 mi) south of Cahuita* ☎ *755–0302* 🎫 *Donation requested at Cahuita entrance; $7 at Puerto Vargas entrance* ⊙ *Weekdays 8–4, weekends 7–5.*

Sports & the Outdoors

BICYCLING   You can bike through Cahuita National Park, but the trail gets pretty muddy at times, and you run into logs, river estuaries, and other obstacles. Nevertheless, mountain bikes are a good way to get around on the dirt roads and trails surrounding Cahuita and Puerto Viejo de Talamanca. Cycling is easiest in the dry season, of course, though many hardy souls are out during the long rainy season. There are several area bike-rental outlets. **Caribbean Flavor** (⊠ Center of town ☎ 755–0017) charges $8 a day for a mountain bike.

HIKING   A serious hiking trail extends as far as Puerto Vargas. If you're staying in Cahuita, you can take a bus or catch a ride into Puerto Vargas and hike back around the point in the course of a day. If you camp at Puerto Vargas, you can also hike south along the beach to Puerto Viejo de Talamanca and bus or cab it back to the park. Be sure to bring plenty of water, food, and sunscreen. Along the trail you might spot Howler and White-faced Capuchin monkeys, coatis, armadillos, and raccoons. Swimming is prohibited here because of the extremely strong current.

SNORKELING & SURFING   Cahuita's reefs are just one of several high-quality snorkeling spots around here. You can rent snorkeling gear in Cahuita or Puerto Viejo de Talamanca or through your hotel; most hotels will also organize trips. It's wise to work with a guide, as the number of good snorkeling spots is limited and they're not always easily accessible. Cahuita established a community lifeguard team in 2002, a real rarity in Costa Rica. As elsewhere up and down the Caribbean coast, the undertow poses risks for even experienced swimmers. Use extreme caution and never swim alone.

Although it's not in town, **ATEC** (☎ 750–0398), an ecotourism organization in nearby Puerto Viejo de Talamanca, has tourism information and can help with travel arrangements, equipment rentals, and much more. The staff at the friendly storefront **Cahuita Tours,** 180 m north of Ricky's Bar, can assist with tourist information, travel arrangements, snorkeling- and surfing-equipment rental, horseback riding, and other tours.

Puerto Viejo de Talamanca

⑬ *16 km (10 mi) south of Cahuita.*

Puerto Viejo de Talamanca was once quieter than Cahuita, but no more—it's one of the hottest spots on the international surf punk circuit. This muddy, colorful little town swarms with surfers, new-age hippies, beaded and spangled punks, would-be Rastafarians of all colors and descriptions, and wheelers and dealers both pleasant and otherwise. Time was when most kids came here with only one thing on their mind: surfing. Today, many seem to be looking only for a party, with or without surf.

But if alternative lifestyles aren't your bag, there are plenty of more "grown-up" offerings on the road heading southeast and northwest out of town. Some locals bemoan the loss of their town's innocence, as the ravages of drugs and other evils have surfaced, but only in small doses: this is still a fun town to visit, with a great variety of hotels, cabinas, and restaurants in every price range.

You have access to the beach right in town, and the Salsa Brava, famed in surfers' circles for its pounding waves, is here off the coast as well. The surfing waves are at their best between December and April and again in June and July. The best strands of Caribbean sand are outside the village. Playa Negra, a black-sand beach, extends northwest from Puerto Viejo for about a kilometer (½ mi). Heading southeast from town, Playa Cocles begins about 2 km (1¼ mi) from Puerto Viejo. A series of small beaches, collectively referred to as Playa Chiquita, runs from 4 to 7 km (2½ to 4½ mi) out of town. Farther-flung Punta Uva extends for the next 2 km (1 mi) beyond Playa Chiquita. In these beach areas, you see some of the region's first luxury tourist developments, though still quite small scale, and some interesting eco-lodges. This is the place for those preferring creature comforts who also wish to see this less frequented part of the country.

In the middle of town, **ATEC** (the Association for Ecotourism and Conservation) plays an important role in the south coast's cultural and ecotourism movement. The agency's small office also serves as a fax, phone, and e-mail center and a general travel-information center for the town and the region. You can arrange walks focusing on Afro-Caribbean or indigenous culture—tours to the nearby Kekoldi indigenous reserve are especially popular—plus rain-forest hikes, coral-reef snorkeling or fishing trips, bird-watching, night walks, and adventure treks. ATEC is also an excellent source for information on volunteer vacations. Of the money collected for tours booked through the agency, 15%–20% goes

to local organizations and wildlife refuges. ✉ *Across from Restaurant Tamara* ☎ *750–0398* 🖶 *750–0191* ⊕ *www.greencoast.com/atec.htm* ⊗ *Mon., Tues., Thurs., and Fri. 8 AM–9 PM; Wed. 8–noon and 2–9; Sat. 8–noon and 1–9; Sun. 8–noon and 4–8.*

Pulpería Manuel León (✉ *Southeast of bus stop* ☎ *750–0422*), a local general store often called El Chino, changes cash or traveler's checks daily 9–8 if there is enough cash on hand. U.S. greenbacks fetch the best rates, but Manuel accepts Canadian dollars, pounds, and euros, too. During the December–May high season, most hotels will also change money. At the **Finca La Isla Botanical Garden** you can wander around a working tropical fruit, spice, and ornamental plant farm. Sloths abound, and you could see a few poison dart frogs. An $8 guided tour includes admission and a glass of the farm's homemade fruit juice. ✉ *½ km (¼ mi) west of Puerto Viejo at Playa Negra* ☎ *750–0046* 💵 *$3* ⊗ *Fri.–Mon. 10–4.*

Cacao once ruled the Talamanca region, but few plantations are left these days. One friendly Swiss couple continues the tradition and gives you a **Chocolate Tour** of their working plantation. Follow the life cycle of this little-known crop, from cultivation to processing. And, of course, there's sampling at the tour's conclusion. There are no fixed tour times; call to reserve (you need a minimum of four people) and to be picked up from the Playa Chiquita School. Since these folks are Swiss, they can tailor the commentary in German, French, or Italian, in addition to English or Spanish. ☒ *Playa Chiquita, 6 km (4 mi) west of Puerto Viejo at Playa Negra* ☎ *750–0075* ☒ *Tour $15/person.*

♻ Unlike most such establishments in Costa Rica, which are for show only, this working **Butterfly Garden** cultivates 60–80 species of butterfly, three of which are unique to the area, for shipment to similar facilities around the world. The knowledgeable staff provides guided tours with bilingual commentary. ☒ *Punta Uva, 7 km (4½ mi) southeast of Puerto Viejo* ☎ *750–0086* ☒ *$5* ☉ *Daily 8–4.*

Where to Stay & Eat

★ **$–$$** ✕ **Amimodo.** The name translates "my way," and the exuberant, multigenerational Italian owners really do it their way, combining the cuisine of northern Italy, from where they came, with Caribbean flavors. Your antipasto might be classic bruschetta or *jamón de tiburón* (shark ham with avocado dressing). Or your ravioli might be stuffed with tropical shrimp, pineapple, and curry, with avocado sauce on the side. The tropical veranda with gingerbread trim spills over onto the beach with abundant greenery, and the restaurant is a popular gathering place for Puerto Viejo's Italian community. ☒ *200 m east of Stanford's* ☎ *750–0257* ☒ *AE, DC, MC, V* ☉ *Closed Wed. No lunch weekdays.*

$–$$ ✕ **Lotus Garden.** Sushi is hard to come by in Costa Rica, period, let alone way out here. This open-air restaurant puts a Caribbean spin on Japanese cuisine, using local ingredients such as sushi-quality marlin whenever possible and, according to the owner, forever experimenting with new dishes. Try the Puerto Viejo roll, much like a California roll only made with snapper and mango. The all-you-can-eat sushi bar at $14 per person draws the crowds. Tropical fruits, miso soup, fried rice, and a good selection of wines and sake round out any meal. ☒ *200 m east of Stanford's* ☎ *750–0232* ☒ *AE, DC, MC, V.*

$–$$ ✕ **La Pecora Nera.** Though the name means "black sheep" in Italian, there's
Fodor'sChoice nothing shameful about this thatch-roof roadside restaurant. There's al-
★ ways a lot more to choose from than what appears on the sparse-looking menu; the owners come out of the kitchen and triumphantly announce which additional light Tuscan entrées, appetizers, and desserts they've decided to concoct that day. Be prepared for a long, leisurely dining experience with attentive, fussed-over service. ☒ *3 km (2 mi) south of Puerto Viejo on road to Manzanillo* ☎ *750–0490* ☒ *No credit cards* ☉ *Closed Mon. Apr.–Nov.*

$–$$ ✕ **Salsa Brava.** The restaurant at Salsa Brava—with sublime surf vistas—has taken the name of this famed surfing locale. Opt for casual counter service or grab a seat at one of the colorful roadside tables. Lunch and dinner center on grilled fish and meat. ☒ *100 m east of Stanford's Disco* ☎ *750–0241* ☒ *No credit cards* ☉ *Closed Mon.*

¢–$ ✕ **Café Coral.** It's a quaint but true tale that Café Coral shocked Puerto Viejo with the introduction of pizza in 1989—those were pre-telephone days here, after all. These folks still do a bang-up job out of their openair, thatch-roof restaurant. The Smoky, with sausage, mushroom, pineapple, chile dulce (red peppers), and more, is the most requested dish. Mornings, Coral transforms itself into the town's quintessential American-style breakfast joint. Feast on pancakes before heading out for the day. ⊠ *45 m south of Adventist church* ☎ *750–0051* ⊟ *No credit cards* ⊘ *Closed Mon. No lunch.*

¢–$ ✕ **Restaurant Tamara.** In the nondescript indoor seating area you're cooled by a fan and entertained by TV; the outdoor seating area—with a large image of Bob Marley on red, yellow, and green walls—has a palpable Jamaican motif. The Caribbean food at this two-story unpretentious place is tasty and authentic: you can't lose with the chicken in Caribbean sauce or virtually any of the fresh fish dishes. And it's near the beach. ⊠ *Across from ATEC* ☎ *750–0148* ⊟ *AE, MC, V.*

¢–$ ✕ **Selvin's.** An old standby at Punta Uva, Selvin's keeps limited hours, especially in the off-season, so head out here if you're fortunate enough to be in town when the place is open. Everyone knows the owner as "Blanca," and she cooks up a menu of rondón, rice and beans, lobster, shrimp, and chicken with sweet mole sauce. This is one of the few places around that accepts traveler's checks as payment. ⊠ *Punta Uva, 7 km (4½ mi) southeast of town* ☎ *750–0664* ⊟ *No credit cards* ⊘ *Closed Mon. and Tues. Dec.–May and Mon.–Thurs. June–Nov.*

¢ ✕ **Soda Miss Sam.** Older women in Caribbean communities here are often addressed as "Miss" regardless of marital status. Miss Sam has been dishing up hearty Caribbean cuisine for years, though she prefers not to divulge how many. She usually has rice and beans going, or can fix a casado with chicken, beef, pork, or fish and freshly squeezed fruit juices as accompaniment. ⊠ *300 m south, 200 m east of bus stop* ☎ *750–0108* ⊟ *No credit cards* ⊘ *Closed Sun.*

$$$ ▦ **Las Palmas Beach Hotel.** The closest thing the area has to a beach resort, the orange Las Palmas is a bit un–Puerto Viejo in that regard. But if relaxing poolside knowing that the beach lies a few steps away appeals to you, then this is the place. Rooms, all with ocean views, have tile floors and bright floral-print spreads and drapes and congregate around the pool. Sliding glass doors that allow you to see out but not in afford a measure of privacy and lead onto individual terraces or balconies. ⊠ *Punta Uva, 9 km (5½ mi) southeast of town* ☎ *759–9090* 🖷 *759–9222* ⊕ *www.laspalmashotel.com* ⊅ *30 rooms, 5 suites* ⟁ *Restaurant, coffee shop, fans, refrigerators, pool, hot tub, beach, horseback riding, bar, shop* ⊟ *AE, DC, MC, V.*

★ $$ ▦ **Shawandha Lodge.** The service is personalized and friendly at Shawandha, whose spacious, beautifully designed bungalows are well back from the road at Playa Chiquita. The thatch-roof bungalows have elegant hardwoods, four-poster beds, and verandas with hammocks. Each bathroom has a unique and gorgeous tile mosaic. Well-known local chef Johana Ramírez crafts her distinctive French-Caribbean cuisine in the open-air restaurant. The hearty breakfast starts off with an impressive fruit plate. A white-sand beach lies 180 m away, across the road. ⊠ *Playa Chiquita, 6 km (4 mi) southeast of town* ☎ *750–0018* 🖷 *750–0037* ⊕ *www.shawandhalodge.com* ⊅ *12 bungalows* ⟁ *Restaurant, fans, in-room safes, bar, laundry service; no a/c, no room phones, no room TVs, no smoking* ⊟ *AE, MC, V* ⊙ *BP.*

$$ **Villas del Caribe.** Right on the beach north of Punta Uva, these multiroom villas are commodious and comfortable, if somewhat pedestrian in design. Each has a blue-tile kitchen, a small sitting room with low-slung couches, a plant-filled bathroom, and a patio with hammock and excellent views of the beach. Upstairs are one or two spacious bedrooms with a wooden deck. ⊠ *4 km (2½ mi) southeast of town* ☎ *750-0202, 233-2200 in San José* 🖷 *750-0203, 221-2801 in San José* ⊕ *www. villascaribe.net* ⟿ *12 villas* △ *Restaurant, fans, kitchenettes, beach; no a/c, no room phones, no room TVs* 🖃 *AE, DC, MC, V* ⟨⊙⟩ *BP.*

$–$$ **Cariblue Bungalows.** Cariblue's finely crafted all-wooden bungalows
are spaciously arrayed on the edge of the jungle, across the road from the splendid white-sand beaches of Punta Cocles. Cabinas are linked to the main ranch-style building by paths that meander through a gently sloping lawn shaded with enormous trees. Expansive verandas and beautiful bathroom-tile mosaics add an air of refinement; hammocks add an air of relaxation. The youthful Italian owners serve a huge breakfast. ⊠ *2 km (1 mi) southeast of town on road to Manzanillo, across road from Playa Cocles* ☎ *750-0035* 🖷 *750-0057* ⊕ *www.cariblue. com* ⟿ *15 bungalows* △ *Restaurant, fans, pool, hot tub, billiards, 2 bars, shop, laundry service; no room phones, no room TVs* 🖃 *AE, MC, V* ⟨⊙⟩ *BP.*

$–$$ **El Pizote Lodge.** El Pizote observes local architectural mores while offering more than most in the way of amenities. All standard rooms have polished wood paneling, reading lamps, mirrors, and firm beds. Each of the two-room bungalows sleeps six. The restaurant serves breakfast, dinner, and drinks all day. Guanábana and papaya grow on the grounds, and hiking trails lead off into the jungle. ⊠ *Right side of road from Cahuita, 180 before entrance to town* ☎ *750-0088* 🖷 *750-0226* ⊕ *www.pizotelodge.com* ⟿ *8 rooms, 4 with bath; 6 bungalows* △ *Restaurant, fans, pool, volleyball, bar, laundry service; no a/c in some rooms, no room phones, no room TVs* 🖃 *V.*

$ **Agapi.** Agapi means "love" in Greek, and Costa Rican–Greek owners Cecilia and Tasso lovingly watch over their guests with some of the most attentive service around. Six furnished apartments overlook the beach and come complete with fully equipped kitchen, hot-water bath, hammock, mosquito nets over the beds, and private balcony. A common area in the back contains a beachside barbecue. ⊠ *1 km (½ mi) southeast of town* ☎ *750-0446* 🖷 *750-0418* ⊕ *www.agapisite.com* ⟿ *6 apartments* △ *Fans, kitchens; no a/c, no room phones, no TV in some rooms* 🖃 *AE, MC, V.*

$ **Casa Camarona.** Though half the rooms have air-conditioning at this secluded lodging, you hardly need it. The abundant shade and sea breezes of the Gandoca-Manzanillo Wildlife Refuge, where the Casa is set, keep the rooms delightfully cool. All the spacious, wooden, rustic rooms front the ocean and have two double beds. Meals are served at the seaside Caribbean restaurant. ⊠ *Playa Cocles, 3 km (2 mi) south of town* ☎ *750-0151 or 283-6711* 🖷 *750-0210 or 222-6184* ⊕ *www. casacamarona.co.cr* ⟿ *17 rooms* △ *Restaurant, fans, bicycles, bar, laundry facilities; no a/c in some rooms, no room phones, no room TVs* 🖃 *AE, MC, V.*

$ ▦ **La Costa de Papito.** Papito's raised cabins are deep in the property's wooded grounds and furnished with whimsical bright tropical-blue and zebra-stripe prints. Breakfast is served at the table and chairs on your porch, which also comes complete with a hammock or swing chair. And here's a real rarity in Costa Rica: the lodging counts one wheelchair-accessible unit, not on stilts and with a detached bath and shower. ⊠ *2 km (1 mi) southeast of town* ☎ *750–0080* ⊕ *www.greencoast.com/ papito.htm* ⇝ *10 cabins* ⚐ *Fans; no room phones, no room TVs* ⊟ *AE, MC, V.*

$ ▦ **Escape Caribeño.** Wonderfully friendly Italian owners Gloria and Mauro Marchiori treat you like family at their lodging just outside of town. A dozen immaculate hardwood bungalows line a pleasant garden area amply populated with hummingbirds. All units come complete with hammocks, mosquito nets, double beds, and even a bunk bed or two for larger groups. Across the road lie two stucco cabins in a wooded area on the beach, both with kitchenette. Breakfast is served in a thatch-roof-covered dining area in the center of the garden. ⊠ *400 m southeast of town* ☎ *750–0103* ⊕ *www.escapecaribeno.com* ⇝ *14 cabins* ⚐ *Fans, some kitchenettes, minibars; no a/c in some rooms, no room phones, no room TVs* ⊟ *AE, DC, MC, V.*

$ ▦ **Hotel La Perla Negra.** The original owners' previous experience as designers is evident in the fine construction of this handsome, two-story wooden structure across a tiny dirt road from Playa Negra. All rooms have balconies, half with ocean views, half with jungle views. The three-meal restaurant features grilled meats and fish. Between the building and the beach is a spacious, inviting pool. ⊠ *Playa Negra, 1 km (½ mi) north of Puerto Viejo* ☎ *750–0111, 800/221–4713 in U.S.* 🖷 *750–0114* ⊕*www.perlanegra-beachresort.com* ⇝*24 rooms, 1 apartment* ⚐ *Restaurant, fans, tennis court, pool, billiards, bar, laundry service; no a/c, no room phones, no room TVs* ⊟ *AE, MC, V* ❢ *CP.*

$ ▦ **Yaré Hotel.** The sound of the jungle is overpowering, especially at night, as you relax in your brightly painted Yaré cabina. All rooms have hot water and verandas with hammocks. The restaurant is open for breakfast, lunch, and dinner. ⊠ *Playa Cocles, 3½ km (2 mi) southeast of town* ☎ *750–0420* ☎ *750–0106* ⊕ *www.hotelyare.com* ⇝ *22 rooms* ⚐ *Restaurant, fans, some kitchenettes, refrigerators, laundry service; no room phones, no room TVs* ⊟ *AE, DC, MC, V* ❢ *BP.*

¢–$ ▦ **Bungalows Calalú.** A French couple operates this budget option on a quiet lane off the main road just outside of town. Five wooden bungalows are scattered around the wooded grounds. Each comes with a porch equipped with a hammock, perfect for relaxing at the end of the day. Breakfast is served overlooking a small butterfly garden. ⊠ *180 m southeast and 75 m west of Stanford's* ☎ *750–0042* ⊕*www.puertoviejo. net/calalu* ⇝ *5 cabins* ⚐ *Fans, some kitchens, pool, Ping-Pong; no a/c, no room phones, no room TVs* ⊟ *AE, MC, V.*

¢–$ ▦ **Cabinas Casa Verde.** Set back a few blocks from the waterfront hustle, the comfortable cabinas at this Swiss–Costa Rican–run hotel in town are decorated with an interesting variety of items such as shell mobiles, watercolor frescoes, and indigenous tapestries. And yet, overall, rooms have a neat-as-a-pin quality. Exotic birds flutter constantly through the lush plantings that screen the cabinas from the street. The place is immensely popular, since the price is low and it's clean and well run; reserve ahead. ⊠ *200 m south and 200 m east of bus stop* ☎ *750–0015* 🖷 *750–0047* ⊕ *www.cabinascasaverde.com* ✆ *Apdo. 37–7304, Puerto Viejo de Talamanca* ↘ *17 rooms, 9 with bath* ⚐ *Cafeteria, fans, some refrigerators, massage, shop, laundry service; no room phones, no room TVs* ▤ *AE, MC, V.*

¢–$ 🔟 **Pachamama.** Within sight of the Puerto Viejo–Manzanillo road, but seemingly deep within the confines of the Gandoca-Manzanillo Wildlife Refuge, Pachamama offers a get-away-from-it-all nature experience at a fraction of the cost of the other Costa Rica eco-lodges. Cozy wood cabins are simply furnished with two beds and mosquito netting and colorful spreads and drapes. A house can be rented by the week or month. Personal touches such as breakfast brought to the porch of your cabin are customary. ⊠ *Punta Uva, 9 km (5½ mi) southeast of town* ☎ *759–9204* ↘ *2 bungalows, 1 house* ⚐ *Fans; no a/c, no room phones, no room TVs* ▤ *No credit cards* ⦿ *BP.*

¢ 🔟 **Coco Loco Lodge.** The cool, forested grounds here lie close to the center of town but seem so far away. The Austrian owners lavish you with lots of personal attention. The bungalows on stilts are simply furnished but contain hot-water baths, mosquito nets over the beds, and hammocks on the porch. There's also one fully furnished house available for short- or long-term rental. Great coffee is included in the room rate; a huge buffet breakfast is extra. ⊠ *180 m south of bridge at entrance to town* ☎🖷 *750–0281* ⊕ *www.cocolocolodge.de* ↘ *5 cabins, 1 house* ⚐ *Fans; no a/c, no room phones, no room TVs* ▤ *MC, V.*

¢ 🔟 **Hotel Pura Vida.** The friendly owners help make this the nicest of the lowest-end budget lodgings in the center of town. Rooms are basic, but clean, bright, and well ventilated and arranged around a center patio. Guests have use of the shared kitchen. ⊠ *270 m south of bus stop* ☎ *750–0002* 🖷 *750–0296* ↘ *10 rooms, 3 with bath* ⚐ *Fans; no a/c, no room phones, no room TVs* ▤ *AE, MC, V.*

Sports & the Outdoors

ATEC (the Association for Ecotourism and Conservation; ⊠ Across from Restaurant Tamara, center of town ☎ 750–0398 🖷 750–0191 ⊕ www. greencoast.com/atec.htm) is a tourist agency that sets up rain-forest hikes, snorkeling or fishing trips to coral reefs, bird-watching excursions, treks, and walking tours. Local organizations and wildlife refuges receive 15%–20% of ATEC's proceeds.

BICYCLING   Everyone gets around via bike here, and everyone has one for rent. Quality varies widely, but **Cabinas Grant** (⊠ 100 m south of the bus stop ☎ 750–0292) rents good-quality bikes for a mere $3 a day.

SURFING   Surfing is the name of the game in Puerto Viejo. There are a number of breaks here, most famously Salsa Brava, which breaks rather far offshore and requires maneuvering past some tricky currents and a shallow reef. Hollow and primarily right breaking, Salsa Brava is one gnarly wave when it gets big. If it gets *too* big, or not big enough, check out the breaks at Punta Uva, Punta Cocles, or Playa Chiquita. Boogieboarders and bodysurfers will also dig the beach-break waves at various points along this tantalizingly beautiful coast. But a surfer's paradise makes for dangerous swimming here. Undertows can carry you far from shore before you realize what's happening; exercise extreme caution.

Nightlife

Ticos come from miles around for the Friday and Monday reggae nights at **Disco Bambú** (⊠ Next to Jhonny's). Play backgammon or billiards, and chow down on pizza or sandwiches at **El Dorado** (⊠ Across from ATEC ☎ 750–0604). **Jhonny's Place** (⊠ 230 m east of bus stop ☎ 750–0623) has nights variously devoted to reggae, jazz, R&B, and hip-hop. The dancing usually gets started after 11 PM. Second-floor organic food restaurant **El Loco Natural** (⊠ Across from ATEC) morphs into a hot reggae-calypso-soul venue most evenings. **Maritza Bar** (⊠ 50 m east of bus stop) is a local favorite, and has karaoke on Saturday night. **Neptune Sports Bar** (⊠ 100 m east of Restaurant Tamara) sees crowds cheering on their favorite televised sporting events, but also hosts live music and has Wednesday-night jam sessions. **Stanford's Disco** (⊠ 100 m from the town center on the road to Manzanillo) is the place to merengue or salsa the weekend nights away.

Shopping

El Calor del Caribe (⊠ Across from ATEC ☎ 750–0434) is a standard souvenir shop with wood carvings, masks, coffee, and banana paper products. Buy your official Puerto Viejo T-shirt at **El Color del Caribe** (⊠ 100 m south of bus stop ☎ 750–0615), which also has a huge selection of Rastafarian clothing, and hammocks, wood carvings, and delightful whimsical mobiles. **Luluberlu** (⊠ 200 m south and 50 m east of bus stop ☎ 750–0394) sells a wonderful selection of local indigenous carvings—balsa and *chonta* wood are especially popular—and jewelry. The sprawling **Tienda del Mar** (⊠ Next to Restaurant Tamara ☎ 750–0355 or 750–0876) specializes in bright, colorful batik clothing of all sizes, as well as more run-of-the-mill T-shirts, sandals, and postcards.

Gandoca-Manzanillo National Wildlife Refuge

⑭ *15 km (9 mi) south of Puerto Viejo de Talamanca.*

The Refugio Nacional de Vida Silvestre Gandoca-Manzanillo stretches along the southeastern coast from the town of Manzanillo to the Panamanian border. Because of weak laws governing the conservation of refuges and the value of coastal land in this area, Gandoca-Manzanillo is less pristine than Cahuita National Park and continues to be developed. However, the refuge still bears plenty of rain forest, *orey* and Jolillo swamps, 10 km (6 mi) of beach where four species of turtles lay their eggs, and almost 3 square km (1 square mi) of *cativo* forest and coral reef. The Gandoca estuary is a nursery for tarpon and a wallowing spot for crocodiles and caimans.

The easiest way to explore the refuge is to hike along the coast south of Manzanillo. You can hike back out the way you came in, or arrange (in Puerto Viejo de Talamanca) to have a boat pick you up at Monkey

REEFS AT RISK

ONE OF THE MOST COMPLEX ORGANISMS IN THE MARINE WORLD, a coral reef is an extraordinary and extraordinarily delicate habitat. Coral reefs are the result of the symbiotic relationship between single-cell organisms called zooxanthellae that grows inside the cells of coral polyps and produce oxygen and nutrients that are released into the coral tissues. Corals secrete calcium carbonate (limestone) that, over time, forms the vast coral reef "superstructure." Zooxanthellae require exposure to sunlight to thrive. The healthiest coral reefs are in clear, clean, tropical seawater at a temperature of 70 to 80°F (20 to 25°C). Healthy coral reefs are biologically rich gardens occupied by a diverse selection of life forms, from microscopic unicellular algae and phytoplankton to a wide range of fish.

Unfortunately, coral reefs in Costa Rica are in danger. Dirt and sediment from banana plantations and logging areas, as well as runoff from pesticide use, are killing them. The dirty runoff literally clogs the pores of the zooxanthellae and smothers them. In Golfo Dulce, 98% of one of the oldest reefs in Costa Rica has been destroyed by this sedimentation. The once-enormous reefs of Cahuita are almost entirely gone.

Human visitors, including careless snorkelers, have also damaged reefs. Just touching a reef damages it. When exploring a coral reef, look but don't touch and snorkel only on its outer side, preferably in calm weather. Can the reefs be saved? With commitment and time, yes. Coral is resilient, and will grow back—if the Costa Rican government makes it a priority.

Point (a three- to four-hour walk from Manzanillo) or Gandoca (six to eight hours). The park administrators, Benson and Florentino Grenald, can tell you more and recommend a local guide; inquire when you enter Manzanillo village and the locals will point you toward them. You can also arrange boat trips to dive spots and beaches in the refuge in Puerto Viejo de Talamanca and Manzanillo. ⊠ *10 km (6 mi) southeast of Puerto Viejo* ☎ *750–0398 ATEC* ☉ *Daily 7–4.*

The nearby village of **Manzanillo** maintains that "end of the world" feel. Tourism is still in its infancy this far down the coast, though with the road paved all the way here, the town is now a popular destination among people in Limón for weekend day trips. The rest of the week, you'll likely have the place to yourself.

| off the beaten path | **HITOY CERERE NATIONAL PARK –** The remote, 90-square-km (56-square-mi) Reserve Biológica Hitoy Cerere occupies the head of Valle de la Estrella (Star Valley). The park's limited infrastructure was badly damaged by the 1991 quake, since the epicenter was precisely here. Paths that do exist are very much overgrown because of limited use—travelers scarcely come here. Jaguars, tapirs, peccaries, porcupines, |

anteaters, and armadillos all carry on, however, along with more than 115 species of birds. Watch for the Common Basilisk Lizard, also called the Jesus Christ Lizard because it walks on water. The moss-flanked rivers have clear bathing pools and spectacular waterfalls. Check with the park service in San José if you want to stay overnight. ⊠ *Catch a bus in Limón for Valle de la Estrella and get off at Finca Seis; then rent a four-wheel-drive vehicle; you can drive to within 1 km (½ mi) of the reserve* ☎ *283–8004* ☜ *Free* ☉ *24 hours.*

Where to Stay & Eat

¢–$$ ✕ **Restaurant Maxi's.** Cooled by sea breezes and shaded by tall, stately palms, this two-story, brightly painted wooden building offers weary travelers cold beer, potent cocktails, and great seafood at unbeatable prices after a day's hike in the refuge. Locals and expatriates alike—and even chefs from Puerto Viejo's fancier restaurants—come here for their lobster fix, and the fresh fish is wonderful, too. Locals tend to congregate in the rowdy but pleasant downstairs bar, where reggae beats into the wee hours. ⊠ *Main road, Manzanillo* ☎ *759–9073* ☐ *No credit cards.*

$$ ▦ **Almonds & Corals Tent Lodge Camp.** Buried in a dark, densely atmospheric beachfront jungle within the Gandoca-Manzanillo Wildlife Refuge, Almonds & Corals takes tent camping to a new level. The "campsites" are freestanding platforms raised on stilts and linked by boardwalks lighted by kerosene lamps. Each safari-style tent is protected by a peaked roof, enclosed in mosquito netting, and has beds, electric lamps, hammocks, and hot water. A fine three-meal restaurant is tucked into the greenery halfway down to the property's exquisite, secluded beach. Your wake-up call is provided by howler monkeys and gossiping parrots. ⊠ *Near end of road to Manzanillo* ☎ *759–9056 or 272–2024* ☐ *272–2220* ⊕ *www.almondsandcorals.com* ✉ *Apdo. 681–2300, San José* ⇌ *25 tent-cabins* ⚐ *Restaurant, fans, hot tub, beach, snorkeling, bar, shop, laundry service, airport shuttle, travel services; no a/c, no room phones, no room TVs* ☐ *AE, MC, V* ⦿ *MAP.*

¢   ▦ **Cabinas Pangea.** The tiny Italian-owned Pangea sits back in a wooded garden on a side street in Manzanillo. The two wood cabins are simply furnished with hardwood floors, two beds covered with mosquito netting, and a porch with an inviting, relaxing hammock. An ample breakfast consists of crepes, fruit, and coffee. ⊠ *100 m south of Aquamor Manzanillo* ☎ *759–9004* ⇌ *2 cabins* ⚐ *Fans; no a/c, no room phones, no room TVs* ☐ *No credit cards* ⦿ *BP.*

¢   ▦ **Cabinas Something Different.** On a quiet street, these shiny, spic-and-span motel-style cabinas are the nicest option in the village of Manzanillo. Each bright tile-floor unit comes with a TV—quite a rarity in these parts—a table, and a small porch and sleeps up to four people. ⊠ *180 m south of Aquamor, Manzanillo* ☎☐ *759–9014* ⇌ *9 cabins* ⚐ *Fans, refrigerators; no a/c in some rooms, no room phones* ☐ *No credit cards.*

Sports & the Outdoors

Aquamor Adventures (⊠ Main road, Manzanillo ☎ 759–9012 ⊕ www.greencoast.com/aquamor.htm) tends to all your water-sporting needs in these parts, with guided kayaking, snorkeling, and scuba-diving tours, as well as equipment rental. It also offers the complete sequence of PADI-certified diving courses. Aquamor is affiliated with the **Talamanca Dolphin Foundation**; its 2½-hour dolphin observation tours are excellent opportunities to see bottlenose, *tucuxi*, and Atlantic spotted dolphins swimming this section of the coast.

Sixaola to Panama

44 km (26 mi) south of the turnoff to Puerto Viejo de Talamanca.

Costa Rica's sleepy border post at Sixaola fronts Guabito, Panama's equally quiet border crossing. Both are merely collections of banana plantation stilt houses and a few stores and bars; neither offers any lodging or dining options. Costa Rican rental vehicles may not leave the country, so crossing into Panama as a tourist is an option only via public transportation. The bus route from San José to Cahuita and Puerto Viejo de Talamanca terminates here at the border approximately six hours after leaving the capital. Disembark and head for the Costa Rican immigration office down a flight of stairs from the west end of a former railroad bridge. Officials place an exit stamp in your passport, after which you walk across the bridge to Panamanian immigration and purchase a $5 tourist card for entry into the country. Crossing into Panama is much easier on weekdays; the bank that sells the tourist cards is frequently not open on weekends. You'll be allowed entry, but will have problems explaining why you have no tourist card when it's time to leave Panama. To avoid entirely the need for a tourist card, obtain a visa free of charge in advance from the **Embassy of Panama in San José** (☎ 257–3251), necessary only if you plan to enter the country on the weekend. The border crossings are open 7 am–5 pm (8 am–6 pm Panamanian time) daily. Set your watch one hour ahead when you enter Panama.

Taxis wait on the Panamanian side to transport you to the small city of Changuinola, the first community of any size, from which there are bus and air connections for travel farther into Panama. Taxis can also take you to Almirante, where you'll find boat launches to Bocas del Toro, the real attraction here in the northwestern part of the country. This archipelago of 68 islands continues the Afro-Caribbean and indigenous themes seen on Costa Rica's Atlantic coast, and offers diving, snorkeling, swimming, and wildlife-viewing. The larger islands are home to a growing selection of hotels and restaurants, everything from funky to fantastic. Bocas has acquired a cult following among long-term foreign visitors to Costa Rica who find it a convenient place to travel when their permitted three-month status as a tourist has expired. A quick 72-hour jaunt out of the country gets you another three months in Costa Rica.

Whatever your destination in Panama, come armed with dollars. Panama uses U.S. currency, but refers to the dollar as the *balboa*. (It does mint its own coins, all the same size as their U.S. counterparts.) No one anywhere will accept or exchange your Costa Rican colónes.

THE CARIBBEAN A TO Z

To research prices, get advice from other travelers, and book travel arrangements, visit www.fodors.com.

AIR TRAVEL

You can fly from San José to the airstrip in either Tortuguero (TTQ) or Barra del Colorado (BCL). At this writing, domestic service is scheduled to begin to the small airport in Limón (LIO) in 2005.

CARRIERS NatureAir flies from San José's Tobias Bolaños Airport to Barra del Colorado daily at 6:15 AM. Flying time is about 30 minutes. Service continues to Tortuguero, arriving at 7:05, and then returns to San José. The airline plans to start service to Limón in 2005, with continuing service to Bocas del Toro, Panama. SANSA flies to Barra del Colorado daily at 6 AM with a second stop at Tortuguero. The SANSA agent in Tortuguero serves as the local contact for NatureAir as well, and can provide information about both airlines.

🛪 Airlines & Contacts **NatureAir** ☎ 220-3054 in San José, 709-8011 or 838-6330 in Tortuguero ⊕ www.natureair.com. **SANSA** ☎ 221-9414 in San José, 709-8011 or 838-6330 in Tortuguero 🖷 255-2176 ⊕ www.flysansa.com.

BOAT & FERRY TRAVEL

From Puerto Viejo de Sarapiquí, boats ply the old route up the Río Sarapiquí to the Río San Juan on the Nicaraguan border. From here you can travel downstream to Barra del Colorado or Tortuguero, but departure times vary—contact Gavilán Sarapiquí River Lodge or negotiate your own deal dockside. Passports are a must: the San Juan forms the boundary between the two countries, but Nicaragua has sovereignty over the river. Many private operators can take you from the docks at Moín, just outside of Limón, up the canals to Tortuguero, but there is no scheduled public transportation. Show up at the docks early and expect to pay around $100 round-trip for up to four people. Modesto Watson, an eagle-eyed Miskito Indian guide, will take you upstream if he has room on his boat. Contact Modesto or his wife, Fran. You can also hire boats to travel between Tortuguero and Barra del Colorado, but prices are quite high.

🛥 Boat & Ferry Information **Fran and Modesto Watson** ☎🖷 226-0986 ⊕ www.tortuguerocanals.com. **Gavilán Sarapiquí River Lodge** ✉ 1 km (½ mi) southeast of Comando Atlántico [naval command] ☎ 766-6743 🖷 253-6556 ⊕ www.gavilanlodge.com.

BUS TRAVEL

All public buses from San José to the Caribbean depart from the Gran Terminal del Caribe (⇨ San José A to Z *in* Chapter 1).

THE NORTHERN LOWLANDS Empresarios Guapileños buses from San José to Guápiles can drop you off in Braulio Carrillo National Park or at the Rain Forest Aerial Tram, a one-hour trip; they leave from San José every half hour between 5 AM and 9 PM daily.

THE NORTHERN CARIBBEAN COAST Empresarios Guapileños buses go to Río Frío and Puerto Viejo de Sarapiquí (a two-hour trip, with stops at Las Horquetas and La Selva en route) via Braulio Carrillo; they depart the capital daily at 6:30, 7:30, 10, and

11:30 AM and at 1:30, 2:30, 3:30, 4:30, and 6 PM. Buses also travel from San José to Puerto Viejo de Sarapiquí via Vara Blanca—a four-hour trip that does *not* pass through Braulio Carrillo—daily at 6:30 AM, 1, and 5:30 PM. Though beautifully scenic, the Vara Blanca route is not one to take if you're prone to motion sickness.

Linaco has daily service to Siquirres with a stop at the entrance to EARTH. Buses depart San José hourly from 9 AM to 5 PM.

COASTAL TALAMANCA   Autotransportes Caribeños offers daily direct service from San José to Limón, a 2½-hour trip, departing hourly from 5 AM to 6:30 PM. The routes alternate between the *directo* (express) service, frequently in double-decker buses, and *corriente,* which stop everywhere. Opt for the former.

Autotransportes Mepe runs daily service to Cahuita and Puerto Viejo de Talamanca, about a four-hour trip, from San José at 6 and 10 AM and 1:30 and 3:30 PM. Buses stop in Puerto Viejo de Talamanca at a covered bus stop next to the ocean near the entrance to town. Service continues to the Panamanian border at Sixaola. Autotransportes Mepe buses depart Limón for Cahuita (1 hour), Puerto Vargas (1¼ hours), and Puerto Viejo de Talamanca (1½ hours) in front of Radio Casino daily at 5, 8, and 10 AM and 1, 4, and 6 PM.

All bus service to this part of the country must take alternate routes on those occasions when heavy rains and landslides close the highway through Braulio Carrillo National Park. The detours can add anywhere from one to three hours to your journey. Check before you set out if you travel during the worst of the rainy season.

SHUTTLE VANS   If you prefer a more private form of travel, consider taking a shuttle. Gray Line Tourist Bus has shuttle service that stops in Cahuita on its daily service between San José and Puerto Viejo de Talamanca. The comfortable, air-conditioned vans leave San José from many hotels at 7 AM and leave from Puerto Viejo for San José at noon. Reserve tickets ($25) a day in advance. Interbus's comfortable air-conditioned vans depart San José hotels daily at 10 AM for Limón, Cahuita, Puerto Viejo de Talamanca, and Manzanillo. Tickets are $25 and should be reserved a day in advance.

🚍 Bus Lines **Autotransportes Caribeños** ☎ 222-0610 or 758-2575. **Autotransportes Mepe** ☎ 257-8129 or 758-1572. **Autotransportes Sarapiquí** ☎ 257-6859. **Empresarios Guapileños** ☎ 222-0610 or 766-6740. **Linaco** ☎ 222-0610 or 768-9484.

🚍 Bus Stations **Cahuita terminal** ✉ Next to Bar Saz, Cahuita ☎ No phone. **Gran Terminal del Caribe** ✉ Avda. 2 and C. 8, across from the soccer stadium, Limón ☎ No phone. **Puerto Viejo de Sarapiquí terminal** ✉ Center of town across from soccer field, Puerto Viejo de Sarapiquí ☎ 766-6740. **Puerto Viejo de Talamanca terminal** ✉ 50 m west of Hotel Maritza, Puerto Viejo de Talamanca ☎ 750-0023.

🚍 Shuttle Van Services **Gray Line Tourist Bus** ☎ 232-3681 or 220-2126 ⊕ www.graylinecostarica.com. **Interbus** ☎ 283-5573 ⊕ www.interbusonline.com.

CAR TRAVEL
There are no rental agencies in the area. Rent in San José.

The Carretera Braulio Carrillo (Braulio Carrillo Highway) runs from C. 3 in San José and passes the Zurquí and Quebrada González sectors of Braulio Carrillo National Park. It branches at Santa Clara, north of the park, with the paved Highway 4 continuing north to Puerto Viejo de Sarapiquí. Alternatively, an older winding road connects San José with Puerto Viejo de Sarapiquí, passing through Heredia and Vara Blanca. The roads in the Sarapiquí part of the Atlantic lowlands are mostly paved, with the usual rained-out dirt and rock sections; road quality depends on the time of year, the length of time since the last visit by a road crew, and/or the amount of rain dumped by the latest tropical storm.

The paved two-lane Guápiles Highway continues from Santa Clara southeast to Guápiles, EARTH, and Limón, a total distance from San José to the coast of about 160 km (100 mi).

You cannot drive to Tortuguero or Barra del Colorado; you must fly or take a boat. South of Limón, a paved road covers the roughly 40 km (25 mi) to Cahuita, then passes the Cahuita turnoff and proceeds for roughly 16 km (10 mi) toward Puerto Viejo de Talamanca. It is paved as far as the village of Manzanillo. Four-wheel drive is always preferable, but the major roads in this region are generally passable by any car. Just watch for potholes and unpaved sections—they can appear on any road at any time, without marking or warning. One-lane bridges appear frequently, especially south of Limón. If the triangular CEDA EL PASO sign faces you, yield first to oncoming traffic.

Road travel to and from this part of the country occasionally becomes more complicated when heavy rains cause landslides blocking the highway near the Zurquí Tunnel in Braulio Carrillo National Park just north of San José. The alternate route is a long, slow journey via Turrialba and Siquirres. Check before you set out when traveling during the heaviest of the rainy season.

Several gas stations flank the highway between Guápiles and Limón, and just outside Puerto Viejo de Sarapiquí. South of Limón, you'll find just one, north of Cahuita. Fill the tank when you get the chance.

EMERGENCIES
In an emergency, dial 911, or one of the numbers below. There are no 24-hour pharmacies in the Caribbean.

🎫 Emergency Services **Ambulance** ☎ 128. **Fire** ☎ 118. **Police** ☎ 911. **Traffic Police** ☎ 227-8030.

🎫 Hospitals **Hospital de Guápiles** ✉ 90 m south of fire station, Guápiles ☎ 710-6801. **Hospital Dr. Tony Facio** ✉ Highway to Portete, Limón ☎ 758-2222.

LANGUAGE
The Atlantic coast's long African-Caribbean heritage makes it the most likely place in the country to find English-speakers, though residents will speak a Caribbean-accented English that may sound unfamiliar to you. "Okay" is a general all-purpose greeting heard on the coast, and is gradually replacing the older generation's traditional *"Wha' happin!"* (What's happening?) With Spanish now the language of instruction in all schools, young people here are less likely to speak English than their elders.

MAIL & SHIPPING

The privatized Correos de Costa Rica provides reasonable postal service from this part of the country, but your best bet is to wait and mail letters and cards from San José. DHL and UPS have offices in Limón for express shipping of packages. There are public computers for Internet use in Cahuita, Limón, Puerto Viejo de Sarapiquí, Puerto Viejo de Talamanca, and Tortuguero. Expect to pay $2–$4 per hour. Connection times are slower than in San José.

▣ Internet Cafés ATEC ⊠ Across from Restaurant Tamara, Puerto Viejo de Talamanca ☎ 750–0398. **Café Caoba** ⊠ Next to police station, Tortuguero. **Café Internet Río Negro** ⊠ Playa Chiquita, Puerto Viejo de Talamanca, 4 km (2½ mi) southeast of town ☎ 750–0801. **Cíber Café** ⊠ Next to Turística Cahuita, Cahuita ☎ 755–0409. **Edutec** ⊠ Avda. 3 and C. 4, Limón ☎ 798–0101. **Internet Sarapiquí** ⊠ Next to Joyería Mary, Puerto Viejo de Sarapiquí ☎ 766–6223. **Video Mundo** ⊠ Across from Restaurant Tamara, Puerto Viejo de Talamanca ☎ 750–0651.

▣ Post Offices Correos de Costa Rica ⊠ East of police station, Cahuita ⊠ Avda. 2 and C. 4, Limón ⊠ 50 m north of soccer field, Puerto Viejo de Sarapiquí ⊠ 50 m west of ATEC, Puerto Viejo de Talamanca.

▣ Shipping Serices DHL ⊠ Across from Terminal de Cruceros, Limón ☎ 758–1256. **UPS** ⊠ West side of Parque Vargas, Limón ☎ 798–5173.

MONEY MATTERS

Most larger tourist establishments are prepared to handle credit cards. Banks are sparse in this region. Changing U.S. dollars or traveler's checks is possible at the few offices of Banco Nacional, but lines are long. The Scotiabank in downtown Limón has an ATM that accepts Plus- and Cirrus-affiliated cards. You're best off taking care of getting cash with your ATM card back in San José before venturing here.

▣ Banks Banco Nacional ⊠ 50 m north of Central Plaza, Puerto Viejo de Sarapiquí ⊠ Avda. 2, between Cs. 3 and 4, Limón ⊠ 400 m east and 50 m north of hospital, Guápiles ☎ 710–7351. **Scotiabank** ⊠ Avda. 3 and C. 2, Limón.

SAFETY

The conditions that make the Caribbean so popular among surfers spell danger for swimmers. Drownings occur each year. Strong riptides can pull you out to sea, even in waist-deep water, before you realize what's happening. Never swim alone in these parts—good advice anywhere, of course.

TAXIS

Official red taxis ply the streets in Limón, Guápiles, and Puerto Viejo de Sarapiquí or hang out at designated taxi stands. Cahuita and Puerto Viejo de Talamanca have a couple of official taxis each, but there and elsewhere, taxi service is much less organized, with private individuals providing rides. To be on the safe side, ask your hotel or restaurant to call one for you.

TOURS

Tortuguero tours are usually packaged with one- or two-night stays in local lodges. Grupo Papagayo offers three-day, two-night tours, including bus and boat transport from San José to the Jungle Lodge in

Tortuguero, for about $240. Mawamba leads a slightly more expensive version of the same tour, with nights at the Mawamba Lodge. Costa Rica Expeditions flies you straight to its rustically charming Tortuga Lodge for three days and two nights, for about $380 a head. Ecole Travel offers a less expensive $95 excursion beginning and ending at the Moín docks and offering lodging at El Manatí, meals not included. Fran and Modesto Watson are experts on the history and ecology of the area; among other tours, they offer a two-day tour on their *Riverboat Francesca,* with the overnight at a nature lodge. The cost is about $190 per person, including meals and transfers. The Watsons can put together made-to-order packages for fishing as well.

The Río Indio Adventure Lodge takes you on organized all-inclusive guided trips from San José for stays in its luxury eco-hotel in the middle of the Río Indio-Maiz Biological Reserve, just over the border near San Juan del Norte, Nicaragua. The Hotel Gavilán Río Sarapiquí offers day excursions from its site near Puerto Viejo de Sarapiquí up to the San Juan for wildlife-viewing and bird-watching.

ATEC conducts such special-interest tours as "Sustainable Logging," "Yorkin Indigenous Tour," and assorted bird-watching, turtle-watching, indigenous culture, and ecologically oriented excursions on the southern coast. Talamanca Adventures leads off-the-beaten-path 1- to 13-day tours of its namesake region, familiarizing you with everything from Caribbean cooking to rain-forest conservation to indigenous farming. Terraventuras leads you around Tortuguero and Gandoca-Manzanillo Wildlife Refuge as well as renting the best-quality surfboards, bicycles, Boogie boards, and snorkeling gear. Aquamor specializes in land- and ocean-focused tours of the Gandoca-Manzanillo Wildlife Refuge.

The excellent Horizontes specializes in more independent tours with as few as eight people, including transport by four-wheel-drive vehicle, naturalist guides, and guest lectures. The Caribbean Conservation Corporation can also recommend good local guides. Aventuras Naturales, Costa Rica Expeditions, and Ríos Tropicales lead tours on the Sarapiquí River. Ríos Tropicales leads rafting excursions on the Pacuare and Reventazón rivers out of its operations center in Siquirres.

Limón's Laura Tropical Tours caters to cruise passengers disembarking from the ships and offers area excursions to banana plantations, Tortuguero, and Cahuita National Park. Mambo Tours has an office in Limón's cruise terminal, and can take you on three- to eight-hour excursions around the region, and even on an all-day trip to San José.

Divers looking for sites off the beaten track can contact Shawn Larkin, a freelance dive guide and columnist who writes about sea life and diving conditions for the *Tico Times,* for information or to sign up for a dive trip.

🔳 Tour Operators **ATEC** ✉ Across from Soda Tamara, Puerto Viejo de Talamanca ☎ 750–0191 ⊕ www.greencoast.com/atec.htm. **Aquamor** ☎ 759–9012 ⊕ www. greencoast.com/aquamor.htm. **Aventuras Naturales** ☎ 225–3939 ⊕ www.adventure-costarica.com. **Caribbean Conservation Corporation** ☎ 710–0547 in Tortuguero, 224–9215 in San José ⊕ www.cccturtle.org. **Costa Rica Expeditions** ✉ C. Central and

Avda. 3, Barrio La Merced, San José ☎ 222-0333 🖷 257-1665 ⊕ www. costaricaexpeditions.com. **Ecole Travel** ⊠ C. 7 and Avdas. Central and 1, San José ☎ 223-2240 🖷 223-4128. **Fran and Modesto Watson** ☎🖷 226-0986 ⊕ www. tortuguerocanals.com. **Grupo Papagayo** ⊠ Paseo Colón and C. 38, Paseo Colón, San José ☎ 233-0133. **Hotel Gavilán Río Sarapiquí** ☎ 766-6743 ⊕ www.gavilanlodge. com. **Horizontes** ⊠ 150 m north of Pizza Hut, Paseo Colón, San José ☎ 222-2022. **Laura Tropical Tours** ⊠ Terminal de Cruceros, Limón ☎ 758-1240. **Mambo Tours** ⊠ Terminal de Cruceros, Limón ☎ 798-1542. **Mawamba** ☎ 710-7280 in Tortuguero, 223-2421 in San José. **Río Indio Adventure Lodge** ☎ 296-3338 ⊕ www.rioindiolodge.com. **Ríos Tropicales** ☎ 233-6455 ⊕ www.riostropicales.com. **Shawn Larkin** ⊠ Near Gandoca-Manzanillo National Wildlife Refuge ☎ 506/770-8021 or 506/391-3417. **Talamanca Adventures** ☎ 224-3570 in San José 🖷 253-7524 ⊕ www.talamanca-adventures. com. **Terraventuras** ⊠ 100 m south of bus stop Puerto Viejo de Talamanca ☎ 750-0489 ⊕ www.terraventuras.com.

VISITOR INFORMATION

The tourist office in San José has information on the Atlantic lowlands. The ATEC office in Puerto Viejo de Talamanca is a great source of information on local tours, guides, and interesting activities. Stop by or contact the Tortuguero Information Center in the village to find out about local tours and activities.

🗐 Tourist Information **ATEC** ⊠ Across from Soda Tamara, Puerto Viejo de Talamanca ☎ 750-0191 ⊕ www.greencoast.com/atec.htm. **Instituto Costarricense de Turismo** (ICT) ⊠ Edificio CINDE, Autopista General Cañas, Barrio La Uruca ⊠ C. 2, between Avdas. 1 and 3, Barrio La Merced ☎ 222-1090. **Tortuguero Information Center** ⊠ Across from Catholic church, Tortuguero village ☎ 709-8011 or 833-0827.

UNDERSTANDING COSTA RICA

COSTA RICA AT A GLANCE

Fast Facts

Name in local language: Costa Rica
Capital: San José
National anthem: "Noble Patria" (Noble Homeland)
Type of government: Democratic republic
Administrative divisions: Seven provinces, divided into 81 cantons, subdivided into 421 districts
Independence: September 15, 1821 (from Spain)
Constitution: November 7, 1949
Legal system: Supreme Court of Justice (22 magistrates elected by Legislative Assembly for renewable eight-year terms). The offices of the ombudsman, comptroller general, and procurator general assert autonomous oversight of the government.

Legislature: 57-deputy unicameral Legislative Assembly, elected at four-year intervals
Population: 3,896,092
Median age: Female 26, male 25
Life expectancy: Female 79, male 74
Infant mortality rate: 10.56 deaths per 1,000 live births
Literacy: 96%
Language: Spanish (official), English
Ethnic groups: White (including mestizo) 94%, black 3%, Amerindian 1%, Chinese 1%, other 1%
Religion: Roman Catholic 76%, Evangelical Protestant 14%, none 5%, other 5%

Geography & Environment

Land area: 50,660 square km (19,560 square mi; approximately the size of the U.S. state of West Virginia)
Coastline: 1,290 km (802 mi)
Terrain: Rugged central range with 112 volcanic craters that separates the eastern and western coastal plains
Natural resources: Hydroelectric power, forest products, fisheries products
Natural hazards: Droughts, flash floods, thunderstorms, earthquakes
Flora: 9,000 species, including 1,200 orchid species and 800 fern species; tidal mangrove swamps, tropical rain forest, subalpine forest
Fauna: 36,518 species, including 34,000 species of insects and 2,000 species of butterflies, the endangered squirrel monkey, manatee, and Three-wattled Bellbird
Environmental issues: Deforestation, rapid industrialization and urbanization, air and water pollution, soil degradation, plastic waste

Economy

Economic reforms have been in place since the 1990s. There are fewer controls on foreign investment and imports, and domestic output is increasingly privatized.
Currency: Colón
GDP: $32 billion
Per capita income: $4,090

Inflation: 9.1%
Unemployment: 6.3%
Work force: 1.9 million
Debt: $4.8 billion
Major industries: Tourism, microprocessors, food processing, textiles and clothing, construction materials, fertilizer, plastic products

Agricultural products: Coffee, pineapple, sugar, bananas, corn, rice, beans, potatoes, beef
Exports: $5.1 billion
Major export products: Bananas, coffee, electronic components, pineapples, sugar, textiles
Export partners: U.S. 51%, Europe 23%, Central America 11%, Japan 2%

Imports: $6.4 billion
Major import products: Chemicals, consumer goods, electronic components, machinery, petroleum products, vehicles
Import partners: U.S. 56%, Europe 10%, Mexico 5%, Central America 5%, Japan 5%, Venezuela 4%

Did You Know?

• Tourism earns more foreign exchange than bananas and coffee combined.

• Costa Rica did away with its military in 1949.

• Costa Rica has 12 distinct "life zones" or ecosystems.

• Five percent of the world's plant and animal species are found in this country.

• Costa Rica is the home of seven active volcanoes—including Volcán Arenal, the second-largest active volcano in the world—and 60 extinct or dormant volcanoes.

• There are more species of birds in Costa Rica than in the United States and Canada combined.

THE LAND OF "PURA VIDA"

PURA VIDA MEANS "PURE LIFE," and is used by Ticos—as Costa Ricans call themselves—to express agreement, greeting, leave-taking, and basically anything positive. Once you set foot in this tiny nation between Panama and Nicaragua in the Central American isthmus, you realize that it's also a philosophy of life in Costa Rica. The spirit of pura vida might explain why more than a million visitors came to this country in 2003 and why Costa Rica continues to gain international popularity as an ecological wonderland. The mere mention of the country conjures up visions of rain forests, volcanoes, tropical beaches, and exotic wildlife. And it delivers on all these and more. This country about the size of the U.S. state of West Virginia is packed with incredible biological diversity, varied landscapes, and a seemingly endless selection of outdoor diversions, from bird-watching and beach trips to thrilling rafting and rain-forest hiking.

Costa Rica's natural beauty and accessibility (it's a 5-hour flight from New York City and 3½ hours from Houston) make it appealing to a broad range of visitors. Whether you want to explore the country's extensive system of national parks and nature reserves, enjoy the amenities of coastal luxury resorts or volcano-view observatory lodges, or seek thrills surfing some of Central America's biggest waves, you'll find that, from nearly every angle, Costa Rica is an exceptionally beautiful place.

Ticos know just how good they have it. Fiercely proud of their history, culture, and achievements, they are also polite and accommodating. They will go to great lengths to *quedar bien*—to leave a good impression, especially with foreigners. Many Costa Ricans, especially younger people who live in and around the capital of San José, as well as those employed in the tourism industry, speak English well. Most visitors return impressed with Tico warmth and hospitality.

A combination of history, politics, and luck explains some of the reasons Costa Rica has managed to avoid the turmoil that has engulfed much of Central America in the last half century, and has achieved a far higher standard of living than its neighbors. Most Latin American countries remain dominated by the "oligarchy," enormously wealthy families that were granted vast tracts of land by the Spanish Crown.

Costa Rica was largely neglected during the colonial era and experienced most of its growth after independence from Spain in the early 19th century. It became a nation of immigrants, who came to work and prospered, creating a large and stable middle class. Ticos have a strong sense of national identity and pride themselves first on being Costa Ricans rather than Central Americans, or even Latin Americans.

The political strife that rocked Central America during the 1970s and '80s left a negative impression of the area in the minds of many North Americans and Europeans. People unfamiliar with Costa Rica often equate the problems in countries such as El Salvador and Nicaragua with the entire region. Surrounded by political unrest, Costa Rica has managed to remain an island of stability and peace. The country has no military—it was abolished in 1949. It's also the region's most sturdy democracy, and the country has a deep-rooted respect for human rights. The functional literacy rate is about 96%. Its telecommunications and health-care systems, although not up to North American standards, are undoubtedly the best in Central America. And except for the area around Limón, the tap water is safe and drinkable.

The key to Costa Rica's booming tourism industry is its astonishing biological diversity, seen in the variety of flora, fauna, landscapes, and microclimates within its frontiers. National parks and preserves cover close to 25% of the country and are home to 876 species of birds, 205 species of mammals, 376 types of reptiles and amphibians, and more than 9,000 different species of flowering plants, among them 1,200 varieties of wild orchids. Landscapes include cool mountain valleys and massive, rumbling volcanoes, hilly coffee *fincas* (farms) and torpid banana groves, and sultry mangrove forests and palm-strewn beaches.

The many rivers that wind through the country's valleys churn through steep stretches that are popular white-water-rafting routes. Some of the rivers end up as languid jungle waterways appropriate for both animal-watching and sportfishing. With mile upon mile of beaches surrounded by coconut palms and thick forest, the Caribbean and Pacific coasts are ideal for swimming and sunbathing, and when the sun goes down, many beaches are visited by nesting sea turtles. The oceans that hug those coasts hold intricate coral formations, rugged islands, colorful schools of fish, and plentiful waves, enticing anglers, surfers, and sea-kayakers.

A BIOLOGICAL SUPERPOWER

OSTA RICA MAY LACK OIL FIELDS and coal deposits, but it's blessed with awesome natural resources. The country's ecological wealth includes fertile volcanic soil, sun-swathed beaches, hundreds of colorful bird species, and massive trees whose branches support elevated gardens of orchids and bromeliads—the kind of priceless commodities that economists have long ignored. Investment bankers may wonder how this tiny nation ended up with so pretentious a name as "Rich Coast," but many a biologist, Tico, and nature-loving visitor understands where the republic's true wealth lies.

Costa Rica's forests hold an array of flora and fauna so vast and diverse that scientists haven't even named thousands of the plant and insect species found here; and of the species that have been identified, few have been thoroughly studied. These forests are among the most diverse and productive ecosystems in the world—although tropical forests cover a mere 7% of the Earth's surface area, they hold more than half the planet's plant and animal species—and few countries offer better exposure to tropical nature than Costa Rica.

The country covers less than .03% of the Earth's surface, yet it contains nearly 5% of the planet's plant and animal species. The variety of native flora and fauna is astonishing: Costa Rica contains at least 9,000 plant species, including more than 1,200 types of orchids, some 2,000 kinds of butterflies, and 876 bird species (more than the United States and Canada combined). But such numbers don't begin to convey the awe you feel when you stare up the convoluted trunk of a centennial strangler fig, listen to the roar of a howler monkey reverberate through the jungle, or watch a delicate hummingbird drink nectar from a multicolored heliconia flower.

Many of Costa Rica's plants and animals are beautiful, others are bizarre, and the ecological web that ties them all together is both complex and fascinating. It may be hard to recognize the richness of a Costa Rican forest at first glance—the overwhelming verdure of the rain forest can give the false impression of uniformity—but if you spend some time exploring one with a qualified nature guide, you come to understand why scientists have dubbed Costa Rica a "biological superpower."

Costa Rica's biological diversity is the result of its tropical location (on a slip of land connecting North and South America), its varied topography, and the many microclimates resulting from the combination of mountains, valleys, and lowlands. But to understand why Costa Rica is so biologically important today, we need to look back to prehistoric times, to a world that human eyes never saw but that scientists have at least partially reconstructed.

Just a Few Dozen Millennia Ago

In geological terms, Costa Rica is relatively young, which explains why there are precious few valuable minerals beneath its soil. Five million years ago, this patch of land didn't even exist: North and South America were separated by a "canal" the likes of which Teddy Roosevelt—father of the Panama Canal—couldn't have conjured up in his wildest dreams. In the area now occupied by Panama and Costa Rica, the waters of the Pacific and Atlantic oceans flowed freely together. Geologists have named that former canal the Straits of Bolívar, after the Venezuelan revolutionary who wrested much of South America from Spain.

Far beneath the Straits of Bolívar, the incremental movement of tectonic plates slowly created the Central American isthmus. Geologists speculate that a chain of volcanic islands appeared in the gap around 30 million years ago; a combination of volcanic activity and plate movement caused the islands to grow and rise from the water, eventually forming a connected ridge. The land bridge was completed around 3 million years ago, closing the interoceanic canal and connecting North and South America for the first time.

Because several tectonic plates meet beneath Central America, the region has long been geologically unstable, experiencing occasional earthquakes, frequent tremors, and regular volcanic eruptions. Although it seems a curse to be hit by one of these natural disasters, there actually wouldn't be a Costa Rica were it not for such frightening phenomena. What is now the country's best soil was once spewed from the bowels of the volcanoes that dominate its landscape, and the jarring adjustments of adjacent tectonic plates actually pushed most of today's Costa Rica up out of the sea.

The intercontinental connection completed 3 million years ago had profound biological consequences: it separated the marine life of the Pacific and Atlantic oceans, and it created a pathway for interchange for the flora and fauna of North and South America. Though hardly the kind of lapse that excites a geologist, 3 million years is a long time by biological standards, and the region's plants and animals have changed considerably since the inter-American gap was spanned. Whereas evolution took different paths in the waters that flank the isthmus, organisms that had evolved on separate continents were able to make their way into the opposite hemisphere, and the resulting interaction determined what lives in the Americas today.

Mind-Boggling Biodiversity

Costa Rica's enormous natural diversity is in many ways the result of the intercontinental exchange, but the country's flora and fauna actually add up to more than what has passed between the conti-

nents. Although it is a biological corridor, the isthmus also acts as a filter, a hospitable haven to many species that couldn't complete the journey from one hemisphere to the other. The rain forests of Costa Rica's Atlantic and southwestern lowlands, for example, are the most northerly home of such southern species as the Crab-eating Raccoon and a dreaded jungle pit viper known as the Bushmaster. The tropical dry forests of the northern Pacific slope, on the other hand, are the southern limit for such North American species as the White-throated Magpie-Jay and the Virginia Opossum. In addition to species whose range extends only as far as Costa Rica in one direction, and those whose range extends into both North and South America, such as the White-tailed Deer and the Gray Hawk, Costa Rica's many physical barriers and microclimates have fostered the development of indigenous plants and animals, such as the Mangrove Hummingbird and Mountain Salamander.

What all this biological babble means to travelers is that they might spot a North American Pale-billed Woodpecker and a howler monkey (of South American descent) in the branches of a rain tree, which is native to Central America. And then there are the tourists—migrants, that is—such as the dozens of northern bird species that spend their winter holidays in Costa Rica, among them the Tennessee Warbler, Western Tanager, and Yellow-bellied Sapsucker. In addition to recognizing some of the birds that migrate here, you'll no doubt be at home with some of the plants, such as the philodendrons and impatiens that grow wild in the country, but cost a pretty penny in the garden shop back home. Costa Rica does have plenty of oak trees, squirrels, and sparrows, but most of its flora and fauna look decidedly tropical. Not only are such common plants as orchids, palms, and ficuses unmistakably tropical, but many of the resident animals are distinctly neotropical—found only in the American tropics—including sloths, iguanas, toucans, and monkeys with prehensile tails.

The wildlife is spread through an array of ecosystems, which biologists have divided into a dozen "life zones," but that actually consist of a biological continuum almost too vast for classification. Though the existence of specific flora and fauna in any given life zone is determined by various physical conditions, the two most important are altitude and rainfall. Average temperatures in the tropics vary very little from month to month, though the temperature does change a good bit during the course of a day, especially in the mountains. The Costa Rican highlands are consistently cooler than the lowlands, which means you can spend a morning sweating in a sultry coastal forest, then drive a few hours into the mountains and find yourself needing a warm jacket.

In more temperate parts of the world, cold weather hits the mountaintops a month or two before the lowlands, but eventually gets his icy grip on everything. In the tropics, however, only the tops of the highest mountains freeze, so the very highest-altitude flora tends to look completely different from that of even nearby valleys. Altitude also plays a substantial role in regulating humidity, since clouds accumulate around mountains and volcanoes, providing regular precipitation as well as shade, which in turn slows evaporation. These conditions lead to the formation of luxuriant cloud forests on the upper slopes of many mountains. In general, the higher you climb, the more lush the vegetation, except for the peaks of the highest mountains, which often protrude from the cloud cover and are thus fairly arid.

Although you may associate the tropics with rain, precipitation in Costa Rica varies considerably, depending on where you are and when you're there. This is a result of the mountainous terrain and regional weather patterns. A phenomenon called rain shadow—when one side of a mountain range receives much more rain than the other—plays an important ecological role in Costa Rica. Four mountain ranges combine to create an intercontinental divide that separates the country into Atlantic and Pacific slopes; and thanks to the trade winds, the Atlantic slope receives much more rain than the Pacific. The trade winds steadily pump moisture-laden clouds southwest over the isthmus, where they encounter warm air or mountains, which make them rise. As the clouds rise, they cool, lose their ability to hold moisture, and eventually dump most of their liquid luggage on the Caribbean side.

During the rainy season—mid-May to December—the role of the trade winds is diminished, as regular storms roll off the Pacific Ocean and soak the western side of the isthmus. Though it rains all over Costa Rica during these months, it often rains more on the Pacific side of the mountains than on the Atlantic. Come December, the trade winds take over again, and hardly a drop falls on the western side until May. The dry season is most intense in the northwestern province of Guanacaste, where most trees drop their foliage and the forests take on a desert visage. That region quickly regains its verdure once the rains return in May, marking the beginning of a springlike season that Costa Ricans nonetheless refer to as *el invierno* (winter).

Climate variation within the country results in a mosaic of forests, from those that receive only a few feet of rain each year to those that experience 100 inches or more annually. The combination of humidity and temperature helps determine what grows where; but whereas some species have very restricted ranges, others seem to thrive just about anywhere. Plants such as strangler figs and bromeliads grow all over Costa Rica, and animals such as the Collared Peccary and coati—a long-nose cousin of the raccoon—can pretty much live wherever human beings let them. Other species have extremely limited ranges, such as the Mangrove Hummingbird, restricted to the mangrove forests of the Pacific coast, and the Volcano Junco, a gray sparrow that lives only around the highest peaks of the Cordillera de Talamanca.

It's a Jungle out There

Costa Rica's incredible biodiversity is part of what makes it such an invigorating vacation spot, but the landscape that travelers most want to see is the tropical rain forest. The protected areas of the Atlantic and southern Pacific lowlands hold tracts of virgin rain forest where massive tropical trees tower more than 33 m (100 feet) over the forest floor. The thick branches of these jungle giants are covered with an abundance of epiphytes (plants that grow on other plants but are not parasites) such as ferns, orchids, bromeliads, mosses, vines, and aroids. Most of the rain forest's foliage and fauna is clustered in the arboreal garden of the canopy.

Although life flourishes in the canopy, the intense sunlight that quickly dries the treetops after downpours results in a recurrent water shortage. Consequently, plants living in the canopy have developed ways to cope with aridity: many orchids have thick leaves that resist evaporation and spongy roots that can quickly soak up large amounts of water when it rains. Tank bromeliads have a funnel shape that enables them to collect and hold water at the center of their leaves. Acting as miniature oases, these plants attract arboreal animals to drink from, hunt at, or—in the case of certain insect larvae and tree-frog tadpoles—live in their pools. In exchange for vital water, the waste and carcasses of these animals give the plants valuable nutrients, which are also scarce in the canopy.

The fact that so many animals spend so much of their time in the canopy can be frustrating for people who come to the rain forest to see wildlife. But by patiently peering through binoculars, you might glimpse the furry figure of a sloth, or the brilliant regalia of a Scarlet Macaw; and it's hard to miss the arboreal acrobatics of monkeys, who leap from tree to tree, hang from branches, and generally make spectacles of themselves. For a closer look at the canopy, you may want to take a ride on the Rain Forest Aerial Tram, near the Guápiles Highway, stroll down Monteverde's Sky Walk, or linger on a tree platform at Hacienda Barú, in Dominical, or at the Corcovado Lodge Tent Camp. For an adrenaline-pumping introduction to treetop ecology, take one of the canopy tours offered throughout the country, but don't expect to see much wildlife as you zip from tree to tree along steel cables.

Because little sunlight reaches the ground in a virgin rain forest, the jungle floor is a dim, quiet place, with not nearly as much undergrowth as in those old Tarzan movies. Still, an array of plants, from ferns to palm trees, has adapted to this shady world. The light level inside a rain forest is comparable to that of the average North American living room, or shopping mall, which is why some of the plant species that grow there have become popular houseplants up north. But the vegetation is not sparse everywhere: whenever an old tree falls, it creates a gap in the canopy, which leads to a riot of growth on the ground, as plants compete for the newfound sunlight.

Few travelers are disappointed by Costa Rica's forests, but some are discouraged by the difficulty of spotting animals. Hikers occasionally encounter such earthbound creatures as the coati or the agouti, a terrier-size rodent that resembles a giant guinea pig, and in most areas you're likely to see iridescent Blue Morpho butterflies, hyperactive hummingbirds, brightly colored poison dart frogs, and tiny lizards standing guard on tree trunks. Most forest dwellers, however, spend much of their time and energy trying *not* to be seen, and the foliage aids them in that endeavor. An untrained eye can miss the details, which is why a naturalist guide is invaluable: in addition to spotting and identifying plants and animals, a good guide can explain some of relationships that weave them together in one of the planet's most complex ecosystems.

The rain forest is characterized by intense predation. Its inhabitants dedicate most of their resources to finding their next meal and avoiding *becoming* a meal in the process. Animals can hide or flee when in danger, but plants have developed such survival tactics as thorns, prickly hairs, and toxic substances that make their leaves unappetizing. Because of the relative toxicity of most rain-forest foliage, many insects eat only a small portion of a leaf before moving on to another plant, so as not to ingest a lethal dose of any one poison. You can see the results of this practice by looking up into the canopy—almost every leaf is full of little holes.

Camouflage is another effective animal defense. The tropical rain forest is full of insects that have evolved to resemble the leaves, bark, moss, and leaf litter around them. Some bugs have adopted the colors of certain flowers, or even the mold that grows on plants. Though they can be a chore to spot, those camouflaged critters are quite intriguing.

Other creatures go to the opposite extreme and advertise themselves with bright colors. Some hues are meant to help find a mate amid the mesh of green; others serve as a danger sign to potential predators. Some species of caterpillar, for example, are not only immune to the toxins of the plant on which they live, but actually sequester that poison within their bodies, making themselves toxic as well. Native tribes have used the toxic secretions from aptly named poison dart frogs to poison the tips of their arrows and blowgun darts. These frogs' typical warning pattern mixes bright colors with black or dark blue, a coloration that conveys a simple message to predators: eat me and die.

As with any successful strategy, there are bound to be copycats. "Mimics" have warning coloration, but lack the poison to follow through with the threat—certain edible caterpillars look like venomous ones, and some harmless serpents have markings similar to those of the deadly coral snake. Such acts of deception often reach amazing levels of intrigue. The cocoons of certain butterflies not only resemble the head of a viper, but if disturbed, begin to move back and forth just as a snake's head would. One large butterfly has spots on its wings that look like eyes, so that when it opens them it resembles an owl. Another butterfly species looks exactly like a wasp.

In addition to eluding predators, plants and animals must compete with other species that have similar niches—the biological equivalents of jobs. This competition fosters cooperation between noncompetitive organisms. Plants need to get their pollen and seeds distributed as far as possible, and every animal requires a steady food supply, which brings us to everyone's favorite subject: the birds and the bees.

Although butterflies and bees do most of the pollinating up north, tropical plants are pollinated by everything from fruit flies and hummingbirds to beetles and bats. The flowers of such plants are often designed so that their nectar is readily available to pollinators but protected from freeloaders. The beautiful hibiscus flower is designed to dust a hummingbird's forehead with pollen and collect any pollen that's already there while the tiny bird drinks the nectar hidden deep in its base; the flower is too long for a butterfly, and the nectar is held too deep for a bee to reach. No system is perfect, though: you may see a Bananaquit—a tiny bird with a short beak—biting holes in the base of a hibiscus flower in an effort to drink its nectar without getting anywhere near its pollen.

Intense competition for limited resources keeps the rain forest's trees growing taller, roots reaching farther, and everything mobile working on a way to get more for less. The battle for light sends most of the foliage sky high, and the battle for nutrients speeds to a breakneck pace the process of decay and recycling that follows every death in the forest. One result of this high-speed decomposition is that most of the nutrients in a rain forest are present in its living things, whereas the earth beneath them retains few essential elements. Rainforest soils consequently tend to be nutrient-poor, less than ideal for farming.

A Mosaic of Ecosystems

Though the rain forest is the most famous region in Costa Rica, there are other types of forests here equally rich in life and well worth exploring. The tropical dry forests of the northwestern lowlands are similar to rain forests during the rainy season, but once the weather turns dry, they change profoundly: most trees lose their leaves, and some burst simultaneously into full, colorful flower. The yellow-blossom buttercup tree and the pink tabebuia, among others, brighten up the arid northwestern landscape in the dry season. The dry forest contains many of the plants, animals, and exclusive relationships found in the rain forest, but it's also home to species often associated with the forests and deserts of Mexico and the southwestern United States, including cacti, coyotes, and diamondback rattlesnakes. Because dry forests are less dense than rain forests, it can be easier to see animals in them; this is especially true in the dry season, when foliage is sparse and animals often congregate around scarce water sources and trees with fruit or flowers.

The cloud forests on the upper reaches of many Costa Rican mountains and volcanoes are even more luxuriant than rain forests, so deeply lush that it can be hard to find the bark on a cloud-forest tree for all the growth on its trunk and branches. Plants grow on plants that are growing on *other* plants: vines, orchids, ferns, aroids, and bromeliads are everywhere, and mosses and liverworts often cover the vines and leaves of other epiphytes. Because of the steep terrain, a cloud forest's trees grow on slightly different levels, and the canopy is more irregular than that of a lowland rain forest. Because more light reaches the ground, there is plenty of undergrowth, including prehistoric-looking tree ferns, a wealth of flowering plants, and "poor man's umbrellas"—made up of a few giant leaves.

Cloud forests are home to a multitude of animals, ranging from delicate glass frogs, whose undersides are so transparent that you can see many of their internal organs, to the legendary Resplendent Quetzal, a bird considered sacred by the ancient Maya. The male quetzal has a crimson belly and iridescent green back, wings, and tail feathers that can grow longer than 2 feet in length. Those tail feathers float behind the quetzal when it flies, a splendid sight that no doubt inspired its ancient name, "the plumed serpent." Although the tangle of foliage and almost constant mist make it hard to see cloud-forest wildlife, you should still catch glimpses of such colorful birds as the Emerald Toucanet, Collared Redstart, and dozens of hummingbird species.

Humidity protects the cloud-forest canopy from the water shortages that often plague the upper reaches of lowland rain forests. In fact, the cloud forest's canopy is often soaking wet. During much of the year, a moisture-laden mist moves through the cloud forest, depositing condensation on the plants; this condensation causes a sort of secondary precipitation, with droplets forming on the epiphytic foliage and falling regularly from the branches to the forest floor. Cloud forests thus function like giant sponges, soaking up humidity from the clouds and sending it slowly downhill to feed the streams and rivers on which many regions and communities depend for water.

On top of high ridges, and near the summits of volcanoes, the cloud forest is transformed by strong, steady winds that topple tall trees and regularly break off branches. The resulting collection of small, twisted trees and bushes is known as an elfin forest. On the upper slopes of the Cordillera de Talamanca, Costa Rica's highest range, the cloud forest gives way to the bleak *páramo*, a high-altitude ecosystem composed of shrubs, grasses, and hardy herbs. Most of these plants are common in the heights of South America's Andes; the Costa Rican páramo defines their most northerly distribution.

On the other extreme, along both coasts, are river mouths and estuaries with extensive mangrove forests. These primeval-looking, often flooded profusions grow in tidal zones all over the tropics. Many of the trees in mangrove forests grow on "stilt" roots, which prop their leaves up out of the saltwater and help them absorb carbon dioxide when the tide is high. The roots also lend protection to various small fish and crustaceans and are often covered with barnacles, mussels, and other shellfish.

Mangrove forests are fairly homogeneous, with stands of one species of tree stretching off as far as the eye can see. They are also extremely productive ecosystems that play an important role as estuaries: many marine animals, such as shrimp, spend the early stages of their lives in mangrove estuaries; other animals spend their entire lives there. Vital to the health of the ocean beyond them, mangroves are attractive sites for animals that feed on marine life, especially fish-eating birds such as cormorants, herons, pelicans, and ospreys.

The forests that line the Caribbean canals, along Costa Rica's northeastern coast, are dominated by the water-resistant *jolillo* palm or *palma real*. This area is home to many of the same animals found in the rain forest—monkeys, parrots, iguanas—as well as river dwellers such as turtles, crocodiles, and anhingas. A boat trip up the canals is thus a great opportunity to observe wildlife, as are similar excursions on jungle rivers such as the Río Frío and the Río Sarapiquí. Seasonal *lagunas* (lagoons) such as Caño Negro and the swamps of Palo Verde National Park,

which disappear during the dry months, are excellent places to see birds during the wet season.

In addition to its varied forests, Costa Rica has 1,224 km (760 mi) of coastline, which consists of beaches separated by rocky points. The points are home to a variety of marine life, but even more remarkable, many of the country's beaches are important nesting spots for endangered sea turtles. And submerged in the sea off both coasts are various reefs—some rocky, some covered with coral—that are home to hundreds of species of colorful fish, crustaceans, and other invertebrates. The diverse coral reefs off the southern Caribbean coast could well be the marine equivalent of the rain forest.

Where Have All the Forests Gone?

All this natural diversity notwithstanding, as you travel through Costa Rica, you see that its predominant landscapes are not cloud and rain forests but the coffee and banana plantations and cattle ranches that have replaced them. The country's pre-Columbian cultures may have revered the jaguar and the Harpy Eagle, but today's inhabitants are largely less illustrious beasts: the cows and the Cattle Egrets that populate countless acres of pasture.

In the last half century, more than two-thirds of Costa Rica's original forests have been destroyed. Forests have traditionally been considered unproductive land, and their destruction was for a long time synonymous with development. In the 1970s and 1980s, international and domestic development policies fueled the destruction of large tracts of wilderness. Fortunately, Costa Rican conservationists grew alarmed by this deforestation, and in the 1970s they began creating what has since grown to become the best national park system in Central America.

In addition to protecting vast natural expanses that make up nearly a quarter of the country, the Costa Rican government has made progress in curbing deforestation outside the national parks. The rate of destruction has dropped significantly, but poaching and illegal logging continue to be problems that, if left uncorrected, could eventually wipe out entire species or wilderness areas.

Deforestation not only spells disaster for the jaguar and the eagle, but can have grave consequences for human beings. Forests absorb rain and release water slowly, playing an important role in regulating the flow of rivers—which is why severely deforested regions often suffer twin plagues of floods during the rainy season and drought during the dry months. Tree covers also prevent topsoil erosion, thus keeping the land fertile and productive; in many parts of the country, erosion has left once-productive farmland almost worthless. Finally, hidden within Costa Rica's boundless living species are countless unknown or understudied substances that might eventually be extracted to cure diseases. The destruction of this country's forests is a loss for the entire world.

Travel Responsibly & Save a Few Trees

With each passing year, more and more Costa Ricans are coming to realize how valuable and imperiled their remaining wilderness is. Costa Ricans visit their national parks in significant numbers, and they consider those protected areas vital to the national economy, both for the natural resources they preserve and for their commercial role as tourist attractions. Local conservationists, however, are still a long way from achieving their goal of involving communities in the protection of the parks around them.

Costa Ricans who cut trees and hunt endangered animals usually do so out of economic necessity, and alas, the people who live near protected areas are often the last to benefit from the tourism that wilderness attracts. Your national park/reserve entrance fee helps support the preservation of Costa Rica's wildlife and places. You can also make your visit beneficial to the people living nearby by hiring local guides, horses, or boats; eating in local restaurants; and buying things (other than wild-animal products, of course) in local shops.

You can go a few steps further by making donations to local conservation groups or to such international organizations as Conservation International, the Rainforest Alliance, and the World Wildlife Federation, all of which support important conservation efforts in Costa Rica. It's also helpful to stray from the beaten path: explore private preserves, and stay at lodges that contribute to environmental efforts and to nearby communities. By planning your visit with an eye toward grassroots conservation efforts, you join the global effort to save the earth's tropical ecosystems and help ensure that the treasures you traveled so far to see remain intact for future generations.

— David Dudenhoefer

A BRIEF HISTORY

First Encounters

I N MID-SEPTEMBER 1502, on his fourth and last voyage to the New World, Christopher Columbus was sailing along the Caribbean coast of Central America when his ships were caught in a violent tropical storm. Seeking shelter, he found sanctuary in a bay protected by a small island; ashore, he encountered native people wearing heavy gold disks and gold bird-shape figures who spoke of great amounts of gold in the area. Sailing farther south, Columbus encountered more natives, also wearing pendants and jewelry fashioned in gold. He was convinced that he had discovered a land of great wealth to be claimed for the Spanish empire. The land itself was a vision of lush greenery; popular legend has it that, on the basis of what he saw and encountered, Columbus named the land Costa Rica, the "rich coast."

The Spanish Colonial Era

The first Spaniard to attempt the conquest of Costa Rica was Diego de Nicuesa in 1506. But his sick and starving troops were not able to surmount the resistance of the indigenous population, and the Spanish were unsuccessful. Similar hardships were encountered by other Spaniards who visited the region. The first "successful" expedition to the country was made by Gil González de Ávila in 1522. Exploring the Pacific coast, he converted more than 6,000 people of the Chorotega tribe to Catholicism. A year later he returned to his home port in Panama with the equivalent of $600,000 in gold, but more than 1,000 of his men had died on the exhausting journey. Of course, just as many native peoples, if not more, died because of disease and skirmishes with the Europeans. Many other Spanish expeditions were undertaken, and, fortunately for the people indigenous

to the area, all were less than successful at colonization, often because of rivalries between various expeditions. By 1560, almost 60 years after its discovery, no permanent Spanish settlement existed in Costa Rica (this name was then in general use, although it incorporated an area far larger than its present-day boundaries), and the indigenous peoples had not been subdued.

Costa Rica remained the smallest and poorest of Spain's Central American colonies, producing little wealth for the empire. Unlike other countries around it, Costa Rica tended to be largely ignored in terms of conquest and instead began to receive a wholly different type of settler—hardy, self-sufficient individuals who had to work to maintain themselves. Costa Ricans, both settlers and native peoples, endured the difficult living conditions of an agriculture-based existence in exchange for Spain's lack of interest. The population stayed at fewer than 20,000 for centuries (even with considerable growth in the 18th century) and was mainly confined to small, isolated farms in the highland Central Valley and the Pacific lowlands.

By the end of the 18th century, however, Costa Rica began to emerge from isolation. Some trade with neighboring Spanish colonies was carried out—in spite of constant harassment by English pirates, both at sea and on land—and the population had begun to expand across the Central Valley.

Seeds of political discord, which were soon to affect the colony, had been planted in Spain when Napoléon defeated and removed King Charles IV in 1808 and installed his brother Joseph on the Spanish throne. Costa Rica pledged support for the old regime, even sending troops to

Nicaragua in 1811 to help suppress a rebellion against Spain. By 1821, though, sentiment favoring independence from Spain was prevalent throughout Central America, and a declaration of independence for all of Central America was issued by Guatemala on September 15 of that year. Costa Rica then became part of the Mexican empire until 1826, when it became part of the United Provinces of Central America. Costa Rica declared its independence as a sovereign nation in 1838. The only major threat to that sovereignty took place in 1856, when the mercenary army of U.S. adventurer William Walker invaded the country from Nicaragua, which it had conquered the year before. Walker's plan to turn the Central American nations into slave states was cut short by Costa Rican president Juan Rafael Mora, who raised a volunteer army and repelled the invaders, pursuing them into Nicaragua and joining troops from various Central American nations to defeat the mercenaries.

It was this conflict that produced national hero Juan Santamaría, a young drummer boy from a poor family who is immortalized today both as the namesake of Costa Rica's international airport and in a monument in the Central Valley city of Alajuela. When the Costa Ricans drove Walker's troops from their country in 1857, they chased the troops to Rivas, Nicaragua. The filibusters took refuge in a wooden fort and Juan Santamaría, with a militia from Alajuela, offered to burn it down to drive them out. Legend says that Santamaría ran toward the fort carrying a torch, and that although he was shot repeatedly, he managed to throw it and to burn the fort down. His bravery wasn't recognized at the time, probably because of his modest origins, but in 1891 a statue depicting a strong and handsome soldier carrying a torch was placed in Alajuela, thus immortalizing Santamaría. For this occasion, Ruben Darío, the great Nicaraguan writer, dedicated a poem to

him. April 11 is now a national holiday in Costa Rica, called Juan Santamaría Day, which celebrates the Costa Rican victory at the Battle of Rivas.

Foundations of Democracy

The 19th century saw dramatic economic and political changes in Costa Rica. For the major part of that century, the country was ruled by a succession of wealthy families whose grip was partially broken only toward the end of the century. The development of agriculture included the introduction of coffee in the 1820s and bananas in the 1870s, both of which became the country's major sources of foreign exchange. First head of state Governor Juan Mora Fernández gave away free land and coffee seeds to any farmer who agreed to cultivate the crop for export, and many citizens prospered thanks to the "grain of gold." The government spent profits from the coffee trade on improving roads and ports, and other projects that included San José's Teatro Nacional. Bananas arrived with U.S. entrepreneur Minor Keith, whom the Costa Rican government hired to build a railroad. In exchange for his work, he was given a land grant on both sides of the track. Keith planted bananas, and the crop has since joined coffee and pineapples as Costa Rica's top agricultural exports.

In 1889 the first free popular election was held, characterized by full freedom of the press, frank debates by rival candidates, an honest tabulation of the vote, and the first peaceful transition of power from a ruling group to the opposition. This event provided the foundation of political stability that Costa Rica enjoys to this day. During the early 20th century each successive president fostered the growth of democratic liberties and continued to expand the free public school system, started during the presidency of Bernardo Soto in the late 1880s.

Booming exports were cut short by the arrival of World War I, followed by the

Great Depression and World War II. Poverty soared and a social revolution threatened in the late 1930s, as the popular Communist Party threatened strikes and violence. Costa Rica's version of the New Deal came in 1940, when conservative president Rafael Angel Calderón Guardia—the son of aristocrats—allied with the Catholic Church and implemented many of the Communist Party's demands. This willingness to compromise led to a wide-ranging system of socialized medicine, minimum wage laws, low-cost housing, and many other laws and constitutional reforms that protected workers.

The success of Calderón's social reforms was tainted by accusations of corruption. In 1944, he left office, only to be replaced by his close associate Teodoro Picado. Calderón and his United Christian Socialist Party were accused of rigging the election. Serious trouble flared when Calderón sought reelection in 1948, and lost to Otilio Ulate. Calderón refused to accept defeat and demanded a recount. Soon after, the local schoolhouse where the ballots were kept mysteriously caught fire. When Calderón's political allies in Congress appointed him president, the result was a civil uprising by outraged citizens, led by the still-revered José Figueres Ferrer, who had been exiled by Calderón as the political leader of the opposition. After a few months of armed conflict, a compromise was reached—Figueres and his "Army of National Liberation" would respect Calderón's social guarantees, and Figueres would preside over an interim government that would end after 18 months. In 1949, José "Don Pepe" Figueres abolished Costa Rica's military and created a national police force, nationalized the banking system and public utilities, and implemented additional health and education reforms. He stepped down after the 18-month period, only to be reelected twice in free elections. Sons of both Calderón and Figueres served four-year terms as president in the 1990s.

The Modern Era

Significant changes took place during the 1950s and 1960s, including greater involvement by the state in economic affairs. Insurance, telecommunications, the railroad system (now defunct), ports, and other industries were nationalized. The state-led economic model, although increasingly inefficient, led to a rising standard of living until the early 1970s, when an economic crisis introduced Costa Ricans to hyperinflation. By the mid-1980s, Costa Rica had begun pulling out of its economic slump, in part thanks to efforts to diversify the economy, which had long been dominated by coffee and bananas. Costa Rica made international headlines in 1987, when President Oscar Arias (1986–90) won the Nobel Peace Prize for his efforts to bring peace to other Central American countries. Arias remains a champion for peace and democracy through the Arias Foundation for Peace and Human Progress in San José. By the mid-1990s, tourism surpassed bananas as the country's largest earner of foreign exchange, and high-tech companies such as Intel, Dell Electronics, and Motorola opened plants and service centers in Costa Rica, providing relatively well-paying jobs for educated, bilingual young professionals.

Recent years have seen the continued growth of the tourism industry, and the establishment of a thriving but controversial Internet-based gambling industry tied to U.S. sporting events. Still, inflation hovers around 9% annually, the per capita income in Costa Rica is only about $4,000 per year, and the country's currency continues to be devalued on a regular basis. Attempts to privatize state-owned industries have been unsuccessful, and many Ticos feel frustrated by their country's resistance to change.

Today the challenge facing Costa Rica is how to conserve its natural resources while still permitting modern development. The government has been unable or unwilling to control illegal logging, an industry that threatens to destroy the country's old-growth forests. Urban sprawl in the Central Valley and the development of megaresorts along both coasts threaten forests, wildlife, and the slow pace of life that makes Costa Rica so enjoyable for visitors. Although tourism provides a much-needed injection of foreign exchange into the economy, the government has not fully decided which direction it should take. The buzzwords now are "ecotourism" and "sustainable development," and it is hoped that Costa Rica will find it possible to continue down these roads rather than opt for something akin to the Acapulco or Cancún style of development.

CHRONOLOGY

1502 BC On his fourth and last journey to the "New World," Christopher Columbus lands on the Caribbean coast of Costa Rica. An estimated 25,000 Indians lived here at that time; few survived the Spanish conquest.

1561 BC Juan de Cavallon leads the first successful Spanish colonizers into Costa Rica.

AD 1808 Coffee plants are brought to Costa Rica from Cuba, and coffee soon becomes the nation's principal export crop and the "coffee barons" (cafeteleros) become the nation's economic and political elite.

1821 On September 15, Central America declares its independence from Spain.

1823 Costa Rica joins the United Provinces of Central America, along with Nicaragua, Honduras, El Salvador, and Guatemala.

1838 Costa Rica declares its independence.

1857 Costa Rica, with the help of Honduras, El Salvador, and Guatemala, defeats American William Walker, who had invaded Nicaragua and installed himself as president and intended to expand slavery throughout Central America.

1859 President Juan Rafael Mora is thrown out of power (and eventually executed) in a coup led by cafeteleros.

1879 American businessman Minor Keith brings the cultivation of bananas to Costa Rica, and establishes what will become the United Fruit Company.

1940 Rafael Angel Calderon Guardia of the United Christian Socialist Party (PUSC) introduces liberal reforms, including recognition of workers' rights and minimum wages.

1948 Rafael Angel Calderon Guardia declines to step down as president. A 40-day civil war, led by José "Don Pepe" Figueres Ferrer, co-founder of the National Liberation Party, who had been exiled by Calderon, topples the government.

1949 President "Don Pepe" Figueres institutes ambitious socialist program, including introducing a social security system, nationalizing banks and utilities, and abolishing the military.

1958–1973 Costa Rica governed by mainly conservative administrations.

1968 Volcano Arenal, in the northern lowlands, dormant for 400-plus years, erupts, killing 87 people and destroying the town of Arenal.

1978 Rodrigo Carazo, a conservative, elected president as the economy continues to deteriorate.

1982 President Luis Alberto Monge institutes austerity measures designed to pull Costa Rica out of a severe economic slump. Costa Rica comes under pressure from the United States to oppose Nicaragua's Sandinista regime.

1986 Oscar Arias Sanchez is elected president on a platform promising peace throughout Central America. In 1987, Nicaragua, El Salvador, and Guatemala sign a peace plan. He is ultimately awarded the Nobel Peace Prize for his efforts.

1990 Rafael Angel Calderon Fournier, son of Rafael Angel Calderon Guardia, is elected president.

1994 José Maria Figueres, son of "Don Pepe," is elected president.

1998 Intel opens its first plant in Costa Rica. By 2003, it accounts for 37% of Costa Rica's exports.

2002 Abel Pachecho, M.D., (PUSC) is elected president. More than 1 million tourists visit Costa Rica.

2003 Energy and telecommunications workers strike over President Pacheco's privatization plans. Primary- and secondary-school teachers strike over nonpayment of their salaries.

BOOKS & MOVIES

Books

Inside Costa Rica, by Tom Barry and Silvia Lara (Interhemispheric Resource Center), is an in-depth factual rundown of the country. For an analysis of Costa Rican culture and society, read *The Ticos* (Lynne Rienner Publishers), by Mavis Hiltunen Biesanz et al. David Rains Wallace's *The Quetzal and the Macaw: The Story of Costa Rica's National Parks* (Sierra Club Books) is an entertaining and informative account of Costa Rica's exemplary conservation efforts. *The Costa Rica Reader* (Grove Weidenfeld), by Marc Edelman and Joanne Kenen, is a critical anthology and comparison of traditional and progressive versions of the country's history.

Some of the most popular books on this country feature its rich natural history. *A Guide to the Birds of Costa Rica,* by F. Gary Stiles and Alexander F. Skutch (Cornell), is a first-rate field guide. Alexander Skutch has also written some entertaining chronicles combining natural history, philosophy, and anecdote, among them *A Naturalist in Costa Rica* (University Press of Florida).

The *Costa Rica: Eco-Traveller's Wildlife Guide,* by Les Beletsky (Academic Press), gives an overview of the most common fauna. For an in-depth look at local ecology, read *A Neotropical Companion,* by John Kricher (Princeton University Press); *Tropical Nature,* by Adrian Forsyth and Ken Miyata (Macmillan); or the encyclopedic *Costa Rican Natural History* (University of Chicago Press), compiled by tropical biology expert Daniel Janzen, Ph. D. *Field Guide to the Wildlife of Costa Rica,* by Carrol L. Henderson (University of Texas Press), offers an in-depth look at some 300 species of birds, mammals, reptiles, amphibians, butterflies, moths, and other invertebrates.

Costa Rica has a rich literary tradition, but few of its writers have been translated into English. Those who have can be hard to find in the United States. For insight on local culture, pick up *Costa Rica: A Traveler's Literary Companion,* edited by Barbara Ras (Consortium), a collection of translated short stories by the country's best writers. *Years Like Brief Days* (Dufour Editions) is one of the most popular novels of Fabián Dobles, famous for his humorous depiction of life in rural Costa Rica in the early 20th century. *The Lonely Men's Island* (Editorial Escritores Unidos, Mexico), the first novel of José León Sánchez, recounts the author's years on Isla San Lucas—the Costa Rican version of Alcatraz—where he was sent for stealing a statue of the country's patron saint, La Virgen de Los Angeles.

Movies

Jurassic Park (1993) was set on Costa Rica's isolated Cocos Island, but the film was actually shot in Hawaii. Oddly enough, much of the film version of *Congo* (1995), another Michael Crichton novel, was shot in Costa Rica. Most of Ridley Scott's *1492: Conquest of Paradise* (1992) was filmed on Costa Rica's Pacific coast. If you're more interested in the waves that break off that coast, check out the surf classic *The Endless Summer* (1966); both the original and remake have Costa Rica footage. An excellent documentary on underwater life in Costa Rica (as well as in the Galápagos and Australia) is *Wonders of the Deep* (1998; Madacy Entertainment).

WILDLIFE & PLANT GLOSSARY

Here is a rundown of some of the most common and attention-grabbing mammals, birds, reptiles, amphibians, plants, and even a few insects that you might encounter. We give the common Costa Rican names, so you can understand the local lingo, as well as the latest scientific terms.

Fauna

Agouti (*guatusa*; *Dasyprocta punctata*): A 20-inch tail-less rodent with small ears and a large muzzle, the agouti is reddish brown on the Pacific side, more of a tawny orange on the Caribbean slope. It sits on its haunches to eat large seeds and fruit.

Anteater (*oso hormiguero*): Three species of anteater inhabit Costa Rica—the Giant (*Myrmecophaga tridactyla*), Silky (*Cyclopes didactylus*), and Collared, or Vested (*Tamandua mexicana*). Only the last is commonly seen, and too often as roadkill. This medium-size anteater, 30 inches long with an 18-inch tail, laps up ants and termites with its long, sticky tongue and has long, sharp claws for ripping into insect nests.

Armadillo (*cusuco*; *Dasypus novemcinctus*): The nine-banded armadillo is widespread in Costa Rica and also found in the southern United States. This nocturnal and solitary edentate roots in soil with a long muzzle for a varied diet of insects, small animals, and plant material.

Bat (*murciélago*): With more than 100 species, Costa Rica's bats can be found eating fruit, insects, fish, small vertebrates, nectar, and even blood, in the case of the infamous Vampire Bat (*vampiro*, *Desmodus rotundus*), which far prefers cattle blood to that of any tourist. As a group, bats are extremely important ecologically, and are essential to seed dispersal, pollination, and controlling insect populations.

Caiman (*caiman*): The Spectacled Caiman (*Caiman crocodilus*) is a small crocodilian (to 7 feet) inhabiting fresh water, subsisting mainly on fish. Most active at night (it has bright-red eye shine), it basks by day. It is distinguished from the American crocodile by a sloping brow and smooth back scales.

Coati (*pizote*; *Nasua narica*): This is a long-nose relative of the raccoon, its long tail often held straight up. Lone males or groups of females with young are active during the day, on the ground, or in trees. Omnivorous coatis feed on fruit, invertebrates, and small vertebrates.

Cougar (*puma*; *Felis concolor*): Mountain lions are the largest unspotted cats (to 8 feet, including the tail) in Costa Rica. Widespread but rare, they live in essentially all-wild habitats and feed on vertebrates ranging from snakes to deer.

Crocodile (*lagarto*; *Crocodylus acutus*): The American Crocodile, up to 16 feet in length, is found in most major river systems, particularly the Tempisque and Tárcoles. It seldom attacks humans, preferring fish and birds. It's distinguished from the caiman by a flat head, narrow snout, and spiky scales.

Ctenosaur (*garrobo*; *Ctenosaura similis*): Also known as the Black, or Spiny-tailed Iguana, this is a large (up to 18 inches long with 18-inch tail) tan lizard with four dark bands on its body and a tail ringed with sharp, curved spines. Terrestrial and arboreal, it sleeps in burrows or tree hollows. It lives along the coast in the dry northwest and in wetter areas farther south. The fastest known reptile (clocked on land), the Ctenosaur has been recorded moving at 21.7 mi per hour.

Dolphin (*delfín*): Several species, including Bottlenose Dolphins (*Tursiops truncatus*), frolic in Costa Rican waters. Often seen off Pacific shores are Spotted Dolphins (*Stenella attenuata*), which are small (up to 6 feet), with pale spots on the posterior half of the body; they often travel in groups of 20 or more and play around vessels and in bow wakes. Tucuxi Dolphins (*Sotalia fluviatilis*) have also been spotted in small groups off the southern Caribbean coast, often with Bottlenose Dolphins.

Frigatebird (*tijereta del mar*; *Fregata magnificens*): A large, black soaring bird with slender wings and forked tail, this is one of the most effortless and agile flyers in the avian world. More common on the Pacific coast, it doesn't dive or swim but swoops to pluck its food, often from the mouths of other birds.

Frog (*rana*): Some 120 species of frog exist in Costa Rica; most are nocturnal, except for the Strawberry Poison Dart Frog (*Dendrobates pumilio*) and Green-and-black Poison Dart Frog. The bright coloration of these two species, either red with blue or green hind legs or charcoal black with fluorescent green markings, warns potential predators of their toxicity. The Red-eyed Leaf Frog (*Agalychnis callidryas*) is among the showiest of nocturnal species. The large, brown Marine Toad (*Bufo marinus*), also called Cane Toad or Giant Toad, comes out at night.

Howler Monkey (*mono congo*; *Alouatta palliata*): These dark, chunky-bodied monkeys (to 22 inches long with 24-inch tail) with black faces travel in troops of up to 20. Lethargic mammals, they eat leaves, fruits, and flowers. The males' deep, resounding howls serve as communication among and between troops.

Hummingbird (*colibrí*): Weighing just a fraction of an ounce, hummingbirds are nonetheless some of the most notable residents of tropical forests. At least 50 can be found in Costa Rica, visiting typically red, tubular flowers in their seemingly endless search for energy-rich nectar. Because of their assortment of iridescent colors and bizarre bills and tail shapes, watching them can be a spectator sport. Best bets are hummingbird feeders and anywhere with great numbers of flowers.

Iguana (*iguana*): Mostly arboreal but good at swimming, the iguana is Costa Rica's largest lizard: males can grow to 10 feet, including tail. Only young Green Iguanas (*Iguana iguana*) are bright green; adults are much duller, females dark grayish, and males olive (with orangish heads in breeding season). All have round cheek scales and smooth tails.

Jacana (*gallito de agua*; *Jacana spinosa*): These birds are sometimes called "lily trotters" because their long toes allow them to walk on floating vegetation. Feeding on aquatic organisms and plants, they're found in almost any body of water. They expose yellow wing feathers in flight. Sex roles are reversed; "liberated" females are larger and compete for mates (often more than one), whereas the males tend to the nest and care for the young.

Jaguar (*tigre*; *Panthera onca*): The largest New World feline (to 6 feet, with 2-foot tail), this top-of-the-line predator is exceedingly rare but lives in a wide variety of habitats, from dry forest to cloud forest. It's most common in the vast Amistad Biosphere Reserve, but it is almost never seen in the wild.

Jesus Christ Lizard (*gallego*): Flaps of skin on long toes enable this spectacular lizard to run across water. Costa Rica has three species: the Lineated Basilisk (*Basiliscus basiliscus*) on the Pacific side is brown with pale lateral stripe; in the Caribbean, the Emerald Basilisk (*Basiliscus plumifrons*) is marked with turquoise and black on a green body; and the Striped Basilisk (*Basiliscus vittatus*), also on the Caribbean side, resembles the lineated basilisk. Adult males grow to 3 feet (mostly tail), with crests on the head, back, and base of tail.

Leaf-Cutter Ant (*zompopas*; *Atta* spp.): Found in all lowland habitats, these are the most commonly noticed neotropical ants. Columns of ants carrying bits of leaves twice their size sometimes extend for several hundred yards from an underground nest to plants being harvested. The ants don't eat the leaves; their food is a fungus they cultivate on the leaves.

Macaw (*lapas*): Costa Rica's two species are the Scarlet Macaw (*Ara macao*), on the Pacific side (Osa Peninsula and Carara Biological Reserve), and the severely threatened Great Green Macaw (*Ara ambigua*), on the Caribbean side. These are huge, raucous parrots with long tails; their immense bills are used to rip fruit apart to reach the seeds. They nest in hollow trees and are victimized by pet-trade poachers and deforestation.

Magpie Jay (*urraca*; *Calocitta formosa*): This southern relative of the blue jay, with a long tail and distinctive topknot (crest of forward-curved feathers), is found in the dry northwest. Bold and inquisitive, with amazingly varied vocalizations, these birds travel in noisy groups of four or more.

Manatee (*manatí*; *Trichechus manatus*): Although endangered throughout its range, the West Indian Manatee can be spotted in Tortuguero, meandering along in shallow water, browsing on submerged vegetation. The moniker "sea cow" is apt, as they spend nearly all their time resting or feeding. Their large, somewhat amorphous bodies won't win any beauty contests, but they do appear quite graceful.

Margay (*caucel*; *Felis wiedii*): Fairly small, this spotted nocturnal cat (22 inches long, with 18-inch tail) is similar to the ocelot but has a longer tail and is far more arboreal: mobile ankle joints allow it to climb down trunks headfirst. It eats small vertebrates.

Morpho (*morfo*): Three Costa Rican species of this spectacular large butterfly have a brilliant-blue upper wing surface, one of which, the Blue Morpho (*Morpho peleides*), is common in moister areas and has an intense ultraviolet upper surface; one

is white above and below; and one is brown and white. Adults feed on rotting fallen fruit; they never visit flowers.

Motmot (*pájaro bobo*): These handsome birds of the understory have racket-shape tails. Nesting in burrows, they sit patiently while scanning for large insect prey or small vertebrates. Costa Rica has six species.

Ocelot (*manigordo*; *Felis pardalis*): Mostly terrestrial, this medium-size spotted cat (33 inches long, with 16-inch tail) is active night and day, and feeds on rodents and other vertebrates. Forepaws are rather large in relation to the body, hence the local name, which means "fat hand."

Oropéndola (*oropéndola*; *Psarocolius* spp.): This crow-size bird in the oriole family has a bright-yellow tail and nests in colonies, in pendulous nests (up to 6 feet long) built by females in isolated trees. Males make an unmistakable, loud, gurgling liquid call. The bird is far more numerous on the Caribbean side.

Parakeet and Parrot (*pericos*, parakeets; *loros*, parrots): There are 15 species in Costa Rica (plus two macaws), all clad in green, most with a splash of a primary color or two on the head or wings. They travel in boisterous flocks, prey on immature seeds, and nest in cavities.

Peccary: Piglike animals with thin legs and thick necks, peccaries travel in small groups (larger where the population is still numerous); root in soil for fruit, seeds, and small creatures; and have a strong musk odor. Costa Rica has two species: the Collared Peccary (*saíno*, *Tayassu tajacu*) and the White-lipped Peccary (*chancho de monte*, *Tayassu pecari*). The latter is now nearly extinct.

Pelican (*pelícano*): Large size, a big bill, and a throat pouch make the Brown Pelican (*Pelecanus occidentalis*) unmistakable in coastal areas (it's far more abundant on the Pacific side). Pelicans often fly in V formations and dive for fish.

Quetzal: One of the world's most exquisite birds, the Resplendent Quetzal (*Pharomachrus mocinno*) was revered by the Maya. Glittering green plumage and the male's long tail coverts draw thousands of people to highland cloud forests for sightings from February to April.

Roseate Spoonbill (*garza rosada; Ajaja ajaja*): Pink plumage and a spatulate bill set this wader apart from all other wetland birds; it feeds by swishing its bill back and forth in water while using its feet to stir up bottom-dwelling creatures. Spoonbills are most common around Palo Verde and Caño Negro.

Sea Turtle. *See* Close-Up: Tico Turtles, *in* Chapter 7.

Sloth (*perezoso*): Costa Rica is home to the Brown-throated Three-toed Sloth (*Bradypus variegatus*) and Hoffmann's Two-toed Sloth (*Choloepus hoffmanni*). Both grow to 2 feet, but two-toed (check forelegs) sloths often look bigger because of longer fur and are the only species in the highlands. Sloths are herbivorous, accustomed to a low-energy diet, and well camouflaged.

Snake (*culebra*): Costa Rica's serpents can be found in trees, above and below ground, and even in the sea on the Pacific coast. Nearly all of the more than 125 species are harmless, but are best appreciated from a distance. Notable members of this group include Costa Rica's largest snake, the Boa Constrictor (*Boa constrictor*), reaching up to 15 feet, and the fer-de-lance (*terciopelo, Bothrops asper*) which is a much smaller (up to 6 feet) but far more dangerous viper.

Spider Monkey (*mono colorado, mono araña*): Lanky and long-tailed, the Black-handed Spider Monkey (*Ateles geoffroyi*) is the largest monkey in Costa Rica (to 24 inches, with 32-inch tail). Moving in groups of two to four, they eat ripe fruit, leaves, and flowers. Incredible aerialists, they can swing effortlessly through branches using long arms and legs and prehensile tails. Caribbean and southern Pacific populations are dark reddish brown; northwesterners are blond.

Squirrel Monkey (*mono titi*): The smallest of four Costa Rican monkeys (11 inches, with 15-inch tail), the Red-backed Squirrel Monkey (*Saimiri oerstedii*) has a distinctive facial pattern (black cap and muzzle, white mask) and gold-orange coloration on its back. The species travels in noisy, active groups of 20 or more, feeding on fruit and insects. Numbers of this endangered species have been estimated between 2,000 and 4,000 individuals. Almost all *Saimiri oerstedii* in Costa Rica are found in Manuel Antonio National Park or in parts of the Osa Peninsula.

Tapir (*danta; Tapirus bairdii*): The largest land mammal in Costa Rica (to 6½ feet), the tapir is something like a small rhinoceros without armor. Adapted to a wide range of habitats, it's nocturnal, seldom seen, but said to defecate and sometimes sleep in water. Tapirs are herbivorous and use their prehensile snouts to harvest vegetation. The best opportunities for viewing wild tapirs are in Corcovado National Park.

Toucan (*tucán, tucancillo*): This bird is familiar to anyone who's seen a box of Froot Loops® cereal. The Aracaris is one, a slender toucan with the trademark bill. Keel-billed (*Ramphastos sulfuratus*) and Chestnut-mandibled Toucans (*Ramphastos swainsonii*) are the largest (18 inches and 22 inches); they are black with bright-yellow "bibs" and multihued bills. The smaller, stouter Emerald Toucanet (*Aulacorhynchus prasinus*) and Yellow-eared Toucanet (*Selenidera spectabilis*) are aptly named.

Three-wattled Bellbird (*pájaro campana; Procnias tricarunculata*): Although endangered, the bellbird can be readily identified in cloud forests where it breeds (around Monteverde, for example) by its extraordinary call, a bold and aggressive "bonk," unlike any other creature in the forest. If you spot a male calling, look for the three pendulous wattles at the base of its beak.

Whales (*ballena*): Humpback Whales (*Megaptera novaeanglia*) appear off the Pacific coast between November and February; they migrate from California and as far as Hawaii.

White-Faced Capuchin Monkey (*mono cari-blanca*; *Cebus capuchinus*): Medium-size and omnivorous, this monkey (to 18 inches, with 20-inch tail) has black fur and a pink face surrounded by a whitish bib. Extremely active foragers, they move singly or in groups of up to 20, examining the environment closely and even coming to the ground. It's the most commonly seen monkey in Costa Rica.

Flora

Ant-acacia (*acacia*; *Acacia* spp.): If you'll be in the tropical dry forest of Guanacaste, learn to avoid this plant. As if its sharp thorns weren't enough, acacias exhibit an intense symbiosis with various ant species (*Pseudomyrmex* spp.) that will attack anything—herbivores, other plants, and unaware human visitors that come in contact with the tree. The ants and the acacias have an intriguing relationship, though, so do look, but don't touch.

Bromeliad (*piña silvestre*): Members of the family Bromeliaceae are *epiphytes*, living on the trunk and branches of trees. They are not parasitic, however, and so have adapted to acquire all the necessary water and nutrients from what falls into the central "tank" formed by the leaf structure. Amphibians and insects also use the water held in bromeliads to reproduce, forming small aquatic communities perched atop tree branches. In especially wet areas, small bromeliads can even be found on power lines.

Heliconia (*helicónia*; *Heliconia* spp.): It's hard to miss these stunning plants, many of which have huge inflorescences of red, orange, and yellow, and leaves very much the size and shape of a banana plant. With luck, you'll catch a visit by a hummingbird—truly a visual treat.

Mangroves (*mangles*): Taken together, this handful of salt-tolerant trees with tangled, above-ground roots make up their own distinct ecosystem. Buttressing the land against the sea, they serve as nurseries for countless species of fish and other marine animals and provide roosting habitat for marine birds. Mangroves are found on the coast in protected areas such as bays and estuaries.

Naked Indian Tree (*indio desnudo*; *Bursera simaruba*): This tree can be found in forests throughout Costa Rica, often forming living fences, and is instantly identifiable by its orange bark that continually sloughs off, giving rise to another common name, the tourist tree. One theory suggests that the shedding of its bark aids in removing parasites from the tree's exterior.

Orchid (*orquídea*): The huge Orchidaceae family has more than 1,200 representatives in Costa Rica alone, with nearly 90% percent living as epiphytes on other plants. The great diversity of the group belies not only examples of great beauty, but exquisite adaptations between flowers and their insect pollinators. With a combination of rewards (nectar) and trickery (visual and chemical cues) orchids exhibit myriad ways of enticing insects to cooperate.

Strangler Fig (*Matapalo*; *Ficus spp.*): Starting as seedlings high in the canopy, these aggressive plants grow both up toward the light, and down to the soil, slowly taking over the host tree. Eventually they encircle and "strangle" the host, killing it, leaving a ring of fig trunk around an empty interior. Figs with ripe fruit are excellent places for wildlife spotting, as they attract monkeys, birds, and an assortment of other creatures.

MENU GUIDE

Rice and beans is the heart of Costa Rica's *comida típica* (typical food). It's possible to order everything from sushi to crepes in and around San José, but most Ticos have a simple diet built around rice, beans, and the myriad fruits and vegetables that flourish here. Costa Rican food isn't spicy, and many dishes are seasoned with the same five ingredients—onion, salt, garlic, cilantro, and red bell pepper.

Spanish	English

General Dining

Spanish	English
Almuerzo	Lunch
Bocas	Appetizers or snacks (literally "mouthfuls") served with drinks in the tradition of Spanish tapas.
Casado	Heaping plate of rice, beans, fried plantains, cabbage salad, tomatoes, *macarrones* (noodles), and fish, chicken, or meat—or any variation thereof; *casado* and *plata del día* are often used interchangeably
Cena	Dinner
Desayuno	Breakfast
Plata del día	Plate of the day
Soda	An inexpensive café; casados are always found at sodas

Especialidades (Specialties)

Spanish	English
Arreglados	Sandwiches or meat and vegetable puff pastry
Arroz con mariscos	Fried rice with fish, shrimp, octopus, and clams, or whatever's fresh that day
Arroz con pollo	Chicken with rice
Camarones	Shrimp
Ceviche	Chilled seafood marinated in lime juice, served with chopped onion and garlic
Chilaquiles	Meat-stuffed tortillas
Chorreados	Corn pancakes, served with *natilla* (sour cream)
Corvina	Sea bass
Empanadas	Savory or sweet pastry turnover filled with fruit or meat and vegetables
Empanaditas	Small empanadas
Gallo pinto	Rice sautéed with black beans (literally, "spotted rooster"), often served for breakfast
Langosta	Lobster

Langostino	Prawns
Olla de carne	Soup of chayote squash, corn, yuca (a tuber), and potatoes
Palmitos	Hearts of palm, served in salads or as a side dish
Pescado ahumado	Smoked marlin
Picadillo	Water squash, potatoes, carrots, or other vegetables chopped into small cubes and combined with onions, garlic, and ground beef
Pozol	Corn soup
Salsa caribeño	A combination of tomatoes, onions, and spices that accompanies most fish dishes on the Caribbean coast

Postres (Desserts) & Dulces (Sweets)

Cajeta de coco	Fudge made with coconut and orange peel
Cajeta	Molasses-flavored fudge
Dulce de leche	Thick syrup of boiled milk and sugar
Flan	Caramel-topped egg custard
Mazamorra	Cornstarch pudding
Melcochas	Candy made from raw sugar
Pan de maiz	Sweet corn bread
Tres leches cake	"Three milks" cake, made with condensed and evaporated milk and cream

Frutas (Fruits)

Aguacate	Avocado
Anon	Sugar apple; sweet white flesh; resembles an artichoke with a thick rind
Banano	Banana
Bilimbi	Looks like a miniature cucumber crossed with a star fruit; ground into a savory relish
Fresca	Strawberry
Cas	A smaller guava
Granadilla	Passion fruit
Guanábana	Soursop; large, spiky yellow fruit with white flesh and a musky taste
Guayaba	Guava
Mamon chino	Rambutan; red spiky ball protecting a white fruit similar to a lychee
Marañone	Cashew fruit; used in juices
Melon	Canteloupe
Mora	Blackberry

Palmito	Heart of palm
Piña	Pineapple
Pipa	Green coconut; sold at roadside stands with ends chopped off and straws stuck inside
Sandia	Watermelon
Tiriguro	Star fruit

Bebidas (Beverages)

Agua dulce	Hot water sweetened with raw sugarcane
Batido	Fruit shake made with milk (con leche) or water (con agua)
Café con leche	Coffee with hot milk
Café negro	Black coffee
Fresca natural	Fresh-squeezed juice
Guaro	Harsh, clear spirit distilled from fermented sugarcane
Horchata	Cinnamon-flavored cornmeal drink
Refrescos	Tropical fruit smoothie with ice and sugar

VOCABULARY

	English	Spanish	Pronunciation

Basics

	English	Spanish	Pronunciation
	Yes/no	Sí/no	see/no
	OK	De acuerdo	de a-**kwer**-doe
	Please	Por favor	pore fah-**vore**
	May I?	¿Me permite?	may pair-**mee**-tay
	Thank you (very much)	(Muchas) gracias	(**moo**-chas) **grah**-see-as
	You're welcome	Con mucho gusto	con **moo**-cho **goose**-toe
	Excuse me	Con permiso	con pair-**mee**-so
	Pardon me	¿Perdón?	pair-**dohn**
	Could you tell me?	¿Podría decirme?	po-dree-ah deh-**seer**-meh
	I'm sorry	Disculpe	Dee-**skool**-peh
	Good morning!	¡Buenos días!	**bway**-nohs **dee**-ahs
	Good afternoon!	¡Buenas tardes!	**bway**-nahs **tar**-dess
	Good evening!	¡Buenas noches!	**bway**-nahs **no**-chess
	Goodbye!	¡Adiós!/¡Hasta luego!	ah-dee-**ohss**/ah -stah-**lwe**-go
	Mr./Mrs.	Señor/Señora	sen-**yor**/sen-**yohr**-ah
	Miss	Señorita	sen-yo-**ree**-tah
	Pleased to meet you	Mucho gusto	**moo**-cho **goose**-toe
	How are you?	¿Cómo está usted?	**ko**-mo es-**tah** oo-**sted**
	Very well, thank you.	Muy bien, gracias.	**moo**-ee bee-**en**, **grah**-see-as
	And you?	¿Y usted?	ee oos-**ted**
	Hello (on the telephone)	Diga	**dee**-gah

Days of the Week

	English	Spanish	Pronunciation
	Sunday	domingo	doe-**meen**-goh
	Monday	lunes	**loo**-ness
	Tuesday	martes	**mahr**-tess
	Wednesday	miércoles	me-**air**-koh-less
	Thursday	jueves	hoo-**ev**-ess

Friday	viernes	vee-**air**-ness
Saturday	sábado	**sah**-bah-doh

Months

January	enero	eh-**neh**-roh
February	febrero	feh-**breh**-roh
March	marzo	**mahr**-soh
April	abril	ah-**breel**
May	mayo	**my**-oh
June	junio	**hoo**-nee-oh
July	julio	**hoo**-lee-yoh
August	agosto	ah-**ghost**-toh
September	septiembre	sep-tee-**em**-breh
October	octubre	oak-**too**-breh
November	noviembre	no-vee-**em**-breh
December	diciembre	dee-see-**em**-breh

Useful Phrases

Do you speak English?	¿Habla usted inglés?	**ah**-blah oos-**ted** in-**glehs**
I don't speak Spanish	No hablo español	no **ah**-bloh es-pahn-**yol**
I don't understand (you)	No entiendo	no en-tee-**en**-doh
I understand (you)	Entiendo	en-tee-**en**-doh
I don't know	No sé	no seh
I am American/ British	Soy americano (americana)/ inglés(a)	soy ah-meh-ree-**kah**-no (ah-meh-ree-**kah**-nah)/ in-**glehs** (**ah**)
What's your name?	¿Cómo se llama usted?	koh-mo seh **yah**-mah oos-**ted**
My name is . . .	Me llamo . . .	may **yah**-moh
What time is it?	¿Qué hora es?	keh **o**-rah es
It is one, two, three . . . o'clock.	Es la una. . . . Son las dos, tres	es la **oo**-nah/sohn lahs dohs, tress
How?	¿Cómo?	**koh**-mo
When?	¿Cuándo?	**kwahn**-doh
This/Next week	Esta semana/ la semana que entra	**es**-teh seh-**mah**-nah/lah seh-**mah**-nah keh **en**-trah

This/Next month	Este mes/el próximo mes	**es**-teh mehs/el **proke**-see-mo mehs
This/Next year	Este año/el año que viene	**es**-teh **ahn**-yo/el **ahn**-yo keh vee-**yen**-ay
Yesterday/today/ tomorrow	Ayer/hoy/mañana	ah-**yehr**/oy/mahn-**yah**-nah
This morning/ afternoon	Esta mañana/ tarde	es-tah mahn-**yah**-nah/**tar**-deh
Tonight	Esta noche	es-tah **no**-cheh
What?	¿Qué?	keh
What is it?	¿Qué es esto?	keh es **es**-toh
Why?	¿Por qué?	pore **keh**
Who?	¿Quién?	kee-**yen**
Where is . . . ?	¿Dónde está . . . ?	**dohn**-deh es-**tah**
the bus stop?	la parada del autobus?	la pah-**rah**-dah del oh-toh-**boos**
the post office?	la oficina de correos?	la oh-fee-**see**-nah deh koh-**reh**-os
the museum?	el museo?	el moo-**seh**-oh
the hospital?	el hospital?	el ohss-pee-**tal**
the bathroom?	el baño?	el **bahn**-yoh
Here/there	Aquí/allá	ah-**key**/ah-**yah**
Open/closed	Abierto/cerrado	ah-bee-**er**-toh/ ser-**ah**-doh
Left/right	Izquierda/derecha	iss-key-**er**-dah/ dare-**eh**-chah
Straight ahead	Derecho	dare-**eh**-choh
Is it near/far?	¿Está cerca/lejos?	es-**tah sehr**-kah/ **leh**-hoss
I'd like . . . a room	Quisiera . . . un cuarto/una habitación	kee-see-ehr-ah oon **kwahr**-toh/ **oo**-nah ah-bee-tah-see-**on**
the key	la llave	lah **yah**-veh
a newspaper	un periódico	oon pehr-ee-**oh**-dee-koh
a stamp	la estampilla	lah es-stahm-**pee**-yah
I'd like to buy . . .	Quisiera comprar . . .	kee-see-**ehr**-ah kohm-**prahr**
cigarettes	cigarrillos	ce-ga-**ree**-yohs
a dictionary	un diccionario	oon deek-see-oh-**nah**-ree-oh
soap	jabón	hah-**bohn**
suntan lotion	loción	loh-see-**ohn** brohn-

	bronceadora	seh-ah-**do**-rah
a map	un mapa	oon **mah**-pah
a magazine	una revista	**oon**-ah reh-**veess**-tah
a postcard	una tarjeta postal	**oon**-ah tar-**het**-ah post-**ahl**
How much is it?	¿Cuánto cuesta?	**kwahn**-toh **kwes**-tah
Telephone	Teléfono	tel-**ef**-oh-no
I am ill	Estoy enfermo(a)	es-**toy** en-**fehr**-moh(mah)
Please call a doctor	Por favor llame a un medico	pohr fah-**vor ya**-meh ah oon **med**-ee-koh
Help!	¡Auxilio! ¡Ayuda! ¡Socorro!	owk-**see**-lee-oh/ ah-**yoo**-dah/ soh-**kohr**-roh
Fire!	¡Incendio!	en-**sen**-dee-oo
Caution!/Look out!	¡Cuidado!	kwee-**dah**-doh

INDEX

NOTES

FODOR'S KEY TO THE GUIDES

America's guidebook leader publishes guides for every kind of traveler.
Check out our many series and find your perfect match.

FODOR'S GOLD GUIDES
America's favorite travel-guide series
offers the most detailed insider reviews
of hotels, restaurants, and attractions
in all price ranges, plus great background information, smart tips, and
useful maps.

COMPASS AMERICAN GUIDES
Stunning guides from top local writers
and photographers, with gorgeous
photos, literary excerpts, and colorful
anecdotes. A must-have for culture
mavens, history buffs, and new residents.

FODOR'S CITYPACKS
Concise city coverage in a guide plus a
foldout map. The right choice for urban
travelers who want everything under
one cover.

FODOR'S EXPLORING GUIDES
Hundreds of color photos bring your
destination to life. Lively stories lend
insight into the culture, history, and
people.

FODOR'S TRAVEL HISTORIC AMERICA
For travelers who want to experience
history firsthand, this series gives in-
depth coverage of historic sights, plus
nearby restaurants and hotels. Themes
include the Thirteen Colonies, the Old
West, and the Lewis and Clark Trail.

FODOR'S POCKET GUIDES
For travelers who need only the
essentials. The best of Fodor's in
pocket-size packages for just $9.95.

FODOR'S FLASHMAPS
Every resident's map guide, with
dozens of easy-to-follow maps of
public transit, restaurants, shopping,
museums, and more.

FODOR'S CITYGUIDES
Sourcebooks for living in the city:
thousands of in-the-know listings for
restaurants, shops, sports, nightlife,
and other city resources.

FODOR'S AROUND THE CITY WITH KIDS
Up to 68 great ideas for family days,
recommended by resident parents.
Perfect for exploring in your own
backyard or on the road.

FODOR'S HOW TO GUIDES
Get tips from the pros on planning the
perfect trip. Learn how to pack, fly
hassle-free, plan a honeymoon or cruise,
stay healthy on the road, and travel
with your baby.

FODOR'S LANGUAGES FOR TRAVELERS
Practice the local language before you
hit the road. Available in phrase books,
cassette sets, and CD sets.

KAREN BROWN'S GUIDES
Engaging guides—many with easy-to-
follow inn-to-inn itineraries—to the
most charming inns and B&Bs in the
U.S.A. and Europe.

SEE IT GUIDES
Illustrated guidebooks that include the
practical information travelers need, in
gorgeous full color. Thousands of
photos, hundreds of restaurant and
hotel reviews, actual prices, and ratings
for attractions all in one indispensable
package. Perfect for travelers who want
the best value, packed in a fresh, easy-
to-use, colorful layout.

OTHER GREAT TITLES FROM FODOR'S
Baseball Vacations, The Complete
Guide to the National Parks, Family
Vacations, Golf Digest's Places to Play,
Great American Drives of the East,
Great American Drives of the West,
Great American Vacations, Healthy
Escapes, National Parks of the West,
Skiing USA.